MAGILL'S ENCYCLOPEDIA OF SOCIAL SCIENCE

PSYCHOLOGY

MAGILL'S ENCYCLOPEDIA OF SOCIAL SCIENCE

PSYCHOLOGY

Volume 3
Memory–Separation and divorce: Adult issues

Editor
Nancy A. Piotrowski, Ph.D.
University of California, Berkeley

Project Editor
Tracy Irons-Georges

SALEM PRESS, INC.
Pasadena, California
Hackensack, New Jersey

Editorial Director: Christina J. Moose
Project Editor: Tracy Irons-Georges
Copy Editor: Leslie Ellen Jones
Assistant Editor: Andrea E. Miller
Acquisitions Editor: Mark Rehn
Photograph Editor: Philip Bader
Research Supervisor: Jeffry Jensen
Production Editor: Cynthia Beres
Page Design/Graphics: James Hutson
Layout: Eddie Murillo

∞ The paper used in these volumes conforms to the American National Standard for Permanence of Paper for Printed Library Materials, Z39.48-1992 (R1997).

Some of the updated and revised essays in this work originally appeared in *Magill's Survey of Social Science: Psychology*, edited by Frank N. Magill (Pasadena, Calif.: Salem Press, Inc., 1993).

Library of Congress Cataloging-in-Publication Data

Magill's encyclopedia of social science: psychology/ editor, Nancy A. Piotrowski.
   p. cm.
Includes bibliographical references and index.
ISBN 1-58765-130-0 (set : alk. paper) — ISBN 1-58765-131-9 (v. 1 : alk. paper) —
ISBN 1-58765-132-7 (v. 2 : alk. paper)— ISBN 1-58765-133-5 (v. 3 : alk. paper) —
ISBN 1-58765-134-3 (v. 4 : alk. paper)
1. Psychology—Encyclopedias. I. Piotrowski, Nancy A.

BF31 .M33 2003
150'.3—dc21

                                                                  2002151146

Second Printing

Table of Contents

MAGILL'S ENCYCLOPEDIA OF SOCIAL SCIENCE

PSYCHOLOGY

Memory

TYPE OF PSYCHOLOGY: Memory
FIELDS OF STUDY: Cognitive processes

Theories of memory attempt to identify the structures and explain the processes underlying the human memory system. These theories give coherence to an understanding of memory and suggest new research needed to extend knowledge about learning and memory.

KEY CONCEPTS
- episodic memory
- iconic memory
- long-term memory
- memory trace
- schemas
- semantic memory
- sensory memory
- short-term memory

INTRODUCTION

Human memory is among the most complex phenomena in the universe. A Russian newspaper reporter once flawlessly recalled a list of fifty unrelated words he had studied for only three minutes fifteen years before. On the other hand, as everyone knows from personal experience, the memory system is also capable of losing information presented only seconds in the past. Errors in memory create so many problems that it seems imperative to know all that is possible about human memory. For that, a theory is needed.

A scientific theory is a systematic way to understand complex phenomena that occur in nature. A theory is judged to be useful insofar as its claims can be supported by the findings of empirical tests, especially experimentation, and insofar as it leads to further research studies. A theory is not right or wrong; it is simply a tool to describe what is known and to suggest what needs further study.

Three major forms of memory are generally described: short-term, long-term, and sensory memory. Short-term memory represents the temporary retention of newly acquired information. Generally, short-term memory lasts no longer than about twenty seconds. This is useful for short-term tasks, such as the recall of speech during discussions or discourse with another person. Short-term memory is rapidly lost, sometimes referred to as a process of decaying. Alan Baddeley, a major researcher in the field of memory, has suggested a concept of "working memory" may be substituted for short-term. Repeat stimulation, or rehearsal, may transfer short-term memory into that of long-term.

Long-term memory involves storage of information over longer periods of time, potentially as long as the life of the individual. Some researchers into the subject consider long-term memory to include two major areas: episodic and semantic. Episodic memory addresses events that have a temporal relationship with a person's life. This may include recall of when events or information appeared. Semantic memory represents the concepts or skills, represented in part by learning, that people acquire through the course of their lives.

Sensory memories are those which can be retrieved as a result of sensory stimuli. For example, a particular odor may result in recall of events from the past. The unusual smell of a cleaning solution may cause recall of a college dormitory from years past. This form of recall has been called olfactory memory. The image of a flower may result in the memory of a teenage boyfriend. Such a visual stimulus is sometimes referred to as iconic memory.

Theories of memory have been important to psychology for a long time, often occupying the time and interest of researchers throughout their careers. Memory, which is always connected to learning, is defined as the mental process of preserving information acquired through the senses for later use. The cognitive approach to memory places emphasis on mental processes, which result in the ability to comprehend or recall what is learned. The basis is found in changes that occur in the regions of the brain, such as the hippocampus, associated with memory. In a sense, memory is the record of the experiences of a lifetime. Without it, a person could not reexperience the past; everything at every moment would be brand-new. A person could not even recognize the face of a loved one or learn from any experience. A person would thus have a greatly reduced chance for survival and would have no sense of personal identity. Memory is, in short, critical to functioning as a human being.

ASSOCIATIONISM, COGNITIVE THEORY, AND NEUROPSYCHOLOGY

The goal of a theory of memory is to explain the structures (hardware) and the processes (software) that make the system work. Explaining how such a complex system works is a massive undertaking. The attempts have taken the form of large-scale theories, which seek to deal with all major operations of the memory systems. The major theories of memory are associationism and theories from cognitive psychology and neuropsychology. The theories differ primarily in views of the retention and retrieval functions of memory. They also differ in terms of their conception of memory as active or passive.

Associationism, the oldest of the three, is the theory that memory relies on forming links or bonds between two unrelated things. This theory stems from the work of Hermann Ebbinghaus, who started the use of laboratory methods in the study of memory in the late nineteenth century. According to this theory, the ability to remember depends on establishing associations between stimuli and responses (S-R). Establishing associations depends on the frequency, recency, and saliency of their pairing. If these bonds become very strong, the subject is said to have developed a habit. Associationism also assumes the existence of internal stimuli that produce behavioral responses. These responses then become stimuli for other unobservable internal responses, thus forming chains. In this way, complex physical behaviors and mental associations can be achieved. Associationists tend to view the memory system as essentially passive, responding to environmental stimuli.

Cognitive theory emphasizes studying complex memory in the real world; it is concerned with the ecological validity of memory studies. Most of this work stems from the research of Sir Frederic C. Bartlett, who was not satisfied with laboratory emphasis on "artificial memory," but rather chose to study what he called meaningful memory. Meaningful memory, he said in his book *Remembering: A Study in Experimental and Social Psychology* (1932), is a person's effort to make sense of the world and to function effectively in it. Cognitive psychology recognizes subjective experiences as inescapably linked to human behavior. It centers on internal representation of past experiences and assumes that intentions, goals, and plans make a difference in what is remembered and how well it is remembered. The focus in memory research is on semantic memory—the knowledge of words, categories, concepts, and meanings located in long-term memory. People have highly complex networks of concepts, which

helps account for their behavior in the real world. These networks are called schemas. New experiences and new information are viewed in light of old schemas so that they are easier to remember. Cognitive theory emphasizes how the individual processes information, and it uses the computer as its working model of memory.

Neuropsychology has contributed the third major theory of memory. Although psychology has always recognized the connection between its concerns and those of biology and medicine, the technology now available has made neuropsychological analysis of brain structure and functioning possible. Karl Lashley was an early researcher who sought to find the location of memory in the brain. He ran rats through mazes until they had learned the correct pathway. His subsequent surgical operations on experimental rats' brains failed to show localization of memory.

The search for the memory trace, the physiological change that presumably occurs as a result of learning, continued with Donald Hebb, who had assisted Lashley. The brain consists of billions of nerve cells, which are connected to thousands of other neurons. Hebb measured the electrical activity of the brain during learning, and he discovered that nerve cells fire repeatedly. He was able to show that an incoming stimulus causes patterns of neurons to become active. These cell assemblies discovered by Hebb constitute a structure for the reverberating circuits, a set of neurons firing repeatedly when information enters short-term memory. This firing seems to echo the information until it is consolidated in long-term memory. Other researchers have found chemical and physical changes associated with the synapses and in the neurons themselves during learning and when the learning is consolidated into long-term memory. The discovery of the memory trace, a dream of researchers for a long time, may become a reality. Neuropsychology sees memory as a neural function controlled by electrical and chemical activity.

CLINICAL APPROACHES TO MEMORY DISORDERS

Human memory is so important to daily life that any theory that could explain its structures and processes and thus potentially improve its functioning would be invaluable. Memory is inextricably tied to learning, planning, reasoning, and problem solving; it lies at the core of human intelligence.

Although memory does decline with age, most older people experience only mild forgetfulness. (CLEO Photography)

None of the three theories is by itself sufficient to explain all the phenomena associated with memory. Over the years, a number of ideas have been developed in the attempt to improve memory functioning through passive means. Efforts to induce learning during sleep and to assess memory of patients for events taking place while under anesthesia have had mixed results, but on the whole have not succeeded. Memory enhancement through hypnosis has been attempted but has not been shown to be very effective or reliable. Pills to improve memory and thereby intelligence have been marketed but so far have not been shown to be the answer to memory problems. Research has begun on the possibility that certain drugs (such as tacrine) may interactively inhibit memory loss in people afflicted with certain kinds of dementia (for example, Alzheimer's disease). Work in neuropsychology has shown the influence of emotion-triggered hormonal changes in promoting the memory of exciting or shocking events (such as one's first kiss or an earthquake). This has led to an understanding of state-dependent memory: Things learned in a particular physical or emotional state are more easily remembered when the person is in that state again. This helps explain the difficulties in remembering events that took place when a person was intoxicated or depressed. In fact, heavy use of alcohol may result in significant memory loss. A person may not even remember having injured someone in a car accident. Although not fully researched, it may be that certain kinds of memory are mood-congruent. Perhaps memories of events that occurred when a person was in a certain mood may become available to the person only when that mood is again induced.

More active means for memory improvement have met with greater success. Associationist theory has demonstrated the value of the use of mnemonics, devices or procedures intentionally designed to facilitate encoding and subsequent recall. The use of rhymes, acronyms, pegwords, and the like enables people to recall factual information such as the number of days in each month ("Thirty days have September . . . "), the names of the Great Lakes (the acronym HOMES), and the colors of the visible spectrum (ROY G. BIV). Visual cues, such as tying a string around one's finger or knotting one's handkerchief, are traditional and effective ways to improve prospective memory. Cognitive psychology has demonstrated the importance of emotional factors—how and why something is learned—to the effectiveness of memory. It has provided the research base to demonstrate the effectiveness of study strategies such as the SQ3R (survey, question, read, recite, review) technique. Cognitive theory has also shown that metamemory, a person's knowledge about how his or her memory works, may be important for the improvement of memory.

In clinical settings, much research has been concerned with memory impairment as a means to test the applicability of theories of memory. Head injuries are a common cause of amnesia in which events immediately prior to an accident cannot be recalled. Damage to the hippocampus, a part of the brain that is vital to memory, breaks down the transfer of information from short-term to long-term memory. One dramatic case concerns "H. M.," a patient who had brain surgery to control epileptic seizures. After surgery, H. M.'s short-term memory was intact, but if he was momentarily distracted from a task, he could not remember anything about what he had just been doing. The information was never transferred to long-term memory. Such patients still remember information that was stored in long-term memory before their operation, but to them everyday experiences are always strangely new. They can read the same paragraph over and over, but each time the material will be brand-new. In H. M.'s case, it was discovered that his intelligence as measured by standardized tests actually improved, yet he was continually disoriented and unable to learn even the simplest new associations. Intelligence tests are made to measure general information, vocabulary, and grammatical associations; these things were stored in H. M.'s long-term memory and were apparently not affected by brain surgery. In cases less dramatic than H. M.'s, damage to particular areas of the brain can still have devastating effects on the memory. Damage can be caused by accidents, violent sports activity, strokes, tumors, and alcoholism. Alzheimer's disease is another area to which research findings on memory may be applied. In this fatal disease a patient's forgetfulness increases from normal forgetting to the point that the patient cannot remember how to communicate, cannot recognize loved ones, and cannot care for his or her own safety needs.

Associationism, cognitive psychology, and neuropsychology can each explain some of the structures and processes involved in these and other real-world problems, but it seems as though none of the theories is sufficient by itself. Memory is such a complex phenomenon that it takes all the large-scale theories and a number of smaller-scale ones to comprehend it. The truth probably is that the theories are not mutually exclusive, but rather are complementary to one another.

Physiological Basis of Memory

Theories of learning and memory have been of great concern to philosophers and psychologists for a long time. They have formed a major part of the history of psychology. Each of the theories has been ascendant for a time, but the nature of theory building requires new conceptions to compensate for perceived weaknesses in currently accepted theories and models. Associationism was the principal theory of memory of stimulus-response psychology, which was dominant in the United States until the mid-1950's. Cognitive psychology evolved from Gestalt psychol-

ogy, from Jean Piaget's work on developmental psychology, and from information-processing theory associated with the computer, and was extremely important during the 1970's and 1980's. Neuropsychology developed concurrently with advanced technology that permits microanalysis of brain functioning. It has resulted in an explosion of knowledge about how the brain and its systems operate.

Formation of memory seems to involve two individual events. Short-term memory develops first. Repeated rehearsal transfers this form of memory into long-term storage. At one time, it was believed both these forms of memory involved similar events in the brain. However, experimental models have shown such a theory to be incorrect. Two experimental approaches have addressed this issue: the separation of memory formation involving "accidental" or intentional interference with brain function, and development of an animal model for the study of memory.

Electroshock treatment of depression in humans has been shown to interfere with short-term memory formation. However, these persons are still perfectly able to recall the memory of earlier events stored within long-term memory. Accidental damage to temporal lobes of the brain does not appear to interfere with short-term memory, but may inhibit the ability to recall events from the past.

The experimental use of an animal model in the study of memory formation was developed by Eric Kandel at Columbia University. Kandel has utilized the sea slug *Aplysia* in his study of memory. The advantage of such a model is its simplicity—instead of approximately one trillion neurons which make up the nervous system of humans, *Aplysia* contains a "mere" twenty thousand.

Using a variety of stimuli on the animal, and observing its response, Kandel has shown that the physiological basis for short-term memory differs from that of long-term. Specifically, short-term memory involves stimulus to only a small number of individual neurons. Long-term memory involves *de novo* (new) protein synthesis in the affected cells, and formation of extensive neural circuits. Kandel was awarded the Nobel Prize in Physiology or Medicine in 2000 for this work.

Memory Retrieval

The basis for memory recall remains an active area of study. Memory retrieval can be of two types: recognition and recall. In recognition, the individual is presented with information that had been previously learned. The subject remembers he or she has already observed or learned that information. In effect, it is analogous to seeing a movie or book for the second time. In recall, information is reproduced from memory, as in response to a question. The physiological basis for retrieval probably involves the activation of regions of the brain which were involved in the initial encoding.

SOURCES FOR FURTHER STUDY

Baddeley, Alan D. *Human Memory: Theory and Practice.* Upper Saddle River, N.J.: Prentice Hall, 1997. Updated edition of a classic text. The original emphasis on history of memory research continues, along with experimental views of consciousness and implicit memory.

Collins, Alan, ed. *Theories of Memory.* Mahwah, N.J.: Lawrence Erlbaum, 1993. Emphasis of the book is on research into theories of memory, particularly that of a cognitive approach. Various explanations are presented.

Hunt, R. Reed, and Henry Ellis. *Fundamentals of Cognitive Psychology.* 6th ed. Columbus, Ohio: McGraw-Hill, 1998. The authors approach the role of cognitive psychology in memory using an experimental problem-solving approach. Updated theories explaining both long-term and short-term memory, as well as retrieval, are included.

Kandel, Eric. "The Molecular Biology of Memory Storage: A Dialogue Between Genes and Synapses." *Science* 294 (2001): 1030-1038. A summary of the Nobel Prize-winning research into the physiological basis of memory. The author provides an experimental approach in differentiating short-term and long-term memory at the molecular level. The article requires some knowledge of neural function.

Neisser, Ulric. *Cognition and Reality: Principles and Implications of Cognitive Psychology.* San Francisco: W. H. Freeman, 1981. This book marked the acceptance of cognitive psychology as a major component within the approach to the study and understanding of memory. The major goals of the approach are described. Many of the author's suggestions as to an experimental approach using real-world models have been applied in subsequent years.

Norman, Donald A. *The Psychology of Everyday Things.* Cambridge, Mass.: Perseus, 1988. An older text, but remains an enjoyable approach to the subject. The author emphasizes the cognitive approach in dealing with problems. Topics include recognition of both good and bad design, as well as ways to improve design based upon psychology of the consumer.

Nyberg, Lars, et al. "Reactivation of Encoding-Related Brain Activity During Memory Retrieval." *Proceedings of the National Academy of Sciences of the United States of America* 97 (September 26, 2000): 11,120-11,124. Description of positron-emission tomography (PET) studies which monitor brain activity during memory recall. The authors demonstrate, through linkage of visual and auditory recall, that recall involves regions of the brain initially involved in memory formation.

R. G. Gaddis;
updated by Richard Adler

SEE ALSO: Artificial intelligence; Brain structure; Concept formation; Encoding; Forgetting and forgetfulness; Kinesthetic memory; Long-term memory; Memory: Animal research; Memory: Empirical studies; Memory: Physiology; Memory: Sensory; Memory storage; Short-term memory.

Memory
Animal research

TYPE OF PSYCHOLOGY: Biological bases of behavior; memory
FIELDS OF STUDY: Biological influences on learning; nervous system; Pavlovian conditioning

Research with nonhuman animals has significantly contributed to an understanding of the basic processes of memory, including its anatomy and physiology. Important brain regions, neurotransmitters, and genes have been identified and this information is now being used to further understand and treat human memory disorders.

KEY CONCEPTS
- anterograde amnesia
- engram
- experimental brain damage

- genetic engineering
- hippocampus
- prefrontal cortex
- retrograde amnesia
- stroke

INTRODUCTION

Nonhuman animals have been used as subjects in memory research since the earliest days of psychology, and much of what is known about the fundamental processes of memory is largely based on work with animals. Rats, mice, pigeons, rabbits, monkeys, sea slugs, flatworms, and fruit flies are among the most commonly used species. The widespread use of animals in memory research can be attributed to the ability systematically to manipulate and control their environments under strict laboratory conditions and to use procedures and invasive techniques, such as surgery and drugs, that cannot ethically be used with humans. A typical research protocol involves training animals on any of a variety of learning paradigms and concurrently measuring or manipulating some aspect of the nervous system to examine its relationship to memory.

Although learning is closely related, a distinction should be drawn between learning and memory. Learning is defined as a relatively permanent change in behavior as a result of experience. Memory is the underlying process by which information is encoded, stored, and retrieved by the nervous system. Contemporary learning and memory paradigms are based on the principles of classical and operant conditioning first established by the early behaviorists: Ivan Pavlov, Edward L. Thorndike, John B. Watson, and B. F. Skinner. These learning paradigms can be used to examine different types of memory and to explore the underlying brain mechanisms that may mediate them. For classical conditioning, widely used paradigms include eyeblink conditioning, taste aversion learning, and fear conditioning. For operant conditioning, memory for objects, spatial memory, context discrimination, and maze learning are among the most frequently used procedures. Two other very simple forms of learning, habituation, the gradual decrease in response to a stimulus as a result of repeated exposure to it, and sensitization, the gradual increase in response to a stimulus after repeated exposure to it, are both simple forms of nonassociative learning also extensively used in animal memory research.

Researchers have at their disposal a number of techniques that allow them to manipulate the nervous system and assess it functions. Historically, experimental brain damage has been one of the most widely utilized procedures. This technique involves surgically destroying (known as lesioning) various parts of the brain and assessing the effects of the lesion on memory processes. Pharmacological manipulations are also frequently used and involve administering a drug known to affect a specific neurotransmitter or hormonal system thought to play a role in memory. Functional studies involve measuring brain activity while an animal is actually engaged in learning. Recordings can be made from individual brain cells (neurons), groups of neurons, or entire anatomical regions. Beginning in the late 1990's, genetic engineering began to be applied to the study of animal memory. These procedures involve the direct manipulation of genes that produce proteins suspected to be important for memory.

By combining a wide variety of memory paradigms with an increasing number of ways to manipulate and/or measure the nervous system, animal research has been extremely useful in addressing several fundamental questions about memory, including the important brain structures involved in memory, the manner in which information is stored in the nervous system, and the causes and potential treatments for human memory disorders.

THE ANATOMY OF MEMORY

One of the first questions about memory to be addressed using animals was its relationship to the underlying structure of the nervous system. American psychologist Karl Lashley (1890-1958) was an early pioneer in this field; his main interest was in finding what was then referred to as the engram, the physical location in the brain where memories are stored. Lashley trained rats on a variety of tasks, such as the ability to learn mazes or perform simple discriminations, and then lesioned various parts of the cerebral cortex (the convoluted outer covering of the brain) in an attempt to erase the memory trace. Despite years of effort, he found that he could not completely abolish a memory no matter what part of the cortex he lesioned. Lashley summed up his puzzlement and frustration at these findings in this now well-known quote, "I sometimes feel, in reviewing the evidence on the localization of the engram, that the necessary conclusion is that learning just is not possible."

While the specific location of the brain lesion did not appear important, Lashley found that the total amount of brain tissue removed was critical. When large lesions were produced, as compared to smaller ones, he found that memories could be abolished, regardless of the location in the cortex where they were made. This led Lashley to propose the concepts of mass action and equipotentiality, which state that the cortex works as a whole and that all parts contribute equally to complex behaviors.

Further research has generally supported Lashley's original conclusions about the localization of the engram. However, better memory tests and more sophisticated techniques for inducing brain damage have revealed that certain brain regions are more involved in memory than others, and that different brain regions are actually responsible for different types of memory. For example, classical conditioning, which is the modification of a reflex through learning, appears primarily to involve the brain stem and/or cerebellum, which are two evolutionarily old brain structures. Specific circuitry within these structures that underlies a number of forms of classical conditioning has been identified.

In the rabbit, a puff of air blown into the eye produces a reflexive blinking response. When researchers repeatedly pair the air puff with a tone, the tone itself will eventually come to elicit the response. The memory for this response involves a very specific circuit of neurons, primarily in the cerebellum. Once the response is well learned, it can be abolished by lesions in this circuit. Importantly, these lesions do not affect other forms of memory. Similarly, taste aversion learning, a process by which animals learn not to consume a food or liquid that has previously made them ill, has been shown to be mediated by a very specific circuit in the brain stem, specifically the pons and medulla. Animals with lesions to the nucleus of the solitary tract, a portion of this circuit in the medulla where taste, olfactory, and illness-related information converge, will not readily learn taste aversions.

More complex forms of learning and memory have been shown to involve more recently evolved brain structures. Many of these are located in either the cortex or the limbic system, an area of the brain located between the newer cortex and the older brain stem. One component of the limbic system believed to be heavily involved in memory is the hippocampus. One of its primary functions appears to be spatial memory. Rats and monkeys with damage limited to the hippocampus are impaired in maze learning and locating objects in space but have normal memory for nonspatial tasks. Additionally, animals that require spatial navigation for their survival, such as homing pigeons and food-storing rodents (which must remember the location of the food that they have stored) have disproportionately large hippocampi. Moreover, damage to the hippocampus in these species leads to a disruption in their ability to navigate and find stored food, respectively.

One area of the cortex that has been shown to be involved in memory is the prefrontal cortex. This area has been implicated in short-term memory, which is the ability to temporarily hold a mental representation of an object or event. Monkeys and rats that received lesions to the prefrontal cortex were impaired in learning tasks that required them to remember briefly the location of an object or to learn tasks that require them to switch back and forth between strategies for solving the task. Studies involving the measurement of brain function have also demonstrated that this area of the brain is active during periods when animals are thought to be holding information in short-term memory.

While experimental brain damage has been one of the predominant techniques used to study structure/function relationships in the nervous system, difficulty in interpretation, an increased concern for animal welfare, and the advent of more sophisticated physiological and molecular techniques have led to an overall decline in their use.

THE MOLECULES OF MEMORY

While lesion studies have been useful in determining the brain structures involved in memory, pharmacological techniques have been used to address its underlying chemistry. Pharmacological manipulations have a long history in memory research with animals, dating back to the early 1900's and the discovery of neurotransmitters. Neurotransmitters are chemical messengers secreted by neurons and are essential to communication within the nervous system. Each neurotransmitter, of which there are over one hundred, has its own specific receptor to which it can attach and alter cellular functioning. By administering drugs that either increase or decrease the activity of specific neurotransmitters, researchers have been able to investigate their role in memory formation.

One neurotransmitter that has been strongly implicated in memory is glutamate. This transmitter is found throughout the brain but is most highly concentrated in the cerebral cortex and the hippocampus. Drugs that increase the activity of glutamate facilitate learning and improve memory, while drugs that reduce glutamate activity have the opposite effect. The neurotransmitter dopamine has also been implicated in memory formation. In small doses, drugs such as cocaine and amphetamine, which increase dopamine activity, have been found to improve memory in both lower animals and humans. Moderate doses of caffeine can also facilitate memory storage, albeit by a less well understood mechanism. Other neurotransmitters believed to be involved in memory include acetylcholine, serotonin, norepinephrine, and the endorphins.

Research with simpler organisms has been directed at understanding the chemical events at the molecular level that may be involved in memory. One animal in particular, the marine invertebrate *Aplysia californica*, has played a pivotal role in this research. *Aplysia* have very simple nervous systems with large, easily identifiable neurons and are capable of many forms of learning, including habituation, sensitization, and classical conditioning. Canadian psychologist Donald Hebb (1904-1985), a former student of Lashley, proposed that memories are stored in the nervous system as a result of the strengthening of connections between neurons as a result of their repeated activation during learning. With the *Aplysia*, it is possible indirectly to observe and manipulate the connections between neurons while learning is taking place. Eric Kandel of Columbia University has used the *Aplysia* as a model system to study the molecular biology of memory for more than thirty years. He demonstrated that when a short-term memory is formed in the *Aplysia*, the connections between the neurons involved in the learning process are strengthened by gradually coming to release more neurotransmitters, particularly serotonin. When long-term memories are formed, new connections between nerve cells actually grow. With repeated disuse, these processes appear to reverse themselves. Kandel's work has suggested that memory (what Lashley referred to as the engram) is represented in the nervous system in the form of a chemical and/or structural change, depending on the nature and duration of the memory itself. For these discoveries, Kandel was awarded the Nobel Prize in 2000.

Modern genetic engineering techniques have made it possible to address the molecular biology of memory in higher mammals (predominantly mice) as well as invertebrates. Two related techniques, genetic knockouts and transgenics, have been applied to the problem. Genetic knockouts involve removing, or "knocking out," a gene that produces a specific protein thought to be involved in memory. Frequently targeted genes include those for neurotransmitters or their receptors. Transgenics involves the insertion of a new gene into the genome of an organism with the goal of either overproducing a specific protein or inserting a completely foreign protein into the animal. Neurotransmitters and their receptors are again the most frequently targeted sites. A remarkable number of knockout mice have been produced with a variety of short- and long-term memory deficits. In many ways, this technique is analogous to those used in earlier brain lesion studies but is applied at the molecular level. Dopamine, serotonin, glutamate, and acetylcholine systems have all been implicated in memory formation as a result of genetic knockout studies. Significantly, researchers have also been able to improve memory in mice through genetic engineering. Transgenic mice that overproduce glutamate receptors actually learn mazes faster and have better retention than normal mice. It is hoped that in the future gene therapy for human memory disorders may be developed based on this technique.

ANIMAL MODELS OF HUMAN MEMORY DISORDERS

Animal research has many practical applications to the study and treatment of human memory dysfunction. Many types of neurological disorder and brain damage can produce memory impairments in humans, and it has been possible to model some of these in animals. The first successful attempt at this was production of an animal model of brain-damaged-induced amnesia. It had been known since the 1950's that damage to the temporal lobes, as a result of disease, traumatic injury, epilepsy, or infection, could produce a disorder known as anterograde amnesia, which is the inability to form new long-term memories. This is in contrast to the more well-known retrograde amnesia, which is an inability to remember previously stored information. Beginning in the late 1970's, work with monkeys, and later rats, began to identify the critical temporal lobe structures that, when damaged, produce anterograde amnesia. These structures include the hippocampus and, perhaps more important, the adjacent, overlying cortex, which is known as the rhinal cortex. As a result of this work, this brain region is now believed to be critical in the formation of new long-term memories.

Memory disorders also frequently develop after an interruption of oxygen flow to the brain (known as hypoxia), which can be caused by events such as stroke, cardiac arrest, or carbon monoxide poisoning. There are a variety of animal models of stroke and resultant memory disorders. Significantly, oxygen deprivation produces brain damage that is most severe in the temporal lobe, particularly the hippocampus and the rhinal cortex. Using animal models, the mechanisms underlying hypoxic injury have been investigated, and potential therapeutic drugs designed to minimize the brain damage and lessen the memory impairments have been tested. One potentially damaging event that has been identified is a massive influx of calcium into neurons during a hypoxic episode. This has led to the development of calcium blockers and their widespread utilization in the clinical treatment of complications arising from stroke.

Alzheimer's disease is probably the most well-known human memory disorder. It is characterized by gradual memory loss over a period of five to fifteen years. It typically begins as a mild forgetfulness and progresses to anterograde amnesia, retrograde amnesia, and eventually complete cognitive dysfunction and physical incapacitation. One pathological event that has been implicated in the development of Alzheimer's disease is the overproduction of a protein known as the amyloid-beta protein. The normal biological function of this protein is not known, but at high levels it appears to be toxic to neurons. Amyloid-beta deposits are most pronounced and develop first in the temporal and frontal lobes, a fact that corresponds well with the memory functions ascribed to these areas and the types of deficits seen in people with Alzheimer's disease. The development of an animal model has marked a major milestone in understanding the disorder and developing a potential treatment. Mice have been genetically engineered to overproduce the amyloid-beta protein. As a result, they develop patterns of brain damage and memory deficits similar to humans with Alzheimer's disease. The development of the Alzheimer's mouse has allowed for a comprehensive investigation of the genetics of the disorder well as providing a model on which to test potential therapeutic treatments. Limited success for potential treatments has been obtained with an experimental vaccine in animals. This vaccine has been shown to reduce both brain damage and memory deficits. As with most experimental drugs, application to the treatment of human Alzheimer's disease is many years away.

Sources for Further Study

Anagnostopoulos, Anna V., Larry E. Mobraaten, John J. Sharp, and Muriel T. Davisson. "Transgenic and Knockout Databases: Behavioral Profiles of Mouse Mutants." *Physiology and Behavior* 73 (2001): 675-689. A summary of an ongoing project to construct a database of genetically engineered mice designed to facilitate the dissemination of findings among researchers. The article contains an exhaustive reference section on mutant mice and their behavioral and physiological profiles.

Cohen, Neil J., and Howard Eichenbaum. *Memory, Amnesia, and the Hippocampal System.* Cambridge, Mass.: MIT Press, 1993. A discussion of memory impairments resulting from damage the hippocampus and adjacent brain regions.

Duva, Christopher A., Thomas J. Kornecook, and John P. J. Pinel. "Animal Models of Medial Temporal Lobe Amnesia: The Myth of the Hippocampus." In *Animal Models of Human Emotion and Cognition,* edited by Mark Haug and Richard E Whalen. Washington, D.C.: American Psychological Association, 1999. A critical evaluation of the role of the hippocampus in memory for objects. The article includes a historical description of human amnesia and attempts to model it in monkeys and rats.

Kiefer, Steven W. "Neural Mediation of Conditioned Food Aversions." *Annals of the New York Academy of Sciences* 443 (1985): 100-109. A comprehensive review of the brain areas and neural systems involved in food aversion learning.

Martinez, Joe L., and Raymond P. Kesner. *Neurobiology of Learning and Memory.* New York: Academic Press, 1998. An overview of information on the neurobiology of learning and memory from developmental, pharmacological, and psychobiological perspectives. A good introductory level source.

Morgan, Dave, et al. "A Peptide Vaccination Prevents Memory Loss in an Animal Model of Alzheimer's Disease." *Nature* 408 (2000): 982-985. This original research report describes a successful attempt to vaccinate mice that had been genetically engineered to develop Alzheimer's disease against the disorder and prevent memory loss.

Squire, Larry R., and Eric Kandel. *Memory: From Mind to Molecules.* New York: Scientific American Library, 1999. An approachable volume summarizing the major developments in understanding the anatomy and physiology of vertebrate and invertebrate learning. This text contains an extensive discussion of Kandel's work with the molecular biology of memory in *Aplysia* and Squires's work on the neuroanatomy of memory with monkeys. An excellent source for people with a limited background in biology and chemistry.

Tang, Ya-Ping, et al. "Genetic Enhancement of Learning and Memory in Mice." *Nature* 401 (1999): 63-69. An original research report that describes how memory was improved in a strain of mice by genetically engineering them to contain an overabundance of glutamate receptors in the hippocampus.

Thompson, Richard F. "The Neurobiology of Learning and Memory." *Science* 233, no. 13 (1986): 941-947. The author summarizes his work on the brain mechanisms involved in classical conditioning of the eyeblink reflex in rabbits.

Tulving, Endel, and Fergus I. M. Craik. *The Oxford Handbook of Memory.* New York: Oxford University Press, 2000. A comprehensive volume dealing with a wide variety of topics related to both animal and human memory. An excellent general reference source.

Christopher A. Duva

SEE ALSO: Animal experimentation; Artificial intelligence; Brain structure; Concept formation; Encoding; Forgetting and forgetfulness; Habituation and sensitization; Kinesthetic memory; Long-term memory; Memory: Empirical studies; Memory: Physiology; Memory: Sensory; Memory storage; Short-term memory.

Memory
Empirical studies

TYPE OF PSYCHOLOGY: Memory
FIELDS OF STUDY: Cognitive processes; general issues in intelligence

Researchers have investigated a variety of experimental variables in order to understand better the structure of the memory storage system and the processes of remembering and forgetting. Key variables studied include the type of materials to be remembered, such as words, sentences, or pictures; the order of presentation; and the order of recall.

KEY CONCEPTS
- episodic memory
- long-term memory
- recall
- recognition
- rehearsal
- semantic memory
- sensory memory
- short-term memory

INTRODUCTION
A number of testing procedures have been devised to determine how much a person can remember. Much information about short-term memory has been obtained through a set of recall tasks in which the subject is presented with items to be recalled. Basically, the short-term memory system is of limited capacity; information is maintained by continued attention and rehearsal (the repetition of memory items). The information in short-term memory may be lost through displacement by incoming information or lost through decay with time; information in short-term memory can also be transferred to long-term memory. The experimental design can be modified to examine different aspects of short-term memory.

RECALL AND RECOGNITION TESTS
In the free recall technique, subjects are presented with items at a fixed rate of presentation; several trials take place, in which the order of presentation is randomized. Recall refers to the retrieval of information from memory, with or without clues.

The important feature of free recall is that subjects are allowed to remember the items in whatever order they wish. In ordered recall tasks, the subjects can report the items in any order, but they must also identify the position of their presentation. The oldest of all the techniques that involve learning a list of items is serial recall, or serial learning. In serial learning, the subject is shown one word from a list at a time, for a limited amount of time, such as two seconds per word. The second time that the list is presented, it is presented one word at a time, and the subject's task is to remember the upcoming word in the series. In some experimental procedures, the list is repeated until the subject can accurately remember every item. In others, the list is presented a fixed number of times.

In probe recall tasks, by comparison, the subject is required to recall particular elements in a sequence of items. A common example of this is the paired-associate technique of list learning, in which subjects are shown pairs of items. The first item in the pair is called the stimulus, and the second is called the response. Recall is tested by showing the stimulus item only, requiring the subject to remember the response. The paired-associate and serial learning techniques both allow the experimenter to have considerable control, in that subjects have only one possible correct response, a limited time in which to make it, and a specific cue to aid in recall.

In another variation of list learning, called distractor recall, a subject is presented with a set of stimulus items, one item at a time. Each item is presented for a fixed period of time. Once each item has been presented a single time, a short period may follow during which the subject is asked to do an irrelevant task. The purpose of the irrelevant task is to create a delay between presentation of the stimulus items and the test in order to minimize the subject's mental repetition of the items. One such task would be to require the subject to count backward, such as by threes (986, 983, 980, and so on), from a predetermined starting point. Finally, the subject is given a test to determine how many of the original items are remembered.

In general, it is more difficult to test recognition than to test recall. Recall, at least when lists of words are used, is easily scored. When recognition (noticing that information is familiar) is tested, however, the old items must be mixed with new items so that the subjects can indicate which they have seen before. One method of testing recognition is to present the old item with one or more new items and require the subject to select one which he or she believes to be the old item. In such tests, the proportion of items correctly identified as having been seen before decreases as the number of alternatives increases. Accuracy also decreases if the alternatives are similar to the originally presented items. Even when recall is perfect, the time required to produce a response varies. Latency in giving a response can also provide information about the memory processes when performance is close to perfect, making the amount recalled an inappropriate measure. Even when recall is less than perfect, time latencies can reveal underlying differences in memory processes.

TESTING LONG-TERM MEMORY

Experimental tests have also been designed to study long-term memory. Long-term memory refers to the storage area that holds permanent memories and is unlimited in capacity. There is overlap between short-term memory and long-term memory, so a test that requires subjects to recall a list of words will include an assessment of both short-term and long-term memory. For example, words at the end of the list will be in short-term storage, while words at the beginning of the list might have entered long-term storage. Two major forms of long-term memory are episodic memory and semantic memory. Episodic memory involves information about where and when some event occurred. In contrast, semantic memory contains stores of words and coded categorical information.

Researchers seeking to determine the characteristics of long-term memory present subjects with tasks that require decisions about the meaning of words. In a semantic decision task, the subject is asked to decide whether the word is a member of a particular category; the phrase "Tigers are felines" might be presented, and the subject would be asked for a true/false decision. In a lexical decision task, the subject decides whether a string of letters forms a word.

MEMORY ORGANIZATION RESEARCH

A number of studies have been described that are concerned with short-term and long-term memory. Memory research has also included diverse studies of the effects of prior activities, everyday activities, sensory modalities, perfect memories, pathological memory losses (caused by surgery, amnesia, or drug usage), and old age on memory.

Memory experiments have been conducted using materials such as cards, pencils, paper, and stopwatches. More complex techniques control the speed of presentation with computers programmed to present material visually or verbally; there are appropriate response-recording keys for voice response or finger press, which analyze the recall correctness as well as the speed of response. Experiments on memory have been conducted with animals, such as pigeons, rats, and primates, as well as with humans.

Laboratory studies of long-term memory organization are of particular interest for real-world applications. Many of these studies use categorized lists of words. The lists often consist of words from the same natural category, such as dog, cat, horse, and sheep from the category "animal." A list might contain forty words with eight words from five categories. Subjects remember categorized lists better than uncategorized ones. Categorized lists are also remembered better when they are presented in blocks rather than when presented randomly. Blocked presentation refers to the fact that all items from a particular category are presented one after another, and then items from another category are presented. In comparison, with random presentation, the items from different categories are completely mixed in the presentation order. Blocked presentation is much more organized than random presentation is. The superior memory for blocked presentation suggests the important role that organization plays in memory.

A further indication of the importance of organization is the finding that people actively rearrange randomly presented lists. That is, even though items from various categories are presented in random order, subjects tend to group the items into their appropriate categories at recall. That is, the items are recalled by category in spite of having been presented randomly. Examining the order of recall led researchers to the realization that learning and memory are influenced by the active strategies of the subject and by the properties of the learning material that allow organization to take place. When the lists consist of a set of items from a limited number of semantic categories (for example, marine animals and means of transportation) scattered throughout the list, words from each category tend to be recalled together. A number of researchers in

cognitive psychology have used these principles for real-world applications. For example, knowing that people tend to recall information in these ways, educators who write textbooks can organize information in ways that will enhance the human memory system. In addition, understanding human memory helps human-factors psychologists devise techniques for the display of information on computer screens (computer interfaces) that make computer presentations more compatible with the way people learn and remember. Furthermore, in this technological age, people commonly need to search through large amounts of information to find what they are seeking. Utilizing what is known about memory, psychologists are working to devise systems for searching large databases, such as computerized card catalogs in libraries, that work in conjunction with the way people search their own memories.

The importance of the relationships among separate elements has also been illustrated with nonverbal materials. It has been shown, for example, that simple line drawings of parts of the face are difficult to recognize when presented separately. The same drawings, however, are quickly recognized when presented in the context of a face. Additional information is provided by the context—the face, in this case—which aids the recognition of each separate element. Organization in the form of relationships among elements is important to the process of storing information in memory. This research has applications in the area of artificial intelligence. It is helping scientists to program computers to recognize human handwriting, fingerprints, and other complex stimuli.

BIOLOGICAL ASPECTS OF MEMORY

Studies on memory that are of a biological nature have also helped psychologists who are concerned with determining how specific parts of the brain are related to the processes underlying the various types of memory. For example, both external and internal stimuli are perceived by an organism as experiences. The organism converts these experiences to a form that the nervous system can understand; they must be stored in an electrical or molecular form in the brain. An understanding of the biological processes involved has helped psychologists devise tests that are used to assess memory deficits. A memory deficit might be caused by a head injury, tumor, or disease such as Alzheimer's disease. Researchers continue to search for clues that will help people with memory deficits in order to overcome those deficits by means of drug therapy or surgical repair.

EVOLUTION OF RESEARCH

Plato thought of memory as something like a block of wax. Aristotle considered the heart to be of primary importance in the memory process. Other ancient Greeks argued that the brain was the seat of memory. Although thinkers have been interested in memory for thousands of years, it was not studied experimentally until fairly recently. Research on human memory was greatly influenced by the work of European psychologists more than a century ago.

The first controlled experiments on memory were conducted in Europe by Hermann Ebbinghaus in 1885. Ebbinghaus was engrossed in finding out how much verbal material that was well learned would be saved by his own memory over a period of time. He served as his own subject. The number of trials required to relearn a list, compared to the time to learn either a new list or the list when it was first acquired, provided a measure of the saving in learning. This experimental method has rarely been used since his time.

In 1890, William James, an American, included a chapter on memory in his renowned book on psychology. Frederic C. Bartlett, in 1932, began a tradition of studying how memories change over time. After Bartlett's time, the primary experimental strategy became to have subjects learn lists of items, such as nonsense syllables, nouns, or adjectives. The concentration on list learning comes from the early theoretical background, which assumed that memory was built from associations. Behaviorists, such as B. F. Skinner, elaborated on memory as one of many parameters involved in learning; they treated the learning process as the association of responses to stimuli. Repeated exposure to stimuli and responses could strengthen the association between them; forgetting was thought to be a weakened association.

Since the advent of the information-processing approach in psychology in the 1960's, a large number of theories and models of memory have been proposed, including the dual-process theory, the levels-of-processing theory, the neurobiological two-phase model, and the neurobiological four-phase model. The experiments that have been conducted on memory have emerged from these unique theoretical approaches. No matter what the theoretical approach, a constant problem facing the psychologist who studies memory is the need to conduct tests using situations that are similar enough to daily life that the results can be generalized beyond the laboratory, while allowing enough control to be maintained that scoring can accurately show the effect of the experimental variables.

SOURCES FOR FURTHER STUDY

Baddeley, Alan. *Human Memory: Theory and Practice.* Rev. ed. Boston: Allyn & Bacon, 1997. A very readable summary of cognitive psychological approaches to memory. Very up-to-date, with good references.

Cowan, Nelson. *Attention and Memory: An Integrated Framework.* New York: Oxford University Press, 1998. Integrates information-processing and parallel/connectionist models of memory with studies of physical brain function.

Lachman, Roy, Janet L. Lachman, and Earl C. Butterfield. *Cognitive Psychology and Information Processing: An Introduction.* Hillsdale, N.J.: Lawrence Erlbaum, 1979. A comprehensive book that discusses human memory at length. In addition, it provides an overall view of cognitive psychology and describes how the various subareas fit together. Although somewhat outdated, it is a classic book, still in print.

Neath, Ian. *Human Memory: An Introduction to Research, Data, and Theory.* Belmont, Calif.: Wadsworth, 1997. An up-to-date undergraduate textbook. Describes experimental procedures and theories; covers historical development of the understanding of memory as well as current approaches.

Tulving, Endel, and Fergus I. M. Craik, eds. *The Oxford Handbook of Memory.* New York: Oxford University Press, 2000. Summarizes memory research from the 1980's and 1990's, especially brain scanning and behavioral studies. A very complete overview of the current state of the field.

Deborah R. McDonald

SEE ALSO: Artificial intelligence; Brain structure; Concept formation; Encoding; Forgetting and forgetfulness; Kinesthetic memory; Long-term memory; Memory; Memory: Animal research; Memory: Physiology; Memory Sensory; Memory: storage; Short-term memory.

Memory

Physiology

Type of psychology: Biological bases of behavior
Fields of study: Biological influences on learning; nervous system; organic disorders

In the early 1990's, scientists developed a better understanding of the molecular basis of memory. Specific genes conserved through evolution allowed for analysis at the level of the gene in determining which proteins are involved in memory formation. Application of this information has resulted in better means of earlier detection of memory dysfunction, as well as improved treatments.

Key concepts
- consolidation
- dendrite
- electroencephalography
- evoked potential
- hippocampus
- lesion
- neuron
- neurotransmitter
- synapse

Introduction

Investigations of the biological basis of memory have proceeded simultaneously at many different levels: individual neurons and synapses, systems of neurons, whole brains, and whole behaving organisms. Isolated cells, slabs of brain tissue, live invertebrates (such as sea slugs), nonhuman vertebrates (often rats), and even awake human patients have been studied. Several strategies have been used to reveal the location of and mechanisms underlying the engram, or memory trace. In one approach, after an animal subject has learned a task very well, lesions are made in specific regions of the brain. If only memory of the task is impaired, the damaged structure is implicated in the memory process.

Trauma, stroke, disease, and even deliberate surgery may produce "natural" lesions in human patients. Resultant amnesia, or memory loss, can be correlated with the damaged structures using magnetic resonance imaging (MRI), positron emission tomography (PET), computed tomography (CT), and other scanning techniques, and with behavioral performance on standardized psychological and neuropsychological tests.

Another approach is to record changes in the nervous system that occur at the same time as a memory process. If such changes occur only when memory is formed, then they may play a role in the process. Such functional changes in the human (and animal) brain may be seen using single-cell or multicell electrophysiology, electroencephalography, and evoked-potential electrical recording techniques. Researchers have studied memory formation by looking at the chemical composition of the brain (for example, neurotransmitters and protein synthesis).

Finally, various techniques may be used to disrupt the memory formation (consolidation) process shortly before or after a subject has learned a task (that is, started to develop permanent memories). Successful disruption may point to the underlying nature of the process. For example, formation of permanent memories can be prevented by giving direct electrical stimulation to the amygdala (a specific brain area associated with emotion and motivation) or enhanced by stimulation of the reticular formation (associated with alertness and waking), suggesting different roles for these areas.

Neuropsychology, a specialty combining clinical neurology and behavioral analysis, has used both "natural" and experimental lesion techniques to explore memory processes. According to some researchers, for the purposes of neuropsychological analysis, memory should be divided into two categories: declarative and procedural. Declarative memories are facts that one can consciously recollect, while procedural memories are skills or operations that one does not have to think about consciously and that are not linked to a particular time or place. Brain damage does not usually impair procedural knowledge. Global permanent anterograde amnesia (inability to form new permanent memories) and temporary retrograde amnesia (inability to remember past events) for declarative knowledge, however, have been correlated consistently with bilateral (left and right side) lesions of both cortical (the highest and most newly evolved) and subcortical (the lower and older) regions of the brain. Memory problems of chronic alcoholics (Korsakoff's syndrome), demented patients (Alzheimer's disease), and patients with some strokes and aneurysms have all been associated with damage to these areas.

Long-term memory deficits produced by temporal cortex lesions (lesions of the lateral brain area) depend on the type of material that is presented: Left lesions interfere with verbal material, while right lesions interfere with nonverbal material. It does not matter by what sensory modality the material was presented or what modality was used to test for its retention. By contrast, lesions of the frontal cortex (the largest and most forward brain area) interfere with only certain components of memory: memory for the order of things and events, short-term memory for the location of things in space, normal resistance to distraction during learning, and the ability to learn new material without being confused by old material. Unusual and discrete types of amnesia can result from damage to other specific cortical areas, such as the parietal, posterior temporal, and occipital lobes. For example, people may be unable to remember and recognize colors, faces, the names of objects, or the location of an object in the environment.

In contrast to this whole-brain approach, neurobiological investigations have focused on short-, intermediate-, and long-term cellular memory mechanisms. The sensory memory, the shortest memory, persists for about 0.5 second and depends on the activity of reverberating circuits. These circuits are loops of interconnected neurons arranged so that stimulating one will activate each successive one, including, eventually, the first one again. The net effect of this arrangement is that the entire loop stays active—and the memory trace of the initial stimulation persists—long after the initial stimulation has ended.

Other, more enduring memories, lasting from days to years, are thought to reside in synaptic (neuron-to-neuron) connections and to result from neuronal plasticity—the creation of new synaptic connections and/or increased capacity or efficiency of old ones. Many mechanisms for this have been proposed. One possibility is that learning causes neurons to sprout new terminals and make new connections directly (this is termed synaptic turnover or reactive synaptogenesis). Another possibility is that learning liberates blocked connections, which can then respond to incoming signals (the Calpain-Fodrin theory). Dendritic branching may also be important. If memories are stored in synaptic connections, brains with thickly branched dendrites could store more memories than those with thinly

branched dendrites. It is known, for example, that brains of healthy elderly people have more dendritic branches than brains of younger people, or of adults with some types of memory disorders. Moreover, animals raised in stimulating learning environments develop more branches and a greater brain mass than do less stimulated control animals. Learning-induced changes in the shape of dendrites may also promote memory: Stubby ones transmit information more readily than long, thin ones.

Among the most important proponents of animal models in the elucidation of the physiological basis for memory has been Eric Kandel. Kandel, a professor at Columbia University in New York, was awarded the Nobel Prize in Physiology or Medicine in 2000 for his discoveries in the molecular basis for memory. Kandel has carried out much of his work studying the nervous system in the sea slug *Aplysia*. This organism contains relatively few nerve cells (approximately twenty thousand); its neural circuitry is simple by comparison with more evolved organisms such as human beings (containing approximately one trillion nerve cells), and thus it serves as an ideal laboratory animal in the study of memory. Behavioral changes in the animal may involve fewer than one hundred nerve cells.

Kandel tested various forms of stimuli on the organism and observed changes in the responding gill withdrawal reflex as the basis for "memory." Since the reflex would remain for various periods of time, it represented a primitive form of memory. An amplification of the synapses connecting sensory nerve cells to motor neurons could be detected as a molecular response to stimuli and represented memory development.

If the stimulus was weak, a form of "short-term memory" would develop. In this case, the reflex lasted only a short period of time. If the stimulus was stronger, "memory" would last for weeks. At the molecular level, the basis for memory was found to be the relative levels of neurotransmitters that would be released at the synapses. Short-term memory was represented by calcium, which originated from specific ion channels, with resultant release of higher levels of neurotransmitters at the synapses. Kandel found phosphates were joined to certain channel proteins, resulting in amplification of the response.

Formation of long-term memory had an analogous mechanism utilizing phosphorylation reactions. The concentration of an enzyme, protein kinase A (PKA), also involved in phosphorylation of protein targets, was increased in neurons following higher levels of stimuli.

Activity of this enzyme was related to formation of a second molecule within the cell, cyclic adenosine monophosphate (cAMP). The result of increasing the activity of PKA and cAMP was to stimulate the cell to increase levels of proteins in the synapse, with the effect of increasing function of that synapse. Another key protein activated by cAMP was called the cAMP response element binding protein (CREB). If synthesis of new proteins was blocked using drugs, no long-term memory would result. Kandel summarized his work in the statement that all memory is "located in the synapse."

ROLE OF NEUROTRANSMITTERS

The brain and body produce a number of substances that have the ability to modify memory in everyday life. Catecholamines, brain neurotransmitters released during emotional states, seem to facilitate memory storage, and damage to brain structures that secrete catecholamines impairs memory. Stress-produced hormones from the pituitary and adrenal glands can also alter memory formation. Even the endorphins, the body's own morphinelike substances released during stress and involved in pain reduction, may play a modulatory role. Drugs can also influence memory function by altering nervous system activity. For example, stimulants of the central nervous system, such as amphetamine, can enhance memory formation, while depressants of the system, such as barbiturates and morphine, can interfere with it.

Kandel believes that the neurotransmitter serotonin is particularly important in regulating activity of both cAMP and PKA, thereby playing a critical role in memory. Addition of serotonin resulted in an increase in excitability of the synapses, similar to that of adding cAMP directly. Serotonin itself was found to cause an increase in cAMP levels.

The same neurotransmitter, serotonin, was found to be involved in development of both short-term, and long-term memory. When a synapse is activated by serotonin, a signal results which activates cAMP and the CREB protein. Newly synthesized proteins move to the terminals of the cells. Only those synapses bound by serotonin undergo development and growth.

The different forms of memory are the result of different forms of stimuli. Short-term memory re-

sults from a synapse-specific increase in the level of neurotransmitter. Preexisting proteins are modified (phosphorylated), and synaptic connections involve a relatively small number of neurons. In contrast, long-term memory results from activation of a protein pathway and requires new protein synthesis. In addition, significantly more connections are formed with other nerve synapses.

UNDERSTANDING MEMORY LOSS

Sometimes an anecdotal observation leads to new understanding of human behavior. Schizophrenia is a severe mental illness, characterized by thought disorder and incoherent speech, that has been extremely resistant to cure and treatment. By chance, the Italian psychiatrist Ugo Cerletti, practicing in the late 1930's, observed that electric shock applied to the heads of pigs in the local slaughterhouse made the pigs easier to manage. This inspired him to apply a small voltage to the temples of one of his schizophrenic patients in the hope that improvement would result. Nothing appeared to change, so he announced his intention to increase the voltage. At this point, to Cerletti's amazement, the patient protested loudly and with perfectly coherent speech. Encouraged by this improvement, Cerletti gave another shock. This time, unfortunately, the patient became unconscious because of a massive brain seizure and, upon awakening, experienced retrograde amnesia—he was unable to recall what had happened to him in the recent and sometimes distant past.

Following this, shock treatment, or electroconvulsive therapy (ECT), became quite popular for treating schizophrenia and was tried for every sort of mental illness. It became clear over the years, however, that only patients with mood disorders (particularly certain severely depressed patients) showed consistent benefits. In suicidal patients, ECT became the life-saving treatment of choice.

Transient and even permanent memory loss associated with ECT was largely ignored by clinicians, but this amnesiac effect became the focus of experimental research with animals. In a typical experiment, rats were trained on a simple learning task. Electroconvulsive shock—electrical shock to the brain—was given either immediately or at various intervals after training. Memory for the task was then tested a day or so later. Memory was poorest if the shocks were given right after training. This observation led to the conclusion that memory does not form instantaneously but takes time to "consolidate," a major development in memory research. Further investigation determined that, in animals, the body convulsions produced by the shocks were not themselves responsible for the retrograde amnesiac effects. Moreover, a variety of brain structures were found to produce amnesia without seizures. Indeed, stimulation of one structure (the hippocampus) disturbed long-term memory, while stimulation of another (the reticular formation) interfered with short-term memory, indicating different roles for each in the memory process.

This consolidation-disruption research strategy has become one of the major approaches used by memory investigators. Experimental work such as this has also led to improvements in ECT: Shocks are given to a smaller brain region; voltages are lower and better controlled (although seizures are still produced); muscle relaxants and sedatives are administered to avoid the hazards of convulsions; drugs are given to minimize heart-rate and blood-pressure changes; and oxygen is given to lessen memory loss.

The interplay between clinical and experimental work is also seen in research on Alzheimer's disease, a slowly debilitating and life-threatening disease that affects 6 percent of the adult population. Once thought to be an inevitable consequence of aging, or senility, caused by multiple "ministrokes," it is now recognized as a distinct and specific disorder. It begins insidiously, with difficulties of concentration, followed by increasing troubles with problem solving, speaking, learning, and remembering. Patients become apathetic and disoriented; even the ability to recognize loved ones is eventually lost.

Much of psychology's meager understanding of the basis for the memory impairment associated with this disease has come from basic research with animals. For example, studies of patients and animals with lesions in the hippocampus suggested early that this was an important site for memory formation but not for permanent storage. The hippocampus also contains mechanisms for neural plasticity. This is significant because postmortem studies of Alzheimer's patients' brains have revealed a selective loss of cells going to the hippocampus and cells in the neocortex, the highest brain area. Many researchers believe that both the number and shape of dendrites and the growth of synaptic endings are important for memory formation. The number of dendrites is reduced in Alzheimer's patients. More-

over, even normal cells contain abnormal strands (neurofibrillary tangles) inside and tangled masses (neuritic plaques) outside the nerve cells.

Basic animal research has also shown that acetylcholine, an important brain neurotransmitter, plays an important modulatory role in memory. Drugs that interfere with acetylcholine function can produce some symptoms of dementia (cognitive impairment, including memory deficits) in normal human subjects. Moreover, if acetylcholine neurons are transplanted from fetal (still-developing) rat brains to the brains of old rats, the old rats regain some of their youthful ability to learn and remember. In view of these findings, it is significant that both acetylcholine and the enzyme needed to make it (choline acetyltransferase) are reduced in Alzheimer's patients. Indeed, the greater the reduction, the worse the patient's symptoms. This observation, coupled with results from animal studies, has encouraged clinicians to treat the memory and other cognitive problems of Alzheimer's patients with drugs that enhance acetylcholine function—so far, however, with limited success.

RESEARCH AND MEMORY

During the 1880's, the fact that learning, memory, and forgetting operate according to laws was revealed by Hermann Ebbinghaus's laboratory investigations in *Über das Gedächtnis* (1885; *Memory*, 1913). Human amnesia and its implications for memory organization were chronicled by Theodule-Armand Ribot in *Les Maladies de la mémoire* (1881; *The Diseases of Memory*, 1883). Sergei Korsakoff first documented alcohol-induced amnesia (Korsakoff's syndrome), and the psychologist William James, in his classic work *The Principles of Psychology* (1890), distinguished primary and secondary memory, key concepts in the search for the engram, or memory trace.

The search for a mechanism began in earnest in the 1930's with the systematic experimental animal (as opposed to purely clinical and correlational) studies in the neuropsychology laboratory of Karl Lashley. Using lesions, he attempted to localize memory in particular brain structures, but he failed. This led him to conclude that the brain is equipotential: that the memory engram is distributed throughout the brain, or is at least distributed equally throughout functional subunits of the brain.

Donald Hebb, who proposed the notion of reverberating circuits in the 1940's, was one in a long line of researchers who, in opposition to Lashley, believed that memory would be found in specific neural circuits. The role of the middle temporal cortex, in particular, was inadvertently revealed by William Scoville in the 1950's. In an effort to eradicate epileptic seizures in his now-famous patient H. M., he performed a bilateral temporal lobe resection. This resulted in permanent anterograde amnesia. Some researchers now propose that both distributed and localized accounts of memory are valid. That is, memory, in the general sense, may be distributed widely throughout the brain, but different areas may store different components of memory. The anatomical details of this theory remain to be worked out.

Rapid advances in computer-based neural network techniques seem to hold particular promise for yielding useful models of how memory works. Data from basic research on cellular memory mechanisms are translated into mathematical formulations. These in turn are transformed into computer programs that simulate or mimic the observed function of selected subsets of neural nets. Comparing the behavior of computer-simulated nets to actual nets permits refinement of the hypothesized mechanisms. Ideas emerging from this work—for example, the notion of parallel distributed processing (PDP)—will provide work for neurobiologists for years to come.

The possible role played by memory suppressor genes is among the newest areas of research into the regulation of memory. Most prior research centered on positive control of memory formation at the molecular level—the activation of genes for formation of neural circuits and resultant memory. Kandel has also found evidence for a negative control, utilizing the products of memory suppressor genes. Products of these genes inhibit development of the synapse and prevent memory formation.

If indeed such regulation exists, pharmacological agents targeted at suppressor proteins might serve to increase development of memory. This would provide additional targets for reversal, or at least slowing, memory loss associated with neurodegenerative illnesses such as Alzheimer's disease.

SOURCES FOR FURTHER STUDY

Abel, Ted, Kelsey Martin, Dusan Bartsch, and Eric Kandel. "Memory Suppressor Genes: Inhibitory Constraints on the Storage of Long-Term Memory." *Science* 279 (1998): 338-341. Led by a Nobel laureate (Kandel), this team describes research into regulation of genes associated with long-term memory.

Allman, William F. *Apprentices of Wonder: Inside the Neural Network Revolution.* New York: Bantam, 1990. This popular book provides easy access to the field of computer modeling and neural networks for the lay reader. It contains one chapter on memory. Both believers' and skeptics' viewpoints on connectionist theory are presented, with illustrations, a general index, selected references, and a bibliography.

Carlson, Neil. *Foundations of Physiological Psychology.* Boston: Allyn & Bacon, 1998. Updated edition of a major text in the field. In addition to chapters dealing with anatomy and function of the brain, a portion of the book addresses concepts of learning and memory. Incorporated are some of Kandel's discoveries.

Eichenbaum, Howard, and Neal Cohen. *From Conditioning to Conscious Recollection: Memory Systems and the Brain.* New York: Oxford University Press, 2000. The authors argue that distinct neural pathways are involved in specific and general systems of memory. The book addresses this theory as the authors describe the role of parallel neural systems in formation of memory.

Kandel, Eric. "The Molecular Biology of Memory Storage: A Dialogue Between Genes and Synapses." *Science* 294 (2001): 1030-1038. A review of changes which occur in the brain at the cellular level which result in memory storage. Emphasis is on how learning results in changes at nerve synapses.

Nancy Oley;
updated by Richard Adler

SEE ALSO: Aging: Cognitive changes; Alzheimer's disease; Brain specialization; Brain structure; Dementia; Memory: Animal research; Neuropsychology; Parkinson's disease; Shock therapy; Synaptic transmission.

Memory

Sensory

TYPE OF PSYCHOLOGY: Memory
FIELDS OF STUDY: Cognitive processes

Sensory memory captures information acquired through the senses and retains it for a brief time. This allows the important information to be selected out and processed further by other memory systems.

KEY CONCEPTS
- echoic memory
- iconic memory
- information-processing model
- long-term memory
- memory decay
- partial-report technique
- short-term memory
- whole-report technique
- word superiority effect

INTRODUCTION

Human senses (such as sight, smell, touch, and hearing) pick up information about the surrounding physical world. Once this information is received, it must be converted by the senses into a code that is transmitted to the brain and eventually interpreted. Sensory memory plays a critical role in this process of transforming the outside world into an inner psychological experience. The sensory memory system stores information acquired through the senses for a brief time in order to allow other memory systems to screen and select which parts of the message will be kept for further processing. Depending on the particular sense modality, the duration that items can be held ranges from 0.25 to 2 seconds. Thus, one primary characteristic of this system is that its retention is very brief.

One important question concerns how much information can fit into sensory memory. Sensory memory has a larger capacity than short-term memory, which can hold five to nine bits of information, yet a smaller capacity than long-term memory, which is limitless. A third and somewhat controversial characteristic of sensory memory is that the information it holds is believed to be "precategorical." That is, the information has not been significantly altered, categorized, or processed, but is believed to be represented in a form that is nearly identical to its original copy. It must be pointed out, however, that research by Phil Merikle published in 1980 has weakened this third distinction of sensory memory from other memory systems.

Merikle performed one experiment in which he demonstrated that subjects could pick out a group of letters from any array of letters and numbers which were being held in sensory memory. Merikle's research provides evidence that information in sensory memory is susceptible to at least some processing. This assumes that the test stimuli were in fact being held in sensory memory and never transferred into short-term memory. If the information had been transferred into short-term memory, this second memory system could have been responsible for the ability to select out a group of letters from a group of letters and numbers.

Each sense modality is believed to have its own distinct sensory memory with its own unique characteristics. Much more is known about visual and auditory sensory memory than any of the other senses, simply because the vast majority of research has focused on these two systems. Ulric Neisser, 1967, coined the terms "iconic memory" and "echoic memory" to refer to these separate systems.

ICONIC AND ECHOIC MEMORY

Much of what is known about iconic memory has come from an experimental procedure originally used by George Sperling in 1959. He wanted to find out how much information could be seen during a rapid, brief exposure of stimuli. To answer this question, he presented subjects, using specialized equipment, with a matrix of twelve letters (four letters placed in three rows) for the duration of 50 milliseconds (one-twentieth of a second). After asking the subjects to recall as many of the letters as they could, Sperling found that, on average, they named about four items. More important, he noticed that his subjects insisted that they had seen more than four items but had forgotten the others. Sperling concluded that perhaps more of the letters were originally seen, yet were held for such a brief time that some of the items were being lost through memory decay as the subjects were calling out the letters.

To explore this possibility further, Sperling altered his experimental procedure. Rather than having subjects call out items from anywhere within the matrix of letters—called the whole-report technique—he presented them with a tone signal that immediately followed the presentation of letters. He used the tone to cue the subjects to call out only items from one row of the matrix. For example, a high tone would signal that the top row should be recalled. Using this partial-report technique, Sperling found that the subjects recalled three to four letters, despite the fact that they did not know in advance which row they would be asked to report. This level of performance was nearly identical to the previously used whole-report technique. This result led him to infer that the subjects saw approximately nine items. He based this conclusion on the fact that three items were being recalled from a row that was not determined until after the display was shown. Since it did not matter which row was being signaled for recall, Sperling found that on average three letters were seen from each of the three rows. Subjects did not call out all nine letters because of the short duration of the memory trace.

Sperling's research provided empirical support for the existence of a brief sensory register. Not only did he find the capacity of sensory memory, but also, by delaying the presentation of the tone during the partial-report technique, he learned about its duration. He found that information in sensory iconic memory lasted only about 250 milliseconds (one-quarter of a second).

Echoic memory has been ingeniously studied using a similar method. Subjects were aurally presented with different letter combinations simultaneously to the right ear, left ear, and both ears (for a total of nine items) using special headphones. Subjects were then visually cued to recall only the items presented to one ear. When this partial-report technique was compared to the whole-report method, the results paralleled what was found with iconic memory. Subjects recalled more items using the partial-report technique, which indicated an echoic memory was present. It is believed that the duration of echoic memory is considerably longer than iconic memory, somewhere between 2 and 3 seconds.

An important question that has received some attention is why people need a sensory memory. Margaret Matlin pointed out in 1989 that humans live in a world where their senses are overwhelmed with stimulation that can change in an instant. A memory system that can rapidly absorb information and retain it for even a brief time allows subsequent memory systems to perform more in-depth analyses. In this way, information deemed to be unimportant can be discarded, while information regarded as important can be passed on to the next processing stage, short-term memory.

USES OF SENSORY MEMORY

Sensory memory plays an important and integral role in a variety of psychological processes. For example, someone who has just returned from Europe might show a friend some of the pictures she has taken. One of these pictures shows her in Rome standing next to a large piece of stone called Trajan's column. The process of pattern recognition gives the friend the ability to recognize her as well as the other objects in the picture. In order for this to occur, the visual system must receive information from the picture by attending to it; then, this information is temporarily stored in iconic memory. At this point, an interaction occurs between information held in sensory memory and memories of previous experience held in long-term memory. As has been mentioned, information in iconic memory must be acted upon quickly or else it is lost. Decision rules must be applied at this stage to determine which pieces of information are relevant and deserving of more complex processing. One way meaningful information can be identified occurs through a matching process of information stored in long-term memory with the contents of iconic memory. One friend can recognize the other in the picture because he "knows" what she looks like. Specifically, he has detected unique features, such as her eyes or the shape of her nose, that tell him for certain that the person in the picture is his friend. Pattern recognition does not end with identifying the friend, but extends to all the other objects in the picture. Although numerous theories have been put forth to explain pattern perception, a common component of many of these theories is the important role sensory memory plays.

The notion of a sensory memory was used by Robert Solman and colleagues in 1981 to explain the phenomenon of the word superiority effect. It has been found that people who are briefly presented with a letter (T) and then asked to choose which letter they have just seen from a set of two letters (D, T) do not perform as well as when they are presented with a word (CART) and have to choose the correct word from a set (CARD, CART). Basically, subjects are better able to discriminate the letter T from D when it is embedded in a word. Solman and colleagues believe that one possible explanation for the word superiority effect is that words are stored longer than individual letters in sensory memory. Thus, the longer the words are retained in iconic memory, the easier it is for subjects to remember the correct response in a subsequent recall test.

Henry Ellis and Reed Hunt, in their book *Fundamentals of Human Memory and Cognition* (4th ed., 1989), describe how research into sensory memory can be used to help solve an important problem associated with a learning disability. They mention a particular reading problem called specific reading disability, which prevents children from reading normally. One unusual characteristic of this reading disorder is that in its early stages, no other intellectual abilities are affected. Once a child matures to the age of approximately twelve years, academic performance in other areas such as mathematics begins to deteriorate. It is not known what causes the specific reading disability.

Ellis and Hunt mention that it was believed that children with the reading problem did not see the same perceptual images as normal readers. The perceptual deficit hypothesis was the name given to the theory that the root of this problem was perceptual in nature. One unfortunate aspect of the perceptual deficit hypothesis was that it implied the problem was occurring at the most basic level of the visual system: the sense receptors. If this were true, then no amount of training, practice, or learning strategies could possibly help overcome the disability.

In 1977, Frederick Morrison and his colleagues performed an experiment using a group of sixth-graders to test this hypothesis. Half the children in the group were normal readers, while the other half were poor readers with a reading disability. Morrison believed that if the problem were caused by a perceptual abnormality, it would become evident after looking at the precise nature of the information held in the sensory memory. By conducting an experiment similar to the one performed by Sperling, Morrison tested the contents of the perceptual stimuli in iconic memory for both the normal and poor readers to find out if they differed.

Morrison found that good readers and poor readers performed equally well on a recognition task for information in sensory memory. This finding goes contrary to the prediction made by the perceptual deficit hypothesis, which assumed that the poor readers would not perform as well since the letters were believed to be abnormally processed. Morrison found that good readers began to outperform poor readers only after the cue that started the recognition test was delayed by at least 300 milliseconds. This revealed that the problem which caused the reading disability was occurring at a higher level of information processing rather than at the sensory memory stage, as was once believed.

INVESTIGATION HISTORY

The notion that humans possess a brief visual sensory storage was first proposed by Wilhelm Wundt as early as 1899. Although he did not have access to the sophisticated equipment needed to demonstrate experimentally the existence of this memory system, perhaps he saw evidence for it by making the following observation. If a hand-held candle is moved rapidly in a circular path in a darkened room, one can see what appears to be a brightly lit ring. Despite the fact that the flame of the candle does not occupy every position on this circle continuously, an illusion occurs whereby one can still "see" the flame after it has moved. This phenomenon occurs as a result of visual sensory memory. It is not unreasonable to think that Wundt proposed a brief visual register after seeing evidence for it with common, everyday examples such as this.

In 1958, Donald Broadbent proposed a theory of attention that incorporated the concept of a sensory register. The sensory register, as Broadbent saw it, was a temporary short-term store for information received by the senses. Information from different senses was transmitted on separate channels. A selective filter was believed to act on the information in the sensory store by conducting a rudimentary analysis of its contents to determine which information should be attended to and processed more thoroughly. The notion of a brief sensory store was an integral part of Broadbent's theory, as well as of other theories of attention which were developed later.

Sperling published his results providing empirical support for a sensory memory in 1960. The scientific community readily embraced them. By 1968, Richard Atkinson and Richard Shiffrin had incorporated sensory memory into their information-processing theory of memory. The Atkinson and Shiffrin theory evolved into one of the most significant and influential models of human memory devised to that time. Sensory memory, according to their model, was viewed as the first stage in a series of information-processing stages. Sensory memory captured and briefly held information while control processes determined which information would be transferred to short-term memory and eventually to long-term memory.

Although at times the concept of a sensory memory has been challenged, it should continue to remain a pivotal psychological construct for the understanding of many perceptual and learning processes.

SOURCES FOR FURTHER STUDY

Anderson, John Robert. *Cognitive Psychology and Its Implications.* 5th ed. New York: Worth, 1999. This unique text introduces the reader to a nontraditional discussion of cognitive psychology. Although the sections on sensory memory are brief, this book contains more thorough discussions of perception and attention.

Best, John B. *Cognitive Psychology.* 5th ed. Belmont, Calif.: Wadsworth, 1998. One of the most complete texts in human cognition, with chapters on perception, attention, pattern recognition, memory, forgetting, and language. The writing is engaging and encourages readers to think for themselves.

Crowder, Robert G. *Principles of Learning and Memory.* Hillsdale, N.J.: Lawrence Erlbaum, 1976. Although less information has been gathered on echoic memory than on iconic memory, this book has a more in-depth discussion of echoic memory than is typically found in other texts. A good discussion of the Atkinson and Shiffrin model of human information-processing is presented, as well.

Ellis, Henry C., and R. Reed Hunt. *Fundamentals of Human Memory and Cognition.* 4th ed. Dubuque, Iowa: Wm. C. Brown, 1989. Includes one of the best descriptions of how sensory memory relates to the processes in pattern recognition, a fine chapter on attention, and separate chapters on short-term and long-term memory. Not as broad in coverage as other texts, but generally discusses topics in greater depth.

Lachman, Roy, Janet L. Lachman, and Earl C. Butterfield. *Cognitive Psychology and Information Processing: An Introduction.* Hillsdale, N.J.: Lawrence Erlbaum, 1979. Includes a wonderful discussion on the history of the stage theory of memory, along with a detailed discussion of the early work in sensory memory initiated by George Sperling.

Matlin, Margaret W. *Cognition.* 5th ed. Pacific Grove, Calif.: International Thomson, 2001. One of the most accessible general cognitive textbooks on the market. A clear writing style, along with phonetic tips to help the reader pronounce difficult words, assists the novice in understanding complex cognitive principles. Includes a number of experiments that the reader can perform to help grasp concepts.

Bryan C. Auday

SEE ALSO: Attention; Hearing; Kinesthetic memory; Long-term memory; Memory: Empirical studies; Pattern recognition; Sensation and perception; Senses; Short-term memory; Smell and taste; Touch and pressure; Visual system.

Memory storage

TYPE OF PSYCHOLOGY: Memory
FIELDS OF STUDY: Cognitive learning

The distinction between episodic and semantic memory provides a useful tool for classifying memory phenomena and methods of measuring memory performance. Separate types of memory models have been proposed for each, but debate continues as to whether episodic and semantic memories constitute distinct memory systems.

KEY CONCEPTS

- anterograde amnesia
- autobiographical memory
- episodic memory
- flashbulb memory
- semantic memory

INTRODUCTION

In 1972, Endel Tulving proposed a distinction between two parallel and partially overlapping memory systems, one for personal experiences and the other for general knowledge of the world. Episodic memory stores personal recollections of episodes or events that one has encountered at a particular time and place. Examples of episodic memories would include remembering such things as one's first airplane trip, eating cereal for breakfast this morning, and seeing the word "August" on a list recently learned in an experiment. Semantic memory stores shared factual information about language and the world, but without reference to when it was learned. For example, knowledge that a Boeing 747 is a type of airplane, that cereal is a common breakfast food, and that August has thirty-one days is all stored in semantic memory.

In his 1983 book, *Elements of Episodic Memory,* Tulving lists twenty-eight differences between episodic and semantic memory. Among them are the source of information (sensation versus comprehension), organization (temporal versus conceptual), emotional content (more important versus less important), vulnerability to forgetting (great versus small), and method of testing in the laboratory (recall of particular episodes versus general knowledge).

Tulving pointed out that up to 1972, most memory research followed in the tradition of Hermann Ebbinghaus, focusing on verbal learning tasks concerned with the accuracy of a subject's performance in remembering personally encountered events (such as the word "bed" on a list). Tulving considered these tasks as tapping episodic memory. A typical episodic memory phenomenon is the serial-position effect, wherein the first and last few items in a series are recalled better than the middle items (the primacy effect and the recency effect, respectively).

Since the early 1970's, memory research has expanded to include tasks designed to uncover the content and organization of information in semantic memory. Some tests assess factual and linguistic knowledge acquired over years of study and experience. Examples include the verbal and quantitative sections of college entrance examinations. A variety of new methods has also been developed to investigate how factual and lexical information is structured and interrelated in long-term memory. For example, subjects have been asked to generate lists of category members, in which the first and most often mentioned instances are interpreted to be the prototypical or best examples available in memory. In a fragment-completion task, the strength of memory traces is indexed by how much of a picture or printed word can be erased from memory and still be identified.

Several semantic memory tasks rely on reaction time as their dependent measure. In a lexical decision task, shorter reaction times to decide whether a string of letters composes a word provide a measure of the item's strength or current level of activation. Similarly, in a semantic verification task, the time to

decide whether a sentence is true (for example, "A tomato is a vegetable") can be interpreted to indicate the strength of the stated fact or the semantic distance "traveled" between the two named concepts to verify or negate the statement. A robust semantic memory phenomenon is priming, which refers to the activation of associations in a memory network. For example, in a lexical decision experiment, subjects identify "nurse" as a word more quickly if it is preceded by the semantically related word "doctor" than by the unrelated word "table" or the nonword "batel." This finding suggests that concepts with similar or shared meanings are stored close to one another in a semantic network, so that accessing one tends to highlight the others.

MEMORY MODELS

Memory models based on episodic tasks have focused on the transition of information from acquisition to storage. For example, the multistore model of Richard Atkinson and Richard Shiffrin distinguished between preattentive sensory registers: a limited-capacity, short-term store (STS) and a semantically organized, long-term store (LTS). Of critical interest were the coding processes used to transfer information from STS to LTS. More recently, Fergus Craik and Robert Lockhart proposed a levels-of-analysis model to account for the increasing trace duration of episodic memories. Both these models were developed to explain the accumulation of memory phenomena from traditional list-learning experiments.

By contrast, semantic memory models have focused exclusively on the organization and retrieval of information already stored in long-term memory (LTM). For example, Lance Rips, Edward Shoben, and Edward Smith proposed a feature-comparison model, in which semantic information is coded as lists of necessary (defining) and descriptive (characteristic) features.

According to this model, subjects verify statements by searching the stored features of the named concepts, looking for matches. Fast reaction times are associated with close matches (resulting in a decision of "true") or the apparent absence of matches (with a decision of "false"). Their model explains why subjects verify sentences with considerable overlap between concepts (for example, "A robin is a bird") or none at all (for example, "A robin is a fish") more quickly than sentences with concepts which have only a few shared features (for example, "A penguin is a bird"). It also accounts for either fast, "false-alarm" errors or slow, correct decisions, when many shared features suggest at first glance that a false statement is true (for example, "A whale is a fish").

Other semantic memory models have suggested that information in LTM is arranged in hierarchical networks of taxonomic categories, or interrelated networks of propositions. These models have been strongly influenced by advances in artificial intelligence and linguistics. A particularly well-developed semantic memory model is John Anderson's modified adaptive control of thought (ACT*, read "act-star") theory. In his schema, Anderson distinguishes between a declarative memory system (with an embedded working memory), which stores and operates on factual knowledge of temporal, spatial, and semantic information, and a procedural memory system of how to do things.

EPISODIC AND SEMANTIC MEMORIES

An issue of critical importance is how information gets from episodic into semantic memory. Marigold Linton has suggested that as the number of experiences with a particular type of event increases, memories of the specific episodes become confused and eventually cannot be distinguished, but the strength of its generalized trace in semantic memory increases. These contrasting functions were suggested by the results of Linton's study of her own memory. Every day for six years, she recorded at least two events from her own life, then periodically tested her ability to remember those specific events. She found that memories of unique events, especially those with high emotional content, were often retained intact in episodic memory, whereas repeated events were transformed into generalized, abstracted memories or facts in semantic memory. Overall, her memories of personal events were forgotten at a rate of about 5 percent a year, in a nearly linear fashion.

A class of episodic memories which do not appear to erode over time has been called flashbulb memories. For example, Roger Brown and James Kulik reported that nearly all the adults they interviewed reported vivid personal memories of where they were, what they were doing, how they heard about it, and their own subsequent feelings and actions when they received the news of President John

Kennedy's assassination in 1963. Previous generations of Americans have reported similar memories regarding the attack on Pearl Harbor in 1941, and younger subjects have reported flashbulb memories for the 1986 explosion of the space shuttle *Challenger.*

The clarity of people's memories for these and similar important historical and personal episodes has suggested to Ulric Neisser that they constitute a special case of episodic memories that are reflected on, repeated to others, and rehearsed countless times. What is finally remembered is a combination of the original episode, other generic information about the event drawn from semantic memory (for example, recalled facts reported by the news media), and the subtle changes that appear with each repetition. Neisser calls these "repisodic memories," and he offers another example in the case of John Dean's testimony at the Senate's Watergate hearings in 1973. Dean had practiced the presentations he made to Richard Nixon in the Oval Office, subsequently rehearsed his memories of those conversations many times, and kept a scrapbook of newspaper accounts of the unfolding tale. By comparing Dean's sworn statements to the tape recordings of the actual White House conversations, Neisser confirmed that Dean's repisodic memory was essentially correct in retaining the gist of the whole chain of events, even though it did not faithfully report the individual encounters.

ACCESSING PERSONAL MEMORIES

Clearly, one's personal and generic memories are often intertwined, as one recalls a compromise between what was and what must have been. From the outset, episodic memories are fashioned by an individual's preexisting knowledge of the world, which is necessary to make sense of experience. As noted above, semantic memories often reflect generalizations constructed from many similar episodes. As one searches one's memory, the retrieval process often assumes the characteristics of problem solving. For example, in answering the question "What were you doing at 2:00 P.M. on the third Monday in September five years ago?," one's retrieval strategy would depend on some abstract factual information from semantic memory (for example, determining that one was a sophomore in high school that year and would have been in school, in an afternoon biology class). One might then reason that since mid-

September is early in the semester, one was probably studying some introductory biological concept such as evolution. That insight then cues an episodic memory of Mr. Brown, the biology teacher, blaming evolution for the football team's loss in their opening game the previous Saturday night.

Autobiographical memories provide a link to one's personal past and help one maintain a coherent sense of self. For elderly persons who may be struggling to preserve their self-respect, keeping access to personal memories can be extremely important. Sharan Merriam has reported that providing cues such as old photographs and objects from the past, as part of a technique known as reminiscence therapy, has proved successful with disoriented persons, as it assists them in remembering who they are. Fortunately, even among those patients suffering dense anterograde amnesia (the inability to enter new information into memory), most retain access to autobiographical memories of events that occurred prior to the onset of amnesia.

PROSPECTIVE VERSUS RETROSPECTIVE MEMORY

Alan Baddeley and Arnold Wilkins have suggested that the episodic-semantic distinction can be meaningfully applied to prospective memory (remembering to perform some act in the future) as well as to retrospective memory (remembering events experienced in the past). An example of a prospective episodic task is remembering to carry out some infrequently performed action on a fixed time schedule, such as recalling to take medication four times a day over the course of a week. In this case, the reference is personal, the organization is temporal, and the occasion of first learning and establishing this intention to act can still be recalled. By contrast, an example of a prospective semantic task is remembering an action sequence of overlearned steps, such as those involved in cooking with a memorized recipe. The reference is cognitive, the organization is cognitive, and the origin of this habitual sequence probably can no longer be recalled.

DEBATE IN RESEARCH

Douglas Hintzman has noted that authors in various fields had applied labels to capture the essence of the episodic-semantic distinction prior to Tulving's landmark article in 1972. In philosophy, Henri Bergson distinguished between "pure memory" and "habit memory," and Don Locke contrasted "personal memory" with "factual memory." In literature, Arthur Koestler differentiated between "picturestrip memory" and "abstractive memory." Neurologist Wilder Penfield distinguished between "experiential record" and "concepts." In psychiatry, Ernest Schactel defined "autobiographical memory"(memory for information and events related to the self from an individual's past) versus "practical memory," and Robert Reiff and Martin Scheerer focused on "remembrances" versus "memoria." In recent years, however, Endel Tulving has been the main standard-bearer of the dichotomy.

While its heuristic value for classifying memory phenomena and methods has gone relatively unchallenged, Tulving's claim for episodic and semantic memories as separate systems has engendered considerable debate. Attempts to validate this position have relied on experimental demonstrations of dissociation, or cases in which a variable affects performance in an episodic task differently than it affects performance in a semantic task. Gail McKoon, Roger Ratcliff, and Gary Dell (in a study published in 1986) reviewed experimental evidence from a variety of studies reporting dissociation, differences during episodic and semantic tasks in blood flow and brain activity patterns, and different memorial consequences of amnesia; they concluded that a theory of separate memory systems is not warranted.

In response to these criticisms, Tulving has proposed a modified framework in which episodic memory is embedded within semantic memory, which is itself a specialized subsystem of procedural memory. These levels are hypothesized to vary in the kinds of conscious awareness associated with their operation. Procedural memory, which encodes learned stimulus-response associations, is characterized as nonknowing (or "anoetic," in Tulving's terminology). Semantic memory, which constructs and stores a person's knowledge of the world, supports introspective awareness or metacognition (the ability to monitor one's own cognitive processes), and in that sense is knowing (noetic). Episodic memory retains knowledge of the individual's personal past, and thus represents self-knowing (autonoetic) consciousness. The verification of this schema remains a goal of future research.

A notable outcome of Tulving's original argument was to shift attention in memory research away from episodic list learning and toward the structure of long-term semantic knowledge. More recently, there has been a growing interest in personal episodic, or autobiographical, memory. These are precisely the kinds of recollections that Ebbinghaus sought to exclude from the study of memory, considering them too personal and difficult to verify. Any comprehensive theory of memory, however, will need to account for the full range of interdependent memories, from highly personal accounts to abstract facts.

SOURCES FOR FURTHER STUDY

Baddeley, Alan D. *Human Memory: Theory and Practice.* Rev. ed. Boston: Allyn & Bacon, 1997. A very readable, comprehensive review of episodic, autobiographical, and semantic memory research and theories. Fully referenced and understandable to college or high school students.

Carruthers, Mary J. *The Book of Memory: A Study of Memory in Medieval Culture.* Reprint. New York: Cambridge University Press, 1993. A fascinating study of medieval memory storage techniques, illustrating the change in memory capacity created by the transition from an oral to a literate culture.

Neisser, Ulric, and Ira E. Hyman, eds. *Memory Observed: Remembering in Natural Contexts.* 2d ed. New York: Worth, 1999. This edited volume includes seminal articles on flashbulb memories, Marigold Linton's account of her personal memory study, and Neisser's case study of John Dean's testimony. A fascinating combination of old and new memory research.

Rubin, David C., ed. *Autobiographical Memory.* Reprint. New York: Cambridge University Press, 1988. An excellent source of theories and research on autobiographical memory. Several chapters focus on memory failures associated with amnesia, considered by some a critical testing ground for the episodic-semantic distinction.

Tulving, Endel. *Elements of Episodic Memory.* Oxford, England: Oxford University Press, 1983. In this book, Tulving intersperses a review of evidence for the episodic-semantic distinction with his personal reflections on the practice of scientific research. An interesting insider's view.

_____. "How Many Memory Systems Are There?" *American Psychologist* 40, no. 4 (1985): 385-398. In this 1984 address for the Distinguished Scientific Contribution Award from the American Psychological Association, Tulving proposes a "monohierarchical" arrangement of episodic memory embedded in semantic memory and argues for the stochastic independence of episodic and semantic memory phenomena.

Tulving, Endel, and Fergus I. M. Craik, eds. *The Oxford Handbook of Memory.* New York: Oxford University Press, 2000. Summarizes memory research since the 1980's, especially brain scanning and behavioral studies. A very complete overview of the current state of the field.

Thomas J. Thieman

SEE ALSO: Amnesia and fugue; Aphasias; Brain structure; Encoding; Forgetting and forgetfulness; Long-term memory; Memory; Memory: Empirical studies.

Mental health practitioners

TYPE OF PSYCHOLOGY: Psychotherapy
FIELDS OF STUDY: Behavioral therapies; cognitive therapies; psychodynamic therapies

Mental health practitioners are those professionals who are involved in the treatment of psychological and emotional disorders. They include clinical psychologists, counseling psychologists, psychiatrists, and psychiatric social workers; their professional preparations differ considerably, but their contributions are all essential.

KEY CONCEPTS
- assessment
- behavioral medicine
- brain dysfunction
- diagnosis
- electroconvulsive therapy (ECT)
- forensic psychology
- neuropsychology
- psychotherapy

INTRODUCTION

Since the beginning of the twentieth century, there has been a growing concern about mental health. Studies have indicated that approximately one out of every five persons in the United States will experience a psychological disorder severe enough to warrant professional help. Given the magnitude of this problem, the question emerges as to who will provide the kind and amount of treatment needed for this large number of individuals.

Mental health practitioners have emerged from different fields of endeavor. The field of medicine produced psychiatrists; the field of psychology produced clinical psychologists and counseling psychologists; and the field of social work produced psychiatric social workers. In some states, such as California, legislation created special mental health practitioners called marriage, family, and child counselors to fulfill the needs that were not met by these large professional groups.

TYPES OF PRACTITIONERS

Psychiatrists are those individuals who have completed four years of college and four years of medical school, including one year of internship. After completion, they continue their studies in a residency in psychiatry for approximately three years and learn the skills of a practicing psychiatrist. This is generally done in a mental hospital or clinic, under the supervision of other psychiatrists. Upon completion, they may choose to take an examination which will award them the status of being certified. This status recognizes that a psychiatrist has demonstrated a level of competence that meets professional standards.

As a physician, the psychiatrist can perform all the medical functions that any physician can perform. In terms of the mental health setting, this means that the psychiatrist's activities can involve the administration of different types of drugs that are designed to alter the way a patient feels, thinks, or behaves. The psychiatrist conducts psychotherapy and is concerned about any physical conditions that might make the patient's psychological disposition more serious. The psychiatrist may use other biological treatments, such as electroshock therapy, in the treatment of severe depression and is qualified to supervise the care of patients requiring long-term hospitalization.

The clinical psychologist emerges from the tradition of psychology rather than that of medicine, with a background in theories of behavior and the ways in which behavior may be changed. After completing four years of undergraduate study—usually, but not necessarily, in psychology—the student studies two more years to obtain a master's degree in psychology and completes a master's thesis, which

provides evidence of research capabilities. This is followed by three more years working toward a Ph.D. degree and the completion of an internship in a mental health setting. After completion of these academic requirements, a psychologist is eligible to take the state licensing examination, which usually requires an oral and a written test. In some states, such as California, the psychologist is required to complete an additional year of supervised experience after receiving a Ph.D. degree before becoming eligible for the licensing examination. After passing the examination for licensing, the psychologist is then able to offer services to the public for a fee. Many clinical psychologists choose to go into private practice, that is, to provide services to private patients in their own offices. About a quarter of all psychologists in the United States list private practice as their primary setting of employment. Other clinical psychologists work in settings such as hospitals, mental health clinics, university counseling centers, or other human service agencies.

After five years of clinical experience, the psychologist may apply for certification by the American Psychological Association. Obtaining certification requires passing written and oral tests as well as an on-site peer examination of clinical skills. Those who succeed are awarded the title of Diplomate in Clinical Psychology. This same award is given in other areas, such as counseling psychology, school psychology, industrial and organizational psychology, and neuropsychology. Board certification clarifies for the general public that the psychologist has demonstrated better-than-average clinical skills and is recognized as such by his or her professional peers. Fewer than 10 percent of all clinical psychologists have been awarded the status of diplomate. This is a useful guide, therefore, for persons who are uncertain about who to see for therapy or assistance. Most telephone directories will designate the diplomate status of individuals, since the American Psychological Association requires that they identify themselves as such.

The counseling psychologist, much like the clinical psychologist, is required to obtain a Ph.D. degree and complete an internship in counseling psychology. Counseling psychologists work in the mental health profession by providing services to those individuals, or couples, who are under stress or crisis but who continue to be functional. These are individuals who have functioned well in their lives but are meeting particularly difficult situations and require professional help to adjust to or overcome the stresses of the moment. These situations could involve loss of job, marital conflict, divorce, separation, parent-child or other family conflicts, prolonged physical illnesses, or academic difficulties. Counseling psychologists may either be in private practice or be employed by a university counseling center, where they provide services exclusively to college students.

A fourth type of mental health worker is the psychiatric social worker. This person completes four years of undergraduate study in the social or behavioral sciences, then completes two additional years of study in a school of social work. Social workers may choose different areas of specialty; the mental health worker usually concentrates in psychiatric social work. This involves recognizing the social environment of the patient and altering it in ways that will reduce stress and help maintain the gains that the patient may have achieved in treatment. The social worker becomes involved with issues such as vocational placements, career choice, and family stresses and is the link between the patient and the outside world. Social workers who are licensed may have their own private practices and may offer counseling and psychotherapy as a form of treatment.

TYPICAL ACTIVITIES

Surveys conducted by the American Psychological Association indicate that clinical psychologists spend most of their professional time with therapy, diagnosis and assessment, and teaching and administration. These categories constitute approximately 70 percent of their daily activity. Additional activities involve research and consultation with other agencies or professionals. Forty percent of their daily activity, however, is devoted to providing direct clinical services to patients either through psychotherapy or psychological testing.

Almost all practicing clinical psychologists engage in some type of diagnosis or assessment. These assessments usually involve the administration of psychological tests, which include intelligence tests, vocational tests, personality tests, attitude tests, and behavioral repertoires. The purpose of the testing is to assess the patient's current status, to determine any disabling conditions, to assess the patient's psychological strengths that can be utilized in therapy, and to determine treatment recommendations

that are specific to the patient's particular problem. Usually these results are discussed with the patient, and a plan of treatment or therapy is recommended by the psychologist and agreed upon by the patient.

Since there are more than two hundred forms of psychotherapy or behavioral interventions, it is the responsibility of the psychologist to determine which of these procedures is best for the patient, taking into consideration the patient's age, physical status, psychological and emotional condition, and the length of time the disorder has been present. Psychologists should have a good knowledge of the research literature, which would tell them which of these many therapeutic approaches is best for the particular clients with whom they are working at the time.

In the course of private clinical work, the clinical psychologist is likely to meet a variety of different types of cases. These clients may be referred for treatment by other mental health workers, hospitals, insurance plans, ministers, or prior patients.

Clients vary as to the severity of their disorders. Some are very seriously disturbed, such as schizophrenic adults who are not receiving treatment in the community and are homeless. They often require hospitalization that provides a complete plan of treatment. Clients with drug or alcohol problems who have had long-standing difficulties with these substances may also require partial hospitalization. The clinical psychologist often acts as the principal or cooperating therapist who plans and participates in the treatment program. Since many clinical psychologists have hospital privileges that allow them to admit their patients to a hospital facility, this procedure is used with severely disturbed persons who are a danger to themselves or to others.

Those psychologists who work principally in private practice tend to see clients who have problems adjusting but who do not require hospitalization. These clients often seek therapy to reduce excessive symptoms of anxiety, depression, or intrusive thoughts that affect their daily lives. Other clients seek help in relationships with others to solve marital, parent-child, employee-supervisor, or sexual conflicts. The clinical psychologist in private practice meets the needs of these clients by providing the best means of resolving these conflicts.

Because psychologists deal with human behavior, they are often involved in many other facets of human activity that require their expertise. For example, psychologists are called upon to testify in court on questions of sanity, in custody cases, and, occasionally, as expert witnesses in criminal cases. Other psychologists are involved in sports psychology, helping athletes to develop the best psychological and emotional conditions for maximum performance. Still others work in the area of neuropsychology, which deals with patients who have experienced head injuries. Psychologists are asked to assess the extent of the injury and to find those areas that could be used to help the patient recover lost skills. Other psychologists specialize in treating of children who have been sexually or physically abused, in providing drug or alcohol counseling, in working in prisons with juvenile delinquents, or in working with patients who have geriatric disorders.

Some psychologists are involved in full- or part-time teaching at a university. These clinical psychologists not only continue their own clinical practices but also help prepare undergraduate and graduate students through direct classroom instruction or through supervision of their intern or field experiences.

DEVELOPMENTS IN THE FIELD

The field of psychology that deals mainly with emotional and psychological adjustment is called clinical psychology. This field began to take root during World War I, when psychologists were asked to screen military recruits for emotional problems and to assess intellectual abilities so that recruits could be placed in appropriate military positions. During World War II, clinical psychologists assumed an even greater role by developing psychological tests that were used in the selection of undercover agents. They were also asked to provide psychotherapy for soldiers who had emotional or neurological disorders.

Following World War II, clinical psychologists became heavily involved in the development and construction of psychological tests to measure intelligence, interest, personality, and brain dysfunction. Psychologists also became more involved in providing psychotherapy. Today, more psychologists spend their time providing psychotherapy than performing any other single activity.

Clinical psychology today regards itself as an independent profession, separate from the field of psychiatry, and sees itself rooted in the discipline of general psychology with the added clinical skills that make its practitioners uniquely capable of providing services to the general public. It is likely that clinical psychologists will continue to move in the direction of independent practice, focusing on new areas such as behavioral medicine, neuropsychology, forensic psychology, and pharmacotherapy. The latter trend is seen in the state of New Mexico's decision to allow psychologists with appropriate training to prescribe psychotropic drugs beginning in 2002.

SOURCES FOR FURTHER STUDY

American Psychological Association. *Graduate Study in Psychology.* Washington, D.C.: Author, 2002. Presents programs of graduate study in psychology in the United States and abroad that lead to a master's or doctorate degree in any field of psychology. Lists the requirements for admission for each school, financial assistance available, degree requirements, and the procedures for submitting applications. Most helpful to any student considering graduate study in psychology.

_____. *Psychology as a Health Care Profession.* Washington, D.C.: Author, 1979. A seventeen-page pamphlet covering psychology in its professional role. Discusses how psychological methods are applied to the health care profession; what psychologists do in various settings; the question of how cost-effective their contributions are; and ways that psychologists have affected public policy in health care issues. Single issues of this pamphlet are available at no cost from the American Psychological Association.

Saccuzzo, Dennis P., and Robert M. Kaplan. *Clinical Psychology.* Boston: Allyn & Bacon, 1984. A textbook in clinical psychology providing a broad introduction to this field. Covers the historical foundation, the acquisition of clinical skills, theoretical models, psychotherapy, psychological testing, community psychology, and behavioral medicine. A useful introduction to the field of clinical psychology which includes a valuable chapter on the way it relates to other branches of psychology such as learning, motivation, perception, and biological factors.

Sternberg, Robert J., ed. *Career Paths in Psychology: Where Your Degree Can Take You.* Washington, D.C.: American Psychological Association, 1997. Presents an overview of career options for psychologists beyond academic research or individual practice.

Gerald Sperrazzo

SEE ALSO: Behavior therapy; Behavioral family therapy; Brief therapy; Clinical interviewing, testing, and observation; Cognitive therapy; Cognitive behavior therapy; Community psychology; Couples therapy; Diagnosis; *Diagnostic and Statistical Manual of Mental Disorders* (DSM); Existential psychology; Gestalt therapy; Group therapy; Health psychology; Music, dance, and theater therapy; Observational learning and modeling therapies; Person-centered therapy; Play therapy; Psychoanalytical psychology; Psychology: Fields of specialization; Psychotherapy: Children; Psychotherapy: Effectiveness; Psychotherapy: Goals and techniques; Psychotherapy: Historical approaches; Rational-emotive therapy; Reality therapy.

Mental retardation

TYPE OF PSYCHOLOGY: Developmental psychology
FIELDS OF STUDY: Childhood and adolescent disorders; organic disorders

Mental retardation occurs about three times per thousand births and usually indicates an intelligence quotient (IQ) of less than 70. Variations in severity may allow some individuals to be virtually independent and capable of retaining simple jobs, whereas more severely affected persons may require lifetime institutional care. The causes of mental retardation are numerous, with many having a clearcut underlying genetic basis, others implicating environmental factors, and still others with no known cause.

KEY CONCEPTS
- congenital
- Down syndrome
- fetal alcohol syndrome
- fragile X syndrome
- idiopathic
- intelligence quotient (IQ)
- mental retardation
- phenylketonuria
- teratogens

INTRODUCTION

The term "mental retardation" conjures up different meanings for different people. A useful definition is provided by the American Association on Mental Retardation: "Mental retardation is a particular state of functioning that begins in childhood and is characterized by limitation in both intelligence and adaptive skills." Mental retardation reflects the "fit" between the capabilities of individuals and the structure and expectations of their environment. It is characterized by significantly subaverage intellectual functioning, existing concurrently with related limitations in two or more of the following applicable adaptive skill areas: communication, home living, community use, health and safety, leisure, self-care, social skills, self-direction, functional academics, and work. It is evident that deficits in intelligence and adaptive skills will be related to the complexity of the society in which the individual lives.

Degrees of severity of mental retardation have been utilized based on IQ scores. The four levels of severity are mild retardation (IQ range 50-70), moderate retardation (IQ range 35-50), severe retardation (IQ range 20-35), and profound (IQ range less than 20). Rather than use a classification based on the severity level, a classification based on the type and intensity of support needed also is now in practice: intermittent, limited, extensive, or pervasive. Persons with mild retardation usually are capable of living with some degree of independence in the community and can usually work successfully at simple jobs. The great majority—85 percent—of cases of mental retardation fall into this category. The remaining 15 percent of cases are at the moderate, severe, and profound levels, with only approximately 1-2 percent at the profound level. These last three levels are sometimes grouped together as severe. Profoundly affected individuals require constant care and supervision.

Several causes of mental retardation are becoming known, although in many cases it may not be possible to ascribe mental retardation in a family member to a specific cause. Just because a disorder is congenital (present at birth) does not necessarily imply that the disorder is genetic. Agents that are capable of affecting the developing fetus such as alcohol, mercury, infections, maternal phenylketonuria, and many other substances may lead to mental retardation. Many single-gene disorders and chromosomal abnormalities produce mental retardation as part of their syndromes, or disorders characterized by multiple effects. A large-scale study of se-

---

DSM-IV-TR Criteria for Mental Retardation

Significantly subaverage intellectual functioning:
- for children and adults, IQ of approximately 70 or below
- for infants, clinical judgment of significantly sub-average intellectual functioning

Concurrent deficits or impairments in adaptive functioning (effectiveness in meeting standards expected for age and cultural group) in at least two of the following areas:
- communication
- self-care
- home living
- social/interpersonal skills
- use of community resources
- self-direction
- functional academic skills
- work

- leisure
- health
- safety

Onset before age eighteen

DSM code based on degree of severity reflecting level of intellectual impairment:
- Mild Mental Retardation (DSM code 317): IQ level of 50-55 to approx. 70
- Moderate Mental Retardation (DSM code 318.0): IQ level of 35-40 to 50-55
- Severe Mental Retardation (DSM code 318.1): IQ level of 20-25 to 35-40
- Profound Mental Retardation (DSM code 318.2): IQ level below 20 or 25
- Mental Retardation, Severity Unspecified (DSM code 319): IQ level Untestable

---

verely mentally retarded patients institutionalized in Wisconsin, summarized by Sarah Bundey in 1997, indicated that 11.8 percent of the cases were due to chromosomal abnormality, 6.5 percent to single-gene defects, 16.3 percent to multiple congenital anomaly syndromes, 14.7 percent to central nervous system malformations such as hydrocephalus, 32.1 percent to central nervous system dysfunction due to perinatal or unidentified prenatal causes including cerebral palsy, 8.5 percent to infectious disease, 3.9 percent to postnatal brain damage, and 1.2 percent to infantile psychosis; 4.3 percent were unclassified. It was noted that the number of patients with Down syndrome was low since they were admitted less frequently. Other surveys have shown that Down syndrome accounts for about one-third of mentally retarded patients.

ETIOLOGY

Although some cases of mental retardation are idiopathic (without a specific known cause), many known causes account for many of the cases of mental retardation. The difficulties in teasing out factors involved in mental and behavioral disorders are seen clearly in the study of children exposed prenatally to radiation following the Chernobyl nuclear plant accident in 1986, as reported by S. Igumnov and V. Drozdovitch. The children who had been exposed to radiation displayed borderline intellectual

functioning and emotional disorders to a greater degree when compared to a control group. Other unfavorable social-psychological and sociocultural factors included a low educational level of the parents and problems associated with relocation from the contaminated areas.

Similar complications are seen in the work of M. S. Durkin and colleagues on prenatal and postnatal risk factors among children in Bangladesh. The study screened more than ten thousand children from both rural and urban areas. Significant predictors of serious mental retardation included maternal goiter and postnatal brain infections. Consanguinity also was a significant factor in the rural areas. For less severe mental retardation, maternal illiteracy, maternal history of pregnancy loss, and small size for gestational age at birth were significant independent risk factors.

It is convenient to separate the known causes of mental retardation into the two categories of genetic and acquired or environmental. However, many cases of mental retardation may be a result of the interaction of several genes and the environment, in which case the disorder is said to be multifactorial.

GENETIC CAUSES

Approximately one thousand genetic disorders are associated with mental retardation and the number increases regularly. If mental retardation is associated with other conditions or features, it is syndromic; if it is the only primary symptom, it is said to be nonspecific. In general, a genetic involvement is more likely to be found in severe forms of mental retardation than it is in milder forms. A few examples of chromosomal and single-gene disorders leading to mental retardation will be discussed as representative examples.

CHROMOSOMAL DISORDERS. Down syndrome was first described by John Langdon Down in 1866, and although heredity was suspected in its etiology, it was not until 1959 that it was discovered that Down syndrome patients had one extra chromosome, for a total of forty-seven instead of the normal forty-six. Down syndrome occurs at a frequency of about one in one thousand births and is the single most important cause of mental retardation. The great majority of Down patients have three chromosomes number 21 instead of two (a condition called trisomy 21). The physical features associated with Down syndrome are easily recognizable: short stature, a short neck with excessive loose skin, thick lips, epicanthal folds of the eye, malformed ears, poor muscle tone, and a flattened facial profile. Major physical problems include heart and kidney defects, deafness, and gastrointestinal blockages. Developmental milestones are delayed, and mental retardation is common. Intelligence varies considerably, with an average IQ of 50 and only a small percentage of patients approaching the lower end of the normal range. It is essential that parents and educators assess the capabilities of each child and provide an educational environment that maximizes achievement.

Although Down syndrome is genetic in the sense that it results from an imbalance in the genetic material—an extra chromosome—it is not hereditary in the sense that it does not run in families. The incidence of Down syndrome also shows a striking increase with maternal age, increasing dramatically (one in fifty births) in women giving birth beyond age thirty-five.

Other cases involving an extra chromosome or a missing chromosome, particu-larly if the missing chromosome is one of the autosomes, usually lead to spontaneous abortion. A normal human has twenty-two pairs of autosomes and one pair of sex chromosomes—XX if a female, XY if a male. The few that survive have severe malformations, including those of the brain, and are likely to have severe mental retardation. Malformations as a result of abnormalities involving the sex chromosomes are usually less severe. Females with an extra X chromosome (XXX) tend to have lower IQs than their siblings. Males with an extra X chromosome (XXY), a condition called Klinefelter syndrome, usually are not mentally retarded but may

In addition to challenges associated with daily living, the mentally retarded often face ostracism or belittlement as a result of societal attitudes and misperceptions. (National Easter Seal Society)

develop psychosocial problems. Males with an extra Y chromosome (XXY) may have speech, language, and reading problems.

Single-Gene Disorders. Fragile X syndrome is the second most common genetic cause of mental retardation. It is the most common inherited form of mental retardation. As is true of other disorders due to sex-linked recessive genes, more males are affected than are females. The frequency of fragile X males is about 1 in 1,000; for females, it is about 1 in 2,500. It is estimated that up to 8 percent of the males in institutions for mental retardation have a fragile X chromosome. Grant R. Sutherland and John C. Mulley in 1996 provided a useful review of the characteristics of fragile X syndrome. Features include a prominent forehead and jaws; prominent, long, and mildly dysmorphic ears; hyperextensible finger joints; enlarged testes (macroorchidism); and mitral value prolapse. About 80 percent of fragile X males have mental retardation. Most of them have moderate retardation, but some are only mildly retarded. They tend to have better verbal than spatial abilities. They show speech abnormalities such as echolalia (compulsively repeating the speech of others). In general, they tend to be hyperactive. Only about one-half of girls with the fragile X chromosome are affected, and limited studies of females estimate that perhaps up to 7 percent of female mental retardation is due to fragile X syndrome. The specific gene involved in fragile X syndrome has been identified: The syndrome is caused by an expanded triplet repeat, a form of mutation in which deoxyribonucleic acid (DNA) nucleotides are repeated a number of times.

Phenylketonuria (PKU) is one of the inborn errors of metabolism that results in mental retardation if left untreated. PKU is a disorder of amino acid metabolism in which individuals cannot metabolize normally the amino acid phenylalanine because they are deficient in the liver enzyme phenylalanine hydroxylase. As a result, phenylalanine and other metabolites accumulate in the blood. At birth, children are normal, but clinical features gradually appear during the first twelve months. Some affected persons have a "mousy" odor about them because of the excretion of phenylacetic acid. They tend to have light skin and hair, seizures, mental retardation, and other neurologic symptoms. PKU occurs in about one in fourteen thousand births and once accounted for about 1 percent of severely re-

tarded individuals in institutions. Some interesting variations in the incidence of PKU are seen among different populations. In Turkey, a very high incidence is seen, 1 in 2,600 births, whereas in Japan the rate is only 1 in 143,000 births. The disorder is inherited as autosomal recessive, and most of the affected children are born to parents who are not affected.

PKU represents the prototype of genetic disorders for which newborn screening can be done: babies with high blood levels of phenylalanine can be identified and treatment can begin immediately. Dietary management of phenylalanine levels does not correct the underlying gene defect, but it keeps the levels sufficiently low that adverse effects on the brain and nervous system do not occur and mental retardation is avoided. It is thought necessary to maintain the special diet through the adolescent years. It also is necessary for women with PKU who become pregnant to resume a diet low in phenylalanine to prevent high intrauterine levels from affecting the developing fetus, even though the latter may not be genetically "programmed" to inherit PKU. Untreated patients with PKU have mean IQs around 50, whereas treated patients will have IQs close to normal.

Environmental Causes

Numerous cases of mental retardation are a result of damage to a fetus during pregnancy. Other problems may arise during birth or after birth. Physical or chemical agents that cause an increase in congenital defects are known as teratogens. Since teratogens affect embryos and fetuses directly, the effects are not likely to produce heritable changes. A woman who uses or is exposed to various teratogens during pregnancy runs the risk of producing a child with a developmental malformation. Potential teratogens include alcohol, drugs, viral infections, radiation, diabetes mellitus, malnutrition, and environmental toxins.

Since its initial clinical delineation in 1973, fetal alcohol syndrome has been noted as a major cause of mental retardation in countries where alcohol is consumed regularly. Estimates indicate that it may be responsible for as many as one to three cases of mental retardation out of every thousand births. Fortunately, fetal alcohol syndrome is easily preventable through abstinence from alcohol during pregnancy. Children affected with fetal alcohol syndrome have a characteristic facial appearance, with a small skull, upturned nose, thin upper lip, underdeveloped upper jaw, epicanthal folds, and a long philtrum (the vertical groove on the median line of the upper lip). There is growth retardation, which has its onset prenatally and continues during the postnatal period with some catch-up growth taking place thereafter. Head and brain size remain well below normal. Children show developmental delays, attention deficits, hyperactivity, and mental deficiency. Although the average IQ of children with fetal alcohol syndrome is low, 60 to 65, there is considerable variation, with some children having normal or near-normal intelligence but experiencing learning disorders. Severe physical defects found in many of these children include cardiac and skeletal defects.

Although it is evident that the risk of fetal alcohol syndrome is related to the amount and timing of the alcohol consumed by the pregnant woman, an exact close relationship has been difficult to establish. Even with moderate consumption (one to two ounces of absolute alcohol), the serious effects of fetal alcohol syndrome have been observed in approximately 10 percent of births. Many physicians now recommend that women practice total abstinence from alcohol during the entire pregnancy.

Prevention and Treatment

Although it is not possible to treat some underlying causes of mental retardation, many of the genetic and teratogenic cases can be prevented through genetic counseling, prenatal diagnosis, and education to alert people of the risk to developing fetuses of teratogens such as alcohol. It also is essential to have an accurate diagnosis of the cause and nature of the problems associated with individual cases of mental retardation in order for parents to be able to undertake the best possible intervention program for their children.

Newborn screening programs can detect certain disorders that will lead to mental retardation, including PKU, congenital hypothyroidism, galactosemia, maple syrup urine disease, and other inherited metabolic disorders. Prenatal testing (such as amniocentesis and chorionic villi sampling) can be used to detect chromosomal disorders, including Down syndrome and several hundred single-gene disorders that may lead to severe physical and/or mental disorders in children. Neural tube defects can be detected prenatally by testing the amniotic fluid for elevated levels of alpha-fetoprotein. Most of the cases of prenatal testing are done for individuals in which there is a reason to suspect that the fetus is at an increased risk for a particular genetic disease or birth defect. These risks include increased maternal age, birth of a previous child with a disorder, and a family history of a disorder. Genetic counseling also is used to aid a couple in understanding genetic risks before a pregnancy has commenced, however, most mentally retarded children are born to parents with no history of mental retardation.

Sources for Further Study

Baroff, George S., and J. Gregory Olley. *Mental Retardation: Nature, Cause, and Management.* 3d ed. Philadelphia: Brunner-Routledge, 1999. This textbook presents information on the biological and psychological causes of mental retardation and its management.

Beirne-Smith, Mary, James R. Patton, and Richard F. Ittenback. *Mental Retardation.* 6th ed. Upper Saddle River, N.J.: Prentice Hall, 2001. A comprehensive book that deals with historical, biological, psychological and sociological aspects of mental retardation.

Burack, Jacob A., Robert M. Hodapp, and Edward Zigler, eds. *Handbook of Mental Retardation and Development.* New York: Cambridge University Press, 1997. This handbook provides comprehensive information emphasizing the developmental aspects of mental retardation.

Durkin, M. S., et. al. "Prenatal and Postnatal Risk Factors for Mental Retardation Among Children in Bangladesh." *American Journal of Epidemiology* 152, no. 11 (2000): 1024-1033. This study examines the role of different factors in causing mental retardation in rural and urban children.

Igumnov, S., and V. Drozdovitch. "The Intellectual Development, Mental, and Behavioural Disorders in Children from Belarus Exposed in Utero Following the Chernobyl Accident." *European Psychiatry* 15, no. 4 (2000): 244-253. The authors report borderline intellectual functioning and emotional disorders in children exposed in utero to fallout from Chernobyl, along with factors thought to contribute (such as relocation).

McKusick, Victor A. *Mendelian Inheritance in Man.* 12th ed. Baltimore: The John Hopkins University Press, 1999. This book is a comprehensive catalog of human genes and genetic disorders including mitochondrial genes.

Rimoin, David L., J. Michael Connor, and Reed E. Pyeritz. *Emery and Rimoin's Principles and Practice of Medical Genetics.* 3d ed. New York: Churchill Livingstone, 1997. This voluminous book includes several chapters dealing with mental and behavioral disorders.

Donald J. Nash

SEE ALSO: Birth: Effects on physical development; Developmental disorders; Down syndrome; Intelligence; Intelligence quotient (IQ); Prenatal physical development; Thought: Study and measurement.

Midlife crises

TYPE OF PSYCHOLOGY: Developmental psychology
FIELDS OF STUDY: Adulthood; coping

Midlife crisis describes the transition from early adulthood to middle age. It can be a stressful time of reevaluation, leading to both external and internal changes in a person's life.

KEY CONCEPTS

- crisis
- empty nest
- generativity
- life structure
- off-time events
- transition

INTRODUCTION

The term "midlife crisis" has become a part of the everyday vocabulary of most people and is often mentioned when explaining the cause of a variety of difficult changes during adulthood, ranging from depression to extramarital affairs. The more generic term of "crisis" can be defined as a period of alienation and confusion during which one feels overwhelmed and dissatisfied with one's life. Most researchers describe the midlife crisis as a period of alienation, stress, and disequilibrium occurring immediately prior to the individual's entrance into middle age. The typical age reported for the midlife crisis varies depending on the researcher.

Some claim that the midlife crisis may begin around age thirty-five and last until age forty, others have identified the late thirties and early forties as the most likely time for crisis, and still others claim that the midlife crisis occurs in the middle to late forties.

The notion of a midlife crisis being a predictable event in people's lives was popularized by Gail Sheehy's *Passages: Predictable Crises of Adult Life* (1976). Sheehy referred to the ages thirty-five to forty-five as the "deadline decade," emphasizing that this is the period during adulthood when people tend to start panicking about running out of time to accomplish the goals and dreams they established in their youth. The midlife crisis described by Sheehy is similar to Daniel Levinson and his coauthors' approach to adult development, outlined in their book *The Seasons of a Man's Life* (1978). Levinson's theory describes the changing "life structures" and transitional periods throughout an adult's development from entering early adulthood to entering late adulthood. Life structures can be defined as the basic pattern of a person's life at a given time that both influences and is influenced by the person's relationship with the environment. During the midlife transition (ages forty to forty-five), Levinson claims that virtually all men experience a stressful period of crisis. Both Sheehy and Levinson, as well as other authors, emphasize the marked shift in time perspective that occurs during the transition into middle adulthood. The authors claim that this is the first time in people's lives when they fully realize that time is finite and that eventual death is a personal reality for them. Facing one's own mortality leads to considerable existential questioning about the meaning of life, one's identity, and one's role in life, somewhat similar to the questions that are first faced during adolescence.

The main reason that this growing awareness of mortality leads to a crisis is that people at this stage reevaluate their lives and tend to question virtually every major value and belief that they have held. Adults may reevaluate their previous decisions regarding career and marriage, question their satisfaction with these decisions, and subsequently make major changes in their lives. All this questioning and change can precipitate a crisis in people's lives because they often do not have sufficient strategies to cope with the changes and are unsure of who they are and what they stand for.

THREE MIDLIFE PSYCHOLOGICAL TASKS

According to Levinson, there are three major psychological tasks that people in midlife must face. First, they must reappraise their past so that they can make the best use of their remaining time. During the process of reappraisal, people often come to realize that many of their assumptions about the world and their lives were idealistic illusions, and they then develop more realistic, balanced views. Another task is to modify their life structures by making both external and internal changes. External changes may include changes in family structure (possibly divorce and remarriage) or changes in career structure. Changes in personal outlook, values, and goals represent internal changes that occur during the midlife transition. Finally, people must integrate into their personalities those aspects of themselves that have previously been ignored or neglected. In particular, the polarities or opposites of being young versus old, destructive versus creative, masculine versus feminine, and attached versus separate must be integrated into the personality to form a broader, more balanced perspective.

TRANSITION VERSUS CRISIS DEBATE

Levinson's view that people inevitably experience a midlife crisis around age forty is shared by some experts in developmental psychology but is firmly disputed by others. Although most theorists agree that there is a transition between young and middle adulthood, many challenge the notion that the transition is experienced as a "crisis." Researchers such as Bernice Neugarten claim that life events, not birthdays, are the basis for crises. In particular, unpredictable or "off-time" events (life events that occur at unexpected or unpredictable times) are more likely to bring on a crisis than events that are predictable and occur at the expected time. If people are prepared for a specific change during adulthood, such as having their children leave home, then Neugarten suggests that the change, though stressful, does not set off a crisis.

PERSONAL APPROACH TO CHANGES

The individual's personal approach to dealing with changes, as well as his or her attitude toward the change, influences whether the change will lead to a crisis. An event is more likely to be experienced as stressful if it is perceived as a negative event over which the person has no control. On the other

hand, if the event is viewed as a challenge, the person is more likely to feel energized and optimistic about coping with any ensuing changes. Other factors that can influence how individuals deal with important life events are physical health, personality style (flexible versus inflexible, resilient versus vulnerable), personal history of coping with previous stressful events, and degree of social support from family, friends, coworkers, and community.

Neugarten suggests that important life events serve to mark the passage of time through one's lifetime. Several such events that often occur during the transition to middle adulthood can contribute to a midlife crisis. One of the main changes faced during this period is the subtle but unmistakable appearance of physical aging. Gray hairs become more abundant, wrinkles around the eyes and face become more pronounced, and parents may find that their adolescent children can now regularly beat them in basketball, races, and other tests of athletic prowess in which the parents once were undisputed champions.

In addition to these physical changes, women entering midlife must face the eventual loss of their ability to have children with knowledge that menopause is rapidly approaching. Even for women who do not wish to have children (or more children), the loss of choice on the matter can be disturbing. Men do not face the same loss of reproductive functioning, but they often start to develop doubts about their "sex appeal"; consequently, a man may seek an affair with a younger woman in order to reaffirm his sense of sexual desirability.

The midlife transition is also a time when people's perspectives toward their careers often change. People begin to realize that their career options have narrowed substantially. They also may find that they have reached a plateau in their current career, as the important tasks and opportunities are frequently assigned to younger, more motivated employees. Finally, the limited time left before retirement may lead to a sense of disappointment when the middle-aged person realizes that he or she has not attained all the goals and dreams of youth.

FAMILY ISSUES

Significant changes can also occur in the family during the midlife transition. Adults in their late thirties to early forties often have adolescent children who are most likely going through identity crises of their own. Two or more corresponding but separate crises occurring in the same family can interfere with communication and family harmony. Another change associated with having children is facing the "empty nest," when grown children begin to leave home for college or to start families of their own. The departure of children from the home often involves a significant role loss for the mother and possibly a lost opportunity for a close relationship for the father. In addition, just as the children are leaving home, adults in midlife may suddenly find themselves saddled with the stress and responsibility of caring for frail, elderly parents. The caregivers (typically middle-aged women) faced with the burden of caring for a dependent parent are referred to as the "sandwich" generation, because they are caught between the competing demands of their ailing parent, grown children, spouse, and their own desire finally to address their own personal needs and dreams. The increasing pressures at this time in life when people often expect to have more time to themselves can create a tremendous amount of stress.

Marital dissatisfaction during midlife is at an all-time high for many couples. The responsibilities of careers and rearing children keep many married couples busy and preoccupied during early adulthood. Once the children leave home and careers plateau, however, couples tend to take a more thorough look at their relationship and often wonder whether they want to maintain it. Not surprisingly, many divorces occur at this time in life.

PSYCHOLOGICAL CHANGES

Given all the important and difficult changes occurring during midlife, it should not be surprising that individuals' lives and perspectives are often qualitatively different after the midlife transition. According to Erik Erikson, people in middle adulthood struggle with opposing tendencies toward generativity and stagnation. Generativity refers to a desire to renew oneself through contributing to future generations. Ways that people typically contribute include rearing their own children, teaching, coaching, serving as a mentor, or making an artistic or creative contribution to society. People who are successful at generativity during this period are more likely to come through the midlife crisis with a stronger sense of identity and greater life satisfaction. On the other hand, those who stagnate at this stage and become self-absorbed tend to become increasingly narrow and rigid in perspective and bitter in attitude.

Another psychological change during this period has to do with the tendency for adults to exhibit characteristics typically associated with the opposite sex. Men who have primarily been aggressive and active in their careers may become more reflective, nurturing, and interested in building closer family relationships with their children and spouse. In contrast, women tend to become more assertive, self-confident, and oriented toward personal achievements at midlife, particularly once the responsibility of child rearing diminishes.

INFLUENCE OF JUNG AND JAQUES

The idea of the midlife crisis can be traced back to the writings of Carl Jung in which he portrayed the second half of life as a time for balance and reflection. Jung claimed that the passing of youth at middle age is marked by psychological changes in the individual. Prominent aspects of the personality become less important and are even gradually replaced by opposite personality traits. In addition, Jung held that one of the primary changes of this period was a greater emphasis on exploration of one's inner self and a search for meaning in one's life. These changes are thought to pave the way for greater acceptance of one's eventual death.

Although Jung's work suggested that an important change occurred at midlife, the London psychoanalyst Elliott Jaques is credited with being the first author to use the term "midlife crisis." His article "Death and the Mid-Life Crisis" (1965) was based on his study of the lives of composers, writers, and artists. Jaques found that there was a marked shift in the themes and styles of these creators from the more straightforward and descriptive work of their early adult years to a much more tragic and philosophical approach during their middle-age years. Later in life, the themes of these writers and artists became more serene and calm. Jaques proposed that the shift in style at midlife was based on the individuals' confrontation with mortality. Similarly, the eventual acceptance of their mortality led to a greater sense of peace in their later years, which was reflected in their work.

The writings of Jung and Jaques were significant in the field of psychology because they heralded a broader focus in the understanding of human development. Initially, the focus of developmental psychology was based solely on the physical, cognitive, and psychological changes during childhood and adolescence. It was assumed that people were finished with important development changes by puberty and that no further changes of significance occurred again in people's lives until the decline in functioning right before death. Regardless of whether one thinks of midlife as a transition or a crisis, the study of midlife changes has contributed much to the understanding of ongoing development during adulthood.

Future work in the area of midlife crisis is likely to lead to a greater understanding of the varied ways different people have of approaching and coping with stressors and changes in midlife. In particular, future research will probably focus on cultural differences in the experience of midlife as well as gender differences, as society's differential expectations and demands regarding gender continue to shift. Finally, changes in the expected age and duration of midlife crises may occur as the average human life span changes and the average age of the population as a whole continues to increase.

SOURCES FOR FURTHER STUDY

Apter, Terry. *Secret Paths: Women in the New Midlife.* New York: W. W. Norton, 1995. Based on interviews with more than eighty women in Britain and the United States. Offers real-world examples of the common experiences of women in midlife.

Farrell, Michael P., and Stanley D. Rosenberg. *Men at Midlife.* Boston: Auburn House, 1981. Based on surveys of three hundred men and in-depth interviews with twenty men and their families, the authors have developed an explanatory model for four different types of midlife experience for men. They challenge the notion that the midlife crisis is typical and emphasize the importance of family relationships.

Hollis, James. *The Middle Passage: From Misery to Meaning in Midlife.* Toronto: Inner City, 1993. A renowned Jungian analyst presents his solution to dealing with midlife crises.

Levinson, Daniel J., Charlotte Darrow, Edward Klein, Maria Levinson, and Braxton McKee. *The Seasons of a Man's Life.* Reissue ed. New York: Ballentine, 1986. Summarizes Levinson's influential theoretical approach to adult development, based on in-depth interviews with forty men, aged thirty-five to forty-five.

Sheehy, Gail. *Passages: Predictable Crises of Adult Life.* New York: E. P. Dutton, 1976. This widely read book describes the predictable crises of adulthood, including the midlife crisis. Sheehy includes many personal experiences and case examples to illustrate the stages of development. Sheehy's engaging writing style and clever chapter titles make the book readable and enjoyable for a wide range of audiences.

Stephanie Stein

SEE ALSO: Analytical psychology: Carl; G. Jung; Career selection, development, and change; Coping: Strategies; Development; Ego psychology: Erik Erikson; Erikson, Erik; Identity crises; Intimacy; Jung, Carl G.; Separation and divorce: Adult issues; Stress.

Miller, Neal E.

BORN: August 3, 1909, in Milwaukee, Wisconsin
DIED: March 23, 2002, in Hamden, Connecticut
IDENTITY: American psychologist, social learning theorist

Dollard, John

BORN: August 29, 1900, in Menasha, Wisconsin
DIED: October 8, 1980, in New Haven, Connecticut
IDENTITY: American sociologist, social psychologist
TYPE OF PSYCHOLOGY: Learning; personality; psychotherapy
FIELDS OF STUDY: Aggression; general constructs and issues; personality theory

Miller and Dollard were pioneers in the scientific study of personality who integrated neobehaviorism with psychoanalysis and established the first social learning theory.

Psychologist Neal E. Miller and sociologist John Dollard began their long-lasting and influential collaboration while members of the Yale University Institute of Human Relations. Their first major publication together, which included several coauthors, was *Frustration and Aggression* (1939). This work stimulated a wide range of studies on aggression. Their next major book, *Social Learning and Imitation* (1941), introduced the first fully articulated social learning theory, including the proposition that models constitute an important determinant of behavior. Unlike many personality theories at the time, Dollard and Miller's propositions were well grounded in experimentation, including research with laboratory animals. Their 1950 book *Personality and Psychotherapy: An Analysis in Terms of Learning, Thinking, and Culture* offered a remarkable synthesis of neobehavioral learning theory and psychoanalysis.

John Dollard was born in Menasha, Wisconsin. He earned an undergraduate degree from the University of Wisconsin in 1922 and his Ph.D. in sociology from the University of Chicago in 1931. He joined Yale University that same year as an assistant professor of anthropology and was trained in psychoanalysis while a research fellow in Berlin. He joined the Institute of Human Relations as a sociologist and, as further evidence of his academic range and depth, from 1948 until his retirement in 1969 served as professor of psychology. In addition to his work with Miller, Dollard is highly regarded for his 1937 book *Caste and Class in a Southern Town*.

Neal Elgar Miller was born in Milwaukee, Wisconsin. He earned a B.S. from the University of Washington, an M.A. from Stanford in 1932, and a Ph.D. in psychology from Yale in 1935, where he worked under Clark Hull, the famous neobehaviorist. He traveled Europe as a research fellow and received psychoanalytic training in Vienna. Miller subsequently joined the Institute of Human Relations at Yale and began his renowned collaboration with Dollard. He conducted research for the U.S. Army Air Force from 1942 to 1946, but returned to Yale and became the James Rowland Angell Professor of Psychology in 1952. He received the Warren Medal for outstanding research in psychology from the Society of Experimental Psychologists in 1957, was elected to the National Academy of Sciences in 1958, and was recognized for Distinguished Scientific Contributions by the American Psychological Association (APA) in 1959. He was elected president of the APA in 1961 and received the National Medal of Science in 1964. Miller moved to Rockefeller University in 1966 to head the laboratory of physiological psychology, where he helped pioneer the field of health psychology, conducting research on such topics as biofeedback and the voluntary control of autonomic nervous system processes. The APA honored him again in 1983 with the Distinguished Professional Contributions to Knowledge Award and in 1991 with the Outstanding Lifetime Contribution to Psychology Award.

SOURCES FOR FURTHER STUDY

Hergenhahn, B. R., and Matthew H. Olson. *An Introduction to Theories of Personality*. 5th ed. Upper Saddle River, N.J.: Prentice-Hall, 1998. The chapter on Dollard and Miller provides one of the most comprehensive summaries of their work, including their classic work on frustration-aggression, social learning, and psychotherapy.

Miller, Neal E. "Obituary: John Dollard (1900-1980)." *American Psychologist* 37, no. 5 (1982): 587-588. Provides an overview of Dollard's life, his professional contributions, and personal reflections from his closest associate.

Phares, E. Jerry, and William F. Chaplin. *Introduction to Personality*. 4th ed. New York: Longman, 1997. The section on reinforcement theory provides an overview of Dollard and Miller's theory and research, including short biographies.

Jay W. Jackson

SEE ALSO: Behaviorism; Conditioning; Habituation and sensitization; Operant conditioning therapies; Pavlovian conditioning; Phobias; Reflexes; S-R theory: Neal E. Miller and John Dollard.

Minnesota Multiphasic Personality Inventory (MMPI)

DATE: First published in 1943; second edition published in 1989
TYPE OF PSYCHOLOGY: Personality; psychopathology
FIELDS OF STUDY: Personality assessment

The Minnesota Multiphasic Personality Inventory is the most widely used and researched personality assessment instrument in clinical practice. It is primarily used to aid in the diagnosis and assessment of the major psychological disorders.

KEY CONCEPTS
• clinical scales
• normative sample

- psychological test
- psychopathology
- restandardization
- validity scales

INTRODUCTION

The Minnesota Multiphasic Personality Inventory (MMPI/MMPI-2) was developed during the late 1930's, reaching publication in 1943. The authors of the test were Starke R. Hathaway, a psychologist, and J. Charnley McKinley, a physician to whom Hathaway reported at the University of Minnesota Hospitals. The test was originally developed to aid in the assessment of adult psychiatric patients, both to describe the type and severity of their disturbance and to measure patient change over time. It quickly grew in popularity to become the most widely used and researched psychological test ever published.

Three characteristics distinguished the MMPI from the psychological tests of the 1930's. First, it was developed as a "broad band" test, that is, a "multiphasic" test that would assess a number of personality attributes in a single administration. Most personality tests up to that time were more narrow in their focus. Second, this was the first personality test to use an empirical method of selecting test questions. This procedure involved selecting test items that differentiated between persons making up a normal population and persons in the clinical group of interest (such as individuals diagnosed with schizophrenia, depression, or other psychiatric disorders) at a statistically significant level. Third, the MMPI incorporated validity scales, or measures of test-taking attitude that identified tendencies to either underreport or overreport psychopathology.

RESTANDARDIZATION

An important limitation of the original MMPI had to do with its normative sample, or the reference group used to represent the normal population (in contrast to the clinical groups). The original normal reference group consisted primarily of a rural, all white, eighth-grade-educated population who were visiting patients at the University of Minnesota Hospital. Over time, a number of criticisms were made that this group, predominantly Scandinavian in origin, was not representative of the broader United States population. Other problems with the MMPI also developed, including outdated test item content, poorly worded items, or item content ob-

jectionable to contemporary test takers (for instance, questions regarding religious beliefs or bodily functions). In response to such concerns, an MMPI restandardization project was begun in 1982, culminating in the publication of the MMPI-2 in 1989. Comparison of the restandardized normal sample to 1990 census data by ethnicity, age, and education indicated that the new normative group was significantly more representative of the United States population than were the original norms, with the exception that well-educated persons were overrepresented. The MMPI-2 also incorporated additional validity measures and newly developed scales reflecting contemporary clinical problems.

DESCRIPTION OF THE TEST

The MMPI-2 is an objectively scored, standardized questionnaire consisting of 567 self-descriptive statements answered as either "true" or "false." Responses can be either hand- or computer-scored and are summarized on a profile sheet. Interpretation is based on both the configuration of scales on the profile sheet and demographic variables characterizing the test-taker. The basic profile sheet is made up of nine validity measures and ten traditional clinical scales. Fifteen additional "content" scales can also be scored, as well as potentially hundreds of supplementary and research scales. The validity scales measure test-taking attitudes, including such characteristics as consistencies in response patterns and tendencies to exaggerate or minimize psychological problems. The clinical scales are labeled both by a number and with traditional psychiatric diagnostic labels such as hypochondriasis, depression, paranoia, and schizophrenia. The specific MMPI scale labels may be misleading in that some diagnostic labels are outdated (such as "psychasthenia" or "hysteria"). In addition, the scales do not effectively differentiate diagnostic groups (for instance, an elevation on the paranoia scale is not exclusive to persons with a paranoia diagnosis). It has thus become standard practice to refer to profiles by characteristic scale numbers (such as a "49" profile) and to interpret them according to relevant research rather than by scale labels. The fifteen content scales reflect the client's endorsement of test items whose content is obvious and descriptive of particular problem areas such as anxiety, health concerns, or family problems. The many supplementary scales measure a wide range of concerns, ranging from addiction proneness to post-traumatic stress disorder to marital distress. The MMPI-2 is appropriate for use only with those aged eighteen years and older. A shorter version of the test, the MMPI-A, is available for use with fourteen- to eighteen-year-old adolescents.

SOURCES FOR FURTHER STUDY

Butcher, James N., ed. *Basic Sources on the MMPI-2.* Minneapolis: University of Minnesota Press, 2000. This text collects in one volume the classic and critical research literature fundamental to a basic understanding and interpretation of the original MMPI and MMPI-2.

_____, ed. *International Adaptations of the MMPI-2.* Minneapolis: University of Minnesota Press, 1996. An edited text by a recognized authority who guided the restandardization of the MMPI-2. Discusses the adaptation of the MMPI-2 into eighteen other languages and general issues relating to cross-national personality assessment.

Caldwell, Alex B. "What Do the MMPI Scales Fundamentally Measure? Some Hypotheses." *Journal of Personality Assessment* 76, no. 1 (2001): 1-17. An edited version of an invited Master Lecture presented to the Society for Personality Assessment Convention in March, 2000. The author shares his views of what the MMPI scales actually measure, based on more than fifty years of interpreting MMPIs through Caldwell Reports, a service highly regarded for its sophisticated computerized interpretations.

Dahlstrom, W. G., D. Lachar, and L. W. Dahlstrom. *MMPI Patterns of American Minorities.* Minneapolis: University of Minnesota Press, 1986. Written by longstanding, esteemed MMPI researchers, this is a classic and still definitive review of MMPI profile patterns among American minority groups.

Friedman, A. F., R. Lewak, D. S. Nichols, and J. T. Webb. *Psychological Assessment with the MMPI-2.* Mahwah, N.J.: Lawrence Erlbaum, 2001. A thorough, detailed introduction to all aspects of the clinical use of the MMPI-2.

David W. Brokaw

SEE ALSO: Beck Depression Inventory (BDI); California Psychological Inventory (CPI); Children's Depression Inventory (CDI); Clinical interviewing, testing, and observation; Depression; Diagnosis; *Diagnostic and Statistical Manual of Mental Disorders* (DSM); Personality interviewing strategies; Personality: Psychophysiological measures; Personality rating scales; State-Trait Anxiety Inventory; Thematic Apperception Test (TAT).

Misbehavior

TYPE OF PSYCHOLOGY: Learning
FIELDS OF STUDY: Attitudes and behavior; biological influences on learning

The association between misbehavior and learning has been addressed by psychoanalytic theorists as well as social learning theorists; both have shed light on the social conditions that precipitate misbehavior, particularly in children.

KEY CONCEPTS
• goals of misbehavior
• imitation
• modeling
• recognition reflex
• social learning

INTRODUCTION

Behavior is called misbehavior when it is found to be unacceptable by others. Those persons who label certain actions as misbehavior are more or less tolerant of a range of behaviors. Furthermore, the people who call certain actions misbehavior are typically adults, and those whose actions are labeled misbehavior are usually children. Within the repertoire of behaviors that are termed misbehavior are noncompliance, defiance, destructiveness, and aggression.

Both psychoanalytic theorists and social learning theorists relate misbehavior to the individual's interpretation of social experiences. A secondary conclusion by theorists in both camps is that misbehavior is purposeful and goal directed. According to both theoretical orientations, the link between social experiences and misbehavior is bridged by an emphasis on the cognition of the individual. What separates the two theoretical views is the role each attributes to human consciousness. The psychoanalytic explanation of why a person misbehaves emphasizes unconscious motivation, whereas social learning theorists assign a larger role to conscious cognitive processes.

DREIKURS'S CONTRIBUTIONS

Rudolf Dreikurs, an early student and colleague of Alfred Adler, was a strong supporter of Adler's school of individual psychology. From the time of his arrival in the United States until his death in 1972, Dreikurs worked to popularize Adler's views. Adler, who believed that the goal of psychology is to educate the whole community toward more effective social living, developed an innovative counseling approach for restricted audiences. This approach focused on a community of committed parents, teachers, and other adults working together toward the fostering of social responsibility in children. This effort resulted in the opening of a number of child guidance centers in Vienna and elsewhere in Europe. Dreikurs participated in the child guidance centers in Vienna and was well known throughout Europe before the Fascists gained power. After escaping to the United States by way of Brazil in 1939, he established a practice in Chicago and thereafter had a profound impact on parent education in this country. Dreikurs placed considerable emphasis on the process by which a person is socialized within the family. By emphasizing this process, Dreikurs provided a basis for understanding how the family atmosphere is played out in the socialization process and how the socialization process contributes to children's misbehavior. Dreikurs's major contributions to Adler's approach consist of the refinement of open-centered family counseling concepts; demonstration of the multiple-therapist concept long before it was presented in the general psychology literature; and the development of a system of democratic conflict resolution to be used in the family, or in any other setting in which people live and interact with one another.

DREIKURS'S FOUR GOALS OF MISBEHAVIOR

Based on his clinical work, Dreikurs discovered four goals that he believed guide all forms of misbehavior: attention, power, revenge, and a display of inadequacy. According to Dreikurs, these goals derive from children's private logic—what they think of themselves, others, life, and the goals they set for themselves. These four categories of misbehavior are seen as goals in that the misbehavior achieves something for the individual.

Persons who misbehave to obtain attention have learned from previous social experiences that a type of misbehavior gains attention from others, even though the attention is typically negative. Those who misbehave with the goal of power have discovered a way of gaining a type of power through actions labeled misbehavior. Individuals whose misbehavior derives from the goal of revenge are those whose bids for attention and power have been met with such negative consequences that they are motivated by the goal of seeking revenge. Finally, people who misbehave with a goal of displaying inadequacy are those who do not try, are often seen as lazy, are unkempt, or appear to be unmotivated. These individuals have given up trying to gain attention and/or power and feel powerless to seek revenge.

The concept of the four goals of misbehavior is premised on the assumption, reflecting the theorizing of Adler, that individuals are social creatures whose behavior is purposeful and whose primary desire is to belong. Thus, the four goals of misbehavior are actually underlying goals, each of which is believed to aid the individual in the quest for belonging. The belief of the person that these goals of misbehavior will secure a place of belonging and acceptance within a family or group is not realized, however, since misbehavior generally alienates one from others. In recognition of this dilemma, Dreikurs emphasized that the goals of misbehavior are mistaken goals. Even though people may be able to observe keenly, accurately, and carefully what goes on around them, they often misinterpret these events, draw mistaken conclusions, and make faulty decisions based on these misinterpretations and mistaken conclusions. This is particularly true of children, whose cognitive understanding of the world differs from that of adults.

RECOGNIZING UNDERLYING GOALS

Although misbehaving persons are generally unaware of the mistaken goals underlying their misbehavior, others can learn to recognize these underlying goals by observing the effects the misbehavior has on others. As noted by Dreikurs, what one is inclined to do in response to another's misbehavior is generally consistent with the goal underlying that misbehavior. Reactions that correspond to and reflect mistaken goals are giving undue attention, engaging in power struggles, seeking retaliation, or giving up in despair. According to this model, others can observe individuals misbehaving according to the logic outlined above, although the misbehaving persons may be unaware of why they are doing so. The key to discerning the person's goal, however, is to take notice not only of that person's behavior but also of others' reactions to that behavior.

Even though the method for recognizing Dreikurs's mistaken goals of misbehavior is clear and simple, the application of this process in decreasing a child's (or an adult's) misbehavior is a bit more complicated. First, if one is attempting to discern the underlying goal motivating another's behavior, one must observe carefully not only that person's misbehavior but also others', including one's own, responses to that behavior. This may require several observations. In observing one's responses, it is necessary to watch not only for actual responses but also for what one is inclined to do in reaction to the misbehavior.

If one's typical response to the misbehavior in question is to give attention (positive or negative) to the person who is misbehaving, then it is logical to assume that attention is the underlying goal (even if one does not actually give attention in that particular instance). If one is inclined to become angry (lose control) in response to misbehavior, there is a good chance that power is the underlying goal. It is important to remember that when one responds to misbehavior by losing one's own control, power is conceded to the misbehaving person.

If one has a tendency to feel hurt by someone else's misbehavior, that instance of misbehavior is probably motivated by a goal of revenge. In this case, the person is responding to feelings of pain and hurt and misbehaves in ways designed to inflict pain on others. This act of revenge, however, is not necessarily directed toward the person or persons who contributed to the pain the individual is acting out. This is a critical point because it emphasizes the necessity of not only observing one's own interactions with the individual but also taking into consideration interactions that person has had with others.

If one experiences a tendency to give up in despair, a display of inadequacy is likely to be the underlying goal of the person who is misbehaving. In this situation, the individual has learned, through repeated experiences, that attempts to gain positive attention and/or power have been relatively fruitless. Rather than continuing to be exposed to painful evaluations and criticisms, a lack of motivation is displayed, others give up in despair, and the person

exhibiting a display of inadequacy is spared the pain of negative evaluation and humiliation.

FOCUS ON AGGRESSION

Social learning theorists also emphasize the process by which the person is socialized within the family. In stressing the relevance of this process to misbehavior, they have addressed various aspects of misconduct. The type of misbehavior that has received the most attention from social learning theorists is aggression, particularly in children. According to this theory, aggressiveness is learned from observing and imitating models. These models include parents who rely on physical punishment as well as other punitive methods of discipline, aggressive siblings and peers, and aggressive models on television. In the case of the parent displaying aggressiveness by the use of physical punishment or verbal attacks, the child is provided a very clear model of aggressive behavior. The child learns from this model that the best way to get people to do what he or she wants is to behave aggressively toward them. Those children who have been exposed to parental models of aggression are more likely to use aggression with siblings and peers. When this occurs, the other child may fight back, decreasing the likelihood that the aggressor will be reinforced for the attack. On the other hand, the victim may cry or run away. In this case, the aggressor succeeds and is thus reinforced for aggressive behavior. Furthermore, other children witnessing the aggression learn that aggression brings reinforcement. In addition to parental, peer, and sibling models of aggression, children are exposed to aggressive models on television that demonstrate vicarious reinforcement for aggression.

STRATEGIES FOR MANAGING MISBEHAVIOR

In the application of theoretical views to the management of misbehavior, Dreikurs (as well as social learning theorists) focuses on the consequences of behavior. Dreikurs's method for decreasing misbehavior consists of three strategies: changing one's responses to the misbehavior so that the unacceptable behavior does not achieve the goal that it is designed to achieve; assisting the misbehaving person in becoming aware of the underlying goal motivating the misbehavior; and making deliberate efforts to assist a person prone to misconduct in achieving a sense of belonging, so that he or she does not resort to misbehavior to satisfy this need.

The first strategy (changing one's response to misbehavior) is simple and straightforward in theory but somewhat more difficult in application. The challenge is to respond differently from the way one is inclined to respond to such behavior. Specifically, this strategy consists of not giving attention to misbehavior designed to attract attention, not reacting angrily or losing control in response to behavior that typically angers or contributes to a loss of control, not focusing on or exposing hurt feelings in response to misbehavior based on a goal of revenge, and not giving up in despair at a person's display of inadequacy.

The second part of the approach (assisting the misbehaving person in becoming aware of the underlying goal motivating the misbehavior) can sometimes be accomplished simply by calling the person's attention to what appears to be the underlying goal. An example of this would be to say to a child, "Do you think that you knock over your sister's blocks to get my attention?" The purpose of this strategy is to assist individuals in becoming conscious of why they behave in ways that others consider unacceptable. If this strategy is to be successful, it must be done in a way that does not communicate a value judgment or sound reproachful. If individuals are not suffering the sting of disapproval, they may be assisted in understanding why they misbehave (which often troubles the person displaying this behavior as much as it does those who are exposed to it). Dreikurs referred to this awareness as the recognition reflex. In emphasizing the value of the recognition reflex for assisting persons in understanding what motivates their misbehavior, Dreikurs pointed out that this tactic is more effective with children than with adolescents and adults, who have had more time to build stronger defense mechanisms.

The third strategy (assisting the misbehaving person in achieving the goal of belonging without resorting to misconduct) is based on an appreciation of every individual's need for attention and power. This understanding suggests an effective approach for decreasing misbehavior by providing sufficient attention to the individual and recognizing the person's need for power.

The strategy of providing attention is uncomplicated. Positive attention should be freely given at any time except when misbehavior is occurring.

Therefore, one does not wait for some specified behavior to occur in order to show attention. Depending on the level of misconduct in which that person is engaging, this could be a long wait. Meanwhile, the misbehavior will probably continue. It is suggested, instead, that attention be generously bestowed in a variety of ways. This could be as casual as recognizing that person's entrance into the room, noticing personal things about that person (haircut, clothes, mood, and so on), and showing interest in ideas, concerns, and questions generated by the person. Based on the relationship one has with the person exhibiting misbehavior, one may choose to design a more structured method of delivering attention, such as engaging the person in projects which provide an opportunity for a large amount of feedback and considerable dialogue.

In order to decrease misbehavior motivated by power needs, it is important to monitor closely experiences of the individual which may diminish the person's sense of power, while simultaneously making deliberate efforts to assist that person in appropriate efforts to gain power. In the case of children misbehaving with an underlying goal of power, one is likely to find that power-assertive methods of discipline are being used with the child. Excessively strict, harsh methods of control, including the use of physical punishment, weaken a child's sense of power and contribute to the likelihood that misbehavior based on power needs will occur. It is reasonable to conclude that any person engaging in misbehavior based on the goal of power has been exposed to some type of experience which contributed to the person's sense of powerlessness.

While monitoring experiences which diminish the person's sense of power is necessary, it is not sufficient for decreasing misbehavior. Persons with a lowered sense of power also require experiences designed to assist them in regaining a feeling of power. According to Dreikurs, the most appropriate group arrangement for meeting the power needs of all individuals within the group is one based on democratic relations. This arrangement, which is based on the concept of equality, does not assume identical responsibilities and privileges to all members. Rather, it is based on a recognition of the equal worth of all members of the group. Within this arrangement, decisions affecting members of the group are made with the needs and well-being of all members in mind. Furthermore, input from all members is encouraged to the degree that it is feasible.

SOCIAL LEARNING APPROACH

The application of the social learning approach to misbehavior is one that focuses on discovering environmental consequences that influence behavior and taking steps to change these consequences, thereby decreasing misbehavior. The misconduct of primary interest to social learning theorists has been aggressiveness. According to their model, since aggressiveness is maintained or increased through the consequence of reinforcement, the recommended approach for dealing with this type of misbehavior is fourfold: Limit exposure to aggressive models in real life and on television; provide models who behave responsibly and considerately, rather than those who behave cruelly or impulsively; be certain that aggression is not reinforced; and reinforce behavior which is incompatible with aggression.

The influence of models on the behavior of individuals was first demonstrated by the work of Albert Bandura in 1962. Since then, social learning theory has been invoked to explain a variety of behaviors. This theoretical approach gets its name from the emphasis it places on social variables as determinants of behavior and personality. Foremost in Bandura's analysis of learning is the role of imitation, which has its conceptual foundation in operant conditioning.

According to social learning theorists, most of a person's learning comes from actively imitating, or modeling, the actions of others. The term "modeling" is used interchangeably with terms such as "observational learning" and "vicarious learning" to mean that one adds to one's repertoire of actions by seeing or hearing someone else perform the behavior, rather than overtly carrying out the behavior oneself.

Bandura's views regarding imitation are reflected in the chief contributions of social learning theory, which consist of an explanation of the way a person acquires a new behavior never attempted before; the identification of the steps involved in the process of learning from models; and explanations of the way consequences influence future actions and of the development of complex behavior.

SOURCES FOR FURTHER STUDY

Brooks, Jane. "Establishing Close Emotional Relationships with Children." In *The Process of Parenting.* 5th ed. Toronto: Mayfield, 1999. Explains Rudoff Dreikurs's view of the democratic family in detail. The focus of his theory, that misbehavior results from faulty goals, is also highlighted. Of particular interest in this chapter is how Dreikurs's views on misbehavior compare with perspectives of other contemporary theorists.

Christensen, Oscar, and Carroll Thomas. "Dreikurs and the Search for Equality." In *Handbook on Parent Education,* edited by Marvin J. Fine. New York: Academic Press, 1980. Presents the views of Alfred Adler and his impact on the work of Rudolf Dreikurs. Dreikurs's views of the child and parent-child relations dominate the chapter. Dreikurs provides a theoretical basis for understanding children's behavior by examining the social context of this behavior.

Crain, William C. "Bandura's Social Learning Theory." In *Theories of Development: Concepts and Applications.* 4th ed. Englewood Cliffs, N.J.: Prentice-Hall, 1999. Social learning theory is presented from a developmental perspective. Although the theory is not covered in depth, the author provides a flavor of the ideas of the theory, including its origins, concepts, and some of its practical applications. Reviews the use of this theory in studies of aggression.

Harris, Judith Rich, and Robert M. Liebert. *The Child: A Contemporary View of Development.* 3d ed. Englewood Cliffs, N.J.: Prentice-Hall, 1991. An excellent summary of social learning theory and its application to the understanding of aggressive behavior. Explains important terms and discusses research focusing on the relation of harsh physical punishment and aggression.

Thomas, R. Murray. *Comparing Theories of Child Development.* 5th ed. Belmont, Calif.: Wadsworth, 1999. Provides an overview of the origins of social learning theory, including how it fits into the behaviorist tradition. A description of key aspects of social learning theory is also presented.

Phyllis A. Heath

SEE ALSO: Aggression; Aggression: Reduction and control; Attention-deficit hyperactivity disorder (ADHD); Cognitive social learning: Walter Mischel; Conduct disorder; Parenting styles; Radical behaviorism: B. F. Skinner; Reinforcement; Social learning: Albert Bandura.

Mischel, Walter

BORN: February 22, 1930, in Vienna, Austria
IDENTITY: Austrian-born U.S. clinical psychologist and personality theorist
TYPE OF PSYCHOLOGY: Personality
FIELDS OF STUDY: Personality assessment; personality theory

Mischel, with Yuichi Shoda, developed a dynamic theory of personality that is an alternative to the traditional, trait-based view.

Walter Mischel was born in Vienna, Austria, on February 22, 1930. His family fled the Nazi regime in 1938 and eventually immigrated to Brooklyn, New York. He earned a B.A. in psychology from New York University in 1951 and an M.A. in clinical psychology from City College of New York in 1953. While a graduate student, he worked as a social worker in the slums of Manhattan. Since the methods of psychoanalysis seemed to have little utility when applied to social work, he sought a more empirically grounded doctoral program. He attained a Ph.D. in clinical psychology in 1956 at Ohio State University, where he studied social learning theory with Julian B. Rotter and personal construct psychology with George A. Kelly. Both men greatly influenced Mischel's subsequent scholarly development.

At Harvard University, he reviewed the empirical research and concluded that most of the studies did not support the prevailing ideas about personality. He levied this serious criticism in a monograph titled *Personality and Assessment* (1968) which was at first disparaged. However, a long debate ensued that revolved around the "personality paradox," a term coined by Daryl Bem and Andrea Allen. At the time, most theorists believed that traits or dispositions characterized a relatively stable personality structure. However, the paradox was that observed behavior was not consistent in a variety of situations. Mainstream psychologists believed that measurement error accounted for the inconsistent data. Mischel believed that the problem was not with flawed measures but with flawed thinking about the nature of personality. The search for the locus of personality consistency and a desire to understand better the organization of personality were major themes for the rest of Mischel's career.

In 1973, he wrote an important paper titled "Toward a Cognitive Social Learning Reconceptualization of Personality." He replaced traits with person variables and considered behavior in context. For example, a person may be shy in some settings and not in others. In 1995, Mischel and Yuichi Shoda wrote "A Cognitive-Affective System Theory of Personality: Reconceptualizing Situations, Dispositions, Dynamics, and Invariance in Personality Structure" that resolved the personality paradox. The surprising resolution was that intra-individual profiles or patterns of responses in a variety of settings were consistent.

Mischel won many awards for his creative work. In 1982 he received the Distinguished Scientific Contribution Award of the American Psychological Association and he held an endowed chair in psychology at Columbia University. In 2000, he was appointed editor of the respected journal *Psychological Review.*

SOURCES FOR FURTHER STUDY

Hall, Calvin S., Gardner Lindzey, and John B. Campbell. *Theories of Personality.* 4th ed. New York: John Wiley & Sons, 1998. Describes major theories and includes a discussion of Mischel's ideas.

Pervin, Lawrence A., and Oliver P. John, eds. *Handbook of Personality: Theory and Research.* 2d ed. New York: Guilford, 1999. Chapters by theoreticians with an introductory chapter describing the history of modern theories.

"Walter Mischel." *American Psychologist* 38, no. 1 (1983): 9-14. Summarizes the life and work of Mischel. Includes an extensive bibliography.

Tanja Bekhuis

SEE ALSO: Cognitive psychology; Cognitive social learning: Walter Mischel; Kelly, George A.; Personality theory.

Mood disorders

TYPE OF PSYCHOLOGY: Psychopathology
FIELDS OF STUDY: Depression

The diagnosis of a mood disorder requires the presence or absence of a mood episode: major depressive episode, manic episode, mixed episode, or hypomanic episode. The mood disorders include major depressive disorder, dysthymic disorder, bipolar I disorder, bipolar II disorder, and cyclothymic disorder. The mood disorders can be specified with seasonal pattern, rapid-cycling, or postpartum onset.

KEY CONCEPTS

- bipolar I disorder
- cyclothymic disorder
- depressive episode
- dysthymic disorder
- hypomanic episode
- major depressive disorder
- manic episode
- postpartum onset
- rapid-cycling
- seasonal pattern

INTRODUCTION

Descriptions of mood disorders can be found in ancient texts such as the Bible and writings of Hippocrates (c. 460-c. 377 B.C.E.). Aulus Cornelius Celsus, a medical writer, described melancholia as a depression caused by "black bile" in about 30 C.E.

Mood disorders are characterized predominantly by a disturbance in mood. The American Psychiatric Association's *Diagnostic and Statistical Manual of Mental Disorders: DSM-IV-TR* (rev. 4th ed., 2000) describes mood episodes that characterize the mood disorders: major depressive episode, manic episode, mixed episode, and hypomanic episode.

In a major depressive episode, a person experiences depressed mood for a period of at least two weeks. For the diagnosis of a depressive episode, the person must experience at least four of the following symptoms: changes in appetite or weight, sleep, and psychomotor activity; decreased energy; feelings of worthlessness or guilt; difficulty concentrating; recurrent thoughts of death or suicide. There is significant impairment in occupational or social functioning.

In a manic episode, a person experiences an abnormally elevated or irritable mood for at least one week. In addition, the person must experience at least three of the following symptoms: inflated self-esteem, decreased need for sleep, pressured (loud, rapid) speech, racing thoughts, excessive planning of or participation in multiple activities, distractibility, psychomotor agitation (such as pacing), or excessive participation in activities that may lead

to negative consequences (such as overspending). There is severe impairment in social or occupational functioning, or there are psychotic features.

A hypomanic episode is characterized by a period of at least four days of abnormally elevated or irritable mood. The affected person must experience at least three of the following symptoms: inflated self-esteem, decreased need for sleep, pressured speech, flight of ideas, increased involvement in goal-directed activities, psychomotor agitation, or excessive participation in activities that may lead to negative consequences. The hypomanic episode is differentiated from the manic episode by less severe impairment in social or occupational functioning and a lack of psychotic features.

A person experiencing a mixed episode displays symptoms of both manic and major depressive episodes nearly every day for a period of one week.

Major depressive disorder is characterized by one or more major depressive episodes. Dysthymic disorder involves at least two years of depressed mood with symptoms that do not meet the criteria for a major depressive episode. Bipolar I disorder includes one or more manic or mixed episodes with major depressive episodes. Bipolar II disorder is characterized by one or more major depressive episodes with at least one hypomanic episode. Cyclothymic disorder is represented by at least two years of hypomanic episodes and depressive symptoms that do not meet the criteria for a major depressive episode.

MAJOR DEPRESSIVE DISORDER

Major depressive disorder involves disturbances in mood, concentration, sleep, activity, appetite, and social behavior. It is much more than temporarily feeling sad. It is estimated that one out of every five women and one in fifteen men will suffer from major depression in his or her lifetime. An estimated 18 million Americans are affected. In 1990, $30.4 billion was lost as a result of the illness.

A major depressive episode may develop gradually or appear quite suddenly, without any relation to environmental factors. The symptoms of major depressive disorder will vary among individuals, but there are some common symptoms. People with major depressive disorder may have difficulty falling asleep, sleep restlessly or excessively, and wake up without feeling rested. They may experience a decrease or increase in a desire to eat. They may crave certain foods, such as carbohydrates. They may be unable to pay attention to things. Even minor decisions may seem impossible to make. A loss of energy is manifested in slower mental processing, an inability to perform normal daily routines, and slowed reaction time. Sufferers may experience anhedonia, an inability to experience pleasure. They lose interest in activities they used to enjoy. They ruminate about failures and feel guilty and helpless. People with major depressive disorder tend to seek negative feedback about themselves from others. They see no hope for improvement and may be thinking of death and suicide. In adolescents, depression may be manifested in acting out, anger, aggressiveness, delinquency, drug abuse, poor performance in school, or running away. Depression is a primary risk factor in the third leading cause of death among young people, suicide.

There is probably no single cause of major depressive disorder, although it is primarily a disorder of the brain. A chemical dysfunction and genetics are thought to be part of the cause. Neural circuits, which regulate mood, thinking, sleep, appetite, and behavior, do not function normally. Neurotransmitters are out of balance. One neurotransmitter implicated in depression is serotonin. It is thought that in major depressive disorder there is a reduced amount of serotonin available in the neural circuits (specifically, in the synapse). This results in reduced or lacking nerve impulse. In many patients with the disorder, the hormonal system that regulates the body's response to stress is overactive. Stress, alcohol or drug abuse, medication, or outlook on life may trigger depressive episodes.

Cognitive theories of depression state that a negative cognitive style, such as pessimism, represents a diathesis (a predisposition) which, in the presence of stress, triggers negative cognitions such as hopelessness. Negative cognitions increase the person's vulnerability to depression. Some common precipitants of depression in vulnerable people include marital conflict, academic or work-related difficulty, chronic medical problems, and physical or sexual abuse.

DSM-IV-TR Criteria for Major Depressive Episode

Five or more of the following symptoms present during the same two-week period and representing a change from previous functioning:

- depressed mood or loss of interest or pleasure (at least one); does not include symptoms clearly due to a general medical condition, mood-incongruent delusions, or hallucinations
- depressed mood most of the day, nearly every day, as indicated by either subjective report or observation made by others; in children and adolescents, can be irritable mood
- markedly diminished interest or pleasure in all, or almost all, activities most of the day, nearly every day, as indicated by either subjective account or observation made by others
- significant weight loss (when not dieting) or weight gain or decrease/increase in appetite nearly every day; in children, consider failure to make expected weight gains
- insomnia or hypersomnia nearly every day
- psychomotor agitation or retardation nearly every day observable by others, not merely subjective feelings of restlessness or being slowed down

- fatigue or loss of energy nearly every day
- feelings of worthlessness or excessive or inappropriate guilt (which may be delusional) nearly every day, not merely self-reproach or guilt about being sick
- diminished ability to think or concentrate, or indecisiveness, nearly every day, either by subjective account or as observed by others
- recurrent thoughts of death (not just fear of dying), recurrent suicidal ideation without a specific plan, or suicide attempt or specific plan for committing suicide

Criteria for Mixed Episode not met

Symptoms cause clinically significant distress or impairment in social, occupational, or other important areas of functioning

Symptoms not due to direct physiological effects of a substance or general medical condition

Symptoms not better accounted for by bereavement, persist for longer than two months, or characterized by marked functional impairment, morbid preoccupation with worthlessness, suicidal ideation, psychotic symptoms, or psychomotor retardation

DSM-IV-TR Criteria for Mixed Episode

Criteria met both for Manic Episode and for Major Depressive Episode (except for duration) nearly every day during at least a one-week period

Mood disturbance sufficiently severe to cause marked impairment in occupational functioning or usual social activities or relationships with others or to necessitate hospitalization to prevent harm to self or others, or psychotic features present

Symptoms not due to direct physiological effects of a substance or general medical condition

Mixed-like episodes clearly caused by somatic antidepressant treatment (medication, electroconvulsive therapy, light therapy) should not count toward diagnosis of Bipolar I Disorder

Criteria for Severity/Psychotic/Remission Specifiers (DSM code in fifth digit; can be applied to Mixed Episode in Bipolar I Disorder only if the most recent mood episode):
  • Mild (.x1): No more than minimum symptom criteria met for both Manic Episode and Major Depressive Episode

  • Moderate (.x2): Symptoms or functional impairment between Mild and Severe
  • Severe Without Psychotic Features (.x3): Almost continual supervision required to prevent physical harm to self or others
  • Severe with Psychotic Features (.x4): Delusions or hallucinations; if possible, specify whether psychotic features are mood-congruent (delusions or hallucinations entirely consistent with the typical manic or depressive themes) or mood-incongruent (delusions or hallucinations that do not involve typical manic or depressive themes; includes persecutory delusions not directly related to grandiose or depressive themes, thought insertion, and delusions of being controlled)
  • In Partial Remission (.x5): Symptoms of Mixed Episode present but full criteria not met, or a period occurs without any significant symptoms of a Mixed Episode lasting less than two months following the end of the Mixed Episode
  • In Full Remission (.x6): No significant signs or symptoms present in the past two months
  • Unspecified (.x0)

In most cases, medication and/or psychotherapy is the treatment of choice. Treatment depends on the severity and pattern of the symptoms. With treatment, 80 percent of people with major depressive disorder return to normal functioning.

Antidepressant drugs influence the functioning of certain neurotransmitters (serotonin, which regulates mood, and norepinephrine, which regulates the body's energy). Tricyclic antidepressants act simultaneously to increase both these neurotransmitters. This type of antidepressant has often intolerable side effects such as sleepiness, nervousness, dizziness, dry mouth, or constipation. Monoamine oxidase inhibitors (MAOIs) increase levels of these same neurotransmitters plus dopamine, which regulates attention and pleasure. MAOIs can cause dizziness and interact negatively with some foods. Selective serotonin reuptake inhibitors (SSRIs) have fewer side effects but can cause nausea, insomnia or sleepiness, agitation, or sexual dysfunction. Aminoketones increase norepinephrine and dopamine, with agitation, insomnia, and anxiety being common side effects. Selective norepinephrine reuptake inhibitors (SNRIs) increase levels of norepinephrine and

can cause dry mouth, constipation, increased sweating, and insomnia. The selective serotonin reuptake inhibitor and blockers (SSRIBs) increase serotonin and elicit the fewest side effects (nausea, dizziness, sleepiness). Herbal remedies, such as St. John's wort, may act like SSRIs. Some drugs blunt the action of a neurotransmitter known as substance P. Other drugs reduce the level and effects of a stress-sensitive brain chemical known as corticotropin-releasing factor (CRF). The hypothalamus, the part of the brain that manages hormone release, increases production of CRF when a threat is detected. The body responds with reduced appetite, decreased sex drive, and heightened alertness. Persistent overactivation of this hormone may lead to depression. The effects of antidepressants are due to slow-onset adaptive changes in neurons. They may take several weeks to have a noticeable effect.

Psychotherapy works by changing the way the brain functions. Cognitive-behavioral therapy helps patients change the negative styles of thinking and behaving associated with depression. Therapies teach patients new skills to help them cope better with life, increase self-esteem, cope with stress, and

DSM-IV-TR Criteria for Manic Episode

Distinct period of abnormally and persistently elevated, expansive, or irritable mood, lasting at least one week or any duration if hospitalization is necessary

During the period of mood disturbance, three or more of the following symptoms have persisted (four if the mood is only irritable) and have been present to a significant degree:
- inflated self-esteem or grandiosity
- decreased need for sleep
- more talkative than usual or pressure to keep talking
- flight of ideas or subjective experience that thoughts are racing
- distractibility
- increase in goal-directed activity (either socially, at work or school, or sexually) or psychomotor agitation
- excessive involvement in pleasurable activities with high potential for painful consequences (such as unrestrained buying sprees, sexual indiscretions, foolish business investments)

Criteria for Mixed Episode not met

Mood disturbance sufficiently severe to cause marked impairment in occupational functioning or usual social activities or relationships with others or to necessitate hospitalization to prevent harm to self or others, or psychotic features present

Symptoms not due to direct physiological effects of a substance or general medical condition

Manic-like episodes clearly caused by somatic antidepressant treatment (medication, electroconvulsive therapy, light therapy) should not count toward diagnosis of Bipolar I Disorder

Criteria for Severity/Psychotic/Remission Specifiers (DSM code in fifth digit; can be applied to Manic Episode in Bipolar I Disorder only if the most recent mood episode):
- Mild (.x1): Minimum symptom criteria met for Manic Episode
- Moderate (.x2): Extreme increase in activity or impairment in judgment
- Severe Without Psychotic Features (.x3): Almost continual supervision required to prevent physical harm to self or others
- Severe with Psychotic Features (.x4): Delusions or hallucinations; if possible, specify whether psychotic features are mood-congruent (delusions or hallucinations entirely consistent with the typical manic themes of inflated worth, power, knowledge, identity, or special relationship to a deity or famous person) or mood-incongruent (delusions or hallucinations that do not involve typical manic themes; includes persecutory delusions not directly related to grandiose ideas or themes, thought insertion, and delusions of being controlled)
- In Partial Remission (.x5): Symptoms of a Manic Episode present but full criteria not met, or a period occurs without any significant symptoms of a Manic Episode lasting less than two months following the end of the Manic Episode
- In Full Remission (.x6): No significant signs or symptoms present in the past two months
- Unspecified (.x0)

---

deal with interpersonal relationships. There is evidence that severe depression responds most favorably with a combination of medication and psychotherapy.

Electroconvulsive therapy (ECT) is an effective treatment for major depressive disorder. The treatment was first developed in 1934. Between 80 and 90 percent of people with the disorder show great improvement with ECT, which produces a seizure in the brain by applying electrical stimulation to the brain through electrodes placed on the scalp. ECT reduces the level of CRF. The treatment is usually repeated to obtain a therapeutic response. Common, yet short-lived, side effects include memory loss and other cognitive deficits.

DYSTHYMIC DISORDER

Dysthymic disorder was first introduced as a category of mood disorder in 1980. Dysthymia means "ill-humored." It is characterized as a mild, chronic depression lasting at least two years and affects 3 to 5 percent of all Americans. The majority of people with dysthymia also develop major depressive disorder, a state called double depression. The disorder is more prevalent in women than in men.

Essentially, dysthymic disorder is a low-grade, chronic depression. Diagnosis of dysthymic disorder requires the impairment of physical and social functioning. Treatment may include cognitive and behavioral therapy as well as pharmacotherapy, especially SSRIs.

BIPOLAR DISORDER

In 1686, Théophile Bonet, a French pathologist, described a mental illness he called *maniaco-melancholicus*. In 1854, Jules Falret, a French physician, described *folie circulaire*, distinguished by alternating moods of depression and mania. In 1899, Emil Kraepelin, a German psychologist, described manic-depressive psychosis. Bipolar disorder has a lifetime prevalence of 1.2 percent. It affects more than 2.3 million adult Americans each year. It is equally common in men and women.

There is a genetic link to bipolar disorder. About 50 percent of all bipolar disorder patients have at least one parent with a mood disorder. An increased level of calcium ions is found in the blood of patients with bipolar disorder. There is also a lowered blood flow in the brain, as well as slower overall metabolism. Some research suggests that bipolar disorder may be caused by disturbed circadian rhythms and related to disturbances in melatonin secretion.

The DSM-IV-TR divides bipolar disorder into bipolar I disorder, bipolar II disorder, and cyclothymic disorder. Bipolar I disorder is characterized by the occurrence of one or more manic episodes or mixed episodes and one or more major depressive episodes. Bipolar II disorder is characterized by the occurrence of one or more major depressive episodes accompanied by at least one hypomanic episode. Cyclothymic disorder is a chronic, fluctuating mood disturbance involving periods of hypomanic episodes and periods of major depressive episodes.

Treatment options include psychotherapy and medication. Mood stabilizers, such as lithium and divalproex sodium, are the most commonly used medications. Lithium is a naturally occurring substance that increases serotonin levels in the brain. Side effects can include dry mouth, high overdose toxicity, nausea, and tremor. Divalproex sodium increases GABA (gamma-amino butyric acid) in the brain. Neurotransmitters trigger either "go" signals that allow messages to be passed on to other cells in the brain or "stop" signals that prevent messages from being forwarded. GABA is the most common message-altering neurotransmitter in the brain. Possible side effects of divalproex sodium include constipation, headache, nausea, liver damage, and tremor. Olanzapine increases levels of dopamine and serotonin. Side effects include drowsiness, dry mouth, low blood pressure, rapid heartbeat, and tremor. Anticonvulsants are also widely prescribed. Carbamazepine, for example, increases GABA and serotonin. Possible side effects include blurred vision, dizziness, dry mouth, stomach upset, or sedation. In the case of severe mania, patients may take a

---

DSM-IV-TR Criteria for Hypomanic Episode

Distinct period of persistently elevated, expansive, or irritable mood, lasting throughout at least four days and clearly different from the usual nondepressed mood

During the period of mood disturbance, three or more of the following symptoms have persisted (four if the mood is only irritable) and have been present to a significant degree:

- inflated self-esteem or grandiosity
- decreased need for sleep
- more talkative than usual or pressure to keep talking
- flight of ideas or subjective experience that thoughts are racing
- distractibility
- increase in goal-directed activity (either socially, at work or school, or sexually) or psychomotor agitation
- excessive involvement in pleasurable activities with high potential for painful consequences (such as

unrestrained buying sprees, sexual indiscretions, foolish business investments)

Episode is associated with unequivocal change in functioning uncharacteristic of the person when not symptomatic

Disturbance in mood and change in functioning observable by others

Episode not severe enough to cause marked impairment in social or occupational functioning or to necessitate hospitalization

No psychotic features present

Symptoms are not due to direct physiological effects of a substance or general medical condition

Hypomanic-like episodes clearly caused by somatic antidepressant treatment (medication, electroconvulsive therapy, light therapy) should not count toward diagnosis of Bipolar II Disorder tranquilizer or a neuroleptic (antipsychotic drug) in addition to the mood stabilizer. During the depressive episode, the person may take an antidepressant. ECT may also be helpful during severe depressive episodes.

SPECIFIERS FOR MOOD DISORDERS

Specifiers allow for a more specific diagnosis, which assists in treatment and prognosis. A postpartum onset specifier can be applied to a diagnosis of major depressive disorder, or bipolar I or II disorder if the onset is within four weeks after childbirth. Symptoms include fluctuations in mood and intense (sometimes delusional) preoccupation with infant well-being. Severe ruminations or delusional thoughts about the infant are correlated with increased risk of harm to the infant. The mother may be uninterested in the infant, afraid of being alone with the infant, or may even try to kill the child (infanticide) while experiencing auditory hallucinations instructing her to do so or delusions that the child is possessed. Postpartum mood episodes severely impair functioning, which differentiates them from the "baby blues" that affects about 70 percent of women within ten days after birth.

Seasonal pattern specifier can be applied to bipolar I or II disorder or major depressive disorder. Occurrence of major depressive episodes is correlated with seasonal changes. In the most common variety, depressive episodes occur in the fall or winter and remit in the spring. The less common type is characterized by depressive episodes in the summer. Symptoms include lack of energy, oversleeping, overeating, weight gain, and carbohydrate craving. Light therapy, which uses bright visible-spectrum light, may bring relief to patients with a seasonal pattern to their mood disorder.

The rapid cycler specifier can be applied to bipolar I or II disorder. Cycling is the process of going from depression to mania, or hypomania, and back or vice versa. Cycles can be as short as a few days or as long as months or years. Rapid cycling involves the occurrence of four or more mood episodes during the previous twelve months. In extreme cases, rapid cyclers can change from depression to mania and back or vice versa in as short as a few days without a normal mood period between episodes. Seventy to ninety pecent of rapid cyclers are both premenopausal and postmenopausal women. Rapid cycling is associated with a poorer prognosis.

SOURCES FOR FURTHER STUDY

Copeland, Mary Ellen. *The Depression Workbook: A Guide for Living with Depression and Manic Depression.* Oakland, Calif.: New Harbinger, 1992. The author has written a workbook for coping with depression based on a study of 120 people with depression and manic depression. She includes sections on possible causes of mood disorders and offers advice about building a support system, finding a health care professional, building self-esteem, and preventing suicide.

Court, Bryan L., and Gerald E. Nelson. *Bipolar Puzzle Solution: A Mental Health Client's Perspective.* Philadelphia: Taylor & Francis, 1996. The authors provide answers to questions asked by support group members about living with manic-depressive illness.

Cronkite, Kathy. *On the Edge of Darkness.* New York: Dell, 1994. This is a collection of celebrity accounts of their personal experiences with depression. The reader is invited into their experiences of what depression feels like, how it is treated, and the consequences to the individual and family.

Dowling, Colette. *You Mean I Don't Have to Feel This Way? New Help for Depression, Anxiety, and Addiction.* New York: Macmillan, 1991. The author presents the biological basis of disorders including bulimia, depression, and panic disorder. She includes a section on getting help through psychotherapy and medication.

Gold, Mark S. *The Good News About Depression: Breakthrough Medical Treatments That Can Work for You.* New York: Bantam Books, 1995. The author, a biopsychiatrist, guides the reader through treatments available to people with depression. He describes conditions that mimic the symptoms of depression.

Ingersoll, Barbara D., and Sam Goldstein. *Lonely, Sad, and Angry.* New York: Doubleday, 1995. The authors provide information about depressive disorders in children and adolescents. They include guidelines on how to react to a crisis, what to expect in the future, and how to get family help. There is also a section on recognizing depression in the classroom.

Moreines, Robert N., and Patricia L. McGuire. *Light Up Your Blues: Understanding and Overcoming Seasonal Affective Disorders.* Washington, D.C.: The PIA Press, 1989. The authors, both biopsychiatrists, describe the symptoms, causes, and effects of seasonal affective disorder. They also describe phototherapy.

Nelson, John E., and Andrea Nelson, eds. *Sacred Sorrows: Embracing and Transforming Depression.* New York: Jeremy P. Tarcher/Putnam, 1996. This is an anthology of personal experiences, biological research, psychological research, and spiritual traditions written by psychiatrists, psychologists, social workers, novelists, philosophers, and teachers. The book provides a firsthand experience of depression and a look at theories about why people become depressed. Some of the essays discuss treatments including medication, physical exercise, psychotherapy, and raising planetary awareness.

Radke-Yarrow, Marian. *Children of Depressed Mothers.* New York: Cambridge University Press, 1998. The author presents a developmental perspective on the children of depressed mothers. The book reports the results of a longitudinal study of children and their families.

Thompson, Tracy. *The Beast: A Journey Through Depression.* New York: Penguin, 1996. A journalist tells the story of how she came to terms with her depression. Good firsthand discussion of symptoms such as short-term memory deficits, anxiety, anhedonia, and changes in sleep patterns, sensation, and perception. Her account includes a frank discussion of feelings of isolation and thoughts of suicide.

Elizabeth M. McGhee Nelson

SEE ALSO: Bipolar disorder; Clinical depression; Depression; Drug therapies; Postpartum depression; Seasonal affective disorder; Shock therapy.

Moral development

TYPE OF PSYCHOLOGY: Developmental psychology
FIELDS OF STUDY: Infancy and childhood; social perception and cognition

Moral development is the process of internalizing society's rules and principles of right and wrong. In order to maintain a stable social order, the achievement of morality is necessary. Acquiring morals is a sequential process linked to a person's stage of moral reasoning and cognitive understanding.

KEY CONCEPTS
- cognitive development
- empathy
- moral development
- moral rules
- morality
- social order

INTRODUCTION

Morality is a set of standards that a person has about the rightness and wrongness of various kinds of behavior. Moral development is the way in which these sets of standards change over a period of time and experiences. Without moral rules—obligatory social regulations based on the principles of justice and welfare for others—society would be chaotic and without order. Most societies, for example, agree that certain behaviors (such as murder and theft) are wrong, and most people follow these moral principles. Not everyone has the same way of reasoning about the morality of a situation, however, as seen in the following two scenarios from the work of psychologist Jean Piaget.

A little boy named John is in his room. He is called to dinner, and he goes into the dining room. Behind the door on a chair is a tray with fifteen cups on it. John does not know this; when he goes in, the door knocks against the tray, and all fifteen cups are broken. There is another boy, named Henry. One day when his mother is out he tries to get some jam from the cupboard. He climbs onto a chair but cannot reach it; he knocks over a cup. The cup falls down and breaks.

When asked which of the above two boys is more naughty, most adults would immediately reply that Henry is more guilty. Conversely, a child between six and ten years of age usually will say that John is more guilty. The differences between the two scenes consist of both the amount of damage done and the intentions of the two children. It is obvious that children and adults do not view the situations in the same way.

INFLUENCE OF FREUD AND PIAGET

Human morality has been an issue in philosophy since the days of Aristotle; psychology primarily began to study the topic in the early twentieth century. At this time, both Sigmund Freud and Piaget addressed the issue of children's moral development.

Freud proposed that children around four years of age assimilate the morals and standards of their same-sex parent, resulting in the onset of the child's superego, which is the storehouse for one's conscience. Thus, children have a rudimentary sense of right and wrong based on the morals of their parental figure. Since Freud's concept was based on his theory of psychosexual development, it was discredited by his European colleagues for most of his lifetime. Thus, his theory of moral acquisition has not generally been the basis of research on the development of morality.

Piaget began observing children when he was giving intelligence tests in the laboratory of Alfred Binet. He observed that children do not reason in the same way that adults do. Thus, by questioning Swiss schoolchildren about their rules in a game of marbles, Piaget adapted his theory of cognitive development to moral development. Lawrence Kohlberg elaborated on Piaget's theory by studying children's as well as adults' reasoning concerning moral dilemmas. Kohlberg is still generally considered the leading theorist of moral development.

STAGES OF MORAL DEVELOPMENT

According to Piaget and Kohlberg, moral judgments are related to the stage of cognitive development from which a person is operating when making these judgments. According to Piaget's theory, the development of morality includes several stages. People cannot progress to higher stages of moral development until they have also progressed through higher stages of cognitive understanding. Cognition refers to the mental processes of thinking, reasoning, knowing, remembering, understanding, and problem solving. During the premoral stage (through five years of age), children have little awareness of morals. As children grow, they learn about cooperative activity and equality among peers. This cognitive knowledge leads to a new respect for rights and wrongs. At this stage (age six to ten), children cannot judge that Henry is more guilty than John, because they are not capable of understanding the differences in the children's intentions. The only understanding is of the degree of damage done. Therefore, the number of cups broken is the basis for the judgment of the wrongness of the act, regardless of the actor's good or bad intentions.

Finally, as children develop, they learn that rules can be challenged and are able to consider other factors, such as a person's intentions and motivation. Once this shift in perception occurs, children's moral development will progress to a higher stage.

ROLE OF REASONING

Kohlberg expanded Piaget's theory by investigating how people reasoned the rightness or wrongness of an act and not how people actually behaved. For example, Kohlberg proposed the following moral dilemma. A man named Heinz had a wife who was dying from a disease that could be cured with a drug manufactured by a local pharmacist. The drug was expensive to make, but the druggist was charging ten times the amount it cost. Heinz could not afford the drug and pleaded with the man to discount the drug or let him pay a little at a time. The druggist refused, so Heinz broke into the pharmacy and stole the drug for his wife. Should Heinz have stolen the drug?

By listening to people's reasoning concerning Heinz's actions, Kohlberg proposed that there are three levels (of two stages each) of moral reasoning. The first level is called the preconventional level; in this stage, a person's feelings of right and wrong are based on an external set of rules that have been handed down by an authority figure such as a parent, teacher, or religious figure. These rules are obeyed in order to avoid punishment and/or to gain rewards. In other words, people at this stage of moral reasoning would not steal the drug—not because they believed that stealing was wrong, but rather because they had been told not to and would fear being caught and punished for their action.

The second level of moral reasoning is the conventional level, at which judgments of right and wrong are based on other people's expectations. For example, at this level there are two substages. One is known as the "good boy/nice girl" orientation, in which morality is based on winning approval and avoiding disapproval by one's immediate group. In other words, people may or may not steal the drug based on what they believe their peers would think of them. The second substage is called the "law and order" orientation, under which moral behavior is thought of in terms of obedience to the authority figure and the established social order. Social order refers to the way in which a society or culture functions, based on the rules, regulation, and standards that are held and taught by each member of the society. The "laws" are usually obeyed without question, regardless of the circumstances, and are seen as the mechanism for the maintenance of social order. A person operating from this stage would say that Heinz should not steal the drug because it was against the law—and if he did steal the drug, he should go to jail for his crime.

The third level of moral reasoning is called the postconventional orientation. At this stage, the person is more concerned with a personal commitment to higher principles than with behavior dictated by society's rules. Disobeying the law would be in some instances far less immoral than obeying a law that is believed to be wrong, and being punished for the legal disobedience would be easier than the guilt and self-condemnation of disobeying the personal ethical principles held by that person. For example, many civil rights workers and Vietnam War conscientious objectors were jailed, beaten, and outcast from mainstream society, but those consequences were far less damaging to them than transgressing their own convictions would have been.

According to Kohlberg, the preconventional stage is characteristic of young children, while the conventional stage is more indicative of the general population. It has been estimated that only about 20 percent of the adult population reach the post-conventional stage. Thus, the course of moral development is not the same for everyone. Even some adults operate at the preconventional level of moral reasoning. Education, parental affection, observation and imitation, and explanations of the consequences of behavior are factors in determining the course of moral development in a child.

ROLE-PLAYING

Moral development is a progression from one stage to a different, higher stage of reasoning. One cannot proceed to a higher stage of morality without the accompanying cognitive understanding. Thus, if a child thinks that John, who broke fifteen cups, is more guilty than Henry, who broke one cup, then merely telling the child that Henry's intentions were not as good as John's, and therefore John is not as guilty, is not going to change the child's perceptions. The child's understanding of the situation must be actively changed. One way of doing this is through role-playing. The child who thinks that John is more guilty can be told to act out the two

scenes, playing each of the two boys. By asking the child questions about his or her feelings while going through each of the scenes, one can help the child gain empathy (the capacity for experiencing the feelings and thoughts of other people) for each of the characters and gain a better understanding of intentions and actions. Once the child has the cognitive understanding of intentions, he or she is then able to reason at a higher level of moral development.

In other words, in trying to elevate someone's moral reasoning, the first goal is to elevate his or her cognitive understanding of the situation. This can also be done by citing similar examples within the person's own experience and chaining them to the event at hand. For example, if last week the child had accidentally broken something, asking the child how he or she remembers feeling when that event happened will remind the child of the emotions experienced at the time of the event. The child must then associate the remembered emotions with the situation at hand. This can be accomplished by asking questions, such as "Do you think that John might have felt the same way as you did when you broke the vase?" or "How do you think John felt when the cups fell down? Have you ever felt the same?" If one merely tells the child that John felt bad, the child may or may not comprehend the connection, but if one asks the child to reason through the situation by having empathy for John, then the child is more likely to progress to the next stage of moral reasoning.

This type of empathetic role-playing can be very important in trying to change deviant behavior. If a child is stealing, then having the child imagine or play a role in a situation where he or she is the one being stolen from is the quickest way for the child to change his or her judgments of the rightness or wrongness of the situation. Punishment may deter the behavior, but it does not result in a change in cognitive understanding or moral reasoning.

In addition to changing moral reasoning powers, this type of role-playing is also more likely to aid the child from an understimulated home environment. The child whose social environment includes many incidents of undesirable behaviors or who lacks examples of positive behaviors must be stimulated in ways that appeal to current cognitive understanding but that show ways of thinking that differ from current examples in his or her life.

STUDY OF SOCIAL COGNITIONS

Other areas of psychological research are concerned with the topic of children's "social cognitions," which subsumes the topic of morals and considers other issues such as empathy, attribution, and motivations. One area that has come to light is the issue of the effect of the emotions on cognitions and their contribution to moral judgments. For example, it has been shown that people in a good mood are more likely to help than those in a bad mood. Expanding on this premise, other research has demonstrated that even the way people perceive an object or situation is closely linked to their psychological or emotional states at the time. Even concrete perceptions can be changed by a person's state of being. One example is that people who are poor actually judge the size of a quarter to be larger than do people who are rich.

As cognitive theories begin to consider the interactive components that emotions have in cognitions, new methods of study and new theoretical predictions will change the way cognitive psychologists study such areas as problem solving, decision making, reasoning, and memory. Each of these areas is independently related to the study of moral development and should affect the way psychologists think about how people acquire and think about morality within society.

In addition, as society increases in sophistication and technology, new issues will emerge that will strain old theories. Issues that are particular to new generations will result in new ways of thinking about morality that were not faced by past generations. The direction that moral development goes is ultimately highly dependent on the problems of the current society.

SOURCES FOR FURTHER STUDY

Duska, Ronald F., and Mariellen Whelan. *Moral Development: A Guide to Piaget and Kohlberg.* New York: Paulist Press, 1975. Presents Jean Piaget's theory and its implications for Lawrence Kohlberg's expansion into his own theory of moral development. All of the moral stories used by Piaget and Kohlberg in their research are replicated in this book. Also includes research findings and ways in which to apply these theories to everyday situations in teaching children. This book can be read easily by the high school or college student.

Gilligan, Carol, Janie Victoria Ward, and Jill McLean Taylor, eds. *Mapping the Moral Domain.* Cambridge, Mass.: Harvard University Press, 1990. A collection of essays presenting the contribution of women's studies to Kohlbergian theories of moral development.

Nucci, Larry P. *Education in the Moral Domain.* New York: Cambridge University Press, 2001. Brings together theoretical and practical approaches to creating a classroom environment that nurtures moral development in children.

Reed, Donald R. C. *Following Kohlberg: Liberalism and the Practice of Democratic Community.* South Bend, Ind.: University of Notre Dame Press, 1998. Offers a comprehensive overview of Kohlberg's research, from an empirical and psychological perspective as well as a more abstract philosophy.

Rich, John Martin, and Joseph L. DeVitis. *Theories of Moral Development.* 2d ed. Springfield, Ill.: Charles C Thomas, 1996. Presents a range of psychologists' theories on moral development, including Sigmund Freud, Alfred Adler, Carl Jung, and David Sears. In addition, it places moral development within the framework of higher education and relates it to a life-span perspective. Certain sections of the book would be difficult for a novice student to follow; however, in terms of a summary review of theoretical positions, the book is a handy reference.

Donna Frick-Horbury

SEE ALSO: Adolescence: Cognitive skills; Birth order and personality; Cognitive ability: Gender differences; Cognitive development: Jean Piaget; Crowd behavior; Development; Gilligan, Carol; Juvenile delinquency; Women's psychology: Carol Gilligan.

Mother-child relationship

TYPE OF PSYCHOLOGY: Developmental psychology
FIELDS OF STUDY: Infancy and childhood

The mother-child relationship is a process of attachment that begins at birth and is usually in place by one year of age. Attachments can be either secure or insecure and are based primarily on the mother's response to the child. However, infants participate in the synchrony of the attachment relationship.

KEY CONCEPTS
- ambivalent attachment
- avoidant attachment
- biological preparedness
- critical periods
- disorganized attachment
- ethological theory of attachment
- resistant attachment
- secure attachment
- separation anxiety

INTRODUCTION

John Bowlby (1907-1990) was one of the first psychologists to be interested in studying attachment patterns in mother and child. He became involved in this when he was working with juvenile thieves and noticed that all such youths had experienced a disruptive relationship with their mothers when they were infants or young children. His studies led him to formulate his theory of attachment, which is considered the most comprehensive theory available. Bowlby's theory is based on the ethological principle that some behaviors are biologically programmed for optimal adaptability to the environment, which in turn increases the probability for survival. According to Bowlby, infants' behaviors are biologically programmed to insure attachment to a primary caretaker and attachment is an optimal strategy for survival.

ETHOLOGICAL THEORY OF ATTACHMENT

Mother and child relationships begin as an interactive dance in which each party responds to the other with a set of behaviors meant to result in a synchronized pattern of love. According to the principles of Bowlby's ethological theory of attachment, all infants are born into the world biologically prepared to respond to attachment behaviors from a primary caretaker. At birth, infants have a set of limited responses, each of which elicit a specific response in an adult. For example, the cries of newborn babies will trigger milk flow in their mothers or increase the physiological arousal of any adult, which in turn increases the probability that the child's needs will be met. Other examples include the fact that a newborn can recognize its mother's voice, will grasp a finger placed in its hand, and will calm down when touched. In turn, an adult is likely to respond to these behaviors with loving and tender caresses and words. As the interactions grow and mature, the patterns of attachment become more canalized until, at about one year old, a child can be classified into one of several attachment patterns.

ATTACHMENT TYPES

Attachment is a pattern of parent-child interactions that determines the overall relationship between the child and its mother or father. Children can have a secure attachment to one or both parents, or they can have an insecure attachment. Bowlby determined that children who are securely attached view their mothers as "secure bases" to which they will return when feeling anxious or threatened.

The attachment classification was enhanced by Mary Ainsworth when she determined that one way to view differences in attachment security was to purposefully expose a baby to a environment that may be distressing. She devised the laboratory procedure of the "strange situation," where infants and mothers were placed into a room full of toys. During a specified time period, the mother left and returned several times. The baby was left either with a stranger or alone. The child's response to the separation and its reunion behaviors to the mother showed several differences in the child's behaviors dependent on its pattern of maternal attachment. This procedure has become the standard operation used to measure attachment and has revealed a great deal about attachment in both the infant and older child.

SECURE ATTACHMENT

In a secure attachment, infants tend to explore the environment more freely and are able to separate from their mothers without too much distress. On reunion, secure children are always happy to see their mothers and respond in a positive way. These children are also able to share their toys with strangers and be comforted by strangers if left alone. As children grow, those with a secure attachment tend to be happier and more stable, have more friends, do better in school, have higher motivation and achievement mastery, be more empathetic and more moral, and more likely to be a leader in school.

Secure attachment begins primarily with mothers responding in a nurturing and gentle manner. They are quick to comfort a crying child, show affection, are sympathetic, and smile at their children frequently. In the context of discipline, they are less likely to nag or punish, especially spank, and are

In most cases, mothers form the closest bonds with children and have considerable impact on their development. (CLEO Photography)

more likely to reinforce positive behavior than focus on negative behavior. When a child does something wrong, this mother will explain to the child why the behavior was wrong and what the consequences are in a context that the child will understand. The mother encourages, helps, nurtures, and disciplines in a firm but gentle manner.

INSECURE ATTACHMENT

There are at least two kinds of insecure attachment. Even though it is called insecure attachment, it is still an attachment. The bonding is not as strong or stable as a secure attachment and there are different consequences. Insecure attachment occurs because the infant has a need to protect himself or herself from some unpleasant parental situation and the only way to do that is to direct its attention away from the parent. All infants have a need for affection and love. If they seek out the mother, for example, and reach out or smile at her and the mother

does not respond, the child's emotional needs are not met and he or she feels distress and anxiety. If this happens enough times, the child learns to expect rejection and a conflict arises between the child's needs and expectations. The child learns to avoid this unpleasant situation by directing attention away from the parent. Thus, the attachment that forms is not one where the child is certain that the parent will respond to his or her needs or make him or her feel secure. The child's emotional development hardwires in the brain differently from the secure child. Thus, the insecure child's emotional responses will be different also.

Generally, the two most widely recognized types of insecure attachment are avoidant attachment and resistant attachment. Children who form a resistant attachment pattern have found that the mother is inconsistent in her response to the child's need. In some situations the mother is available and helpful, while at other times she is unresponsive or unavailable and may even use abandonment as a means of controlling the child. According to Mary Ainsworth, this results in the child having a severe emotional response when separated from the mother, and separation anxiety results in clinging and anxious behavior. However, when the mother returns, the child will resist any overtures of contact that the mother might make and does not easily calm down. The child may even show signs of anger or aggressive behavior toward the mother. About 10 to 15 percent of American infants show this pattern. Ainsworth refers to this type of attachment as ambivalent. Because the mother sometimes shows positive reactions to the child, the child does not totally disengage and still desires contact with the mother. Thus, these children show a mixture of desire for and rejection of the mother. They will be intimate one second and hostile the next. If the mother joins them after a separation, these children will focus on the toys or tasks at hand and will greet the mother briefly, but distantly.

The second pattern of insecure attachment is avoidant. An avoidantly attached infant does not expect the mother to respond in a helpful manner, and the child learns that he or she may even be rebuffed when approaching the mother for protection or comfort. The mother of this child is usually rejecting of the child and shows little affection to the child. In order to protect himself or herself, the child distances from the mother and is not distressed during parental separation. When the mother returns, the child avoids the mother and does not greet her positively or affectionately. As the child ages, he or she attempts to live without love and support from others by becoming emotionally self-sufficient. About 20 percent of American babies show this type of attachment.

An avoidant attachment can also occur with the mother who shows too much attention to a child, who overreacts to everything, who is too exuberant in responses of even a positive expression, or who is too possessive or protective of the child. This overreactive response is too overwhelming for the child, who will react by directing attention away from the mother and thus become insecurely attached.

Another pattern of insecure attachment is disorganized/disoriented attachment. This attachment illustrates the most severe pattern of insecurity for the child. When young, these children display confused, contradictory behaviors toward the mother when reunited with her. For example, they may approach her but their facial expressions will relate no element of pleasure. In fact, these children more likely will display a flat, unemotional, or depressed expression. As these children age, their behavior toward their mother changes, responding to their mother at reunion with either a controlling or a dominating attitude, possibly trying to humiliate or reject the parent. They may also respond with an attitude of role-reversal, where the parent is treated as if he or she had become the child.

ATTACHMENT STABILITY

Although attachment patterns for the most part are stable over the life span, attachment patterns can be changed. It is never too late to forge a secure attachment. However, the emotional patterns of the child tend to be hardwired during early development and some of the child's emotional responses will be automatic. The critical period is thought to be within the first three years of life. In other words, when a parent comforts a hurt child, there is a corresponding neural loop that goes from the emotional centers of the brain to the cerebral cortex of the brain and reduces anxiety. When this occurs enough times there is an automatic response in the brain that allows the child to comfort himself or herself. However, if the child is hurt and seeks comfort but gets instead a rebuke or even more physical pain, then the brain wires up differently so that physical hurts are associated with emotional hurts or vice versa. This does not necessarily indicate that the brain neural networks are abnormal, but they are different from children whose parents meet their emotional needs. There is still much research that needs to be done before it can be said for sure that the neural pattern is irrevocable, but some things can be changed.

SOURCES FOR FURTHER STUDY

Ainsworth, Mary, M. Blehar, Everett Waters, and S. Wall. *Patterns of Attachment: A Psychological Study of the Strange Situation.* Hillsdale, N.J.: Lawrence Erlbaum, 1978. This work is the first book to describe the work of Ainsworth in other countries and how the attachment measurement originated.

Bowlby, John. *Attachment and Loss.* Vol. 1. New York: Basic Books, 1969. This is the original book on Bowlby's work with juvenile thieves. This book looks at the affects of maternal separation and loss in infants and children.

_____. *A Secure Base: Parent-Child Attachment and Healthy Human Development.* New York: Basic Books, 1988. An excellent overview of Bowlby's theory and his observations of parent-child attachment.

Karen, Robert. *Becoming Attached.* New York: Oxford University Press, 1994. The authors discussed all issues concerning the history and current literature of attachment in parent and child relationships.

Main, Mary, and Donna Weston. *The Place of Attachment in Human Behavior, Avoidance of the Attachment Figure in Infancy: Descriptions and Interpretations.* New York: Basic Books, 1982. A descriptive overview of case studies and early interpretation of the reactions of children in various clinical settings.

Donna Frick-Horbury

SEE ALSO: Archetypes and the collective unconscious; Attachment and bonding in infancy and childhood; Child abuse; Family life: Adult issues; Family life: Children's issues; Father-child relationship; Gender-identity formation; Oedipus complex; Parenting styles; Parental alienation syndrome; Separation and divorce: Adult issues; Separation and divorce: Children's issues; Sibling relationships; Stepfamilies.

Motivation

TYPE OF PSYCHOLOGY: Biological bases of behavior; emotion; learning; memory; motivation; social psychology

FIELDS OF STUDY: Attitudes and behavior; aversive conditioning; behavioral and cognitive models; cognitive learning; methodological issues; motivation theory; Pavlovian conditioning; personality theory; social motives

Central to the study of psychology is motivation, which is fundamentally concerned with emotion, personality, learning, memory, and with gaining an understanding of how behavior is most effectively activated, organized, and directed toward the achievement of goals.

KEY CONCEPTS
- activation theory
- behavioral approach
- cognitive approach
- hedonistic theory
- humanistic approach
- hydraulic model
- incentive theory
- Pavlovian conditioning
- psychodynamic approach
- teacher expectations

INTRODUCTION

Research in motivation is pivotal to such fields as educational psychology, social psychology, behavioral psychology, and most other subareas of psychology. Motivation is centrally concerned with the goals people set for themselves and with the means they take to achieve these goals. It is also concerned with how people react to and process information, activities directly related to learning. People's motivation to process information is influenced by two major factors: the relevance of the topic to the person processing the information, which affects their willingness to think hard about the topic; and the need for cognition, or people's willingness to think hard about varied topics, whether they are directly relevant to them or not. The relevance of a topic is central to people's motivation to learn about it.

For example, if the community in which a person lives experiences a severe budgetary crisis that will necessitate a substantial increase in property taxes, every resident in that community, home owners and renters alike, is going to be affected directly or indirectly by the increase. Because this increase is relevant to all the residents, they will, predictably, be much concerned with the topic and will likely think hard about its salient details. If, on the other hand, a community in a distant state faces such a crisis, residents in other communities, reading or hearing about the situation, will not have the motivation to do much hard thinking about it because it does not affect them directly.

The second category of motivation rests in the need of some individuals for cognition. Their inherent curiosity will motivate them to think deeply about various topics that do not concern them directly but that they feel a need to understand more fully. Such people are deliberate, self-motivated thinkers possessed of an innate curiosity about the world that surrounds them. They generally function at a higher intellectual level than people who engage in hard thinking primarily about topics that affect them directly. One of the aims of education at all levels is to stimulate people to think about a broad variety of topics, which they will do because they have an inherent curiosity that they long to satisfy.

EARLY CONCERNS WITH MOTIVATION

During the late nineteenth century, Austrian psychoanalyst Sigmund Freud (1856-1939) developed theories about motivation that are usually categorized as the psychodynamic approach. He contended that people have psychic energy that is essentially sexual or aggressive in its origins. Such energy seeks results that please, satisfy, or delight. This pleasure principle, as it was called, had to function within the bounds of certain restraints, identified as the reality principle, never violating the demands of people's conscience or of the restrains or inhibitions that their self-images imposed. In Freudian terms, the superego served to maintain the balance between the pleasure principle and the reality principle. In *Beyond the Pleasure Principle* (1922), Freud reached the conclusion that all motivation could be reduced to two opposing sources of energy, the life instinct and the death instinct.

Heinz Hartmann (1894-1970) went a step beyond Freud's psychodynamic theory, emphasizing the need for people to achieve their goals in ways that do not produce inner conflict, that are free of actions that might compromise or devastate the ego. More idealistic was Robert White, who denied Freud's contention that motivation is sexual or aggressive in nature. White contended that the motivation to achieve competence is basic in people. Everyone, according to White, wishes to be competent and, given proper guidance, will strive to achieve competence, although individual goals and individual determinations of the areas in which they wish to be competent vary greatly from person to person.

Such social psychologists as Erik Erikson (1902-1994), Carl Jung (1875-1961), and Karen Horney (1885-1952) turned their attention away from the biological and sexual nature of motivation, focusing instead upon its social aspects. They, like Freud, Hartmann, and White before them, sought to understand the unconscious means by which psychic energy is distributed as it ferrets out sources of gratification.

THE BEHAVIORISTS

The behavioral approach to motivation is centrally concerned with rewards and punishments. People cultivate behaviors for which they are rewarded. They avoid behaviors that experience has shown them will result in pain or punishment. B. F. Skinner (1904-1990) was probably the most influential behaviorist. Many educators accepted his theories and applied them to social as well as teaching situations.

Clark Hull (1884-1952), working experimentally with rats, determined that animals deprived of such basic requirements as food and/or punished by painful means such as electric shock, develop intense reactions to these stimuli. John Dollard (1900-1980) and Neal Miller (1909-2002) extended Hull's work to human subjects. They discovered that the response elicited by these means depends on the intensity of the stimulus, not on its origin. The stimuli employed also evoke previously experienced stimulus-response reactions, so that if subjects are hurt or punished following a volitional act, they will in future avoid such an act. In other words, if the negative stimuli are rapidly reduced, the responses that immediately preceded the reduction are reinforced. These researchers concluded that physiological needs such as hunger are innate, whereas secondary drives and the reaction to all drives, through conditioning, are learned.

Ivan Pavlov (1849-1936) demonstrated the strength of conditioned responses in his renowned experiments with dogs. He arranged for a bell to sound immediately before the dogs in his experiment were to be fed. The dogs came to associate the sound of a bell with being fed, a pleasurable and satisfying experience. Eventually, when Pavlov rang the bell but failed to follow its ringing with feeding, the dogs salivated merely on hearing the sound because they anticipated the feeding to which they had become conditioned. Over time, the motivation to satisfy their hunger came to be as much related to hearing the bell as it was to their actually being fed. Pavlovian conditioning is directly related to motivation, in this case the motivation to satisfy hunger.

KONRAD LORENZ'S HYDRAULIC MODEL

Freud argued that if instinctive urges are bottled up, they will eventually make the individual ill. They demand release and will find it in one way or another as the unconscious mind works to direct the distribution of people's psychic energy.

Konrad Lorenz (1903-1989) carried this notion a step beyond what Freud had postulated, contending that inherent drives that are not released by external means will explode spontaneously through some inherent releasing mechanism. This theory, termed Lorenz's hydraulic model, explains psychic collapses in some people, particularly in those who are markedly repressed.

Erich Fromm (1900-1980), carried Freud's notions about the repression of innate drives one step beyond what Lorenz espoused. Fromm added a moral dimension to what Freud and Lorenz asserted by postulating that humans develop character as a means of managing and controlling their innate physiological and psychological needs. He brought the matter of free will into his consideration of how to deal in a positive way with innate drives.

THE HEDONISTIC THEORY OF MOTIVATION

Hedonism emphasizes pleasure over everything else. The hedonistic theory of motivation stems from Freud's recognition of the pleasure principle, which stipulates that motivation is stimulated by pleasure and inhibited by pain.

Laboratory experiments with rats demonstrated unequivocally that, given a choice, rats work harder to get food that tastes good to them than to get food that is nutritious. Indeed, laboratory animals will take in empty calories to the point of emaciation as long as the food that contains such calories tastes good. It is thought that hedonistic motivation is directly related to pleasure centers in the brain, so that organisms work both consciously and unconsciously toward stimulating and satisfying these pleasure centers.

THE INCENTIVE THEORY OF MOTIVATION

Alfred Adler (1870-1937), the Austrian psychologist who founded the school of individual psychology, rejected Freud's emphases on sex and aggression as fundamental aspects of motivation. Breaking from Freud, who had been among his earliest professional associates, Adler contended that childhood feelings of helplessness led to later feelings of inferiority. His means of treating the inferiority complex, as this condition came to be known, was to engage his patients in positive social interaction. To do this, he developed an incentive theory of motivation, as articulated in his two major works, *Praxis und Theorie*

der Individual psychologie (1920; *The Practice and Theory of Individual Psychology,* 1924) and *Menschenkenntnis* (1927; *Understanding Human Nature,* 1927).

Adler's theory focused on helping people to realize the satisfaction involved in achieving superiority and competence in areas in which they had some aptitude. The motivation to do so is strictly personal and individual. Adler's entire system was based on the satisfactions to be derived from achieving a modicum of superiority. The incentive approach views competence as a basic motivation activated by people's wish to avoid failure. This is a reward/punishment approach, although it is quite different from that of the behaviorists and is in essence humanistic. The reward is competence; the punishment is failure. Both factors stimulate subjects' motivation.

THE ACTIVATION THEORY OF MOTIVATION

Drive reductionists believed that if all of an organism's needs are fulfilled, that organism will lapse into a lethargic state. They conclude that increasing needs will cause the organism to have an increased drive to fulfill those needs. Their view is that the inevitable course that individual organisms select is that of least resistance.

Donald O. Hebb, however, takes a more sanguine view of motivation, particularly in humans. In his activation theory, he contends that a middle ground between lethargy at one extreme and incapacitating anxiety at the other produces the most desirable level of motivation. This theory accounts for states of desired arousal such as that found in such pursuits as competitive sports.

The drive reductionists ascribe to the reward/punishment views of most of the behaviorists, who essentially consider organisms to be entities in need of direction, possibly of manipulation. The drive inductionists, on the other hand, have faith in the innate need of organisms to be self-directive and to work individually toward gaining competence. Essentially they accept the Greek ideal of the golden mean as a guiding principle, which has also been influential in the thinking of such humanistic psychologists.

THE HUMANISTIC APPROACH TO MOTIVATION

Abraham Maslow (1908-1970) devised a useful though controversial hierarchy of needs required to satisfy human potential. These needs proceed from low-level physiological needs such as hunger, thirst, sex, and comfort, through such other needs as safety, love, and esteem, finally reaching the highest level, self-actualization. According to Maslow, human beings progress sequentially through this hierarchy as they develop. Each category of needs proceeds from the preceding category and no category is omitted as the human develops, although the final and highest category, self-actualization, which includes curiosity, creative living, and fulfilling work, is not necessarily attained or attainable by all humans.

The humanists stipulate that people's primary motives are those that lead toward self-actualization, those that capitalize on the unique potential of each individual. In educational terms, this means that for education to be effective, it must emphasize exploration and discovery over memorization and the rote learning of a set body of material. It must also be highly individualized, although this does not imply a one-on-one relationship between students and their teachers. Rather than acting a fonts of knowledge, teachers become facilitators of learning, directing their students individually to achieve the actualization of the personal goals that best suit them.

Carl Rogers (1902-1987) traced much psychopathology to conflicts between people's inherent understanding of what they require to move toward self-actualization and society's expectations, which may run counter to individual needs. In other words, as many people develop and pass through the educational system, they may be encouraged or required to adopt goals that are opposed to those that are most realistic for them. Humanistic views of human development run counter to the views of most of the psychodynamic and behaviorist psychologists concerned with learning theory and motivation as it relates to such theory.

COGNITIVE APPROACHES TO MOTIVATION

The research of Kurt Lewin (1890-1947) in the subjective tension systems that work toward to resolution of problems in humans along with his research, done in collaboration with Edward C. Tolman (1886-1959), that emphasizes expectancies and the subjective value of the results of actions has led to a cognitive approach to motivation. Related to this research is that of Leon Festinger (1919-1989), whose theory of cognitive dissonance stipulates that if people's beliefs are not in harmony with each other, they will experience a discomfort that they will attempt to eliminate by altering their beliefs.

People ultimately realize that certain specific behaviors will lead to anticipated results. Behavior, therefore, has a purpose, but the number of goals related to specific behaviors is virtually infinite. People learn to behave in ways that make it most likely to achieve expected results.

Robert Rosenthal and Lenore Jacobson demonstrated that teacher expectations have a great deal to do with the success of the students with whom they work. Their experiment, detailed fully in *Pygmalion in the Classroom* (1968), relates how they selected preadolescent and adolescent students randomly and then told the teachers of those students that they had devised a way of determining which students were likely to show spurts of unusual mental growth in the coming year.

Each teacher was given the names of two or three students who were identified as being on the brink of rapid intellectual development. The researchers tested the students at the end of the school year and found that those who had been designated as poised on the brink of unusual mental development tested above the norm even though they had been selected randomly from all the students in the classes involved. In this experiment, teacher motivation to help certain students succeed appears to have been central to those students' achieving goals beyond those of other students in the class.

SOURCES FOR FURTHER STUDY

Boekaerts, Monique, Paul R. Pintrich, and Moshe Zeidner. *Handbook of Self-Regulation.* San Diego, Calif.: Academic Press, 2000. Chapters 5 and 15 deal specifically with motivation, offering unique perspectives that are both physiological and social. The approach of this volume is essentially humanistic.

Ferguson, Eva Dreikurs. *Motivation: A Biosocial and Cognitive Integration of Motivation and Emotion.* New York: Oxford University Press, 2000. This book requires some background in the field of motivation. It is carefully researched and accurately presented. Its focus is more on the physiological aspects of motivation than on the social.

Glover, John A., Royce R. Ronning, and Cecil R. Reynolds, eds. *Handbook of Creativity.* New York: Plenum, 1989. Of special interest to those seeking information about motivation will be chapter 7, "Cognitive Processes in Creativity," and those parts of chapter 5, "The Nature-Nurture Problem in Creativity," that deal with cognitive and motivational processes.

Greenwood, Gordon E., and H. Thompson Fillmer. *Educational Psychology: Cases for Teacher Decision-Making.* Columbus, Ohio: Merrill, 1999. Of particular value in this book of case studies is part 5, which deals with motivation and classroom management. In this section, chapter 25, "Motivation or Control?," is particularly relevant to readers interested in motivation. The approach in this book is eminently practical. The writing is easily accessible to beginners in the field.

Kendrick, Douglas T., Steven L. Neuberg, and Robert B. Cialdini. *Social Psychology: Unraveling the Mystery.* Boston: Allyn & Bacon, 1999. This is one of the best-written, most accessible books in introductory psychology. It is replete with examples to illustrate what is being said. The prose style is enticing and the intellectual content is exceptional. The chapter entitled "The Motivational Systems: Motives and Goals" is particularly relevant to those studying motivation. Strongly recommended for those unfamiliar with the field.

Lawler, Edward E., III. *Rewarding Excellence: Pay Strategies for the New Economy.* San Francisco: Jossey-Bass, 2000. Approached from the standpoint of a professor of management, this book discusses various motivational protocols employed by industry. Some of them are easily transferable to broader contexts. The tactics suggested are largely behavioral. They deal extensively with reward/punishment scenarios.

Lesko, Wayne A., ed. *Readings in Social Psychology: General, Classic, and Contemporary Selections.* Boston: Allyn & Bacon, 2000. Among the most cogent selections in this collection for those pursuing information about motivation are "Cognitive, Social, and Physiological Determinants of Emotional States" by Stanley Schachter and Jerome E. Singer; "Cognitive Reactions to Smoking Relapse: The Reciprocal Relation between Dissonance and Self-Esteem" by Frederick X. Gibbons, Tami J. Eggleston, and Alida C. Benthin; and "Behavioral Study of Obedience" by Stanley Milgram. This entire collection is worth reading. Nearly every selection in it relates in some way to motivation.

Rosenthal, Robert, and Lenore Jacobson. *Pygmalion in the Classroom.* New York: Holt, Rinehart and Winston, 1968. This report of an experiment that deals with teacher expectations and their relation to student achievement is compelling and provocative.

Wagner, Hugh. *The Psychobiology of Human Motivation.* New York: Routledge, 1999. Wagner demonstrates how humans can adapt to complex social environments by controlling and channeling their basic physiological drives. Wagner points out the fallacy of attempting to explain human motivation in terms of models based on animal physiology. He also questions in an intelligently critical manner Abraham Maslow's hierarchy of needs. Wagner's skepticism is at once challenging, thought-provoking, and refreshing.

Wong, Roderick. *Motivation: A Biobehavioural Approach.* New York: Cambridge University Press, 2000. Wong's focus is sharply on behaviorism and on the physiological aspects of motivation, although chapter 9, "Social Motivation: Attachment and Altruism," moves into the area of social psychology. This is not a book for beginners, although its ideas are well presented, often with cogent examples.

R. Baird Shuman

SEE ALSO: Achievement motivation; Adler, Alfred; Affiliation motive; Behaviorism; Conditioning; Drives; Ego, superego, and id; Freud, Sigmund; Fromm, Erich; Incentive motivation; Lewin, Kurt; Lorenz, Karl; Miller, Neal E., and John Dollard; Pavlov, Ivan; Pavlovian conditioning; S-R theory: Neal E. Miller and John Dollard; Work motivation.

Motor development

TYPE OF PSYCHOLOGY: Developmental psychology
FIELDS OF STUDY: Infancy and childhood

Motor development refers to the development of voluntary control over one's body and its parts, as in crawling, walking, reaching, and grasping. Motor development parallels brain growth and development and is influenced by both biological and environmental factors.

KEY CONCEPTS
- central nervous system
- cephalo-caudal development
- cerebral cortex

- fine motor movements
- gross motor movements
- mass-to-specific development
- maturation
- proximo-distal development

INTRODUCTION

Motor development refers to the development of voluntary control over the body and its parts. Gross motor development refers to the development of skills or behaviors that involve the large muscle masses and large body movements (such as crawling, walking, running, and throwing), whereas fine motor development refers to the development of small muscle movements, usually in reference to the hands (as in grasping, writing, and fastening buttons). Motor skills develop rapidly during the early years of life and follow a predictable sequence of stages.

Motor development proceeds according to three developmental principles: from head to toe (cephalo-caudal development), from the center of the body to the body's periphery (proximo-distal development), and from large to small muscle control, with actions becoming more refined and directed (mass-to-specific development). Cephalo-caudal development is illustrated by the fact that infants gain control over their heads and shoulders before their legs. Proximo-distal development is shown by young children gaining control over their arms before their hands and fingers, and mass-to-specific development is illustrated by the fact that infants reach for an object with both arms extended before they can reach out with one arm at a time.

The development of both gross and fine motor skills depends on the maturation (development attributable to one's genetic timetable and not to experience) of the nervous system. Voluntary movements develop as the cortex, which is the outer layer of the brain, matures. Whereas the cortex is barely functioning at birth, the "lower" parts of the brain—such as the brain stem and the midbrain—that control basic, nonthinking functions such as breathing, heartbeat, digestion, and reflexes are mature at birth. This is part of the reason that newborns have only reflexive, involuntary movements during the first few months of life. Voluntary control over the body develops gradually as connections between the muscles and the higher brain centers such as the cortex become established. The parts of the brain concerned with posture and balance also develop

gradually over the first year of life; they contribute to infants being able to sit up, stand, and then walk.

The gradual acquisition of fine and gross motor skills has a number of important implications for a child's social, cognitive, and personality development. The development of fine motor skills allows infants to examine and experiment with objects, explore their environment, and even communicate with others by showing objects or by pointing. Gross motor milestones provide children with a new and progressively complex perspective of the world, more opportunities to explore and learn about the physical and social environment, and increasing degrees of independence—which have implications for children's developing sense of mastery and competence. These motor milestones in turn affect parents' interactions with, and treatment of, their increasingly independent children.

SEQUENCES OF DEVELOPMENT

Gross motor and fine motor skills follow a specific sequence of development. Gross motor (or locomotor) development eventually results in a young child being able to walk and run. To reach this point, a child must first develop control of his or her head, sit up, and then develop enough balance and strength to stand. By approximately two months of age, most infants can lift their heads, and by three to four months of age they are usually able to roll over. At five or six months they can sit up, and by seven to nine months they usually begin crawling. Infants may be able to stand while holding onto an object at six months, pull themselves to standing between eight and ten months, and walk independently at around twelve to fourteen months. By eighteen months of age, toddlers are usually able to run, walk backward, throw a ball, and climb stairs; between twenty-four to thirty-six months, they may be able to ride a tricycle. From two to six years of age, children continue to refine their movements. For example, a two-year-old's awkward gait and poor balance change by three years of age to a more stable and balanced gait, allowing the child to hop, jump, and run back and forth. By four years of age, children's walking movements are similar to adults', allowing them to move easily up and down stairs and even to hop on one foot. By age five, children are well coordinated, have good balance, and are able to move skillfully and gracefully while walking, running, climbing, and throwing.

Fine motor development eventually results in refined eye-hand coordination, which will enable a child to write. To achieve this, children must first be able to reach, grasp, and manipulate objects voluntarily and possess refined finger (especially thumb-to-index-finger) control. At birth, no voluntary control exists. By three months of age, babies begin to make poorly directed swiping movements with their entire arms (fists closed). At around four months, infants use an open-handed, scooping movement with a slightly better aim; by five months, infants can reach and grasp objects with both hands, holding the object in the center of the palm by all fingers. Between nine and ten months, infants can hold objects by the palm and middle fingers in a palmar grasp. The ability to use the thumb and index finger together (pincer grasp) typically develops between nine and fifteen months. Infants who have developed this skill usually enjoy practicing it and will pick up tiny objects such as lint or bugs from the floor. By eighteen months of age, toddlers are able to hold crayons and to open drawers and cupboards; by twenty-four months, the development of full thumb-to-index-finger control makes it easier for them to turn doorknobs, unscrew lids, scribble, and feed themselves. By age three, children may be able to put some puzzle pieces together. They also have better control when using forks and can begin to dress themselves. (The ability to lace shoes, fasten buttons, and pull zippers, however, generally does not appear until age six or seven.) By age four or five, eye-hand coordination and fine motor skills improve. Children may be able at this time to print large letters that look pieced together; they are typically placed anywhere on a piece of paper. Many can print their first names and a few numbers by age five. From age six on, hand movements become more fluid and refined; writing is characterized by more continuous strokes and is less choppy.

Although the sequence of stages of motor development is uniform in normal individuals, there is wide variation among individuals in the ages at which certain skills are acquired. This normal variation is attributable to both biological and environmental factors, including maturation, heredity, neurological maturity, health, activity level, experience, and nutrition.

ROLE OF BIOLOGICAL MATURATION

Learning to walk, achieving bowel and bladder control, and even learning to read and write are not physiologically possible until the child's nervous and motor systems are sufficiently developed. Although normal experience (such as that offered by an average home environment) appears to be necessary for normal motor development, biological maturation places limits on what can be achieved through experience or practice. In fact, efforts by parents or other adults to teach or push young children to learn particular skills before they are maturationally ready may actually be harmful to their development.

Learning to walk, for example, requires central nervous system maturity, postural balance, muscular and skeletal strength, and well-developed sight and hearing. Studies have suggested that practicing the early walking reflex in infants to speed up their learning to walk may actually be harmful, because it may interfere with the development of the "higher" (cortical) areas of the brain that gradually take over the

---

DSM-IV-TR Criteria for Developmental Coordination Disorder (DSM code 315.4)

Performance in daily activities requiring motor coordination substantially below that expected given chronological age and measured intelligence

May be manifested by the following:
- marked delays in achieving motor milestones such as walking, crawling, or sitting
- dropping things
- clumsiness
- poor performance in sports
- poor handwriting

Disorder interferes significantly with academic achievement or activities of daily living

Symptoms not due to a general medical condition such as cerebral palsy, hemiplegia, or muscular dystrophy

Criteria for pervasive developmental disorder not met

If mental retardation is present, motor difficulties exceed those usually associated with it

control of mature, independent walking. Early walking movements, which are evident between birth and three months of age, are actually a reflex that is controlled by the "lower" parts of the brain that control involuntary behavior. In addition, other studies have found that using walkers (seats on frames with wheels) too early or too often may damage infants' hip sockets.

Toilet training is also dependent on nervous system maturation. The neurons (nerve cells) controlling bowel and bladder movements mature at about the same time that children generally achieve voluntary control, around eighteen to twenty-four months of age. Bowel control is achieved before bladder control, and girls typically achieve bowel and bladder control before boys do.

Being able to ride a tricycle (which usually occurs around age three) or a bicycle (which typically occurs by age six or seven) also requires that a certain level of muscle strength, posture, and balance be achieved before these skills are possible. Catching a ball is usually too difficult and complex for four-year-olds because it requires timing, distance perception, quick reactions, and coordinated movements of the arms, hands, eyes, and body. A successful way of playing "catch" with children of this age is to roll the ball on the ground.

Fine motor skills (such as pouring juice from a pitcher, writing with a pencil, assembling a puzzle with many small pieces, cutting food with a knife and fork, or fastening small buttons) develop more slowly than gross motor skills during infancy and early childhood and are therefore more difficult for young children to master. Children lack the motor control necessary to complete these tasks successfully because the central nervous system is not completely developed at this age—the parts of the brain governing fine motor coordination take years to mature fully.

Reading and writing also depend on maturational readiness. Reading requires focused attention, controlled coordination between the eye muscles and the brain, and a certain level of nervous system maturity. Children younger than six years of age usually are not physiologically capable of moving their eye muscles slowly and deliberately across lines of small letters. They also have a difficult time sustaining controlled and systematic focusing and are farsighted. Because reading depends on maturity of the nervous system, it is generally recommended that formal reading be delayed until age six or seven. Writing, on the other hand, depends on the eyes, brain, and small muscles of the fingers working together. As nervous system maturation progresses, greater fine motor control is achieved, and children's hand strokes become more fluid and continuous during the school-age years.

Finally, hand preference ("handedness") is also biologically based. Hand preference in reaching, grasping, and writing may be found even in infancy. Hand preference appears to be determined partly by heredity but also by the organization of the brain, with structural and functional differences between the left and right sides of the brain evident at birth. Most children develop hand preferences by age three or four, with the majority (85 to 90 percent) showing a right-hand preference. It may, however, take some children several years after this to solidify their hand preference. Forcing children to change their handedness may create a number of problems, including stuttering and other language problems, fine motor skill deficits, and emotional problems.

EVOLUTION OF RESEARCH

Early interest in motor development focused primarily on outlining the sequence of stages of motor development, identifying approximate ages at which these milestones occur, and speculating about the relative contributions of biology and the environment to motor development. These themes mirror two principal concerns of developmental psychology: the sequence of stages of development and the influence of biology versus experience on development.

Interest in, and observations of, early motor development date back at least to the eighteenth century. The earliest accounts of children's development, known as "baby biographies," were detailed descriptions of the developmental sequence of behavior during the early years of life. A more methodical approach to outlining behavioral milestones began around the early 1900's, when normative studies (studies investigating the typical performance of children at different ages) were undertaken. In 1911, for example, Arnold Gesell founded the Yale Clinic of Child Development and constructed norms for such motor skills as grasping, crawling, swimming, standing, and walking. His norm charts were used throughout most of the twentieth century.

The general conclusion of Gesell and others during the 1930's and 1940's was that motor development is under biological control; however, studies have since shown that severe environmental deprivation can retard motor development and that environmental improvement by age two is necessary for infants to recover fully. Most researchers today believe that both maturation and experience play important roles in the course of motor development.

Although there was interest in motor development during the first half of the twentieth century, this interest declined somewhat from the 1950's until the 1980's. During this lull, however, motor development was still considered an integral part of Jean Piaget's well-known theory of cognitive development in young children. Whereas motor development was originally viewed as the gradual acquisition of isolated skills, motor skill acquisitions are currently viewed as parts of a complex, interrelated motor system that parallels brain growth and development. It is likely that future research will continue to examine these issues as well as the relationship of motor development to cognition, language acquisition, and social development.

SOURCES FOR FURTHER STUDY

Fitzgerald, Hiram E., et al. "The Organization of Lateralized Behavior During Infancy." In *Theory and Research in Behavioral Pediatrics*. Vol. 5, edited by Hiram E. Fitzgerald, B. Lester, and M. Yogman. New York: Plenum, 1991. A good overview on the lateralization of motor skills and behaviors in early development. Covers the influence of brain development on lateralized motor skills.

Gallahue, D. L. *Motor Development and Movement Experiences*. New York: John Wiley & Sons, 1976. A well-written resource on the theory, research, and practical applications of motor development and movement from age three to seven years.

Payne, V. G., and L. D. Isaacs. *Human Motor Development: A Lifespan Approach*. 5th ed. Mountain View, Calif.: Mayfield, 2001. This book is a comprehensive, in-depth overview of motor development from birth to maturity.

Piper, Martha C., and Johanna Darrah. *Motor Assessment of the Developing Infant*. Philadelphia: W. B. Saunders, 1994. A collection of tests for physical therapists who are assessing an infant's motor skill development. Includes score sheets.

Rosenblith, Judy F., and Judith E. Sims-Knight. *In the Beginning*. Monterey, Calif.: Brooks-Cole, 1985. A very readable resource on early development that has excellent chapters on developmental milestones and the influence of the environment on development.

Laura Kamptner

SEE ALSO: Birth: Effects on physical development; Brain specialization; Cognitive development: Jean Piaget; Physical development: Environment versus genetics; Prenatal physical development; Reflexes in newborns.

Multiple personality

TYPE OF PSYCHOLOGY: Psychopathology
FIELDS OF STUDY: Coping; models of
   psychopathology; personality disorders

Multiple personality is the name of abnormal behavior in which a person behaves as if under the control of distinct and separate parts of the personality at different times. It is caused by severe childhood abuse and responds to long-term psychotherapy that addresses the past abuse and the resulting symptoms of dissociation.

KEY CONCEPTS
• alternate personality
• dissociation
• dissociative identity disorder
• integration
• repression

INTRODUCTION

Multiple personality has had considerable research and clinical attention focused on it since the early 1980's, and this interest has increased significantly from that point on. However, multiple personality was known and studied even prior to the famous Sigmund Freud (1856-1939), the Austrian psychiatrist and founder of psychoanalysis. Well-known French psychologists Pierre Janet (1859-1947) and Alfred Binet (1857-1911), among others, had written about it in the late nineteenth century, prior to Freud's writings. With the rise of psychoanalysis in the early twentieth century, the study of multiple personality and dissociation waned dramatically for many years. Two famous multiple personality cases in the United States were popularized by books and then films: *The Three Faces of Eve* in 1957 and *Sybil* in 1973.

In 1980, multiple personality disorder (MPD) was officially sanctioned as a legitimate psychiatric disorder by its inclusion in the third edition of the *Diagnostic and Statistical Manual of Mental Disorders* (DSM-III) published by the American Psychiatric Association. The official diagnostic label was changed in the fourth edition, DSM-IV, to dissociative identity disorder (DID), though it is still commonly known as multiple personality.

CAUSE

Research has shown that multiple personality is most probably caused by severe childhood abuse, usually both physical and sexual. Psychotherapists who specialize in treating disorders caused by trauma hypothesize that the human mind or personality divides to cope with the terror of the trauma. It is as if one part of the mind handles the abuse to protect another part of the mind from the pain. This splitting of consciousness is a psychological defense called dissociation. Instead of memory, bodily sensation, emotions, and thoughts all being associated with an experience (which is the normal process of human experience), these aspects lose their association and seem to separate. A common example would be that a person who was sexually abused as a child loses the memory of those events and may have no recall of them until later in adulthood. In this case, the whole experience is dissociated. For example, in multiple personality, a so-called alternate personality ("alter" for short) named Ann experienced the abuse, while alter Jane, who deals with normal, everyday living, was not abused. Thus, Jane has no memories of abuse. A variation is that only certain aspects of the experience are dissociated, so that, for instance, the abused person has the memory that the sexual abuse happened but has no emotions regarding the pain and trauma of it. Freud coined the term "repression" to describe the process by which emotions that are too threat-

ening to be admitted into consciousness are pushed into the unconscious.

DIAGNOSIS

Several well-researched psychological tests and structured interviews aid in diagnosing a client. For a formal diagnosis of DID, the DSM-IV-TR states that the following four criteria must be present: two or more distinct identities or personality states (each with its own relatively enduring pattern of perceiving, relating to, and thinking about the environment and self); at least two of these identities or personality states recurrently take control of the person's behavior; there is an inability to recall important personal information that is too extensive to be explained by ordinary forgetfulness; and the disturbance is not due to the direct physiological effects of a substance (such as blackouts due to alcohol, drugs, or seizures).

The central paradox of multiple personality is that it is both real and not real at the same time. It is not real in that the mind or personality does not literally split. There is only one brain and one body. It is a creation of a person's imagination. At the same time, however, the person with DID experiences very real separations and is not faking them. The perceived separate parts must be dealt with as if they were separate while teaching them the reality that they must live in the same body and jointly suffer the consequences of the actions of any one part.

Multiple personality goes unrecognized too often as a result of several reasons. First, it has only received considerable attention since the early 1980's.

DSM-IV-TR Criteria for Multiple Personality

DISSOCIATIVE IDENTITY DISORDER (DSM CODE 300.14)

Presence of two or more distinct identities or personality states (each with its own relatively enduring pattern of perceiving, relating to, and thinking about the environment and self)

At least two of these identities or personality states recurrently take control of the person's behavior

Inability to recall important personal information too extensive to be explained by ordinary forgetfulness

Disturbance not due to the direct physiological effects of a substance (such as blackouts or chaotic behavior during alcohol intoxication) or a general medical condition (such as complex partial seizures); in children, the symptoms are not attributable to imaginary playmates or other fantasy play

Chris Costner Sizemore, the subject of the book and film The Three Faces of Eve *about multiple personality disorder.* (AP/Wide World Photos)

Second, it was wrongly thought to be extremely rare, so psychotherapists were previously taught that they would probably never see a case of it. Third, the trauma that causes DID produces so many symptoms, such as depression, anxiety, hearing voices, and mood changes, that it is wrongly diagnosed as schizophrenia, bipolar disorder, or something else. Fourth, there is skepticism about its validity as a true diagnosis.

Alters can be categorized in various ways. Some are victims who took most of the abuse. Some are persecutors who identified with the abuser and try to control other alters internally. Some are functioning alters who handle work or school. Alters may believe they are the opposite sex of the body and can see themselves as almost any age. Some may know a great deal about other alters. Others may only know of themselves and have no knowledge that others even exist.

Because at least some alters are usually dissociated from other alters, the person with DID will typically experience time loss when one alter has had control of the body and a different alter takes control who does not know what has happened previously. Dissociation is experienced in degrees. When it is present to a lesser degree, DID patients hear voices inside their heads. They are hearing alters talking. This may scare them when they first experience it, or it may be so normal for them that they mistake these voices for their own thoughts.

TREATMENT

Clinical experience and research have shown that this disorder is treatable to full remission and therefore the prognosis is more hopeful than with some other psychiatric disorders. The negative side of treatment is that it takes a long time, usually five to seven years and in some cases longer. The guidelines for treatment established by the International Society for the Study of Dissociation call for psychotherapy two to three times a week for several years.

The initial goal of psychotherapy is stabilization, to stop any destructive behaviors such as suicide or other forms of self-harm. The intermediate goal is to become aware of the alters, counsel their individual needs, and then bring about cooperation and communication between alters to make daily functioning more effective. The long-range goal is to bring about the integration of all split personalities into one unified personality. Integration is the combining of all aspects of the self, even the ones that may seem destructive or feel great pain. The goal is not to get rid of certain alters, as every part is an aspect of the self and needs to be integrated into the self.

Part of treatment consists of recounting and processing the memories of abuse. Ignoring past abuse is not helpful. However, this memory work needs to be done slowly and carefully, going at a pace that does not overwhelm the client. One goal is to keep the client functioning as normally as possible in daily life. Mistakes have been made by therapists who go too fast, too far, and who focus on talking about memories without addressing other needs, such as helping clients stabilize, encouraging cooperation and communication of alters, gradually integrating alters, teaching toleration of uncomfortable emotions, and instilling new coping mechanisms other than dissociating. The therapist should not suggest to the client that he or she was abused but should let the client discover this on his or her own.

Hypnosis may be used as part of the treatment, but it is not required. Experienced trauma therapists talk easily with the various alters and usually learn to recognize the different parts with little trouble. The switch between alters most often but not always is subtle and not dramatic. Psychiatric medications are often used as an adjunct to talking therapy, to help with the symptoms accompanying DID such as depression and anxiety. Since DID is a disorder caused by personal experience, it is not cured by medications.

What does not work is ignoring or denying the presence of alters, focusing only on the present and ignoring the past, trying to get rid of so-called bad alters, and exorcising alters who are psychological entities. Obviously, a person with DID will succeed best in counseling with a psychotherapist who is experienced and has specialized training in the treatment of trauma disorders.

IMPACT

People who suffer from multiple personality are adults who live with a coping mechanism that worked well to survive the horrors of abuse in childhood but is not working as well in a normal adult environment. All patients with DID suffer to some extent, which usually drives them to find relief. Some of these forms of relief are healthy, such as psychotherapy, and some may be unhealthy, such as addictions used to drown the painful feelings.

Some people with multiple personality appear to function normally and may not even know themselves that they have more than one personality. They may be able to function at a very high level at a job, for instance, while those close to them sense things are not normal. They may function normally for years and then have a crisis that seems to develop very rapidly. Other people with DID have trouble functioning normally and have a long history of psychological problems. These people may be unable to work to support themselves and need multiple hospitalizations. It is common for someone with DID to function at an extremely high level in one area or at one time and conversely to function at a very low level in another area or at another time. This leaves those around them very puzzled and confused.

CONTROVERSY

Unfortunately, there is controversy regarding multiple personality. Some critics inside and outside the mental health profession claim that it is not a legitimate psychiatric disorder, perhaps because the idea of having multiple personality and repressed memories does not make common sense to them. They may believe that this disorder is created by people seeking attention through being dramatic, caused by incompetent therapists suggesting this diagnosis to their clients, or used by people wanting an excuse for irresponsible or even criminal behavior. Some of these critics also attack the concept of recovered memories of child sexual abuse. They believe this profound loss of memory is not real and that these recovered memories are actually false memories that serve the same purposes mentioned above.

The result is that the trauma field has tended to become polarized into true believers and extreme skeptics. A balanced position has sometimes been lost. Trauma experts with a balanced view will admit that some memories are inaccurate, that some clients labeled as having DID have indeed been misdiagnosed for the reasons the critics offer, and that some therapists do a poor job. However, these experts argue that the research base and clinical evidence supporting the existence of a distinct diagnosis called DID is strong and that the repression of memories of childhood abuse is real.

SOURCES FOR FURTHER STUDY

Cohen, L., J. Berzhoff, and M. Elin, eds. *Dissociative Identity Disorder: Theoretical and Treatment Controversies.* Northvale, N.J.: Jason Aronson, 1995. This book gives the differing views regarding the controversies around DID. Each chapter offers both sides of the position on the topic at hand. It is somewhat technical.

Hocking, Sandra J. *Living with Your Selves: A Survival Manual for People with Multiple Personalities.* Rockville, Md.: Launch Press, 1992. This is a self-help book written by and for someone who has multiple personality. It contains helpful and accurate information.

Putnam, Frank. *Diagnosis and Treatment of Multiple Personality Disorder.* New York: Guilford, 1989. A leading textbook meant for professionals written by an expert at the National Institute of Mental Health.

Ross, Colin A. *Dissociative Identity Disorder: Diagnosis, Clinical Features, and Treatment of Multiple Personality.* New York: John Wiley & Sons, 1997. Perhaps the leading textbook on DID. Everything you wanted to know and more by an international psychiatric expert. It is written for the professional, though it is very readable. It also contains the author's psychological test called the DDIS to help diagnose DID.

_____. *The Osiris Complex: Case Studies in Multiple Personality Disorder.* Toronto: University of Toronto Press, 1994. This international expert writes an interesting and readable book for both lay and professional audiences giving specific cases with details that illustrate features of DID.

Dennis Bull

SEE ALSO: Child abuse; Hallucinations; Hypnosis; Personality disorders.

Murray, Henry A.

BORN: May 13, 1893, in New York, New York
DIED: June 23, 1988, in Cambridge, Massachusetts
IDENTITY: American physician and psychologist
TYPE OF PSYCHOLOGY: Personality
FIELDS OF STUDY: Personality theory

Murray is well known as the developer of personology, the integrated study of the individual from physiological, psychoanalytical, and social viewpoints, and the primary developer of the Thematic Apperception Test (TAT). In addition, his concept of motivation has had a major influence on the theories of psychology.

Henry A. Murray was born in New York City in 1893. He entered Harvard University in 1911 as a history major. However, in 1915 he entered the Columbia College of Physicians and Surgeons in New York, earning a degree in medicine in 1919.

In 1925, Murray first met the Swiss psychiatrist Carl Jung, who had a lasting influence on his work. Drawing on the writings of Herman Melville, the author of the novel *Moby Dick* (1851), Murray began to develop his theory of personality, using Melville as a case study. Though never published, the biography of Melville, according to Murray, had a major influence on the scholars of that time. Also during this period, Murray's published articles and book chapters introduced the application of Jung's "depth psychology" to the American community of scholars.

After earning his Ph.D. in 1927, Murray became an instructor at Harvard under Morton Prince (1854-1929), a psychopathologist who had founded the Harvard Psychological Clinic. Murray became an assistant professor at Harvard in 1929, associate professor in 1937, and professor of clinical psychology in 1948. Murray continued his work with the Harvard Psychological Clinic after the death of Prince, and with the assistance of a neuropsychiatrist colleague, Stanley Cobb, Murray moved the focus of the clinic from experimental research in hypnosis and multiple personality to Freudian and Jungian psychoanalysis. He also introduced these subjects into the Harvard curriculum. Under the umbrella of personology, Murray and his interdisciplinary research team studied single individuals on a variety of levels. With his staff, Murray published *Explorations in Personality: A Clinical Study of Fifty Men of College Age* in 1938. For decades, this remained the principal text for personality theory.

As interest in the newly emerging field of psychoanalysis grew in the 1930's, two important projective techniques introduced systematic ways to study unconscious motivation: the Rorschach or inkblot test, developed by the Swiss psychiatrist Hermann Rorschach (1884-1922), and the Thematic Apperception Test (TAT), developed by Murray and C. D. Morgan, an American psychologist. Both of these tests are frequently included in contemporary personality assessment. The TAT, an important tool in clinical psychology, requires the subject to tell stories about a series of pictures from which interpretations are made by the therapist.

Murray served in the Army from 1943 until 1948, selecting personnel for the Office of Strategic Services, later known as the Central Intelligence Agency (CIA), and training agents in the United States and abroad. After his discharge from the Army as a lieutenant colonel, Murray joined Gordon Allport (1897-1967) in the newly established department of social relations at Harvard. There, with anthropologist Clyde Kluckhohn (1905-1960), he began studying personality in society and from the viewpoint of the dyadic interaction, the idea that a relationship between two people could be viewed as a single system with equal input from both partners. He also studied the role of mythology in personality and in society. At this time, Murray was best known for his development of a human motivational system of social needs. He described behavior as a function of the interaction of individual needs, such as a need for achievement or a need for affiliation, and the "press" of the environment.

Murray held numerous honorary doctorates and was a member of the American Academy of Arts and Sciences. He retired from Harvard in 1962 as a professor emeritus. Murray died in Cambridge, Massachusetts, in 1988, at the age of ninety-five. In his memory, Radcliffe College established the Henry A. Murray Research Center for the Study of Lives.

SOURCES FOR FURTHER STUDY

Robinson, Forrest G. *Love's Story Told: A Life of Henry A. Murray.* Cambridge, Mass.: Harvard University Press, 1992. A biography of Murray.

Schneidman, Edwin S., ed. *Endeavors in Psychology:*

Selections from the Personology of Henry A. Murray. New York: Harper & Row, 1981. A collection of Murray's psychological writings.

Mary E. Carey

SEE ALSO: Allport, Gordon; Jung, Carl G.; Personology: Henry A. Murray; Rorschach inkblots; Thematic Apperception Test (TAT).

Music, dance, and theater therapy

DATE: The 1920's forward
TYPE OF PSYCHOLOGY: Psychotherapy
FIELDS OF STUDY: Psychodynamic therapies

Music, dance, and theater therapies utilize various media such as movement and creative expression to accomplish the desired therapeutic goals; these therapies reflect a focus on the therapeutic value of artistic experiences and expression.

KEY CONCEPTS
- adaptive patterns
- creativity
- developmental task
- improvisation
- movement therapy
- philosophical models

INTRODUCTION

Music, dance, and theater therapies employ a wide range of methods to accomplish the goal of successful psychotherapy. "Psychotherapy" is a general term for the wide variety of methods psychologists and psychiatrists use to treat behavioral, emotional, or cognitive disorders. Music, dance, and theater therapies are not only helpful in the observation and interpretation of mental and emotional illness but also useful in the treatment process. Many hospitals, clinics, and psychiatrists or therapists include these types of therapy in their programs. They are not limited to hospital and clinical settings, however; they also play important roles in a wide variety of settings, such as community mental health programs, special schools, prisons, rehabilitation centers, nursing homes, and other settings.

Music, dance, and theater therapies share a number of basic characteristics. The therapies are generally designed to encourage expression. Feelings that may be too overwhelming for a person to express verbally can be expressed through movement, music, or the acting of a role. Loneliness, anxiety, and shame are typical of the kinds of feelings that can be expressed effectively through music, dance, or theater therapy. These therapies share a developmental framework. Each therapeutic process can be adapted to start at the patient's physical and emotional level and progress from that point onward.

Music, dance, and theater therapies are physically integrative. Each can involve the body in some way and thus help develop an individual's sense of identity. Each therapy is inclusive and can deal with either individuals or groups and with verbal or nonverbal patients in different settings. Each is applicable to different age groups (children, adolescents, adults, the elderly) and to different diagnostic categories, ranging from mild to severe. While music, dance, and theater therapies share these common characteristics, however, they also differ in important respects.

DANCE THERAPY

Dance therapy does not use a standard dance form or movement technique. Any genre, from ritual dances to improvisation, may be employed. The reason for such variety lies in the broad spectrum of persons who undergo dance therapy: Neurotics, psychotics, schizophrenics, the physically disabled, and geriatric populations can all benefit from different types of dance therapy. Dance therapy may be based on various philosophical models. Three of the most common are the human potential model, the holistic health model, and the medical model. The humanistic and holistic health models have in common the belief that individuals share responsibility for their therapeutic progress and relationships with others. By contrast, the medical model assumes that the therapist is responsible for the treatment and cure.

Dance therapy is not a derivative of any particular verbal psychotherapy. It has its own origin in dance, and certain aspects of both dance and choreography are important. There are basic principles involving the transformation of the motor urge and its expression into a useful, conscious form. The techniques used in dance therapy can allow many different processes to take place. During dance therapy, the use of movement results in a total sensing of submerged states of feeling that can serve to eliminate inappropriate behavior. Bodily integration is another process that can take place in dance therapy. The patient may gain a feeling of how parts of the body are connected and how movement in one part of the body affects the total body. The therapist can also help the patient become more aware of how movement behavior reflects the emotional state of the moment or help the patient recall earlier emotions or experiences. Dance therapy produces social interaction through the nonverbal relationships that can occur during dance therapy sessions.

MUSIC THERAPY

Music therapy is useful in facilitating psychotherapy because it stimulates the awareness and expression of emotions and ideas on an immediate and experiential level. When a person interacts musically with others, he or she may experience (separately or simultaneously) the overall musical gestalt of the group, the act of relating to and interacting with others, and his or her own feelings and thoughts about self, music, and the interactions that have occurred. The nonverbal, structured medium allows individuals to maintain variable levels of distance from intrapsychic (within self) and interpersonal (between people) processes. The abstract nature of music provides flexibility in how people relate to or take responsibility for their own musical expressions. The nonverbal expression may be a purely musical idea, or it may be part of a personal expression to the self or to others.

After the activity, the typical follow-through is to have each client share what was seen, heard, or felt during the musical experience. Patients use their musical experiences to examine their cognitive and affective reactions to them. It is then the responsibility of the music therapist to process with the individual the reactions and observations derived from the musical experience and to help the person generalize them—that is, determine how they might be applied to everyday life outside the music therapy session. Group musical experiences seem to stimulate verbal processing, possibly because of the various levels of interaction available to the group members.

THEATER THERAPY

Theater therapy, or drama therapy, uses either role-playing or improvisation to reach goals similar to those of music and dance therapy. The aims of the drama therapy process are to recognize experience, to increase one's role repertoire, and to learn how to play roles more spontaneously and competently.

The key concepts of drama therapy are the self and roles. Through role taking, the processes of imitation, identification, projection, and transference take place. Projection centers on the concept that inner thoughts, feelings, and conflicts will be projected onto a relatively ambiguous or neutral role. Transference is the tendency of an individual to transfer his or her feelings and perceptions of a dominant childhood figure—usually a parent—to the role being played.

USES AND GOALS OF PSYCHOTHERAPIES

New approaches and applications of music, dance, and theater therapies have been and are being developed as these fields grow and experiment. The goal of theater or drama therapy is to use the universal medium of theater as a setting for psychotherapeutic goals. Opportunities for potential participants include forms of self-help, enjoyment, challenge, personal fulfillment, friendship, and support. The theater setting helps each individual work with issues of control, reality testing, and stress reduction.

David Johnson and Donald Quinlan conducted substantial research into the effects of drama therapy on populations of schizophrenics. Their research addressed the problem of the loss of the self and the potential of drama therapy in recovering it. They found that paranoid schizophrenics create more rigid boundaries in their role-playing, while nonparanoid schizophrenics create more fluid ones. They concluded that improvisational role-playing is an effective means to assess boundary behaviors and differentiate one diagnostic group of schizophrenics from another.

Drama therapy has also been used in prison environments to institute change and develop what has been termed as a therapeutic community. The Geese Theatre Company, founded in the United States in 1980, works to change the institutional thinking, metaphors, responses, and actions unique to the prison environment, to allow both staff and prisoners to change and convert prisoner images and metaphors. The therapists found that drama therapy, or role play, intensifies the affect necessary to challenge beliefs. The method requires strong support from staff and the institution. Drama therapy, they point out, provides an unexpected format, action-based, and driven by people in relationship with one another. Their work in prison settings in both Australia and Romania helped in continuing development of process and principles for transforming prison cultures into effective therapeutic communities.

Dance therapy has been found to be extremely useful in work with autistic children, as well as children with minimal brain dysfunction (MBD). The symptoms of a child with MBD may range from a behavioral disorder to a learning disability. Though the symptoms vary, and some seem to vanish as the child matures, the most basic single characteristic seems to be an inability to organize internal and external stimuli effectively. By helping the child with MBD to reexperience, rebuild, or experience for the first time those elements upon which a healthy body image and body scheme are built, change can be made in the areas of control, visual-motor coordination, motor development, and self-concept.

The goals of dance therapy with a child with MBD are to help the child identify and experience his or her body boundaries, to help each child master the dynamics of moving and expressing feelings with an unencumbered body, to focus the hyperactive child, to lessen anxiety and heighten the ability to socialize, and to strengthen the self-concept.

Music therapy has been used successfully with patients who have anorexia nervosa, an eating disorder which has been called self-starvation. Anorexia nervosa represents an attempt to solve the psychological or concrete issues of life through direct, concrete manipulation of body size and weight. Regardless of the type or nature of the issues involved, which vary greatly among anorectic clients, learning to resolve conflicts and face psychological challenges effectively without the use of weight control is the essence of therapy for these clients. To accomplish this, anorectics must learn to divorce their eating from their other difficulties, stop using food as a tool for problem solving, face their problems, and believe in themselves as the best source for solving those problems. Music therapy has provided a means of persuading clients to accept themselves and their ability to control their lives, without the obsessive use of weight control, and to interact effectively and fearlessly with others.

Many health professionals have acknowledged the difficulty of engaging the person with anorexia in therapy, and music has been found to work well. Because of its nonverbal, nonthreatening, creative characteristics, music can provide a unique, experiential way to help clients acknowledge psychological and physical problems and resolve personal issues.

Music and dance therapies are being used to improve quality of life for older victims of dementias, including Alzheimer's disease. The number of cases of Alzheimer's is expected to increase as the population ages. It has been found that both music and movement can be used to reach these patients when other methods fail. The keys to this therapy include song preference of the client and the use of music specific to the client's life and youth. This music has been most effective if presented live, using the same rhythms and syncopations as the original music. Such therapy can be used to support and encourage behaviors that allow patients with dementia access to a higher quality of life, and to the expression of feelings and enjoyment.

Dynamic play therapy is another approach which combines concepts and techniques of drama and dance improvisation. It has been used in clinical settings involving foster, adoptive, and birth families with troubled children. This type of family play therapy emerged from sessions which often included adult caretakers of foster children and addressed specific problems concerning abuse and family-related expressive activities.

INTERDISCIPLINARY RELATIONSHIPS

The interdisciplinary sources of dance, music, and drama therapies bring a wide range of appropriate research methodologies and strategies to the discipline of psychology. These therapies tend to defy conventional quantification. Attempts to construct theoretical models of these therapies draw on the disciplines of psychology, sociology, medicine, and the arts. There is no unified approach to the study and practice of these therapies.

Dance therapy has its roots in ancient times, when dance was an integral part of life. It is likely that people danced and used body movement to communicate long before language developed. Dance could express and reinforce the most impor-

tant aspects of a culture. Societal values and norms were passed down from one generation to another through dance, reinforcing the survival mechanism of the culture.

The direct experience of shared emotions on a preverbal and physical level in dance is one of the key influences in the development of dance or movement therapy. The feelings of unity and harmony that emerge in group dance rituals provide the basis of empathetic understanding between people. Dance, in making use of natural joy, energy, and rhythm, fosters a consciousness of self. As movement occurs, body sensations are often felt more clearly and sharply. Physical sensations provide the basis from which feelings emerge and become expressed. Through movement and dance, preverbal and unconscious material often crystallizes into feeling states of personal imagery. It was the recognition of these elements, inherent in dance, that led to the eventual use of dance or movement in psychotherapy.

Wilhelm Reich was one of the first physicians to become aware of and utilize body posturing and movement in psychotherapy. He coined the term "character armor" to describe the physical manifestation of the way an individual deals with anxiety, fear, anger, and similar feelings. The development of dance into a therapeutic modality, however, is most often credited to Marian Chace, a former dance teacher and performer. She began her work in the early 1940's with children and adolescents in special schools and clinics. In the 1950's and 1960's, other modern dancers began to explore the use of dance as a therapeutic agent in the treatment of emotional disturbances.

There is a much earlier history of music therapy; the use of music in the therapeutic setting dates back to the 1700's. The various effects of different types of music on emotions were recognized. Music could be used to restrain or inflame passions, as in examples of martial, joyful, or melancholic music. It was therefore concluded that music could also have positive healing effects, although these would vary from person to person. Early research showed music therapy to be useful in helping mental patients; people with physical disabilities; children with emotional, learning, or behavioral problems; and people with a variety of other difficulties. Music could be used to soothe and to lift the spirits, but it required experimentation and observation.

Although its theatrical roots are ancient, drama or theater therapy is still in early stages of professional development. The field developed out of clinical experience in the 1920's, and its use and value as a psychotherapeutic tool is well documented. As a profession, drama therapy now requires the articulation and documentation of theories and methods as well as intensive case studies as support. Four challenges have been identified for the field: to develop new university programs and to increase the supply of students, to expand opportunities for advanced learning and to use mentors to help internalize a professional identity, to produce books and texts to attract new students and to establish the field academically, and to participate with other creative arts therapy organizations to protect legislatively professional interests and the needs of clients. All these forms of therapy can thus be best understood in terms of their backgrounds, relationships, and individual contributions to therapeutic applications in both mental and physical healing.

BIBLIOGRAPHY

Gilroy, Andrea, and Colin Lee, eds. *Art and Music: Therapy and Research.* New York: Routledge, 1995. A comprehensive introduction to art therapy and music therapy in the United Kingdom. It gives an excellent overview of research in both therapies, and contributors describe various research projects such as music therapy with offenders and with people living with AIDS and art therapy for people with learning disabilities and psychotic illness. The book is quite readable and valuable for its presentation of application of the research process in two therapeutic contexts.

Landy, Robert J. *Drama Therapy: Concepts and Practices.* Springfield, Ill.: Charles C Thomas, 1986. Particularly valuable in identifying the relationship between drama therapy and other psychotherapies. Contains numerous examples and illustrations of drama therapy as it has been used to address various psychological problems.

Lewis, P., and D. Johnson, eds. *Current Approaches in Drama Therapy.* Springfield, Ill.: Charles C Thomas, 2000. This is an excellent compilation of articles on the field of drama therapy and the variety of approaches taken by therapists. The volume is quite readable, even though professional vocabulary and terms are used. The book is directed to drama therapists, and those who might consider the profession. A number of case studies are used which point to the efficacy of drama therapy in various contexts.

Schneider, Erwin H., ed. *Music Therapy.* Lawrence, Kans.: National Association for Music Therapy, 1959. One of a series of annual publications of the proceedings of the National Association for Music Therapy. While somewhat old, this volume covers a wide variety of applications and settings of music therapy through case studies. It is a classic in the field of music therapy.

Siegel, Elaine V. *Dance-Movement Therapy: Mirror of Our Selves.* New York: Human Sciences Press, 1984. Strong theoretical framework and applied theory of dance and psychotherapy. This is a very scholarly investigation of dance therapy; includes movement as well.

Robin Franck;
updated by Martha Oehmke Loustaunau

SEE ALSO: Group therapy; Humanism; Person-centered therapy; Play therapy; Psychoanalytic psychology; Psychotherapy: Children; Psychotherapy: Goals and techniques.

N

Narcissistic personality

TYPE OF PSYCHOLOGY: Personality; psychopathology
FIELDS OF STUDY: Personality disorders; personality theory

Narcissistic personality consists of a constellation of traits that include an exaggerated sense of self-importance, a preoccupation with being admired, and a lack of empathy for the emotions of other people. Narcissistic personality disorder is a long-standing, inflexible way of behaving that has developed from childhood.

KEY CONCEPTS
- entitlement
- grandiosity
- perspective-taking ability
- temperament

INTRODUCTION

A person with a narcissistic personality shows a pattern of grandiosity, which is manifested by a strong tendency to overestimate one's abilities and accomplishments. Together with this grandiosity is a central feature of entitlement. This produces an exaggerated sense of self-importance and preoccupation with being admired. Persons with a narcissistic personality expect other people to give them their undivided attention and admiration. It is their belief that unlimited success, power, intelligence, and beauty are due them regardless of their actual accomplishments. Their behavior is marked with repeated self-references and bragging. These actions make them the center of attention, and they fully expect that others comply with their fantasy of entitlement.

Narcissistic personality disorder is one of the psychiatric disorders described by the American Psychiatric Association. The behaviors associated with the condition are persistent and lead to difficulties in maintaining mutually respectful and satisfying interpersonal relationships.

POSSIBLE CAUSES

An additional central feature of the narcissistic personality relates to the inability to take the perspective of others. Persons with this personality cannot empathize with the feelings of others, since it is only their own emotions that are important. Although very young children have this narcissistic tendency, it usually disappears through the course of development as they acquire perspective-taking ability. This capacity allows people to look at the world through the eyes of other people. With perspective-taking ability, a person can sympathize for the hardships endured by others, empathetically feel the pain of and commiserate with the joy felt by others. Children who do not show the typical pattern of emotional development grow to become adult narcissistic personalities. As adults, these individuals often take advantage of others to achieve their own goals and become arrogant and snobbish toward other people. Envy is found among persons with a narcissistic personality, as they resent the success of others.

Basic personality traits or temperaments are factors in the development of narcissistic personality disorder. Temperament emerges early in infancy and affects how the child interacts with the environment. Some infants show shyness or are inhibited around novel situations, while others are outgoing and playful. Such temperaments are an early foundation for the development of an adult personality. Genetics may play a role in the formulation of these infant temperaments or character traits. The maladaptive style of the narcissistic personality may evolve from a disturbed parent-child attachment due to the particular early temperament found in the infant.

DIAGNOSIS

A diagnosis of narcissistic personality disorder requires that a person shows a pervasive pattern of grandiosity, need for admiration, and lack of empathy beginning in early adulthood. Grandiosity produces a sense of unlimited power and intelligence and the feeling that only successful, high-status persons are worthwhile as friends and associates. The narcissistic personality disorder is described by an exaggerated sense of self-importance, a preoccupation with fantasies of unlimited success, a belief in being special, an exploitative style toward other people, a sense of entitlement, and arrogance. Formal diagnosis of narcissistic personality disorder by mental health professions is often difficult because the diagnostic criteria are inferred from behavior rather than through direct observation. Personality characteristics exist on a continuum from normal to pathological. It is difficult to determine at what point particular behavioral tendencies have become the sign of a psychiatric disorder.

TREATMENT AND IMPACT

The narcissistic personality disorder is very resistant to the traditional methods used for treatment. Patients do not believe that they need to change and typically enter treatment only at the insistence of someone else. Persons with narcissistic personality disorder put responsibility for treatment on other people and will avoid being the focus of therapy. Individual psychotherapy (talk therapy) and group therapy have been used for persons with this disorder. The psychotherapy approach is called cognitive-behavioral therapy. This therapy assumes that problem behaviors are caused by faulty ways of thinking about the environment and other people, and the focus of treatment is on the modification of the troublesome beliefs. However, psychotherapy and even the use of medications such as antidepressants have been found to be of limited value for persons with narcissistic personality disorder. No treatment has yet produced a cure. Since persons with this disorder seldom seek therapy themselves, they may become involved with treatment in conjunction with another person's therapy.

The negative impact of the disorder often falls on the family and friends of persons with a narcissistic personality. A narcissistic spouse may cause great difficulty in a marriage through constant demands and expectations of admiration. Conflicts may emerge when these expectations are not realized. A parent with narcissistic personality disorder may prevent a child from receiving adequate care and nurturance, as personal demands for attention dominate the child's needs.

DSM-IV-TR Criteria for Narcissistic Personality Disorder (DSM code 301.81)

Pervasive pattern of grandiosity (in fantasy or behavior), need for admiration, and lack of empathy, beginning by early adulthood and present in a variety of contexts

Indicated by five or more of the following:
- grandiose sense of self-importance (exaggerates achievements and talents, expects to be recognized as superior without commensurate achievements)
- preoccupation with fantasies of unlimited success, power, brilliance, beauty, or ideal love
- belief that he or she is "special" and unique and can only be understood by, or should associate with, other special or high-status people (or institutions)
- need for excessive admiration
- sense of entitlement (unreasonable expectations of especially favorable treatment or automatic compliance with his or her expectations)
- interpersonal exploitation (takes advantage of others to achieve his or her own ends)
- lack of empathy (unwilling to recognize or identify with feelings and needs of others)
- envy of others or belief that others are envious of him or her
- arrogant, haughty behaviors or attitudes

SOURCES FOR FURTHER STUDY

Blais, M. "Content Validity of the DSM-IV Borderline and Narcissistic Personality Disorder Criteria Sets." *Comparative Psychiatry* 38 (1997): 31-37. This study describes the basic symptoms associated with the narcissistic personality disorder and how they relate to a formal diagnosis of the disorder.

Golomb, M., M. Fava, and J. Rosenbaum. "Gender Differences in Personality Disorders." *American Journal of Psychiatry* 152 (1995): 579-582. This disorder is seen in men more often than women. The authors discuss some of the issues surrounding this difference.

Kernberger, O. "A Psychoanalytic Theory of Personality Disorders. In *Major Theories of Personality Disorder,* edited by J. F. Clarkin and M. Lenzenweger. New York: Guilford Press, 1996. This chapter suggests the possible psychodynamics in the early parent-child interactions that lead to the development of narcissistic personality disorder.

Ronningstam, E., and M. Lyons. "Changes in Pathological Narcissism." *American Journal of Psychiatry* 152 (1995): 253-257. The authors discuss the most significant characteristics that define the narcissistic personality. Grandiosity was found to be of particular significance as a predictive factor.

Frank J. Prerost

SEE ALSO: Addictive personality and behaviors; Antisocial personality; Borderline personality; Histrionic personality; Intimacy; Multiple personality; Personality disorders; Personality theory.

Nearsightedness and farsightedness

TYPE OF PSYCHOLOGY: Sensation and perception
FIELDS OF STUDY: Vision

Nearsightedness and farsightedness result from an inability of the lens of the eye to focus the image of far or near objects on the retina. In the inherited form of the disability, the eyeball is too long or short in the anterior-posterior direction to allow correct focusing by the lens. In the form of the disability that is related to age, the lens becomes too inflexible to focus nearby objects.

KEY CONCEPTS
- emmetropia
- hyperopia
- laser-assisted in situ keratomileusis (LASIK)
- myopia
- photorefractive keratectomy (PRK)
- presbyopia
- refractive surgery

INTRODUCTION
Several disabilities affecting vision involve defects in the lens or cornea or the focusing mechanism of the eyes. By far the most common of these disabilities are nearsightedness and farsightedness, the inability to focus the eyes on objects that are either far from or close to the viewer.

Light reflected or originating from distant objects enters the eye in essentially parallel rays. In a person with normal vision, the lens of the eye brings these rays to a point of focus on the retina. The focusing creates an image of distant objects on the retina, much like the image focused by a film or slide projector on a screen. The image focused on the retina by the lens of the eye, however, is inverted and greatly reduced in size. The image of a person's head and shoulders at a distance of 20 feet from the viewer, for example, is focused upside down on the retina in a spot only 0.5 millimeter wide.

Many persons suffer from disabilities in vision caused by an inability to focus on near or far objects. In such persons, the distance between the lens and retina of the eye is too long or short to allow correct focusing. When the distance from the lens to the retina is too long, the point of focus of the lens falls in front of the retina when parallel rays from distant objects enter the eye. Such persons cannot focus clearly on distant objects and are said to be nearsighted or myopic. When the distance between the lens and the retina is too short, the diverging rays from near objects are focused on a point that would fall behind the retina. Individuals with this disability cannot focus on nearby objects and are said to be farsighted or hyperopic. An individual with normally shaped eyeballs, who is neither nearsighted nor farsighted, is emmetropic. Myopia and hyperopia are inherited conditions in many individuals.

Another form of farsightedness, presbyopia, occurs with advancing age and results from a gradual loss of flexibility in the lens with advancing age. The lens of the eye differs from the lens of an optical device such as a telescope or camera in being flexible and able to change in surface curvature. Instead of focusing primarily by moving the lens forward or backward with respect to the retina, the eye contracts small muscles surrounding the lens, the ciliary muscles, to change the curvature of the lens, thereby changing its focal length. (The focal length is the distance from the center of the lens to the point of focus.)

LENSES AND FOCUS
The focusing process, first worked out by Hermann von Helmholtz, has some characteristics that at first

seem unexpected. If it were removed from the eye, the fully flexible lens of a young person would assume an approximately spherical shape, with the maximum possible surface curvature. In this form, the lens would have maximum converging or focusing power. This is a result of the fact that the lens consists of a jellylike internal substance enclosed and held under pressure by a tough but elastic surface capsule. A spherical shape would allow the lens to assume a conformation of minimum surface area per volume.

In the eye, the lens is placed under constant tension by fibers that radiate from the lens and attach to the sides of the eye. These nonelastic fibers stretch the lens into a maximally flattened state. In this form, the lens has minimum converging or focusing power. When in its fully flattened form, the lens is considered relaxed. In a person with normal vision, the parallel light rays reflected from distant objects are brought to a point of perfect focus on the retina by the relaxed lens.

Light rays reflected from objects closer than about 6 meters diverge too widely to be focused on the retina by the relaxed lens. In response, a group of ciliary muscles surrounding the lens contracts. These muscles collectively form a sphincter, in a form similar to the pupil of the eye or to the lips compressed to form the letter O. Contraction of the ciliary muscles has the effect of opposing the zonular fibers, compressing the lens and allowing it to assume a more spherical shape. This increases the converging power of the lens, allowing the diverging rays reflected from nearby objects to be brought to a point of perfect focus on the retina.

There is a limit to the ability of the lens to round up under the action of the ciliary muscles, so that objects held too closely cannot be clearly focused. As individuals age, several interacting factors modify this ability. One factor is the consistency of the lens, which becomes less flexible with age and loses its ability to round up under the action of the ciliary muscles. Other factors, analyzed by Jane F. Koretz and George H. Handelman, include growth of the lens and changes in the tension and arrangement of the zonular fibers. These combined factors have the effect of moving the limit of nearest vision steadily farther from the eye—that is, of making the individual more farsighted—as the individual ages. In a newborn baby, the lens is so flexible that objects placed as close as 7 centimeters can be clearly fo-

cused. In young children, the nearest focusing distance lengthens to about 8.5 centimeters. By the twenties to thirties, the point of nearest focus has extended to about 10 to 15 centimeters. By age forty, the point of clearest focus has receded to about 22 centimeters for the average person. By this time, most people need glasses or contact lenses to converge light strongly enough to see nearby objects in clear focus. By age fifty, the nearest point of focus lies at about 40 centimeters, so that objects must be held at arm's length to be seen clearly without the aid of glasses. By age seventy, the point of nearest focus has receded to hundreds of centimeters. (These figures are for people who are neither nearsighted nor farsighted in their twenties and thirties.)

DIAGNOSIS

In order to test an individual's eyes for nearsightedness or farsightedness, the ability of the lens to accommodate, or change in focus, must be eliminated. Otherwise, the condition of nearsightedness or farsightedness might be hidden by the eye's ability to change its focus. For example, in mild farsightedness, in which the fully relaxed lens would focus light rays slightly behind the retina, the ciliary muscles can easily contract enough to bring the rays into focus on the retina. As a result, the farsightedness will pass undetected. This is an undesirable condition, because in such persons the ciliary muscles are under a constant state of contraction, which can lead to eyestrain and headaches.

To eliminate accommodation as a source of error, drops are usually added to paralyze the ciliary muscles temporarily. The point of focus of the fully relaxed lens can then be accurately determined. The ability of the eye to accommodate and conceal inherent nearsightedness or farsightedness is one of several reasons that it is not advisable to correct faulty vision by trying on the glasses available at drugstores and department stores until a pair is found that apparently provides clear vision.

TREATMENT

Nearsightedness and farsightedness have been problems for the human population since long before recorded history. In ancient times, people noticed that glass spheres, or a spherical bottle filled with water, could magnify objects and make them more clearly visible. Crude lenses of this type were probably used, at least by farsighted persons, to provide a partial correction from the earliest times. More highly developed, handheld lenses correcting for nearsightedness and farsightedness were used during the early history of both Europe and China; by the fourteenth century, the first eyeglasses had been invented in Italy. Credit for this invention is generally given to Alessandro di Spina of Florence, Italy. A portrait painted in Italy in 1352 is the first known depiction of a person wearing eyeglasses.

Nearsightedness and farsightedness can be corrected by lenses placed in front of the eye or directly on the cornea. For correction of farsightedness, a converging lens is placed in front of the eye. This lens bends parallel rays reflected from distant objects into converging pathways. Because the rays are now converging rather than parallel, the lens can bring the rays to focus precisely on the retina rather than behind the lens. For the correction of nearsightedness, a diverging lens is placed in front of the eye. The diverging rays are focused precisely on the retina rather than off the retina, as they would be in the uncorrected eye. The degree of convergence or divergence needed to correct for farsightedness or nearsightedness is usually determined simply by trial and error, by the selection of progressively stronger or weaker lenses until the correcting lens that gives maximal visual acuity is found.

In 1784, Benjamin Franklin invented bifocals by combining lenses correcting for near and far vision. The lenses were cut in half, placed one above the other, and held in a common frame. By the early twentieth century, bifocals were cut from a single piece of glass. In more recent years, trifocals have allowed correction for near, intermediate, and far vision. The ultimate correction is now obtained by multifocal lenses, which have a complex surface curvature that increases the power of the lens continuously from the top to the bottom. The top of the lens corrects for distant vision and the bottom for near vision. By tilting the head, the wearer can find a point on the lens that gives clear vision for any distance between near and far vision.

Because eyeglasses are fixed in place on the head, they cannot move with the eyes. As a consequence, the distance from the eye to the lens changes as the eyeball rotates. This change in distance is compensated for by a difference in curvature in the front and back of the eyeglass lens, so

that the power of the lens varies from the center to the edges. The correction is imperfect even in modern glasses, so that objects viewed through off-center regions of the lenses appear distorted and slightly out of focus. This has the effect of reducing the clarity of peripheral vision. To compensate for this deficiency, most persons wearing glasses learn to turn the head instead of the eyes to view objects in the periphery. Eyeglasses present another problem because they are located several centimeters from the lens of the eye. Because of their position, lenses correcting for nearsightedness or farsightedness have the effect of changing the size or magnification of the image.

Whether the correcting lens is placed a few centimeters in front of the eye, as it is in glasses, or directly on the cornea, as it is in contact lenses, makes essentially no difference to the correction of nearsightedness or farsightedness. Contact lenses, however, have the advantage of automatically correcting astigmatism caused by defects in the curvature of the cornea. Because the cornea has a curved surface, it acts as a fixed lens and contributes to the focus of the eye. In corneal astigmatism, the cornea, rather than having a spherical shape, is slightly flattened or rounded too greatly in one direction over the surface. The effect makes one region of the cornea converge light rays more strongly than other regions. As a result, not all parts of the field of view can be placed in focus. If a series of lines radiating from a point is viewed by an astigmatic individual, some of the lines are seen in focus and some out of focus. Usually, the in-focus and out-of-focus lines are 90 degrees apart. When a contact lens is placed over the cornea, the contact lens, in effect, becomes the cornea. Because a contact lens is constructed with a perfectly spherical surface curvature, any astigmatism caused by imperfections in the cornea is relieved. Because most astigmatism is corneal, rather than caused by imperfections in the lens of the eye, contact lenses are usually effective in eliminating astigmatism as well as nearsightedness.

Since contact lenses are seated directly on the cornea of the eyes, they turn with the eye. As a result, they provide a wide field of undistorted view comparable to normal vision. Because they are placed close to the lens of the eye, in a position that is essentially the same as the cornea itself, they correct for nearsightedness and farsightedness without significantly affecting the size of the image. The several advantages of contact lenses are offset for many persons, however, by their greater expense and irritation of the eyes.

Refractive Surgeries

Newer state-of-the-art vision correction is available to the nearsighted, the farsighted, and the astigmatic in the form of refractive surgery. Refractive surgeries include all procedures that reduce refractive errors, correcting myopia, hyperopia, and astigmatism. Currently, there are many refractive procedures available to those with impaired vision.

Photorefractive keratectomy (PRK) has been used since 1989, when clinical trials began. This procedure employs a laser to modify the curvature of the cornea, thereby correcting nearsightedness, farsightedness, or astigmatism.

Laser-assisted in situ keratomileusis (LASIK) is a newer type of refractive surgery, which was first studied in clinical trials in 1995. Using a microkeratome, the surgeon creates a thin layer of cornea that can be folded back. The laser correction is then applied underneath the flap. When this technique is used, there is little scarring, recovery of vision is quick, and minimal pain occurs.

There are currently many new procedures being evaluated by the Food and Drug Administration (FDA) for treatment of nearsightedness and farsightedness. These procedures include intraoccular rings and laser thermokeratoplasty. Which procedure is best for any individual depends on the subject's age, type and degree of refractive error, and the risks and benefits for each person as well as the subject's personal circumstances.

Sources for Further Study

Brint, Stephen F., Corrine Kuypers-Delinger, and D. Kennedy. *The Laser Vision Breakthrough: Everything You Need to Know Before Making a Decision.* Roseville, Calif.: Prima, 2000. This book, coauthored by the first U.S. surgeon to perform LASIK, gives a detailed account of laser vision correction. It includes a discussion of everything from pre-op examination to follow-up care, detailing pros and cons of the procedure.

Masland, Richard H. "The Functional Architecture of the Retina." *Scientific American* 255 (December, 1986): 102-111. This clearly written article describes the types of cells in the retina and how they are arranged and organized into a system functioning in light absorption and the transmission of nerve impulses. Outlines the author's research in tracing the shapes of individual retinal nerve cells, and shows how his and other techniques will eventually lead to a complete three-dimensional reconstruction of the organization of the retina. Many diagrams and photos, including both light and electron microscope pictures, illustrate the text.

Neisser, Ulrich. "The Process of Vision." *Scientific American* 259 (September, 1988): 204-214. Analyzes the interaction between the retinal image and the brain in the perception of visual images, including factors that affect visual perception, such as memory and attention. Clearly and simply written; includes interesting illustrative examples. Demonstrates that what is perceived in vision is vastly more complex than the initial image projected on the retina.

Schnapf, Julie L., and Denis A. Baylor. "How Photoreceptor Cells Respond to Light." *Scientific American* 256 (April, 1987): 40-47. Explains the techniques used to detect and record the responses to stimulation by single rods and cones in the retina, and the patterns in which the photoreceptors respond to light absorption. Describes the differences between rods and cones, and outlines the roles of cones in color vision. Clearly and simply written, with a wealth of illustrations, some in full color.

Sherwood, Lauralee. *Human Physiology: From Cells to Systems.* 4th ed. Pacific Grove, Calif.: Brooks/Cole, 2001. This college physiology text outlines the structure and function of the human visual system from the receptors in the eye through the thalamus and the occipital lobe of the brain. This topic is clearly explained in Chapter 6, covering the Special Senses.

Slade, Stephen G., R. N. Baker, and D. K. Brockman. *The Complete Book of Laser Eye Surgery.* Napierville, Ill.: Sourcebooks, 2000. A complete guide to the state of the art refractive procedures currently being used to correct myopia, hyperopia, presbyopia, and astigmatism. This book answers questions on LASIK, PRK, and other new surgical options.

Vander, Arthur, James Sherman, and Dorothy Luciano. *Human Physiology: The Mechanisms of Body Function.* 8th ed. Boston: McGraw-Hill, 2001.

Chapter 9 of this college physiology text, entitled "The Sensory Systems," includes a clear overview of the human visual system as it normally functions.

Stephen L. Wolfe;
updated by Robin Kamienny Montvilo

SEE ALSO: Brain specialization; Brain structure; Pattern vision; Sensation and perception; Vision: Brightness and contrast; Vision: Color; Visual system.

Nervous system

TYPE OF PSYCHOLOGY: Biological bases of behavior; language; learning; memory; sensation and perception

FIELDS OF STUDY: Auditory, chemical, cutaneous, and body senses; biological treatments; endocrine system; nervous system; organic disorders; schizophrenias; thought; vision

The nervous system represents the interconnections of cells that recognize and coordinate the senses of the body. The nervous system is divided into two major components: the central nervous system, which includes the brain and spinal cord, and the peripheral nervous system, which communicates impulses to and from the regions of the body.

KEY CONCEPTS
- central nervous system
- endocrine system
- endorphins and enkephalins
- limbic system
- neuron
- neurotransmitters
- peripheral nervous system

INTRODUCTION

The functions of the human nervous system are in many ways analogous to that of a computer. The brain receives information in the form of stimuli from the senses open to the outside world. Within the brain are specific regions, analogous to programs, that interpret the stimuli and allow for a response. More specifically, such responses take the form of physiological or behavioral changes.

Some of these stimuli result from activation of tissues or organs within the endocrine system, a network of glands which secrete hormones directly into the bloodstream for regulation of target organs.

The functional unit of the nervous system is the neuron, a cell which receives or sends information in the form of electrical impulses. The major component of the neuron is the cell body, the portion which contains the nucleus and most of the internal organelles. Two major forms of neurons are found within the nervous system: sensory neurons, which transmit the impulse toward the central nervous system (brain and spinal cord), and motor neurons, which receive impulses from the brain or spinal cord and transmit the impulse to muscles or other tissues.

Depending upon the type of neuron, a variety of processes may emanate from the cell body. Axons transmit the impulse away from the cell body and toward the target cell or tissue. Dendrites receive the impulse from other neurons or other sources of stimuli. The actual nerve consists of bundles of thousands of axons wrapped within a form of connective tissue.

The surface of a resting, or unstimulated, neuron has a measurable electrical potential across the membrane. When the nerve is stimulated, whether mechanically such as by pressure or electrically as in the sense of sight, an influx of electrically charged ions such as sodium occurs; the result is referred to as an action potential. The electrical discharge flows along the axon until it reaches the end of the neuron. Eventually the resting potential is restored, and the neuron may again undergo stimulation.

At its tip, the axon divides into numerous terminal branches, each with a structure called a synaptic bulb on the end. Within the bulb are vessels containing chemicals called neurotransmitters, molecules which transmit the electrical signal from one neuron to another, or to target tissues such as those in the endocrine system.

There exist within the nervous system a large number of different forms of neurons, many of which respond to different types of neurotransmitters. Alterations in production of these chemicals, or in the ability of nerves to respond to their stimuli, form the physiological basis for a variety of psychological problems.

CENTRAL NERVOUS SYSTEM

The central nervous system is composed of two principal structures: the brain and the spinal cord. The brain is one of the largest organs in the body, weighing on average about three pounds and consisting of one trillion neurons by early adulthood.

The brain is subdivided into four major functional areas. The cerebrum, the largest portion of the brain, regulates sensory and motor functions. The convolutions characteristic of the human brain represent the physical appearance of the cerebrum. The brain stem connects the brain with the spinal cord, carrying out both sensory and motor functions. The diencephalon consists of the thalamus,

the relay center for sensory functions entering the cerebrum, and the hypothalamus, which controls much of the peripheral nervous system activity and regulates endocrine processes. The fourth portion of the brain is the cerebellum, the rear of the brain where voluntary muscle activity is controlled.

PERIPHERAL NERVOUS SYSTEM

The peripheral nervous system consists of the sensory receptors such as those that recognize touch or heat in the skin or visual stimuli in the retina of the eye, and the nerves which communicate the stimuli to the brain. The peripheral nervous system is often subdivided into two parts, according to function: the somatic portion, which recognizes stimuli in the external environment such as on the skin, and the autonomic portion, which recognizes changes in the internal environment, such as hormone or mineral concentrations in the bloodstream.

The somatic portion of the peripheral nervous system in humans consists of twelve pairs of nerves which originate in the brain and which transmit sensory input from the body. For example, nerve endings in the retina of the eye transmit images to the brain; sensory fibers in the face transmit impulses affecting the skin or teeth. An additional thirty-one pairs of nerves emerge from the spinal cord, subdivide into branches, and innervate various regions of the body.

The autonomic nervous system maintains homeostasis, or constancy, within the body. For example, receptors measure heart rate, body temperature, and the activity of hormones within the bloodstream and tissues. Any abnormality or change results in a signal sent to the brain.

The most notable of the functions of the autonomic nervous system occur in the sympathetic and parasympathetic systems. The sympathetic arm of the system is primarily associated with the stimulation tissues and organs. For example, during times of stress, hormones are released that increase the heart rate, constrict blood vessels, and stimulate the sweat glands, a phenomenon often referred to as "fight or flight." By contrast, the parasympathetic system counteracts these effects, decreasing the heart rate, dilating blood vessels, and decreasing the rate of sweating.

ROLE OF NEUROTRANSMITTERS

Neurons communicate with one another through the release of neurotransmitters, chemical sub-

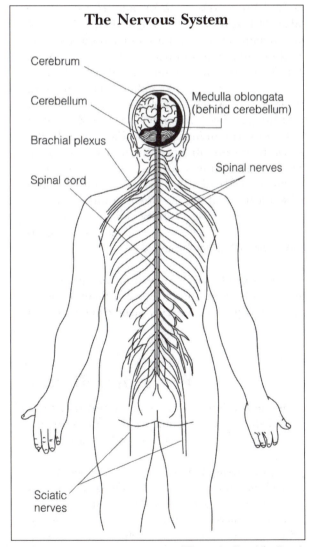

The Nervous System

Cerebrum

Cerebellum

Medulla oblongata
(behind cerebellum)

Brachial plexus

Spinal nerves

Spinal cord

Sciatic
nerves

(Hans & Cassidy, Inc.)

stances that transmit nerve impulses between nerve cells. Numerous types of neurotransmitters have been identified. Some of these transmitters act to excite neurons, while others inhibit neuronal activity. The particular type of transmitter is synthesized within the cell body of the neuron, travels along the axon, and is released into the space between neurons, known as the synapse.

Among the most prominent neurotransmitters involved in the excitation of neurons is acetylcholine. The same transmitter bridges the junctions between nerves and skeletal muscles as well as glandular tissues in the body. In the brain, acetylcholine bridges the synapses between neurons throughout the central nervous system. The amino acids glutamic acid and aspartic acid are also known to be involved in excitation of some neurons within the brain. The neurotransmitter serotonin is released mainly within the brain stem, where it appears to regulate activities such as sleep, moods, and body temperature.

Certain neurotransmitters serve in the inhibition of neuronal activity. The most common of these is gamma-aminobutyric acid (GABA), found primarily in the diencephalon region of the brain. Here GABA acts to reduce the activity within the region. Antianxiety drugs such as valium or librium appear to work by enhancing the activity of GABA, resulting in the relaxation of skeletal muscles. Antidepression compounds such as Prozac and Zoloft appear to function through blockage of serotonin uptake by neurons.

ENDORPHINS AND THE PLACEBO EFFECT

Persons who receive treatments with agents that possess no pharmacological activity for various illnesses or conditions have often been known to show improvement. Such a reaction is called the placebo effect. Whether the placebo effect is real has long been controversial. A 1955 study published in the prestigious *Journal of the American Medical Association* was the first significant report that the effect was real. More recent work has suggested the placebo effect may be sometimes more myth than reality. Nevertheless, there is evidence that such an effect may indeed occur and may be associated with forms of neurotransmitters called endorphins (endogenous morphines) and enkephalins. Endorphins and enkephalins represent a class of neurotransmitter-like chemicals called neuropeptides, small molecules which consist of between two and forty amino acids.

Enkephalins, discovered in 1975, block pain impulses within the central nervous system in ways similar to the drug morphine. The second class of molecules, subsequently called endorphins, was discovered soon afterward. They appear to act through suppression of pain impulses through suppression of a chemical called substance P. Substance P is released by neurons in the brain, the result of pain impulses from receptors in the peripheral nervous system. By inhibiting the release of substance P, these neuropeptides suppress sensory pain mechanisms. In support of a physiological basis for the placebo effect, patients treated with the endorphin antagonist naloxon produced no discernable response to placebo treatment.

Endorphins have been shown to play a role in a wide variety of body functions, including memory and learning and the control of sexual impulses. Abnormal activity of endorphins has been shown to play a role in organic psychiatric dysfunctions such as schizophrenia and depression. Deficits in endorphin levels have been observed to correlate with aggressiveness; endorphin replacement therapy results in the diminishment of such behavior. Abnormal levels of endorphins in the blood have also been found in individuals suffering from behavioral disorders such as anorexia or obesity.

LIMBIC SYSTEM AND EMOTIONS

The limbic system is the label that applies to regions of the diencephalon such as the thalamus and hypothalamus that are associated with behaviors such as emotions, learning, and sexual behavior. Stimulation of various areas within the limbic system during surgery has resulted in the patient feeling a variety of conflicting emotions, such as happiness and pleasure or fear and depression, depending upon the area being tested.

Some of these emotions or behaviors are associated with survival. For example, stimulation of certain areas results in feelings of rage or sexual excitement. Such patterns of behavior, accompanied by increased heart rate and blood pressure, have suggested that the limbic system plays a role in the "fight or flight" phenomenon.

Neurotransmitters such as serotonin and dopamine are believed to play roles in these behaviors. The effects of recreational drugs on behaviors and emotions may in part be due to the similarity of action between these drugs and neurotransmitters. For example, the high associated with amphetamine use or abuse may result from stimulation of these neurotransmitters. Cocaine blocks the movement of dopamine, resulting in the continual activation of neurons which use dopamine as a neurotransmitter. The addiction associated with cocaine results from alterations in the affected neurons, resulting in an increase in need for stimulation by these pathways.

The disorder schizophrenia may also be the result of impaired transmission of dopamine. The symptoms of schizophrenia—hallucinations or delusions—may be decreased through the use of drugs which inhibit dopamine release. Likewise, drugs which stimulate dopamine activity increase the severity of symptoms.

SOURCES FOR FURTHER STUDY

Becker, J., S. Breedlove, and D. Crews. *Behavioral Endocrinology*. Cambridge, Mass.: MIT Press, 2000. Emphasis is on the role of the endocrine system and neurotransmitters on physiology of the nervous system, as well as effect on behaviors.

"The Brain." *Scientific American* 241 (September, 1979). The issue was devoted entirely to the nervous system. Though new information has subsequently become available, the issue remains an excellent general source for the subject. Excellent photographs and diagrams are included in the articles.

Kolb, Bryan, and Ian Whishaw. *An Introduction to Brain and Behavior*. New York: Worth, 2001. Textbook on the subject. In addition to thorough coverage of brain structure and function, the authors describe the role of neurophysiology and behavior.

Sherwood, Lauralee. *Human Physiology: From Cells to Systems*. Pacific Grove, Calif.: Brooks/Cole, 2001. Drawing on recent experimentation, the author provides extensive background material for those chapters which explain the function of the nervous system. The text includes extensive details, but tables and diagrams clarify the material and provide numerous examples.

Richard Adler

SEE ALSO: Adrenal gland; Brain damage; Brain specialization; Brain structure; Endocrine system; Endorphins; Gonads; Hormones and behavior; Neurons; Neuropsychology; Pituitary gland; Psychobiology; Reticular formation; Sensation and perception; Senses; Sex hormones and motivation; Split-brain studies; Synaptic transmission; Synesthesia; Thyroid gland; Visual system.

Neurons

TYPE OF PSYCHOLOGY: Biological bases of behavior
FIELDS OF STUDY: Nervous system

The basic cellular units of the nervous system are glial cells and neurons. Thinking, emotions, and behavior are made possible by electrochemical messages transmitted from one location to another—a process that is only accomplished by neurons.

KEY CONCEPTS
- action potential
- axon
- dendrite
- long-term potentiation
- myelin
- neuron
- resting potential
- soma
- synapse

INTRODUCTION

In the latter part of the nineteenth century, there were two competing theoretical approaches toward explaining the composition of the brain. The reticular theory, championed by the Italian scientist Camillo Golgi (1843-1926), proposed that the brain consisted of a dense, netlike structure of nerve wires with no individual cells. The neuron doctrine, as advocated by the Spanish scientist Santiago Ramón y Cajal (1852-1934), asserted that the brain was composed of individual cells, just like other structures of the body, and that these cells were separated from one another by small gaps. The best microscopic views of that era could not provide evidence to determine which theory was correct, and a contentious debate ensued.

Ironically, it was a staining technique developed by Golgi in the late 1800's that enabled Ramón y Cajal eventually to demonstrate the existence of individual cells in the brain, confirming the neuron doctrine. Ramón y Cajal called these cells neurons, nerve cells that are specialized to receive information and electrochemically transmit it to other cells. In 1906, the gaps between these neurons were termed "synapses" by Charles Sherrington, who deduced many of the properties of synaptic functioning.

NEURONAL STRUCTURE AND TYPES

There are an estimated one trillion neurons in the human nervous system, with somewhere around one hundred billion in the brain. Neurons share many of the same features as other cells. For example, they are surrounded by a membrane, have a nucleus which contains the chromosomes, are provided metabolic energy by mitochondria, and synthesize proteins at sites called ribosomes. What makes neurons structurally different from other cells is a unique tripartite structure.

Most neurons contain a soma, many dendrites, and only one axon. The soma or cell body is a rounded swelling of the neuron that contains the cell nucleus. Electrical messages, also called impulses or action potentials, are collected in the soma which, in turn, may cause the discharge of electricity to another cell.

Input to the soma usually comes from dendrites. Most neurons have many of these branching fibers whose surface is lined with receptors specialized to receive impulses. Some dendrites have small outgrowths called spines on them. Spines increase the places available for connection to other cells.

The axon is a thin fiber, usually longer than the dendrites, that is specialized to send messages from the soma to other cells. Axons have many branches, each of which enlarges at the tip forming the terminal end bulb. It is from this end bulb that chemicals are released into the synaptic cleft (gap).

Neurons can be distinguished from one another in several ways. Axonal length is long in projection neurons, but short or even absent in local neurons. The function of neurons is different in sensory neurons, which are specialized to detect physical information from the environment, than it is in motor

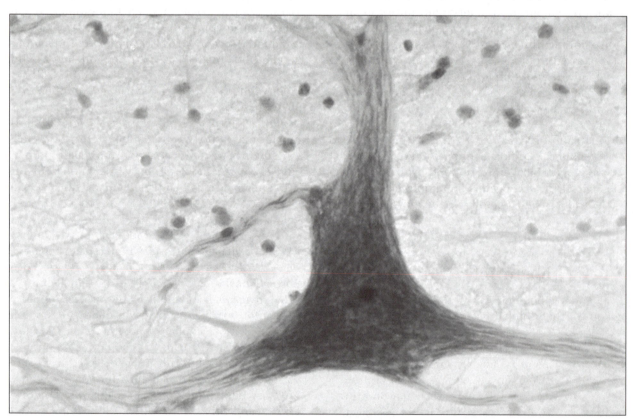

A nerve cell. (Digital Stock)

neurons, which are specialized to activate muscles and glands. A third function of neurons, found in interneurons, is to communicate only with other neurons. The direction of the neural impulse is toward a structure in afferents, away from a structure in efferents, and within a structure in intrinsic neurons. Finally, neurons can be distinguished on the basis of polar dimensions. Unipolar neurons carry a message in one direction only, bipolar neurons convey an impulse in two directions, and multipolar neurons can transmit information in many directions.

THE RESTING POTENTIAL

Each neuron has the capability of producing an electrical charge called the resting potential. Neurons in their resting (nondischarging) state generate voltage by creating an imbalance of positive (sodium, potassium, and calcium) and negative (chloride) electrically charged particles called ions. Four factors contribute to this ion imbalance between the inside and the outside of the neuron's membrane. First, the membranes of neurons have small gaps in them called ion channels. Potassium and chloride ions pass through these channels more readily than sodium ions, resulting in more negative ions on the inside of the neuron than on the outside. Second, the sodium-potassium pump forces three sodium ions out of the neuron for every two potassium ions allowed inside the cell, resulting in less positively charged ions inside the neuron. Third, proteins on the inside of the neuron carry a negative charge. Finally, the gradient balance between entropy—ions will move toward a place of less density—and enthalpy—ions will move toward a place of opposite electrical charge—results in a further negatively charged environment inside the neurons. Combining these four factors together yields approximately a –70 millivolt resting potential for each neuron. In other words, the neuron is like a battery that carries a charge of –70 millivolts.

THE ACTION POTENTIAL

Stimulation from the environment or other neurons can disturb the balance that creates the neuron's resting potential and produce a reversal of electrical polarity that leads the neuron to discharge an electrical impulse. This process is called the action potential and occurs in three phases. The first phase begins with a depolarization—a reduction of

the electrical charge toward zero—of the neuron. When this depolarization is sufficient to cause the neuron to be approximately 10 to 15 millivolts less negative, the threshold of excitation is reached and the sodium ion gates, responding to the voltage change, will be opened. This results in a sudden influx of positively charged ions resulting in a reversal of polarity. One millisecond after the sodium gates open, they immediately shut, cutting off the sodium influx, and the gates cannot be opened for another millisecond or so, ending the first phase of the process.

The second phase begins with the opening of the potassium ion channels. Because the inside of the neuron is now positively charged and dense with potassium ions, the positively charged potassium ions flow out of the neuron. Unlike the sodium gates, the potassium gates do not snap shut quickly, and this results in less potassium ions inside the neuron than during the resting state. The net effect is that the second phase produces a hyperpolarization, which means that the neuron has an increased charge of approximately –110 millivolts.

In the third phase, the sodium and potassium gates return to their normal conditions, restoring the ion flow conditions that create the resting potential. As a result of the action potential, slightly more sodium ions and slightly fewer potassium ions are found in the neuron at the beginning of the third phase. The sodium-potassium pump eventually corrects this small imbalance and restores the original resting potential conditions.

Between the peak of the action potential and the restoration of the resting potential, the neuron resists generating an action potential. This resistance of refractory period is first absolute—it is impossible for an action potential to occur—and then relative—action potentials can happen, but require stronger-than-normal stimulation.

AXONAL CONDUCTION

In motor neurons, but not all interneurons or sensory neurons, the action potential begins where the axon exits the soma, a place called the axon hillock. Basically, each point along the axon regenerates the sodium ion influx as it travels down the axon like a ripple caused by throwing a stone in a pond. Because the sodium ion gates snap shut shortly after they open, the action potential will not travel back to the soma and the impulse is ensured to move toward the synapse. Unlike the small ripple on the pond, the traveling wave down the axon does not diminish in size or velocity and is independent of the size of the stimulus that generates it. This axonal (not dendritic or somatic) phenomenon is called the "all-or-none" law.

The speed of the impulse down the axon is affected by two factors. First, the larger the diameter of the axons, the more rapidly the impulse is transmitted. Second, many axons are covered with an insulating material called myelin. In myelinated axons, neural impulses "jump" from one break in the myelin sheath—called a node of Ranvier—to another break, resulting in conduction speeds of up to 270 miles per hour. This node-to-node jumping, called saltatory conduction, is much faster than conduction in unmyelinated axons, which produces speeds of only 2 to 22 miles per hour.

SYNAPTIC TRANSMISSION

Because a small gap separates one neuron from another, the traveling electrical charge down the axon cannot affect the next neuron electrically—the "wire" is cut. What allows the gap to be bridged is a chemical process that can be described as a sequence that begins with presynoptic events (what occurs in the sending neuron) and ends with postsynaptic events (what occurs in the receiving neuron).

Presynaptically, when the action potential reaches the terminal end bulb, it opens ion channels for calcium ions which then enter the axon. Calcium activates tiny bubbles called vesicles, which contain chemicals called neurotransmitters. The neurotransmitters are chemicals synthesized in the somas of sending neurons that will cause changes in receiving neurons. The activated vesicles will then excrete neurotransmitters into the synaptic cleft. These chemicals will diffuse across the cleft to the postsynaptic neuron. The total process takes approximately two milliseconds.

Postsynaptically, neurotransmitters attach to places on the receiving neuron called receptors. Different receptors are specialized to pick up different kinds of neurotransmitters. Additionally, most of the many kinds of neurotransmitters will have several different types of receptors with which they can interact. Once the neurotransmitter activates the receptor, it may have an excitatory effect, making the postsynaptic cell more likely to produce an impulse, or an inhibitory effect, making the receiv-

ing neuron less likely to generate an action potential. While most neurotransmitters are predominantly excitatory or inhibitory, the ultimate effect of the neurotransmitter depends on the particular receptor. Furthermore, neurotransmitters can alter the activity of the postsynaptic neuron iontropically, by opening ion gates (a quick but brief process), or metabotropically, by initiating metabolic changes (a slow but long-lasting process). Neurotransmitters that do not bind to receptors are usually reabsorbed into the presynaptic neuron or enzymatically broken down, thereby preventing overactivity of the postsynaptic neuron.

Most neurons are on the receiving end of input from many other neurons. How often a synapse is activated (temporal summation), how many innervating synapses are activated (spatial summation), what neurotramsitters are released, and what receptors are involved all combine to determine whether a neuron will produce an action potential.

BRAIN, MIND, AND NEURON

The synaptic network that links neurons is a dynamic system that is highly responsive to the organism's experience. The more synapses are stimulated, the more efficient they become in their activity. Furthermore, repeated synaptic stimulation increases the number of synapses and induces dendritic branching. This phenomenon, called long-term potentiation, is the neuronal substrate of learning. Long-term potentiation is one reason that those who frequently engage in intellectually stimulating habits, such as reading, develop denser brains than less intellectually stimulated individuals. In other words, an active mind makes for a better brain.

SOURCES FOR FURTHER STUDY

Huguenard, John, David A. McCormick, and Gordon M. Shepherd. *Electrophysiology of the Neuron: An Interactive Tutorial/Book and Disk.* New York: Oxford University Press, 1997. This disk and manual presents seventeen interactive demonstrations of neuronal properties and interactions. Also available in Macintosh format (1999 edition).

Kalat, James W. *Biological Psychology.* 7th ed. Belmont, Calif.: Wadsworth/Thomson Learning, 2001. This best-selling book in the field of physiological psychology presents an accessible introduction to neurons and their functioning in second and third chapters.

Levitan, Irwin B., and Leonard K. Kaczmarek. *The Neuron: Cell and Molecular Biology.* New York: Oxford University Press, 2001. The biochemical and physiological attributes of neurons are investigated in this book. The authors present high-level knowledge in a readable fashion.

McKim, William A. *Drugs and Behavior: An Introduction to Behavioral Pharmacology.* Upper Saddle River, N.J.: Prentice Hall, 2000. The impact of drugs, neurophysiologically and psychologically, are explored in this excellent book.

Nicholls, John G., A. Robert Martin, Paul A. Fuchs, and Bruce G. Wallace. *From Neuron to Brain.* Sunderland, Mass.: Sinauer Associates, 2001. The authors describe various attributes of neuronal communication and functioning in a book accessible to the general reader.

Paul J. Chara, Jr.

SEE ALSO: Adrenal gland; Brain damage; Brain specialization; Brain structure; Endocrine system; Endorphins; Gonads; Hormones and behavior; Nervous system; Neuropsychology; Pituitary gland; Psychobiology; Reticular formation; Sensation and perception; Senses; Sex hormones and motivation; Split-brain studies; Synaptic transmission; Synesthesia; Thyroid gland; Visual system.

Neuropsychology

TYPE OF PSYCHOLOGY: Biological bases of behavior
FIELDS OF STUDY: Behavioral and cognitive models; cognitive processes; nervous system; organic disorders

Neuropsychology is the study of the relationship between the brain and behavior. It has provided insights into the workings of the normal brain as well as innovations for diagnosing and assisting individuals with an injury to or disease of the brain.

KEY CONCEPTS
- assessment
- cognition
- lesion
- norm
- rehabilitation

INTRODUCTION

Neuropsychology is the study of the relationships between the brain and behavior. More fully, it is the study of both human and animal cerebral organization as it relates to behavior. Considerable attention is directed toward investigating the workings of both healthy and damaged neural systems; specifically, there is interest in obtaining a more complete understanding of disorders of language, perception, and motor action. While the field of neuropsychology can be divided into a number of specialty areas, a discussion of experimental neuropsychology and clinical neuropsychology may be the most productive. While this distinction is not absolute, it serves to classify the types of work in which neuropsychologists are involved.

BRAIN LESIONS

Clinical neuropsychology refers to the study of individuals who have lesions of the brain. These lesions are often produced by tumors, cerebral vascular accidents (strokes), or trauma (for example, an automobile accident). The clinical neuropsychologist is heavily involved in the assessment of cognitive deficits brought on by these brain lesions. By evaluating the patient's performance on a variety of paper-and-pencil tests, the neuropsychologist can make valuable diagnostic inferences. The clinician can begin to develop hypotheses concerning the location, extent, and severity of the lesion.

Similarly, an attempt is made to discern the functional significance of the brain lesion on the patient. Damage to the same part of the brain may affect two individuals very differently. Because of this fact, it is vital that the clinical neuropsychologist assess the effect of the lesion on the patient's daily functioning at work, at home, and in social contexts as well as the relatively artificial environment of the testing room. Furthermore, it is important that evaluation consider the patient's current strengths in addition to weaknesses or impairments. Intact abilities can assist the patient in coping and compensating for the loss of some other function.

BRAIN BATTERIES

A comprehensive neuropsychological test battery should assess the integrity of the entire brain. To assure the thoroughness of the evaluation, the neuropsychologist generally administers a large number of diverse tests to the patient. The tests typically demand different mental or cognitive abilities, which are subserved by different regions of the brain. These different cognitive abilities are commonly referred to as cognitive domains and include functions such as attention, memory, perception, movement, language, and problem solving. A number of comprehensive test batteries have been created to assess the various cognitive domains. The Halstead-Reitan and Luria-Nebraska are two such batteries that have been used to diagnose the location and severity of brain damage in neurological patients.

These batteries consist of a variety of subtests that are believed to tap into different cognitive abilities. For example, the Halstead-Reitan contains subtests that have proved to be helpful in localizing brain damage. This is done by first administering the Halstead-Reitan to a large number of patients with previously diagnosed brain damage. The researcher then looks at those patients with damage to a particular region of the brain (for example, right frontal) and observes which subtests gave them difficulty. By repeating this process on each patient group (left frontal, right posterior, and so on), the researcher can establish norms.

When a patient with suspected damage is tested with the battery, his or her scores can be compared to those in each patient group. Thus, if he or she performs similarly to the right-frontal norms, damage may be diagnosed to this region. While this is an oversimplification, it provides a general model of how test batteries are used in neuropsychology to evaluate patients with suspected brain damage.

EXPERIMENTAL NEUROPSYCHOLOGY
Experimental neuropsychology focuses on answering theoretical questions rather than solving clinical or practical ones. Because of the invasive nature of these questions, experimental neuropsychologists often use animals rather than humans in their research. Typically, animals are used in the initial stages of a line of research. After the research procedure has been proved to be safe and effective, however, it is then confirmed on a human sample. Experimental neuropsychologists have shed light on a number of cognitive functions and the parts of the brain involved in those functions.

The methods that experimental neuropsychologists use to study cognitive abilities in humans can be quite creative. The tachistoscope is a device that projects a visual image to either the right or the left

half of the visual field very quickly, so that the right or left hemisphere of the brain has preferential access to the visual image. Thus, the importance of the left or right hemisphere of the brain in a given task can be identified.

While the daily routines of clinical and experimental neuropsychologists are quite different, their work can be considerably intertwined. For example, the insights of experimental neuropsychologists often improve clinicians' ability to assess and treat individuals with neurological impairment. Similarly, clinicians' descriptions of interesting patients can often open the road for further theoretical investigation by experimental neuropsychologists.

PRACTICE AND THEORY
The fields of clinical and experimental neuropsychology have been useful in solving a number of practical problems as well as more theoretical ones. For example, clinical neuropsychological procedures have been applied in the assessment and treatment of individuals suspected of having Alzheimer's disease. This disease is difficult to confirm unless a sample of brain is removed and inspected microscopically, a procedure that is quite invasive and is rarely attempted until after the patient's death. Neuropsychological test procedures have contributed dramatically to the accurate diagnosis of Alzheimer's disease without the use of invasive measures such as surgery.

Typically, a series of memory, language, perceptual, and problem-solving tasks are given to the individual when the disease is first suspected. The patient is then tested serially at six-month intervals, and the overall pattern of test scores across time is evaluated. If the patient tends to display a decremental pattern of performance across two or more cognitive domains (for example, memory and language), a diagnosis of dementia is supported.

Along with the measurement of various cognitive functions, neuropsychology also seems particularly equipped to investigate other aspects of the disease. While a patient's performance on a test battery is helpful, other features must be examined in diagnosing the disorder. For example, depression, hallucinations, delusions, and verbal or physical outbursts are often common with the disease. Conversely, the appearance of certain other signs or symptoms make a diagnosis of Alzheimer's disease unlikely. Because of this diverse collection of psychological and behavioral symptoms, clinical neuropsychology may be the best manager of services for these patients.

A second application of neuropsychological techniques concerns the recent surge in rehabilitation efforts with the brain-injured. Many individuals who have sustained an injury to or have a disease of the brain have great difficulty returning to their premorbid jobs or avocations. Neuropsychological rehabilitation attempts to assist these patients with ongoing cognitive difficulties as they reenter the work and home setting. Very often, people who have brain injuries do not have problems with all cognitive domains, but rather with a select few (for example, attention or language). Because of this selective impairment, clinical neuropsychologists can focus their efforts on improving an individual's attentional abilities or use of language.

A specific example of neuropsychological rehabilitation can be seen in the case of an individual who has been involved in a motor vehicle accident. These patients tend to sustain primary damage to the frontal aspects of the brain because they withstand the initial impact. Damage to the frontal regions normally produces individuals who are very unaware of their surroundings. Furthermore, they typically lack appropriate social skills as well as planning and organizational abilities. These abilities can be improved, however, if the patient works with a neuropsychologist who knows what to expect from each patient based on the exact area of damage.

Generally, rehabilitation involves intensive exposure to the problematic cognitive task. In the case of a patient with damage to the frontal area of the brain, this might entail placement in a group situation in which the patient practices social skills. Specific activities might include working on conversation skills, role-playing a job interview or asking for a date, or working on a group project. Individual sessions with the patient might be better suited for the treatment of the organizational and planning deficits experienced by frontal patients. Here, the neuropsychologist might teach the patient to use a diary to plan the week's activities and learn to solve problems to get things done.

While neuropsychologists often assist patients in acquiring compensation strategies to work around their particular difficulties, there are other rationales for rehabilitative efforts. Many researchers and psychologists believe that practicing the impaired function assists the repairing brain in doing

that task. There appears to be a six- to twelve-month period immediately after a brain injury when the brain is developing pathways around the damaged tissue. Many believe that during this critical period, it is important to engage the patient in activities that were most compromised by the injury. Thus, if the injury took a major toll on memory abilities, the patient should be exposed to exercises and activities that demand he or she remember things.

In general, neuropsychology has tremendous applied value for persons who have sustained a neurological insult such as a stroke or brain injury. Furthermore, it is useful in the initial assessment and accurate diagnosis of a given neurological disorder, as well as in the continued care and treatment of individuals with known brain pathology.

Brain Study

Neuropsychology rapidly emerged as a separate branch of the neurosciences in the 1970's and 1980's. During that time, there was an explosion of training programs for neuropsychologists and scientific research concerning the relationships between the brain and behavior. While the field has only recently evolved, however, the discipline's underpinnings can be traced back thousands of years. Egyptian writings dating to 2500 B.C.E. describe trauma to the brain and the behavior of the patient sustaining this damage.

A second early milestone occurred with the anatomical studies and illustrations of the 1800's. In 1861, Paul Broca demonstrated that a lesion of the left frontal lobe of the brain caused a disruption of the production of speech. Soon after this revelation, researchers became quite consumed with localizing all cognitive functions to some discrete part of the brain.

Those who believed that each function could be neatly contained in a small region of the brain came to be known as localizationists. Those who believed that all areas of the brain were equally involved in all cognitive abilities were labeled equipotentialists. A third group known as interactionists suggests that more basic cognitive functions are relatively localized but interact to allow for more complex cognitive processes. This perspective was derived from the late nineteenth century research of Hughlings Jackson in his clinical work as a neurologist. In many ways, Jackson's ideas were quite advanced for his time and the available research methodology.

The twentieth century witnessed a steady accumulation of knowledge concerning the relationships between the brain and behavior. These developments occurred primarily because of the need to assist soldiers who had sustained wartime brain injuries. In the process of treating these individuals, much was learned about the role of various brain regions in carrying out various behaviors. The systematic study of brain-injured persons by Aleksandr Luria contributed tremendously to the process of assessing and localizing brain dysfunction.

This new awareness provided psychology with a better understanding of how the physical brain can produce very atypical behaviors. Before this time, it was believed that behavioral disturbance was universally caused by disruption of the nonphysical "mind." The new knowledge has given clinical psychologists much more sophisticated answers about how best to treat patients with behavioral difficulties. It has also served to remove some of the stigma attached to mental illness or dysfunction. The lay public seems more willing to tolerate atypical behavior from an individual with physical damage to the brain than from a patient labeled as being mentally ill.

The future of neuropsychology appears to be full of promise. It is expected that investigators will continue to conduct research that sheds light on the workings of the healthy brain as well as assisting those with neurological damage. Furthermore, it appears that neuropsychology will continue to advance the larger field of psychology by providing physiological explanations for behaviors and disorders that now have only hypothetical ones.

SOURCES FOR FURTHER STUDY

Beaumont, J. Graham. *Introduction to Neuropsychology.* New York: Guilford Press, 1983. A very accessible reference for the student who is new to the field. Particularly helpful in describing the methods used to investigate experimental neuropsychological phenomena.

Ellis, Andrew W., and Andrew W. Young. *Human Cognitive Neuropsychology.* Rev. ed. Hillsdale, N.J.: Lawrence Erlbaum, 1996. Presents ideas and research from the mid-1980's on the integrated workings of the brain. Particularly helpful in establishing a theoretical framework that assists the student in integrating the often divergent research findings in a more holistic manner.

Kolb, Bryan, and Ian Q. Whishaw. *Fundamentals of Human Neuropsychology.* 4th ed. New York: W. H. Freeman, 1995. A very comprehensive textbook that fully covers the fields of clinical and experimental neuropsychology. Lengthy, but clear and well written. Best suited to the student who has previously read an introductory work in the field (for example, Beaumont).

Ledoux, Joseph. *Synaptic Self: How Our Brains Become Who We Are.* New York: Viking Press, 2002. Written for a lay audience, explains the neuroscience of personality and the brain. Focuses on the working of the synapses in the brain's communication system.

Luria, Aleksandr Romanovich. *The Working Brain: An Introduction to Neuropsychology.* New York: Basic Books, 1973. Considered by many to be the seminal work in the field. Presents many of Luria's most dramatic insights about normal and damaged brains. Although the title suggests this is an introduction, the ideas presented in this source are often highly complex.

Sacks, Oliver. *The Man Who Mistook His Wife for a Hat.* New York: Summit Books, 1985. Sacks is a gifted writer as well as successful neurologist, and he displays the best of both these talents in this work. Reads more like a novel than a textbook. Based on actual neurological cases seen by Sacks.

Jeffery B. Allen

SEE ALSO: Alzheimer's disease; Brain damage; Brain specialization; Brain structure; Cognitive psychology; Computer models of cognition; Dementia; Nervous system; Neurons; Parkinson's disease; Psychosurgery; Split-brain studies.

Neurotic disorders

TYPE OF PSYCHOLOGY: Consciousness; personality; psychopathology; psychotherapy

FIELDS OF STUDY: Psychodynamic and neoanalytic models; psychodynamic therapies

Neurotic disorders are defined by the form and type of symptoms that become manifest. The various neurotic disorders include anxiety neurosis, depressive neurosis, obsessive-compulsive neurosis, phobic neurosis, and hysterical neurosis. These disorders are the

result of unconscious mental conflict and are shaped by early experience, coupled with innate temperament.

KEY CONCEPTS
- anxiety
- depression
- emotional conflict
- hysteria
- mental conflict
- obsessive compulsiveness
- Oedipus complex
- phobia
- psychoanalytic psychotherapy
- transference

INTRODUCTION

"Neurosis" is a general term used to describe various forms of mental disorders that involve symptoms of anxiety, depression, hysteria, phobia, and obsessive compulsiveness. The Scottish physician and researcher William Cullen (1710-1790) first used the term during the eighteenth century. At that time, a whole range of symptoms and diseases were referred to as neurotic and were thought to be organically based, with specific, localized points (for example, digestive neurosis). The Austrian psychiatrist Sigmund Freud (1856-1939) coined the term "psychoneurosis" to denote and describe his discovery that neurotic disorders do not have localized organic origins but are psychological in nature and caused by early emotional trauma, the results of which are psychological and emotional conflict. Based on his research into neurotic disorders with colleague and physician Josef Breuer (1842-1925), Freud created the theory and mental health discipline of psychoanalysis. The psychoanalytic understanding of mental disorders is based on the observation that early life experience, in combination with an individual's biological givens, affects later emotional development and that many of the sources of one's psychological symptoms (for example, unhappiness and anxiety) stem from early experiences with parents and other caregivers. These early interpersonal experiences, coupled with one's early temperament, have emotional consequences that are largely unconscious in nature.

The symptomatology associated with various neurotic disorders, then, stems from emotional conflicts originating in early life. Although the sources of these conflicts are unconscious, the consequences of this unrecognized emotional turmoil lead to various psychological symptoms.

EARLY CONCEPTION OF NEUROTIC DISORDERS

During the end of the nineteenth century and the early part of the twentieth century, Freud described the two broad types of neuroses, transference neuroses and narcissistic neuroses. He thought that patients with psychotic symptoms or severe depression were incapable of forming a relationship with their treating psychoanalyst; they were narcissistic, autistic-like, and consequently unable to be held by psychotherapeutic means. He believed that patients with hysterical, phobic, or obsessive-compulsive symptoms, however, were capable of developing an emotional tie to the analyst. He referred to the special nature of the patient-doctor relationship as transference and referred to patients with hysterical, phobic, or obsessive-compulsive symptoms as suffering from transference neuroses. These patients were amenable to "the talking cure."

Freud first began to formulate his theory of psychoneurosis, his discovery that symptoms had psychological meaning, after studying in France with the famous French neurologist Jean-Martin Charcot (1825-1893), who demonstrated that patients' symptoms under hypnosis could be displaced and/or eliminated. For example, a woman with an arm paralysis could be hypnotized and the paralysis transferred from one arm to another. This observation, coupled with his experience of treating sexually repressed upper-middle-class Viennese patients in the late nineteenth and early twentieth centuries in Vienna led Freud to the conclusion that neurotic symptoms stem from early sexual wishes and desires that were unacceptable and therefore rendered unconscious. Psychological defense mechanisms such as repression are used to eliminate unacceptable thoughts or feelings or painful inner emotional conflicts.

Freud believed that, around the age of three or four, the child wanted to possess the parent of the opposite sex and get rid of the same-sex parent (the Oedipus complex in boys, the Electra complex in girls). Because of basic physical limitations and fear of retaliation, these desires had to be repressed. Unresolved sexual conflict and less-than-successful repression of these wishes and desires led to the various forms of neurotic symptoms. These symptoms represented repressed sexual conflict that was striving for release and gratification ("the return of the repressed"). The particular symptom both symbolized and disguised the nature of the conflict. The specific fixation point at which the individual's sexual development was arrested dictated the "choice" of a particular neurotic disorder or symptom. Heightened sexual pleasure was localized at three bodily areas, corresponding to three different stages of development. The three stages of childhood sexuality were labeled oral, anal, and phallic, with the Oedipus complex culminating at the phallic stage of development. Healthy negotiation of these stages and the Oedipus complex dictated normal heterosexual relationships. Fixation or arrest during these stages of development culminated with problems in intimate heterosexual relationships as an adult, as well as in the development of neurotic symptomatology.

The symptoms associated with hysterical neurosis have been recognized since antiquity. They include unstable and tense emotional experience, hypochondrias, overreaction to external demands, sexual conflict coupled with heightened flirtatiousness toward the opposite sex, and lack of psychological insight. Hysterical neurosis may lead to a conversion of anxiety into physical symptoms.

Freud also discovered that the hysteric's predominant mode of defense against conflict and distress is repression. With repression, an individual is unable consciously to remember or experience disturbing feelings, thoughts, or wishes. In hysterical neurosis, unacceptable thoughts and feelings have been eliminated from consciousness via this mechanism of defense. The presence, however, of a neurotic symptom reflects the fact that repression was incomplete. Unacceptable anger at a loved one, for example, will be repressed from consciousness, but one may be left with the symptom of paralysis of the arm. A psychological conflict is converted into a physical symptom.

The obsessive neurotic is seen as utilizing his or her intellect excessively, so as to avoid emotional conflicts or experience. These individuals, therefore, will excessively ruminate, be hyperrational, and avoid their emotions completely. They use the defense mechanism of intellectualization and also of reaction formation, whereby one behaves the opposite of what one truly but unacceptably feels. The obsessive neurotic, therefore, may be overly kind

and rational toward someone at whom she or he is enraged but also loves.

Freud also wrote about phobia as a neurosis whereby an individual utilizes the defense mechanism of displacement, transferring a danger that is internal (castration anxiety, for example) onto an external danger that symbolizes the inner anxiety. Castration anxiety due to Oedipal conflict may lead to a displacement of that fear onto an external danger, with the phobic child, for example, manifesting a seemingly irrational fear of being bitten by a horse.

CONTEMPORARY UNDERSTANDING

Modern psychoanalytic understanding of neurotic disorders is broader than the early Freudian classifications of hysteria, obsessive-compulsiveness, and phobia, with less emphasis on sexual conflict as the sole causative feature. Conflicts involving a range of early emotions and impulses are seen as implicated in the development of neurotic disorders. Modern psychoanalysts utilize scientific approaches to enhance theory and practice. The University of Michigan research psychoanalyst Howard Shevrin, for example, has provided empirical brain-based evidence for the presence of unconscious psychological conflict and has enhanced the understanding of the role of unconscious conflict in the formation of psychological symptoms.

Sexuality and aggression continue to be seen as essential driving forces that shape development and are central factors in the construction of neurotic symptoms. Additionally, the modern psychoanalyst considers factors associated with later points of development, when examining neurotic symptomatology.

The developing child is seen as possessing immature intellectual, emotional, and imaginative capacities. He or she is faced with managing inner fears, as well as negotiating relationships with primary caretakers. Frustration and conflict inevitably emerge, and patterns of emotional experience, fantasy, and behavior develop in response to these early experiences. Modern psychoanalysis emphasizes the position that character, behavior, and the imagination of the child all reflect, in part, solutions to the inevitable conflicts experienced by the child as a result of his or her wishes, urges, and fantasies that are unacceptable to caretakers and also ambivalently felt by the child (hateful feeling toward one's mother, for example). Emotional conflict, guilt, and self-condemnation inevitably result to some degree or other and necessitate the mobilization of various psychological defense mechanisms, including repression. Fears, wishes, and thoughts that are unacceptable and censored take on a dangerous, forbidding dimension. These unresolved, repressed thoughts and feelings lead to the creation of unconscious fantasies that are in conflict with the more conscious self and may cause seemingly senseless or unreasonable emotional turmoil. For example, a young boy who is frightened, ashamed, and guilt-ridden by his hateful impulses toward his father will repress these urges. As an adult, he may inexplicably feel like a "monster" (an unconscious fantasy of himself when angry) whenever he naturally asserts himself, without consciously understanding why self-expression is so difficult.

Modern psychoanalysis differentiates a range of neurotic disorders within two broad classifications, symptom neurosis and character neurosis. The symptom neuroses are specific and tied to specific symptoms. Hysterical neurosis, obsessive neurosis, depressive neurosis, and anxiety neurosis all reflect underlying emotional conflicts but are manifested through different symptoms. For example, the hysteric converts emotional turmoil into somatic complaints. The obsessive is emotionally cut off from self and others and is ritualistic, while the depressive is sad, with chronic self-esteem problems. The anxiety neurotic ruminates and may have a specific irrational fear (phobia).

With symptom neurosis, the neurotic is distressed and the symptoms are ego-dystonic; that is, the symptoms are felt to be alien, unwanted, and foreign to the self. With character neurosis, however, symptoms are not present and the character neurosis is reflected by maladaptive and enduring personality patterns of behavior and experience that, although neurotic, are accepted features of the individual's self or identity (ego-syntonic). Others may perceive an obsessive neurotic personality, for example, as unemotional and excessively avoidant of feelings, but he will see himself as objective and fastidious. The hysterical neurotic personality will view herself as spontaneous and not excessively emotional, whereas the depressive neurotic personality may realize he is always depressed, but believe that it is for good reasons. Because the neurotic pattern of behavior is ego-syntonic, neurotic personalities are more difficult to treat.

Psychoanalytic Treatment

Psychoanalytic psychotherapy seeks not only to relieve current symptoms but also to deal with root emotional conflicts and causes of the symptoms or behavioral patterns. Because the sources of one's conflicts, symptoms, and behavior patterns are essentially unconscious, and because defenses have been constructed to help one adapt as effectively as possible, psychoanalytic treatment takes time, is intensive, and lasts from one to three or more years. The therapeutic relationship that develops is intimate and intense. The psychoanalyst and patient collaborate in the exploration of the patient's symptoms and style of relating. This leads to the patient becoming aware of his or her underlying sources of conflict, not only intellectually but also emotionally. The emotional understanding occurs predominantly through the understanding of feelings, thoughts, and fantasies that arise out of the realistic and unrealistic (transference) dimensions of the therapeutic relationship. It is through the relationship that the patient can reexperience, in the here-and-now, how his or her inner conflicts and unconscious difficulties have been creating symptoms and dysfunctional repetitive patterns of behavior. The analyst and patient work together to understand how and why certain wishes and desires, feelings, thoughts, and unconscious fantasies have developed and contribute to the patient's emotional and behavioral difficulties. Over the course of treatment, the patient's capacity for emotional integration improves, as does his or her capacity to function without self-defeating behaviors, emotions, and thoughts.

Sources for Further Study

Kligman, D. *The Development of Freud's Theories: A Guide for Students of Psychoanalysis.* Madison, Conn.: International Universities Press, 2001. The author organizes Sigmund Freud's theoretical contributions into six major thematic areas. In addition, this guide helps the reader understand the development of psychoanalytic ideas from Freud's early notions through contemporary psychoanalytic conceptualization.

Mitchell, L. S., and M. Black. *Freud and Beyond: A History of Modern Psychoanalysis.* New York: Basic Books, 1995. Psychoanalysts Steven Mitchell and his wife, Margaret Black, outline the history of psychoanalysis and provide the reader with an explanation on the evolution of psychoanalytic concepts and important classical and contemporary theorists. The book is well written and an excellent introduction to psychoanalytic theory and practice.

Moore, B., and E. Fine. *Psychoanalytic Terms and Concepts.* New Haven, Conn.: Yale University Press, 1990. This glossary of psychoanalytic terms and concepts provides both the scholar and the layperson with basic definitions of the language of psychoanalysis.

Neressian, E., and R. Copff, eds. *Textbook on Psychoanalysis.* Washington, D.C.: American Psychiatric Press, 1996. A sophisticated introduction into the discipline of psychoanalysis, this volume provides a detailed explanation into psychoanalytic theory and how psychoanalysts conceptualize diagnosis and treatment.

Sandler, J., A. Holder, C. Dare, and A. Dreher. *Freud's Model of the Mind: An Introduction.* Madison, Conn.: International Universities Press, 1997. The authors provide a clear explication of the historical basis of classical Freudian theory as well as a clear description of the post-Freudian formulations of how the mind functions.

Westen, D. "The Scientific Legacy of Sigmund Freud: Towards a Psychodynamically Informed Psychological Science." *Psychological Bulletin* 124, no. 3 (1998): 331-371. In this article, published in one of the American Psychological Association's most prestigious journals, the author considers Freud's legacy by considering the relevance of contemporary psychoanalytic theory and practice to modern twenty-first century psychological science.

Richard Lettieri

SEE ALSO: Ego defense mechanisms; Freud, Sigmund; Hysteria; Oedipus complex; Phobias; Psychoanalytic psychology: Sigmund Freud; Women's psychology: Sigmund Freud.

Nonverbal communication

TYPE OF PSYCHOLOGY: Language
FIELDS OF STUDY: Interpersonal relations; social perception and cognition

Nonverbal communication describes all the wordless messages that people exchange, either intentionally or unintentionally. It plays an important role in the way that people interact and is the primary means for communicating emotion, forming impressions, and communicating about relationships.

KEY CONCEPTS
- chronemics
- haptics
- kinesics
- leakage
- olfaction
- paralanguage
- proxemics
- violation of expectations

INTRODUCTION

Most researchers accept Ray Birdwhistell's approximation that nonverbal communication accounts for at least 60 to 70 percent of what humans communicate to one another, although psychologist Albert Mehrabian estimates that as much as 93 percent of the emotional meaning of messages is transmitted nonverbally. Studies have shown that nonverbal messages are generally more believable than verbal ones; when verbal and nonverbal messages contradict, most people believe the nonverbal. Nonverbal communication is at least as important as verbal communication; however, the formal study of nonverbal communication is still in its infancy when compared to verbal communication.

Charles Darwin's *The Expression of the Emotions in Man and Animals* (1872) was one of the first studies to associate nonverbal behaviors of humankind with other species and to emphasize its function of indicating mood, attitude, and feeling. His research initiated the modern study of nonverbal communications, an interdisciplinary field that calls upon scholars from linguistics, anthropology, sociology, physical education, physiology, communication, and psychology. The early works on nonverbal communication tended to be speculative, anecdotal, and tentative, but by 1960, major works began emerging that organized and synthesized the existing data from these diverse fields. Theoretical issues became clarified, and many methodological problems were solved.

IMPLICIT COMMUNICATION CODES

One of the most influential researchers in the nonverbal communication area has been Mehrabian, who calls this "implicit communication" because it is usually done subtly; people are generally not aware of sending or receiving nonverbal messages. Mehrabian found that nonverbal communication is used to communicate attitudes, emotions, and preferences, especially the following four: pleasure/displeasure; arousal/nonarousal; dominance/submissiveness; and liking/nonliking.

Each of these emotions is associated with a cluster of nonverbal actions that is communicated in one of seven different codes. Codes are organized message systems consisting of a set of symbols and the rules for their use. The eight nonverbal codes are physical appearance (especially height and body type); kinesics (the study of body movements, gestures, posture, and facial expressions); proxemics (the use of space as a special elaboration of culture); haptics (the study of touch and touching); chronemics (the study of how people use and structure time); olfactics; paralanguage (tone, pitch, accents, emphases, yawns, voice qualities, rate of speaking, and pauses) and silence; and artifacts (objects, such as clothing, jewelry, furniture, and cars, that are associated with people).

FUNCTIONS

Joseph DeVito and Michael Hecht state that nonverbal messages perform seven important functions. First, they provide information; this can occur deliberately or through leakage, as when a person reveals that he or she is lying by talking overly fast and in short sentences. Second, they regulate interaction, by telling people when to begin a conversation, whose turn it is to speak, and when the conversation is over. Kinesics, especially eye contact, is the main code used for this function. Third, nonverbal communication is the primary means of expressing emotions. Researchers have identified the nonverbal cues used in expressing the basic emotions of happiness, surprise, fear, anger, sadness, disgust, contempt, and interest. Paul Ekman and Wallace Friesen found that the expression and interpretation of emotions is universal; therefore, the nonverbal expression of emotion is probably biologically determined.

The fourth function of nonverbal communication is in exercising social control. Nonverbal messages of power and dominance can be used to control people and events. Fifth, nonverbal communication helps to accomplish specific tasks or goals (such as

Body language can reveal much information about a person's mood and attitude. (CLEO Photography)

hitchhiking using the familiar hand gesture). Sixth, nonverbal messages are very important in telling the listener how to interpret a message; for example, sarcasm is signaled through paralanguage, and kinesics help to communicate empathy, as when the speaker leans forward and touches the listener while giving bad news. Finally, nonverbal messages present a person's self-image. Physical appearance is usually the major code used in forming first impressions; artifacts such as clothing, office furniture, hairstyle, and glasses can be used to create a variety of self-images. Paralanguage, such as a squeaky voice or a certain accent, may also help to create a particular image of a person.

CHARACTERISTICS

Just as verbal messages are often misunderstood, so are nonverbal messages. Three characteristics of nonverbal communication are important in understanding the potential for confusion that may exist in both sending and interpreting nonverbal messages. First, nonverbal communication is different from nonverbal behavior. Nonverbal communication consists of messages that are symbolic, that stand for something other than themselves. Nonverbal behavior does not stand for anything else. For example, if a listener avoids eye contact with a speaker because of an emotional response to the message or to the person, or if the speaker interprets the action that way, the action is nonverbal communication. If the listener avoids eye contact because the sun is in her eyes, and the speaker does not interpret it as meaningful, then the action is nonverbal behavior.

Second, nonverbal communication is rule-guided activity. These rules are arbitrary and unwritten; they are learned by observing others. Breaking these rules can provoke unpleasant emotional reactions; for example, staring at someone in an elevator can result in hostility. Because the nonverbal rules are arbitrary and may change from situation to situation (such as at home versus on the job), it is important to be a careful observer and learn the rules before acting.

The third characteristic is that nonverbal communication is strongly influenced by culture. Although all cultures interpret some nonverbal behaviors (such as smiling) in the same way, they also differ from one another in interpreting other nonverbal messages, such as proxemics. Many cultures, for example, allow a closer standing distance than does the culture of the United States, and this difference can often result in misunderstandings. Hand gestures which are innocent in one culture may be highly offensive in another.

INTERPERSONAL RELATIONSHIPS

Nonverbal communication has been used to examine almost every aspect of human behavior. Two of the most widely researched areas are interpersonal relationships and nonverbal communication in the workplace.

Nonverbal communication plays an important role in initiating, maintaining, and terminating relationships. One study identified fifteen cues that express a woman's interest in dating; almost all of these were nonverbal cues, including high amounts of eye contact, smiling, forward lean, shoulder orientation, close (about 45 centimeters, or 18 inches) proximity, and frequent touching. The men and women participants all agreed that a woman who displays these cues to a man is probably interested

in dating him. More than two-thirds of the males surveyed said they prefer women to use these nonverbal messages to convey their interest in dating; less than one-third said they preferred a verbal approach. A similar study observed flirting behavior in a singles bar and catalogued fifty-two different nonverbal acts; the most frequently occurring were eye gaze, forward lean, smiles, and touch.

Nonverbal cues are also used to develop and maintain relationships. On dates, sexual intimacy is regulated by nonverbal cues, and increasing intimacy is marked through intimate physical contact. Desmond Morris, in his book *Intimate Behaviour* (1971), suggested twelve stages of contact in animal courtship that he believes apply generally to human beings: eye to body, eye to eye, voice to voice, hand to hand, arm to shoulder, arm to waist, mouth to mouth, hand to head, hand to body, mouth to breast, hand to genitals, and genitals to genitals. Finally, nonverbal cues are involved in relationship termination. There are many nonverbal signs that a relationship is ending, including chronemics (less time spent together), less touching and mutual eye contact, and fewer smiles.

UNDERSTANDING POWER IN THE WORKPLACE

Nonverbal communication on the job can determine who is hired, promoted, and fired. Power plays an important role in business organizations, and, as Mehrabian demonstrated, nonverbal communication is the implicit communication system through which power is manifested. The nonverbal codes that are most often used in communicating power are physical appearance, artifacts, kinesics, proxemics, haptics, and chronemics.

A person's height and physical size is an important component of power and status. Research shows that taller men get better jobs, are paid larger salaries, and are perceived as having more status; overweight people have more problems getting hired and being accepted to colleges. Attractive people are more persuasive than unattractive people and are more likely to receive assistance and encouragement. Body shape is associated with a wide range of personality characteristics: For example, mesomorphs (bony, muscular, athletic) are identified as being dominant, confident, and adventurous; ectomorphs (tall, thin, fragile) with being shy, tense, and awkward; and endomorphs (soft, round, fat) with being dependent, sluggish, and sympathetic.

People make these judgments unconsciously, and the impressions are usually difficult to overcome.

Artifacts function as symbols of power in four ways: First, they are symbols of the power structure within the organization; second, individuals who have access to them may rise to more powerful positions in the formal power structure; third, certain artifacts may be the actual rewards that maintain the organization through material reinforcement; and finally, artifacts of power may produce self-expectancies that actually cause the individual to act in a more powerful manner. Some examples of artifacts that symbolize power are large corner offices, reserved parking places, and expensive company cars and office furnishings. Clothing is an artifact that helps others determine a person's status, credibility, and persuasiveness; for example, in one study, job interviewers rated applicants who dressed in darker colors as more competent than applicants with the same qualifications who dressed in light colors. Kinesic postures and positions correspond to organizational positions in that superiors tend to be more kinesically expansive than subordinates. One kinesic sign of power is upright posture; another is a comfortable, relaxed seated position with the legs crossed, arms asymmetrically placed, and body leaning sideways and reclining slightly.

Numerous dominance and submission messages are sent via facial expressions because they convey emotional states and evaluations better than any other part of the body; the human face is capable of more than 250,000 different expressions. Among both primates and humans, smiling is a submissive gesture often displayed to appease a dominant aggressor. Eye gaze is another indicator of power; many researchers have found that higher-status persons look more when speaking and look less when listening than do lower-status persons. Apparently the high-status individual has both the ability and the prerogative to maintain visual attentiveness while speaking but is not obligated to reciprocate eye contact when listening. These gaze patterns during interactions may severely undercut or augment an individual's power.

In proxemics, as Nancy Henley points out in *Body Politics: Power, Sex, and Nonverbal Communication* (1979), dominant animals and dominant humans follow the same pattern: They control greater territory; they are free to move in territory belonging to others; subordinates yield space to them when ap-

proached, or in passing; they are accorded greater personal space; and they take up more space with their bodies and possessions. Haptic behavior is the most intimate form of nonverbal communication. Power and control are communicated through the initiation of touch. Empirically, touchers have been found to be significantly more dominant than recipients of touch, higher-status persons more frequently will touch lower-status persons, and direct poking with an index finger is a dominant act.

ROLE IN HUMAN DEVELOPMENT

Nonverbal communication was of interest primarily to elocutionists until 1872, when Charles Darwin published his findings. Darwin aroused interest in nonverbal communication among researchers in many different fields, especially psychology. Nonverbal communication is of particular interest to the field of psychology for two reasons: its role in the development of human personality and its usefulness in treating patients with psychological disturbances.

Nonverbal communication, especially touch, plays an essential role in human development. Of the available forms of communication, haptics is the first form developed in infants. Babies explore their own bodies and their environment through touch. Psychologically, the infant, through self-exploration, begins the process of achieving self-identity, environmental identity, security, and well-being. The development of healthy individuals seems related to the amount of touch they receive as infants; for example, tactile deprivation has been associated with learning problems and lack of trust and confidence.

RELATIONSHIP WITH DISORDERS

Clinical psychologists have become increasingly interested in the relationship between psychological disorders and nonverbal behavior, and they have relied on a knowledge of the behavioral symptoms of maladjustment in diagnosing and treating psychological problems. Sigmund Freud believed that a patient's physical actions were at least as important as verbal actions in communicating the sources of psychological trauma.

Wilhelm Reich used relaxation exercises with his obsessive-compulsive patients; his belief was that actions and feelings are connected, and if feelings cannot be changed through discussions and insight, maybe they can be modified by simply changing a person's postures, gestures, and facial and vocal expressions. More recently, Reich's premise has been elaborated extensively by action-oriented therapies such as dance or body-awareness therapy. In some cases, the therapist tells the client to express different emotions through movement. By observing these movements, the therapist is able to find out which emotions the client typically and easily conveys and which he or she has trouble expressing. The latter are symptomatic of a more general difficulty, and the client is encouraged to express these particular feelings in movements. The improved ability to express such feelings in action can then provide the stimulus for a more explicit discussion of feelings.

OLFACTORY RESEARCH

In the 1990's, psychologists and other nonverbal researchers became interested in the role of olfaction (the study of how people use and perceive odors) and olfactory memory in affecting mood and behavior and in improving the learning process. They found that strong fragrances such as musk can cause mood changes. Synthetic aroma chemicals which are often used seem to be the culprit, but researchers have not yet discovered why smelling these chemicals would cause a person's mood to change. Researchers also discovered that olfaction affects behavior; for example, workers exposed to stimulating scents such as peppermint set higher goals and are more alert and productive than workers who were not exposed to the scents.

Finally, olfactory memory seems to play a role in learning. In one study, fragrance was sprayed in the classroom while the professor was lecturing. When students were tested, the same fragrance was sprayed. Students in the experimental group scored much higher and seemed to retain more of the knowledge than did students in the control group, who had not smelled the fragrance. The area of olfaction appears to be a promising one for nonverbal communication researchers.

SOURCES FOR FURTHER STUDY

Guerrero, Laura, Joseph A. DeVito, and Michael L. Hecht, eds. *The Nonverbal Communication Reader.* 2d ed. Prospect Heights, Ill.: Waveland Press, 1999. Presents a readable and interesting discussion of nonverbal communication, including several areas that are not generally studied, such as olfactics (smell) and artifactual communication, such as clothing, cars, and jewelry. Applications to interpersonal relationships are discussed extensively. A very useful publication.

Harper, Robert Gale, Arthur N. Wiens, and Joseph D. Matarazzo. *Nonverbal Communication: The State of the Art.* New York: John Wiley & Sons, 1978. Reviews a large number of studies on various areas of nonverbal communication. The material in this book has been organized and presented to give the reader an idea of how the findings were obtained as well as what the findings were. Very thorough and detailed.

Henley, Nancy M. *Body Politics: Power, Sex, and Nonverbal Communication.* 1979. Reprint. Englewood Cliffs, N.J.: Prentice-Hall, 1986. Focuses on the power aspect of nonverbal communication, both on the interpersonal and on the intergroup level, with particular reference to male dominance. Presents some interesting and well-researched findings.

Hickson, Mark L., Don W. Stacks, and Nina-Jo Moore. *NVC: Nonverbal Communication Studies and Applications.* 4th ed. Los Angeles: Roxbury, 2002. Emphasizes the interaction between biological functions and sociopsychological functions and discusses the influence of sociology on nonverbal communication. Provides an extensive discussion of nonverbal research, but the language is not technical and is easily understood.

Mehrabian, Albert. *Silent Messages: Implicit Communication of Emotions and Attitudes.* 2d ed. Belmont, Calif.: Wadsworth, 1981. Mehrabian discusses how nonverbal communication is used to communicate attitudes, emotions, and preferences implicitly; people are usually unaware of sending or receiving these nonverbal messages. Discusses the use of nonverbal communication in areas such as selling, persuasion, deceit, political campaigns, and advertising.

Ting-Toomey, Stella. *Communicating Across Cultures.* New York: Guilford Press, 1999. Examines differences and similarities in nonverbal communication across cultures. Offers many tables and charts to assist readers in putting theory into practice.

Karen Anding Fontenot

SEE ALSO: Attraction theories; Couples therapy; Emotional expression; Emotions; Facial feedback; Self-presentation; Strategic family therapy.

O

Obesity

TYPE OF PSYCHOLOGY: Motivation
FIELDS OF STUDY: Physical motives; substance abuse

Obesity is a condition in which body fat mass is at least 20 percent higher than the standard value. It is an important promoting factor in diseases such as coronary heart disease and diabetes; it also interferes with normal social relationships and can induce depression as a result of distorted self-image. Many people suffer from this condition, and millions of dollars are spent on its treatment.

KEY CONCEPTS
- adipose tissue
- adrenals
- basal metabolism
- corticosteroids
- endocrine
- hyperplasia
- hypertrophy
- lipids
- metabolism
- thyroid

INTRODUCTION

Obesity is a form of disordered nutrition. The word is derived from the Latin *obesus*, meaning "eaten away," which shows that long ago it was realized that overeating may cause disease and even death.

A distinction should be drawn, however, between being overweight and being obese. A person is called overweight when his or her weight in relation to his or her height is greater than the normal value recorded in statistical body frame weight tables. Being overweight, in some cases, can be the consequence of an exaggerated development of muscle and bone tissue as well as an excess amount of water. In contrast, an obese person is someone who has abnormal amounts of body fat. As a rule of thumb, in medical terms, people are considered obese when they are 20 percent above the normal weight, based on height, sex, and body frame.

Fat (adipose tissue containing lipids) is a normal, necessary part of the human body structure. It is an important form of energy storage, and it has a role as a protecting layer surrounding vulnerable organs (such as the kidneys), cushioning them against damage; in addition, when fat is broken down in the body, it is a source of water and of essential fatty acids necessary for survival. During embryonic development, the human fetus accumulates fat deposits as it grows. Whereas the fat content of the fetal body is only 0.5 percent of body weight at twenty weeks' gestation, it reaches 16 percent at birth. The baby continues to accumulate adipose tissue, which reaches a peak value of 26 percent at six months. Then there is a decrease until age eight, when again the child starts to accumulate more adipose tissue until he or she reaches puberty.

Fat is stored in adipose tissue, made up of special cells filled with lipid. During the first year of life, the number of adipose cells increases with the amount of fat available for deposition. That is known as hyperplasia. Later in life, the number of adipose cells no longer changes; rather, the size of the existing cells enlarges. This is called hypertrophy. It has been reported that the early years of life are the most crucial in determining the body weight of a person, because the adipose cells formed during this period are never lost. This suggests that avoidance of adipose tissue hyperplasia in early infancy could prevent adult obesity. It has been demonstrated that adult body weight usually correlates with the weight at five years of age. Eighty percent of overweight children will develop into obese or overweight adults.

TYPES OF OBESITY

The types and causes of obesity can be classified as hypertrophic obesity, hyperplastic obesity, obesities of endocrine origin, genetic obesities, metabolic abnormalities, drug-related obesities, special psychological obesities, obesity resulting from socioeconomic factors, and obesity resulting from nutritional factors as such. Hypertrophic obesity is also known as adult-onset obesity. It is the most common type and is caused by an imbalance between the intake of energy (food) and the expenditure of energy (physical work) in an otherwise healthy person. Usually, the individual maintains a fairly stable normal weight until middle age, when the weight slowly starts to increase. In particular, these persons go on periodic diets, losing some weight only to regain even more when they stop dieting.

Hyperplastic obesity, also known as juvenile-onset obesity, is of two types: one in which the energy imbalance is caused by an excessive intake of food and one caused by inactivity. If a child has a higher energy intake than required to counterbalance the energy output represented by his or her basal metabolism, activity level, and potential for growth, the child will not grow faster or develop more muscle but instead will deposit the excess energy as fat. This is seen especially in bottle-fed infants whose mothers feed them larger volumes or more concentrated formula than required.

The endocrine-related obesities are, as the name shows, caused by dysfunctions of the hormone-secreting glands—for example, a lack of thyroid hormone—resulting in a much-reduced basal metabolic rate, or an excessive production of adrenal corticosteroid hormones. Genetic obesities are inherited diseases in which obesity is only one of a number of abnormalities. Metabolic abnormalities refer to disturbances of the normal metabolic processes, such as circulatory deficiency or an excessive conversion of sugar into fat. A drug-related obesity is one induced as a secondary effect of a drug taken for medical or other reasons. Examples of such drugs are antidepressants, female hormones, and even monosodium glutamate.

The special psychological obesities are of three types. The night eater is a person who abstains from food during the day but overeats in the evening and late at night and usually suffers from insomnia. Binge eaters undergo random bouts of compulsive overeating; these people are prone to develop anorexia nervosa or bulimia. The depressive overeater suffers from periodic states of depression from which he or she seeks alleviation in food.

Socioeconomic factors may be economic or ethnic. They induce obesity either because highly caloric food is cheaper than less-fattening food or because the traditional food preparation of a particular ethnic group provides more calories than that of another group. For example, Italian cuisine is much higher in caloric content than Japanese cuisine.

The last category consists of obesities caused by nutritional factors per se. The obvious factor is a diet high in calories; another is faulty meal distribution. It has been demonstrated convincingly that many small meals during the day are much less fattening then a few large meals. This can be explained by human heritage. Because humans originated from primate ancestors, their digestive system is adapted to frequent, small meals. Their metabolism is not prepared to process large amounts of food in a short time. When a person eats a large dinner, most of the glucose absorbed into the bloodstream will be deposited first in the liver, then in the muscles, but the excess all goes to the adipose tissue. Therefore, six small meals a day are preferable to two or three large meals.

PHYSICAL DANGERS

Life insurance statistics demonstrate clearly a correlation between above-average body weight and higher mortality rates. The lowest rate was found in persons weighing 10 percent less than average body weight. As a corollary, weight reduction may prolong life. It has been shown that mortality was reduced to normal values in persons who succeeded in losing weight and maintaining the lower weight. There are a number of reports associating obesity with high blood pressure and weight loss with a reduction in blood pressure. Another organ adversely affected by obesity is the lungs. Pulmonary function is impaired as a result of the abnormal functioning of the respiratory muscles and also as a result of obesity itself, which may cause intermittent cessation of breathing during sleep (sleep apnea).

Another consequence of obesity is gastrointestinal diseases, including the formation of gallstones. In people whose body weight is 25 percent above average, the incidence of gastrointestinal ailments has been shown to be 150 percent higher than in the population at large. The explanation lies in the fact that cholesterol production is directly related to body weight. P. J. Nestle, P. H. Schreibman, and E. H.

Ahrens in 1977 found that for each kilogram of body weight above the average, cholesterol production increased by 22 milligrams. A well-known consequence of obesity is the development of diabetes. The incidence of diabetes is in direct correlation with the duration and the degree of the obese status. Weight reduction can, in many cases, decrease the severity of diabetes.

The fact that obesity is associated with high blood pressure, diabetes, and high blood cholesterol levels makes it an obvious causal factor in the development of the primary killer in Western societies, coronary heart disease. Given that obesity is basically an imbalance of energy intake versus output, it can be assumed that obese persons consume a diet higher in calories and also in saturated fat, cholesterol, and sugar. All these substances are considered to promote the development of atherosclerosis, the main cause of coronary heart disease. Overnutrition, in particular the overconsumption of fats, has been linked also to the development of malignant tumors. Although a number of cancers, such as uterine, ovarian, breast, and prostate as well as those of the colon, urinary bladder, and kidney, appear to be correlated with nutrition, only two, cancer of the kidney and of the uterus, have been associated with obesity in women.

These data show clearly that body-weight control—in other words, the fight against obesity—is an important problem of public health. Therefore, it is not surprising that governments put high priority on studies that could yield efficient programs of intervention to ensure that the population will be in good health, which depends on a normal body weight, healthy nutrition, and exercise. In 1962, the Midtown Manhattan study showed a correlation between socioeconomic status and obesity. It found that socioeconomic status defined by education, occupation, and income was inversely related with obesity. This association was especially pronounced in women but in a lesser degree was true also for men. To avoid a misinterpretation of the results (one possibility was that obesity could have determined the socioeconomic status, instead of the reverse), the study took into consideration the status of the parents when the subjects were eight years old. The correlation was the same as in the case of the subjects themselves. A consequence of the finding that social forces have the ability to influence body weight was the institution of organized intervention programs by government, educational institutions, and industry that aimed at behavior modification in the population at large. The treatment of obesity gave rise to a billion-dollar industry which includes low-caloric and health foods, diet pills, home exercise apparatuses, a huge literature covering diets (including some outlandish ones), "fat farms" where people can lose excess pounds for sometimes astronomical fees, and even surgical interventions such as liposuction, jejunoileal bypass, and wiring of jaws. Psychological means to modify the behavior of compulsive overeaters include, among others, individual psychotherapy, group therapy, and hypnotherapy.

GENETIC COMPONENTS

Obesity is not a new condition. As far back as the Stone Age, some humans had large amounts of fat stores, as is proved by primitive sculptures, carvings, and paintings found in caves and archaeological excavations. Even in historical times, in many cultures, obese women have been considered desirable. The reason for this may be the fact that nomadic human groups experienced periods of famine in which only those with adequate energy reserves could survive. The continuing existence of the group depended on females who could resist starvation and still breast-feed their babies. Therefore, males learned to select as mates women who, in a sedentary society, would be considered obese, perpetuating the genetic trait of a tendency toward obesity.

This genetic trait determined a particular type of metabolism that responded to food deprivation by lowering its basal metabolic rate, thus burning less fuel, allowing longer survival during starvation. When times of plenty returned, that low metabolism, paired with a large energy intake, induced obesity, which ensured a better survival during the next famine. This type of metabolism is still present in members of Western societies. Therefore, the tendency toward obesity is innate in many people.

This statement is supported by an interesting study done by Albert J. Stunkard and his collaborators in 1986, in which they examined the roles played by genetics and environment in the development of overweight children. Their subjects were adopted children, their biological parents, and their adoptive parents. Based on body-mass index (the weight in kilograms divided by the square of the height in meters), Stunkard divided the children and the parents into four classes: thin, medium, overweight, and obese. The results of the study showed that there was a strong correlation between the body-mass index of the biological parents and that of their children; in contrast, no correlation was found between the children and ther adoptive parents. That is, obese children had overweight biological parents but thin adoptive parents and vice versa.

In modern Western societies, slim bodies have become the preference; one reason for this is the realization that being obese causes ill health and shortened life span. The striving for a slender body shape has, in fact, become a major preoccupation and sometimes an obsession, giving rise to a billion-dollar industry that caters to the dreams and desires of people trying to lose weight.

SOURCES FOR FURTHER STUDY

Bernell, Bonnie. *Bountiful Women: Large Women's Secrets for Living the Life They Desire*. Berkeley, Calif.: Wildcat Canyon Press, 2000. One of several books emerging from the fat-acceptance movement, written by a psychologist. Offers advice on coming to terms with one's body shape and self-image, dealing with negative feedback from family and society, and living life now rather than waiting until the weight is off.

Hirschmann, Jane R., and Carol H. Munter. *When Women Stop Hating Their Bodies: Freeing Yourself from Food and Weight Obsessions*. New York: Fawcett, 1997. A follow-up to the authors' *Overcoming Overeating* (1988), reviews the psychological based for compulsive eating and provides alternative strategies to persons who have an addictive relationship with food. Presents convincing arguments against dieting and proposes that self-acceptance, physical activity, and health are more appropriate long-term solutions to the problem of overeating.

Lockwood, D. H., and T. G. Heffner, eds. *Obesity: Pathology and Therapy*. New York: Springer-Verlag, 2000. Reviews current theories of the etiology and health impacts of obesity, as well as cutting-edge pharmacological treatments.

Schwartz, Hillel. *Never Satisfied: A Cultural History of Diets, Fantasies, and Fat*. New York: Free Press, 1986. Schwartz, a historian, looks at diets and eating from the perspective of American social and cultural history. Begins with the first weight watchers, in the early nineteenth century; exam-

ines how "shared fictions" about the body fit with various reducing methods and fads in different eras.

Schwartz, Robert. *Diets Don't Work*. 3d ed. Oakland, Calif.: Breakthru, 1996. Practical "how-to" guide to dismantling the diet mentality. This book is a good, basic, and sensible guide for taking stock of the self-defeating weight-loss attitudes and behaviors prevalent in temporary diets versus long-term attitudinal and behavior strategies for permanent weight control.

Thorne, Ruth Raymond. *Fat—A Fate Worse than Death? Women, Weight, and Appearance*. New York: Haworth, 1997. Analyses the social psychology of obsession with women's weight, discusses the insidious nature of fat prejudice, and contests the health rationale for social insistence upon women being thin.

Tribole, Evelyn, and Elyse Resch. *Intuitive Eating: A Recovery Book for the Chronic Dieter*. 5th ed. New York: St. Martin's, 1996. Advocates and advises how to listen to authentic hunger cues and avoid emotion-based overeating.

René R. Roth

SEE ALSO: Addictive personality and behaviors; Anorexia nervosa and bulimia nervosa; Eating disorders; Emotions; Hunger; Nervous system; Obsessive-compulsive disorder; Self-esteem; Self-perception theory.

Observational learning and modeling therapy

TYPE OF PSYCHOLOGY: Learning; personality; psychotherapy

FIELDS OF STUDY: Aggression; anxiety disorders; attitudes and behaviors; behavior therapy; cognitive learning; personality theory; prosocial behavior

Many behaviors are acquired through observing the behaviors of others, and this phenomenon, known as observational learning, has been the subject of extensive scientific theorizing and research. Modeling therapies are a major application of observational learning theory and principles. These therapies pri-

marily have been used to alleviate skill deficits that are associated with psychiatric disorders and to treat fear and anxiety.

Key concepts

- imitation
- modeling
- skills training
- vicarious consequences
- vicarious extinction
- vicarious punishment
- vicarious reinforcement

Introduction

Observational learning refers to acquiring information and changing one's behaviors as a consequence of having observed another's behaviors. It is a major form of learning for humans and primates (hence the expression, "Monkey see, monkey do"). Humans can and do acquire the gamut of behaviors they are capable of performing through observational learning, including verbal and motor skills, attitudes, preferences, values, body language and mannerisms, and emotional responses such as fear. Whereas many behaviors can be learned through Pavlovian and instrumental conditioning, frequently they are acquired more quickly through observational learning. Moreover, it is doubtful that some behaviors, such as language skills, could be acquired without observational learning.

Observational learning requires two parties: a model who explicitly or implicitly demonstrates some behavior and an observer who is exposed to the demonstration. The components of the model's behavior are known as modeling cues, which can be either live or symbolic. Live modeling occurs when the model is physically present; symbolic modeling occurs when the model is not physically present, as in movies, books, television, and any oral description of a person's behaviors. For instance, myths and fairy tales provide archetypal models of roles (such as mother and hero) and values (such as loyalty and honesty) that constitute the fabric of human existence.

Stages

There are three sequential stages of observational learning: exposure, acquisition, and acceptance. First, the observer must be exposed to a model. Every day, people are exposed to countless models, but they pay attention to and remember only a small subset of those modeling cues. The second stage involves the observer's learning (acquiring) the modeling cues and storing them in memory. If the second stage is reached, observational learning has taken place. However, this does not necessarily mean that the observer's behaviors will change because of the acquired modeling cues. In fact, people act on relatively few of the modeling cues that they acquire.

If one's behavior changes based on modeling cues one has acquired, this occurs in the third stage of observational learning, which is called acceptance because one accepts a model's behaviors as a guide for one's own. Acceptance can consist of imitation, which involves acting as the model has, or counterimitation, which involves acting differently than the model has. In each case, the outcome can be direct or indirect. Thus, acceptance can take one of four forms, illustrated by a child observing a parent putting coins in a street beggar's cup.

In direct imitation, the observer copies or does virtually the same thing as the model has done (for example, the child puts change in a beggar's cup). In direct counterimitation, the observer does virtually the opposite of what the model did (the child passes by a beggar without donating change). With indirect imitation, the observer generalizes the model's behavior and acts in a similar, but not exactly the same, way (at school the child donates a toy to a fund for needy children). With indirect counterimitation, the observer generalizes from the model's behavior and acts differently, but not exactly the opposite way (the child does not donate to the toy fund).

During exposure, observers are exposed not only to the model's behavior but also to the consequences of the model's behavior. These consequences influence the observer indirectly or vicariously, which is why they are known as vicarious consequences. Vicarious reinforcement refers to a positive or favorable outcome for the model's behaviors, and vicarious punishment refers to a negative or unfavorable outcome. Vicarious consequences influence both the acquisition and acceptance stages of observational learning. By focusing the observer's attention on the model's actions, vicarious consequences enhance acquisition. In the acceptance stage, vicarious reinforcement increases the likelihood that the observer will imitate the model's actions, whereas vicarious punishment increases the likelihood that the observer will counterimitate. These effects occur because observers believe that they are likely to receive similar consequences for imitating the model.

There are other factors than vicarious consequences that can influence acceptance. For example, in general, imitation is more likely to occur when observers perceive models to be similar to themselves, prestigious, competent, and attractive (factors that are well known to the advertising industry).

SCIENTIFIC RESEARCH

The formal, scientific study of observational learning was begun in 1941 with the publication of *Social Learning and Imitation* by Yale University psychologist Neal Miller and sociologist John Dollard. However, their studies and theorizing essentially were restricted to direct imitation. It was psychologist Albert Bandura at Stanford University who spearheaded the broad study of observational learning with the publication in 1963 of a small but highly influential book titled *Social Learning and Personality Development* (coauthored by Canadian psychologist Richard Walters).

Among Bandura's most influential investigations is the now-classic Bobo doll study. Nursery school boys and girls were shown a five-minute modeling film depicting an adult engaging in discrete, novel, aggressive acts toward an adult-sized inflated plastic Bobo doll (shaped like a bowling pin). The physically aggressive acts (for example, hitting Bobo with a mallet) were accompanied by verbal expressions of aggression ("Soceroo . . . stay down"). One group of children saw the model reinforced for her aggressive behaviors, a second group saw the model punished, and a third group saw her receive no consequences. Next, to ascertain the degree to which the children in each group would spontaneously imitate the model (a measure of acceptance), each child was left alone in a room with a Bobo doll and a variety of toys, including all those used by the model in her assault of Bobo. The child was observed unobtrusively from behind a one-way observation glass. Following this free-play period, the experimenter reentered the room and offered the child juice and stickers as incentives for showing the experimenter what the model had done (a measure of acquisition). The incentives were given to overcome any inhibitions the child might have had for acting aggressively (which is not socially acceptable behavior).

The results of the experiment showed that all of the children learned more aggressive behaviors than they spontaneously performed, and this was especially true for the children exposed to vicarious punishment. Bandura's study supported the critical distinction between the behaviors one learns from models (acquisition) and the behaviors one subsequently engages in (acceptance). Moreover, one of the most remarkable findings of the study was that many of the children engaged in precisely the behaviors they observed the model perform (direct imitation). Subsequently, the effects of violence in television programs on the aggressive behaviors of children and adolescents have been studied extensively. Not surprisingly, the general findings have been that viewing television violence is related to and can be the cause of aggressive behaviors.

Prosocial behaviors also are influenced by modeling. For example, psychologists James Bryan and Mary Ann Test demonstrated that exposure to a model engaging in altruistic behavior in a naturalistic setting would increase imitation for people who observe the model. In one study titled "Lady in Distress: A Flat Tire Study," a college-aged woman stood beside her Ford Mustang that had a flat left rear tire and a spare tire leaning against the car. In the modeling period, a quarter of a mile before reaching the disabled Mustang, motorists passed another car with a flat tire and a man changing the tire as a woman looked on. In the control period, the modeling scene was absent. The presence of the model significantly increased the number of motorists that stopped to offer assistance. In another of Bryan and Test's naturalistic experiments titled "Coins in the Kettle," once every sixty seconds a man approached a Salvation Army kettle outside a large department store and donated money. The first twenty seconds after the model made his donation was considered the modeling period and the third twenty-second period after the modeling sequence was considered the no-modeling period. Donations occurred significantly more often in the modeling periods than in the no-modeling periods.

MODELING THERAPIES

A major practical application of modeling theory and principles has been to provide psychotherapy and remediation for psychiatric disorders and other problem behaviors. Modeling therapies have primarily been used for two problems: to alleviate skill deficits that are associated with psychiatric disorders and to treat fear and anxiety. Modeling also is employed extensively in training psychotherapists.

Treatment of Skill Deficits

Modeling is a major component of skills training; other components include direct instruction, behavior rehearsal, feedback, prompting (providing cues as to how to perform a behavior), and shaping (being reinforced for closer and closer approximations of a behavior). Modeling often is essential because direct instruction may not convey the subtleties of complex skills ("seeing" the behavior may be necessary) and prompting and shaping may not be adequate. One of the earliest applications of skills training was in teaching language and other social skills to children who completely lacked these skills. In the eighteenth century, Jean-Marc-Gaspard Itard attempted to socialize the "Wild Boy of Aveyron," a child who grew up without human contact. More recently, in the 1960's, psychologist Ivar Lovaas pioneered the most successful treatment yet developed for ameliorating some of the massive social skills deficits shown by children with autistic disorder. Modeling has played an essential role in this treatment, although children with autistic disorder often have not learned to imitate in the course of their development. Accordingly, they must first be taught to imitate, which is accomplished through prompting and shaping. Other clinical populations that have serious social skill deficits and have benefitted from skills training include children who rarely interact with peers or interact inappropriately (for example, only aggressively); children and adolescents with physical and language disabilities; people of all ages who are not acting assertively in their lives; hospitalized adults with schizophrenia; and the elderly in nursing homes.

Self-modeling is a unique technique in which clients serve as their own models of adaptive behaviors. Self-modeling capitalizes on the similarity of the model and the observer, which enhances imitation. Developed by psychologist Peter Dowrick, the technique involves preparing a videotape of the client performing the desired behavior (such as appropriately approaching peers and asking them to play a game), and then having the client watch the videotape. Because the client is having difficulty performing the behavior, various "tricks" are used to create the videotape. For instance, clients may be assisted in performing the behavior by the therapist's prompting and modeling the behaviors off-camera, but the final video does not show the assistance. When sustaining a behavior is the problem, brief segments of the client engaging in the behavior are taped and then strung together so that the final videotape shows the client performing the behavior for an extended period.

Treatment of Fear and Anxiety

Fear or anxiety may consist of an emotional component and a behavioral component; the former involves anticipation of negative consequences (such as getting into an accident while driving in traffic) while the latter involves a skill deficit (not knowing how to drive in traffic). Both of these issues can be dealt with when a model performs a feared behavior (such as demonstrating how to drive in traffic) with no negative consequences occurring (the model does not have an accident). This process, known as vicarious extinction, is facilitated by a coping model who, like the observer, is initially fearful and incompetent. The coping model engages in the fear-evoking behavior and gradually becomes less fearful and more competent. Both live and symbolic models are suitable.

The use of a live coping model is illustrated by participant modeling in which the therapist first demonstrates the fear-evoking behavior for the client and then encourages and physically guides the client in performing it. One case involved a forty-nine-year-old woman who had been intensely afraid of crossing streets for ten years and, as a consequence, had withdrawn from social interactions almost completely. The therapist first crossed a street with little traffic while the woman watched. Then, in graduated steps, the therapist, with her arm around the woman's waist, walked with the woman across the street. This was repeated until the woman felt comfortable. With each crossing, the therapist decreased the amount of physical contact with the client until the therapist just walked beside and then behind the woman. Finally, the therapist gradually reduced the distance she accompanied the woman across the street until the woman was able to cross on her own.

Film and Video Modeling

While live modeling can be customized to the client and can be highly efficacious, it may not be cost-effective in terms of therapist time. Symbolic modeling in the form of films and videos, once they are made, can be shown to many people with little or no therapist time required. A major application of film or video modeling has been in the prevention and treatment of fear of medical and dental procedures.

This work was begun by psychologist Barbara Melamed in the 1970's with her modeling film *Ethan Has an Operation*. The sixteen-minute film depicts the experiences of a seven-year-old boy who is about to have surgery to repair a hernia. In its fifteen scenes, the film shows all of the events children who undergo elective surgery are likely to encounter, from admission to discharge. These included Ethan having blood samples taken; the surgeon and anesthesiologist's preoperation consultation with Ethan; Ethan being separated from his mother when wheeled to the operating room; the operating room with all its potentially frightening apparatus; and being in the recovery room. Ethan serves as a coping model who initially exhibits apprehension and fear and then gradually copes with these emotions and successfully goes through each stage of the surgical process. The film has been demonstrated to reduce children's anxiety as well as behavioral problems related to surgery.

Ethan Has an Operation has been widely distributed, and in one survey it was estimated that one-third of all pediatric hospitals in the United States use modeling films to prepare children for surgery and related medical procedures. Other specific modeling films for children, adolescents, and adults have been designed to target fear and distress related to specific medical procedures ranging in severity from receiving an injection to undergoing a bone marrow transplant. Similar films have been produced to help children and adults cope with dental procedures, such has having one's teeth cleaned for the first time. Other, less expensive forms of symbolic modeling, such as coloring books that depict children undergoing medical and dental procedures, have been published. In all cases, coping models are used.

EVALUATION

In general, modeling therapies have been shown to be at least as effective as alternative treatments with which they have been compared; in some cases, such as in reducing children's fears, they are more effective. Modeling therapies are very efficient interventions and sometimes can result in significant changes after only one or two exposures to appropriate models. A number of factors may account for this. Modeling is simultaneously able to teach clients adaptive behaviors, prompt and motivate their performing them, and reduce anxiety clients have about engaging in the adaptive behaviors (such as fear of being rebuffed when acting assertively). Reinforcement need not be administered because observational learning can occur without reinforcement. Standard symbolic modeling in the form of films or videos and pamphlets can be used with many clients, thereby rendering such interventions highly cost-effective once they have been produced. Nonprofessional change agents, such as parents, can easily be trained to administer modeling treatments at home. Finally, therapists can instruct clients to expose themselves, on their own, to natural models, people in their everyday environments who would serve as good exemplars because they exhibit the adaptive behaviors that would benefit the clients.

Clients consider modeling therapies to be an acceptable form of treatment. Because modeling is inherently subtle and unintrusive, clients do not feel manipulated or coerced, as they might in more directive forms of therapy. When clients feel freer and in control of their treatment, they are more likely to change.

SOURCES FOR FURTHER STUDY

Bandura, Albert. *Social Foundations of Thought and Action: A Social Cognitive Theory.* Englewood Cliffs, N.J.: Prentice-Hall, 1986. Observational learning plays a major role in Bandura's social cognitive theory of personality. Despite Bandura's sometimes cumbersome writing style, this large volume contains numerous examples of the role of observational learning in personality development.

Bandura, Albert, and Richard H. Walters. *Social Learning and Personality Development.* New York: Holt, Rinehart, and Winston, 1963. This classic work describes in detail the early studies of and theorizing about observational learning that set the stage for the scientific investigation of observational learning over the next four decades.

Hearold, Susan. "A Synthesis of 1,043 Effects of Television on Social Behavior." In *Public Communication and Behavior,* edited by George Comstock. New York: Academic Press, 1986. A review of one of the most striking effects of modeling in American society.

Lovaas, O. Ivar. *The Autistic Child: Language Development Through Behavior Modification.* New York: Irvington, 1977. Written by the pioneer in behavioral treatment of autistic disorder, this book describes in detail how modeling and other behavioral methods are used to teach language to children well beyond speaking age who do not speak.

Striefel, Sebastian. *How to Teach Through Modeling and Imitation.* 2d ed. Austin, Tex.: Pro-Ed, 1998. A brief practical guide to implementing modeling techniques for developing skills. The book is interactive with numerous exercises that readers can perform to learn the techniques.

Michael D. Spiegler

SEE ALSO: Anxiety disorders; Bandura, Albert; Learning; Observational methods; Phobias; Social learning: Albert Bandura; Violence and sexuality in the media.

Observational methods

TYPE OF PSYCHOLOGY: Psychological methodologies
FIELDS OF STUDY: Descriptive methodologies; methodological issues

Humans are poor observers: They omit, overemphasize, and distort various aspects of what they have seen. Observational methods in psychology have been devised to control or eliminate this problem. These methods increase the accuracy of observations by reducing the effects of perceptual distortion and bias. The development of this methodology has been central to the evolution of scientific psychology.

KEY CONCEPTS
- behavioral taxonomy
- interrater reliability
- operational definition
- reliability
- validity

INTRODUCTION
Humans have tremendous difficulty making accurate observations. Different people will perceive the same event differently; they apply their own interpretations to what they see. One's perception or recollection of an event, although it seems accurate, may well be faulty. This fact creates problems in science, because science requires objective observation.

In large part, this problem is eliminated through the use of scientific instruments to make observations. Many situations exist, however, in which the experimenter is still the recorder. Therefore, methods must be available to prevent bias, distortion, and omission from contaminating observations. Behavior may be observed within natural settings. When using naturalistic observation, scientists only watch behavior; they do not interfere with it.

HISTORY OF RESEARCH
The need for an observational methodology that ensures objective data became apparent early in the history of scientific psychology. In fact, in 1913, John B. Watson, an early American behaviorist, stated that for psychology to become a science at all, it must eliminate the influence of subjective judgment. Watson's influence caused psychology to shift from the subjective study of mental processes to the objective study of behavior. Shifting the focus to behavior improved the reliability of observation dramatically. Behavior is tangible and observable. In the 1920's, the operational definition—a description of behavior in terms that are unambiguous, observable, and easily measured—was introduced. Through using such definitions, communication between psychologists improved greatly. Psychologists were then able to develop experiments that met the scientific criterion of repeatability. Repeatability means that different researchers must be able to repeat the experiment and get similar results.

It soon became apparent, however, that this was not enough. It was discovered that the expectations of researchers biased their observations. This was true even when observations were focused on operationally defined behavior. Methods had to be developed to eliminate these effects, and this led to the development of techniques to reduce or control for experimenter bias. The technique of interrater reliability is an example of one such method. Using observers uninformed about the researchers' expectations also reduces experimenter bias.

In 1976, Robert Rosenthal reported results which showed that subject expectations can also contaminate observational data. It was found that simply observing subjects alters their behavior. How it changes depends on the subjects' interpretation of the situation and their motivation. If subjects could discover what the experimenters' expectations were, they could decide to help, or hinder, the progress of the research. This type of reactivity severely contaminates the accuracy of observational data. Although this is a problem associated primarily with human research, animals also react to observers. This is why it is important to allow sufficient time for animals under observation to habituate to one's presence. Efforts to refine and improve observational methodology continue. Attention is now primarily directed at developing equipment to automate the observational process. The goal is to improve objectivity by removing the experimenter from the situation altogether.

BEHAVIORAL TAXONOMY

To make observation as accurate and objective as possible, researchers use behavioral taxonomy. A behavioral taxonomy is a set of behavioral categories that describe the behavior of the subjects under study. To develop a behavioral taxonomy, the experimenter must first spend time simply watching the population of interest. The observer's presence will alter the subjects' behavior at first. Organisms are reactive, so their initial behavior in the presence of an observer is not typical. Once they become accustomed to being observed, however, behavior returns to normal. This initial observation period, called the habituation period, is important for two reasons. First, it allows the subjects time to become accustomed to the observer's presence. Second, the researcher learns about the subjects by observing them in as many different situations as possible. During this time a diary is kept. Behaviors and their possible functions are jotted down as they are seen. This diary would not be entirely accurate. The observer might distort how often a behavior occurred or perhaps overemphasize interesting behaviors. To overcome these problems, a behavioral taxonomy must be developed.

The taxonomy will include several behavioral categories. Each category describes a specific behavior. During observation, when the behavior is seen, the category is scored. Categories can be either general or specific. Broad categories permit very consistent, and hence reliable, scoring of behavior, but they are

less precise. Specific categories are more precise but make scoring behavior more difficult and less reliable. Whether categories of behavior are general or specific, there are three criteria that all taxonomies must meet: A taxonomy must be clearly defined, mutually exclusive, and exhaustive.

All categories within the behavioral taxonomy must be operationally defined. Operationally defining a category means that one will describe, in concrete terms, exactly what one means by the category name. Operational definitions are used to indicate exactly what one must see to score the category. This serves to eliminate subjective judgment when scoring observations. It also permits scientists to communicate precisely about which behaviors are being studied.

DETERMINING RELIABILITY AND VALIDITY

The next step is to determine whether category definitions are reliable and valid. The term "reliable" refers to whether the definitions permit one to score the behavioral category consistently. To determine whether a definition is reliable, interrater reliability is established. This tells whether two independent observers agree in scoring behavioral categories. If the rate of agreement is high, the category is reliable. For the taxonomy itself to be reliable, all its categories must be reliable. Validity is established when one can show that one is really measuring what one thinks one is. This is very important, as it is not unusual to infer the function of a behavior, only to discover later that the behavior served an entirely different purpose. One way to establish validity is to show a relationship between the category definition and independent assessments of the same behavior.

EXCLUSIVE AND EXHAUSTIVE CATEGORIES

Once taxonomic categories are clearly defined, one must be sure that they are mutually exclusive. This means that each behavior one observes should fit into one, and only one, category; there should be no overlap of meaning between categories. With overlap, the observer will get confused about which behavioral category to score. Such a judgment is subjective, and it will reduce the reliability of the taxonomy and objectivity of the observations.

Finally, the categories should be exhaustive. This means that the categories, as a group, must cover all the behaviors capable of being demonstrated by subjects. Ideally, there should be no behavior that cannot be scored. If the categories are not exhaustive, one will get a distorted idea of how often a particular behavior occurs. Taxonomy must not be developed so as to overrepresent behaviors one finds interesting. Mundane behaviors must be included as well. In this way one can calculate how often each behavior occurs. Although efforts to develop an exhaustive taxonomy must be made, in reality this is impossible. New behaviors will invariably be seen throughout the course of extended observation. To control for this problem, observers will include a category entitled "other." In this way, one can score a behavior even if one has never seen it before. By examining the number of times the "other" category is scored, one can get an idea of how exhaustive the taxonomy is.

TAXONOMY APPROACHES

In measuring behavior with a taxonomy, one can take several approaches. For example, one could use a clock to measure how long each behavior is observed. Using a duration approach is most useful when low-frequency, high-duration behavior is present. One could also quantify how often each behavioral category is scored. The frequency approach is most useful for scoring high-frequency, short-duration behaviors. One could use either the duration or the frequency approach separately or combine the two. Finally, the length and number of observational periods must be determined. In general, the more observational periods used, the better. With respect to length, the observational period must be long enough to permit adequate observation of behavior, but short enough so that one does not become tired and miss important behavior.

APPLIED RESEARCH

An applied example of behavioral taxonomy is its use by researchers to describe monkey behavior. The first step would be to spend many days watching the monkeys' behavior. During this time, the observers would be writing down, in diary form, the behaviors that they see. They would also indicate the function they believe that each behavior serves. The monkeys may appear disturbed or agitated during these initial observations; as time goes by, however, their behavior would become less agitated and they would pay less attention to the observers' presence. Here one can see the importance of

the habituation period. If observers had begun recording behavior from the start, they would probably have described the monkeys inaccurately in some respect.

With the information acquired during the habituation period, the researchers would begin to develop a behavioral taxonomy. They must decide how general or specific the categories in the taxonomy will be. This depends primarily on their purpose. If the categories must be very sensitive to change in behavior, they should be specific. If not, broader categories can be used. Once categories are selected, they are operationally defined. A category for "aggression," for example, could be operationally defined as "grabbing and shaking the cage fence while maintaining eye contact with the experimenter." Note that this definition is clear and concrete. That is, it is based on observable behavior.

In developing the list of behavioral categories, researchers must be sure they are mutually exclusive and exhaustive. To be mutually exclusive, categories must be defined so there is no overlap in meaning between them. To illustrate, the vocalization category might be defined as "any discernible vocal output." It would be unlikely, however, that this category would be mutually exclusive. For example, what if a monkey showed aggression, but while doing so was also vocalizing? Would this be scored as an instance of aggression or vocalization? Because these categories are not mutually exclusive, one would not know. When this occurs, at least one of the categories must be redefined. The listing of categories must also be exhaustive. Observers must form a category for every possible behavior the monkeys might show; also, an "other" category must be included.

Once category definitions have been developed, it must be determined whether they are reliable, valid, mutually exclusive, and exhaustive. This can be determined by having two observers score monkey behavior using the taxonomy. If interrater agreement is high (above 85 percent agreement), the definitions can be considered reliable. If it is low, researchers will revise the necessary category definitions. These observers can also determine if categories are mutually exclusive and exhaustive. They are mutually exclusive if observers found no confusion about which category to score. They are exhaustive if they did not need to score the "other" category. Finally, to establish the validity of category definitions, researchers could ask people familiar with monkey behavior to describe what they would expect to see within each of the categories. If their descriptions agree with the researchers' definitions, there is some evidence that the taxonomy is valid.

With the taxonomy developed, the researchers must decide how many observational periods to use and how long each period will be. In general, the more observational periods used, the more reliable the results. Twenty observational periods is adequate to produce reliable data in most cases. In deciding how long the observational period should be, the purpose of the study must be considered. If high-frequency behavior that falls into very specific categories is being observed, a short observational period should be used. For example, if eye blinks are being counted, the observational period should be no longer than two minutes. Any longer than this and observers would get tired and make inaccurate observations. On the other hand, if low-frequency behavior that is scored in broader categories (for example, tool use) is being watched, longer observational periods should be used.

Finally, researchers must decide how behavior will be quantified. They can measure how long each category of behavior is seen, how often each category of behavior is seen, or both. If they are interested in how much of the monkeys' time is spent engaging in each behavior, they will use the duration approach. If, on the other hand, researchers are more interested in determining the likelihood that a particular behavior will occur, they will use the frequency approach.

With an appropriately developed behavioral taxonomy, the behavior of the monkeys can be described accurately and objectively. Researchers can make statements about the likelihood of various behaviors, what the behaviors mean, and how much time the monkeys spend engaged in each type of behavior. From this information, they obtain an in-depth understanding of the monkeys. For example, through the use of behavioral taxonomies it is known that rhesus monkeys have a dominance hierarchy, are very social, can show tool use and other creative adaptations of behavior when necessary, and show rudimentary forms of communication.

IMPLICATIONS FOR OTHER FIELDS
Humans simply do not record events like video cameras. At the scientific level, much care has to be used to ensure that observations are accurate and objec-

tive. Understanding how human limitations affect observational capabilities has important implications beyond the field of psychology—for example, in law. Tremendous weight is placed on eyewitness testimony in a court of law. Even though eyewitness accounts are probably biased, distorted, and imperfect, the courts recognize them as the best evidence available. Because of what has been learned about the human capacity to make accurate and objective observations, people are well advised to evaluate eyewitness testimony very carefully.

SOURCES FOR FURTHER STUDY

Bakeman, Roger. *Observing Interactions: An Introduction to Sequential Analysis.* 2d ed. New York: Cambridge University Press, 1997. A comprehensive guide to research methods involving the observation of behavior, with guidance for using them. Well-organized, with many tables and summaries.

Bordens, Kenneth S., and Bruce B. Abbott. *Research Design and Methods: A Process Approach.* 4th ed. Mountain View, Calif.: Mayfield, 1998. Presents a discussion of how to develop and use various types of observational methods in psychology. Emphasis is placed on tailoring the methods to fit the investigators' purpose. The relationship between these methods and the statistical analysis of obtained results is also discussed conceptually.

Leahey, Thomas Hardy. *A History of Psychology: Main Currents in Psychological Thought.* 5th ed. Englewood Cliffs, N.J.: Prentice-Hall, 1999. Leahey summarizes the evolution of observational methods in psychology. Philosophical underpinnings are discussed, along with the logic behind the observational strategies selected for use in psychology. Can be understood by beginning college students.

Alan J. Beauchamp

SEE ALSO: Animal experimentation; Archival data; Case-study methods; Complex experimental designs; Data description; Experimental psychology; Experimentation: Ethics and subject rights; Experimentation: Independent, dependent, and control variables; Eyewitness testimony; Field experimentation; Hypothesis development and testing; Quasi-experimental designs; Sampling; Scientific methods; Statistical significance tests; Survey research: Questionnaires and interviews; Within-subject experimental designs.

Obsessive-compulsive disorder

TYPE OF PSYCHOLOGY: Psychopathology
FIELDS OF STUDY: Anxiety disorders

Obsessions and compulsions are the cardinal features of a chronic anxiety disorder known as obessive-compulsive disorder. The identification of repetitive, anxiety-provoking thoughts known as obsessions and of associated compulsive, ritualistic behaviors is critical in the diagnosis and assessment of this debilitating condition.

KEY CONCEPTS
- anxiety
- checking ritual
- cleaning ritual
- compulsions
- fear of contamination
- obsessions
- response prevention

INTRODUCTION

Obsessive thinking and urges to engage in ritualistic compulsive behaviors are common phenomena that most individuals experience to some extent throughout their lives. It is not uncommon, for example, for a person to reexperience in his or her mind involuntary, anxiety-provoking images of circumstances surrounding a traumatic accident or embarrassing moment. Similarly, behaviors such as returning home to make sure the iron is turned off or refusing to eat from a spoon that falls on a clean floor represent mild compelling rituals in which many persons engage from time to time. It is only when these patterns of obsessive thinking and behaving become either too frequent or too intense that they may escalate into a distressing clinical condition known as obsessive-compulsive disorder.

According to the American Psychiatric Association's *Diagnostic and Statistical Manual of Mental Disorders: DSM-IV-TR* (rev. 4th ed., 2000), the primary feature of this disorder is the presence of distressing obsessions or severe compulsive behaviors that interfere significantly with a person's daily functioning. Although diagnosis requires only the presence of either obsessions or compulsions, they typically are both present in obsessive-compulsive disorder. In most cases, persons with this diagnosis spend more time on a daily basis experiencing obsessive thinking and engaging in ritualistic behaviors than other constructive activities, including those pertaining to occupational, social, and family responsibilities. Therefore, it is not uncommon for obsessive-compulsive patients also to experience severe vocational impairment and distraught interpersonal relationships.

OBSESSIONS

The word "obsession" comes from the Latin word *obsidere* ("to besiege") and can be defined as a recurrent thought, impulse, idea, or image that is intrusive, disturbing, and senseless. Among the most common types are themes of violence (for example, images of killing a loved one), contamination (for example, thoughts of catching a disease from a doorknob), and personal injury or harm (for example, impulses to leap from a bridge). Obsessional doubting is also characteristic of most patients with obsessive-compulsive disorder, which leads to indecisiveness in even the most simple matters such as selecting a shirt to wear or deciding what to order at a restaurant. The basic content of obsessive thinking distinguishes it from simple "worrying." Worrying involves thinking about an event or occurrence that may realistically result in discomfort, embarrassment, or harm and has a likely probability of occurring; obsessive thinking is typically recognized by the patient as being senseless and not likely to occur. An example of a worry is thinking about an event that possesses a strong likelihood of occurring, such as failing a test when one has not studied. Imagining that one might leap from the third-floor classroom during the exam, a highly unlikely event, is considered an obsession. Furthermore, because the obsessive-compulsive patient is aware that these intrusive thoughts are senseless and continuously attempts to rid the thought from his or her mind, obsessive thinking is not delusional or psychotic in nature. Although both delusional and obsessive patients may experience a similar thought (for example, that they have ingested tainted food), the obsessive patient recognizes that the thought is unlikely and is a product of his or her mind and struggles to get rid of the thought. The delusional patient adheres to the belief with little to no struggle to test its validity.

COMPULSIONS

Most obsessive-compulsive patients also exhibit a series of repetitive, intentional, stereotyped behaviors known as compulsions, which serve to reduce the anxiety experienced from severe obsessive thinking. The most common forms include counting (for example, tapping a pencil three times before laying it down), cleaning (for example, hand washing after shaking another person's hand), checking (for example, checking pilot lights several times a day), and ordering (for example, arranging pencils from longest to shortest before doing homework). Compulsions are different from simple habits in that attempts to resist urges to engage in them result in a substantial increase in anxiety, eventually forcing the patient to engage in the compelling behavior to reduce the tension. Urges to engage in simple habits, on the other hand, can often be resisted with minimal discomfort. Furthermore, most habits result in deriving some degree of pleasure from the activity (for example, shopping, gambling, drinking), while engaging in compulsive behaviors is rarely enjoyable for the patient. Compulsions must also be distinguished from superstitious behaviors, such as an athlete's warm-up ritual or wearing the same "lucky" shoes for each sporting event. In contrast to superstitious people, who employ their rituals to enhance confidence, obsessive-compulsive patients are never certain their rituals will result in anxiety reduction. This typically forces these patients continually to expand their repertoire of ritualistic behaviors, searching for new and better ways to eliminate the anxiety produced by obsessive thinking.

It is estimated that approximately 2 percent of the adult population in the United States—a larger percentage than was once believed—has at some time experienced obsessive-compulsive symptoms severe enough to warrant diagnosis. Typically, obsessive-compulsive symptoms begin in adolescence or early adulthood, although most patients report symptoms of anxiety and nervousness as children. Regarding early developmental histories, many obsessive-compulsive patients report being reared in very strict, puritanical homes. The disorder occurs equally in males and females, although cleaning rituals occur more frequently among women. While the course of the disorder is chronic, the intensity of symptoms fluctuates throughout life and occasionally has been reported to remit spontaneously. Because of the unusual nature of the symptoms, obsessive-compulsive patients often keep their rituals hidden and become introverted and withdrawn; as a result, the clinical picture becomes complicated by a coexisting de-

---

DSM-IV-TR Criteria for Obsessive-Compulsive Disorder (DSM code 300.3)

Either obsessions or compulsions

Obsessions defined by all of the following:
- recurrent and persistent thoughts, impulses, or images experienced, at some time during disturbance, as intrusive and inappropriate and cause marked anxiety or distress
- thoughts, impulses, or images not simply excessive worries about real-life problems
- attempts made to ignore or suppress thoughts, impulses, or images, or to neutralize them with some other thought or action
- recognition that thoughts, impulses, or images are product of his or her own mind (not imposed from without, as in thought insertion)

Compulsions defined by both of the following:
- repetitive behaviors (hand washing, ordering, checking) or mental acts (praying, counting, repeating words silently) that individual feels driven to perform in response to an obsession or according to rules that must be applied rigidly
- behaviors or mental acts aimed at preventing or reducing distress or preventing some dreaded event or situation; behaviors or mental acts either are not connected in a realistic way with what they are designed to neutralize or prevent or are clearly excessive

At some point, individual recognizes obsessions or compulsions as excessive or unreasonable; this does not apply to children

Obsessions or compulsions cause marked distress, are time-consuming, or interfere significantly with normal routine, occupational or academic functioning, or usual social activities or relationships

If another Axis I disorder is present, content of obsessions or compulsions not restricted to it

Disturbance not due to direct physiological effects of a substance or general medical condition

Specify if with Poor Insight (most of the time during current episode, obsessions and compulsions not recognized as excessive or unreasonable)

pressive disorder. It is typically the depression which forces the patient to seek psychological help.

ETIOLOGY AND TREATMENTS

Because of the distressing yet fascinating nature of the symptoms, several theoretical positions have attempted to explain how obsessive-compulsive disorder develops. From an applied perspective, each theoretical position has evolved into a treatment or intervention strategy for eliminating the problems caused by obsessions and compulsions. According to psychoanalytic theory, as outlined by Sigmund Freud in 1909, obsessive-compulsive rituals are the product of overly harsh toilet training which leaves the patient with considerable unconscious hostility, primarily directed toward an authoritarian caregiver. In a sense, as uncomfortable and disconcerting as the obsessions and compulsive behaviors are, they are preferable to experiencing the intense emotions left from these childhood incidents. Obsessions and compulsions permit the patient to avoid experiencing these emotions. Furthermore, obsessive-compulsive symptoms force the patient to become preoccupied with anxiety-reduction strategies which prevent them from dealing with other hidden impulses, such as sexual urges and desires. Based upon the psychoanalytic formulation, treatment involves identifying the original unconscious thoughts, ideas, or impulses and allowing the patient to experience them consciously. In his classic case report of an obsessive patient, Freud analyzed a patient known as the "rat man," who was plagued by recurrent, horrifying images of a bucket of hungry rats strapped to the buttocks of his girlfriend and his father. Although periodic case reports of psychoanalytic treatments for obsessive-compulsive disorder exist, there is very little controlled empirical work suggesting the effectiveness of this treatment approach.

Behavioral theorists, differing from the psychoanalytic tradition, have proposed that obsessive-compulsive disorder represents a learned habit that is maintained by the reinforcing properties of the anxiety reduction that occurs following ritualistic behaviors. It is well established that behaviors that are reinforced occur more frequently in the future. In the case of compulsive behaviors, the ritual is always followed by a significant reduction in anxiety, therefore reinforcing the compulsive behavior as well as the preceding obsessive activity. Based upon the behavioral perspective, an intervention strategy called response prevention, or flooding, was developed to facilitate the interruption of this habitually reinforcing cycle. Response prevention involves exposing the patient to the feared stimulus (for example, a doorknob) or obsession (for example, an image of leaping from a bridge) in order to create anxiety. Rather than allowing the patient to engage in the subsequent compulsive activity, however, the therapist prevents the response (for example, the patient is not permitted to wash his or her hands). The patient endures a period of intense anxiety but eventually experiences habituation of the anxiety response. Although treatments of this nature are anxiety provoking for the patient, well-controlled investigations have reported significant reductions in obsessive thinking and ritualistic behavior following intervention. Some estimates of success rates with response prevention are as high as 80 percent, and treatment gains are maintained for several years.

Theories emphasizing the cognitive aspects of the obsessive-compulsive disorder have focused on information-processing impairments of the patient. Specifically, obsessive-compulsive patients tend to perceive harm (for example, contamination) when in fact it may not be present, and to perceive a loss of control over their environment. While most individuals perceive a given situation as safe until proved harmful, the obsessive-compulsive patient perceives situations as harmful until proved safe. These perceptions of harm and lack of control lead to increased anxiety; the belief that the patient controls his or her life or the perception of safety leads to decreased anxiety. Accordingly, compulsive rituals represent a patient's efforts to gain control over his or her environment. Cognitive interventions aim to increase the patient's perception of control over the environment and to evaluate realistically environmental threats of harm. While cognitive approaches may serve as a useful adjunct to behavioral treatments such as response prevention, evidence for their effectiveness when used in treating obsessions and compulsions is lacking.

Finally, biological models of obsessive-compulsive disorder have also been examined. There is some indication that brain electrical activity during information processing, particularly in the frontal lobes, is somewhat slower for obsessive-compulsive patients in comparison to other people. For example, metabolic activity of the frontal brain regions measured using positron emission tomography (PET) scans differentiates obsessive-compulsive patients from both normal people and depressive patients. Further, a deficiency in certain neurotransmitters (for example, serotonin, and norepinephrine) has been implicated in the etiology of the disorder. Several interventions based upon the biological model have been employed as well. Pharmacotherapy, using antidepressant medications that primarily act to facilitate neurotransmitter functioning (for example, clomipramine), has been shown to be effective in treating from 20 to 50 percent of obsessive-compulsive patients. More drastic interventions such as frontal lobotomies have been reported in the most intractable cases, with very limited success.

Among the interventions employed to rid patients of troublesome obsessions and compulsions, response prevention holds the most promise. Because of the intensity of this treatment approach, however, the cost may be substantial, and many patients may not immediately respond. A number of predictors of poor treatment response to behavioral interventions (characteristic of those most refractory to treatment) have been identified. These include a coexisting depression, poor compliance with exposure/response-prevention instructions, the presence of fears that the patient views as realistic, and eccentric superstition. In these cases, alternative forms of treatment are typically considered (for example, pharmacotherapy).

PREVALENCE AND RESEARCH

Obsessions and compulsions represent human phenomena that have been a topic of interest for several centuries; for example, William Shakespeare's characterization of the hand-washing Lady Macbeth has entertained audiences for hundreds of years. Prior to the first therapeutic analysis of obsessive-compulsive disorder, then called a neurosis—Freud's description of the "rat man"—obsessive thoughts were commonly attributed to demoniac influence and treated with exorcism. Freud's major contribution was delivering the phenomenon from the spiritual into the psychological realm. Although initial case reports employing psychoanalysis were promising, subsequent developments using behavioral and pharmacological formulations have more rapidly advanced the understanding of the phenomenology and treatment of this unusual condition. In addition, with the public revelation that certain

prominent individuals such as the aircraft designer and film producer Howard Hughes suffered from this condition, the prevalence estimates of this disorder have steadily increased. Although a number of patients have sought help for this debilitating disorder since the time it was first clinically described, it has been confirmed that this problem is far more prevalent than initially thought. The increase is probably related not to an actual increase in incidence but to individuals becoming more willing to seek help for the problem. Because of the increasing number of individuals requesting help for problems relating to obsessions and compulsions, it is becoming more and more important to foster the maturation of appropriate treatment strategies to deal with this disorder.

Further, it has become increasingly important to understand the manifestation of obsessions and compulsions from a biological, psychological, and socio-occupational level. Ongoing investigations are examining the biological makeup of the nervous systems peculiar to this disorder. Research examining the specific information-processing styles and cognitive vulnerabilities of obsessive-compulsive patients is also being conducted. Both response-prevention and biochemical-intervention strategies (for example, clomipramine) are deserving of continued research, primarily in the examining characteristics of obsessive-compulsive patients that predict treatment efficacy with either form of intervention. Finally, early markers for this condition, including childhood environments, early learning experiences, and biological predispositions, require further investigation so that prevention efforts can be provided for individuals who may be at risk for developing obsessive-compulsive disorder. With these advances, psychologists will be in a better position to reduce the chronic nature of obsessive-compulsive disorder and to prevent these distressing symptoms in forthcoming generations.

SOURCES FOR FURTHER STUDY

American Psychiatric Association. *Diagnostic and Statistical Manual of Disorders: DSM-IV-TR.* Rev. 4th ed. Washington, D.C.: Author, 2000. The DSM-IV-TR provides specific criteria for making psychiatric diagnoses of obsessive-compulsive disorder and other anxiety disorders. Brief summaries of research findings regarding each condition are also provided.

Emmelkamp, Paul M. G. *Phobic and Obsessive Compulsive Disorders: Theory, Research, and Practice.* New York: Plenum, 1982. A somewhat dated but classic work outlining the importance of behavioral strategies in overcoming obsessive-compulsive, as well as phobic, conditions.

Jenike, Michael A., Lee Baer, and William E. Minichiello. *Obsessive-Compulsive Disorders: Theory and Management.* 2d ed. Littleton, Mass.: PSG, 1990. A comprehensive overview of the topic that does not burden the reader with intricate details of analysis. Readable by the layperson. Covers the topic thoroughly.

Mavissakalian, Matig, Samuel M. Turner, and Larry Michelson. *Obsessive-Compulsive Disorders: Psychological and Pharmacological Treatment.* New York: Plenum, 1985. An exceptionally well written text based upon a symposium held at the University of Pittsburgh. Issues pertaining to etiology, assessment, diagnosis, and treatment are covered in detail.

Rachman, S. J. "Obsessional-Compulsive Disorders." In *International Handbook of Behavior Modification and Therapy,* edited by Alan S. Bellack, Michel Hersen, and Alan E. Kazdin. 2d ed. New York: Plenum, 1990. Rachman's work using behavioral strategies with obsessive-compulsive patients is unparalleled. No bibliography would be complete without a contribution from Rachman, one of the most respected authorities in the field.

Steketee, Gail, and Andrew Ellis. *Treatment of Obsessive-Compulsive Disorder.* New York: Guilford, 1996. A comprehensive resource for mental health professionals. Covers behavioral and cognitive approaches, biological models, and pharmacological therapies.

Turner, S. M., and L. Michelson. "Obsessive-Compulsive Disorders." In *Behavioral Theories and Treatment of Anxiety,* edited by Samuel M. Turner. New York: Plenum, 1984. Summarizes information regarding diagnostic issues, assessment strategies, and treatment interventions for obsessive-compulsive disorder. Provides an excellent review of intervention efforts employing response prevention and clomipramine.

Kevin T. Larkin and Virginia L. Goetsch

SEE ALSO: Abnormality: Biomedical models; Anxiety disorders; Aversion, implosion, and systematic desensitization; Cognitive therapy; Drug therapies.

Oedipus complex

TYPE OF PSYCHOLOGY: Biological bases of behavior; developmental psychology; emotion; memory; personality; psychopathology; psychotherapy; social psychology

FIELDS OF STUDY: Adolescence; attitudes and behavior; behavioral therapies; childhood and adolescent disorders; classic analytic themes and issues; group and family therapies; infancy and childhood; interpersonal relations; personality assessment; personality disorders; sexual disorders

Oedipus, a character from Greek mythology who inadvertently killed his father and married his mother, became a model comparison figure for Sigmund Freud as he began the recognition of infantile sexuality and the Oedipus complex during his period of self-analysis, starting in 1897.

KEY CONCEPTS
- abandonment
- aggression
- depression
- family dynamics
- guilt
- incest
- infantile sexuality
- murder
- psychoanalysis
- rage
- self-mutilation
- suicide

INTRODUCTION

The classic presentation of the myth of Oedipus is the play *Oidipous Tyrannos* (c. 429 B.C.E.; *Oedipus Tyrannus,* 1715), by the Greek playwright Sophocles. The play begins when Laius, ruler of Thebes, is told he will one day be murdered by a son. When Jocasta, his wife, gives birth to a son, the couple orders him killed. Instead, the baby is abandoned, then found and adopted by Polybus, king of Corinth. The boy, named Oedipus, grows up believing Polybus is his biological father.

As an adult, Oedipus is told that he is fated to kill his father and, in an attempt to evade the prophecy, leaves Corinth. On the road, he meets an old man driving a wagon who refuses to move and let Oedipus pass. In a rage, Oedipus unknowingly kills Laius, his biological father.

The throne of Thebes is now vacant, and through a series of circumstances Oedipus becomes king of Thebes and marries the widow of the former king—his biological mother, Jocasta. The two have four daughters. Thebes is then beset with a terrible plague. Oedipus vows to save his kingdom and puts a curse on the person who must have committed the sin that has caused the plague. Through an entanglement of circumstances and the confession of Polybus, Oedipus learns the truth of his murder of his father and marriage to Jocasta, his mother. Jocasta hangs herself in shame. Oedipus takes the brooches from her dress and thrusts the pins into his eyes, blinding himself so he cannot see the evil around him. Oedipus is taken to Mount Cithaeron, where he was originally abandoned, and left to die as the gods originally intended.

OEDIPUS IN THE HUMAN PSYCHE

Sigmund Freud, the Austrian founder of psychoanalysis, first turned his attention to the Oedipus myth while undertaking his own self-analysis in the late 1890's, as he was attempting to puzzle out the dynamics of infant sexuality. After studying the Oedipus myth, Freud truly believed he had gained insight into the human mind, revealing a basic tenet of the human psyche based on persons dealing with family dynamics. Freud believed all male children deal with aggression toward their fathers and dream of making love to their mothers at some point in their development. Freud felt that Oedipus was the perfect model for this example because of his extreme behaviors.

Improper infantile sexual feelings that are not dealt with cause neuroses that affect daily life. These neuroses complications can cause disabilities later on. However, historical data now prove incestuous behaviors are extremely rare in all societies worldwide. Psychiatrists have dismissed much of what Freud had to say on the subject.

Diagnosing this complex is difficult in the light of psychological research since Freud first used the term and began treatment using psychoanalysis. Versions of what might still be termed Oedipal conflicts may be found in psychiatric patients exhibiting sexual disorders as a result of childhood incestuous experiences. Serial murders most often have suffered abnormal sexual experiences, and case histo-

ries show that child molesters also have often been sexually abused as children. However, the idea that the incestuous relations between children and adults are the result of (unconscious) desire on the part of the child is now discredited. Most references to the Oedipus complex now take place in the realm of literary studies.

SOURCES FOR FURTHER STUDY

Blazina, Chris. "Mythos and Men: Toward New Paradigms of Masculinity." *The Journal of Men's Studies* 5, no. 4 (May, 1997): 285-295. Blazine states that while stories such as Green Man and Odysseus offer an alternative view of gender roles and male identity, stories such as Heracles and Oedipus can offer detrimental messages to men concerning family and profession. She discusses the social aspects of masculinity and the influence of Greek mythology through modern times.

Slater, Philip. *The Glory of Hera*. Reprint. Princeton, N.J.: Princeton University Press, 1992. Applies Freudian psychoanalytical theory to ancient Greek society in an attempt to explain its family dynamics through its myths. Fascinating, though somewhat dated and anthropologically suspect.

Sophocles. *The Oedipus Cycle*. Translated by Dudley Fitts and Robert Fitzgerald. San Diego, Calif.: Harvest, 1987. Knowing the story of Oedipus helps understand what Sigmund Freud means by the Oedipus complex.

Young, Robert M., ed. *Oedipus Complex: Ideas in Psychoanalysis*. New York: Totem Books, 2001. Comparison of opinions of Melanie Klein and Sigmund Freud concerning the Oedipal phases and issues.

Virginiae Blackmon

SEE ALSO: Ego, superego, and id; Freud, Sigmund; Penis envy; Psychoanalytic psychology and personality: Sigmund Freud; Psychosexual development.

Operant conditioning therapies

TYPE OF PSYCHOLOGY: Psychotherapy
FIELDS OF STUDY: Behavioral and cognitive models; behavioral therapies

Operant conditioning therapies are based on the assumption that operant behavior is shaped by its consequences; therapists use reinforcement, extinction, punishment, and discrimination training to overcome behavioral problems. Operant conditioning techniques have been applied to individual and group behavior in a variety of settings, including hospitals, prisons, schools, businesses, and homes.

KEY CONCEPTS
- aversive stimulus
- discrimination training
- extinction
- negative punishment
- operant conditioning
- positive punishment
- positive reinforcement
- successive approximations

INTRODUCTION

Behavior therapy uses principles of learning to modify human behavior. One orientation within behavior therapy is the operant conditioning approach, also called behavior modification. This approach modifies operant behavior by manipulating environmental consequences. The term "operant" refers to voluntary or emitted behavior that operates on the environment to produce consequences. The basic premise of operant conditioning is that operant behavior is controlled by its consequences. What happens to an individual after he or she performs some behavior determines the likelihood of that behavior being repeated. Pleasant or reinforcing consequences strengthen behavior, while unpleasant or punishing consequences weaken behavior.

THERAPEUTIC APPROACHES

There are several characteristics that distinguish the operant approach to therapy. One is the manner in which clinical problems are conceptualized and defined. Traditional psychotherapy tends to view disturbed behavior as a symptom of an internal psychological conflict; the goal of therapy is to help the individual gain insight into this inner problem. Therapists with an operant orientation, however, view maladaptive behavior as the problem itself. They believe that, just as normal or adaptive behavior is shaped by environmental consequences, so too is abnormal or maladaptive behavior. Therefore, by carefully arranging events in the client's environ-

ment, it should be possible to modify maladaptive behavior and help the client learn more appropriate ways of behaving.

The behavior therapist defines problems in terms of specific behaviors that can be observed and quantified. Behavioral excesses involve too much of a specific behavior that can be specified in terms of frequency, intensity, or duration. Chain-smoking, overeating, and physically abusing another person are examples of behavioral excesses. The opposite difficulty is a behavioral deficit. In the case of a behavioral deficit, a behavior either does not occur or occurs at an extremely low rate. A man who cannot feed or dress himself and a child who rarely talks to other children exhibit behavioral deficits. Still other behaviors are problematic because they are inappropriate when performed in a particular setting. Taking one's clothes off in public or laughing during a solemn funeral service illustrates behavioral inappropriateness.

Behavioral monitoring is an integral component of operant conditioning therapies. The problem behavior is first observed and recorded as it naturally occurs in a variety of settings, and no attempt is made to modify the behavior. The therapist, a parent, a teacher, a spouse, a peer, or the client may conduct the observation and record the behavior. This part of the behavior-modification program, which is called baseline observation, provides a record of where and when the behavior occurred as well as information about its topography or form, such as duration and intensity. Behavioral measures are often plotted on a graph to provide a visual record of behavior. The baseline data are used to define the problem or target behavior as precisely as possible. The client and therapist also define the desired changes in this target behavior and set up specific behavioral goals to be met during treatment.

TREATMENT TECHNIQUES

Operant techniques that are appropriate for modifying the target behavior are then selected. Therapists begin by selecting the least intrusive and restrictive procedures demonstrated to be effective for treating a specific problem. Since these techniques are based on years of experimental research and evaluation, it is possible for therapists to define explicitly their methods and their rationale to the client. This degree of precision, rarely found in traditional psychotherapy, makes it easier for clients and those working with clients to understand and implement therapeutic procedures.

Behavioral observation continues throughout the treatment phase of the modification program. Behavior is monitored on a regular basis, and changes from the baseline level are recorded. Examination of this ongoing record of behavioral progress allows both therapist and client to evaluate the effectiveness of the treatment at any given time. If behavior is not changing in the desired direction or at the desired pace, the treatment program can be altered or adjusted.

Behavior modifiers often include a follow-up phase as part of the modification program. After termination of treatment, the client may be contacted on a periodic basis to assess whether treatment gains are being maintained. Behavior therapists have discovered that generalization of behavior changes from the therapeutic setting to the natural environment does not occur automatically. An increasing emphasis is being placed on incorporating procedures to facilitate behavior transfer into modification programs. Some therapists have reduced their reliance on tangible reinforcers, such as food or toys, and have stressed the use of social and intrinsic reinforcers, such as positive attention from others and personal feelings of pride and mastery. These are the kinds of reinforcers that are likely to maintain positive behavioral changes in the client's natural setting. Therapists also devote attention to training individuals who will interact with the client after the termination of treatment in the effective use of operant procedures.

Ethical guidelines are followed when conducting a behavior-modification program. Since behavior therapists insist on explicit definition of problem behaviors and treatment methods, this approach facilitates public scrutiny of ethical conduct. Educating the client in the rationale and application of procedures greatly reduces the possibility that operant conditioning techniques will be used in an exploitive or harmful fashion.

POSITIVE REINFORCEMENT

The treatment of behavioral deficits typically involves the application of positive-reinforcement techniques. Positive reinforcement increases the frequency of a response by immediately following the response with a favorable consequence. If the desired behavior does not occur at all, it can be developed by us-

ing the shaping procedure. In shaping, successive approximations—responses that more and more closely resemble the desired response—of the desired behavior are reinforced. Wayne Isaacs, James Thomas, and Israel Goldiamond provided an impressive demonstration of the use of shaping to reinstate verbal behavior in a schizophrenic patient who had been mute for nineteen years. Chewing gum was used as the positive reinforcer, and gum delivery was made contingent first upon eye movements in the direction of the gum, then upon lip movements, then upon any vocalization, and finally upon vocalizations that increasingly approximated actual words. Within six weeks, the patient was conversing with the therapist.

Positive reinforcement is also used to strengthen weak or low-frequency behaviors. Initially, the desired behavior is placed on a continuous reinforcement schedule in which each occurrence of the behavior is followed by reinforcer delivery. Gradually, an intermittent schedule can be introduced, with several responses or a time interval required between successive reinforcer deliveries.

Since people get tired of the same reinforcer and different people find different commodities and activities reinforcing, a token economy system provides another means of programming positive reinforcement. A system that delivers tokens as rewards for appropriate behaviors can be used with a single individual or a group of individuals. Tokens are stimuli such as check marks, points, stickers, or poker chips, which can be accumulated and later exchanged for commodities and activities of the individual's choosing. Tokens can be delivered on a continuous or intermittent schedule of reinforcement and are often accompanied by praise for the desired behavior. Ultimately, the goal of the program is to fade out the use of tokens as more natural social and intrinsic reinforcers begin to maintain behavior.

EXTINCTION AND PUNISHMENT PROCEDURES

Extinction and punishment procedures are used to treat behavioral excess. If the reinforcer that is maintaining the excessive behavior can be identified, an extinction program may be effective. Extinction is a procedure that is used to eliminate a response by withholding the reinforcer following performance of the response. A classic demonstration of extinction is a study by Carl Williams designed to eliminate intense tantrum behavior at bed-time in a twenty-one-month-old child. Observation revealed that parental attention was reinforcing the tantrums, so the parents were instructed to put the child to bed, close the bedroom door, and not re-turn to the child's room for the rest of the night. This extinction procedure eliminated the tantrums in seven nights. Tantrums were then accidentally reinforced by the child's aunt, and a second extinc-tion procedure was instituted. Tantrums were re-duced to a zero level by the ninth session, and a two-year follow-up revealed that no further tantrums had occurred.

Punishment procedures decrease the frequency of a response by removing a reinforcing stimulus or by presenting an aversive stimulus (a painful or un-pleasant event) immediately following the response. Removal of a positive reinforcer contingent upon performance of the target behavior is called neg-ative punishment or response cost. Some token economy systems incorporate a response cost com-ponent, and clients lose tokens when specified in-appropriate behaviors are performed. In another form of negative punishment, time-out or sit-out, an individual is moved from a reinforcing environment to one that is devoid of positive reinforcement for a limited amount of time. For example, a child who misbehaves during a classroom game might be seated away from the other children for a few min-utes, thereby losing the opportunity to enjoy the game.

The most intrusive behavior-reduction technique is positive punishment, which involves the presenta-tion of an aversive stimulus contingent upon perfor-mance of the undesirable behavior. This procedure is used only when other procedures have failed and the behavioral excess is injurious to the client or to others. Thomas Sajwaj and his colleagues em-ployed a positive punishment procedure to reduce life-threatening regurgitation behavior in a six-month-old infant. Within a few minutes of being fed, the infant would begin to bring up the milk she had consumed, and regurgitation continued until all the milk was lost. Treatment consisted of filling the infant's mouth with lemon juice immediately following mouth movements indicative of regurgita-tion. Regurgitation was reduced to a very low level after sixteen lemon-juice presentations.

Extinction and punishment techniques can pro-duce side effects that include aggressive behavior and fear, escape, and avoidance responses. These can be reduced by combining behavior-reduction procedures with a program of positive reinforce-ment for desirable alternative behaviors. In this way, the behavioral excess is weakened and the client is simultaneously learning adaptive, socially approved behaviors.

STIMULUS-DISCRIMINATION TRAINING
Behaviors that are labeled as inappropriate because of their place of occurrence may be treated using stimulus-discrimination training. This involves teach-ing the client to express a behavior in the presence of some stimuli and not express the behavior in the presence of other stimuli. For a preschooler who takes his clothes off in a variety of public and private places, discrimination training might involve prais-ing the child when he removes his clothes in his bedroom or the bathroom and using extinction or punishment when clothing removal occurs in other settings. Verbal explanation of the differential con-tingencies also helps the client learn discrimina-tion.

EVOLUTION OF RESEARCH
Operant conditioning therapies evolved from the laboratory research of B. F. Skinner. In 1938, Skin-ner published *The Behavior of Organisms*, which out-lined the basic principles of operant conditioning that Skinner had derived from the experimental study of the effects of environmental consequences on the lever-pressing behavior of rats. This work stimulated other psychologists to analyze operant behavior in many animal species.

Most early studies with human subjects were de-signed to replicate and extend this animal research, and they served to demonstrate that operant tech-niques exerted similar control over human behav-ior. A literature of operant principles and theory be-gan to accumulate, and researchers referred to this approach to learning as the experimental analysis of behavior.

Some of these human demonstrations were con-ducted in institutional settings with patients who had not responded well to traditional treatment ap-proaches. The results of such studies suggested that operant procedures could have therapeutic value. In 1959, Teodoro Ayllon and Jack Michael de-scribed how staff members could use reinforcement principles to modify the maladaptive behaviors of psychiatric patients. In the 1960's, Sidney Bijou pioneered the use of operant procedures with mentally retarded children and Ivar Lovaas developed an operant program for autistic children.

The 1960's also saw applications in noninstitutional settings. Operant techniques were introduced into school classrooms, university teaching, programs for delinquent youth, marriage counseling, and parent training. Universities began to offer coursework and graduate training programs in the application of operant principles. By the late 1960's, the operant orientation in behavior therapy became known by the terms "behavior modification" and "applied behavior analysis."

During the 1970's, many large-scale applications were instituted. Psychiatric hospitals, schools, prisons, and business organizations began to apply operant principles systematically to improve the performances of large groups of individuals. Another important trend that began in the 1970's was an interest in the self-modification of problem behaviors. Numerous books offered self-training in operant procedures to deal with problems such as smoking, drug abuse, nervous habits, stress, sexual dysfunction, time management, and weight control.

INTEGRATION WITH BEHAVIORAL MEDICINE

Since the 1980's, operant conditioning therapies have become an integral component of behavioral medicine. Reinforcement techniques are being used in the treatment of chronic pain, eating and sleeping disorders, cardiovascular disorders, and neuromuscular disorders. Operant procedures are also effective in teaching patients adherence to medical instructions and how to make healthy life-style changes.

Behavior modifiers continue to direct attention toward public safety and improvement of the physical environment. Therapists are evaluating the effectiveness of operant procedures to combat crime, reduce traffic accidents, and increase the use of seat belts, car pools, and public transportation. Programs are being designed to encourage energy conservation and waste recycling.

Throughout the history of its development, behavior modification has emphasized the use of operant conditioning principles to improve the quality of life for individuals and for society as a whole. Behavior therapists actively support efforts to educate the public in the ethical use of operant techniques for social betterment.

SOURCES FOR FURTHER STUDY

Karoly, Paul, and Anne Harris. "Operant Methods." In *Helping People Change: A Textbook of Methods*, edited by Frederick H. Kanfer and A. P. Goldstein. 4th ed. Boston: Allyn & Bacon, 1991. A concise and easy-to-follow description of operant methods. Each technique is accompanied by illustrative case studies and recommendations for effective use.

Kazdin, Alan E. *Behavior Modification in Applied Settings*. 6th ed. Belmont, Calif.: Wadsworth, 2000. An introduction to behavior modification that can be understood by the high school or college student. Operant techniques are clearly described, with the emphasis on how they are applied in a wide range of settings. Excellent discussion of recent developments in the field.

Martin, Garry, and Joseph Pear. *Behavior Modification: What It Is and How to Do It*. 6th ed. Englewood Cliffs, N.J.: Prentice-Hall, 1998. One of the best introductions to behavior modification. The book offers clear explanations of the principles underlying techniques and detailed guidelines for their effective application. Study questions, practical exercises, and self-modification exercises facilitate mastery of concepts.

Watson, David L., and Roland G. Tharp. *Self-Directed Behavior: Self-Modification for Personal Adjustment*. 8th ed. Belmont, Calif.: Wadsworth, 2001. This do-it-yourself guide to behavior changes makes extensive use of principles of reinforcement to help the lay reader improve behaviors in areas such as time management, smoking, overeating, assertiveness, insomnia, budgeting, and social behavior.

Linda J. Palm

SEE ALSO: Aversion, implosion, and systematic desensitization; Behaviorism; Conditioning; Habituation and sensitization; Learned helplessness; Learning; Pavlovian conditioning; Phobias; Reflexes.

Optimal arousal theory

TYPE OF PSYCHOLOGY: Motivation
FIELDS OF STUDY: Motivation theory

Optimal arousal theory suggests that arousal prompts human behavior. Arousal theorists hypothesize that each human has a level of arousal at which he or she generally performs best and that the individual strives to maintain that level of arousal in much the same way that the body homeostatically controls its temperature.

KEY CONCEPTS

- construct
- hedonic
- homeostatic
- motivation
- reticular activating system

INTRODUCTION

Optimal arousal theory is a "push" or internal motivation theory. Arousal, like drive, is thought to energize and direct behavior. Arousal theory enjoys some advantages over drive theory, however; it is able to explain behavior that continues at the same level and intensity or increases, and it is not a hypothetical construct but a measurable phenomenon. A construct can be defined as a formal concept representing the relationships between variables such as motivation and behavior. The latter fact permits empirical testing.

Arousal is both physiological and behavioral in its makeup. The physiological component is generally objective and measurable; the psychological component is subjective and observable. The central nervous system controls physiological arousal. The brain stem, for example—particularly the reticular activating system (RAS)—controls levels of consciousness from coma or deep sleep to complete wakefulness, while the cerebral cortex (the outer layer of the brain that controls complex voluntary functions such as thinking, reasoning, motor coordination, memory, and language), in coordination with the RAS and by way of the autonomic nervous system and the endocrine system, provides for moment-to-moment, "gut-level" differences in levels of arousal. According to various theorists, moment-to-moment differences in arousal relate to the type, intensity, quality, and effectiveness of individual behavior—including stable aspects of behavior that make up a significant part of individual personality.

The individual's arousal level at any given moment is a function of stimulation (in the near past and the present), the individual's baseline (resting) level of arousal, and his or her stimulus sensitivity. A stimulus is whatever impinges on and is processed by any of the senses (for example, the warmth of a campfire on one's skin or the sound of a car horn in one's ears). The effects of stimulation are generally cumulative, persist over time, and have a direct effect on behavior.

THEORETICAL PERSPECTIVES

The Yerkes-Dodson law provides a starting point for understanding the arousal-behavior relationship. According to that early twentieth century law, there is an inverted-U relationship between motivation and performance; that is, as motivation increases, performance improves up to some point at which performance is maximized. Thereafter, increases in motivation lead to decreases in performance. Thus, the peak of the inverted U is analogous to the point of diminishing marginal returns.

Since arousal is a motivational concept, it is a simple matter to replace the motivation of the Yerkes-Dodson law with arousal, a substitution that was formalized by Donald O. Hebb in 1955. D. E. Berlyne developed this relationship further when he proposed that each individual has an optimal level of arousal (OLA) at which he or she typically feels and performs best and that each individual engages in activities that are calculated to maintain the OLA in a homeostatic (referring to the maintenance of balance or equilibrium in bodily processes) manner.

Arousal both prompts and is the consequence of behavior; for example, a person who is experiencing a low level of arousal is motivated to engage in behavior that has a high stimulus value—that will result in increased overall arousal approaching the optimum. People with chronically low resting levels of arousal will tend to be able to tolerate noise, crowds, excitement, and the like. An individual with a chronically high resting level of arousal, however, will tend to engage in behavior of modest to low stimulus value in order to avoid exceeding or deviating from his or her OLA. Such individuals tend to engage in more solitary pastimes, avoid noise, avoid crowds, and shun sensation-seeking behavior. According to Hans Eysenck, these differences in behavior, which are attributable to differing resting levels of arousal—particularly cortical arousal—are the hypothetical basis for the dimension of personality called extroversion.

ROLE OF TIME AND CIRCUMSTANCES

An individual is, however, more than a simple product of his or her mean resting arousal level. Time and circumstances can cause any individual at any given moment to be above or below the OLA and engage in behavior that is either typical or atypical. An extrovert, for example, might feel overwhelmed or become too busy and consequently seek a period of atypical peace and solitude. In addition, while some theorists have posited a single OLA for all behavior, others espouse the idea that there is a separate OLA for each possible behavior, including tasks and/or problems with different degrees of difficulty. Certain latter-day theorists have noted cogently that the extremes of arousal have both positive and negative hedonic values; that is, low arousal corresponds to boredom or relaxation depending on the situation, and high arousal similarly corresponds to either anxiety or excitement.

Arousal is, in summary, a ubiquitous, continuous, and persistent aspect of human life. It has the theoretical potential to affect—to a greater or lesser extent—virtually all behavior. Practical interests in the arousal-behavior link cover a variety of topics, including the role of arousal in performance, decision making, moods and emotions, and personality formation.

EFFECT ON TASK PERFORMANCE

Arousal affects performance in several ways: It affects how well one is able to complete difficult tasks, perform in the presence of others, and make effective decisions. In the first case, research has generally supported the idea that people perform difficult tasks best at moderate levels of arousal (at the peak of the inverted "U"), although it is possible to perform easy or moderately difficult tasks effectively over a wider range of arousal. For example, when taking an important examination, one will likely be able to answer easy test questions correctly even if one is very tired, relaxed, or anxious, whereas one will probably find more complex test items difficult to answer if one is only moderately tired or anxious. As a matter of fact, challenging questions often induce the very arousal that interferes with answering them expeditiously and correctly.

The mere presence of others seems to add another measure of difficulty to task performance. Since 1898, social psychologists have studied a phenomenon known as social facilitation. Social facilitation is the tendency of people to perform easy or well-learned tasks more effectively and difficult or poorly learned tasks less effectively in the presence of one or more other persons. Robert B. Zajonc has posited that the mere presence of others (whether they pay attention to the performer or not) is stimulating, hence arousing, and that it is this increase in arousal that causes social-facilitation effects. Thus, the presence of others might facilitate the performance of a runner but impair the performance of someone attempting to solve a complex crossword puzzle or pass a difficult exam.

AROUSAL AND DECISION-MAKING RESEARCH

Because life is full of pressure-filled and arousing moments and because there is always a demand for people who can remain coolheaded and effective under stressful conditions, researchers have been very interested in the relationship between arousal and decision making. In 1959, J. A. Easterbrook observed that increasing arousal leads to an increasing restriction of cues (stimuli/information), perhaps as a result of a narrowing of attention to essential information. Continued increases in arousal may, however, begin to narrow attention too much and thus interfere with the proper consideration of essential information. Thus, according to the combined results of several researchers, increased arousal actually facilitates the decision-making process up to a point by focusing attention on relevant information and eliminating distraction caused by extraneous detail. Increases in arousal beyond that point begin to screen out crucial information and impair decision making. Again, the Yerkes-Dodson law applies. From a practical standpoint, it seems that practice and training best enable an individual to counteract the effects of increased arousal on decision making.

RELATIONSHIP TO EMOTION

Though emotion theorists and scholars differ regarding the precise process of human emotion, they hold at least one belief in common: Autonomic nervous system arousal is central to the experience of emotion. Autonomic arousal provides the subjective physical coloring of the experience of emotion. Therefore, even the novice should not be surprised that there is an interplay between emotion and other arousal-related phenomena. For example, Dolf Zillmann noted that people who had been riding bicycles for exercise and who were angered after they ceased exercising displayed an anger that was considerably greater than might otherwise have been expected considering the circumstances. Physical exercise activates the sympathetic nervous system. After one finishes exercising, the sympathetic nervous system returns to its normal level of activation at a measured pace; thus, for some time after the completion of exercise, one is in a state of decreasing neural arousal. If one is angered during this period, the neural arousal "piggybacks" the arousal generated as the result of becoming angry, causing the anger to be inappropriately intense. This piggybacking of residual neural arousal on subsequently induced emotional arousal, which Zillmann calls the excitation-transfer process, provides a plausible explanation for the human tendency to overemote occasionally about trifling matters or events.

Individuals manifest stable differences in mean arousal level as a function of their typical arousal levels' proximity to their OLAs. People who are chronically overaroused have only a modicum of room for increased arousal before they exceed their optimal level, while those who are chronically underaroused seem to engage almost constantly in stimulus-seeking behavior. It is reasonable to posit that enduring differences in mean arousal levels lead to more or less stable patterns of behavior that are predictable and intended to optimize arousal. Thus, individual differences in baseline arousal and sensitivity to further arousal may lead to personality formation in the way that Eysenck suggests.

Eysenck has hypothesized that extroversion is composed of two first-order factors: sociability and impulsivity. Extroversion, sociability, and impulsivity are supposed to relate to arousal negatively and linearly, which suggests, for example, that the less aroused a person typically is, the more sociable and impulsive he or she will be; the more aroused someone is, the less sociable and more controlled he or she will be. Eysenck's theory has inspired considerable research that has yielded illuminating and theory-consistent results. In addition to a large body of research that, when synthesized, finds substantial support for the predicted relationships between various indices of physiological arousal and extroversion, other experimental studies provide theory-consistent results such as the ability of extroverts to tolerate significantly higher levels of noise and pain than introverts and the ability of introverts to detect

audio or video signals at a significantly lower intensity threshold than extroverts (an indication of greater stimulus sensitivity). Such findings have useful applications in determining individual occupational and situational suitability.

NEWER RESEARCH

Though the inverted U of the Yerkes-Dodson law was an early twentieth century conceptualization, it was not until the 1950's that arousal theory emerged to adopt the inverted U. Following the 1949 discovery of the reticular formation's "arousing" function, a number of arousal theories of motivation, including Hebb's, were developed. All these theories incorporated the idea that the human being could be underaroused or overaroused. The reticular activating system, in conjunction with the cerebral cortex, was viewed as the homeostatic mechanism for maintaining a balance—or optimal level—of arousal. As a result, optimal arousal theory had a describable and measurable theoretical basis.

The early arousal theories touted a simplified notion of the relationship between indices of arousal and human behavior. There was a tendency to believe that virtually any of a variety of measures of physiological arousal would correlate well with behavioral measures of arousal as well as with one another. The results of research sometimes confirmed and sometimes contradicted this simplistic approach. Behavioral-level measures of arousal were not always well conceptualized: The central nervous system clearly did not act in simple unison with arousal. The results of research varied with the particular choice of cortical and/or autonomic arousal measure. Using heart rate as a measure, for example, has generally resulted in equivocal results in the study of the relationship between extroversion and arousal. This probably does not mean that the theory is invalid. The heart rate apparently has no simple relationship with cortical arousal. In addition, problems were caused by the design of the behavior measures, the types of experimental activity in which the subjects were engaged, the time of day, and the simplified notion that too much and too little arousal take on only negative hedonic (associated with the seeking of pleasure and the avoidance of pain) significance.

The results of research through the early 1970's suggested that arousal theory had validity but contradicted the simple theoretical connection between behavior and physiology that had been postulated. Such research has led to the modification of some theories and the formation of others. Eysenck, for example, shifted his theoretical focus from chronic or resting levels of arousal underlying extroversion to differences in underlying arousal potential (for example, stimulus sensitivity). Michael J. Apter, on the other hand, offered a new theoretical formation that accounts for the dual hedonic nature of high and low arousal. Apter posited two biological arousal systems, the telic and paratelic, which are roughly equivalent to introversion and extroversion and which underlie the dual metamotivational states. The future of optimal arousal theory seems to lie with the further development of theories that account for the ambiguities of past research, the apparent complexities of biological arousal systems, and the revision of behavioral-level arousal measures to fit the data that have been gathered.

SOURCES FOR FURTHER STUDY

Apter, Michael J., David Fontana, and Stephen J. Murgatroyd. *Reversal Theory: Applications and Developments.* Hillsdale, N.J.: Lawrence Erlbaum, 1986. Reviews Apter's theory, applicable research results, applications to individual and social phenomena, and theoretical developments.

Berlyne, D. E. *Conflict, Arousal, and Curiosity.* New York: McGraw-Hill, 1960. Berlyne presents his theoretical propositions for a motivation of perceptual and intellectual activities, including his notions about intermediate/optimal arousal levels.

Evans, Phil. *Motivation and Emotion.* New York: Routledge, 1989. In a chapter entitled "An Energizing Force," Evans covers the development of arousal theory, critiques the theory, notes its strengths and weaknesses, summarizes the findings of related research, and concludes with an assessment of Apter's latter-day reversal theory.

Eysenck, Hans Jurgen. *Personality, Genetics, and Behavior.* New York: Praeger, 1982. Eysenck presents selected papers dealing with his arousal-based theory of personality—especially extroversion. The opening chapter provides an excellent review of the development of his theory and its basis in arousal.

Geen, R. G. "Human Motivation: New Perspectives on Old Problems." In *The G. Stanley Hall Lecture Series.* Vol. 4. Washington, D.C.: American Psychological Association, 1984. In this 1984 state-of-motivation lecture, Geen primarily addresses latter-day arousal theories such as the dual arousal model and reversal theory and discusses trends in the field of motivation.

Ronald G. Ribble

SEE ALSO: Brain structures; Decision making; Emotions; Hormones and behavior; Motivation; Nervous system; Neurons.

P

Pain

TYPE OF PSYCHOLOGY: Biological bases of behavior; sensation and perception

FIELDS OF STUDY: Auditory, chemical, cutaneous, and body senses; biological treatments; nervous system

Pain is an extremely important sensation or perception, warning a person of actual or potential injury or disease. Chronic pain may debilitate and distress a person far beyond the condition that triggered it. Theories of pain and analgesia have provided an understanding of diverse psychological phenomena, ranging from phantom limb pain to the placebo effect, and led to new psychological and biological treatments for both acute and chronic pain.

KEY CONCEPTS
- analgesia
- endorphin
- nociceptor
- opiate
- placebo effect
- primary afferent neuron
- receptor

INTRODUCTION

Pain is the physical or mental suffering caused by injury or disease. It is characterized variously as a sensation of pricking, burning, aching, stinging, or soreness. It is a highly individual and plastic (changeable) experience, influenced by factors such as drugs, surgery, hypnosis, fear, joy, stress, social ritual, status, sex, social interaction, and even culture. Pain is not a uniquely human experience; it is common to almost all animals.

Pain sensations may be triggered by a wide variety of stimuli—anything that causes tissue injury (for example, intense heat or cold, excessive pressure or stretching, cutting or piercing). Tissue in-

jury is not required, however. For example, damaging X and gamma radiation causes tissue injury but not pain, while touching the eyeball or eardrum causes pain without tissue injury. Furthermore, psychological states can cause pain in the absence of tissue injury. Examples include stress manifesting as stomach pain or memories of a trauma experienced as recurring pain in an involved body part. Some rare individuals are born without the ability to feel pain, and often injure themselves severely without knowing it.

The pain experience begins with the primary afferent neurons. Their specialized receptor endings, the free nerve endings, are triggered by painful stimuli and send their messages to the spinal cord via two distinct bundles of fibers—A delta and C fibers. The A delta fibers, most sensitive to mechanical pressure and damaging heat, are associated with the sensation of sharp, pricking pain. The C fibers (polymodal nociceptors), most sensitive to chemical stimuli, are associated with long-lasting, burning pain. When stimulated, these fibers release multiple neurotransmitters, including Substance P and glutamate, onto secondary neurons in the dorsal horn of the spinal cord. Finally, there are small interneurons, which run between dorsal horn neurons and release opioids, GABA (an inhibitory neurotransmitter), and other chemicals to decrease the pain signal.

These secondary dorsal horn neurons then transmit pain signals to the brain. One component of this system, the neo- or lateral spinothalamic tract (pathway), carries messages to the thalamus and may enable a person to localize sharp or acute pain. The thalamus is a set of structures in the forward part of the brain (forebrain) that receives and forwards messages from all sensory systems.

Another component, the paleospinothalamic (or spinoreticular) tract, carries pain messages to the brain stem (lower brain) reticular formation, with only a few cells going to the thalamus. Since the reticular formation is responsible for maintaining wakefulness and alertness, pain and other noxious (dangerous) stimuli may alert a person via this pathway. Paleospinothalamic fibers, also called multireceptive or wide dynamic range nociceptors, react to both noxious and non-noxious stimuli, and may be responsible for carrying the diffuse pain messages of chronic pain.

A third component, the spinotectal tract, sends fibers to the midbrain (middle brain), especially an area called the periaqueductal gray. Both the periaquaductal gray and the thalamus connect to the limbic system, an area of the brain associated with emotions. Scientists suspect that limbic input influences the emotional part of the pain experience.

Pain messages are sent finally to the cortex (the highest forebrain area): from the forebrain thalamus to specific areas of the cortex; from the midbrain reticular formation to the cortex in a diffuse, nonspecific way; and from the midbrain periaqueductal area to the cortex indirectly, through connections with the limbic system.

A simple ascending model of the pain system, however, does not account for a variety of human pain experiences. For example, rubbing an injured limb can reduce pain, as can strong emotions. To account for such phenomena, in 1965, Ronald Melzack and Patrick Wall postulated a "gating mechanism" within the spinal cord that would prevent pain signals from traveling from the spinal cord to the brain. Rubbing the skin would presumably close the gate. Most important, Melzack and Wall hypothesized that the brain itself could send signals down to the spinal cord to close the gate directly, thus shutting off pain messages at their source.

Although incorrect in its details, this theory was of great significance because it drew attention to the psychological aspects of pain—the role of emotion and motivation in the pain experience—and integrated these psychological aspects with the traditional, purely sensory account of pain. It also encouraged scientists to look for descending components of the pain system. It is now known that the pain signal is heavily modified by descending tracts at the spinal cord level. Under conditions of external threat, injury, or emotional stress, descending tracts from the brain release opioids and hormones, such as cortisol, that decrease the pain signal that is perceived. This phenomenon may be observed in wounded soldiers who continue to function under

fire with minimal perception of pain until the attack ceases. Two of the most important of these tracts use the neurotransmitters norepinephrine and serotonin to reduce the pain signal. These tracts malfunction in people with depression, increasing their experience of pain.

PAIN RESEARCH

Basic animal research has been successfully applied to the treatment of pain in people. For example, in experiments with rats, electrical stimulation of the periaqueductal gray made the animals less sensitive to pain. When other brain areas were similarly stimulated, no such pain reduction occurred. Subsequently, electrical stimulation techniques for both the brain and spinal cord were developed to reduce chronic pain in human patients. Former Alabama governor George Wallace, crippled with chronic pain by an attacker's bullet, had electrodes implanted over the pain pathways in his spinal cord. Using a dorsal column stimulator, a cigarette-packsized device, he was able to send small amounts of electrical current into the spinal cord. Pain relief occurred without the undesirable drowsiness and constipation associated with pain-killing drugs such as morphine. Similarly, cancer patients with chronic pain can sometimes gain relief with electrical stimulation delivered through electrodes implanted directly into their brains. Unfortunately, the effects of electrical brain and spinal cord stimulation are relatively short-lived, and, like traditional, addictive pain-killing medications, their analgesic effects tend to lessen with time.

Pain research has led to a better understanding of acupuncture, a technique used for centuries in China to relieve pain. Acupuncturists insert fine needles through the skin and rotate them. The specific points stimulated, however, do not correspond to any known neural pathways. For this reason, Western physicians categorically rejected this approach as nonscientific for many years. During the 1960's, however, American scientists visited China and observed painless surgery using only acupuncture anesthesia in awake patients. Convinced that the phenomenon was real, they began searching for new explanations.

Animal research provided an answer. Two groups of rats were first given a painful (but not injurious) heat stimulus to their tails. The control group was then given acupuncture stimulation to relieve the pain. The experimental group was first treated with naloxone and then given acupuncture. Naloxone is a substance which acts in the brain as an opiate antagonist; that is, it can bind to the brain receptor sites normally reserved for the body's own opiates and thus block the normal action of the opiates. Pain was reduced in the control but not the experimental group, suggesting that acupuncture analgesia is mediated by an endogenous opiate analgesia system. With this new understanding, acceptance of the technique for the management of pain has grown significantly. Some clinics now offer this noninvasive method of pain relief to women during labor.

External events and even mental states can affect the experience of pain. Soldiers severely injured during battle often fail to notice the injury until long after the battle is over, and patients given a sugar pill (a placebo) for pain often obtain relief. Basic research has provided further insights into the mechanisms by which this occurs.

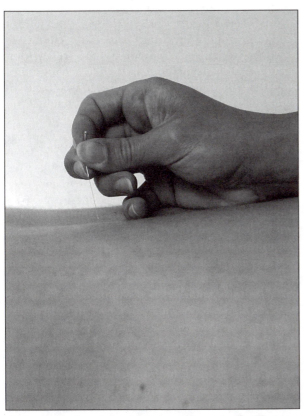

Acupuncture has gained some acceptance in the West as a method of pain relief. (PhotoDisc)

In one laboratory study, rats were placed in a steep-walled container filled with cold water from which escape was impossible. They had to swim to avoid drowning. After a few minutes, they were removed from the water and their pain thresholds were tested using a heat stimulus applied to their tails. The thresholds were found to be significantly elevated (they felt less pain) for several hours compared to before the swim. Thus, environmental stressors were shown to produce pain relief. Other studies have shown that some of the analgesic effects of stress (and the placebo effect) result from the release of endogenous opiates. If the opiate antagonist naloxone is given to the rats before they are exposed to cold-water stress, the elevation in their pain thresholds is blocked.

Researchers have also found that stress, opiate analgesia, and immunity are related. Large doses of the drug morphine can suppress immunity. Moreover, stress can trigger the release of endorphins both to reduce pain and to suppress the immune system (by reducing the number of natural killer cells released from the spleen).

PAIN STUDY

The study of pain must have emerged from the human desire to eliminate it. Various folk remedies for pain have existed since the time of Scribonius Largus, the Roman physician (43 C.E.) who used electric eels to reduce pain, often killing his patients in the process. Formal scientific study of the causes and treatment of pain, however, was practically unknown until the 1970's. Progress in this area was hampered by several factors. Researchers were reluctant to acknowledge that studies of animal pain might be relevant for the study of human pain, particularly since human pain appeared to be so plastic. Adequate techniques for accurately measuring pain in humans or animals were also slow to develop. Interest in pain research reached critical mass in 1974, leading to the appearance of *Pain*, the first journal entirely dedicated to reporting pain research. The 1970's also brought two key discoveries in pain research: Neurochemist Candace Pert found opiate receptors in the rat brain, and neurochemist Choh Li subsequently identified endogenous opiates (endorphins and enkephalins).

In 1971, psychologist Huda Akil discovered that brain stimulation with electrical current or opiates could reduce pain in animals. This finding, taken together with the discovery of endogenous opiates and their receptors, quickly led scientists to realize that in addition to the well-known ascending pathways that mediated pain, there were also descending, perhaps opiate-related, pathways that could modify pain. This realization revolutionized the study of pain, focusing attention sharply on the interaction between ascending and descending pain systems.

Interest in pain research and treatment received a further boost in the 1980's, when the World Health Organization, under its chief Jan Stjermsward, launched a series of major initiatives to increase international awareness of pain, improve training in pain management, and provide access to pain medication in underserved countries.

Psychologists have been concerned with pain from both the clinical and basic research perspectives. Pain as a topic has supplied the context and motivation for much productive interdisciplinary work. The efforts of molecular biologists, pharmacologists, electrophysiologists, neurochemists, neurosurgeons, biomedical engineers, and computer modelers, as well as physiological and clinical psychologists, have combined to propel the investigation of pain ahead at a rapid rate.

Psychologists have had a profound impact on the study of pain by other scientists and, in turn, have been influenced by them. They have carefully documented the behavioral phenomena to be explained (for those seeking to understand the chemistry and anatomy of pain), such as phantom limb pain (pain seeming to come from a limb that has been removed), analgesia associated with sex and defeat, the placebo effect, the "high" of the long-distance runner, the modifiable pain of childbirth, the analgesic effects of stress, and the role of emotions, cognition, and motivation in modifying sensory experience. Psychologists have also provided the sophisticated psychophysical techniques needed to assess pain, and framed the behavioral questions to be considered by nonbehavioral researchers. Psychologists have been at the forefront in developing behavioral and biological techniques to manage pain.

Reciprocally, neurochemical, neurophysiological, and neuroanatomical studies have guided psychologists toward a new understanding of how behavioral systems are organized in the brain. Opiate receptors of various types have been identified in many brain areas, not only those associated with pain. They appear to have a broad range of behavioral functions, ranging from the regulation of food intake to sex, emotion, vision, hearing, biological rhythms, aggression, and sleep.

Fortunately, advances in the study of pain have had a rapid and direct impact on human health. They have already revolutionized the medical treatment of pain and have also contributed to the improved psychological treatment of pain. Ultimately, a more coherent picture of the complex interactions of pain and the cognitive, emotional, and motivational systems of the brain will emerge, and with it a more enlightened approach to both the biological and psychological treatments of pain.

SOURCES FOR FURTHER STUDY

Basbaum, Allan J., and Thomas M. Jessell. "The Perception of Pain." In *Principles of Neural Science*, edited by Eric R. Kandel and James H. Schwartz. 4th ed. New York: McGraw-Hill, 2000. An excellent neuroscience text geared toward the upper-level undergraduate, graduate student, or professional, with detailed chapters on neuroanatomy, neurophysiology, and other cutaneous senses (touch), in addition to the well-written and clear pain chapter. Extensive bibliography, pictures and diagrams, and subject and name indices, bring the reader quickly to seminal research in the field.

Melzack, Ronald, and Patrick D. Wall. *The Challenge of Pain*. 3d ed. New York: Penguin, 1996. A detailed and thorough treatment of the subject for a nontechnical audience, written by major theorists in the field. Discusses types of clinical pain, physiological mechanisms, the evolution of pain theories, and pain control techniques. Contains references, glossary, index, and illustrations.

_____, eds. *Textbook of Pain*. 4th ed. New York: W. B. Saunders, 2000. A 1,588-page textbook with exhaustive coverage of all aspects of pain physiology and treatment.

Neal, Helen. *The Politics of Pain*. New York: McGraw-Hill, 1978. Discusses pain from the patient's rather than the scientist's point of view. Explores the religious, psychological, and cultural aspects of pain; neglect of pain in children; the cancer industry; patient activism in the face of medical ignorance and unwillingness to respond to patients' pain; and the role of pharmaceutical companies. Dated in some respects, but places pain research and clinical practice in their proper political, social, and economic contexts.

Nancy Oley;
updated by Elizabeth Haase

SEE ALSO: Biofeedback and relaxation; Emotions; Endorphins; Nervous system; Pain management; Sensation and perception; Senses; Stress; Touch and pressure.

Pain management

TYPE OF PSYCHOLOGY: Biological bases of behavior; cognition; emotion; sensation and perception; stress

FIELDS OF STUDY: Auditory, chemical, cutaneous, and body senses; behavioral therapies; biological treatments; cognitive processes; coping

Pain is not simply a physical sensation; it also has important psychological components, including attention and the significance of the injury to the person. In addition, various secondary reinforcers may serve to sustain the pain experience. Psychological approaches to pain management take these factors into account. These approaches include hypnosis, biofeedback, operant conditioning, and the cognitive behavioral therapy.

KEY CONCEPTS

- acute pain
- biofeedback
- chronic pain
- cognitive behavioral therapy
- hypnosis
- psychopharmacology
- reinforcement
- secondary reinforcers

INTRODUCTION

Contemporary attempts to define pain specify the inclusion of both physiological and psychological components. That is, at least in higher species, pain is not simply a function of bodily damage alone. The amount and quality of pain are also influenced by a number of psychological factors. These include the focus of one's attention, one's thoughts concerning the pain (including one's understanding of its consequences), one's culture, and the degree to which one feels that one can, at least partially, control the pain. These elements, originating from the cortex, thalamus, and limbic system, modulate pain in the body via descending neural tracts in the spinal cord.

The interaction of psychology and physiology is demonstrated by the phenomenon of stress-induced analgesia. Stress brought on by swimming in cold water, by running a marathon, or perhaps by being wounded in battle results in the production of the body's own chemical pain suppressors, the endorphins (endogenous morphines), to help suppress the pain.

The influence of psychological factors on pain is also demonstrated in research on the effects of placebos. Although not all people respond to placebos, about one-third do obtain relief comparable to the effects of the drug presumed to be administered. Research has shown that the pain suppression effect of a placebo is influenced by several factors. These include the assumed strength of the drug being administered as well as the dosage—that is, two placebo capsules produce twice the effect of one capsule. Factors that have been found to influence the level of placebo analgesia include the level of anxiety of the patient (anxious persons are more responsive) and the doctor-patient relationship. The placebo effect may, in some cases, be mediated by the production of endorphins.

Cognitive factors may also be critical in the perception and control of pain. In a classic study conducted by Richard Nisbett and Stanley Schachter, participants were given a pill that presumably contained a drug. Some of the participants were led to believe that this drug would produce pain-associated sensations: heart palpitations, breathing irregularities, and butterflies in the stomach. That is, they were led to believe that the pill they had taken would cause the same physical reactions as a painful stimulus. Other participants were led to believe that the drug would produce pain-irrelevant effects such as an itching sensation, numb feet, and possibly a mild headache. After taking the pill, participants received electric shocks. Those participants who had received the pain-relevant instructions were able to tolerate four times as much shock as those in the pain-irrelevant condition, suggesting that intellectual knowledge of what to expect decreased how much the shocks "hurt." This study clearly indicates that people's attributions and thoughts can influence the experience of pain.

The importance of cognition to the experience of pain is also demonstrated in a study conducted by Philip Zimbardo and others. These researchers found that those participants in their study who were led to believe they had little justification for experiencing pain not only reported less pain but actually experienced less pain (as reflected by galvanic skin response) than those who had greater justification.

A number of cultural differences have also been found with respect to the experience of pain. These differences indicate the importance of expectations—that is, whether one has learned that a particular experience is painful—on the experience of pain. Using childbirth as an example, Americans expect labor and delivery to be painful. Yet, as Ronald Melzack mentions in his book *The Puzzle of Pain* (1973), women in many other cultures have much less distress during childbirth. In some cultures, it is the husband who gets in bed and moans and groans as if in pain. Even in Scandinavia, which enjoys a standard of living comparable to that of the United States, women are far less likely to require medication when delivering a child than are American or English women.

The meaning of the situation is also a critical psychological variable influencing the experience of pain. A dramatic example of the importance of this was observed on the battlefields of World War II. While many of the casualties had experienced considerable physical trauma, only a minority complained of enough pain to require morphine, even though they were sensitive enough to feel the pain of an injection. The vast majority of persons experiencing similar injury in civilian life, however, do require morphine. The difference is the significance of the event. For soldiers, the injury meant that they would be sent home—not whole, perhaps, but at least alive.

Finally, pain states can be caused by or modulated by many psychiatric illnesses. Somatoform disorder is an illness in which the patient has pain in at least six body organs, none of which show tissue injury. In conversion disorders, patients develop physical symptoms such as blindness, paralysis, or paresthesias (painful tingling in the limbs) in response to a stress—again, without physical injury.

Patients with major depression develop a general increase in pain sensitivity, as well as more acute pains such as headaches and backaches, due to dysregulation of neurotransmitters which play a role in both pain and depression. Psychotic illnesses and anxiety disorders can also be associated with pain states.

PAIN MANAGEMENT TECHNIQUES

Several techniques have been found to be effective for the management of acute or recurring pain. Two of these are hypnosis and biofeedback.

Hypnosis has been found to be effective as the sole or supplementary anesthetic for a variety of painful procedures including tooth extractions, surgery, and the pain of childbirth. Two important factors influencing the effectiveness of hypnosis in pain relief are the patient's ability to be hypnotized and the therapist's ability to elicit responses appropriate and adequate to bring about useful perceptual alterations. According to Josephine Hilgard, the best candidates for hypnosis are those people who have a rich imagination, enjoy daydreaming, and can generate vivid mental images. Hypnotic management of pain includes specific suggestions of dissociation (reducing emotional involvement), distraction, changing interpretation of body signals, displacing pain to a different body part, and/or suggestions of numbness.

Psychologists have used biofeedback to help people control recurrent pain. The object of this technique is for the person to learn to use higher mental processes to regulate physiological functioning. To do this, the person must learn to discriminate subtle internal cues associated with desired physiological changes and reproduce these cues at will. Biofeedback also facilitates the learning of relaxation, which may reduce chronic pain involving muscle contraction. Biofeedback encourages involvement (therefore, distraction) and provides the person with a coping strategy. The effect is to increase the person's perception of his or her control of the pain.

The most frequent use of biofeedback involves the use of electromyography (EMG) for reducing muscle tension associated with a variety of conditions including tension headache, chronic back pain, and muscle tension pain in the neck and shoulders. EMG measures the electrical activity of muscle fibers, thus serving as an index of muscle contraction or relaxation. EMG can be effective if the pain is in the muscle being monitored (rather than referred pain) and is sufficiently close to the surface that the muscle activity can be sensed.

Temperature feedback is used to assist people who suffer from vascular (migraine) headaches. A thermometer is put on the index finger and the person is told that blood is flowing to the periphery, or that his or her hand is warming. The effect of this is to bring about the suggested change and, thus, reduce pressure within the blood vessels surrounding the brain, which, in turn, reduces pain.

BEHAVIORAL APPROACHES

Psychological approaches have also been adapted to help people deal with chronic pain. These include operant and cognitive behavioral approaches.

The object of the operant approach is to reduce the excessive disability associated with the pain problem, rather than to reduce the pain itself. The first step in this procedure is one of confrontation and education, that is, to convince the person that he or she can do more even if the pain continues. Typically, it is the family that serves as the primary reinforcer of disability and activity. Therefore, their cooperation and involvement are essential if this approach is to be effective in the long term. The most common reinforcers used in the treatment are praise and attention. Rest may also be used as a reinforcer following the completion of activities. Undesirable behaviors, such as talking about the pain or screaming, are not rewarded with attention. Desired behaviors are broken down into small increments. The pain patient is encouraged to do more and more over time. This gradually results in the person being able to engage in more normal activities. As activity increases, there is a progressive withdrawal from pain medications.

The focus of the cognitive behavioral approach is to convince the person that the pain is at least partially under his or her control. The person is provided with a range of coping skills to help deal with maladaptive thoughts and noxious sensations that may contribute to the suffering. In contrast to the behavioral approach, the cognitive approach does not view the person as passive. Instead, it places emphasis on the fact that people are active processors of their environment. This approach generally employs relaxation training, either for its direct effects (the reduction of arousal) or for its cognitive

effect (distraction). Deliberate attempts to distract are also employed. This may involve having the person listen to an interesting talk show rather than to music; it may involve having the person engage in an activity that requires close attention and thus serves to direct his or her attention outward. This approach also uses cognitive restructuring. First, the therapist elicits the unique thoughts and feelings the individual associates with pain—for example, that his or her continued pain signals a life-threatening condition. The therapist then attempts to elicit competing thoughts from the person, perhaps that the pain has always subsided in the past and will this time as well. In addition, coping imagery is often employed. This involves having the person imagine he or she is becoming anxious and is beginning to experience pain. The person then is asked to imagine himself or herself successfully coping with the pain using the techniques that have been learned.

PHARMACEUTICAL TREATMENTS

Medications are used to augment psychological management strategies. Over-the-counter nonsteroidal anti-inflammatory drugs such as acetaminophen, aspirin, and stronger prescription drugs like them are the most widely used pain medications. The World Health Organization recommends that they be used throughout a pain treatment. For more severe pain, such as cancer pain, long-acting opiate drugs, such as oxycodone, morphine sulfate, and methadone, are added. Shorter-acting opiates are then added for pain that "breaks through" this core treatment.

Antidepressant drugs are commonly used to treat pain. Since the 1960's, tricyclic antidepressants such as amitriptyline and imipramine have been shown to be beneficial adjuvants to a pain treatment. These medicines act on noradrenergic pathways. Serotonin reuptake inhibitor drugs, such as paroxetine and citalopram, are effective for pain due to their action on serotonin receptors in inflamed tissue, the descending serotonergic tract of the spinal cord, and the serotonergic neurons that modulate opiate pathways in the peri-aquaductal gray. Many other types of medicine, acting on the multiple systems that modulate pain, are also used in pain control.

NECESSITY OF PAIN RESEARCH

With the exception of a very few individuals, every person occasionally experiences acute pain. This may be the result of a toothache, cuts or bruises received while engaging in an athletic event, or countless other sources of injury. In addition, tens of millions of people in America, and probably hundreds of millions of people around the world, suffer from the effects of chronic pains, lower-back pain, arthritis, and various forms of headache. Migraine headaches alone are thought to cost up to seventeen billion dollars in lost productivity annually. In addition to the financial costs, untreated pain has a host of negative health consequences, including lower immune function, increased tumor growth, and the health consequences of self-medication through substance abuse.

Despite these deleterious effects, pain remains an underrecognized and undertreated social problem. On medical wards, up to half of patients suffer with untreated pain. Reasons include patient stoicism and fears of addiction, and doctors' lack of pain management training. Although studies have repeatedly shown that pain treatment does not lead to addiction, fears persist. Psychological methods of pain control can help lessen fears of dependency on medication and enhance appropriate medication use.

Pain management is a truly interdisciplinary concern. Future development will be dependent upon the cooperation of people in the fields of neurology, neurosurgery, psychology, psychiatry, and many other disciplines. This cooperation will undoubtedly result in an increased understanding of pain and a reduction of human suffering, and will also facilitate efforts to gain a better understanding of the interaction of mind and body.

Sources for Further Study

Barber, Joseph, and Cheri Adrian, eds. *Psychological Approaches to the Management of Pain.* New York: Brunner/Mazel, 1982. A compilation of selections, written by authorities from both research and applied areas, concerned with psychology of pain control. Major topics include the use of hypnosis (including self-hypnosis) for the control of pain, the management of acute pain, and the treatments used in interdisciplinary pain clinics.

Bresler, David E., and Richard Trubo. *Free Yourself from Pain.* New York: Awareness Press, 1999. Discusses the nature and control of pain, as well as a number of both traditional and unconventional therapies used in pain management. Numerous self-help forms are included.

Hiesiger, Emile, and Kathleen Brady. *Your Pain Is Real: Free Yourself from Chronic Pain with Breakthrough Medical Discoveries.* New York: HarperCollins, 2001. Neurologist and pain management specialist Hiesiger seeks to empower the chronic pain sufferer. Similar in content to *The Pain Relief Handbook* but more recent.

Nown, Graham, and Chris Wells. *The Pain Relief Handbook: Self-Help Methods for Managing Pain.* New York: Firefly Books, 1998. A comprehensive layman's guide to understanding and managing chronic pain, with illustrations and an elaborate resource guide.

Robert D. Johnson;
updated by Elizabeth Haase

See also: Attention; Biofeedback and relaxation; Hypnosis; Meditation and relaxation; Pain; Stress: Physiological responses.

Paranoia

Type of psychology: Psychopathology
Fields of study: Psychosis

Paranoia is a term that has been generally used by the public to indicate any type of suspiciousness. Professionals reserve the use of the term for persons showing extreme suspicion of other people and their motives. The level of suspiciousness is delusional. Paranoia was once used as a diagnosis, but currently the diagnosis of delusional disorder has been developed to signify delusional paranoia.

Key concepts
- delusional disorder
- delusional system
- erotomanic type
- grandiose type
- jealous type
- paranoid social cognition
- persecutory type
- repression
- schizophrenia
- somatic type

INTRODUCTION

Paranoia is defined as a psychiatric disorder in which a person has a group of false beliefs or delusions. The person with paranoia cannot be argued out of believing that the delusions are true. Usually when paranoia is present, a network or system of interconnecting false beliefs is present in the person's mind. Paranoia is no longer used as a diagnosis. Today when a person has been found to show paranoia, a diagnosis of delusional disorder is made.

The use of the term "paranoia" has a long history that extends back to the ancient Greeks and Romans. The word "paranoia" derives from the Greek words meaning "beside" and "mind." The Greeks and Romans used the term to describe a wide variety of mental disorders, and their use does not reflect the current utilization of the term.

During the 1800's, paranoia began to be defined by experts in the field of psychiatry as a mental condition influencing how a person conceptualized the surrounding environment. In 1863, Karl Kahlbaum (1828-1899) used the term "paranoia" to describe a state of partial insanity that affected the intellect, but not other areas of mental functioning. In the view of Kahlbaum, a person with paranoia held a group of false beliefs to be true. Emil Kraepelin (1856-1926) expanded on this concept by characterizing paranoia as a condition with a persistent delusional system of false belief that a person held to be true despite evidence to the contrary. Eugen Bleuler (1857-1939) believed that paranoia was a distinct but rare psychiatric disorder.

Sigmund Freud (1856-1939) wrote that paranoia developed from homosexual impulses that caused a person great distress. Because of the anxiety, the person would use repression to force the impulses into the unconscious mind. Once in the unconscious mind, the threatening impulses would show themselves in the form of suspiciousness and fear of being persecuted. Today the ideas of Freud are useful only as suggestions of how the unconscious may affect behavior, but the sexual connotations are no longer seen as significant in the development of paranoia.

EXTENT OF THE PROBLEM

Paranoia or delusional disorder has been found to be a rare condition with an annual incidence of one to three new cases per 100,000 persons each year in the United States. Usually the age of onset for the disorder is around forty years of age, but persons have been diagnosed with the condition from adolescence to late adulthood. Females show a slight edge in the number of persons diagnosed with delusional disorder. In general, it is believed that the condition is unreported because few people with delusional disorder seek professional help.

DIAGNOSIS

It can be difficult to diagnose paranoia because of the imprecise nature of the symptoms. Many people believe ideas that cannot be proven empirically or that are definitely false. To assist with the diagnosis of paranoia, the psychiatric community suggests that formal identification of delusions requires consideration of the beliefs and ideas in a person's own community. If the community would label a belief as preposterous, then paranoia can be considered as a diagnosis.

For a diagnosis of delusional disorder to be made, the false beliefs must not appear to be bizarre. This means that the delusional ideas could be possible. For example, a person believing a flying hamburger is attempting to devour him would have a bizarre delusion. Bizarre delusions are usually associated with schizophrenia, which is a severe psychiatric disorder in which a person loses reasoning capacity, has a severe disruption in mood state, shows disorganized speech, and may experience hallucinations.

Delusional disorder exists in the form of different types that indicate the content of the delusions. The persecutory type is found when a person falsely believes that someone is spying, stalking, or spreading false rumors about him or her. Sometimes the person with a persecutory type of delusional disorder can be dangerous to others, threatening or carrying out acts of violence. The jealous type is found when a person is convinced that a sexual partner is unfaithful. The grandiose type believes that he or she has unusual powers, talents, or a special relationship with someone with a celebrity status. Another type of delusional disorder is the erotomanic type. This type involves the false belief that someone of high status or importance is in love with the delusional person. The somatic type has an extreme belief that he or she has some physical illness or medical condition.

DSM-IV-TR Criteria for Paranoia

DELUSIONAL DISORDER (DSM CODE 297.1)

Nonbizarre delusions (involving situations occurring in real life, such as being followed, poisoned, infected, loved at a distance, or deceived by spouse or lover, or having a disease) of at least one month's duration

Symptoms for schizophrenia not met; tactile and olfactory hallucinations may be present if related to delusional theme

Apart from impact of delusion(s) or its ramifications, functioning not markedly impaired and behavior not obviously odd or bizarre

If mood episodes have occurred concurrently with delusions, their total duration has been brief relative to duration of delusional periods

Disturbance not due to direct physiological effects of a substance or general medical condition

Type based on predominant delusional theme:
- Erotomanic Type: Delusions that another person, usually of higher status, is in love with individual
- Grandiose Type: Delusions of inflated worth, power, knowledge, identity, or special relationship to deity or famous person
- Jealous Type: Delusions that individual's sexual partner is unfaithful
- Persecutory Type: Delusions that person (or someone to whom person is close) is being malevolently treated in some way
- Somatic Type: Delusions that person has some physical defect or general medical condition
- Mixed Type: Delusions characteristic of more than one of above types but no one theme predominates
- Unspecified Type

PARANOID PERSONALITY DISORDER (DSM CODE 301.0)

Pervasive distrust and suspiciousness of others such that their motives are interpreted as malevolent, beginning by early adulthood and present in variety of contexts

Indicated by four or more of the following:
- suspects, without sufficient basis, that others are exploiting, harming, or deceiving him or her
- preoccupied with unjustified doubts about loyalty or trustworthiness of friends or associates
- reluctant to confide in others because of unwarranted fear that information will be used maliciously against him or her
- reads hidden demeaning or threatening meanings into benign remarks or events
- persistently bears grudges (unforgiving of insults, injuries, or slights)
- perceives attacks on his or her character or reputation not apparent to others and quick to react angrily or counterattack
- has recurrent suspicions, without justification, regarding fidelity of spouse or sexual partner

Does not occur exclusively during course of schizophrenia, a mood disorder with psychotic features, or another psychotic disorder and not due to direct physiological effects of a general medical condition

(SCHIZOPHRENIA) PARANOID TYPE (DSM CODE 295.30)

Type of Schizophrenia involving preoccupation with one or more delusions or frequent auditory hallucinations

None of the following is prominent:
- disorganized speech
- disorganized or catatonic behavior
- flat or inappropriate affect

POSSIBLE CAUSES

The causes of delusional disorder are not known, but delusional disorder appears to develop slowly over a period of time. The person who develops the disorder usually has a group of personality characteristics including being standoffish, unfriendly, and emotionally cold. Usually a pattern emerges in which the person blames others for their failures and disappointments. This leads to a paranoid social cognition as a constant interpretation of the world.

TREATMENT

There is no one treatment for persons with delusional disorder. It has been found that once the delusional system has been established, it is extremely difficult to remove or modify it. In order for psychotherapy to be effective, a relationship needs to be developed between the patient and the therapist. However, communication with a person who has a delusional disorder is very difficult, and such a patient will usually refuse offers of medication. The group of drugs called antipsychotic medications, including haloperidol and pimozide, are often tried for treatment, but the medications are usually not taken with any regularity. Many persons with this disorder are hospitalized if they become a threat to other people, but once the person renounces the delusion, he or she will be discharged. The long-term prognosis for the successful treatment of delusional disorder has been poor.

SOURCES FOR FURTHER STUDY

Chadwick, Paul, M. J. Birchwood, and Peter Trower. *Cognitive Therapy for Delusions, Voices, and Paranoia.* New York: John Wiley & Sons, 1996. Written for psychologists and therapists, offers guidelines for diagnosing paranoia and delusional disorders and analyses the usefulness of cognitive therapy for dealing with them.

Gabbard, G., S. Lazar, and D. Spiegel. "The Economic Impact of Psychotherapy: A Review." *American Journal of Psychiatry* 154 (1997): 147-155. This is a study on the benefits of attempting psychological treatment with persons who have delusional disorder. Although it is a difficult process, the long-term benefits are significant.

Kinderman, P., and R. Bentall. "Causal Attributions in Paranoia and Depression: Internal, Personal, and Situational Attributions for Negative Events." *Journal of Abnormal Psychology* 106 (1997): 341-345. The underlying cognitive processes found in delusional disorder are reviewed. The authors discuss how the delusional person generalizes small negative events to a broader context.

Kramer, M. "Paranoid Cognition in Social Systems: Thinking and Acting in the Shadow of Doubt." *Personality and Social Psychology Review* 4 (1998): 251-275. The author provides an excellent description of the cognitive framework used by paranoid individuals to interpret the world. This is a good source to understand how the delusional person thinks.

Munro, Alistair. *Delusional Disorder: Paranoia and Related Illnesses.* New York: Cambridge University Press, 1999. A thorough overview of the current thinking on paranoia. Reviews the classic literature and considers the 1987 DSM-III-R revisions of the diagnosis of paranoia.

Oltmans, Thomas, and Brendan Maher, eds. *Delusional Beliefs.* New York: John Wiley & Sons, 1988. A collection of papers from a number of disciplines on delusional disorders.

Siegel, Ronald K. *Whispers: The Voices of Paranoia.* New York: Touchstone, 1996. A psychopharmacologist relates the delusional beliefs of paranoids, attempting to communicate the experience of suffering from paranoid disorders.

Frank J. Prerost

SEE ALSO: Cognitive psychology; Hallucinations; Jealousy; Personality disorders; Psychoanalytic psychology and personality: Sigmund Freud

Parental alienation syndrome

DATE: The 1960's forward

TYPE OF PSYCHOLOGY: Biological bases of behavior; developmental psychology; emotion; motivation; personality; psychopathology; psychotherapy; social psychology; stress

FIELDS OF STUDY: Adolescence; aggression; attitudes and behavior; childhood and adolescent disorders; coping; depression; interpersonal relations; personality disorders; prejudice and discrimination; problem solving; social motives

Parental alienation syndrome is the systematic denigration of one parent by the other with the intent of alienating the child against the other parent, with no justification. The purpose of the alienation is usually to gain or retain custody.

KEY CONCEPTS
- abandonment fear
- absent parent
- arbitration/family counseling
- brainwashing/programming
- discussed alienation
- dysfunctional families
- gender-specific political issues
- joint custody laws
- physical abuse
- systematic denigration

INTRODUCTION

Parental alienation syndrome (PAS) has arisen primarily in the context of child custody in divorce actions. Divorcing parents getting joint custody find that the interactions that must take place in transferring the child between households further complicates emotions for both parents. There is an ongoing confusion in both the legal and the medical professions as to the syndrome's nature and dimensions and how PAS can be detected. The courts have four main criteria to guide attorneys in establishing PAS.

Criterion I must show active blocking of access or contact between the child and the absent parent for the protection of the child.

Criterion II establishes that permanent termination of visitation has occurred as the result of accusations of physical abuse against the absent parent.

Criterion III establishes that a positive relationship existed between the child and the absent parent before the divorce or separation, but has severely deteriorated since then. Healthy established parental relationships do not erode naturally.

Criterion IV establishes that the alienating parent is creating a fear-based environment, causing a child to fear abandonment by the resident parent.

These criteria seem easy to identify separately. However, when coupled with actual court cases, absolutes of the human behaviors involved are difficult to establish.

POSSIBLE CAUSES

Courts have become the arena for determining what the legal system believes to be "the best interest of the child" because PAS arises primarily from child-custody disputes. Parents who initiate PAS seem to be psychologically stuck in the first stage of child development, when survival skills are learned. The initiating parent needs total control of his or her environment and the people in it. These parents expect emotional recompense for any attempt on their part to please other people; they do not know how to give, and are not likely to obey court rules because they do not play by the rules. Through many studies, these traits have been shown to be intergenerational in dysfunctional families. PAS can be a very effective tool in obtaining complete custody. Numerous motivations are involved, such as a desire for money in the form of child support, or because the alienating parent wants to remarry and not have the first spouse in the picture.

DIAGNOSING PARENTAL ALIENATION SYNDROME

Actual diagnosis of PAS in a legal proceeding is left to a mental health professional. The diagnosis by a physician or psychologist called to testify might be presented in clinical terms that are not always clear to the layman, especially to the emotionally biased parents involved. The diagnosis is therefore open to interpretation and argument by opposing attorneys. There is an ongoing argument among medical professionals regarding whether PAS is a syndrome (a number of symptoms occurring together, constituting a distinct clinical picture) or a disorder (a disruption or interference with normal functions or established systems).

One parent turning a child against another parent is not a complicated concept on its own. Historically, however, PAS has been hard to prove because of the unpredictable, often untruthful human behaviors involved. There is also attempted PAS, when the legal criteria are not met, but the parent has tried, without success, to alienate the child from the other parent. Attempted alienation is very harmful to the child. Therefore the courts should not view these children as neutral.

WHO SUFFERS?

Children who are caught in the middle between feuding parents suffer, as most do not understand what is wrong. These children often feel the parental break-up is their fault. The alienated parent suffers greatly, especially when forbidden to see the child (or children) due to false and unfair accusations. The situation causes a wave effect involving grandparents and other family members.

TREATMENT OPTIONS

Arbitration by a family counseling specialist must be ordered before court proceedings begin. False accusations can psychologically damage a child for life. As adults, these children often seek out the alienated/absent parent, only to find that the accusations were unfounded. If severe guilt and emotional distress do exist, professional help is recommended immediately.

HISTORY OF TREATMENT

Feminists in the 1960's and 1970's demanded that fathers take a more active role in rearing their children. Rigidity of the parental roles fell away while the "tender years" doctrine was still in place. This legal doctrine states that the mother gave birth to the child and therefore the woman must be the superior parent. The 1970's brought "no-fault" divorce laws that caused a historically unprecedented increase in divorce. Joint custody laws were successfully passed and custody became a highly gender-specific political issue. The programming or brainwashing of a child to denigrate the other parent became a frequent occurrence, and was named parental alienation syndrome in the 1980's by forensic psychiatrist Richard A. Gardner.

SOURCES FOR FURTHER STUDY

Clawar, S. S., and B. V. Rivlin. *Children Held Hostage: Dealing with Programmed and Brainwashed Children.* Chicago: American Bar Association, 1991. An in-depth study of long-term effects.

Gardner, Richard A. *Parental Alienation Syndrome: A Guide for Mental Health and Legal Professionals.* 2d ed. Cresskill, N.J.: Creative Therapeutics, 1998. Covers the etiology, manifestations, and treatment of PAS, as well as distinguishing between PAS and bone fide child abuse or neglect. Written by the leader in the field.

_____. "Should Courts Order PAS Children to Visit or Reside with the Alienated Parent?" *The American Journal of Forensic Psychology* 19, no. 3 (2001): 61-106. Advocates changing access or custody away from an alienating parent.

Turkat, Ira Daniel. "Questioning the Mental Health Expert's Custody Report." *American Journal of Family Law* 7 (1993): 175-177. Suggestions relevant in selecting an expert in legal cases.

Virginiae Blackmon

SEE ALSO: Divorce and separation: Adult issues; Divorce and separation: Children's issues; Family life: Adult issues; Family life: Children's issues; Law and psychology; Parenting styles.

Parenting styles

TYPE OF PSYCHOLOGY: Developmental psychology
FIELDS OF STUDY: Adolescence; infancy and childhood

Parenting styles have a significant impact on the development of children in terms of competence and independence. Numerous studies have identified differences in parenting styles according to how parents combine various aspects of responsiveness and demandingness. The most commonly identified styles of parenting are authoritarian, permissive, authoritative, and uninvolved.

KEY CONCEPTS
- authoritarian style of parenting
- authoritative style of parenting
- demandingness
- independence
- induction
- parenting style
- permissive style of parenting
- responsiveness
- social responsibility
- uninvolved style of parenting

INTRODUCTION

The research on parenting styles has examined patterns of child-rearing behavior exhibited by parents and corresponding behavior and personality characteristics found in their children. Parenting style can be categorized by two components: responsiveness, a parent's response to the child's needs and wishes, and demandingness or behavioral control, a parent's approach to discipline and the level of demands placed on the child. Numerous researchers have found that parenting style influences the development of children.

Although parenting styles have been described in a variety of terms by different authors, the most commonly identified styles of parenting were labeled by developmental psychologist Diana Baumrind during the early 1960's. Through extensive observation, interviews, and psychological testing, she identified three different approaches to child rearing and discipline as authoritarian, permissive, and authoritative. According to Baumrind, parenting style is the pattern of normal variations in parents' attempts to control and socialize their children. It represents the overall approach to child rearing rather than situation-specific practices by parents.

Each of the three parenting styles identified by Baumrind has been described in terms of high or low levels of emotional support and high or low levels of control or demandingness. Following Baumrind's early research, a fourth style labeled as uninvolved or neglectful is often included.

SPECIFIC STYLES OF PARENTING

The authoritarian style of parenting is a combination of low levels of emotional support and high levels of control. Authoritarian parents have a rigid set of absolute standards for child behavior which are strictly enforced through physical punishment. They expect instant and unquestioning obedience from their children. Respect for authority, work, and tradition is very important to authoritarian parents, and challenges to the parents' authority or questioning of rules is simply not tolerated. These parents exert restrictive control over their children's self-expression and independent behavior.

Parents with a permissive (or indulgent) style provide emotional support but exercise little control over their children. These parents are nonpunitive and make very little attempt to discipline their children or otherwise control their behavior. They place very few demands on their children for household chores and allow the children to make their own decisions about basic family policies such as television viewing and bedtime. Permissive parents are very responsive to their children and are accepting of their children's impulses, desires, and activities. Rather than purposefully directing, shaping, or altering their children's behaviors or decisions, they prefer to see themselves as resources that their children may consult if they wish.

The third style of parenting is referred to by Baumrind as authoritative. Authoritative (or democratic) parents set clear standards for mature and responsible behavior and expect their children to meet these standards. They firmly enforce rules but they do not unduly restrict their children's activities or self-expression. In fact, authoritative parents recognize their children's individual rights, interests, and unique style, and encourage them to think for themselves. These parents encourage verbal give-and-take regarding family rules, will listen to reasonable requests from their children, and are open to some degree of negotiation. When disciplining their children, authoritative parents rely on induction rather than coercion. Induction refers to the use of reasoning to explain and enforce parental expectations.

The uninvolved or neglectful style is a fourth possible parenting approach used by a significant minority. Some view this style as an extension of permissive parenting, but it lacks the high degree of involvement and represents instead a low level of both emotional support and control. Parents who are uninvolved tend to minimize the time and energy devoted to parenting. They know very little about their children's activities, show little interest in their children's experiences, and rarely talk to their children or consider their opinions when making decisions.

DIMENSIONS OF PARENTING BEHAVIOR

The prototypical styles of child rearing can be clearly distinguished from one another on the basis of two dimensions of parenting behavior: demandingness and responsiveness. Demandingness can be defined as the degree to which parents use control to demand that their children meet their high expectations with regard to mature, responsible behav-

---

Men and Parenting

Although a majority of the research literature on parenting focuses on mothers, an increased interest in fathers as involved parents is emerging. During the 1990's, an accumulation of studies on the role of fathers in child rearing suggested that when fathers are more involved, children experience the benefits in many areas. Some of the findings from this research literature include the following:

- The influence of fathers may be more indirect and long-term than the mothers' influence, which is often directly involved in day-to-day activities.
- Fathers are more likely to be involved in childcare activities when they have more child-centered beliefs about child rearing and more egalitarian perspectives on gender roles.
- Fathers tend to relate to young children through a vigorous style of play ("rough and tumble"), as opposed to the tendency of mothers to provide caregiving behaviors. Children whose parents tend to play with them are more likely to be popular with other children because they are better at recognizing and interpreting social and emotional expressions of others.
- The impact of fathers' involvement may be more important for sons during preadolescence and for daughters during adolescence.
- Father involvement during the childhood years may result in greater educational and occupational success for the children as adults.
- Fathers bring different assets to child rearing than mothers and complement rather than compete with the mother-child relationship.

ior. Parental responsiveness refers to the degree of warmth, acceptance, and noncoerciveness evident in the parents' interactions with their children. The authoritarian parenting style has been described as high in demandingness and low in responsiveness. In contrast, the permissive parenting style is thought to be low in demandingness and high in responsiveness. The authoritative parenting style is high in the dimensions of both demandingness and responsiveness. The least effective parenting style, the uninvolved, is low in both demandingness and responsiveness. Parents with this style combine the emotional aloofness of authoritarian parenting with the disciplinary parenting of permissive parenting.

A further distinction can be made between the aspects of demandingness emphasized by authoritarian and authoritative parents. The demandingness displayed by authoritative parents is high in the use of firm control with their children; that is, they firmly and consistently enforce rules but do not extensively or intrusively direct their children's activities. On the other hand, authoritarian parents, also high in demandingness, tend to rely more on restrictive control, which involves the extensive use of rules that cover most aspects of their children's lives and severely restrict their autonomy to develop skills on their own.

CONSEQUENCES FOR CHILD DEVELOPMENT

In her research on child-rearing practices, Baumrind not only identified patterns of parenting styles but also identified characteristics of children reared by these parents. She found that parents' approaches to child rearing have important implications in terms of the degree of autonomy and responsible social behavior exhibited by children. The children of authoritative parents, in comparison to other peers, were found to be more self-reliant, self-controlled, content, and explorative. They were also energetic, friendly, curious, cooperative; they got along well with peers, and they exhibited high self-esteem. Furthermore, these children exhibited more mature moral judgments than their peers and were better able to control their own aggressive impulses and channel them into more appropriate, prosocial behaviors.

In contrast, authoritarian parenting is associated with children who are unhappy, socially withdrawn, distrustful, and moody. In addition, they tend to lack spontaneity and be overly dependent on adults

for directions and decision making. Finally, these children are more likely to be rejected by their peers and suffer from low self-esteem. Parents who rely on a permissive style of child rearing tend to have children who are immature, lacking in impulse control, less exploratory, more dependent, and aggressive.

Children with uninvolved parents, labeled by some researchers as "disengaged" parents, may experience the most negative consequences. Although researched less than the other three styles, parents with this style are rarely there for their children in terms of either discipline or support. The largest differences in competence in general are found between children with unengaged parents and their peers with more involved parents. Children with disengaged parents are frequently absent from school, earn lower grades, and are less motivated to perform well in the classroom.

When these children become adolescents, they tend to overconform to the pressures of the peer group because there is very little pressure at home to conform to parents' values and expectations. Those adolescents who have parents low in both demandingness and responsiveness (indifferent parents) are more likely to become engaged in delinquent behavior, as well as in early experimentation with drugs, alcohol, and sex.

Baumrind's original goal in her research was to identify the specific aspects of child-rearing practices that lead to instrumental or optimal competence in children. She described competence as a combination of social responsibility and independence. A socially responsible child is friendly and altruistic toward peers and cooperative with adults. In contrast, a socially irresponsible child would behave in a hostile and selfish fashion toward other children and be resistive with adults. Independence in a child is characterized by assertiveness, leadership, and confident, purposeful activity. Children low in independence are described as suggestible, submissive followers engaged in disorganized and aimless activity. Children who were high in both social responsibility and independence were considered to be optimally competent. Competent children are mostly likely to be able to resolve social conflicts in a way that is both effective and fair as well as being sensitive and compassionate to the needs of others.

During the last half of the 1990's, many researchers published their studies on the relationship between parenting style and adolescent development. Originally, studies were conducted with preschool and elementary school children, but equal attention was not given to later development. The results from studies with adolescents have consistently shown the superiority of authoritative parenting over the other styles.

GENDER DIFFERENCES

Not surprisingly, when the factor of children's competence was examined and matched with parenting style, Baumrind found that children from authoritative homes were much more competent than their peers. In particular, she found that girls with authoritative parents were more likely to exhibit behavior which was assertive, purposeful, and achievement-oriented. Boys from authoritative homes were more likely to be friendly and cooperative in comparison to other boys their age. Lower levels of competence were observed in children coming from authoritarian and permissive households. Boys with authoritarian parents were low in social responsibility and tended to be hostile and resistive, whereas girls tended to be lower in independence and assertiveness. Permissive parenting was associated with low levels of social assertiveness in girls and low achievement orientation in both sexes.

It is clear from this research that parenting styles affect boys and girls in different ways. Differences in parenting styles appear to have a stronger impact on the development of social responsibility in boys than in girls, most likely because there is normally less variability between girls on this attribute. According to the literature on sex roles, cooperation and compassion toward others in an attribute most frequently associated with females, regardless of how they were reared. Similarly, child-rearing practices have a consistent and stronger impact on the development of independence and social assertiveness in girls than in boys. The characteristics of dominance, assertiveness, and leadership associated with the attribute of independence are more often found in males, regardless of their upbringing. In a sense, what authoritative parenting appears to do is strengthen the otherwise less developed component of competence in each sex and lead to a more balanced combination of both social responsibility and independence. Sandra Bem, a leading researcher in the area of sex roles, has used the term "androgynous" to refer to individuals who are high in positive

characteristics typically associated with both males and females. There is much research to indicate that androgynous individuals are more likely to be competent and psychologically well adjusted in adulthood.

SOURCES FOR FURTHER STUDY

Baumrind, Diana. "Rearing Competent Children." In *Child Development Today and Tomorrow*, edited by William Damon. San Francisco: Jossey-Bass, 1989. Baumrind summarizes her earlier and more recent work on parenting styles. Much of the focus is on the differential effects of demandingness and responsiveness on child development. Provides an excellent overview of the parenting styles research; can be understood by the beginning college student.

Darling, Nancy, and Lawrence Steinberg. "Parenting Style as Context: An Integrative Model." *Psychological Bulletin* 113 (1993): 487-96. Argues that social context and the cultural meaning of specific dimensions of parenting style will have an effect upon the degree of influence that parenting styles have upon children. Important reading for those who desire a serious study of parenting styles.

Huxley, Ron. *Love and Limits: Achieving a Balance in Parenting*. New York: Singular Publishing Group, 1999. Huxley writes about the four styles of parenting in terms of love and limits, suggesting an appropriate balance between the two. This book is written for parents and is especially helpful for readers who are seeking a practical application of parenting styles rather than just theoretical information.

Pruett, Kyle D. *Fatherneed: Why Father Care Is as Essential as Mother Care for Your Child*. New York: Free Press, 2001. The author focuses on the distinct contributions which fathers make in the lives of their children. Attention is given to the lifelong benefits of the mutually dependent relationship between children and fathers that the author calls "Fatherneed." Fathers are encouraged to become involved in caring activities from infancy to adolescence.

Steinberg, Lawrence. *Beyond the Classroom: Why School Reform Has Failed and What Parents Need to Do*. New York: Simon & Schuster, 1996. Steinberg is a recognized expert on psychological development and family relations during adolescence.

This book provides excellent information for both educators and families relative to the effect that parenting styles have upon adolescent development.

Steinberg, Lawrence, Nancy Darling, and Anne C. Fletcher. "Authoritative Parenting and Adolescent Adjustment: An Ecological Journey." In *Examining Lives in Context: Perspectives on the Ecology of Human Development*, edited by Phillis Moen, Glen H. Elder, Jr., and Kurt Luscher. Washington, D.C.: American Psychological Association, 1995. Stresses the importance of considering parenting style within context. The positive influence that authoritative parenting has upon academic performance is not found in the same degree across ethnic cultures.

Strauss, Murray. *Beating the Devil Out of Them: Corporal Punishment in American Families*. New York: Lexington, 1994. Strauss, a recognized authority on domestic abuse, is possibly the most outspoken critic of spanking, He argues that studies show a link between childhood spanking and aggressive behavior in later life because spanking teaches a child violence. Some of the consequences he notes are increased risks of depression, suicide, criminality, and substance abuse.

Teyber, Edward. *Helping Children Cope with Divorce.* San Francisco: Jossey Bass, 2001. Although the primary purpose of this book is to help children cope with divorce, good information is included relative to parenting and particularly to how divorce affects parenting styles. The author discusses "parentification" or role reversal that often occurs with divorce. Chapter 6 is on the need children have for both mothers and fathers

Smith, Charles A., ed. *The Encyclopedia of Parenting Theory and Research*. Westport, Conn.: Greenwood Press, 1999. An excellent source which provides a comprehensive summary of current information on parenting. Synthesizes research on parenting in alphabetically arranged entries. Draws on the disciplines of psychology, education, and sociology.

Stephanie Stein;
updated by Lillian J. Breckenridge

SEE ALSO: Attachment and bonding in infancy and childhood; Behavioral family therapy; Birth order and personality; Child abuse; Father-child relationship; Juvenile delinquency; Mother-child relationship; Self-esteem; Strategic family therapy.

Parkinson's disease

TYPE OF PSYCHOLOGY: Psychopathology
FIELDS OF STUDY: Nervous system; organic disorders

Parkinson's disease is a chronic, progressive, neurodegenerative disorder of the nervous system that usually has its onset in middle age. Characteristic symptoms include tremor, rigidity, and slowness of movement. Although the exact causes are not known, both genetic and environmental factors are implicated.

KEY CONCEPTS
- akinesia
- bradykinesia
- dementia
- depression
- dopamine
- levodopa
- rigidity
- substantia nigra
- transplantation of dopamine neurons
- tremor

INTRODUCTION

Parkinson's disease is one of the most common neurological disorders, affecting one person in every thousand. James Parkinson, in 1817, aptly described some of the classic symptoms in his book *An Essay on the Shaking Palsy*. Parkinson reported the patients as having a chronic and progressive disorder of the nervous system that had a late age onset with the first mild symptoms not appearing until middle age. He also noted a tremor or shaking which typically appeared in the hand or one side and later spread to the other side. The disease progressed for a variable number of years, eventually leading to invalidism and death. A significant contribution was his ability to recognize the disorder as a disease distinct from previously described diseases.

Although Parkinson's disease is thought of as a disease with its onset in middle age, there is a considerable variation in the age of onset and there are other forms of the disease in addition to the classical form. The average age of onset is somewhere in the sixties. About 15 percent of patients develop symptoms between the ages of twenty-one and forty years. An extremely rare form of the disease, juvenile Parkinsonism, begins before the age of twenty-one. In addition to the severe neuromuscular symptoms, dementia may occur in some patients. In addition to tremors, other major symptoms are muscle stiffness or rigidity and bradykinesia or slow movement and even a difficulty in starting movement. Akinesia, an impairment of voluntary activity of a muscle, also occurs. A number of other symptoms may appear as a consequence of the major symptoms, such as difficulties with speech, bowel and bladder problems, and a vacant, masklike facial expression. There are striking variations among patients in the number and severity of the symptoms and the timing of the progression.

CLINICAL FEATURES

The disease that subsequently became known as Parkinson's disease was called "shaking palsy" by Parkinson. The shaking refers to the tremor which, although it is thought by many people to be invariably associated with Parkinson's disease, may be completely absent or present to a minor degree in some patients. Four symptoms which are present in many patients are a progressive tremor, bradykinesia and even akinesia, muscular rigidity, and loss of postural reflexes. There still is no specific test that can be used to diagnose Parkinson's disease. No biochemical, electrophysiologic, or radiologic test has been found to be completely reliable. As a result, misdiagnosis and underdiagnosis have been common with the disease. The situation is complicated further as a number of other diseases and conditions share some of the same symptoms, including Wilson's disease, familial Alzheimer's disease, Huntington's disease, and encephalitis, as well as responses to certain drugs. Symptoms of Parkinson's disease may also develop consequent to trauma to the brain.

A slight tremor in the hands may indicate the first symptoms of Parkinson's disease, and the tremor may or may not also be found in the legs, jaws, and neck. An interesting symptom that may appear in later stages of the disease is seborrhea or acne. Intellectual functioning usually remains normal, but approximately 20 percent of the patients may experience dementia and have a progressive loss of intellectual abilities and impairment of memory. It is not yet clear how the dementia of Parkinson's disease is related to the dementia associated with Alzheimer's disease. Depression also may occur in patients, with approximately one-third of them having depression at any one time. The depression may be directly related to the disease or it may be a reaction to some of the medication.

It has been convenient to divide the progression of symptoms of Parkinson's disease into five stages, according to the severity of the symptoms and the degree of disability associated with them. Stage 1 is marked by mild symptoms. In this stage, the symptom that brings the patient to a physician is likely to be a mild tremor usually limited to one hand or arm. The tremor usually is reduced or disappears during activity but it may increase during periods of emotional stress. During this early stage of the disease, mild akinesia of the affected side and mild rigidity may be evident. Overall, many of these changes are subtle enough that the patient is not aware of them or, at least does not complain of them. Usually, symptoms are confined to one side, but as the disease progresses, it becomes bilateral in most patients in one or two years. In Stage 2, there now is bilateral involvement. Postural changes lead to the patient having a stooped posture and a shuffling walk with little extension of the legs. All body movements become slower and slower (bradykinesia). The difficulty and slowness of movements may cause patients to curtail many of their normal activities and, in many cases, may lead to depression. Stage 3 is characterized by an increase in the postural changes and movements, leading to retropulsion, a tendency to walk backwards, and propulsion, a tendency when walking forward to walk faster and faster with shorter and shorter steps. As the disease progresses, movements occur more and more slowly and there are fewer total movements. By Stage 4, symptoms have come so severe as to lead to significant disability and the patient usually needs constant supervision. The course of the disease leads to Stage 5, a period of complete invalidism in which the patient is confined to a chair or bed. Interestingly, the tremor which is so characteristic of the initial onset of Parkinson's disease tends to lessen considerably during the later stages of the disorder. In addition to the dementia associated with aging, patients with Parkinson's disease show an increased risk of dementia, occurring six to seven times more frequently compared to age-matched controls.

CAUSES

The most striking pathological change noted in Parkinson's disease is a loss of nerve cells in a region of the brain known as the substantia nigra, a layer of deeply pigmented gray matter located in the midbrain. The region contains nerve cells that produce dopamine, a neurotransmitter associated with the control of movement. The levels of dopamine are normally in balance with another neurotransmitter, acetylcholine. In Parkinson's disease, the loss of dopamine-producing cells causes a decrease in the levels of dopamine, with a consequent imbalance with acetylcholine. This leads to the symptoms of Parkinson's disease.

The factors that lead to an upset of the dopaminergic system in the disease are complex. The disease is found throughout the world and occurs in nearly equal frequency in males and females, with slightly more males being affected than females. Parkinson's disease is found in all ethnic groups, although there are some striking ethnic differences. The disease is relatively high among whites and relatively low among African blacks and Asians. Ethnic differences may reflect genetic and environmental differences. It is of interest to note that American blacks have a higher incidence than African blacks, indicating a likely role of local environmental factors.

The role of genetics in Parkinson's disease has been difficult to establish. A family history of Parkinson's disease appears to be a strong indicator of an increased risk of the disease. As part of its comprehensive genetic profiling of its entire population, the country of Iceland has gathered an immense amount of data on genetic diseases, including Parkinson's disease. In the study of late-onset Parkinson's disease, the risk ratio increased with increase in degree of relatedness, giving from 2.7 for nephews and nieces of patients to 3.2 for children of patients to 6.7 for brothers and sisters of patients. Much research remains to be done to determine whether single genes are playing a major causative role or whether the disorder is multifactorial, involving genetic and environmental factors.

TREATMENT

Once it became known that dopamine was depleted in patients with Parkinson's disease, a rationale opened for a potential treatment. Levodopa was the first drug to be used to treat Parkinson's disease successfully and is still the most effective treatment available. Dopamine can pass from the blood into the brain and the drug increases the synthesis of dopamine. The drug does not cure the disease, but it is used in the attempt to control the symptoms. Although the effectiveness of levodopa may diminish somewhat after several years, most patients continue to benefit from its use. It is necessary to monitor patients closely to maintain proper dose levels as well as to register the appearance of new symptoms, side effects, and other complications.

A number of other drugs, alone or in combination, are being used or being tested. Drugs that enhance the action of dopamine are dopaminergic medications. Such drugs may increase dopamine release or may inhibit the breakdown of dopamine. Other drugs are known as anticholinergic medications, and these drugs inhibit the action of acetylcholine.

Surgery has also been used to treat symptoms of Parkinson's disease but results have been somewhat mixed. Surgical techniques include, thalamotomy, a procedure producing a lesions in the thalamus gland for relief of severe unilateral tremor, and pallidotomy, the removal of part of the globus palledus region of the brain, which is used to treat severe rigidity and akinesia. More recently, transplantation of dopamine neurons from human embryos directly into the brain of a patient with Parkinson's disease has been utilized. More trials are required, but results seem to indicate some improvement in symptoms including bradykinesia and rigidity. The use of human tissue has raised many ethical issues, since the tissue is taken from aborted human fetuses. Attempts to use tissues from cultured cells are in progress. It should be stressed that none of the current treatments involving medication and/or surgery produced a complete reversal of the symptoms of Parkinson's disease.

SOURCES FOR FURTHER STUDY

Cram, David L. *Understanding Parkinson's Disease: A Self-Help Guide.* Omaha, Nebr.: Addicus Books, 1999. A physician himself, Cram provides a well-written account of the symptoms and progression of the disease from his personal perspective and also discusses present and future treatments.

Jahanshahi, Marian, and C. David Marsden. *Parkinson's Disease: A Self-Help Guide.* New York: Demos Medical Publishing, 2000. This book is an excellent self-help guide. In addition to chapters on the basic medical facts about Parkinson's disease, there are chapters dealing with living and coping with the disease from the personal and family point of view.

Kondracks, Morton. *Saving Milly: Love, Politics, and Parkinson's Disease.* New York: Public Affairs, 2001. The author provides a moving memoir of his life with his wife, Milly, and the development and impact of Parkinson's disease.

Lanad, Anthony E., and Andres M. Lozano. "Parkinson's Disease: The First of Two Parts." *The New England Journal of Medicine* 339, no. 15 (1998): 1044-1052. A comprehensive review of Parkinson's disease that information on diagnosis and clinical features, pathology, epidemiology, genetics, and list of ninety-three references.

_____. "Parkinson's Disease: Second of Two Parts." *The New England Journal of Medicine* 339, no. 16 (1998): 1130-1143. The second part of a two-part review on Parkinson's disease. The article covers the pathophysiology and various types of treatment and includes a list of 199 references.

Weiner, William J., Lisa M. Shulman, and Anthony E. Land. *Parkinson's Disease: A Complete Guide for Patients and Families.* Baltimore: The Johns Hopkins University Press, 2001. This book does an excellent job not only of giving current information on the features and management of Parkinson's disease but also of providing valuable information on how families and patients can deal with the practical and emotional aspects.

Donald J. Nash

SEE ALSO: Alzheimer's disease; Brain damage; Brain structure; Neuropsychology; Stress: Chromic illness.

Pattern recognition

TYPE OF PSYCHOLOGY: Cognition
FIELDS OF STUDY: Cognitive processes; vision

Making sense of the visual world is a difficult job, but it is one that human beings perform very well. Every three-year-old has pattern-recognition capabilities far beyond those of the most sophisticated computer. The information processing that the human visual system uses to accomplish this feat has many features in common with logical problem solving.

KEY CONCEPTS
• convergence
• fixation
• fovea
• retina
• template

INTRODUCTION

How are objects recognized? This simple question encapsulates a difficult problem for the human visual system: taking a pattern of light from the world and finding in it surfaces, objects, other people, dangers, and pleasures. A paradox of the pattern recognition process is that it all seems so easy—a person simply looks, and all the complexities of the world seem to jump out. One school of psychologists, typified by James J. Gibson, emphasizes direct perception, which to Gibson means that the first thing of which a person is aware in the perceptual process is objects themselves. All the intermediate stages, including the retinal image and numerous levels of physiological processing in the brain, simply do not matter to psychology.

That is how things appear, but there is considerable information processing between the light that strikes the eye and the recognition of a table or a friend. After the light is converted into electrical signals by the retina at the back of the eye, millions of nerve cells process the visual information. At the later stages of processing, many of the strategies used by the visual system are similar to the logical processes that one uses consciously in solving problems. Because the visual system performs these processes unconsciously, its operation has been called "unconscious inference." This term was coined by Hermann von Helmholtz in the mid-nineteenth century to refer to the logical processes that occur in vision.

Perspective illusions provide an example of this unconscious processing. An image of a small bar can be placed on a photograph of railroad tracks that converge in the distance. The bar will appear small if it is over the near part of the tracks, but larger if it is over the more distant tracks. On the photograph, one's visual inference process fails, because it is using a scheme that ordinarily works very well in the real world: Near objects must produce a larger image on the retina to have the same real-world size as more distant objects. The human visual system puts distance and retinal size together so effectively that one normally experiences object constancy—the perception that objects at different distances are the same size even though they project as different sizes on the retina.

DISTANCE AND PATTERN

One part of pattern recognition involves the distance of the pattern. Perception of distance is a good example of the unconscious inference that occurs in vision, because so many different sources of information go into a distance estimate. One source, based on binocular vision, is particularly useful because it can provide an estimate of absolute range. If one fixates an object with both eyes, the convergence of the eyes tells the brain how far away the object is. This is called the stereoscopic cue, and it depends on coordination of the two eyes.

Other distance cues are effective even in a single eye. One is superposition: If one object partly covers another, the covered object must be more distant. This cue gives only relative distance, not absolute distance, as does the stereoscopic cue. Superposition works at any distance, however, while stereoscopic vision is useful only for objects within a few meters of the head. Another cue works only at very long distances—very distant objects, such as mountains, will look blue and hazy, while closer objects are sharp.

Still another source of distance information is motion. When one moves one's head, nearby objects will sweep by faster than more distant ones. If the brain knows the distance to any one point of this sweeping texture (such as the distance to the pavement beneath one's feet), it can calculate the distances to all other objects. These calculations would be difficult to do consciously even if one knew the mathematics required, but the brain performs the operations almost instantly.

Add to these distance cues other information such as familiar distance (one knows how far away the other side of one's living room is without measuring it), and one has a large palette of information

sources that can provide information about the distance of an object. These cues are put together and weighted according to their reliability, and the brain produces a composite distance estimate. A similar process occurs in recognizing objects. The visual image, sound and touch information, and one's knowledge of the situation all combine to identify objects, even if they are at unfamiliar angles or if they cannot be seen clearly. It is the combination of many information sources, including memory, that makes the process quick and reliable.

A powerful theory of pattern recognition by psychologist Irving Biederman holds that people analyze objects into components that he calls geons. These can be simple shapes, such as cylinders and cones, or patterns of edges. Each object has a characteristic set of geons, often not more than two or three, that define it.

PATTERN AND COGNITION

Pattern recognition stands at the center of human activity—it is essential for all aspects of mental life. In appreciating art, one is recognizing patterns, but the process also extends to the most mundane activities, such as recognizing coins when making change. The traditional way to study mental processes is to make a task requiring those processes more difficult until a subject can no longer perform it. In finding where and how the processes fail, psychologists can learn about their structures.

One way psychologists make pattern recognition break down is to degrade images until they can no longer be seen. A classic experiment by Jerome Bruner presents a good example. Bruner presented out-of-focus slides to groups of students, asking them to identify the objects in the slides as soon as they could. At first no one could name the objects, but as they became sharper and the visual information improved, the task became easier. The first guesses about the identities of the objects, however, were frequently wrong. Then Bruner played a trick on his subjects. Half of them saw the slides beginning in a very unfocused state, and many made wrong guesses about the objects presented. When most subjects had a guess but were still uncertain, the other half of the subjects were allowed to see the same slides for the first time. As the pictures came into focus, the second group was able to identify the objects sooner than the first, who had seen the unfocused images longer. The reason was that the first group had a lot of incorrect assumptions about the pictures, and these assumptions hindered their ability to change their minds as new information became available. The experiment shows the value of the information that one brings to a perceptual situation.

Another set of experiments, by Irving Biederman, showed the key role of context and situation in identifying objects. A common object such as a sofa could be easily identified in a familiar setting such as a living room, but the same object in an unexpected setting, such as in a street scene, was very difficult to find. Subjects took several seconds to find the sofa in the street, even though they found it immediately in the living room. The sofa was identical in the two pictures—only the context was changed.

These examples show a contrast between two different types of information used to identify patterns. One begins with signals from the senses, called "bottom-up" information. It originates at the eyes, ears, and skin, and is processed before arriving at the visual cortex. There the bottom-up information meets attention, motivation, and memory, the "top-down" sources of information. It is the meeting of top-down and bottom-up information that defines perception.

Another application of pattern recognition is in clinical medicine, where some patients suffer from brain damage that interferes with their pattern-recognition abilities. The damage is usually from strokes (interruptions of the blood supply to part of the brain), surgery, or accidents. Damage in different parts of the brain interferes with different aspects of the pattern-recognition process. It is clear that an injury that interrupts the nerve fibers linking the eye and the brain, for example, would interrupt pattern recognition by causing blindness. More interesting cases leave visual thresholds intact while disturbing recognition. Patients with this kind of damage have no difficulty in knowing that an object is present, or in avoiding it if it comes toward them, but do not know what it is.

One such case, described by Oliver Sacks in his book *The Man Who Mistook His Wife for a Hat and Other Clinical Tales* (1987), concerns a professor of music who remained productive and valued as a teacher although he had difficulty in recognizing things using vision alone. He would fail to recognize his students, for example, until he heard their voices. Then everything would snap into place and the les-

sons could begin. The professor suffered from visual agnosia, the inability to recognize objects. Milder forms of agnosia involve symptoms such as the difficulty in telling one person from another by looking at their faces or the inability to identify particular things in similar categories, such as the identities of flowers. These patients cannot be cured, but knowledge of the many sources of information in pattern recognition can help them cope with their handicaps. They can be taught to take more advantage of other information sources, such as sounds and context.

PATTERN AND PERCEPTION

Interest in pattern recognition is as old as the ancient Greeks, but little progress was made in explaining its mechanisms until well into the nineteenth century. During that century, mostly in Germany, methods were invented to investigate perception. Visual illusions, such as the railroad track illusion described above, revealed some of the shortcuts that the visual system used to interpret scenes. These illusions are examples of the technique of stressing perception until it breaks down, and learning about the process from the behavior of the system when it fails. The railroad track illusion shows that vision uses perspective, among other things, to judge distance. Even when perspective cannot work, as in viewing a photograph or a drawing on a flat sheet, the system tries to use it anyway.

Perception is more than bringing a pattern into the brain. A pattern without a meaning is of no practical use. Perception, then, is the attaching of meaning to a pattern, a link of top-down with bottom-up information. At the core, it is a matching process. This has been described as template matching, like putting a stencil over a pattern. If the stencil (the template or concept in the head) matches the pattern (the signal from the eyes), then the world contains what was in the stencil, and the pattern is recognized.

There are many theories of perceptual recognition, but they all boil down to some form of template matching. Some machines, such as dollar-bill changing machines, recognize patterns in this way. They look for exactly the required pattern—no variation is allowed. If the bill is dirty or upside down, it is rejected. The system works well at rejecting counterfeit bills, but it is not flexible enough to do the sort of recognition in many contexts that humans do.

Simple templates do not work very well when the pattern varies, as in identifying both "e" and *e* as the same letter. A template that matched the first letter would not recognize the second and would interpret the two patterns as having different meanings.

One solution to the matching problem is to match not the geometric pattern itself but some transformation of it. The pattern in the head would then have the same transformation. The letter "e," for example, could be recognized by its features, as "closed pattern above a curved tail running from upper left to lower right." This pair of features would identify both *e* and "e," without picking other letters falsely. Some modern computer-based pattern-recognition machines use features in this way. The future of pattern-recognition research will be directed toward identifying the features that nature uses to recognize patterns and toward designing machines that use effective features. The human use of context and probability in recognition will also be built into more powerful recognition systems.

SOURCES FOR FURTHER STUDY

Biederman, Irving. "Perceiving Real World Scenes." *Science* 177 (July 7, 1972): 77-80. This article in a nonspecialized journal introduces Biederman's experiments on the role of context in recognizing patterns, with illustrations of expected and unexpected contexts.

Bridgeman, Bruce. *The Biology of Behavior and Mind.* New York: John Wiley & Sons, 1988. Chapter 5 explores the physiological mechanisms of perception, while chapter 6 treats perception as an active process—something one does rather than something that happens to one.

Gregory, Richard Langton. *Eye and Brain.* 5th ed. Princeton, N.J.: Princeton University Press, 1997. This short book, rich with illustrations, leads in a readable way from the optics of the eye to pattern recognition, with stops for nervous system operation and illusions on the way. Highly recommended.

Sacks, Oliver W. *The Man Who Mistook His Wife for a Hat and Other Clinical Tales.* New York: Perennial Library, 1987. This is a fascinating look behind neurological deficits that reveals the humanistic side of medicine. Sacks reviews not only the symptoms of the patients but also their adaptations to their problems.

Solso, Robert L. *Cognitive Psychology.* 6th ed. Boston: Allyn & Bacon, 2000. Various schemes of pattern recognition are described simply and powerfully. The chapter on pattern recognition reviews all the major theories, with extensive illustrations.

Bruce Bridgeman

SEE ALSO: Attention; Logic and reasoning; Pattern vision; Sensation and perception; Visual system; Vision: Brightness and contrast; Vision: Color.

Pattern vision

TYPE OF PSYCHOLOGY: Sensation and perception
FIELDS OF STUDY: Cognitive processes; nervous system; vision

Human pattern vision and machine pattern vision have many properties in common. After extracting lines and other elements from a visual scene, pattern vision devices extract depth using many kinds of cues, and identify objects by interactions with memory. The knowledge can be applied in such settings as virtual reality.

KEY CONCEPTS
- algorithm
- fovea
- receptive field
- retina
- virtual reality

INTRODUCTION

The human visual system is designed to see patterns. In fact, the system uses light only as a medium for detecting patterns; the actual intensities of light in various parts of the visual field are discarded at the first stage of visual processing, and only relative intensities remain. The fate of these patterns of intensities in the visual brain is the concern of pattern vision.

Vision relies upon two kinds of information: patterns of intensity and patterns of color. Intensity patterns are resolved into objects in a number of steps. The steps can be conceived either in terms of the responses of single neurons at various levels of the visual pathways, or as a series of rules, or algorithms, governing the transformations that visual information undergoes. The process begins in the retinas of the two eyes, where each receptor cell is exposed to a tiny sample of the visual world, a small spot of sensitivity. The receptor cells pass their messages to other cells at higher levels, and the visual image is reorganized, or recoded, at each step.

VISION PROCESSING

From the point of view of pattern vision, a particularly significant step occurs when the signals enter the visual cortex, after several stages of processing. Each neuron in the cortex is excited by signals from many receptors lying in a straight line, so that the neuron responds best to a line in the visual field. The line is a receptive field, an area of the world to which the neuron responds. The line must have a particular location and orientation. The neuron responds best, in fact, to a group of parallel lines at a particular spacing. This helps to improve the reliability of the system. Other neurons at the same time respond to lines at other locations, orientations, and spacings.

From this set of line-shaped receptive fields, the visual system constructs an internal model of the visual world. First, the outlines of objects can be recognized from patterns of lines. Next, particular patterns of lines are assigned particular meanings. For example, sometimes two lines will meet at a T junction. In this case, the visual system generally assumes that the crossbar of the T is in front of the upright part, because the crossbar interrupts a line. From an image that contains many such lines and intersections, the visual system reconstructs the surfaces and objects of the world.

MOTION AND SHADING

Often, however, this is not enough. There may remain ambiguities, unanswered questions about what objects are present in the world. The visual system has several additional methods by which to interpret the image. One of them is motion, which is usually present in the visual field. If there is no motion of objects in the world, there is often motion of the observer, so that objects move past the observer at different rates. The visual system can take any group of lines that is moving in the same way and conclude that they represent a single object moving relative to other parts of the visual world.

Objects can also reveal their shapes by their motion. A circular image, for example, might be either a disk or a sphere. A rotating sphere, however, will not change its shape, while a flipping disk will appear round, then elliptical, then flat as it tumbles. Other objects have characteristic changes in appearance as they rotate, providing the visual system with information about their structure. How the system decodes this information is the shape-from-motion problem.

The shading of objects also reveals something about their structure. A surface that is facing a source of illumination will be brighter than a surface at another angle. A rounded object will have continuous changes in shading. This is the shape-from-shading problem, and solving it gives still more information about the structure of the visual world. In this way, the visual system combines information from many cues, or sources of input from the image, and normally the brain does a remarkably good job of interpreting the visual world quickly and accurately.

Color gives still more information about visual patterns, helping the system to distinguish surfaces and textures. It is handled by separate visual mechanisms and cannot resolve as much detail as the form-processing mechanism.

MACHINE VISION

One reason it is important to know how pattern vision works is that an understanding of visual processing is necessary in order to enable machines to interact effectively with the visual environment. As humans interact more with patterns generated in graphics-oriented computers and in art, it becomes important to understand what goes on in the human mind when patterns are processed. One necessity for building robots to do many tasks is to give them the ability to recognize objects in their surroundings. Generally, the robots are computer-based and use television cameras for visual input; interpretation of the image comes next. This has proved to be more difficult than anticipated; even the first step in the process, abstracting lines and edges from the world, remains imperfect in existing systems. One of the efforts in the area of artificial pattern recognition, then, has been to investigate the pattern recognition mechanisms of humans and animals, and to try to build similar mechanisms into the machines. Every three-year-old has far better pattern recognition capabilities than the most sophisticated machines.

One of the problems facing machine vision is that, although the identifying of lines, edges, and patterns might work well in the laboratory, the process is less successful in the real world. Humans have a remarkable ability to recognize patterns even in "noisy" environments, despite shadows, occlusions, changes in perspective, and other sources of variation. The emerging discipline of artificial intelligence is concerned with such problems.

VIRTUAL REALITY

Another application of visual pattern recognition is in the area of virtual reality, the effort to design displays that create in a computer user the illusion that one is actually in a different environment. Usually, the observer wears goggles that present images to the two eyes, reproducing everything that the observer would see in another environment. When the user's head turns, the environment presented in the goggles rotates in the opposite way just as it would in the real world. The system might present an undersea or space environment, for example, and can even include an artificial image of the observer's own hand calculated from the position of an electronically equipped glove worn by the user. Here the difficulty is in deciding what the display should offer to the user; it is impractical to reproduce an entire visual world in all its richness and detail. The designer of a virtual-reality system must select the patterns that will be presented, and must know what information is essential to pattern vision and what can be left out. Again, knowledge of what information the human visual system will extract from the scene is essential to guide decisions about what to present.

An example of how research in pattern vision can influence the design of virtual-reality systems is in the amount of detail that must be presented to the observer. The fovea of the eye, at the center of vision, sees much finer detail than the rest of the retina, and the farther from the fovea one goes, the less detail can be resolved. Engineers take advantage of this property of human vision by designing systems that present rich detail near objects of interest, and less detail elsewhere. It is easier to update the information in this kind of display than to recalculate a finely detailed image for the whole visual field. Similarly, color information need not be presented in great detail over the entire visual field.

Other economies in design can be used in virtual-reality systems as well as in other computer displays. One such shortcut takes advantage of more subtle properties of visual pattern processing. The shading cues that are used to give an object the appearance of depth need not be accurate ones. The visual system is not sensitive to some kinds of distortions in shading, and will accept an object as appropriately shaded even if the mathematics that generate the computer's shading are simplified and distorted.

Another example of a simplification that engineers can make is in the presentation of motion. Humans are not very sensitive to differences in rates of acceleration, so these differences need not be presented accurately. In summary, the human visual system uses shortcuts in interpreting the visual image, and artificial systems can use similar shortcuts in constructing the image.

THEORETICAL DEVELOPMENTS

The beginnings of research on pattern vision can be traced to the work of René Descartes in the seventeenth century. Descartes dissected a cow's eye and found that a small upside-down image of the world was projected on the back of the eye. All the information that comes from vision passes through a similar stage in human eyes as well. For more than two centuries, however, little progress was made in deciphering what happened to visual information after it left the retina. Anatomists learned where in the brain the visual fibers led, but they could not find out what was happening there.

One of the advances in the twentieth century that has made work on pattern vision possible is the realization that vision must be studied at many levels of analysis. One level is neurophysiology, the understanding of what goes on in the nerve cells and in the fibers that connect them. Another level is the algorithm, the set of internal rules for coding and interpreting visual information. Researchers at this level ask what steps the visual system must take to interpret a pattern. The steps themselves are taken care of at the neurophysiological level. A third level is behavior; researchers investigate the capabilities of pattern vision in the intact human. At this more global level, one studies visual pattern processing as a whole rather than dissecting its pieces. It is relating one level to another that advances understanding: At the behavior level, it is observed that people are capable of recognizing patterns from lines alone, as in cartoons. At the algorithmic level, it is found that extracting lines from an image is a useful step in interpreting the image. At the neurophysiological level, it is found that some neurons are sensitive to lines in the visual world.

Modern theories of pattern vision all share several ideas. First, information is transformed in small steps, not all at once, from the image to its meaning. The early steps are largely independent of the use to be made of the visual pattern. Later steps involve interactions with memory and with the use to be made of the visual information. At these later stages, even single nerve cells code information from a wide region of the visual field, as these cells have the job of integrating images from large areas. At the algorithmic level, the brain engages a number of assumptions about the structure of the visual world and the objects in it to interpret a scene quickly and reliably. The visual field is represented over and over in the brain as information passes to more specialized regions that emphasize movement, pattern recognition, visual-motor interactions, and other uses that the brain makes of visual inputs.

Another common idea in pattern vision is that the image is analyzed in several different ways at once. Depth, for example, might be sought in stereoscopic vision (small differences in the images arriving at the two eyes), in superpositions (using the T junctions described above, among other methods), in shading, and in other clues. If one method does not come up with a meaningful interpretation, another one will. In this way, a reliable pattern vision system can be created from unreliable components.

Sources for Further Study

Bridgeman, Bruce. *The Biology of Behavior and Mind.* New York: John Wiley & Sons, 1988. Chapter 5 explores the physiological mechanisms of perception, while chapter 6 treats perception as an active process—something a person does rather than something that happens to a person.

Gregory, R. L. *Eye and Brain.* 5th ed. Princeton, N.J.: Princeton University Press, 1997. This short book, rich with illustrations, leads in a readable way from the optics of the eye to pattern recognition, with stops for nervous system operation and illusions on the way. Highly recommended.

Hubel, David H., and Torsten N. Wiesel. "Brain Mechanisms of Vision." In *The Brain.* San Francisco: W. H. Freeman, 1979. The anatomy and workings of the visual parts of the brain are reviewed from the point of view of two Nobel Prize winners. Beautiful color illustrations illuminate the text, based mostly on the visual system of the cat.

Humphreys, G. W., and M. J. Riddoch. *To See but Not to See: A Case Study of Visual Agnosia.* London: Lawrence Erlbaum, 1987. The mysterious symptoms of a patient who could see everything but recognize nothing are analyzed with intelligence and compassion. From such patients, it is possible to learn about pattern vision in normal people.

Solso, Robert L. *Cognitive Psychology.* 6th ed. Boston: Allyn & Bacon, 2000. Various schemes of pattern recognition are described simply and powerfully. The chapter on pattern recognition reviews all the major theories with extensive illustrations.

Waltz, David L. "Artificial Intelligence." *Scientific American* 247 (October, 1982): 118-133. Several computer programs are reviewed in a relatively nontechnical way. Among them are programs that find the three-dimensional structure in line drawings.

Bruce Bridgeman

SEE ALSO: Brain structure; Logic and reasoning; Pattern recognition; Vision: Brightness and contrast; Vision: Color; Visual system.

Pavlov, Ivan

BORN: September 27, 1849, in Ryazan, Russia
DIED: February 17, 1936, in Leningrad, U.S.S.R.
IDENTITY: Russian physiologist and psychologist
TYPE OF PSYCHOLOGY: Biological bases of behavior; cognition; learning
FIELDS OF STUDY: Endocrine system; Pavlovian conditioning

Pavlov developed the concept of the conditioned response, which indicated that living organisms could continuously adapt their behavior to changing circumstances.

Ivan Petrovich Pavlov was born in the central Russian city of Ryazan. As the son of a parish priest, he was assured of access to education and, after graduating from the local church school and briefly attending Ryazan Seminary, studied natural sciences at St. Petersburg University.

Pavlov was a promising student and, under the influence of professor I. F. Tsion, developed a strong interest in physiology. After graduation from St. Petersburg University in 1875, he continued his physiological studies at the Military Medical Academy, working with Sergei. P. Botkin and K. N. Ustimovich. In 1879, he received an M.D. degree and, three years later, completed a doctoral dissertation on the nerves found in the heart.

From 1884 to 1886, Pavlov lived in Germany, studying on the physiology of invertebrates. In 1890, he was appointed professor in the department of pharmacology and director of the physiology section of the Institute of Experimental Medicine in St. Petersburg. It was there that he established a reputation as an exacting researcher. In 1904, he won the Nobel Prize in Physiology or Medicine by focusing on the difficult problem of digestion, which involved the interplay of the circulation of the blood, the activities of the nervous system, and the workings of enzymes.

The conditioned reflex (CR) was Pavlov's most important discovery. Through a number of carefully controlled experiments, he demonstrated the conditions under which dogs came to associate the appearance of food with signals such as ringing bells, thereby converting a normally unconditioned response such as salivation to a conditioned one. This breakthrough, described in *Dvadtsatiletnii opyt obektivnogo izucheniia vysshei nervnoi deiatelnosti zhivotnykh* (1923; *Conditioned Reflexes*, 1927), showed how living creatures could learn to respond physiologically to non-physiologically-based signals. The ramifications of this discovery occupied him for the rest of his scientific career.

The implications of the conditioned reflex were enormous. Its extension to a whole chain of associations (called higher-order conditioning) reinforced materialistic philosophies such as Marxism, supported the idea that nurture was more important than nature, and buttressed behaviorist psychology. Its central concept, that living beings could continuously adapt their behavior to a changing environment, challenged both biological and psychological theories of determinism.

Ivan Pavlov. (© The Nobel Foundation)

Because of the political significance of Pavlov's theory, the Soviet regime provided him with financial support. He also received strong international recognition; most notably, he was awarded France's Order of the Legion of Honor. His death on February 17, 1936, was widely mourned by Russians and non-Russians alike.

SOURCES FOR FURTHER STUDY

Babkin, B. P. *Pavlov: A Biography.* Chicago: University of Chicago Press, 1971. Written by a former colleague, it provides useful information on Pavlov's life and personality.

Gray, Jeffrey Alan. *Ivan Pavlov.* New York: Viking Press, 1980. Grey offers an excellent summary of Pavlov's achievements and examines his place in the behaviorist tradition.

Todes, Daniel. *Ivan Pavlov: Exploring the Animal Machine.* New York: Oxford University Press, 2000.

Aimed at young adults, Todes's work reviews Pavlov's accomplishments, emphasizing the thought processes involved in his investigations.

Michael J. Fontenot

SEE ALSO: Behaviorism; Conditioning; Pavlovian conditioning; Reflexes.

Pavlovian conditioning

DATE: 1890's forward
TYPE OF PSYCHOLOGY: Learning
FIELDS OF STUDY: Pavlovian conditioning

Pavlovian conditioning is a basic process of learning that relates especially to reflexes and emotional behavior. Interest in this form of learning has been long-standing and continues to the present day. Pavlovian principles apply to a very wide range of organisms, situations, and events.

KEY CONCEPTS
- conditioned emotional reaction (CER)
- conditioned response (CR)
- conditioned stimulus (CS)
- discrimination
- extinction
- flooding
- second-signal system
- spontaneous recovery
- stimulus generalization
- systematic desensitization
- unconditioned response (UR)
- unconditioned stimulus (US)

INTRODUCTION

Pavlovian conditioning, also known as respondent conditioning and classical conditioning (to distinguish it from instrumental or operant conditioning), is an elementary learning process and has been of major interest to psychologists ever since the Russian physiologist Ivan P. Pavlov (1849-1936) discovered that a dog could learn to salivate to a neutral stimulus after the stimulus was paired repeatedly with food.

Pavlov's early career focused on the study of heart circulation and digestion in animals (usually dogs), for which he received the Nobel Prize in Physiology or Medicine in 1904. However, by that time Pavlov had already turned his attention to experiments on conditioned reflexes, from which flowed a new psychological nomenclature.

CONDITIONING

The core of Pavlovian conditioning is the pairing (association) of stimuli to elicit responses. Food (meat powder) placed in a dog's mouth naturally produces salivation. Pavlov called the food an unconditioned stimulus (US) and salivation, elicited by the food, the unconditioned response (UR). When a neutral stimulus—for example, a tone that does not naturally elicit salivation—is repeatedly followed by food, the tone alone eventually evokes salivation. Pavlov labeled the tone a conditioned stimulus (CS) and the response (salivation) elicited by it the conditioned response (CR).

Pavlov's formulation can be summarized as follows:

Before conditioning:

Food (US) elicits Salivation (UR)

Conditioning procedure:

Neutral Stimulus (Tone) plus Food (US) elicits Salivation (UR)

After conditioning:

Tone (CS)—elicits—Salivation (CR)

Pavlov believed that conditioned responses were identical to unconditioned responses. That is usually not the case. For example, conditioned responses may be less pronounced (weaker) or a bit more lethargic than unconditioned responses.

Several phenomena turn up in studies of Pavlovian conditioning. Extinction, generalization, and discrimination are among the most important. Extinction refers to the procedure as well as to the elimination of a CR. If the CS is repeatedly presented without the US, extinction occurs: The dog stops salivating to the tone. During the course of extinction, the CR may return from time to time until it is finally extinguished. Pavlov called the occasional return of the CR "spontaneous recovery."

Stimulus generalization refers to responding not only to a particular CS but also to similar but different stimuli. Further, the magnitude (amount of salivation) of a generalized response tends to decline as stimuli become less and less like the CS. For example, a dog trained to salivate to a 5,000-cycle-per-second (cps) tone is likely to salivate also to 5,300 cps and 4,700 cps tones without specific training to do so (stimulus generalization). Responses tend to weaken in an orderly way as tones become more and more unlike the CS—that is, as the tones move away from the CS in both directions, say, to 4,400 cps from 4,100 cps, and 5,600 cps to 5,900 cps, the flow of salivation becomes less and less.

Stimulus generalization in effect extends the number of stimuli that elicit a conditioned response. Discrimination procedures restrict that number by conditioning a subject not to generalize across stimuli. The procedure involves two processes: acquisition and extinction. The CS is paired repeatedly with the US (acquisition) while the US is withheld as generalized stimuli are presented repeatedly (extinction). If the dog now salivates to the CS and not to the generalized stimuli, the dog has learned to discriminate or to act discriminatively. Pavlov reported that some dogs displayed a general breakdown in behavior patterns (experimental neurosis) when called upon to make discriminations that were too difficult for them to make.

Pavlov's work on what he called the second-signal system implies that conditioning principles are relevant to human as well as to animal learning. Once, say, a tone is established as a CS in first-order conditioning, the tone can be paired with a neutral stimulus to establish a second-order CS. Thus, in the absence of food, a light might precede the tone (CS) several times until the light itself begins to function as a CS. Second-order conditioning appears to follow many of the same rules as first-order conditioning.

Pavlov's work has clearly provided one way to study the learning process in great detail. It has also provided the kind of data and theory that have affected research in other areas of learning, such as instrumental conditioning and, subsequently, cognitive science and neuroscience.

RANGE OF PAVLOVIAN CONDITIONING

Pavlovian phenomena have been demonstrated with different kinds of organisms and a wide variety of stimuli and responses far beyond those studied by Pavlov. Stimuli that precede such unconditioned stimuli as sudden loud noises (leading to rapid heart rate), a puff of air delivered to the eye (evoking

blinking), or a large temperature increase (eliciting sweating) may become conditioned stimuli capable of eliciting conditioned responses on their own. The idea of second-order (higher-order) conditioning is profoundly important because it suggests how rewards such as words of praise and money are established apart from primary (biologically necessary) rewards, such as food and water. It also may in part explain the power of films, plays, novels, and advertisements to evoke strong emotion in the absence of direct experience with primary (unconditioned) stimuli. Studies concerned with conditioned emotional reactions (CER), especially fear and anxiety in people—a subject much more complex than simple reflexes—have been of special interest to researchers and therapists for many years.

ADDITIONAL RESEARCH FINDINGS

Studies of conditioning essentially look at how various unconditioned and conditioned stimuli influence responses under different arrangements of time and space. Following are a few general findings.

Pavlovian conditioning tends to be readily established when stimuli or responses or both are strong rather than weak. For example, in response to a near-drowning experience, some people promptly learn to fear such conditioned stimuli as the sight of water, boats, palm trees, bathing suits, and so on. In such cases, relevant stimuli and responses (panic) are presumably quite strong.

Conditioned stimuli are most likely to elicit conditioned responses when unconditioned and conditioned stimuli are paired consistently. If a mother always hums when she rocks her infant daughter to sleep, humming is likely to become a potent and reliable CS, which soothes and comforts her daughter. This outcome is less likely if mother hums only occasionally.

When several stimuli precede a US, the one most often paired with the US will likely emerge as the strongest CS. If, for example, both parents threaten to punish their young son, but only father always carries out the threats, father's threats are more likely than mother's to evoke apprehension in the child.

For some responses, such as eye blinking, conditioned stimuli tend to be strongest when they precede the US by about one-half second. The optimal interval for other responses varies from seconds to fractions of seconds: A neighbor's dog barks immediately before little Sophie falls from her swing, bumping her nose very hard. She cries. If the dog's bark subsequently makes Sophie feel uneasy, the bark is functioning as a CS. This outcome becomes less and less likely as the bark and fall increasingly separate in time.

Conditioned responses are usually not established if a US and CS occur together (simultaneous conditioning)—the potency of the UC overshadows the potential CS—or when a neutral stimulus follows the US (backward conditioning).

SOME PRACTICAL APPLICATIONS

In a widely cited study reported in 1920, American researchers John B. Watson and Rosalie Rayner conditioned a phobic reaction in an eleven-month-old infant named Albert. The researchers discovered that Albert feared loud noises but seemed unafraid of a number of other things, including small animals.

Watson and Rayner subsequently placed a white rat in Albert's crib. When Albert reached for it, the researchers struck a piece of resonate metal with a hammer, making a "loud sound." After a few such presentations, presenting the rat alone elicited crying and various avoidance reactions. Albert also showed signs of fear to similar things, such as a rabbit, a furry object, and fluffy clumps of cotton (stimulus generalization). Thus, Watson and Rayner provided early experimental evidence that Pavlovian principles are involved in the acquisition of human emotional reactions.

While this study induced a phobic reaction in the subject, systematic desensitization is a procedure designed to eliminate phobias and anxieties. The procedure was largely developed and named by South African-born therapist Joseph Wolpe. Noting that it is very difficult to have pleasant and anxious feelings simultaneously, Wolpe fashioned a systematic technique to teach clients to engage in behavior (relaxation) that competes with anxiety.

Therapy typically begins with an interview designed to identify specific sources of the client's fears. The therapist helps the client assemble a list of items that elicit fear. Items associated with the least amount of fear are positioned at the bottom of the list; most feared items are placed near the top. For example, if a client has a strong fear of dogs, the therapist and client would develop a list

of scenes that make the client fearful. Situations may vary from hearing the word "dog" to seeing pictures of dogs, being in the vicinity of a dog, hearing a dog bark, being close to dogs, and patting a dog.

The client is next taught to relax by tensing and releasing various groups of muscles—shoulders, face, arms, neck, and so on. This phase of treatment ends when the client has learned to fully relax on his or her own in a matter of minutes.

The client and therapist now move on to the next phase of therapy. While remaining fully relaxed, the client is asked to imagine being in the first situation at the bottom of the list. The image is held for several seconds. The client then relaxes for about twenty seconds before imagining the same situation again for several seconds. When the client is able to imagine an item and remain fully relaxed, the therapist presents a slightly more fearful situation to imagine. This procedure continues until an image causes distress, at which time the session ends. The next session begins with relaxation, followed by the client slowly moving up the list. As before, the client stops at the point of distress. Therapy is successful when the client can imagine all the items on the list while remaining fully relaxed. The technique is less helpful when clients have difficulty identifying fearful situations or calling up vivid images.

In the hands of a skillful therapist, systematic desensitization is an effective technique for reducing a wide variety of fears. Its Pavlovian features involve pairing imagined fearful scenes with relaxation. When relaxation successfully competes with fear, it becomes a new CR to the imagined scenes. As relaxation becomes sufficiently strong as a CR, anxiety is replaced by calmness in the face of earlier aversive stimuli.

Extinction offers a more direct route to the reduction of fear than systematic desensitization. The technique called flooding makes use of extinction. Flooding exposes the client to fear-arousing stimuli for a prolonged period of time. Suppose a child is afraid of snakes. Although fear is likely to increase initially , flooding would require the child to confront the snake directly and continuously—to be "flooded" by various stimuli associated with the snake—until the conditioned stimuli lose their power to elicit fear. Some therapists think that the application of this technique is probably best left to professionals.

SOME EVERYDAY EXAMPLES

Pavlovian principles may be plausibly applied to daily life, as the following examples illustrate.

Couples sometimes refer to a certain tune as "our song." A plausible interpretation is that Pavlovian conditioning has been at work. The favored tune may have been popular and repeated often at the time of the couple's courtship and marriage. The tune has since become a CS that evokes a variety of pleasant feelings associated with initial love.

A babysitter notes that giving a young child a blue blanket in the absence of his mother markedly reduces his irritability. Most likely the blanket has been sufficiently associated with the soothing actions of his mother (US) and now functions as a calming stimulus (CS).

An adolescent steadfastly avoids the location where he was seriously injured in an automobile accident. He says that just thinking about the highway makes him nervous. The location doubtless contains a number of conditioned aversive stimuli that now trigger unpleasant feelings (CR) and avoidance.

After a bitter divorce, a woman finds that the sight of household items (CS) associated with her former husband is terribly upsetting (CR). She has reduced her resentment by getting rid of the offending items.

A wife often places flower arrangements in her husband's den. The flowers (CS) now bring him a measure of comfort (CR) when she is away on trips.

RESPONDENT CONDITIONING AND REINFORCEMENT

Pavlovian behaviors are principally elicited by antecedent events (just as low temperatures elicit shivering), while many behaviors are strengthened (in reinforcement) or weakened (in punishment) by what follows behavior. In Pavlovian conditioning, two stimuli are presented, one following another, regardless of what a subject does. What follows behavior is usually not important in this form of conditioning. In studying the role of reinforcement on behavior (instrumental or operant conditioning), the consequences that follow a person's actions often determine what the person is likely to do under similar circumstances in the future. What follows behavior is important in this type of conditioning.

The topic of reinforcement is introduced here because Pavlovian conditioning and reinforcement are intricately related in that any Pavlovian conditioning is likely to contain elements of instrumental conditioning, and vice versa. For example, if someone has a near-drowning experience and now avoids bodies of water, it is plausible to say that conditioned stimuli associated with the experience evoke unsettling feelings. The person reduces the unpleasant feelings by avoiding bodies of water. In this example, negative feelings are conditioned according to Pavlovian principles. The avoidance reaction is maintained by (negative) reinforcement and involves instrumental learning. Virtually all the previous examples can be analyzed similarly.

SOURCES FOR FURTHER STUDY

Baldwin, John D., and Janice I. Baldwin. *Behavior Principles in Everyday Life*. 4th ed. Upper Saddle River, N.J.: Prentice-Hall, 2001. Written by two sociologists, this book provides an overview of psychological principles of behavior, including many details about Pavlovian conditioning. The authors provide hundreds of plausible and interesting examples of how behavior principles show up in everyday life. An excellent book for those interested in an interpretation of how Pavlovian and instrumental conditioning work together in daily life.

Hergenhahn, B. R., and Matthew Olson. *Introduction to Theories of Learning*. 6th ed. Upper Saddle River, N.J.: Prentice-Hall, 2001. This book describes the work of fifteen major figures in the area of learning. There are chapters about associative theorists such as Pavlov and functionalist theorists such as the American psychologist B. F. Skinner. A useful elementary survey of learning research and theory spanning one hundred years of development.

Rescorla, Robert A. "Pavlovian Conditioning: It's Not What You Think It Is." *American Psychologist* 43, no. 3 (May, 1988): 151-160. A critical analysis of Pavlovian conditioning by a leading researcher in the field. A major point is that traditional descriptions of Pavlovian conditioning are at best misleading and have failed to incorporate many important developments in the field. The author questions orthodox descriptions of conditioning because they imply that organisms form associations blindly. His view is that organisms actually seek out information using logic and perception to form sophisticated representations of the environment. Rescorla provides a sophisticated examination of the intricacies of conditioning, concentrating on the various outcomes of conditioning and on the circumstances that create them, while citing some of his own work in support of his position.

Watson, John B., and Rosalie Rayner. "Conditioned Emotional Reactions." *Journal of Experimental Psychology* 3 (1920): 1-14. Although this research has been questioned on methodological and ethical grounds—for example, concerns have been raised about the deliberate creation of a phobic reaction in a young child—it is nonetheless a historically important experiment that provided information about how human emotions are learned.

Wolpe, Joseph. *The Practice of Behavior Therapy.* 4th ed. New York: Pergamon, 1990. A significant book by the behavior therapist largely responsible for the development of systematic desensitization. Wolpe discusses behavior therapy as it applies to simple and complex cases of fear and anxiety. Therapeutic approaches discussed include flooding, systematic desensitization, assertiveness training, and the interaction of Pavlovian and operant conditioning. Wolpe is highly critical of the view that therapy consists of little more than information processing and cognitive correction.

Frank J. Sparzo

SEE ALSO: Aversion, implosion, and systematic desensitization; Behaviorism; Conditioning; Habituation and sensitization; Learned helplessness; Learning; Operant conditioning therapies; Phobias; Reflexes.

Peabody Individual Achievement Test (PIAT)

DATE: 1970 forward
TYPE OF PSYCHOLOGY: Intelligence and intelligence testing
FIELDS OF STUDY: Ability tests; intelligence assessment

The Peabody Individual Achievement Test is a widely used, individually administered achievement test for children and adolescents from kindergarten through high school. It provides overall age-equivalent and grade-equivalent scores and subtest scores. It is used in many educational and assessment settings.

KEY CONCEPTS
• achievement
• basal level
• ceiling level
• educational testing

INTRODUCTION

The Peabody Individual Achievement Test is a widely used, individually administered achievement test. Developed in 1970 by Lloyd M. Dunn and Frederick C. Markwardt, it was revised in 1989 by Markwardt. The original version, often called the PIAT, and the revision, often called the PIAT-R, are for children aged five through eighteen. The PIAT measures widely expected educational outcomes, not specific to any particular curriculum.

The PIAT measures achievement in five areas: general information, reading recognition, reading comprehension, mathematics, and spelling. The revision added one more area, written expression. For the general information portion, the examiner reads questions aloud, and the child answers aloud. For reading recognition, the child reads aloud. For reading comprehension, the child reads a sentence silently and then chooses a picture that best illustrates the sentence. For mathematics, the child answers multiple-choice questions on topics ranging from recognizing numbers to solving geometry and trigonometry problems. For spelling, the child chooses the correct spelling of the word that the examiner speaks. For written expression, depending on the child's level, the child either copies and writes words or writes a story in response to a picture.

The items are arranged in increasing order of difficulty. For each child, the examiner starts with some sample items and then obtains basal and ceiling levels. The basal level is the point where the child correctly answers five items in a row. The ceiling level is the point where the child misses five items out of seven. The number of items answered correctly between the basal and ceiling levels determines the child's score. The child's score is matched with scores of children of the same chronological age. The PIAT provides an overall score, percentile ranks, and age-equivalent, grade-equivalent, and standard scores for the overall score and for each portion.

An adult, who is typically an educator or psychologist or someone working under supervision, administers the PIAT to one child at a time. No formal training is required, but the adult must be able to follow the instructions precisely. Typically, testing occurs in a private, quiet, well-lit room and takes about an hour to complete. The items are not timed, except for written expression. Although it is typically given in one session, the child may take a break or come back for a second session if needed.

USES AND LIMITATIONS

The PIAT has several uses. PIAT scores can be useful whenever someone needs an assessment of scholastic achievement or insight into the individual's specific strengths and weaknesses. For the child, this information might be useful in designing a program, providing guidance and counseling, making admissions and placement decisions, and grouping students. In terms of research, the PIAT can be used for evaluation of an educational program. Also, because the test assesses individuals from preschool to post-high school, the PIAT can be used in longitudinal studies on achievement and human development. It could also be used for basic research questions, such as how two achievement areas are related, or the relationship between academic achievement and other traits.

As is true of any test, the PIAT has limitations. One potential limitation is that sometimes people forget that it is a score that the individual made on one specific test on one specific day. They mistakenly believe that the score defines them. Children or adolescents who are ill, distracted, or having an off day for other reasons may perform well below their typical level. Another potential limitation is that the PIAT is limited to English-speaking children in America. Children who have other backgrounds would typically be at a disadvantage. Also, the PIAT must be administered in a standardized way. An examiner who deviates from the instructions might quickly inflate or deflate the child's score.

SOURCES FOR FURTHER STUDY

Costenbader, Virginia K., and John W. Adams. "A Review of the Psychometric and Administrative Features of the PIAT-R: Implications for the Practitioner." *Journal of School Psychology* 29 (Fall, 1991): 219-228. Compares the original PIAT with the revision, discusses new test features (such as providing an expanded protocol form and confidence intervals for raw and derived scores), and outlines procedures for administration and scoring.

Grimley, Liam K. "Academic Assessment of ADHD Children." In *Handbook of Hyperactivity in Children*, edited by Johnny L. Matson. Needham Heights, Mass.: Allyn & Bacon, 1993. Covers the PIAT and other instruments that would be used in an educational assessment of hyperactive children.

Luther, James B. "Review of the Peabody Individual Achievement Test—Revised." *Journal of School Psychology* 30 (Spring, 1992): 31-39. Compares the original PIAT with the revision, noting problems with the new written expression subtest.

Sattler, Jerome M. *Assessment of Children*. 4th ed. San Diego, Calif.: Author, 2002. This book is an excellent resource for assessment. A chapter on "Assessment of Academic Achievement and Special Abilities" thoroughly covers the PIAT-R.

Smith, Douglas K. *Essentials of Individual Achievement Assessment*. New York: John Wiley & Sons, 2001. Written by a school psychologist, this book covers the PIAT and other individually administered achievement tests used in educational planning, transitional programming for students with disabilities, and career/vocational planning.

Lillian M. Range

SEE ALSO: Ability tests; Assessment; Career and personnel testing; Career Occupational Preference System (COPS); College entrance examinations; Creativity: Assessment; General Aptitude Test Battery (GATB); Human resource training and development; Intelligence tests; Interest inventories; Kuder Occupational Interest Survey (KOIS); Race and intelligence; Scientific methods; Stanford-Binet test; Strong Interest Inventory (SII); Survey research: Questionnaires and interviews; Testing: Historical perspectives; Wechsler Intelligence; Scale for Children-Third Edition (WISC-III).

Penis envy

TYPE OF PSYCHOLOGY: Developmental psychology; personality; psychopathology; psychotherapy; social psychology

FIELDS OF STUDY: Childhood and adolescent disorders; classic analytic themes and issues; infancy and childhood; interpersonal relations; models of abnormality; personality disorders; personality theory; psychodynamic and neoanalytic models; sexual disorders

Penis envy was a concept formulated by Sigmund Freud based on his theory that girls experienced deep envy of boys for their possessing a penis and suffered emotionally from this lack. The theory was the basis of his biological frame of reference. Later analysts included the social environment in their concept of personality development and saw social and cultural conditions as more important in female personality development.

KEY CONCEPTS
- castration
- culture
- masculine protest
- masochism
- psychoanalytic treatment
- psychosexual development

INTRODUCTION

Sigmund Freud (1856-1939), the Austrian founder of psychoanalysis, formulated a theory of psychosexual development. The energy that drove this development was called libido, sexualized energy. This theory was biologically oriented and rested on the assumption that the goal of female development was to achieve what the male possessed, namely a penis. Discovering its absence caused profound emotional injury and became the basis for future personality development in the female.

FREUD'S BIOLOGICAL THEORY

In 1905, in "Three Essays on the Theory of Sexuality," Freud stated that girls notice that boys have penises and, as a result, experience intense feelings of envy and wish to be boys. Later he added that both boys and girls develop a sexual theory in which both originally had a penis, and boys assume that girls originally possessed a penis but lost it through castration. This fear in boys of meeting the same fate leads to the resolution of the Oedipus complex, where the boy relinquishes his sexual feelings toward his mother and identifies with his father. Males then adopt a low opinion of females due to their lack of penises.

This envy that girls experience is supposed to profoundly influence their future personality development in several ways. Overcome by powerful feelings of envy, they feel unfairly treated. According to Freud, anatomy is destiny, in that girls want to possess the male sex organ. First they seize on the idea that the clitoris can serve as a penis substitute. Eventually, they are forced to concede that the clitoris is not adequate as a substitute and experience a profound trauma as a result.

One of the possible outcomes of this trauma is the development of the masculine protest. Girls may assume masculine personality characteristics or, as adults, may withdraw from sexual experience entirely to avoid powerful feelings of inadequacy.

When girls discover that all females lack a penis, hostility develops toward the mother, who is seen as having deprived them of this sex organ. They then wish for their father to give them either a penis or a baby, which serves as a penis substitute. The discovery of this wish is considered critical by Freud, who viewed it as a sign that bedrock had been reached in psychoanalytic treatment and that termination was at hand.

Another example of the importance that Freud placed on penis envy was his postulating a direct connection between masochism (the sexual pleasure derived from pain) and female personality development. In his attempt to demonstrate this connection, he selected penis envy as the first experience leading to this conclusion.

POST-FREUDIAN ELABORATION

Erik Erikson (1902-1994), a pupil of Sigmund Freud who emigrated to the United States, combined ego psychology with what he called life-span theory. In this theory, drives or instincts are significant, but the emphasis is on the interaction with the significant people in one's own environment. Erickson accepted Freud's formulation that the girl experiences a trauma at discovering her lack of a penis, but he differed from Freud in that he did not emphasize abnormal behavior but rather the healthy, adaptive processes in the ego of the girl. His shift was away from the trauma of loss to the healthy ego resources that lead to a woman having a positive view of herself. Anatomy is important to Erickson because it provides a framework for male and female experience, but group membership, history, and individual personality all contribute to female personality development. He felt that while male and female ego processes have much in common, the differences in male and female experience and development should be identified and studied.

Karen Horney (1885-1952), a German-born psychoanalyst who emigrated to the United States, began as a classical psychoanalyst. However, she felt that this model was too restrictive and needed to expand in order to include the role of culture in personality development. She recognized that it was entirely possible that girls experience some feelings of envy due to their lack of a penis. However, she also noticed in her clinical practice that boys also experience envy in relation to girls. She found that boys envied girls' breasts and their ability to produce children when adult.

Horney stated that in classical psychoanalysis, the libidinal development of women was evaluated from a male perspective, and questioned whether, since observations are gender influenced, these formulations could be accurate. She emphasized that basing female development on male standards was at best incomplete, since female development included events not found in male development, such as pregnancy and childbirth.

Horney stated that some penis envy may be entirely normal. Having the opportunity to contact his genitals through urination, the boy may find it easier to satisfy his sexual curiosity; the fact that the boy routinely contacts his genitals may make it more acceptable to take the steps toward masturbation. However, she felt that these feelings of envy in women would ordinarily not lead to feelings of inferiority or toward the development of the masculine protest. She found that Freud's formulation of the masculine protest was based upon his study of neurotic women.

Horney stated that conditions other than penis envy would be necessary for a female to reject her gender. One such condition was when the father rejected his daughter's femaleness. Another condition was when mother projected such a negative image of the female role that the girl did not wish to identify with that image.

Horney emphasized that the culture plays a significant role in female personality development. She felt that girls are often subtly and sometimes harshly made to feel inferior, and due to the masculine nature of the culture, girls may be excluded from occupations and other opportunities, which would contribute to feelings of inferiority. She pointed out that in a culture that demeans women sexually, makes it unacceptable for women to be assertive, and makes it difficult for women to be economically independent, it will be easier for women to feel inferior, not because of a lack of a penis, but because of the prevailing attitudes that culture holds toward women.

SOURCES FOR FURTHER STUDY

Blanton, S. *Diary of My Analysis with Sigmund Freud.* New York: Hawthorn Books, 1972. A small volume but a gem of an opportunity to hear Freud discuss his theories while treating a patient. In addition, it points out how important it is to have exact dates in mind when researching his psychosexual theory, as it changed over time.

Erikson, Erik. *Childhood and Society.* New York: W. W. Norton, 1963. This is a clearly written and enjoyable introduction to Erikson, which includes his earliest and latest statements of his developmental model.

Freud, Sigmund. *The Complete Psychological Works of Sigmund Freud.* London: Hogarth Press, 1975. The core of his developmental theory relating to penis envy is well covered in volumes 7, 9, 10, 11, 12. These papers include important statements about his views of women and leave the reader to wonder how these views affected his clinical behavior.

Horney, Karen. *Feminine Psychology.* New York: W. W. Norton, 1967. This book illustrates how Horney was ahead of her time in being able to see how culture shapes individual and group personality, especially for women. She takes Freud's biological theory and interprets it in social-cultural terms. An excellent example of the interpersonal approach to the relationship of marriage.

Monte, Christopher. *Beneath the Mask: An Introduction to Theories of Personality.* 6th ed. Orlando, Fla.: Harcourt Press, 1999. Presents classic psychological theories of human nature, including Freud's theories and their critics.

Leonard Feinberg

SEE ALSO: Ego, superego, and id; Freud, Sigmund; Oedipus complex; Personality theory; Psychoanalytic psychology; Psychoanalytic psychology: Sigmund Freud; Psychosexual development; Women's psychology: Karen Horney; Women's psychology: Sigmund Freud.

Person-centered therapy

TYPE OF PSYCHOLOGY: Psychotherapy
FIELDS OF STUDY: Humanistic therapies

Person-centered therapy is based on a philosophy that emphasizes an inherent human tendency for growth and self-actualization. Psychologist Carl Rogers developed and described person-centered therapy as a "way of being."

KEY CONCEPTS
- congruence
- empathy
- genuineness
- self
- self-actualization
- unconditional positive regard

INTRODUCTION

Psychologist Carl R. Rogers (1902-1987) was the leading figure in the development of phenomenological therapy, and his name has been used synonymously ("Rogerian" therapy) with person-centered therapy. Phenomenological theory is a method of exploration that emphasizes all aspects of human experience. In particular, it highlights the importance of an individual's creative power, in addition to genetics and environment. Moreover, this theory focuses primarily on a person's subjective experience (opinions, viewpoints, and understandings) and defines therapy on the basis of a good human-to-human relationship.

Rogers remained primarily concerned with the conditions for personal growth rather than with the development of personality theory; he focused on personality functioning rather than on personality structures. He did, however, offer formal conceptions of personality. The central concepts and key formulations of person-centered therapy were published in Rogers's *Counseling and Psychotherapy: Newer Concepts in Practice* (1942), *On Becoming a Person* (1961), and his landmark book *Client-Centered Therapy* (1951). Rogers presented nineteen propositions about personality development. These propositions included the following concepts: Each individual exists in a continually changing world in which he or she is the center. Individuals react to the world as they experience and perceive it; thus, "reality" is defined by the person's phenomenal field.

Behavior is basically the goal-directed attempt of the organism to satisfy its needs as experienced in the phenomenal field. Each individual has a unique perspective—his or her own private world—and to comprehend a person one must assume a frame of reference from the person's perspective. Emotion facilitates goal-directed behavior. The structure of the self is formed as a result of evaluative interactions with others; the self is an organized, fluid, yet consistent pattern of perceptions about oneself.

The phenomenal field refers to everything experienced by an individual at any given time. The term "internal frame of reference" refers to the process by which therapists attempt to perceive clients' experiences and "reality" as closely as they can. An individual's reality is essentially that which the person perceives. Moreover, it is the person's subjective experience and perceptions that shape the person's understanding of reality and guide behavior. Events are significant for an individual if the individual experiences them as meaningful. In treatment, therapists strive to understand clients by understanding their views of themselves and the environment in which they live.

IMPORTANCE OF SELF

A central concept within phenomenological theory is the "self" (a structure derived from experiences involving one's own body or resulting from one's own actions). The self (or self-concept), then, is a self-picture or self-awareness. It is a changing process that incorporates the individual's meaning when he or she refers to the characteristics of "I" or "me" in isolation or in relationships with others. The concept of self is also considered to be an organized, consistent, and learned attribute composed of thoughts about self. Rogers views the need for positive regard to be universal. The self-concept depends, in large part, on the "conditions of worth" that a child has learned through interactions with significant others. According to Rogers, the child's need to maintain the love of parents inevitably results in conflict with his or her own needs and desires. For example, as young children assert greater autonomy, a growing awareness of individuality and uniqueness follows. Quite often, the young child demonstrates a negativistic pattern wherein conflicts become more common as the child's needs are in conflict with parent desires.

Maladjustment occurs when there is a lack of consistency between one's concept of self and one's sensory and visceral experiences. If the self-concept is based on many conditions of worth and includes components of failure, imperfection, and weakness, then a lack of positive self-regard will be evident. When such incongruence occurs, individuals are viewed as being vulnerable to psychological problems. Of particular importance is self-esteem (feelings about self), which is often negative or problematic in clients. Poor self-esteem occurs when the phenomenal self is threatened. A threat for one person is not necessarily a threat for another. A person will experience threat whenever he or she perceives that the phenomenal self is in danger. For example, if a well-adjusted athlete misses the final shot at the buzzer in a close basketball game, he or she will not blame the referees or claim physical illness, but instead will examine this experience and perhaps revise his or her self-concept.

SELF-DIRECTION, SELF-ACTUALIZATION, AND CONGRUENCE

Other key principles that underlie person-centered theory involve the processes of self-direction and self-actualization. According to Rogers, humans have an innate tendency to maintain and enhance the self. In fact, all needs can be summarized as the urge to enhance the phenomenal self. Although the process of self-actualization may become disrupted by a variety of social, interpersonal, and cultural factors (determined in large part by the actions of parents, teachers, and peers), Rogers states that the positive growth tendency will ultimately prevail. This actualizing tendency is what produces the forward movement of life, the primary force upon which therapists rely heavily in therapy with clients. Self-actualization refers to the concept that unhampered individuals strive to actualize, enhance, and reach their full potential.

Via self-actualization, a person becomes a fully functioning individual. The qualities of a fully functioning person include being open to experience all feelings while being afraid of none; demonstrating creativity and individual expression; living in the present without preoccupation with past or future; being free to make choices and act on those choices spontaneously; trusting oneself and human nature; having an internal source of evaluation; demonstrating balance and realistic expressions of anger, ag-gression, and affection; exhibiting congruence between one's feelings and experience; and showing a willingness to continue to grow.

Congruence is the term used by Rogers and others to imply the correspondence between awareness and experience. If a client is able to communicate an awareness of feelings that he or she is currently experiencing, the behavior is said to be congruent or integrated. On the other hand, if an individual attempts to communicate a feeling (love, for example) to another person while experiencing incongruence (hostility toward that person), the recipient of that individual's expression of feelings may experience an awareness of miscommunication.

EVOLUTION OF STUDY

Person-centered theory and therapy have evolved since the 1940's. When Rogers published *Counseling and Psychotherapy*, the predominant view among mental health professionals was that the therapist should act as an expert who directs the course of treatment. Rogers, however, described counseling as a relationship in which warmth, responsiveness, and freedom from coercion and pressure (including pressure from the therapist) are essential. Such an approach to treatment emphasized the client's ability to take positive steps toward personal growth. This phase, from 1940 to 1950, has been called Rogers's non-directive period. The second phase, reflective psychotherapy, spanned the years from 1950 to 1957. During this period, Rogers changed the name of his approach to "client-centered counseling" and emphasized the importance of reflecting (paraphrasing, summarizing, and clarifying) the client's underlying feelings.

The third phase, experiential psychotherapy, has been described as lasting from 1957 to 1970. During this phase, Rogers focused on the conditions that would be necessary and sufficient for change to occur. Results of his studies demonstrated that the most successful clients were those who experienced the highest degree of accurate empathy, and that client ratings, rather than therapist ratings, of the quality of the therapeutic relationship were most closely associated with eventual success or failure. Also evident during this phase of development was Rogers's deemphasis of psychotherapy techniques, such as reflection. Instead, he focused more on the importance of basic therapist attitudes. By so doing, he encouraged a wider range of therapist behaviors in order to establish the essential relationship components of empathy, positive regard, and congruence. Therapists were encouraged to attend to their own experiences in the session and express their immediate feelings in the therapy relationship.

In 1974, Rogers changed the name of his approach to person-centered therapy. Rogers believed that person-centered therapy more appropriately described the human values that his approach incorporates. Since the 1970's, an additional phase of person-centered therapy, incorporating a more eclectic approach to treatment, has evolved. Specifically, person-centered therapists frequently employ strategies that focus on thoughts, feelings, and values from other schools of psychotherapy within the framework of a productive, accepting relationship. Person-centered approaches have been successfully incorporated into teaching and educational curricula, marriage programs, and international conflict-resolution situations.

THERAPEUTIC RELATIONSHIPS

Person-centered therapy aims to increase the congruence, or matching, between self-concept and organismic experience. As Rogers described it, psychotherapy serves to "free up" the already existing capacity in a potentially competent individual, rather than consisting of the expert manipulation of techniques designed to change personality. The primary mechanism for reintegration of self and experience is the interpersonal relationship between therapist and client. In fact, the therapeutic relationship is viewed as being of primary importance in promoting healing and growth. Thus, it is this relationship in and of itself that produces growth in the client. Rogers argues that the process of therapy is synonymous with the experiential relationship between client and therapist; change occurs primarily as a result of the interaction between them.

As described by N. J. Raskin and Rogers in 1989, the most fundamental concept in person-centered therapy is trust—that is, trust in clients' tendency to grow toward actualization and trust in clients' ability to achieve their own goals and run their own lives. Similarly, it is important that the therapist be seen as a *person* in the relationship (not as a role), and that the therapist be appreciated and regarded with trust. Rogers stated that clients enter treatment in a state of incongruence, often resulting in vulnerability and anxiety. For treatment to be effective, he

identified three necessary and sufficient ingredients for constructive change: The counselor experiences empathic understanding of the client's internal frame of reference, the counselor experiences unconditional positive regard for the client, and the counselor acts congruently with his or her own experience, becoming genuinely integrated into the relationship with the client. It is also essential to the therapy process that the counselor succeed in communicating unconditional positive regard, genuineness, and empathic understanding to the client.

Of particular importance is empathy. Empathy reflects an attitude of interest in the client's thoughts, feelings, and experiences. Moreover, Rogers describes empathy as "a way of being" that is powerfully curative because of its nonevaluative and accepting quality. In fact, the process of conveying accurate empathic understanding has been described as the most important aspect of the therapeutic endeavor. Therapists who convey this form of sensitivity to the needs, feelings, and circumstances of the client can in essence climb inside the client's subjective experience and attempt to understand the world as he or she does. Empathy facilitates a process through which clients assume a caring attitude toward themselves. Moreover, empathy allows clients to gain a greater understanding of their own organismic experiencing, which in turn facilitates positive self-regard and a more accurate self-concept.

In perhaps all of their previous relationships, clients have learned that acceptance is conditional upon acting in an acceptable manner. For example, parents typically accept children if they do as they are told. In therapy, however, Rogers argued that no conditions of worth should be present. Acceptance of the client as a fallible yet essentially trustworthy individual is given without ulterior motives, hidden causes, or subtle disclaimers. The primary challenge of the therapist's unconditional positive regard comes with clients whose behavior and attitude run strongly counter to the therapist's beliefs. A sex offender, an abusive parent, or a lazy client can test a therapist's level of tolerance and acceptance. Rogers's position is that every individual is worthy of unconditional positive regard.

Genuineness refers to the characteristic of being congruent—the experience of therapists who appropriately express the behavior, feelings, and attitudes that the client stimulates in them. For example, a person does not laugh when sad or angry. Similarly, acting congruently with one's own emotional experience does not mean hiding behind a mask of calm when a client makes upsetting statements. Rogers believed that, in the long run, clients would respond best to a "real person" who is dedicated to the client's welfare and acts in an honest and congruent manner.

SEVEN STEPS OF THERAPY

In person-centered treatment, sessions are usually scheduled once or twice a week. Additional sessions and telephone calls are typically discouraged in order to avoid dependency on the therapist that will stifle personal growth. Rogers has described the general process of therapy as involving a series of seven steps. Step one is an initial unwillingness to reveal self and an avoidance of feelings; close relationships may be perceived as threatening or dangerous. In step two, feelings are described briefly, but the person is still distant from his or her own personal experience and externalizes issues; the person begins to show recognition that conflicts and difficulties exist. In step three, describing past feelings becomes unacceptable; there is more self-disclosure and expression, and the client begins to question the validity of his or her constructs and beliefs.

Step four involves the description of personal feelings as owned by the self and a limited recognition that previously denied feelings may exist; there is an increasing expression of self-responsibility. Step five involves the free expression and acceptance of one's feelings, an awareness of previously denied feelings, a recognition of conflicts between intellectual and emotional processes, and a desire to be who one really is. In step six, there is an acceptance of feelings without the need for denial and a willingness to risk being oneself in relationships with others. In step seven, the person is comfortable with his or her self, is aware of new feelings and experiences, and experiences minimal incongruence.

INFLUENCES

As Rogers began his career during the late 1930's, psychoanalysis was the primary approach to psychotherapy and the dominant model in personality theory. Though Rogers was subjected to traditional psychoanalytic influences, his perspective was nearly the exact opposite of Sigmund Freud's theory; Rogers tended to reject the notion of unconscious pro-

cesses. Instead, he was strongly influenced by the therapeutic approach of psychoanalyst Otto Rank (and his followers at the University of Pennsylvania School of Social Work), the relationship therapy of social worker Jessie Taft, and the feeling-focused approach of social worker Elizabeth Davis. Rank believed that clients benefit from the opportunity to express themselves in session, exhibit creativity in treatment, and even dominate the therapist. Taft emphasized that there are key components to the therapeutic relationship (including a permissive therapeutic environment and a positive working relationship between the therapist and client) which are more important than psychoanalytic explanations of the client's problems. Davis focused almost exclusively on the feelings being expressed in treatment by her clients. From his association with Davis, Rogers developed the therapy component referred to as reflection of feelings. Rogers believed strongly that no individual has the right to run another person's life. Thus, his therapeutic approach was generally permissive and accepting, and he generally refused to give advice to clients.

CONTRIBUTIONS TO PSYCHOLOGY

Person-centered approaches have made major contributions to therapy, theory, and empirical research. In fact, Rogers was responsible for the first systematic investigations of the therapeutic process. He was the first to employ recordings of therapy sessions to study the interactive process and to investigate its effectiveness. Although the use of such recordings is now commonplace in most training programs, Rogers's willingness to open his approach to such scrutiny was unusual for its time.

Person-centered therapy has generated numerous research contributions. A 1971 review of research on "necessary and sufficient" conditions concluded that counselors who are accurately empathic, genuine, and nonpossessively warm tend to be effective with a broad spectrum of clients regardless of the counselors' training or theoretical orientation. The authors also concluded that clients receiving low levels of such conditions in treatment showed deterioration. Many researchers have questioned the "necessary and sufficient" argument proposed by Rogers, however; they suggest that the therapeutic conditions specified by Rogers are neither necessary nor sufficient, although such therapeutic approaches are facilitative.

Although Rogers's approach was developed primarily for counseling clients, the person-centered approach has found many other applications. Person-centered approaches are frequently used in human relations training, including paraprofessional counselors, YWCA/YMCA volunteers, crisis center volunteers, Peace Corps and VISTA workers, and charitable organization workers. Small group therapy programs and personal growth groups also make frequent use of person-centered approaches.

SOURCES FOR FURTHER STUDY

Prouty, Gary. *Theoretical Evolutions in Person-Centered/Existential Therapy.* Westport, Conn.: Praeger, 1994. Good overview of the origin and development of person-centered therapy. Proposes modifications to make it more useful in the treatment of schizophrenia and mental retardation.

Raskin, N. J., and Carl R. Rogers. "Person-Centered Therapy." In *Current Psychotherapies*, edited by Raymond J. Corsini and Danny Wedding. 4th ed. Itasca, Ill.: F. E. Peacock, 1989. One of the last projects that Rogers worked on prior to his death in 1987. Raskin knew Rogers for forty-seven years, and in this chapter he summarizes many of the key principles and concepts associated with person-centered therapy.

Rogers, Carl R. *Client-Centered Therapy.* Boston: Houghton Mifflin, 1951. A landmark text wherein Rogers highlights many of the key components of his evolving approach. The book describes aspects of the therapeutic relationship and the process of therapy.

_____. *Counseling and Psychotherapy: Newer Concepts in Practice.* Boston: Houghton Mifflin, 1942. Rogers's first book-length description of his approach to therapy. This book is of historical significance because it presents a revised version of Rogers's address at the University of Minnesota on December 11, 1940, at which time client-centered therapy was "officially" born.

_____. *On Becoming a Person.* Boston: Houghton Mifflin, 1961. One of Rogers's best-known and most highly regarded books. Presents valuable insight into Rogers, his approach, and the uses of client-centered approaches in education, family life, and elsewhere.

_____. *A Way of Being.* Boston: Houghton Mifflin, 1980. Rogers wrote this book as a follow-up to *On Becoming a Person*, and in it he updates his

theory and therapeutic approach. An excellent bibliography is also included.

Thorne, Brian, and Elke Lambers, eds. *Person-Centered Therapy: A European Perspective.* Thousand Oaks, Calif.: Corwin, 1998. A collection of papers by European therapists. Offers both theoretical analyses and practical advice on dealing with difficult clients.

Gregory L. Wilson

SEE ALSO: Abnormality: Psychological models; Existential psychology; Gestalt therapy; Humanism; Humanistic trait models: Gordon Allport; Psychotherapy: Effectiveness; Psychotherapy: Goals and techniques; Rogers, Carl R.; Self-actualization.

Personal constructs
George A. Kelly

TYPE OF PSYCHOLOGY: Personality
FIELDS OF STUDY: Behavioral and cognitive models

Personal construct theory examines the way each person thinks about the world; it attempts to provide avenues for understanding and making use of one's subjective experiences. It demonstrates how cognitions change when one incorrectly predicts the future on the basis of those cognitions.

KEY CONCEPTS
- construct
- constructive alternativism
- dichotomy
- fixed role therapy
- fundamental postulate
- role
- Role Construct Repertory Test

INTRODUCTION

Personal construct theory maintains that all people are motivated to reduce uncertainty in their lives. In this manner, each person is like a scientist who is attempting to solve complex problems. Instead of dealing with complex equations in chemistry and physics, however, one is attempting to unravel the complexities of one's own life and the relationships that one has developed. Just as scientists are constantly making changes in their theories and research claims based on the availability of new evidence, people change the way they look at their subjective worlds on the basis of new evidence. That evidence appears in the form of new interactions with significant others in people's lives, such as spouses, children, parents, and bosses. When new evidence is made available, a person will alter his or her thought patterns in order to reduce uncertainty in the future. This view forms the basis of George Kelly's principle of constructive alternativism—the view that people are entitled to their own views of the world and that they will make use of those views in order to reduce uncertainty in the future.

George Kelly became involved in personal constructs theory late in his career. Ironically, Kelly's early experiences as a psychologist did not even involve the study of personality. It was only in 1955, twelve years prior to his death, that he published *The Psychology of Personal Constructs: A Theory of Personality*. In this work, he defined and discussed the concept of a construct. For Kelly, a construct is a thought that a person has for the purpose of attempting to interpret events; these interpretations may prove to be accurate or inaccurate. In those situations in which a construct leads to an incorrect prediction of an event, the person is likely to change the construct. All of Kelly's constructs are dichotomous in nature. That is, they are made of pairs of polar opposites that cannot be simultaneously correct when referring to the same person. For example, one cannot view one's boss as both intelligent and unintelligent at the same time. Similarly, one's boyfriend or girlfriend cannot be seen as cruel and kind at the same moment.

FUNDAMENTAL POSTULATE AND COROLLARIES

Kelly claimed that constructs operate according to a fundamental postulate. This postulate maintains that each person directs thoughts and cognitions in a way that permits the most accurate prediction of future events. If a woman has a personal construct which states that her boyfriend is a thoughtful person, and he sends her flowers while she is in bed with the flu, her construct would be regarded as an accurate one. If, however, that same boyfriend used her illness as an opportunity to date other women and ignored her illness in the process, it would be necessary to adjust her construction system because it does not accurately predict her boyfriend's be-

havior. This process of changing one's construction system in order to predict future events more accurately is an ongoing one designed to decrease uncertainty in the future.

While the fundamental postulate is critical to Kelly's attempts to predict and explain behavior, it is not sufficient to cover all aspects of a person's behavior and the choices that are made which cause that behavior. In order to address this additional detail, Kelly provided a series of eleven corollaries to his fundamental postulate. These corollaries are supporting statements that provide a detailed analysis of thoughts and behaviors which cannot be directly derived from the fundamental postulate.

The construction corollary maintains that people continue to learn as they are presented with similar events in life. For example, if a man's mother has given him a birthday present for the last thirty years, his prediction that he will receive another present from her on his next birthday makes sense. Similarly, if one has watched a particular television program such as *Nightline* at 11:30 P.M. on weekdays for the past several years, one's prediction that it will again be on television at the same time tonight is a reasonable one.

Another important corollary to Kelly's fundamental postulate is the dichotomy corollary. This states that all constructs consist of pairs of opposites. That is, a college course may be either interesting or uninteresting, but it cannot be both at the same time. One important aspect of the dichotomy corollary is that each construct must include three members or items, with two of the members having the same characteristic and the third member having the opposite characteristic. For example, breathing and not breathing would not be a legitimate construct in evaluating three friends. Since all of them breathe, the proposed construct would not tell how the three individuals are different as well as alike. Therefore, it would not reduce uncertainty in the future.

A third corollary to Kelly's system that is particularly important is the range corollary. This maintains that a construct is only relevant in dealing with a finite number of events. The events for which a construct is deemed applicable is called its range of convenience. Terms such as "happy" and "sad" would not be within the range of convenience in depicting the characteristics of a tree or a book, while they might be critical in evaluating one's relatives.

Varying degrees of applicability can be found within a series of constructs. For example, the construct "kind versus cruel" would be more relevant in evaluating a relative or girlfriend than it would be in considering the qualities of an elevator operator one occasionally encounters. Kelly's fundamental postulate and supporting corollaries provide considerable information. The theory also provides some interesting applications in terms of personality assessment and therapeutic intervention.

USE WITH CAREER GOALS

Kelly's personal construct theory has been used to explain, predict, and attempt to modify behavior in a wide range of circumstances. One interesting application involves the use of personal constructs in formulating career goals. A high school student, for example, may establish a goal of becoming a successful surgeon in the future. The nature of her constructs can then be examined to determine whether her constructs (as they relate to her own characteristics) are likely to lead to a medical career. She currently views herself as unintelligent rather than intelligent, dedicated to immediate gratification rather than delayed gratification, and lazy rather than hardworking. If she is eventually to become a successful physician, she must reject those constructs and develop a new construction system which is consistent with her career goals. The application of Kelly's theory to career choice is important. While one does not expect first-grade children to examine their own characteristics realistically in considering career options, much more is required of high school and college students. It is not sufficient to state that one wants to pursue a given career: The nature of one's constructs must be evaluated to determine if they are consistent with one's career goals. In those circumstances in which inconsistencies exist, either the constructs or the career goals must change.

ROLE CONSTRUCT REPERTORY TEST

One of the most interesting applications of Kelly's personal construct theory involves the development of an assessment device, the Role Construct Repertory Test. This test defines a role as a set of behaviors that are performed by a person in response to the construction systems and behaviors of others. The test itself determines the nature of a person's system of constructs as it is related to the significant others in that person's life. The test can be used as a means of evaluating progress during psychotherapy or as a vehicle for detecting changes in interpersonal relationships.

The test involves the creation of a grid in which significant others in the life of the person are listed. Examples would be self, mother, spouse, boss, friend, and successful person. The client then considers these individuals in groups of three provided by the therapist. The client comes up with a word that typifies two of these individuals, and a second word that is the opposite of the first word but typifies the third person. This procedure is followed for a group of twenty sorts, or sets of comparisons. This enables the therapist to determine the behaviors and thoughts of the client concerning the significant others in her life.

One of the determinations that can be made involves the flexibility of the client in dealing with others. That is, in listing those individuals on the grid who possess certain positive characteristics, the therapist would examine whether the same individuals on the grid are given credit for all the positive characteristics listed while a second group is always viewed negatively. This would indicate a lack of flexibility in the client and might offer an area for needed change in the future.

FIXED ROLE THERAPY

As an application of Kelly's theory, the Role Construct Repertory Test is an initial step in the therapeutic process. An interesting follow-up provided by Kelly is fixed role therapy. This technique begins by asking the client to develop an in-depth description of himself or herself, written in the third person. This is called a self-characterization sketch. The third-person style is used to produce greater objectivity than would be achieved with first-person narratives. This gives the therapist a clear look at the client from the client's own perspective. The therapist then establishes a role for the client which is directly opposite many of the characteristics in the self-characterization sketch. The client is asked to act out that new role for a period of time. The role would include positive characteristics not found in the self-characterization sketch. The ultimate goal of the technique is to have the client maintain many of those new positive characteristics on a long-term basis.

In evaluating applications of Kelly's work, the emphasis must be placed on the importance of knowing one's own construction system and, when appropriate, taking steps to change that system. While this may be handled through formal techniques such as fixed role therapy, many therapists make use of Kelly's emphasis upon cognitive change without strictly employing his terminology. To this extent, the influence of Kelly's work should increase in the future.

KELLY'S CAREER

George Kelly did not begin his career with the intention of developing personal construct theory. In fact, his initial training was not even in the field of personality psychology. Kelly's original specialty in graduate school was physiological psychology, and his dissertation was concerned with the areas of speech and reading disabilities. Having received his degree around the time of the Great Depression, however, Kelly came to the conclusion that the principles and concepts contained within his areas of specialization offered little solace to those who were emotionally and financially devastated in the aftermath of the Depression. He turned to clinical psychology, with an initial emphasis on the psychoanalytic approach. He noted that concepts such as the id and the libido seemed of no use in dealing with victims of the Depression.

Kelly's initial academic position was at Fort Hays State College in Kansas. While at Fort Hays, he developed a series of traveling psychological clinics designed to treat the emotional and behavioral problems of students. This experience was crucial in the eventual formulation of personal construct theory. Kelly tried numerous forms of treatment with the students and determined that the optimal technique varied across cases. This led him to conclude that any clinical technique that is successful should be retained, while techniques that result in repeated treatment failure should be discarded. This flexibility, reflected in his later theoretical claims regarding constructive alternativism and his fundamental postulate, has made Kelly unique among personality theorists. Kelly's willingness to respect subjective reality as determined by each human being is reflective of his unwillingness to commit himself totally to any one theoretical perspective. Although Kelly was influenced by many theorists, he clearly traveled his own path in the development of his psychology of personal constructs.

SOURCES FOR FURTHER STUDY

Bannister, Donald, and Fay Fransella. *Inquiring Man: The Theory of Personal Constructs*. 3d ed. New York: Routledge, 1986. Provides an excellent introduction to Kelly's theory. In addition, a wide range of applications are provided within the overall field of clinical psychology as well as social psychology. It should be noted that the authors are dedicated advocates of Kelly's perspective.

Bannister, Donald, and J. M. M. Mair, eds. *The Evaluation of Personal Constructs*. New York: Academic Press, 1968. This excellent work is unique in that it provides insights into the types of theoretical and research efforts that have been undertaken as a result of Kelly's contributions. Particularly relevant because it was published shortly after Kelly's death and therefore provides an interesting analysis of Kelly's influence at that time.

Kelly, George Alexander. *Clinical Psychology and Personality: The Selected Papers of George Kelly*. Edited by Brendan Maher. New York: John Wiley & Sons, 1969. This offering is unique in that it contains many of Kelly's last papers. Includes papers that account for the origins of the theory and depicts Kelly's analysis of his work shortly before his death. The presentation is accurate, and it faithfully depicts the essence of Kelly's work.

_____. *The Psychology of Personal Constructs: A Theory of Personality*. New York: W. W. Norton, 1955. This two-volume series, still in print after almost half a century, provides the essence of Kelly's theory. Covers the theoretical basis for the theory by presenting an analysis of personal constructs, constructive alternativism, and the fundamental postulate, as well as the Role Construct Repertory Test and fixed role therapy. Kelly's views of the appropriate place of assessment in the therapeutic process are particularly interesting.

Neimeyer, Robert A. *The Development of Personal Construct Psychology*. Lincoln: University of Nebraska Press, 1985. Looks at the origins, development, and impact of Kelly's theory. Includes many relevant insights into Kelly's early work, while including applications of the theory in areas such as personality, clinical psychology, and social psychology.

Lawrence A. Fehr

Personality disorders

TYPE OF PSYCHOLOGY: Psychopathology
FIELDS OF STUDY: Personality assessment; personality disorders

The personality disorders are a cluster of psychological disorders characterized by inflexible and longstanding patterns of relating to others and the environment that create significant impairment in functioning.

KEY CONCEPTS
- antisocial personality disorder
- avoidant personality disorder
- borderline personality disorder
- dependent personality disorder
- histrionic personality disorder
- narcissistic personality disorder
- paranoid personality disorder
- personality
- obsessive-compulsive disorder
- schizoid personality disorder
- schizotypal personality disorder

INTRODUCTION

Personality is a term used to describe long-standing patterns of thinking, behaving, and feeling. A group of traits which are consistently displayed are considered to be part of a person's personality. A person's mood, for example, is considered to be a more fleeting expression of one's overall personality. Personality comprises traits, attitudes, behaviors, and coping styles which develop throughout childhood and adolescence. Personality can be thought of as a relatively consistent style of relating to others and the environment, developing as a result of genetic and environmental influences. Psychologists have developed several theories to explain personality development. Austrian psychoanalyst Sigmund Freud (1856-1939) believed that personality development originates in early childhood. Freud proposed that personality emerges as a result of unconscious conflicts between unacceptable aggressive and hedonistic instincts and societal mores. According to Freud, unresolved unconscious conflicts from childhood later influence personality development. In contrast to Freud's psychoanalytic theories about personality, other researchers focused on specific traits as the building blocks of personality development. Many classification systems have been developed in an attempt to organize and categorize personality traits and styles. The Big Five system proposes that five basic trait dimensions underlie personality structure: extroversion versus introversion, agreeableness versus disagreeableness, conscientiousness versus impulsiveness, emotional stability versus neuroticism, and openness to experience versus rigidity. Personality disorders may reflect extreme variants of these basic personality dimensions.

The personality disorders are a group of psychological disorders characterized by inflexible and maladaptive patterns of relating to others which result in impairments in day-to-day functioning. The personality disorders are reflected by personality traits which are significantly extreme or exaggerated, making it difficult to establish functional relationships with others. According to the *Diagnostic and Statistical Manual of Mental Disorders: DSM-IV-TR* (rev. 4th ed., 2000), the personality disorders are defined by an enduring pattern of inner experience and behavior which is consistently dysfunctional and creates impairment in functioning. Symptoms of personality disorders are usually evident by early adulthood, coinciding with the developmental period when personality patterns have become established in most people. The DSM-IV-TR identifies ten major personality disorders: paranoid personality disorder, schizoid personality disorder, schizotypal personality disorder, borderline personality disorder, antisocial personality disorder, narcissistic personality disorder, histrionic personality disorder, avoidant personality disorder, dependent personality disorder, and obsessive-compulsive personality disorder. The personality disorders are broken down into three groups, or clusters, based upon similar symptomatology.

CLUSTER A

The personality disorders in Cluster A consist of paranoid personality disorder, schizoid personality disorder, and schizotypal personality disorder. The behavior of people with a cluster A personality disorder is described as odd or eccentric.

Paranoid personality disorder is characterized by a pervasive distrust of others, chronic suspicion about others' motives, and paranoid thinking. Others often avoid individuals with paranoid personality disorder, which reinforces their mistrust of others. The suspicion is chronic and creates a difficulty in establishing and maintaining interpersonal relationships. Paranoid personality disorder is more prevalent in males than females.

Schizoid personality disorder is characterized by a pervasive and long-lasting indifference toward others. The term "schizoid" was initially chosen to refer to the preliminary symptoms, or latent symptoms of schizophrenia. A person with this disorder has little or no interest in interacting with others and is viewed as a loner. People with schizoid personality disorder have little interest in intimacy and tend to display a limited range of emotions. These individuals often are dull and lack a sense of humor. They are perceived by others as being aloof or apathetic and may appear disheveled or unkempt.

Schizotypal personality disorder is characterized by peculiar patterns of behaving and thinking. A person with this disorder may express superstitious beliefs or may engage in fantasy-based thinking. Although their thought processes might be unusual, their beliefs are not considered to be of delusional proportions. Because the symptoms of cluster A personality disorders resemble symptoms of schizophrenia, researchers believe these disorders may be genetically related to schizophrenia.

CLUSTER B

The personality disorders of cluster B are borderline personality disorder, antisocial personality disorder, narcissistic personality disorder, and histrionic personality disorder. The cluster B personality disorders are described as dramatic, erratic, and emotional. The behavior of people with such a disorder creates significant impairment in establishing and maintaining interpersonal relationships. Borderline personality disorder (BPD) is the most prevalent personality disorder. It is diagnosed twice as often among women as men and is characterized by a long-standing and inflexible pattern of emotional instability and unstable personal relationships. Individuals with BPD have an intense fear of abandonment and tend to form intense and unstable relationships with others. They tend to fluctuate between having positive and negative feelings about significant people in their lives. This behavior is referred to as splitting and may contribute to the emotional instability displayed by these people. People with BPD often engage in self-destructive behavior, such as self-mutilation, suicidal acts, or drug abuse. Those with BPD report chronic feelings of emptiness.

Antisocial personality disorder is exemplified by an enduring pattern of behavior that disregards and violates the rights of others. The term "antisocial" refers to behaviors that are antisociety. Antisocial personality disorder is preceded by conduct disorder in the adolescent stages of

---

DSM-IV-TR General Criteria for a Personality Disorder

Enduring pattern of inner experience and behavior deviating markedly from expectations of individual's culture

Manifested in two or more of the following areas:
- cognition (ways of perceiving and interpreting self, other people, and events)
- affectivity (range, intensity, lability, and appropriateness of emotional response)
- interpersonal functioning
- impulse control

Enduring pattern inflexible and pervasive across a broad range of personal and social situations

Enduring pattern leads to clinically significant distress or impairment in social, occupational, or other important areas of functioning

Pattern stable and of long duration, and its onset can be traced back at least to adolescence or early adulthood

Enduring pattern not better accounted for as manifestation or consequence of another mental disorder

Enduring pattern not due to direct physiological effects of a substance or general medical condition

DSM-IV-TR personality disorders:
- Cluster A: Paranoid; Schizoid; Schizotypal
- Cluster B: Antisocial; Borderline; Histrionic; Narcissistic
- Cluster C: Avoidant; Dependent; Obsessive-Compulsive

development. People with antisocial personality disorder often appear initially to be charming and intelligent, yet are also manipulative and grandiose. They lack a moral code which would disallow unacceptable or hurtful behaviors. Therefore, an individual with antisocial personality disorder is likely to engage in criminal acts, manipulative behavior, and the exploitation of others.

Freud coined the term "narcissistic personality disorder" in reference to the Greek myth of Narcissus, who fell in love with his own reflection in a pool of water, preventing him from forming relationships with others. The essential feature of narcissistic personality disorder is an exaggerated sense of self-importance. This disorder is characterized by a need to be the center of attention and a preoccupation with fantasies of one's success or power. A person with narcissistic personality disorder has difficulty understanding the feelings of others and constantly is demanding of attention. These grandiose behaviors typically mask feelings of insecurity.

Symptoms of histrionic personality disorder include excessive emotionality and attention-seeking behavior. A person with histrionic personality disorder is overly dramatic and emotional, and inappropriately seductive in order to gain the attention of others. Histrionic personality disorder is more prevalent among females than males.

CLUSTER C

Cluster C disorders include avoidant personality disorder, dependent personality disorder, and obsessive-compulsive personality disorder. The behavior of people with a cluster C personality disorder is described as anxious or fearful.

People with avoidant personality disorder display a pervasive pattern of social discomfort and a fear of being disliked by others. Because of these feelings, a person with this disorder avoids social interactions with others. People with avoidant personality disorder are extremely shy and have great difficulty establishing interpersonal relationships. They want to be liked by others, but their social discomfort and insecurities prevent them from engaging in interpersonal relationships with others.

Dependent personality disorder is characterized by a chronic pattern of dependent and needy behavior, with an intense fear of being alone. People with this disorder attempt to please other people in order to avoid potential abandonment. They may

say certain things just to be liked by others. They have difficulty making their own decisions and are submissive with others. Individuals with this disorder have difficulty separating from others.

Obsessive-compulsive personality disorder is characterized by an inflexible and enduring need for control and order. People who suffer from obsessive-compulsive personality disorder are so preoccupied with order and organization that they may lose sight of the main objective of an activity. People with this disorder are usually excessively work-oriented and have little patience for leisure time. They are intolerant of indecisiveness or emotionality in others and favor intellect over affect. People with this disorder are perceived as difficult to get along with and unwilling to be a team player. Obsessive-compulsive personality disorder is different from obsessive-compulsive disorder (OCD), which is categorized as an anxiety disorder and involves obsessive thoughts and compulsive behaviors.

DIAGNOSIS

A number of issues have created debate related to the difficulty in and reliability of the diagnosis of personality disorders. The distinction between "normal" personality characteristics and a personality disorder is not necessarily clear in the clinical definition of a personality disorder. The DSM-IV-TR notes that when personality traits are inflexible and create distress or impairment in functioning they constitute a personality disorder. Some argue that there is considerable room for debate about the point at which a trait is considered to create impairment.

The personality disorders have been the subject of criticism by researchers because of the difficulty in diagnosing them reliably. Individuals with a personality disorder often display symptoms of other personality disorders. For example, researchers have debated about the distinction between schizoid personality disorder and avoidant personality disorder, as both disorders are characterized by an extreme in social isolation. Individuals with personality disorders are more likely than the general population to suffer from other psychological disorders, such as depression, bulimia, or substance abuse. This overlap of symptoms may lead to difficulty with diagnostic reliability. The personality disorders occur so frequently with other types of psychological disorders that it is challenging to sort through symptoms to determine what is evidence of each disorder. It is difficult to estimate the prevalence of personality disorders in the United States, as individuals with these disorders do not recognize that they are dysfunctional and are therefore less likely to seek treatment for their disorder.

Researchers have explored the problem of gender bias in the diagnosis of personality disorders. It is believed that some of the symptoms of certain personality disorders are more characteristic of one gender than the other. For example, the aggression and hostility associated with antisocial personality disorder may be traits associated more frequently with the average male population, thus affecting the diagnosis among men compared to women. This supposed gender bias is theorized to be related to the greater prevalence of borderline personality disorder and histrionic personality disorder among women compared to men. Perhaps some of the diagnostic symptoms of this disorder, such as emotionality or fears of abandonment, are behaviors more characteristic of the female population than the male population to begin with.

CAUSES

Various theories have been developed to explain the etiology of personality disorders. The biological perspective examines the roles of genetics and brain functioning in the development of personality disorders. Evidence suggests that the cluster A disorders (paranoid, schizoid, and schizotypal personality disorders) are more prevalent among first-degree relatives of individuals suffering from schizophrenia, suggesting a possible genetic commonality among those disorders.

The underlying symptoms of borderline personality disorder (impulsivity and emotionality) are inherited. Much research confirms that borderline patients are more likely to report a childhood family history that included sexual abuse, domestic violence, and the early loss (either through death or abandonment) of a parental figure. It is believed that this history may be related to the later development of borderline personality disorder. According to developmental theorist Erik Erikson (1902-1994), a sense of basic trust during childhood is an essential component of normal personality development. Erikson stated that a basic sense of trust or mistrust in the self and the world develops in the first year of life. The experience of being abandoned by a par-

ent, then, would foster a sense of mistrust in the world and would affect personality development. In the 1950's, University of Wisconsin psychologist Harry Harlow (1905-1981) explored the effects of attachment on later personality development. Harlow concluded that rhesus monkeys who were separated from their mothers shortly after birth displayed abnormal behaviors later in life, such as unusual fear or aggression, difficulty engaging in mating behaviors, and difficulty with parenting their offspring. Maternally deprived animals, therefore, were more likely to display dysfunction, as is seen in individuals with disorders associated with maternal deprivation, such as borderline and antisocial personality disorders.

Genetic factors may be influential in the development of antisocial personality disorder, as children of biological parents who engage in criminal behavior are more likely to engage in criminal behavior themselves. Learning theorists propose that antisocial behaviors may be learned by mimicking parents with similar behaviors. Individuals with antisocial personality disorder have displayed an abnormally low arousal level, which might enable them to ignore physiological cues that indicate danger or punishment. Research has also suggested that the unusually low level of arousal may cause the antisocial individual to engage in behaviors which increase physiological arousal, or create a "rush."

TREATMENT

Treatment of a personality disorder is difficult due to certain key issues related to these disorders. People with personality disorders tend to lack insight about their dysfunctional ways of interacting with others. Because they do not see themselves as having a problem, they are unlikely to pursue treatment. When a person with a personality disorder does seek treatment, it is usually for some secondary issue, such as alcoholism or depression. People suffering from personality disorders tend to end therapy prematurely, due to their perception that their behavior is not the source of problems. One of the central features of the personality disorders is an impaired ability to maintain relationships with others; therefore, developing a relationship with a therapist is difficult. When the opportunity for treatment does arise, treatment approaches differ depending on the unique characteristics of each of the personality disorders.

The treatment of borderline personality disorder has received much research attention. American psychologist Marsha M. Linehan is credited with the development of dialectical behavior therapy (DBT), a treatment approach for borderline personality disorder which integrates cognitive, behavioral, and Zen principles to help the patient to develop essential coping skills. One of the basic tenets of DBT is that individuals with borderline personality disorder may react abnormally to a normal stimulus (such as an interaction with another person) due to negative or traumatic past experiences (such as sexual abuse). Such individuals may quickly display an increase in emotion and may take a longer period of time to reduce their emotional arousal. Treatment focuses on decreasing self-destructive behaviors and helping individual to regulate their emotions.

People with antisocial personality disorder who participate in treatment usually are made to do so by the legal system. Efficacy of treatment interventions for the person with antisocial personality disorder is often measured in terms of the number of crimes committed by the person after treatment, rather than by any significant change in personality characteristics. Treating any substance abuse issues is an integral component of treatment of antisocial personality disorder. Some believe that prevention is the most important part of managing antisocial behavior.

Researchers have found that low levels of antipsychotic medications are effective in alleviating some symptoms of schizotypal personality disorder. Several studies suggest that antipsychotic medications such as haloperidol may decrease symptoms of depression and impulsivity in the schizotypal individual. People with narcissistic personality disorder are more apt than those with other personality disorders to seek out treatment, using the therapist's office as yet another stage to be the center of attention.

SOURCES FOR FURTHER STUDY

Claridge, Gordon. *Origins of Mental Illness.* 2d ed. Cambridge, Mass.: Malor Books, 1996. The author explores the basic dimensions of personality, personality theories, and basic research and treatment of mental disorders.

Erikson, Erik H. *Identity: Youth and Crisis.* New York: W. W. Norton, 1968. A compilation of Erikson's notable essay about adolescent identity crisis. Articles explore theories of personality development and intrapersonal conflict.

Linehan, Marsha M. *Cognitive-Behavioral Treatment of Borderline Personality Disorder.* New York: Guilford Press, 1993. The author provides an overview of the symptoms of borderline personality disorder followed by an extensive description of an exploration of the foundations of dialectical behavioral therapy. Specific treatment strategies are clearly described, and the book consists of several helpful charts and checklists.

Livesley, W. John, Marsha L. Schroeder, Douglas Jackson, and Kerry L. Jang. "Categorical Distinctions in the Study of Personality Disorder—Implications for Classification." *Journal of Abnormal Psychology* 103, no. 1 (1994): 6-17. This article focuses on the foundation of the classification of personality disorders and challenges some of the empirical evidence regarding the effectiveness of classification.

Maxmen, Jerrold S., and Nicholas G. Ward. *Essential Psychopathology and Its Treatment.* New York: W. W. Norton, 1995. The authors provide a comprehensive overview of the various forms of psychopathology and treatment approaches.

Nathan, Peter E., Jack M. Gorman, and Neil J. Salkind. *Treating Mental Disorders: A Guide to What Works.* New York: Oxford University Press, 1999. Outlines current standards of care for mental illnesses in a question-and-answer format. Offers guides for further information.

Paris, Joel. "A Diathesis-Stress Model of Personality Disorders." *Psychiatric Annals* 29, no. 12 (1999): 692-697. The author explores the possible relationship between life stressors and the development of personality disorders.

Widiger, Thomas A., and Paul T. Costa. "Personality and Personality Disorders." *Journal of Abnormal Psychology* 103, no. 1 (1994): 78-91. The authors review the belief that personality disorders are representative of extreme variants of normal personality traits. Using the five-factor model, the authors explore the correlation between personality and personality disorders.

Janine T. Ogden

SEE ALSO: Antisocial personality; Borderline personality; Conduct disorder; Histrionic personality; Narcissistic personality; Obsessive-compulsive disorder; Paranoia; Schizophrenia: Background, types, and symptoms.

Personality interviewing strategies

Type of psychology: Personality
Fields of study: Personality assessment

There are various approaches to interviewing that are used to determine a person's personality; interviewing is valuable to assess both the healthy personality and the unhealthy one.

Key concepts
- objectivity
- reliability
- theoretical orientation
- validity

Introduction

The assessment of personality is an activity that occurs frequently and can be very important. On an informal level, one makes decisions about someone's personality based on experiences with that person. If one has had positive experiences, one might say the person has a "nice personality." While these informal assessments have significant implications for one's friendships, more formal personality assessments may have far-reaching impact on a person's life. Formal personality assessment is used in making employment decisions as well as decisions about the status of people's mental health. In this latter category, personality interview strategies are widely used. Interview strategies used to assess personality usually are seen as either structured or unstructured. Interview questions are influenced by the theoretical orientation—the psychological theory in which a psychologist has a strong belief (such as Sigmund Freud's theory of psychoanalysis)—of the interviewer.

Fred Kerlinger's discussion of the use of interviews in *Foundations of Behavioral Research* (3d ed., 1986) goes beyond using interviews to assess personality. In personality research, the interview is used to obtain information about the person's thoughts, beliefs, behavior, and feelings to determine how they combine into what is called personality, as well as how they are influenced by or influence other life events. From the research perspective, the personality interview is an in-depth study of all facets of a person's psychological and behavioral makeup.

Structured and Unstructured Interviews

Personality interviews may be placed on a continuum from highly structured at one extreme to highly unstructured at the other. In actuality, few interviews occupy extreme positions. Most interviews are designed to elicit as much useful information as possible from the person being interviewed. Therefore, there is a propensity to prefer one style over the other, although there is no rigid adherence to this tendency. Both structured and unstructured (or standardized and unstandardized) interviews are used in psychology to assess a number of things, including personality. As an approach to assessment, personality interview strategies must conform to expectations of reliability (the quality of delivering the same basic results after each of several interview sessions), validity (the quality of assessing the content that the interviewer intends to assess), and objectivity (the quality of being free of bias or prejudice).

Structured interviews are designed to obtain specific information about the interviewee. In the most highly structured type of interview, there is a list of questions that is presented in its entirety to every person completing the interview. The questions are always presented in the same way and in the same order. The interviewer is not allowed the flexibility to pursue topics of interest; however, the structured interview is actually conducted with somewhat more flexibility in most applied settings. The interviewer is given a list of topics about which information is desired. In gathering the information, the interviewer is free to vary the order of the topics and is able to request elaboration of specific points as needed. This flexibility increases the likelihood that the desired information will be obtained, because the interviewer can vary the order of the interview to put the interviewee at ease while still covering all topics. Structured interviews are sometimes called standardized interviews, because the interview topics and procedures are established in advance. Another name for the structured interview is the directive interview (the interviewee is directed into areas that interest the interviewer).

Unlike structured interviews, unstructured interviews, also called nondirective or unstandardized interviews, place control of the interview with the interviewee. Instead of asking, "How many people are in your family?" for example, interviewers using unstructured approaches use open-ended questions such as "Tell me about your family." By using the open-ended question, the interviewer has the opportunity to learn more about the person's family than with the structured interview. The unstructured interview may produce considerable information yet does not ensure that all topics are covered, as in the structured interview.

Regardless of the type of interview used, the interviewer is charged with observing and interpreting interviewee behavior. Changes in body posture, eye contact, and length of time between question and response are all suggestive of different emotional reactions to the interview. It is up to the interviewer to determine the accuracy of what is being reported by looking for patterns of consistency and inconsistency in the person's behavior. Some determination must be made about whether the person is trying to minimize certain facets of his or her personality in order to save face or, conversely, is exaggerating facets for their inherent shock value. It is important for the interviewer to test various hypotheses about why the interviewee answers in a certain way if an accurate assessment of personality is to take place.

OBSTACLES

A number of common obstacles must be overcome in an interview. One of these is resistance, or the interviewee's reluctance to talk about certain topics, perhaps because the topics are too painful or embarrassing. Resistance may be overcome by allowing the interviewee time to become more comfortable with the interviewer and time to broach the difficult topics in his or her own way. Other complications of the interview are interruptions from other people, distracting settings, and the interviewer's emotional reactions to the person being interviewed.

A new approach to personality interviewing is the use of a computer-administered interview. When a computer is used to administer the interview, a branching program is used. Answering "yes" or "no" to a question may lead to additional questions on that topic or to entirely new topics. Some people have found that computerized interviewing leads to more complete answers. This may be especially true when the subject matter is intimate and potentially embarrassing.

USE IN CLINICAL SETTINGS

Typically, personality interviews are used in clinical settings or to make employment decisions; they are usually used in conjunction with formal psychological testing. Occasionally they are used for research purposes; however, the training necessary to develop a skilled interviewer and the expense involved in the interview process usually limit the settings where they are used to those where they are particularly significant for one reason or another.

In clinical settings, interviews are used for two reasons. First, they are used to gather information about the client or patient's life and about the reason the person is seeking services at this time. Second, the interview is the vehicle for intervention in most forms of psychotherapy. Gary Groth-Marnat discusses the role of the interview within the larger context of psychological assessment in his *Handbook of Psychological Assessment* (1990). In clinical settings, the interview is used to gather intake information (the intake interview) and to establish the person's current emotional and cognitive state (the mental status examination). The intake interview is sometimes known as the initial interview, and it is the first significant contact with the interviewee. The purpose of the intake interview is to determine the reason the person has sought psychological services. This involves determining the person's symptoms or chief complaint.

Once this information is obtained, the interviewer tries to learn more about the person's life. In addition to asking about specific areas of one's life—for example, educational experience and relationship history—the interviewer begins to assess the personality of the interviewee. The personality assessment requires careful observation and integration of both verbal and nonverbal behavior. The interviewer must be aware of how the person reacts to different questions or topics. Some people will always try to please the interviewer, while others may appear nervous, sad, or angry at different times during the interview. Integrating all this information helps the interviewer understand the personality and circumstances of the person being interviewed.

MENTAL STATUS EXAMINATION

The mental status examination is an extension and elaboration of information necessary to understand the personality of the interviewee. While some of the information included in the mental status examination is acquired through direct questioning, much of it is learned through careful listening and observation of the person during the intake interview. The fourth edition of Harold Kaplan and Benjamin Sadock's *Comprehensive Textbook of Psychiatry* (2000) provides a detailed description of the mental status examination. Typically, this examination includes information in the following ten areas: physical appearance and how the person is dressed; attitude toward the interviewer and others; any unusual motor behavior or movements; oddities of speech and language, including accents, speech impediments, and unusual words; disturbances in thought content and process such as delusional beliefs or difficulties expressing thoughts; perceptual problems in the form of hallucinations or illusions; changes in cognition, which may include memory impairments and other intellectual changes; disturbances in orientation and sensorium, which refers to the person's knowledge of who and where he or she is, as well as to a determination of the level of alertness; the current affective or emotional state; and the degree of insight into the person's current cirumstances.

Each aspect of the mental status examination contributes information which helps in the understanding of a person's personality. Information obtained through this part of the interview is also valuable in the diagnosis of psychological disorders. Certain deviations from the norm that may be revealed by the mental status examination are associated with disorders such as anxiety, depression, schizophrenia, and personality disorders. Thus, the intake interview and the mental status examination used together provide the foundation for understanding a person's personality and psychological disorders.

USE IN EMPLOYMENT SETTINGS

Personality interviewing is also an integral part of employment interviews. One important area in which personality interviews are used to help make employment decisions is in the selection of law enforcement officers. The goals of the interview are twofold. First, it is used to identify those candidates who, because of their personality, are likely to make good or effective police officers. These are people with good coping skills, well-developed intellectual abilities, and good observational abilities. Second, the personality interview is used to identify candidates who are likely to make poor law enforcement officers. In the area of law enforcement, it is crucial to consider liability issues and the protection of the public in making hiring decisions. Personality inter-

views provide information that can help to improve the quality of the hiring decisions and ultimately the quality of law enforcement agencies.

Personality interviewing is also used in other employment settings. The interview is a significant part of the application process; used either informally or formally, it yields important information about the applicant's motivation and suitability for the position. Information from the interview helps an employer decide whether the applicant's personality will mesh or clash with coworkers, will convey the appropriate image for the position, or will satisfy other considerations salient to the job. As in clinical settings, the use of the personality interview in employment decisions is frequently combined with formal psychological testing. In both employment and clinical uses, it is important to note areas of similarity and difference between the interview and the testing.

ROLE IN THERAPEUTIC PROCESS

The use of interviewing, in various guises, has been central to psychological investigations of personality as well as to psychotherapeutic approaches to helping interviewees—whether they are called interviewees, patients, or clients. Sigmund Freud called one of the central aspects of psychoanalytic interviewing "free association"—a highly unstructured effort to obtain information that is as uncensored as possible. The interviewee is told to talk about whatever comes to mind without concern for its relevance or appropriateness. Following this uncensored revelation by the interviewee, the interviewer eventually makes interpretations about personality and unconscious conflicts. While personality interviewing and free association remain hallmarks of psychoanalysis, the interview has also been important to others in psychology and psychotherapy.

Carl Rogers, the founder of client-centered or nondirective therapy, considered the interview critical to the therapeutic process. He and his followers believed that, without controlling the direction of the interview, they could learn more about the person that would be useful in helping resolve the person's problems. Rogerian psychologists are firm believers in the nondirective approach because it allows the client to discover, independent of someone else's opinion, the solution to the problem.

Behavioral psychologists, as exemplified by Kenneth P. Morganstern, place their emphasis on a person's observable behavior. Personality is not defined as something a person has but rather as the perceptions of other people based upon the person's behavior. Thus, personality interviewing from a behavioral perspective focuses heavily on observations of the person's behavior in different situations. Many behavioral psychologists believe that a person's personality is modifiable if his or her prior learning experiences can be identified and if it is possible to ensure that specifiable consequences can follow behaviors which the client is trying to change.

Many psychologists, including Gary Groth-Marnat, believe that in the future computers will be used more frequently to administer interviews. Assessment interviews will be more important in determining accountability for treatment decisions and therefore are likely to become more structured. As interviews become increasingly structured, it is also likely that they will represent an integration of different theoretical positions rather than the parallel interview styles that have been developing among psychologists adhering to different theories.

SOURCES FOR FURTHER STUDY

Cormier, William H., and L. Sherilyn Cormier. *Interviewing Strategies for Helpers.* 4th ed. Belmont, Calif.: Wadsworth, 1997. The fourth edition of this book on interviewing represents a major revision and extension of the authors' work. A detailed guide to all facets of interviewing and overcoming obstacles to effective interviews, presented within the context of clinical applications. Includes using the interview to develop and implement intervention strategies. Exercises, worksheets, and other learning activities are provided.

Gay, Peter, ed. *The Freud Reader.* Reprint. New York: W. W. Norton, 1995. Gay presents many of Freud's original essays in chronological order, inserting clearly identified comments of his own as he places a particular writing in its historical and cultural context. While there is no specific essay on or reference to personality interviewing, this work is valuable in understanding the precedent for interviewing set by Freud.

Groth-Marnat, Gary. *Handbook of Psychological Assessment.* 3d ed. New York: John Wiley & Sons, 1997. A presentation of the most widely used psychological tests. Of particular value to the person new to psychological testing is the inclusion of as-

sets and limitations of various tests and discussion of how the various tests were developed. Devotes two chapters to interview strategies, "The Assessment Interview" and "Behavioral Assessment." Recommended readings are included in each chapter.

Kerlinger, Fred Nichols, and Howard B. Lee. *Foundations of Behavioral Research.* 4th ed. Pacific Grove, Calif.: International Thomson, 2000. An excellent and thorough presentation of experimental design issues in psychological research. Kerlinger provides a very good chapter on the use of interviews and how to design good interview schedules. The use of interviews in both applied and research settings is discussed. Examples of well-designed interviews are given.

Kleinmuntz, Benjamin. *Personality and Psychological Assessment.* New York: St. Martin's Press, 1982. Kleinmuntz's book is an introductory-level presentation of psychological assessment. He discusses test construction and the statistics involved in developing and using psychological tests as well as a brief discussion of various categories of tests. One chapter is devoted to interviewing techniques and applications.

Morganstern, Kenneth P. "Behavioral Interviewing." In *Behavioral Assessment: A Practical Handbook,* edited by Alan S. Bellack and Michel Hersen. New York: Pergamon Press, 1988. Morganstern describes the full process of the behavioral interview from beginning to end. He includes a discussion of factors which may facilitate or inhibit the interview. Both the conceptual basis and the ethical considerations of the interview are discussed. Interview examples and references are provided.

Rogers, Carl R. *On Becoming a Person.* Boston: Houghton Mifflin, 1961. One of several books by Rogers that describe his approach to psychotherapy and the use of interviewing within the client-centered framework. It is not a highly technical book and does not presuppose a sophisticated knowledge of psychological theory.

Sadock, Benjamin J., and Virginia Sadock, eds. *Kaplan and Sadock's Comprehensive Textbook of Psychiatry.* 7th ed. Philadelphia: Lippincott, Williams & Wilkins, 2000. This massive textbook covers every major area of psychiatry in its more than three thousand pages. Four essays directly address personality interviewing in the clinical setting. Much of what is presented assumes a background in psychology or medicine.

Wise, Paula Sachs. *The Use of Assessment Techniques by Applied Psychologists*. Belmont, Calif.: Wadsworth, 1989. A short book written for the person with a limited background in psychology. The author devotes some space to defining applied psychology and then proceeds to discuss the use of various assessment approaches by clinical, counseling, industrial/organizational, and school psychologists. She gives examples, presents controversies, and suggests additional readings.

James T. Trent

SEE ALSO: Behavioral assessment; Case-study methodologies; Clinical interviewing, testing, and observation; Diagnosis; *Diagnostic and Statistical Manual of Mental Disorders* (DSM); Survey research: Questionnaires and interviews.

Personality

Psychophysiological measures

TYPE OF PSYCHOLOGY: Personality
FIELDS OF STUDY: Personality assessment

> *Psychophysiological studies comparing individuals with different personality traits have sought to determine the physical characteristics of particular behavioral characteristics. Such research can provide information that helps clarify the importance of various personality types with regard to risk of psychological and physical disorders.*

KEY CONCEPTS
• anxiety sensitivity
• locus of control
• personality
• psychophysiology
• Type A behavior pattern

INTRODUCTION

A broad definition of personality typically includes the dimensions of stability, determinism, and uniqueness. That is, personality changes little over time, is determined by internal processes and ex-

ternal factors, and reflects an individual's distinctive qualities. Personality also can be thought of as unique, relatively stable patterns of behavior, multiply determined over the course of an individual's life. There are many theories for understanding the development of these patterns of behavior.

Twin studies have provided evidence that biological factors help to shape personality; such studies support Hans Eysenck's theory that personality is inherited. The psychodynamic perspective holds that personality is determined primarily by early childhood experiences. Some of the most influential contributions to this perspective came from Sigmund Freud. He argued that unconscious forces govern behavior and that childhood experiences strongly shape adult personality via coping strategies people use to deal with sexual urges. B. F. Skinner, founder of modern behavioral psychology, assumed that personality (or behavior) is determined solely by environmental factors. More specifically, he believed that consequences of behavior are instrumental in the development of unique, relatively stable patterns of behavior in individuals. According to Albert Bandura's social learning perspective, models have a great impact on personality development. That is, patterns of behavior in individuals are influenced by the observation of others. Finally, the humanistic perspective of Carl Rogers suggests that personality is largely determined by the individual's unique perception of reality in comparison to his or her self-concept.

PERSONALITY ASSESSMENT

Assessment of personality can be accomplished from three domains: subjective experience, behavior, and physiology. Traditional means for assessing personality have included objective and projective paper-and-pencil or interview measurements that tap the domain of subjective experience. Behavioral assessment techniques such as direct observation of behavior, self-monitoring (having the individual record occurrences of his or her own behavior), self-report questionnaires, role-play scenarios, and behavioral avoidance tests (systematic, controlled determination of how close an individual can approach a feared object or situation) tap the domains of subjective experience and objective behavior. These techniques have been used in clinical settings to aid in the diagnosis and treatment of deviant or abnormal behavior patterns.

Although psychophysiological measurement of personality has not gained popular use in clinical settings, it complements the techniques mentioned above and contributes to understanding the nature and development of psychological and physical disorders. Just as patterns of responding on traditional personality tests can indicate the possibility of aberrant behavior, so too can tests of physiological patterns. Typical measures taken during this type of assessment include heart rate, blood pressure, muscle tension (measured via electromyography), brainwave activity (measured via electroencephalography), skin temperature, and palmar sweat gland or electrodermal activity. These measures of physiological activity are sensitive to "emotional" responses to various stimuli and have been instrumental in clarifying the nature of certain psychological and physical conditions. One of the fundamental assumptions of psychophysiology is that the responses of the body can help reveal the mechanisms underlying human behavior and personality.

Physiological responsivity can be assessed in a number of different ways. Two primary methodologies are used in the study of the relations between personality and physiology. The first method simply looks at resting or baseline differences of various physiological measures across individuals who either possess or do not possess the personality characteristic of interest. The second method also assesses individuals with or without the characteristic of interest, but does this under specific stimulus or situational conditions rather than during rest. This is often referred to as measuring reactivity to the stimulus or situational condition. Resting physiological measures are referred to as tonic activity (activity evident in the absence of any known stimulus event). It is postulated that tonic activity is relatively enduring and stable within the individual while at rest, although it can be influenced by external factors. It is both of interest in its own right and important in determining the magnitude of response to a stimulus. On the other hand, phasic activity is a discrete response to a specific stimulus. This type of activity is suspected to be influenced to a much greater extent by external factors and tends to be less stable than tonic activity. Both types of activity, tonic and phasic, are important in the study of personality and physiology.

Standard laboratory procedures are typically employed to investigate tonic activity and phasic responses to environmental stimuli. For example, a typical assessment incorporating both methodologies might include the following phases: a five-minute baseline to collect resting physiological measures, a five-minute presentation of a task or other stimulus suspected to differentiate individuals in each group based on their physiological response or change from baseline, and a five-minute recovery to assess the nature and rate of physiological recovery from the task or stimulus condition. Investigations focusing on the last phase attempt to understand variations in recovery as a response pattern in certain individuals. For example, highly anxious individuals tend to take much longer to recover physiologically from stimulus presentations that influence heart rate and electrodermal activity than individuals who report low levels of anxiety.

Studies of physiological habituation—the decline or disappearance of response to a discrete stimulus—also have been used to investigate personality differences. Physiological responses to a standard tone, for example, eventually disappear with repeated presentations of the tone. The rate at which they disappear varies across individuals; the disappearance generally takes longer in individuals who tend to be anxious. Thus, individuals who tend to have anxious traits may be more physiologically responsive, recover from the response less rapidly, and habituate to repeated stimulation more slowly than those who tend to be less anxious. Such physiological differences may be an important characteristic that determines anxious behavior and/or results from subjective feelings of anxiousness.

RELATIONSHIP TO PHYSIOLOGY AND HEALTH

Research has demonstrated that there is considerable variability across individuals in their physiological response patterns, both at rest and in response to various situational stimuli or laboratory manipulations. Evidence indicates that part of this variability across individuals may in some cases be attributable to certain personality traits or characteristic patterns of behavior. Furthermore, research suggests that these personality traits may also be related to the development of psychological or physical disorders. Although the causal links are not well understood, a growing body of research points to relations among personality, physiological measures, and psychopathology/health.

Examples of these relationships are evident in the field of psychopathology, or the study of abnormal behavior. Hans Eysenck proposed that the general characteristics of introversion and extroversion lead individuals to interact very differently with their environment. Some psychophysiological studies support this notion and suggest that the behaviors characteristic of these traits may be driven by physiological differences. Anxiety sensitivity and locus of control are two personality traits that some suggest are related to the development of anxiety disorders and depression, respectively. To varying degrees, anxiety disorders and depression have been investigated in the psychophysiology laboratory and have been found to differentiate individuals with high and low levels of the personality trait, based on their physiological responses.

Introversion describes the tendency to minimize interaction with the environment; extroversion is characterized by the opposite behaviors, or the tendency to interact more with the environment. Eysenck proposed that such traits reflect physiological differences that are genetically determined and reflected in the individual's physiology. Introverted individuals are thought to be chronically physiologically hyperaroused and thus to seek to minimize their arousal by minimizing external stimulation. Extroverted individuals are believed to be chronically physiologically underaroused and to seek a more optimal level of arousal through increased environmental stimulation. It should be easy to confirm or disprove such a theory with psychophysiological studies of resting physiological activity in introverts and extroverts. Electroencephalograph (EEG) studies have produced contradictory evidence about the validity of Eysenck's theory, however; problems in EEG methodology, experimental design, and measurement of the traits themselves have led to considerable confusion about whether the traits actually do have a physiological basis.

ANXIETY SENSITIVITY

Anxiety sensitivity describes the tendency for individuals to fear sensations they associate with anxiety because of beliefs that anxiety may result in harmful consequences. Research in the development and assessment of this construct was pioneered by Steven Reiss and his associates in the late 1980's. They developed a sixteen-item questionnaire, the Anxiety Sensitivity Index (ASI), to measure anxiety sensitivity and

found it to be both reliable and valid. Anxiety sensitivity has been most closely related to panic disorder, an anxiety disorder characterized by frequent, incapacitating episodes of extreme fear or discomfort. In fact, as a group, individuals with panic disorder score higher on the ASI than individuals with any other anxiety disorder. Furthermore, some researchers have demonstrated that individuals scoring high on the ASI are five times more likely to develop an anxiety disorder after a three-year follow-up.

Research investigating responses to arithmetic, caffeine, and hyperventilation challenge in the laboratory has demonstrated that individual differences in anxiety sensitivity levels are probably more closely related to the subjective experience of anxiousness than to actual physiological changes. Individuals high and low on anxiety sensitivity, however, have exhibited differential heart-rate reactivity to a mental arithmetic stressor. That is, individuals high on anxiety sensitivity show a greater acceleration in heart rate than individuals low on anxiety sensitivity when engaging in an arithmetic challenge. Individuals scoring high on the ASI also more accurately perceive actual changes in their physiology when compared with their low-scoring counterparts. Such heightened reactivity and sensitivity to physiological change may partially explain how anxiety sensitivity influences the development of anxiety disorders. Individuals high in anxiety sensitivity may be more reactive to environmental threat; therefore, their increased sensitivity may have a physiological basis. They also may be more likely to detect changes in their physiology, which they are then more likely to attribute to threat or danger.

On a more general note, cardiovascular and electrodermal measures can differentiate between anxiety patients and other people at rest. The differences become greater under conditions of stimulation. Delayed habituation rates in anxiety patients are also part of the pattern of physiological overarousal typically seen in individuals with heightened anxiety. Indeed, heightened physiological arousal is one of the hallmark characteristics of anxiety.

LOCUS OF CONTROL

Locus of control, made popular by Julian Rotter in the 1960's, refers to individuals' perceptions of whether they have control over what happens to them across situations. This personality construct has been related to the development of depression.

Specifically, it is believed that individuals who attribute failures to internal factors (self-blame) and successes to external factors (to other people or to luck) are more susceptible to developing feelings of helplessness, often followed by despair and depression. Locus of control also is hypothesized to have implications in the management of chronic health-related problems.

In oversimplified categorizations, individuals are labeled to have an "internal" or "external" locus of control. "External" individuals, who believe they have little control over what happens to them, are said to be more reactive to threat, more emotionally labile, more hostile, and lower in self-esteem and self-control. Psychophysiological assessment studies have revealed heart-rate acceleration and longer electrodermal habituation for "externals" in response to the presentation of tones under passive conditions. When faced with no-control conditions in stress situations such as inescapable shock, "internals" show elevated physiological arousal, while findings for "externals" are mixed. Thus, the locus of control has varying effects on physiology, depending on the circumstances. Such effects may play a role in psychological disorders such as depression and anxiety. Heightened physiological reactivity may also inhibit recovery from acute illness or affect the course of chronic health problems such as hypertension.

In addition to the relevance of personality to physiological reactivity and psychopathology, research has demonstrated that certain personality types may be risk factors or serve protective functions with regard to physical health. Type A behavior pattern and hardiness are two examples. Type A behavior pattern is characterized by competitiveness, time urgency, and hostility. It has been identified as a potential risk factor for the development of coronary heart disease. Psychophysiological studies have suggested that, under certain laboratory conditions, males who exhibit the Type A pattern are more cardiovascularly responsive. This reactivity is the proposed mechanism by which Type A behavior affects the heart. More recent research has suggested that not all components of the Type A pattern are significantly associated with heightened cardiovascular reactivity. Hostility seems to be the most critical factor in determining heightened reactivity. Males who respond to stress with hostility tend to show greater heart-rate and blood-pressure increases than individuals low in hostility. Some re-

search suggests that hostility is also a risk factor for heart disease in women.

In contrast to hostility, hardiness is proposed to buffer the effects of stress on physiology. Hardy individuals respond to stressors as challenges and believe that they have control over the impact of stressors. They also feel commitment to their life, including work and family. Psychophysiological studies have supported the buffering effect of hardiness. Individuals who are more hardy tend to be less physiologically responsive to stressors and to recover from stressors more rapidly. Again, the construct of hardiness seems to be more relevant for males, partially because males have been studied more often.

These studies show that various personality types can be distinguished to varying degrees by psychophysiological measurement. The implications of such findings include possible physiological contributions to the development of various psychological problems, and personality contributions to the development or course of physical disease.

EVOLUTION OF RESEARCH

Although the sophisticated techniques and instruments that have enabled psychologists to study physiological events were not developed until the twentieth century, the notion that physiology and psychology (body and mind) are linked dates back as far as ancient Greece. Hippocrates, for example, described four bodily humors or fluids thought to influence various psychological states such as melancholy and mania. Although the link between mind and body has received varying degrees of emphasis in scientific thinking across the centuries, it regained prominence in the mid-1900's with the development of the field of psychosomatic medicine along with the widespread influence of Sigmund Freud's theories of personality.

Psychosomatic medicine embraced the notion that personality and physiology are intertwined. Psychosomatic theorists believed that certain diseases, such as diabetes, asthma, and hypertension, were associated with particular personality characteristics. They suggested that personality influenced the development of specific diseases. Although much of this theorizing has been disproved, these theorists did return the focus to investigating the interactive nature of a person's psychological and physiological makeup.

Psychophysiologists acknowledge the influence of personality characteristics on physiology and vice versa, and they are working to characterize these relationships. Future work will better measure particular personality constructs and will clarify the interaction of gender with personality and physiology. Psychophysiologists also must be concerned with the external validity of the data they obtain in the laboratory. It has not been satisfactorily demonstrated that physiological responses measured in a given individual in the laboratory are at all related to that individual's response in the natural environment. Thus, in order to establish fully the usefulness of laboratory findings, psychophysiologists must also study individuals in their natural environments. Recent technological advances will enable ongoing physiological measurement, which should achieve this goal and further establish the relations among personality, physiology, and behavior.

Sources for Further Study

Cacioppo, John T., Louis G. Tassinary, and Gary G. Berntson, eds. *Handbook of Psychophysiology.* 2d ed. New York: Cambridge University Press, 2000. A general guidebook, aimed at advanced students and professionals.

Eysenck, Hans J. *The Biological Basis of Personality.* Springfield, Ill.: Charles C Thomas, 1967. This older book provides a thorough, in-depth discussion of Eysenck's theories of the relations between neuroticism, introversion, and extroversion with physiology.

Stern, Robert Morris, William J. Ray, and Karen S. Quigley. *Psychophysiological Recording.* 2d ed. New York: Oxford University Press, 2000. The authors provide an excellent, readable introduction to basic principles of psychophysiology. Part 2, the main body of the text, covers physiology of and recording procedures for the brain, muscles, eyes, respiratory system, gastrointestinal system, cardiovascular system, and skin. Illustrations depicting typical recordings and a glossary of psychophysiological terms are helpful additions.

Surwillo, Walter W. *Psychophysiology for Clinical Psychologists.* Norwood, N.J.: Ablex, 1990. This text provides basic knowledge of psychophysiology and highlights some areas of application. Surwillo also incorporates helpful diagrams and relevant references for research in the area.

Weiten, Wayne, Margaret A. Lloyd, and R. L. Lashley. "Theories of Personality." In *Psychology*

Applied to Modern Life: Adjustment at the Turn of the Century. 6th ed. Belmont, Calif.: Wadsworth, 1999. This text, written for undergraduate students, provides the reader with a very readable chapter on personality and theories of personality development. Other chapters highlight the dynamics of adjustment, interpersonal factors, developmental transitions, and the impact that personality and styles of coping can have on psychological and physical health.

Virginia L. Goetsch and Lois Veltum

See also: Behavioral assessment and personality rating scales; Clinical interviewing, testing, and observation; Emotions; Nervous system; Neuropsychology; Projection.

Personality rating scales

Type of psychology: Personality
Fields of study: Personality assessment; personality theory

Personality rating scales are used to describe personality trait systems through the measurement of psychological individual difference dimensions, or traits along which people can be ordered, although not all represent explicit theories. They can include rating oneself (self rating) or rating by a peer (observer rating). Their utility in research and applied settings has been demonstrated and their use has become commonplace and widespread.

Key concepts
- bandwidth
- extroversion
- factor analysis
- factor level
- introversion
- neuroticism
- personality traits
- prediction
- primary, secondary, and superfactors
- psychometrics
- psychoticism
- rating scales
- taxonomy

INTRODUCTION

Personality rating scales represent one approach that is used by psychologists and others to measure scientifically dimensions of personality for purposes of summarizing, predicting, and explaining human behavior. In recent history, there has been considerable research on and application of the use of personality rating scales, typically to measure psychological individual difference dimensions or traits along which people can be ordered, such as extroversion or neuroticism. Traits are consistent patterns in the way individuals behave, feel, and think.

Trait psychology can be considered as the theoretical underpinnings for measurements of personality, including personality rating scales. However, the use of rating scales does not provide a sufficient explanation of personality, and there is more to personality than traits. Personality traits must be inferred through measurement, since they are hypothetical constructs that cannot be observed directly, although some trait psychologists, such as Hans Eysenck and Gordon Allport, view traits as "neuropsychic entities." Support for this view has been provided by recent advances in neuroscience which have suggested a genetic link to the major dimensions of personality traits; however, the findings are still preliminary, with half of the variance, at the most, being attributed to traits, while the environment or the interaction of traits with the environment accounting for the rest.

Strictly speaking, a personality rating scale is a subset of items that all describe the same personality characteristic, variable, or trait along a continuum, with multiple categories that are assigned a number and can therefore yield a score. For example, in assessing the extent to which the item "cautiousness" describes a person, Likert scales may be used, such as "very much like the person"; "somewhat like the person"; "uncertain"; "somewhat unlike the person"; "not at all like the person." The rater makes an evaluative judgment by choosing which category along the continuum most accurately depicts the person who is being rated (the ratee). Like physical and mental attributes, traits vary in the population in a continuous and normal distribution (bell-shaped), with most falling within the middle range and fewer lying within the extremes.

Since traits are pervasive across situations, scores on trait measures should be relatively consistent across time, and ratings on scale items measuring the same underlying trait should be in agreement, as should ratings on items assessing different aspects of the same trait, such as test retest and internal consistency reliability respectively; both represent criteria for scientific soundness of scales set forth by psychometricians.

Personality can be described by rating oneself (self ratings). Also, persons can be described based on the impressions that they make on others who observe them. Thus, informants rate another person based on their observations and perceptions of the individual that they are assessing. These are referred to as observer ratings and can be made by a peer, supervisor, teacher, or counselor. Recent research has shown consistency between the different methods of assessing personality, providing support for the scale's reliability validity (that is, that the scale is measuring the construct that it is intended to measure, an additional criterion set forth by psychometricians in order to evaluate the scientific soundness of personality assessment measures).

Lewis Aiken noted in 1997 that personality rating scales are included in inventories and may be a part of questionnaires. Both inventories and questionnaires are sometimes commercially labeled as "scales." Regardless of what form they take and how they are labeled, personality rating scales are widely used in both research and applied settings. Various subdisciplines of psychology, such as personality, social, developmental, educational, school, industrial, clinical, and forensic psychology, rely extensively on rating scales for the scientific assessment of personality for research purposes. They may be used in applied settings such as medical and health care, to assess behavioral risk factors; mental health treatment, to measure psychopathology; colleges, to assist with vocational guidance; business and industry, to aid in personnel selection; the armed services, to aid in selection of those who are the most fit; and criminal justice, in the area of profiling.

ORIGIN, DEVELOPMENT, AND HISTORY

The foundation for the family of paper-and-pencil methods (of which personality rating scales are members) to obtain scientific information about people, products, and/or events evolved out of work in a variety of disciplines. Pierre-Simon Laplace and Karl F. Gauss conducted seminal research on probability theory—the bell-shaped, normal distribution now termed Gaussian distribution—in the early eighteenth century, which made it possible to infer logically the characteristics of populations (whether physical, mental, or personality traits) from the analysis of sample data. Adolphe Quetelet extended of Laplace's and Gauss's work to biological and social data, which marked the beginnings of vital statistics, that is, data pertaining to human life. Gustav Fechner's work in the nineteenth century in the area of psychophysics (subjective mental events) and the mathematical measurement of physical stimuli that gave rise to them produced Fechner's law, that sensation increases with the log of the stimulus. Sir Francis Galton worked in the 1880's with Karl Pearson in the area of statistical methods, and also contributed pioneering methodologies in the area of individual differences. The Woodworth Personal Data Sheet, the first formal, self-report, multi-item, scale personality inventory that assessed psychoneurotic tendencies, was constructed by R. S. Woodworth in 1918 for purposes of weeding out unfit military personnel in World War I. Other early personality measures constructed in the first half of the twentieth century include the attitude inventories of Louis Leon Thurstone and his colleagues, the Strong's Vocational Interest Blank for Men, the Vernon and Allport Study of Values, the Bernreuter Personality Inventory, and the Minnesota Multiphasic Personality Inventory.

CURRENT STATUS AND APPLICATIONS

Since 1960, a number of scales have been created to try to measure traits and organize them into a coherent structure or taxonomy. This effort was significantly advanced by the successful use of factor analysis in the development of a taxonomy of mental abilities and the use of high-speed computers in psychological research. This increased the efficiency and precision of factor analysis in grouping correlated items into factored scales that purportedly map the personality sphere.

Some have regarded trait systems as the theoretical model and scales and inventories as their application, although not all scales and inventories represent explicit theories. Raymond B. Cattell used an empirical approach in which he defined the "personality sphere" with words in the language that are used by observers to describe behavior. Others, such as J. Paul Guilford and Hans Eysenck, have been influenced by existing theory (Carl Jung's psychological types) and their own factoring of existing

items and scales in addition to the research of others. On the other hand, Andrew Comrey and Douglas Jackson have been less concerned with covering the total domain of personality. Instead, psychometric soundness has been the priority in their development of explicit procedures for item selection, scale construction, and validation in defining sets of primary trait scales that best define those areas of the domain that had been well researched.

These approaches have all yielded different numbers of factored scales: Cattell has sixteen; Eysenck, three; Guilford, thirteen; and Comrey, eight. A review and critical analysis by Saul Sells and Debra Murphy of the dimensions of personality represented by these factored scales pointed out considerable difference across systems, yet extensive overlap and common content. The differences are partially due to whether lower-order (narrower) versus higher-order (more general) factors have been the focus, with Eysenck emphasizing the higher-order ones, that is, the superfactors of psychoticism, extroversion, and neuroticism, and Cattell, Guilford, and Comrey focusing on lower-order or primary factors. Some psychologists hold that separate scales based on the lower-order primary factors have greater richness and predict better than those with two scores which compress all of the information. Further, the utility of the levels may depend on the situation; for instance, for Eysenck's psychophysiological experiments, the higher-order factors may be better and the primaries may be more suitable in the fields of clinical and personnel.

In attempts to resolve the discrepancies, there have been several investigations of congruences among the personality factor-trait systems, including one by Saul Sells, Robert G. Demaree, and D. P. Will (the most ambitious project ever attempted in personality questionnaire research at that time) in which they administered Cattell's and Guilford's items to a sample of 2,500 individuals and factored them in the same analysis. The findings yielded eighteen factors, with five being common to both the Cattell and Guilford systems (emotional stability, social extroversion, conscientiousness, relaxed composure versus suspicious excitability and general activity). With the inclusion of agreeableness, all but one (openness to experience) of the five broad bipolar dimensions that P. T. Costa, Jr., and R. R. McCrae have deemed the "Big Five" were reflected in their results.

Currently, the Big Five are posited as accounting for most of the personality-attributable variation in human behavior, although at least thirteen other non-Big Five factors (six attributable to Guilford, five attributable to Cattell, and two attributable to neither) were extracted in the Sells, Demaree, and Will analysis. The two factors attributable to neither contained items that were similar in content but were dissimilar in terms of the source factors from which they were drawn. Expansion of the Big Five to include traits that are represented by combinations of pairs of factors has been suggested by some.

The research of Jackson and colleagues has yielded results that suggest that there are many dimensions of behavior beyond the Big Five, and further, that the narrower facets, thought to be subsumed under the broader Big Five factors, may provide more accurate behavioral prediction than the Big Five alone.

Further, the review by Sells and Murphy found that "two factors with labels similar to those emphasized by Eysenck, neuroticism and extroversion-introversion, were addressed across all five of the systems (Cattell, Eysenck, Jackson, Comrey, and Sells, Demaree, and Wills), although not exactly in the same manner or in the same terms." They additionally point out that factor level can be "an artifact of the composition of the variables in the matrix" and that bandwidth of the various factors produced may be more important; that is, the extent to which the factors are very broad (made up of dissimilar items) or very narrow (made up of tautological items) may be more important than factor level in understanding the relationships among these factors.

In light of the fact that personality factors and their measures are manmade constructs, research to determine the predictive validity of scales that already exist and those that are developed continues to be critical in assessing their theoretical and practical utility. Furthermore, debates on whether broad bandwidth factors or narrower band components have more predictive and explanatory power can best be served by examining each one's specific situational utility within a hierarchical framework of the domain that encourages choice of assessment level.

SOURCES FOR FURTHER STUDY

John, O. P. "The Big Five Factor Taxonomy: Dimensions of Personality in the Natural Language and in Questionnaires." In *Handbook of Personality Theory and Research*, edited by L. Pervin. New York: Guilford Press, 1990. The development of the five-factor model for personality traits is reviewed.

Paunonen, S. V., and M.C. Ashton. "Big Five Factors and Facets and the Prediction of Behavior." *Journal of Personality and Social Psychology* 81, no. 3 (2001): 524-539. Paunonen and Ashton found that their "theoretically guided selection" of predictor facets accounted for large portions of criterion variance not predicted by the Big Five factors, which support exploiting traits not well represented within the Big Five inventory to reduce error and increase accuracy in behavioral explanation in personnel programs and other areas.

Paunonen, S. V., and D. N. Jackson. "What Is Beyond the Big Five? Plenty!" *Journal of Personality* 68 (2000): 821-835. The authors reanalyze Saucier and Goldberg's work (which concluded that so-called non-Big Five personality dimensions are mostly subsumed within the Big Five factor space) and provide evidence supporting the existence of considerable important personality variance and dimensions not accounted for by the Big Five that have theoretical and predictive significance that is worthy of investigation.

Saucier, G., and L. R. Goldberg. "Evidence for the Big Five in Analyses of Familiar English Personality Adjectives." *European Journal of Personality* 10 (1996): 61-77. The authors analyzed many clusters of so-called non-Big Five dimensions of personality reflected in English person-descriptive adjectives and concluded that they can adequately be subsumed under the Big Five factor space.

Sells, S. B., and Debra Murphy. "Factor Theories of Personality." In *Personality and the Behavior Disorders*, edited by N. S. Endler and J. M. Hunt. New York: John Wiley & Sons, 1984. The authors conduct an extensive critical review of factor theories of personality and present findings from a factor analytic study with a sample size of 2,500 individuals; the most ambitious project ever attempted in personality questionnaire research at that time. The recommendation that a new concept "bandwidth" be substituted for "order of factor" is presented.

Debra L. Murphy

SEE ALSO: Beck Depression Inventory (BDI); Behavioral assessment; California Psychological Inventory

(CPI); Children's Depression Inventory (CDI); Clinical interviewing, testing, and observation; Diagnosis; *Diagnostic and Statistical Manual of Mental Disorders* (DSM); Minnesota Multiphasic Personality Inventory (MMPI); Personality: Psychophysiological measures; Personality interviewing strategies; State-Trait Anxiety Inventory; Thematic Apperception Test (TAT).

Personality theory

TYPE OF PSYCHOLOGY: Personality
FIELDS OF STUDY: Personality theory

Personality theories seek to describe and explain the characteristics of thought, feeling, and behavior that differ among individuals, and the coherence of these characteristics within a single individual. Personality theories describe approaches to human nature and provide the foundation for psychological therapies.

KEY CONCEPTS
- attribution theory
- humanistic theory
- personality trait
- psychoanalytic theory
- social learning theory

INTRODUCTION

Psychologists who study personality are interested in explaining both the coherence of an individual's behavior, attitudes, and emotions, and how that individual may change over time. To paraphrase Clyde Kluckhohn, personality theorists seek to describe and explain how each individual is unique, how groups of people meaningfully differ from one another, and how all people share some common attributes. In developing answers to these questions, theorists use widely varying definitions of personality that may differ greatly from the way the term "personality" is used in everyday language. Indeed, if there is a single overriding basic issue in personality theory it is, What is personality?

PERSONALITY AND ESSENCE

Theorists agree that people have an internal "essence" that determines who they are and that guides their behavior, but the nature of that essence differs from theory to theory. Psychoanalytic theories such as Sigmund Freud's see the essence of personality as arising from conflict among internal psychic processes. For Freud, the conflict is viewed as occurring among the urges for instinctual gratification (called the id), the urges for perfection (the superego), and the demands of reality (the ego). Humanistic theories such as those of Carl Rogers and Abraham Maslow also see people as often engaged in conflict. For these theorists, however, the conflicts are between an internal self which is striving for positive expression and the constraints of a restrictive external social world. In general, the humanists have a much more optimistic outlook on human nature than do psychoanalytic theorists.

Still other theorists are more neutral with respect to human nature. George Kelly's cognitive personality theory, for example, views people as scientists, developing and testing hypotheses to understand themselves better and to predict events in their world. Social learning theorists such as Walter Mischel, Albert Bandura, and Julian Rotter see people as developing expectations and behavioral tendencies based on their histories of rewards and punishments, and their observations of others.

To some extent, the question of "essence" is also the question of motivation. Psychoanalytic theorists view people as trying to achieve a balance between instinctual urges and the demands of reality. In contrast, humanistic theorists view people as motivated toward personal growth rather than homeostatic balance. Social learning theorists view people as motivated to avoid punishments and obtain rewards.

Related to the question of the "essence" of personality is the notion of whether part, or all, of the personality can be hidden from the person him- or herself. Psychoanalytic theorists believe that the driving forces of the personality are in the unconscious and thus are not directly accessible to the person except under exceptional circumstances such as those which arise in therapy. Humanists are much more optimistic about the possibility of people coming to know their inner selves. According to Carl Rogers, parts of the self which were once hidden can, when the individual receives acceptance from others, become expressed and incorporated into self-awareness. Social learning theories do not place much weight on hidden personality dynamics. From the social learning perspective, people are viewed as unable to verbalize easily some of their expectations, but no special unconscious processes are hypothesized.

PERSONALITY CHANGE

Theories also differ in the degree to which a person's personality is seen as changing over time. Most personality theories address the development of personality in childhood and the possibility for change in adulthood. Psychoanalytic theorists believe that the most basic personality characteristics are established by the age of five or six, although there are some minor further developments in adolescence. While the person may change in adulthood in the course of psychotherapy and become better able to cope with the conflicts and traumas experienced during the early years, major personality transformations are not expected. Again, humanists are more optimistic than psychoanalytic theorists about personality change, although humanists, too, see the childhood years as important. For example, Rogers suggests that during childhood the parents may communicate their approval of some of the child's feelings and their disapproval of others, leaving the child with a distorted self-concept. Yet, from the humanistic point of view, the person's true inner self will constantly strive for expression. Thus, positive personality change is always seen as possible. Social learning theorists also see personality as changeable. Behaviors learned in childhood may later be changed by direct training, by altering the environment, or by revising one's expectations.

A final issue is the relationship between personality and behavior. For social learning theorists, behaviors and related expectations are personality. A person's behaviors are taken as a sample of a full behavioral repertoire which forms who the person is. Both psychoanalytic and humanistic theorists view behavior as a symptom or sign of underlying, internal personality dynamics rather than a sample of the personality itself. According to this viewpoint, a person's behaviors reflect personality only when interpreted in the light of the underlying traits they reveal. Diverse behaviors may thus be related to a single internal characteristic.

PERSONALITY MEASURES

The study of personality is a scientific discipline, with roots in empirical research; a philosophical discipline, seeking to understand the nature of people; and the foundation for the applied discipline of

psychological therapy. While these three aspects of personality often support and enrich one another, there are also tensions as the field accommodates specialists in each of these three areas.

The approach which focuses on personality as a scientific discipline has produced an array of methods to measure personality characteristics. They range from projective tests, such as having people tell stories inspired by ambiguous pictures, to more standardized paper-and-pencil personality tests in which people respond on bipolar numerical or multiple-choice scales to questions about their attitudes or behaviors. Methodologically, personality testing is quite sophisticated; however, people's scores on personality tests often are rather poor predictors of behavior. The poor record of behavioral prediction based on personality traits, coupled with evidence that suggests that behavior does not have the cross-situational consistency that one might expect, has led Walter Mischel and many other personality specialists to question the utility of most traditional personality theories. Social learning approaches, which emphasize the power of the situation in determining a person's behavior, tend to fare better in these analyses.

PREDICTING BEHAVIOR

Yet research has found circumstances under which people's behavior can be predicted from knowledge of their underlying personality characteristics. If one classifies personality characteristics and behaviors at a very general level, combining observations and predicting to a group of behaviors, prediction improves. For example, predictions would be more accurate if several measures of a person's conscientiousness were combined, and then used to predict an overall level of conscientious behavior in a variety of situations, than if one measured conscientiousness with a single scale and then attempted to predict behavior in one specific situation. Prediction on the basis of personality traits also improves when the situations in which one seeks to predict behaviors allow for individual variation as opposed to being highly constrained by social norms. Five basic personality traits often emerge in investigations: extroversion, agreeableness, conscientiousness, emotional stability, and culture (high scores on culture reflect characteristics such as intelligence and refinement). Some researchers view these trait terms as accurately describing consistent personality differences among people, while others view them as reflecting the "eye of the beholder" more than the core of personality.

Ultimately, people's personality traits and situations interact to produce behavior. Situations may often determine behavior, but people choose to place themselves in specific situations that elicit their traits. A child with a predisposition to aggression may provoke others and thus set the stage for the expression of aggression; one who is highly sociable may seek out others in cooperative situations. The relation between personality and behavior is very complex, and it is difficult to describe fully using standard research methods.

Research is highly unlikely to answer philosophical questions concerning human nature; however, considering people from the different points of view offered by various theories can be an enriching experience in itself. For example, a Freudian perspective on former United States president Lyndon Johnson might see his leadership during the Vietnam conflict as guided by aggressive instincts or even sublimated sexual instincts. On the other hand, a humanist might look at Johnson's presidency and find his decisions to be guided by the need for self-fulfillment, perhaps citing his vision of himself as the leader of the "Great Society" as an example of self-actualization. Social learning theorists would view Johnson's actions as president as determined by the rewards, punishments, and observational learning of his personal learning history, including growing up relatively poor in Texas and accruing power and respect during his years in the U.S. Senate, as well as by the reinforcements and punishments Johnson perceived to be available in the situations in which he found himself during his presidency. In the final analysis, none of these interpretations could be shown to be blatantly false or absolutely true. Historians, biographers, and others might find each to be an enriching viewpoint from which to consider this complex individual.

THERAPY

Multiple points of view also characterize the therapies derived from theories of personality. Most therapists take an eclectic approach, sampling from the ideas of various theories to tailor their treatment to a specific client. Each therapist, however, also may have her or his own biases, based on a particular theoretical orientation. For example, a client who

often feels anxious and seeks help from a psychoanalytic therapist may find that the therapist encourages the client to explore memories of childhood experiences to discover the unconscious roots of the anxiety. Slips of the tongue, dreams, and difficulty remembering or accepting therapeutic interpretations would be viewed as important clues to unconscious processes. The same client seeking treatment from a humanistic therapist would have a different experience. There, the emphasis would be on current experiences, with the therapist providing a warm and supportive atmosphere for the client to explore feelings. A behavioral therapist, from the social learning orientation, would help the client pinpoint situations in which anxiety occurs and teach the client alternative responses to those situations. Again, no one form of therapy is superior for all clients. Successes or failures in therapy depend on the combination of client, therapist, and mode of treatment.

THEORIES AND EXPERIMENTATION

While people have long speculated on the causes and types of individual differences in personality, the theory of Sigmund Freud was the first and most influential psychological personality theory. All subsequent theories have directly or indirectly addressed the central concerns of motivation, development, and personality organization first proposed by Freud. Psychoanalytic theorists such as Carl G. Jung and Alfred Adler, while trained by Freud, disagreed with Freud's emphasis on sexual instincts and developed their own theories, emphasizing different motivations. Similarly, Karen Horney, Erich Fromm, and others developed theories placing greater emphasis on the ego and its interaction with society than did Freud's.

Psychoanalytic theory has had somewhat less of an influence in the United States than it did in Europe. Personality psychology in the United States is relatively more research-oriented, practical, and optimistic. In the United States, Gordon Allport developed one of the first trait approaches to personality. The humanistic theories of Carl Rogers and Abraham Maslow, social learning theories of Albert Bandura and Julian Rotter, and cognitive theory of George Kelly flourished in the 1950's and 1960's and continue to have their advocates. Modern personality psychologists, however, are much more likely to confine themselves to personality measurement and research than to propose broad theories of personality.

Many have questioned personality's status as a scientific subdiscipline of psychology. In 1968, Walter Mischel's *Personality and Assessment*, arguing that the consistency and behavior-prediction assumptions inherent in all personality theories are unsupported by the evidence, was published. At the same time, attribution theories in social psychology were suggesting that personality traits are largely in the "eye of the beholder" rather than in the person being observed. For example, Edward Jones and Richard Nisbett argued that people are more inclined to see others as possessing personality traits than they are to attribute traits to themselves. The continued existence of personality as a subdiscipline of scientific psychology was debated.

The result has been a refined approach to measurement and personality analysis. Current research on personality does not boldly assert the influence of internal personality characteristics on behavior. There are no new theories purporting to explain all of personality or the nature of all people. Rather, attention is paid to careful assessment of personality and to the complex interactions of persons and situations. For example, research on loneliness has found that people who describe themselves as lonely often lack social skills and avoid interactions with others, thus perpetuating their feelings of loneliness. All personality characteristics, including loneliness, are most meaningfully seen as the product of a complex interrelationship between the person and the environment.

SOURCES FOR FURTHER STUDY

Hall, Calvin Springer, Gardner Lindzey, and John Campbell. *Theories of Personality*. 4th ed. New York: John Wiley & Sons, 1997. A classic textbook describing personality theories. Personality research is mentioned, but not discussed in detail. Includes particularly readable, thorough, and accurate descriptions of psychoanalytic theories. Chapter 1 introduces the topic of personality theories, and describes many dimensions upon which theories can be contrasted.

Hampden-Turner, Charles. *Maps of the Mind*. New York: Macmillan, 1981. Presents brief descriptions and pictorial representations (termed "maps") of basic psychological and philosophical concepts. The organization and presentation are a bit idiosyncratic; the summaries are very good, and the diagrams helpful in synthesizing complex information. Descriptions and maps relevant to the theories of Sigmund Freud, Carl Jung, Erich Fromm, Rollo May, Hans Eysenck, Carl Rogers, Harry Stack Sullivan, and Erik Erikson are particularly relevant to basic issues in personality theory.

Mischel, Walter. *Introduction to Personality*. 6th ed. Belmont, Calif.: Wadsworth, 1998. A college-level personality textbook with an emphasis on contemporary issues and research. Each major orientation to personality—psychodynamic, trait, phenomenological (humanistic), and behavioral—is presented with thorough discussions of measurement and research. The reader may find that this text alone is incomplete in its description of personality theories per se, but it makes an excellent companion reading to Hall and Lindzey's *Theories of Personality*. Mischel's own approach to social learning theory is presented.

_____. *Personality and Assessment*. 1968. Reprint. Hillsdale, N.J.: Analytic Press, 1996. The text that inspired debate about the utility of traditional personality theories. Readable but detailed; primarily of historical importance. Contemporary summaries of this issue can be found in Mischel's *Introduction to Personality* and in the *Handbook of Personality: Theory and Research*, edited by Pervin.

Pervin, Lawrence A., and Oliver John, eds. *Handbook of Personality: Theory and Research*. 2d ed. New York: Guilford Press, 2001. A compilation of personality theory and research for the sophisticated reader. Chapters by Walter Mischel ("Personality Dispositions Revisited and Revised: A View After Three Decades"), David Magnusson ("Personality Development from an Interactional Perspective"), and Bernard Weiner ("Attribution in Personality Psychology") may be of particular interest.

Storr, Anthony. *Churchill's Black Dog, Kafka's Mice, and Other Phenomena of the Human Mind*. New York: Grove Press, 1988. This fascinating book demonstrates how personality theories can be used to interpret lives. Storr describes the creative process in general, and the lives of Churchill, Kafka, and others in particular, from his psychological point of view, primarily psychoanalytic in orientation. The perspectives of Freud, Jung, and Erikson are featured.

Susan E. Beers

SEE ALSO: Analytical psychology: Carl G. Jung; Behavioral assessment; Cognitive social learning: Walter Mischel; Humanistic trait models: Gordon Allport; Psychoanalytic psychology; Psychoanalytic psychology and personality: Sigmund Freud; Psychosexual development; Self-actualization; Social learning: Albert Bandura.

Personology

Henry A. Murray

TYPE OF PSYCHOLOGY: Personality
FIELDS OF STUDY: Humanistic-phenomenological models; personality theory

Henry A. Murray's study of personality, or personology, as he preferred to call it, highlights the uniqueness of the individual and the interaction between individual needs and environmental constraints. His theory precipitated the in-depth study of human needs and provided an instrument for assessing human personality.

KEY CONCEPTS
- alpha press
- beta press
- need
- need for achievement
- press
- thematic apperception test (TAT)

INTRODUCTION

Henry A. Murray was born into a wealthy family in New York City in 1893. His early life was unremarkable, and unlike numerous other personality theorists, he experienced no major traumas that obviously influenced his theory. He was not trained in psychology (in fact, he greatly disliked psychology classes); rather, he was trained as a biologist and later received his Ph.D. in biochemistry from the University of Cambridge. His interest in psychology and personality processes was ignited during a three-week stay with Carl G. Jung, the eminent Swiss psychoanalyst. This meeting led to a change in careeraspirations, whereupon Murray was brought to Harvard University to engage in personality research and establish the Harvard Psychological Clinic.

Murray's biomedical training is reflected in his belief that personality processes are dependent on brain functioning. He did not believe that personality actually existed; he believed that descriptions of personality were shorthand methods of describing various aspects of individuals and their behaviors. He thought that personality helped explain and predict an individual's actions, drives, needs, goals, and plans. He stated that his system of personality, "personology," was a tentative theory, as psychologists did not yet know enough to capture completely the essence of each individual.

As opposed to personality theorists who developed their ideas in the clinic, working with emotionally disturbed individuals, Murray believed that the best way to investigate personality was to study normal individuals in their natural environments. While at Harvard, he undertook an intensive study of fifty-one male undergraduates during a six-month period. The undergraduates were examined by a council of twenty-eight specialists of various training and expertise so they might fully understand the personality of the students.

From these studies, Murray developed his ideas about human needs. He believed that these needs helped individuals focus their attention on certain events and guided their behaviors to meet those needs. There are primary needs that originate from internal bodily processes (for example, air, water, food, and sex) and secondary needs that are concerned with mental and emotional satisfaction (for example, achievement, dominance, understanding, and affiliation). He proposed a hierarchy of needs, a concept later elaborated on by Abraham Maslow, in which more basic needs such as food must be met before others can be addressed. Murray originally proposed a list of twenty basic human needs, although this list was later revised and expanded by his students and followers.

"PRESS" CONCEPT

Although Murray's elaboration and description of human needs was one of his major contributions to psychology, his focus on the situational context for behavior foreshadowed psychology's future emphasis on environmental events. He proposed the concept of "press," or forces provided by situations or events in the environment. These forces may help

Psychologist and Harvard University professor David Mc-Clelland, who investigated the need of individuals to overcome obstacles and accomplish difficult tasks. (AP/Wide World Photos)

or hinder individuals in reaching their goals. For example, a student may have a need for achievement that would result in her attending college and receiving a degree. Environmental events such as poverty, however, may hinder her progress or pressure her away from these goals and necessitate that she take a job to support her family. In this situation, Murray also distinguished between "alpha press," or actual pressure resulting from environmental situations, and "beta press," or subjective pressure that results from individual interpretation of the events. In the example of going to college given above, alpha press might be the college board scores or the money necessary to go to certain colleges. These are real, and they involve little interpretation. Beta press might be the interpretation that if the student does not get into a certain college, she will be viewed as an embarrassment and a failure. This type of pressure comes from an internal evaluation of environmental events.

USE OF THE TAT

A final major contribution of Murray's personology theory comes from the device he used to determine individual needs and more generally measure personality. Along with Christiana Morgan, Murray developed the Thematic Apperception Test (TAT), which continues to be a widely used instrument for assessing human personality. The TAT consists of thirty ambiguous black-and-white pictures for which an individual is instructed to make up a story. The test subject is asked to tell what led up to the event in the picture, what is happening in the picture, including how the characters are thinking and feeling, and what will happen to the characters in the future. Murray's idea was that test subjects will project their needs into the picture, much as individuals who are on a diet will notice food in most situations that they encounter. It is similar to the children's game of identifying the shapes of clouds. Children may identify clouds with children's themes of dragons, monsters, or dinosaurs. Adolescents may view these same clouds as other boys and girls, cars, or sports figures. Murray hypothesized that certain themes would emerge from individuals' responses to the figures and that themes and expectations for the future would become evident. Mental health professionals continue to use the TAT for this purpose.

ACHIEVEMENT NEED

Henry A. Murray's theoretical focus was to catalog all possible human needs. This led to a wide range of understanding; however, it was left to later researchers to add depth to the understanding of needs. One of the best researched of the secondary needs is the need for achievement. This need of individuals to overcome obstacles and accomplish what often are very difficult tasks has been investigated in detail by David McClelland and his colleague John Atkinson. They developed a system for scoring individuals' responses to TAT cards to abstract achievement-oriented themes. They observed that individuals who had a high need for achievement completed more tasks under competitive conditions, were more productive in their jobs, and tended to get better grades. They used this information and measuring system to develop a training program for industry that has been shown to increase employees' need for achievement and job productivity. Their system was found to be working even two years after the program was begun. Interesting questions remain, however; for example, at what level does the need for achievement become unproductive? At some point it will lead to unrealistic expectations, unnecessary stress, and related health problems.

One of the fascinating things about the McClelland and Atkinson method of assessing an individual's need for achievement is that it is not restricted to measuring responses from TAT cards. Their scoring system can be used with any written material; therefore, it can be adapted to a vast amount of literary, historical, and biographical information. McClelland conjectured that he could predict the economic growth and decline of a country from the number of achievement themes evident in its children's stories. He looked at the economic conditions of twenty-three countries from 1929 to 1950 and scored its children's stories from the prior decade (1920-1929). While it is apparent that children's stories are not the only factor related to economic well-being, McClelland did discover that those countries with a higher number of achievement themes in the children's stories experienced the most economic growth.

Gender Differences in Achievement

Another example of the importance of Murray's pioneering work on the need for achievement comes from research on how this need is demonstrated differently by men and women. It has been evident for many years that the expression of achievement has been more acceptable for men than for women. It has only been in recent years that the issues surrounding the achievement of women have been investigated. It is clear that these issues, in general, have been experienced much differently by women from the way they have been experienced by men. The paths for understanding and expressing ideas of achievement for men and women clearly differ very early in life. A series of studies supports the idea that women with a high need for achievement come from relatively stressful and difficult home lives, whereas men with a similar level of achievement strivings come from supportive, nonstressful homes. Additionally, girls tend to evidence their needs for achievement because of a desire for adult approval, while boys do not demonstrate this motivation.

One of the more interesting as well as distressing findings regarding sex differences in the need for achievement comes from the research of Matina Horner. She found that women experience considerable conflict and distress when faced with their need to achieve, whereas men do not experience a similar state. She proposed that the "smart girl" faced the prospect of considerable loss of social status and peer rejection as a result of her strivings to achieve. This may result in the behavior of acting "dumb" in order to prosper socially. Horner elaborated on Sigmund Freud's original idea that women actually may fear success because of its social consequences.

In a famous study by Horner, she had men and women write a story after being given an opening line. The women were to write a story about a woman who found herself at the top of her medical school class after the first semester. The men had the same story, except that it was a man who was at the top of the class. Far more women wrote stories of the unappealing and sometimes tragic consequences for the smart woman in class. They wrote about possible rejections and losses of friends and indicated that she would have a poorer chance of getting married. Many of the females came up with situations related to removing the student from the conflict situation, such as dropping out of medical school or settling for becoming a nurse. Finally, some of the students even indicated that she might receive bodily harm as a result of her stellar performance.

The conflicting messages of society regarding achievement for women are clearly shown by this study. It is apparent that women face considerable struggles in their attempts to compete and achieve equally with men. The factors that will alleviate this internal distress and aid women in the full expression of their abilities await further investigation. It was Murray's pioneering study of human needs that laid the groundwork for these types of investigation, which have the potential to inspire long-overdue social changes.

Theoretical Contributions

Murray's theory of personology was a unique contribution to the early years of personality theorizing. His system differed from those before it (for example, Freud's psychoanalytic theory) in that it was not developed in a clinic as a result of working with clients. Murray studied normal individuals in great detail and gained knowledge from experts in a number of disciplines. This gave personality theory a certain degree of academic respectability it had not had previously acquired. Murray was also a highly influential teacher, with many students who in turn made significant contributions to psychology.

Murray's description of "needs" was a major contribution to the psychological study of motivation. His research spurred many investigations of individual human needs. Additionally, his complementary emphasis on environmental events (that is, "press") was later to become a major shift in American psychology. The behavioral school of psychology, with its leaders John B. Watson and B. F. Skinner, was to become the dominant force for many years. Their focus on the manipulation of environmental events (for example, rewards and punishments) was to have a major influence on education, therapy, and child-rearing. The subjective interpretation of environmental events (that is, "beta press") also was a precursor to a major shift in theory. The cognitive school of psychology now focuses on these mental rearrangements of events and makes predictions based on individuals' expectations and fears. Murray's emphasis on the fact that the idiosyncratic perception of an event is not always the same as what actually happened is the foundation for this approach.

Finally, Murray's development of the TAT (with Christiana Morgan) was an early and influential contribution to the area of personality assessment. It and similar tests, such as the Rorschach inkblot test and the incomplete sentences blank, are frequently used for gathering personality information in the clinic. Even the weaknesses of the TAT (for example, different investigators may score it very differently) led to the development of more objective personality tests with standardized questions and scoring. Murray's influence, both in the classroom and in the clinic, was substantial.

SOURCES FOR FURTHER STUDY

Anderson, James W. "Henry A. Murray's Early Career: A Psychobiographical Exploration." *Journal of Personality* 56, no. 1 (1988): 139-171. An interesting presentation of the factors that led Murray to become a psychologist and of how his experiences interacted with his theory. An excellent example of how one's life cannot be extricated from one's beliefs about human nature.

Boring, Edwin G., and Gardner Lindzey, eds. *A History of Psychology in Autobiography.* Vol. 5. New York: Appleton-Century-Crofts, 1967. In an auto-biographical essay in volume 5 of this survey, Murray presents a detailed view of his concepts and the influence of his work.

Hall, Calvin Springer, and Gardner Lindzey. *Introduction to Theories of Personality.* 3d ed. New York: John Wiley & Sons, 1985. A definitive reference for information on most personality theorists. A thorough book that gives a detailed explanation of most of Murray's concepts. Not recommended for the casual reader.

Schultz, Duane P. *Theories of Personality.* 4th ed. Belmont, Calif.: Brooks/Cole, 1990. A review of the major aspects of Murray's theory in an easy-to-read format. Provides substantial biographical information about Murray and how this influenced his theory.

Smith, M. B., and J. W. Anderson. "Henry A. Murray (1893-1988)." *American Psychologist* 44 (1989): 1153-1154. This obituary is a personal account of Murray's career and his impact on his students as well as on psychology. Covers not only the facts of Murray's work but also his perceptions of his work.

Brett L. Beck

SEE ALSO: Achievement motivation; Affiliation motive; Aggression; Behavioral assessment; Personality interviewing strategies; Projection; Psychoanalytic psychology; Work motivation.

Phobias

TYPE OF PSYCHOLOGY: Psychopathology
FIELDS OF STUDY: Anxiety disorders

Phobias are exaggerated, unjustified fears of everyday objects or situations, such as fear of certain types of animals or fears of doing things in front of other people. Though many people experience irrational fears or phobias, few seek treatment; as a result, they suffer emotional pain and may find their lives limited by their phobias.

KEY CONCEPTS
- conditioned response (CR)
- conditioned stimulus (CS)
- instrumental conditioning
- Pavlovian conditioning

- unconditioned response (UR)
- unconditioned stimulus (US)

INTRODUCTION

Phobias are a type of anxiety disorder characterized by a persistent, exaggerated, irrational fear of certain objects or situations and by efforts to avoid the object or situation. In many cases, the distress and the avoidance efforts significantly interfere with an individual's daily life. Phobias are common in the general population; approximately one person in ten suffers from mild phobias, and severe, disabling phobias are found in one person in five hundred.

The three major types of phobias are agoraphobia (a fear of situations in which escape is perceived to be difficult or assistance unavailable), social phobias, and specific (or "simple") phobias. In social phobias, being observed by others may elicit anxiety and the desire to avoid such situations. The person fears doing something which will lead to embarrassment or humiliation, such as being unable to speak or showing nervousness through trembling hands or other signs. Persons with specific phobias avoid a certain type of object or situation or suffer extreme anxiety when in the presence of these objects or situations. Some examples of common specific phobias are acrophobia, fear of heights; arachnophobia, fear of spiders; claustrophobia, fear of being in small, enclosed spaces; pathophobia, fear of diseases and germs; and xenophobia, fear of strangers.

In the presence of the feared object or situation, the severely phobic person's experience and reaction differ dramatically from the average person's. Physiologically, changes in the body cause an increase in heart rate and blood pressure, tensing of muscles, and feelings of fear. In many cases, a panic state develops, characterized by muscular trembling and shaking, rapid, shallow breathing, and feelings of unbearable anxiety and dizziness. Behaviorally, the person will stop or redirect whatever activity in which he or she is engaged, then try to escape from or avoid the phobic object or situation. Cognitively, a phobic person at a distance from the object or situation can recognize it as posing little actual danger; but upon approaching it, fear rises, and the estimation of risk increases.

THEORETICAL EXPLANATIONS

The many theories which attempt to explain how phobias develop can be grouped under three general headings: those which stress unconscious emotional conflicts, those which explain phobias based on the principles of learning, and those which consider biological factors. For Sigmund Freud, phobias represented the external manifestation of unconscious internal emotional conflicts which had their origin in early childhood. These conflicts typically involved the inhibition of primitive sexual feelings.

Learning-theory explanations of phobias are based on Pavlovian conditioning, instrumental conditioning, and social learning theory. According to a Pavlovian conditioning model, phobias result when a neutral stimulus—a dog, for example—is paired with an unconditioned stimulus (US), for example, a painful bite to the leg. After this event, the sight of the dog has become a conditioned stimulus (CS) which elicits a conditioned response (CR), fear; thus, a dog phobia has been learned. Instrumental conditioning (the modification of behavior as a result of its consequences) has been combined with Pavlovian conditioning in the two-factor model of phobias. After the establishment of the phobia by Pavlovian conditioning, as above, a person will attempt to escape from or avoid the phobic object or situation whenever it is encountered. When this is successful, the fear subsides. The reduction in fear is a desirable consequence which increases the likelihood of escape/avoidance behavior in the future (that is, the escape/avoidance behavior is reinforced). The two-factor model thus accounts for both the development and maintenance of phobias. Social learning theory suggests that human learning is based primarily on the observation and imitation of others; thus, fears and phobias would be acquired by observing others who show fearful behavior toward certain objects or situations. This learning occurs primarily during childhood, when children learn many behaviors and attitudes by modeling those of others.

Two theories suggest that inherited biological factors contribute to the development of phobias. The preparedness theory suggests that those stimuli which are most easily conditioned are objects or situations which may have posed a particular threat to humans' early ancestors, such as spiders, heights, small spaces, thunder, and strangers. Thus, people are genetically prepared to acquire fear of them quickly. Similarly, people vary in susceptibility to phobias, and this is also thought to be based at least partly on an inherited predisposition. A phobia-prone person may be physiologically highly arousable; thus, many more events would reach a threshold of fear necessary for conditioning.

Stressful life situations, including extreme conflict or frustration, may also predispose a person to develop a phobia or exacerbate an existing phobia. Further, a sense of powerlessness or lack of control over one's situation may increase susceptibility; this may partly explain why phobias are more common in women, as these feelings are reported more often by women than by men. Once initiated, phobias tend to persist and even worsen over time, and the fear may spread to other, similar objects or situations. Even phobias which have been successfully treated may recur if the person is exposed to the original US, or even to another US which produces extreme anxiety. Thus, many factors—unconscious, learned, and biological—may be involved in the onset and maintenance of phobias. As every person is unique in terms of biology and life experience, each phobia is also unique and represents a particular interaction of the factors above and possibly other, unknown factors.

CASE STUDIES AND THERAPY TECHNIQUES

The following two case studies of phobias illustrate their onset, development, and the various treatment approaches typically used. These studies are fictionalized composites of the experiences of actual clients.

Ellen P. entered an anxiety disorders clinic requesting large amounts of tranquilizers. She revealed that she wanted them to enable her to fly on airplanes; if she could not fly, she would probably lose her job as a sales representative for her company. Ellen described an eight-year history of a fear of flying during which she had simply avoided all airplane flights and had driven or taken a train to distant sales appointments. She would sometimes drive through the night, keep her appointments during the day, then again drive through the night back to the home office. As these trips occurred more often, she became increasingly exhausted, and her work performance began to decline noticeably.

A review of major childhood and adolescent experiences revealed only that Ellen was a chronic worrier. She also reported flying comfortably on many occasions prior to the onset of her phobia, but remembered her last flight in vivid detail. She

was flying to meet her husband for a honeymoon cruise, but the plane was far behind schedule because of poor weather. She began to worry that she would miss the boat and that her honeymoon, and possibly her marriage, would be ruined. The plane then encountered some minor turbulence, and brief images of a crash raced through Ellen's mind. She rapidly became increasingly anxious, tense, and uncomfortable. She grasped her seat cushion; her heart seemed to be pounding in her throat; she felt dizzy and was beginning to perspire. Hoping no one would notice her distress, she closed her eyes, pretending to sleep for the remainder of the flight. After returning from the cruise, she convinced her husband to cancel their plane reservations, and thus began her eight years of avoiding flying.

Ellen's psychologist began exposure therapy for her phobia. First she was trained to relax deeply. Then she was gradually exposed to her feared stimuli, progressing from visiting an airport to sitting on a taxiing plane to weekly flights of increasing length in a small plane. After ten weeks of therapy and practice at home and the airport, Ellen was able to fly on a commercial airliner. Two years after the conclusion of therapy, Ellen met her psychologist by chance and informed her that she now had her own pilot's license.

In the second case, Steve R. was a high school junior who was referred by his father because of his refusal to attend school. Steve was described as a loner who avoided other people and suffered fears of storms, cats, and now, apparently, school. He was of above-average intelligence and was pressured by his father to excel academically and attend a prestigious college. Steve's mother was described as being shy like Steve. Steve was her only child, and she doted on him, claiming she knew what it felt like to be in his situation.

When interviewed, Steve sat rigidly in his chair, spoke in clipped sentences, and offered answers only to direct questions. Questioning revealed that Steve's refusal to attend school was based on a fear of ridicule by his classmates. He would not eat or do any written work in front of them for fear he was being watched and would do something clumsy, thus embarrassing himself. He never volunteered answers to teachers' questions, but in one class, the teacher had begun to call on Steve regularly for the correct answer whenever other students had missed the question. Steve would sit in a near-panic state, fear-

DSM-IV-TR Criteria for Phobias

SPECIFIC PHOBIA (DSM CODE 300.29)

Marked and persistent fear that is excessive or unreasonable and cued by presence or anticipation of specific object or situation (flying, heights, animals, receiving an injection, seeing blood)

Exposure to phobic stimulus almost invariably provokes immediate anxiety response, which may take the form of situationally bound or situationally predisposed panic attack; in children, anxiety may be expressed by crying, tantrums, freezing, or clinging

Person recognizes fear as excessive or unreasonable; in children, this feature may be absent

Phobic situation(s) avoided or endured with intense anxiety or distress

Avoidance, anxious anticipation, or distress in feared situation(s) interferes significantly with normal routines, occupational (or academic) functioning, or social activities or relationships, or marked distress about phobia present

In individuals under age eighteen, duration of at least six months

Anxiety, panic attacks, or phobic avoidance associated with specific object or situation not better accounted for by another mental disorder, such as Obsessive-Compulsive Disorder, Post-traumatic Stress Disorder, Separation Anxiety Disorder, Social Phobia, Panic Disorder with Agoraphobia, or Agoraphobia Without History of Panic Disorder

Specify:
- Animal Type
- Natural Environment Type (such as heights, storms, water)
- Blood-Injection-Injury Type
- Situational Type (such as airplanes, elevators, enclosed places)
- Other Type (such as phobic avoidance of situations that may lead to choking, vomiting, or contracting an illness; in children, avoidance of loud sounds or costumed characters)

SOCIAL PHOBIA (DSM CODE 300.23)

Marked and persistent fear of one or more social or performance situations involving exposure to unfamiliar people or to possible scrutiny by others; individual fears that he or she will act in a way (or show anxiety symptoms) that will be humiliating or embarrassing

In children, evidence requires the capacity for age-appropriate social relationships with familiar people and anxiety must occur in peer settings, not just in interactions with adults

Exposure to feared social situation almost invariably provokes anxiety, which may take the form of situationally bound or situationally predisposed panic attack; in children, anxiety may be expressed by crying, tantrums, freezing, or shrinking from social situations with unfamiliar people

Person recognizes fear as excessive or unreasonable; in children, this feature may be absent

Feared social or performance situations avoided or endured with intense anxiety or distress

Avoidance, anxious anticipation, or distress in feared social or performance situation(s) interferes significantly with normal routines, occupational (academic) functioning, or social activities or relationships, or marked distress about phobia present

In individuals under age eighteen, duration of at least six months

Fear or avoidance not due to direct physiological effects of a substance or general medical condition

Not better accounted for by another mental disorder such as Panic Disorder with or Without Agoraphobia, Separation Anxiety Disorder, Body Dysmorphic Disorder, a Pervasive Developmental Disorder, or Schizoid Personality Disorder

If general medical condition or another mental disorder present, fear unrelated to it

Specify if Generalized (fears include most social situations)

---

ing he would be called on. After two weeks of this, he refused to return to school.

Steve was diagnosed as having a severe social phobia. His therapy included a contract with his teachers in which it was agreed that he would not be called upon in class until therapy had made it possible for him to answer with only moderate anxiety. In return, he was expected to attend all his classes. To

help make this transition, a psychiatrist prescribed an antianxiety drug to help reduce the panic symptoms. A psychologist began relaxation training for use in exposure therapy, which would include Steve volunteering answers in class and seeking social interactions with his peers. Steve finished high school, though he left the state university at the end of his first semester because of a worsening of his phobias. His therapy was resumed, and he graduated from a local community college, though his phobias continued to recur during stressful periods in his life.

These cases illustrate many of the concepts related to the study of phobias. In both cases, it is possible that a high emotional reactivity predisposed the person to a phobia. In Ellen's case, the onset of the phobia was sudden and appeared to be the result of Pavlovian conditioning, whereas in Steve's case, the phobia likely developed over time and involved social learning: modeling of his mother's behavior. Steve's phobia may also have been inadvertently reinforced by his mother's attention; thus, instrumental conditioning may have been involved as well. Ellen's phobia could be seen to involve a sense of lack of control, combined with a possibly inherited predisposition to fear enclosed spaces. Steve's phobia illustrated both a spreading of the phobia and recurrence of the phobia under stress.

HISTORICAL VARIATIONS IN PERSPECTIVES

As comprehensive psychological theories of human behavior began to emerge in the early 1900's, each was faced with the challenge of explaining the distinct symptoms, but apparently irrational nature, of phobias. For example, in 1909, Sigmund Freud published his account of the case of "Little Hans," a young boy with a horse phobia. Freud hypothesized that Hans had an unconscious fear of his father which was transferred to a more appropriate object: the horse. Freud's treatment of phobias involved analyzing the unconscious conflicts (through psychoanalysis) and giving patients insight into the "true" nature of their fears.

An alternative explanation of phobias based on the principles of Pavlovian conditioning was proposed by John B. Watson and Rosalie Rayner in 1920. They conditioned a fear of a white rat in an infant nicknamed "Little Albert" by pairing presentation of the rat with a frightening noise (an unconditioned stimulus). After a few such trials, simply presenting the rat (now a conditioned stimulus) produced fear and crying (the conditioned response).

EXPERIMENTAL MODELS

As B. F. Skinner's laboratory discoveries of the principles of instrumental conditioning began to be applied to humans in the 1940's and 1950's, experimental

models of phobias in animals were developed. In the 1950's, Joseph Wolpe created phobia-like responses in cats by shocking them in experimental cages. He was later able to decrease their fear by feeding them in the cages where they had previously been shocked. Based on this counterconditioning model, Wolpe developed the therapy procedure of systematic desensitization, which paired mental images of the feared stimulus with bodily relaxation.

Social learning theory as advanced by Albert Bandura in the 1960's was also applied to phobias. Bandura conducted experiments showing that someone might develop a phobia by observing another person behaving fearfully. It was later demonstrated that some phobias could be treated by having the patient observe and imitate a nonfearful model. Cognitive approaches to phobias were also developed in the 1970's and 1980's by therapists such as Albert Ellis and Aaron T. Beck. These theories focus on the role of disturbing thoughts in creating bodily arousal and associated fear. Therapy then consists of altering these thought patterns.

APPLICATIONS TO PSYCHOLOGY

Phobias can thus be seen as providing a testing ground for the major theories of psychology. Whether the theorist adopts a psychodynamic, learning/behavioral, or cognitive perspective, some account of the development and treatment of phobias must be made. No one theory has been shown to be completely adequate, so research continues in each area. The study of phobias also illustrates the importance to psychology of animal research in helping psychologists to understand and treat human problems. For example, Susan Mineka has used monkeys to demonstrate the relative importance of social learning versus biology in the development of phobias. Future research will also likely consider the interactions among the various models of phobias and the conditions that might predict which models would be most effective in explaining and treating specific cases of phobias. As the models mature and are integrated into a comprehensive theory of phobias, this knowledge can then be applied to the prevention of phobias.

SOURCES FOR FURTHER STUDY

Beck, Aaron T., and Gary Emery. *Anxiety Disorders and Phobias: A Cognitive Perspective.* Reprint. New York: Basic Books, 1990. Though cognitive explanations and treatments for phobias are stressed, this book considers other perspectives as well, and it could serve as an introduction to the topic for the interested high school or college student.

Bourne, Edmund. *The Anxiety and Phobia Workbook.* 3d ed. Oakland, Calif.: New Harbinger, 2000. An excellent self-help book for the general reader who suffers from an anxiety disorder. Also an accessible introduction to the causes and treatments of phobias for high school and college students. Contains self-diagnostic and therapy exercises, as well as other resources for the phobia sufferer.

Gold, Mark S. *The Good News About Panic, Anxiety, and Phobias.* New York: Random House, 1989. For a general audience. Outlines many biological factors which may be associated with phobias. Presents a one-sided approach, heavily promoting a biopsychiatric view of phobias and their treatment.

Marks, Issac Meyer. *Fears, Phobias, and Rituals.* New York: Oxford University Press, 1987. With more than five hundred pages and a bibliography with more than two thousand references, this text provides comprehensive coverage of all aspects of phobias. Written for the professional and researcher, but accessible to college students who are interested in pursuing some aspect of phobias in detail.

Mineka, Susan. "Animal Models of Anxiety-Based Disorders: Their Usefulness and Limitations." In *Anxiety and the Anxiety Disorders,* edited by A. Hussain Tuma and Jack Maser. Hillsdale, N.J.: Lawrence Erlbaum, 1985. The phobia portion of this chapter reviews the major experiments done with animals which demonstrate the many similarities between human phobias and experimental phobias in animals. Clearly illustrates the relevance of animal research to human behavior. Difficult, yet indispensable for a thorough understanding of phobias.

Wilson, R. Reid. *Breaking the Panic Cycle: Self-Help for People with Phobias.* Rockville, Md.: Anxiety Disorders Association of America, 1987. A publication of a nonprofit organization which is dedicated to disseminating information and providing help to phobia sufferers. The ADAA also publishes the *National Treatment Directory,* which lists treatment programs throughout the country.

David S. McDougal

SEE ALSO: Agoraphobia and panic disorders; Anxiety disorders; Aversion, implosion, and systematic desensitization; Conditioning; Learning; Nervous system; Observational learning; Operant conditioning therapies; Pavlovian conditioning; Preparedness; Reflexes.

Physical development
Environment versus genetics

TYPE OF PSYCHOLOGY: Developmental psychology
FIELDS OF STUDY: Infancy and childhood

Physical development includes a child's physical characteristics, motor development, growth, and brain and nervous system development; the dramatic changes that occur in these areas during the early years of life result from the combined influences of a child's genetic makeup and environmental factors.

KEY CONCEPTS
- chromosome
- critical period
- dominant gene
- gene
- genotype
- phenotype
- polygenic trait
- recessive gene
- sex chromosomes
- sex-linked trait

INTRODUCTION
Physical development generally refers to a child's physical characteristics (such as eye or hair color), growth (changes in height, weight, and bodily proportions), motor development (increasing control over movement, as in the progression from sitting up to standing to walking), and brain and nervous system development (an increase in the size and complexity of the brain, and an increase in the efficiency of message transfers). Dramatic changes take place in these four areas during the early years of life because of the combined influence of a child's genetic makeup and the environment.

Genes provide a master plan, or "blueprint," for development. Genes are chemical bases that form small sections of threadlike structures called chromosomes. Each chromosome is made of thousands of genes, and every cell in the human body has twenty-three pairs of chromosomes. Encoded in the genes are those traits common to the human race (such as the ability to walk upright) as well as those traits that make each child unique (such as the rate of maturation). Genes direct the form and sequence of development, including setting limits on a child's potential and predisposing him or her toward either a normal or an abnormal course of development.

GENETIC TRAITS

Parents pass traits along to their offspring in chromosomes. During the process of fertilization, the twenty-three chromosomes in the mother's ovum unite with the twenty-three chromosomes in the father's sperm. The resulting baby's traits depend on which genes from the mother are matched with which genes from the father. In some cases, certain genes are "dominant" or "recessive." For example, the gene for brown eyes is dominant over the gene for blue eyes, which is recessive. If a child inherits the dominant gene for brown eyes from one parent and the recessive gene for blue eyes from the other parent, the child will have brown eyes. A child must receive the recessive gene for blue eyes from both parents in order to have blue eyes. In other cases, certain traits appear to be a mixture. These "polygenic" traits are the result of the combined influence of many genes; skin color is one example of a polygenic trait. Traits may also be "sex linked," which means that the genes for certain traits (color blindness, for example) are carried in the sex chromosomes. Sex chromosomes constitute the twenty-third pair of chromosomes and function to determine a person's sex. (Females have two X chromosomes, whereas males have one X and one Y chromosome.)

ENVIRONMENTAL INFLUENCE

Whereas genes provide a blueprint for development, the environment may modify the extent to which the blueprint is followed by influencing the direction and speed of a child's physical development, and the expression of certain traits. Environmental influences are those that exist outside the person;

they generally include a person's physical and sociocultural surroundings and the time in history in which she or he is born. The physical environment includes such aspects of a child's immediate environment as the exposure of a fetus to drugs taken by its mother or the exposure of a young child to such environmental hazards as lead or mercury. The sociocultural environment refers to the influence that the people in a child's life may have on its development. For example, the parent-child relationship and the parents' ethnic background have been found to influence a child's physical development. Finally, the time in history in which a child is born may have various consequences for his or her development. For example, the availability of the polio vaccine today prevents the ravaging effects that this disease once had on children.

GENOTYPE AND PHENOTYPE RELATIONSHIP

Although some "genotypes" (a person's genetic makeup) are expressed directly in a person's "phenotype" (observable traits and behavior), as in the case of eye color or blood type, most phenotypes are the result of an interaction between genes and the environment. Some researchers, in fact, have stated that development is the expression of one's genotype in the context of one's environment. For example, a child may inherit a genetic tendency toward obesity or toward being athletic. Whether the child becomes obese, however, may depend on the eating behaviors of the family; similarly, whether a child develops his or her full athletic potential may depend on the child's nutritional status, opportunities available to participate in athletic activities, and the amount of parental support and encouragement received.

Genetic and environmental factors affect many aspects of physical development, ranging from common physical traits and everyday bodily functions to diseases and disorders. A child's physical features (such as hair and eye color), blood type, amount of body fat, body build, metabolism, weight, health, activity level, sensitivity, blood pressure, timing and rate of maturation, hormonal regulation, sequence of motor development, and hand preference are all examples of genetically based traits. Dominant gene traits include brown eyes, brown hair, curly hair, thick lips, and normal color vision, whereas blue eyes and blond hair are examples of recessive gene traits. Height and weight are two types of polygenic traits; color blindness is an example of a sex-linked trait.

GENETIC CAUSE OF DISORDERS

Defective (or absent) genes can cause genetic disorders and diseases that are acquired through these same inheritance patterns. Achondroplasia (a type of dwarfism that is apparent at birth) and Huntington's chorea (a genetic disease that affects the central nervous system and causes progressive neural degeneration), for example, are dominant gene disorders. Sickle-cell anemia (a painful blood disorder that often leads to heart or kidney failure), congenital deafness, phenylketonuria (PKU, the lack of an enzyme to complete the metabolism of milk protein), cystic fibrosis (a metabolic error leading to sticky fluid in the lungs that clogs the airways), and galactosemia (defective carbohydrate metabolism) are all recessive gene disorders. Many disorders are polygenic; among them are cleft palate and cleft lips, childhood diabetes, spina bifida, hip dislocation, and allergies. Color blindness, hemophilia (the inability of the blood to coagulate), and fragile X syndrome (a leading cause of mental retardation among newborns) are all sex-linked disorders.

Developmental disorders may also result from faulty chromosome distribution. Down syndrome, for example, results when a child has three instead of the normal two number 21 chromosomes. Children with Down syndrome have distinct physical features and are moderately to severely retarded. Errors of sex-chromosome distribution can also occur—females may lack a second X chromosome, or males may have an extra X or Y chromosome. These sex-chromosome disorders generally result in infertility, some type of mental retardation, or both.

ENVIRONMENTAL CAUSES OF DISORDERS

Some of the physical, social, and historical influences of the environment begin exerting their effects on a child's development even before birth. Diseases of the mother during pregnancy, such as syphilis, German measles, herpes, gonorrhea, and acquired immunodeficiency syndrome (AIDS), may have consequences for the fetus ranging from blindness, deafness, and brain damage to death. Also, drugs ingested by the mother during pregnancy (including alcohol and the nicotine in cigarettes) may affect the unborn child in mild or severe ways. Maternal emotional stress, inadequate medical care, in-

compatible blood types between the mother and the fetus, exposure to high levels of radiation, and malnutrition all have the potential for adversely affecting the developing fetus.

The impact of some of these environmental influences on development (especially drugs, disease, and malnutrition) depends in part on the timing and the "dosage" involved. "Critical periods" are specific times in development when developing organs, structures, or abilities are most vulnerable to environmental influences. During prenatal development, the first three months of pregnancy is a critical period because all the basic structures (the eyes, ears, brain, heart, and limbs) and organ systems of the fetus are being formed. Shortly after birth, there is another critical period for brain development, as it is developing rapidly. Serious damage to the fetus or infant can result if it is exposed to harmful environmental influences during this time, since the parts of the body that are developing the most rapidly are the most vulnerable. If exposed to the same influences later, the child would likely suffer less serious consequences.

After a child is born, health, medical care, nutrition, and disease continue to influence physical development. Exposure to environmental hazards such as lead or toxic mercury levels can also cause deformities, retardation, and poor muscular development and control.

ROLE OF "PRACTICE"

Normal development not only requires the absence of genetic and environmental difficulties; it also requires practice. In studies of children, normal experience or "practice" has been found to be necessary for normal motor development. In addition, studies using animals have found that normal, everyday visual experience is necessary for the development of normal vision and that enriched or deprived sensory environments can affect brain development (for example, the weight of the cortex and the number of interconnections between the brain cells). In some instances, experience has also been found to speed up development. Philip Zelazo and his colleagues reported in the early 1970's that practice of the walking reflex early in life led to earlier walking in infants; other studies suggest that such practice can be harmful. Some studies have reported that infants who have experience sitting in someone's lap are able to sit alone earlier. Although some skills may be influenced by practice, physical and neural maturation limit what can be achieved.

SOCIOCULTURAL FACTORS

Sociocultural factors, such as family interaction patterns and ethnicity, affect development in a number of ways. Studies have found, for example, that parental attentiveness and encouragement are important factors influencing whether infants take an interest in and explore their environments. Studies of maternal deprivation have found that mothers who are emotionally neglectful, nonnurturant, cold, and unaffectionate toward their children can predispose their children toward a condition called deprivation dwarfism. This condition is characterized by growth retardation and abnormally low levels of growth hormone in spite of the fact that these children have received proper food, have been given adequate medical care, and do not have an illness or physical defect. (Researchers believe that emotional deprivation affects normal hormonal functioning in the body, thereby inhibiting growth.) Physical development may also vary across cultures and ethnic backgrounds—the rate of maturation of African infants, for example, is such that they tend to reach motor milestones such as sitting and walking before European or American infants.

The time in history in which a child is born can also affect a number of factors in a child's life that are related to physical development. For example, societal health practices, daily activities, the extent of medical knowledge available, and nutrition have changed over time. Because of better nutrition, for example, children in Western nations and Japan are taller and reach motor milestones earlier compared with children living a hundred years ago.

HISTORIC DEVELOPMENT OF STUDY

The question of the respective contributions of genes and the environment to development reflects a centuries-old debate by philosophers, psychologists, and others concerning human nature: whether inborn differences or the environment contributes more to human development.

Throughout most of the twentieth century, the predominant view in American psychology emphasized the role of the environment as the predominant influence on human development and behavior. At least part of the reason for this may be attributable to a lack of technology available for in-depth investigation and measurement of human biological processes. Advances in science and technology, however, have allowed better research that has greatly increased knowledge about such processes as brain development and its role in normal and abnormal development and behavior; the role of hormones in development, including the regulation of growth, maturation, sex differences, and other developmental processes and behaviors; and the identification of specific genes and their respective functions in normal and abnormal development. Significant advances in knowledge will continue to be made in these areas in the future.

Whereas the genes versus environment debate has historically focused on the relative contribution of each to development, that view has recently been abandoned in favor of a focus on how genes and the environment interact. This is partly a result of the fact that most developmental psychologists today accept that both factors are necessary for development. Robert Plomin's work in the late 1970's and Sandra Scarr's work in the early 1980's address this focus by suggesting that a person's genetic makeup may influence the kinds of environments that he or she experiences. For example, a child who is athletically inclined may spend more time in athletics than in other kinds of activities, receive more attention and encouragement from coaches (compared with those not so gifted), associate frequently with sports-minded people, and (through increased athletic activity) further develop and refine his or her talents. This emphasis on how genes and the environment interact will continue to be a major focus of research in the field of developmental psychology.

IMPLICATIONS FOR PSYCHOLOGY

The examination of the determinants of physical development is important for a number of reasons. First, it sheds light on the causes (and consequences) of normal and abnormal growth patterns, motor development, and brain and nervous-system development. Second, it may provide insight into some of the causes of normal and abnormal psychological development and behavior because of the relationship between physical development and behavior. Third, it helps explain individual variations in development. Finally, this area of study asserts that human development is not based solely on either the environment or genetics, but rather is caused by the mutual influence of genes and the environment.

Sources for Further Study

Bateson, Patrick, and Paul Martin. *Design for a Life: How Behavior and Personality Develop.* New York: Simon & Schuster, 2000. Written for a general audience, describes current thinking on the nature-nurture debate. Particular attention is paid to the question of genetic influences on behavior.

Falkner, Frank, and J. M. Tanner. *Human Growth.* 2d ed. New York: Plenum, 1986. A three-volume edited set on human growth. The third volume in particular has much work on the genetic, nutritional, and other environmental influences on human growth before and after birth.

Harper, Lawrence V. *The Nurture of Human Behavior.* Norwood, N.J.: Ablex, 1989. An excellent review of the biological mechanisms underlying growth and behavioral development. Includes discussions on evolutionary origins of behavioral development, developmental genetics and embryology, and ways in which experience may influence development. Excellent reference section.

Scarr, Sandra, Richard A. Weinberg, and Ann Levine. *Understanding Development.* San Diego, Calif.: Harcourt Brace Jovanovich, 1986. Reviews human development from conception through adolescence. Excellent chapters on genetic and environmental factors in development. Very readable for the high school or college student.

Tomlinson-Keasey, Carol. *Child Development: Psychological, Sociocultural, and Biological Factors.* Homewood, Ill.: Dorsey Press, 1985. A standard book on child development that covers the prenatal through adolescent periods. Has excellent chapters on human behavioral genetics and the brain. Very readable for the high school or college student.

Wagner, Daniel A., and Harold W. Stevenson, eds. *Cultural Perspectives on Child Development.* San Francisco: W. H. Freeman, 1982. This small edited volume provides a variety of chapters on cross-cultural child development written by leading researchers in the field for a nonprofessional audience.

Laura Kamptner

SEE ALSO: Hormones and behavior; Motor development; Prenatal physical development; Reflexes in newborns.

Piaget, Jean

BORN: August 9, 1896, in Neuchâtel, Switzerland
DIED: September 17, 1980, in Geneva, Switzerland
IDENTITY: Swiss child psychologist
TYPE OF PSYCHOLOGY: Cognition; developmental psychology; learning
FIELDS OF STUDY: Adolescence; behavioral and cognitive models; cognitive development; infancy and childhood; problem solving; thought

Piaget's ideas have had a profound influence on American educators, which is ironic in light of the fact that, though he wrote extensively on growth and development, he rarely addressed himself to the topic of schooling.

Jean Piaget was the son of a professor of medieval literature and acquired his father's taste for hard intellectual work at an early age. He was awarded a Ph.D. in natural history from the University of Neuchâtel in 1918. Wishing to further his studies, Piaget traveled to Paris and spent two years at the

Jean Piaget. (Hulton Archive)

Sorbonne, where he began working with early forms of intelligence tests. Piaget discovered that children could not perform many of the logical tasks that adults find to be commonplace. Why, he asked himself, is this the case? This question led him into his life's work: studying how children develop logical patterns of thought.

Piaget held a number of important posts during his long, scholarly career. In 1921, at the age of twenty-five, he was appointed as director of studies at the Jean-Jacques Rousseau Institute in Geneva, where he served for the next fifty-four years. He also held faculty positions at the Universities of Geneva and Lausanne. Piaget published many books and articles on child growth and development. Among his better-known works are *Le Langage et le pensée chez l'enfant* (1923; *The Language and Thought of the Child*, 1926), *La Construction du réel chez l'enfant* (1937; *The Construction of Reality in the Child*, 1954), and *L'Équilibration des structures cognitives: Problème central du développement* (1975; *The Development of Thought: Equilibration of Cognitive Structures*, 1977).

In 1955, Piaget founded the International Center for Genetic Epistemology at the University of Geneva. The theory of knowledge, he believed, should be grounded in the biological sciences. Learning is the process by which the human organism establishes a working balance with the environment. Piaget called this balance equilibration, which is achieved in two ways: assimilation, where new information is absorbed into an already existing intellectual structure; and accommodation, where the intellectual structure is modified by new experiences.

Piaget is best known for his division of children's cognitive growth into four stages: sensorimotor (birth to age two), preoperational (ages two to seven), concrete operational (ages seven to eleven), and formal operational (age eleven through adulthood). All children pass through these four stages. There are no skips, jumps, or gaps along the way. Children before the age of two years learn by manipulating objects. Preoperational children have acquired language, but they cannot grasp the idea of reversibility in number sets. Concrete operational children can solve reversibility problems in concrete situations. Formal operational children are able to manipulate concepts similar to those found in abstract mathematics.

SOURCES FOR FURTHER STUDY

Ginsburg, Herbert P., and Sylvia Opper. *Piaget's Theory of Intellectual Development.* Englewood Cliffs, N.J.: Prentice Hall, 1987. A concise guide to Piaget's theories and his influence on modern educational practices.

Vidal, Fernando. *Piaget Before Piaget.* Cambridge, Mass.: Harvard University Press, 1994. A thorough though somewhat heavy-going biography.

Stanley D. Ivie

SEE ALSO: Cognitive development: Jean Piaget; Cognitive psychology; Concept formation; Thought: Inferential.

Pinel, Philippe

BORN: April 20, 1745, in Jonquieres, France
DIED: October 25, 1826, in Paris, France
IDENTITY: French physician and founder of scientific psychiatry
TYPE OF PSYCHOLOGY: Psychopathology; psychotherapy
FIELDS OF STUDY: Anxiety disorders; evaluating psychotherapy; experimental methodologies; models of abnormality; personality disorders; psychodynamic therapies; schizophrenias

Pinel, a pioneer in the humane treatment of "the insane," brought the study, care, and cure of the mentally ill into the field of medicine.

Philippe Pinel was born in a small village in southwestern France. His mother came from a family of physicians, and his father was a surgeon who practiced in St.-Paul-Cap-de-Joux, where Philippe grew up. After a time at the Collège de Lavaur, he received a humanistic education from the Fathers of the Christian Doctrine at their Collège de l'Esquille in Toulouse, receiving the degree of master of arts in mathematics. Having decided on a religious career, he enrolled in the faculty of theology at the University of Toulouse in 1767, but, opting for the family profession, he later switched into the faculty of medicine, and he received his M.D. in 1773.

In 1774, he traveled to Montpellier, where, for four years, he studied at France's most famous medical school. Supporting himself by giving private lessons, he frequented hospitals, where he built trusting relationships with patients and began making detailed records of the histories and courses of their illnesses.

Pinel went to Paris in 1778. There, for fifteen years, he made a living by teaching mathematics, editing a medical newspaper, and translating medical works into French. In 1793, he became "physician of the infirmaries" at Bicetre, a Parisian asylum with over four thousand male inmates. The severely insane, believed to be demoniacally possessed, had been kept chained in dark dungeons for years, but Pinel, insisting that they be treated as patients, not outcasts, unchained these unfortunates and housed them in sunny rooms. Then, through warm baths and occupational therapy, he was able to mitigate their mental illness and return many, now cured, to the world.

His successes at Bicetre led to his becoming, in 1795, chief physician of the Hospice de la Salpétrière, where he assumed responsibility for eight thousand women suffering from various chronic illnesses. Salpétrière was the scene of his research for the rest of his life. Though Pinel's fame derives from his compassionate treatment of the mentally ill, his greatest contributions to medical science were his falsification of such traditional ideas as personal wickedness causing insanity and his championing of a new therapeutic approach that he called "moral treatment." This involved improving his patients' food, hygiene, and physical surroundings while helping them to "balance their passions" through exercise, small-group living, and purposeful work.

Pinel published the results of his experiments in several books, the most important of which was his *Traité médico-philosophique sur l'aliénation mentale ou la manie* (1801; *A Treatise on Insanity*, 1806). His writings contributed to making the mentally ill part of medicine, and his ideas constituted the foundations of modern psychiatry. He died at Salpétrière in 1826, and he was buried in Père Lachaise cemetery, the final resting place for many of France's luminaries.

Sources for Further Study

Ackerknecht, Erwin H. *Medicine at the Paris Hospital, 1794-1848*. Baltimore: The Johns Hopkins University Press, 1967. Ackerknecht, a well-known historian of medicine, treats Pinel as a teacher and systematizer of internal medicine in the first part of this book.

Grange, Kathleen M. "Pinel and Eighteenth-Century Psychiatry." *Bulletin of the History of Medicine* 35, no. 5 (September/October, 1961): 442-453. Grange's goal is to show how the new field of psychiatry emerged from Pinel's moral and medical discussions of the emotions.

Riese, Walther. *The Legacy of Philippe Pinel: An Inquiry into His Thought on Mental Alienation*. New York: Springer, 1969. Riese, a physician and medical historian, explores the roots of Pinel's ideas and concludes from an analysis of his writings that Pinel, as a scientist, philosopher, psychotherapist, and psychologist, is a pivotally important figure in the founding of psychiatry.

Woods, Evelyn A., and Eric T. Carlson. "The Psychiatry of Philippe Pinel." *Bulletin of the History of Medicine* 35, no. 1 (January/February, 1961): 14-25. The authors provide a description of Pinel's career and a lucid exposition of his contributions.

Robert J. Paradowski

See also: Madness: Historical approaches; Psychology: Historical approaches.

Pituitary gland

Type of psychology: Biological bases of behavior
Fields of study: Endocrine system; organic disorders

Located at the base of the brain, the pituitary gland is central to the endocrine system; the production and regulation of hormones that play a role in certain behaviors are the primary functions of the pituitary.

Key concepts

- adrenal gland
- anterior pituitary
- endocrine system
- hormone
- hypothalamus
- posterior pituitary

Introduction

Hormones are loosely defined as chemical substances that are produced in certain parts of the body and then carried elsewhere by the bloodstream to perform their function. They include three general chemical types: short chains of amino acids, or proteins; derivatives of amino acids; and steroids. Many behaviors are regulated by hormones. Arguably, the most obvious behaviors are those associated with reproduction. For example, steroids secreted by the sex organs, or gonads, regulate both paternal and maternal behavior: aggression (testosterone), attraction for the opposite sex (pheromones), uterine contraction (oxytocin), and so on.

The system that regulates hormone production is the neuroendocrine system, a series of ductless glands that secrete these chemicals directly into the blood. The pituitary gland is the central organ of the endocrine system. Slightly larger than a centimeter in diameter, it is located at the base of the brain in a bony cavity called the sella turcica. The gland is involved in the secretion of some ten different hormones.

The pituitary is formed from two distinct structures, the adenohypophysis (in the anterior portion of the gland) and the neurohypophysis, which forms the posterior lobe of the pituitary. Not only do the two portions function independently, but they also form independently during embryonic development. The adenohypophysis originates from the outer layer of embryonic tissue, while the neurohypophysis is an outgrowth of the developing forebrain. Not surprisingly, the neurohypophysis receives neurosecretions directly from the hypothalamus region of the brain. Therefore, one might not consider the posterior pituitary to be a gland at all, but rather a neural outgrowth of the brain.

NEUROSECRETIONS AND THE HYPOTHALAMUS

Sets of secretions from the anterior pituitary play various roles in the body. The first set, which includes hormones such as adrenocorticotropic hormone (ACTH), thyroid-stimulating hormone (TSH), follicle-stimulating hormone (FSH), and luteinizing hormone (LH), regulate secretions from the adrenal gland, the thyroid, and the gonads. Two additional hormones from the anterior pituitary, prolactin and growth hormone (GH), have a variety of effects on breast tissue and bone growth, respectively.

Regulation of hormone secretion by the anterior pituitary is primarily the function of the hypothalamus. The hypothalamus is connected through a portal circuit, a connection involving two capillaries

from the brain that merge to form the vein that feeds directly into the adenohypophysis. Neural secretions from the hypothalamus either stimulate or inhibit the appropriate cells in the adenohypophysis, allowing for a finely tuned method of regulation. For example, if a person's fingers touch a hot stove, a sensory reflex allows the person to remove the hand quickly. At the same time, the anterior pituitary is "instructed" to secrete ACTH. The ACTH travels through the blood to the adrenals, which then secrete the appropriate steroids, which have an anti-inflammatory action. The rise in steroid level in the general circulation is monitored by the hypothalamus. At the appropriate level, a negative feedback results, in which ACTH secretion is stopped. The regulation of each hormone produced by the anterior pituitary is performed in an analogous manner.

As described above, the posterior pituitary is directly connected to the hypothalamus; it is not actually a gland. The neurons that make up the neurohypophysis originate in the hypothalamus. Extensions called axons then extend into, and become, the posterior pituitary. These neural structures are closely associated with a capillary network. The result is that neurosecretions produced in the hypothalamus pass through the posterior pituitary directly into the bloodstream.

There are two general types of neurosecretions in humans associated with the neurohypophysis: oxytocin and vasopressin. Oxytocin plays several roles in muscle contraction. For example, during childbirth, it causes the contraction of uterine muscle. Later, it becomes associated with the release of milk through the nipple. Vasopressin is the general name for a series of hormones that regulate blood pressure; it is often referred to as antidiuretic hormone (ADH). Regulation of these hormone levels is similar to that described for the adenohypophysis.

Despite the independent formation and function of the two lobes of the pituitary, regulation of each is carried out coordinately. For example, sucking at the nipple by an infant induces the release of oxytocin through the posterior pituitary. The same stimulus causes an inhibition of the follicle-stimulating hormone by the anterior pituitary. The result is that a nursing mother should be less fertile.

The neuroendocrine system is thus intimately involved with a variety of processes within the body.

These include cell metabolism, development of organ systems such as the gonads, and certain kinds of behaviors. The role played by the pituitary is central to each of these processes, both in their induction and in their regulation. While the master gland in all these endeavors is ultimately the brain, it is through the pituitary gland that the appropriate messengers are sent throughout the body, controlling the function of most body tissues.

ROLE IN PHYSIOLOGY OF BEHAVIOR

Hormones of the endocrine system—in particular, those hormones associated with the pituitary gland—play a vital role in the physiology of behavior. This role may take several forms. For example, among the most obvious effects are those that result from systems that regulate body metabolism. TSH is produced within the anterior pituitary and is involved in regulating the secretion of thyroxin and triiodothyronine by the thyroid. Since thyroxin is particularly important in controlling the metabolic rate, overproduction of TSH may cause symptoms of nervousness, hyperactivity, and loss of sleep. On the other hand, lack of TSH production may result in hypothyroidism, an underactive thyroid. Individuals suffering from this condition are often mentally sluggish. It should be kept in mind, however, that an overactive or underactive thyroid may result from reasons other than inappropriate pituitary activity.

The activity of ACTH, the source of which is the anterior pituitary, is particularly illustrative of the multitude of effects associated with an individual hormone. The major activity of ACTH involves its effects on the adrenal glands. In response to ACTH production, the adrenal cortex (the outer region of the adrenal glands) begins production of a variety of steroid hormones. Several of these steroids, including cortisol, increase the rate of protein and fat metabolism. As in the example presented earlier, cortisol may also act as an anti-inflammatory agent. The pharmaceutical hydrocortisone, used as an anti-inflammatory application to the skin, is based upon the chemical formulation of cortisol.

The production of aldosterone by the adrenal cortex, again regulated by ACTH from the pituitary, promotes resorption of sodium from urine as it passes through the kidney. A variety of sex steroids produced within the adrenal cortex are also regulated through ACTH production. These include

adrenal androgen, principally found in males but also produced in the female. Among older women, for example, higher than normal levels of adrenal androgen may result in the growth of facial hair. Thus, many sexual behaviors and characteristics indirectly come under the control of the anterior pituitary gland.

ACTH secretion exhibits a diurnal rhythm, with increasing production following the onset of sleep. The level continues to increase until the person awakens. ACTH secretion is also influenced by fever, surgery, or stress. In fact, many of the physiological responses to stress—elevation of glucose levels in the blood, elevation of blood pressure, and suppression of the immune response—result from increases in the output of ACTH.

Regulation of ACTH production is another example of the finely tuned "negative feedback" that the body uses to suppress pituitary activity. For example, when corticoid hormone levels in the blood rise, perhaps as the result of a stressful situation, they are monitored within the hypothalamus. At the appropriate time, such as during relaxation, ACTH production is turned off and adrenal activity slows down.

SEXUAL BEHAVIORS

Directly or indirectly, sexual behaviors are also the result of pituitary activity. Production of FSH and LH influences the sex organs to produce sperm or eggs and a variety of sex hormones. Well-known mating and sexual behaviors among humans are therefore influenced by pituitary hormones. In the male, this results from testosterone activity—sexual aggressiveness being a prime example. Whether aggressiveness in general among human males is primarily attributable to hormonal action or to environmental conditioning is not completely clear. Among other primates, however, fighting behavior is definitely a result of testosterone production. Sex hormones also regulate maternal activity among a variety of mammals. The "nesting instinct" and huddling behaviors exhibited by primates, including some humans, are controlled in this manner.

Communication behaviors that result from gonadal hormone production are well known. Visual signals include changes in skin color among female chimpanzees at the time of ovulation and the production of fat pads on the shoulders of male squirrel monkeys during mating season. Production of pheromones, chemicals that exhibit distinct odors, is also used to exhibit sexual receptivity. A male dog may be aware of any receptive female within a radius of hundreds of meters. The use of perfumes or musk is based, in part, on the belief that analogous odors may also influence human activity.

OXYTOCIN

The release of oxytocin by the posterior pituitary is also influenced by a variety of sexual and maternal behaviors. As described above, oxytocin is actually a neuropeptide, a short chain of amino acids that are released into the posterior pituitary from neural axons that originate in the hypothalamus. Oxytocin causes contraction of smooth muscle. During sexual intercourse, release of oxytocin may result in the uterine contraction known as "tenting." This process may draw sperm into the uterus, increasing the likelihood of fertilization. In addition, the smooth muscle contraction in the male that occurs during ejaculation may be caused, in part, by the effects of oxytocin. The contraction of the uterus during labor and delivery is also caused by the effects of oxytocin. Finally, both oxytocin and prolactin, produced within the anterior pituitary, are activated by stimulation associated with suckling and result in milk production and letdown.

The pituitary gland is a principal component of the endocrine system. Hormones that originate within the anterior pituitary act upon a variety of tissues and organs. The posterior pituitary, in turn, serves primarily as a "way station" for neuropeptides produced in the hypothalamus. In this manner, numerous physiological activities and behaviors are regulated by this set of glands.

HISTORY OF STUDY

Knowledge of pituitary function, like that of most tissues and organs in the body, evolved over the period of a millennium. Aristotle (in the fourth century B.C.E.) believed that the pituitary, as an extension of the brain, played a role in regulation of body temperature. He believed that the body humor known as phlegm (Latin *pituita*) passed through the gland into the nasal cavity. (Hence a person's attitude, or humor, was related to the relative qualities of the four body fluids, or humours.) It was on this basis that Andreas Vesalius, the sixteenth century physician considered to be the founder of

modern anatomy, named the gland "pituitary" in his classic work *De humani corporis fabrica* (1543; on the structure of the human body). This view continued to be held into the mid-nineteenth century.

The understanding of body functions is often associated with the correlation of behavioral or physiological changes with organ pathology. Such was the case with the pituitary gland. By 1850, it was recognized that pituitary tumors, particularly in children or young adults, often resulted in conditions such as gigantism, acromegaly, or sexual dysfunction. Furthermore, surgical removal of the gland, first in experimental animals and then in humans, resulted in numerous pathological changes. By the early twentieth century, it was clear that the pituitary played a key role in monitoring a variety of systems in the body.

MODERN RESEARCH AND UNDERSTANDING

As knowledge of pituitary hormones increases, the interaction of these molecules with target sites on other organs or glands can be better understood at the molecular level. At the very least, this can allow treatment or prevention of behavioral or physiological changes associated with abnormalities of the endocrine system. This can include, for example, an improvement in the effectiveness or safety of birth control techniques; a pill that would inhibit sperm production could be used by men.

Oxytocin and ADH, the hormones released through the neurohypophysis, are functionally neurotransmitters. This example illustrates the close structural and functional relationship between different systems—in this case, the endocrine and nervous systems. Clearly, hormonal control is complex and finely controlled. Precise mechanisms of control, however, remain to be worked out. For example, negative feedback was discussed earlier as a means by which adrenal hormones regulate their own secretion. The exact region in the brain that responds to elevated levels of adrenal hormones remains a source of controversy. A similar situation exists for other hormones. Presumably, regulation involves a specific series of neurons with specialized neurotransmitters. As the control mechanisms become better understood, modulation of behavior through proper drug treatment will become more of a reality. For example, use of the drug chlorpromazine results in an increase in prolactin production by the anterior pituitary. Further understanding of the integration of these systems will allow for additional applications in the future.

Sources for Further Study

Cotman, Carl W., and James L. McGaugh. *Behavioral Neuroscience.* New York: Academic Press, 1980. Originally developed as part of a course in neuroscience. The authors provide a broad overview of the topic without becoming bogged down in detail. Several chapters deal specifically with the endocrine system and associated clinical disorders.

Guillemin, Roger, and Roger Burgus. "The Hormones of the Hypothalamus." *Scientific American* 227 (November, 1972): 24-33. An excellent article that deals primarily with the regulation of the pituitary gland. The methods by which hormones of the neurohypophysis have been isolated and studied are highlighted. Particularly useful are the clear diagrams. Description of experimental approaches is minimized.

Holmes, Clarissa S., ed. *Psychoneuroendocrinology: Brain, Behavior, and Hormonal Interactions.* New York: Springer-Verlag, 1990. Presents a thorough discussion of the interdependence of hormonal and psychological factors. Includes discussion of endocrine disease on growth disorders, academic development, and social interactions in children. A section also discusses effects of replacement hormone treatment.

Holmes, R. L., and J. N. Ball. *The Pituitary Gland: A Comparative Account.* Cambridge, England: Cambridge University Press, 1974. A detailed text on the structure and function of the pituitary gland in a variety of vertebrates. Though not written for the casual reader, the text is profusely illustrated and contains an extensive bibliography.

Konner, Melvin. *The Tangled Wing: Biological Constraints on the Human Spirit.* Rev. ed. New York: W. H. Freeman, 2001. An informal discussion dealing with the biological basis for a variety of human behaviors and emotions, such as love, lust, and fear. Included are sections that discuss modifications of behavior and effects of differences in sex.

Wallace, Robert A., Gerald P. Sanders, and Robert J. Ferl. *Biology: The Science of Life.* 4th ed. Reading, Mass.: Addison-Wesley, 1996. A textbook of biology. Several chapters deal with the function of the pituitary gland and its effects on behavior.

Extensive color illustrations and diagrams, and a text that is not overly detailed, allow easy comprehension of the subject.

Richard Adler

See also: Adrenal gland; Endocrine system; Gonads; Hormones and behavior; Stress: Physiological responses; Thyroid gland.

Play therapy

Type of psychology: Psychotherapy
Fields of study: Humanistic therapies; psychodynamic therapies

Play therapy is a method of treating children who have emotional problems, psychological difficulties, or mental disorders. It is conducted in a room specifically equipped for this purpose with toys and activity materials to aid the child in solving problems and to enhance mental health. It most commonly involves one child and one therapist, though it can be conducted with groups of children.

Key concepts
- communication
- empathy
- interpersonal matrix
- limit setting
- symbolism

Introduction

Children of all ages learn about their environment, express themselves, and deal with relationships with others through their play activity. Play is an integral part of childhood, an activity that must be allowed to a child to facilitate the child's development. In fact, play is seen as such an important aspect of a child's life that the United Nations made the right to play an inalienable right for children across the world. Some adults have labeled play a child's "work," and this may be an appropriate way of looking at children's play. Just as work fosters self-esteem for adults, so does play enhance the self-esteem of children. Just as adults learn to solve problems through their work, so do children learn to cope with and invent solutions to problems through their play. Just as adults spend a bulk of their time in work activity, so do children spend most of their waking hours engaged in play.

GROWTH THROUGH PLAY

Through play, children grow in a number of ways. First, they grow emotionally; children learn to express their feelings, understand their feelings, and control their emotions. A child may hit a Bobo doll in an angry manner, then become very friendly and peaceful. The activity of hitting the doll helped the child act out her or his feeling of anger and then turn to more positive emotions. Through play, children grow cognitively. They learn to count in efforts to master sharing with other children; they learn about different functions of the same object; they learn that things can break and be repaired; they learn to think in symbols; and they learn language. Children also learn morality. They act out rules and regulations in play with other children; they learn to share; they learn that some things hurt other people and should therefore not be done; and they realize that rules often serve a purpose of protection or safety. All these growth processes are extremely important by-products of play, but perhaps the most important aspect of play is that of communication—defined here as the sharing of information with other people, either through language or through other ways of interacting. Children tell about themselves and their lives through play. Even when they do not yet have the language, they possess the ability to play.

ROLE OF THERAPIST AND SETTING

This aspect of communication through play is perhaps the most important ingredient of play therapy. In play therapy, a therapist uses a child's play to understand the child and to help the child solve problems, feel better about herself or himself, and express herself or himself better. Children often have difficulty telling adults what they feel and experience, what they need and want, and what they do not want and do not like. Often they lack the language skills to do so, and sometimes they are too frightened to reveal themselves for fear of punishment.

In play therapy, however, the therapist is an adult who is empathic, sensitive, and—above all—accepting and nonthreatening. The child is made to feel comfortable in the room with this adult and quickly recognizes that this person, despite being quite old

(at least from the child's perspective), understands the child and accepts her or his wishes and needs. Children learn to play in the presence of this therapist, or even with the therapist, and through this play communicate with the therapist. They reveal through their activity what they have experienced in life, how they feel, what they would like to do, and how they feel about themselves.

The toys and activities that therapists use vary significantly, though they take great care to equip the room in which they work with the child in such a way as to allow maximum freedom and creativity on the child's part. Therapists generally have puppets, clay, paints, dolls, dollhouses, and building blocks in the room. All these materials share several important traits: They all foster creativity; they have many different uses; they are safe to play with; and they can be used easily by the child for communication. On the other hand, therapists rarely have things such as board games, Slinkies, or theme toys (for example, television "action" heroes), because these toys have a definite use with certain rules and restrictions, are often used merely to re-create stories observed on television, or are not very handy for getting the child to express herself or himself freely. Most of the time, the toys are kept in an office that is specifically designed for children, not a regular doctor's office. As such, the room generally has a child-size table and chairs but no adult-size desk. It usually has no other furniture but may have some large cushions that child and therapist can sit on if they want to talk for a while. Often the room has a small, low sink for water play, and sometimes even a sandbox. Floor and wall coverings are such that they can be easily cleaned so that spills are not a problem and can be easily wiped up and taken care of. The room is basically a large play area; children generally like the play therapy room because it is unlike any other room they have ever encountered and because it is equipped specifically with children in mind.

THERAPEUTIC PROCESS

There are many reasons a child may be seen in play therapy. For example, a referral may come from a teacher who is concerned about a drop in the child's academic performance; from day-care personnel who are concerned about the child's inability to relate to other children; from the child's pediatrician, who believes the child is depressed but cannot find a physical cause; or from parents who think the child is aggressive. Whatever the reason, therapy begins with an intake interview. The intake is a session during which the therapist meets not only with the child but also with the parents and siblings in an attempt to find out as much about the child as possible to gain an understanding of what is wrong. Once the therapist knows what is happening with the child, recommendations for treatment are made. Sometimes the recommendation is for the entire family to be seen in family therapy. Sometimes the recommendation is for the parents to be seen. Sometimes the recommendation is for play therapy for the child.

Once a child enters play therapy, she or he will meet with the therapist once weekly for fifty minutes (sometimes, for very young children, sessions can be as short as thirty minutes) for several weeks or months. During the sessions, the child decides what is played with and how, and the therapist is there to understand the child, help the child solve problems, and facilitate growth and self-esteem for the child. Often, while the child is seen, her or his parents are seen in some type of therapy as well. Children's problems often arise because of problems in the family, which is why it is rare that only the child is in treatment. Parents are often seen in order to work on their relationship either with each other or with the whole family, or to learn parenting skills.

The first thing that happens in play therapy is that the therapist and the child get to know each other and develop a positive relationship. Once the child begins to trust the therapist, she or he starts to reveal concerns and problems through play. The therapist observes and/or interacts with the child to help work out problems, deal with strong feelings, accept needs, and learn to deal with often difficult family or environmental circumstances. All this work is done through the child's play in much the same way as children use play while growing up. In addition to using play activity, however, the therapist uses the trusting relationship with the child.

EXAMPLE OF THERAPY

The process of play therapy is best demonstrated by an example of an actual play therapy interaction between a child and therapist. A nine-year-old boy was referred by his teacher because he was very depressed and frightened, had difficulty making friends, and was not able to trust people. In the intake interview, the therapist found out that the boy had been severely physically abused by his father and that he was abandoned by his birth mother at age two. His stepmother had brought three children of her own into the blended family and did not have much time for this child. In fact, it appeared as though he was left to his own devices most of the time. The family had a number of other problems but refused family therapy. Thus, the child was seen in play therapy. He had considerable difficulty starting to trust the therapist and showed this reluctance in his play. He would often start to play, then check with the therapist for approval, and then stop before he became too involved in any one activity. After six weeks, he realized that the therapist was there to help him, and he began to communicate about his family through play.

The following exchange is a good example of what happens in play therapy. One day, the boy picked up a large wooden truck and two small ones. He proceeded to smash the large truck into the small red one over and over. He took the other small truck and put it between the large one and the small red one, as though to protect the red truck from being hit by the large one. In the process, the blue small truck was hurt badly and had to retreat. The boy repeated this activity several times. The therapist picked up a toy truck of her own and drove between the large truck and both of the small trucks, indicating that she had a truck that was tough enough to stop the large truck from hurting the small ones. The child was visibly relieved and turned to another activity.

What had happened? Before the session, the therapist had received a call from the child's social worker, who told her that the night before, the boy's father was caught sexually abusing his four-year-old stepdaughter, who shared this boy's room. The boy had awakened and unsuccessfully tried to stop his father. He ran to a neighbor's house, and this woman called the police. The father was arrested but threatened to get revenge on both children before he was taken away. The boy had playacted this entire scene with the toy trucks. The father was the large truck; the red truck, his sister; the blue one, himself. The relief sensed by the boy after the therapist intervened is understandable, as her truck communicated to the boy that he would be protected from his father.

EVOLUTION OF PLAY THERAPY

Children use their play in play therapy not only to communicate but also to solve problems and deal with overwhelming feelings. How this happens has been explained and described by many different therapists and theorists since play came to be viewed as an acceptable means of conducting therapy in the early 1930's, based upon the work of Melanie Klein and Anna Freud. These women developed play therapy methods that were based upon earlier psychoanalytic theories proposed by Sigmund Freud. In this approach, free play was considered most important, and the therapist did not generally become engaged at all in the play. The therapist merely reflected back to the child what was seen and occasionally interpreted to the child what the play may have meant.

In the 1940's, Virginia Axline developed her approach to play therapy, which was similar to Klein and Freud's. Axline also believed in free play and did not play with the child. She interpreted and emphasized an environment that put no limits or rules upon the child. She introduced the idea that children in play therapy need to experience unconditional acceptance, empathic concern, and a nondirective atmosphere. In other words, Axline's approach to play therapy was to sit and observe and not be involved with the child.

TYPES OF PLAY THERAPISTS

Since then, the lack of limit setting (imposing rules or regulations upon another person and then enforcing them in a predictable way), as well as the lack of active involvement with children in play therapy, has been criticized by play therapists. Nowadays, play therapists are more likely to get involved in play and to respond to children through play activity (as in the example above), as opposed to using language to communicate with them. There are two major groups of therapists who use play therapy. Traditional psychoanalytic or psychodynamic therapists who are followers of Klein or Axline make up one group; however, even within this group, there is much diversity with regard to how involved the therapist becomes with the child's play. The second group is composed of therapists who focus on the human interaction that takes place—that is, humanistic therapists.

Regardless of which group a play therapist belongs to, however, the primary ingredients that were proposed many years ago remain intact. Free play is still deemed important, and empathy is stressed in the relationship with the child. Many therapists believe that the interpersonal matrix—the environment and the relationship between two or more people who spend time together, along with all the occurrences within it—that exists between the child and the therapist is critical to changes noted in the child. Further, a primary focus remains on the symbolism (the use of indirect means to express inner needs or feelings; a way of sharing oneself without doing so directly or in words) and metaphor expressed by children through play. It is unlikely that the nature of play therapy will change much in the next decades. Play therapy has become one of the most accepted modes of treating children and is likely here to stay.

SOURCES FOR FURTHER STUDY

Axline, Virginia Mae. *Dibs: In Search of Self.* Reprint. New York: Ballantine Books, 1990. Written for the layerson, this book represents a case-study example of a successful play therapy sequence. Outlines the treatment of a severely disturbed boy, providing an excellent example of what happens in a child therapy room.

_____. *Play Therapy: The Inner Dynamics of Childhood.* Boston: Houghton Mifflin, 1947. Provides a thorough look at play therapy from a very nondirective perspective. Written in the 1940's, but has survived as an important reference for therapists who work with children in play therapy. The writing style is accessible to the layperson.

Dodds, J. B. A. *Child Psychotherapy Primer.* New York: Human Sciences, 1985. Provides very practical suggestions and guidelines for persons who are beginning to work with children in a therapy context. Relatively brief (150 pages). A good first resource or overview of the topic.

Landreth, G. L. *Play Therapy.* Muncie, Ind.: Accelerated Development, 1991. Provides a fairly detailed look at the practical aspects of child psychotherapy from a humanistic, person-centered perspective. Easy to read, even for the layperson, despite having been written primarily for the professional or the student of psychology.

Nemiroff, M. A., and J. Annunziata. *A Child's First Book About Play Therapy.* Washington, D.C.: American Psychological Association, 1990. Written for children who may be in need of treatment. A great introduction to the principles of play therapy, best used by parents to read to their children before seeing a child therapist. A picture storybook that holds children's attention well.

Schaefer, Charles E., and S. E. Reid. *Game Play.* New York: John Wiley & Sons, 1986. Puts children's games into the context of therapy. While traditional play therapists use toys, these authors introduce the use of games for therapeutic reasons. Written for the professional but also has implications for parents with regard to making choices of games for children; for example, discusses games that can be used to enhance a child's self-esteem. Somewhat long (more than three hundred pages) and perhaps a bit complicated for the layperson; therefore not a good choice for someone who has not read anything else on the topic.

Christiane Brems

SEE ALSO: Attachment and bonding in infancy and childhood; Child abuse; Family life: Children's issues; Freud, Anna; Music, dance, and theater therapy; Psychotherapy: Children; Psychotherapy: Goals and techniques; Separation and divorce: Children's issues; Strategic family therapy.

Positive psychology

DATE: The 1970's forward
TYPE OF PSYCHOLOGY: Origin and definition of psychology; social psychology
FIELDS OF STUDY: General constructs and issues; prosocial behavior

Positive psychology is the field of study dealing with the human experiences and strengths that make life most worth living. This field encompasses the understanding and facilitation of valued qualities, such as happiness and well-being, optimal experiences, good health, optimism, responsibility, and good citizenship, that enable both individuals and the broader culture to thrive.

KEY CONCEPTS
- flow
- happiness

- optimal experience
- optimism
- resilience
- subjective well-being

INTRODUCTION

Positive psychology emerged as a defined field in the 1990's as a reaction against American psychology's better-known emphasis on psychopathology, or what might be called "negative" psychology, since about World War II. This is based in part on the founding of two major institutions at the end of the war. In 1946, the Veterans Administration (VA) was established, soon to become the largest single training site for and employer of psychologists. Thousands of clinical psychologists earned their living by diagnosing and treating the mental disorders of armed services veterans at VA hospitals. In 1947, the National Institute of Mental Health (NIMH) was founded. Academic psychologists soon discovered that NIMH looked favorably upon funding grants that proposed research on pathology. The benefits of this "negative" focus became clear through the late 1990's as much was learned about helping those who suffered from mental illness. On the other hand, one consequence of this emphasis on fixing what was wrong with people was that psychologists neglected two additional missions of American psychology prior to World War II: the enhancement of fulfillment and productivity in normal people's lives and the nurture of exceptional human potential.

The widespread awareness of positive psychology among American psychologists would probably be dated to 1998. In that year, Martin E. P. Seligman, then- president of the American Psychological Association and a professor at the University of Pennsylvania, determined that the theme of the national convention would be on positive psychology. His vision was to revive and relaunch the scientific study of the best dimensions of human nature.

A basic definition of positive psychology is the study of average people and their virtues and strengths. Overall, the field focuses on topics dealing with the nature of effectively functioning people: what works well, what facilitates improvement, and what is right. Some of the well-researched areas in this field include subjective well-being, optimal experience and the related concept of flow, positive personal traits, good mental and physical health, resilience, and the nurture of excellence.

WELL-BEING, HAPPINESS, AND LIFE SATISFACTION

Subjective well-being may be understood as a combination of personal happiness and life satisfaction. David G. Myers, a social psychologist and professor at Hope College in Michigan, suggests two questions to frame this area. The first has to do with how happy people are in general, the second with the characteristics and circumstances of happy people. Myers reports global data on over a million people in forty-five nations indicating that most people self-report that they are at least moderately happy. The average person rates himself or herself at 6.75 on a ten-point scale where 5 is neutral and 10 the highest extreme of well-being.

The second question deals with a number of variables: age, gender, wealth, relationships, religious faith, personality traits, and more. Despite a common belief that certain times of life (such as adolescence or old age), are less happy than others there is no significant relationship between age and life satisfaction. Likewise, no difference can be found in self-reported happiness between men and women. Research on the relationship between wealth and happiness finds that with the exception that happiness is lower among the very poor, enduring personal happiness does not rise appreciably with increasing personal wealth or a stronger national economy.

By contrast, close, committed, and supportive relationships are strongly associated with both physical and psychological well-being. Looking at physical health, close attachments are associated with decreased rates of illness and premature death, and increased survival rates for those with severe disease. Similarly, social support is associated with positive mental health measures, including greater self-reported happiness and improved coping with a variety of life stressors, including rape, divorce, and job loss. Marriage, one form of a committed intimate relationship, has been repeatedly associated with greater happiness and life satisfaction as well as less depression and loneliness when compared to being divorced, separated, or never having been married. Likewise, more intrinsically motivated, religiously active persons report higher levels of life satisfaction and better coping with adversity, whether measured by level of spiritual commitment or religious attendance.

Finally, a number of studies identify four personality traits that characterize happy people. First, they like themselves and often even demonstrate a self-serving bias, indicating that they view themselves as more ethical, intelligent, healthy, and sociable than average. Second, they tend to be more extroverted, reflecting a genetic predisposition. Third, they experience a stronger sense of personal control over their lives. Fourth, they are optimistic. Contrary to popular notions, optimism has very little to do with "positive thinking" or repeating positive-self phrases. Optimism has much more to do with explanatory style or habitual ways of thinking about why good and bad things happen. Optimistic people are more likely to explain negative experiences in terms of external, temporary, specific causes ("I failed the test because I just did not have time to study this week—next week it will be different"). Positive experiences are likely to be understood in terms of internal, stable, global causes ("I received a high score on the exam because I'm smart").

FLOW AND OPTIMAL EXPERIENCE

Another important area in positive psychology has been the study of optimal human experiences. Mihaly Csikszentmihalyi, director of the Quality of Life Research Center at Claremont Graduate University in California, built his career on research examining the moments in time that people feel most happy. His first studies of optimal experience were based on interviews with several hundred experts in their fields—musicians, chess masters, mountain climbers, artists, surgeons—people who appeared to spend their time doing exactly what they wanted to do just for the joy of the experience. As he probed into their descriptions of what it felt like to engage in these highly valued activities, he began to conceptualize their optimal moments as times of "flow." Flow is a concept describing a state of deep enjoyment in which people are so engaged in a desired activity that nothing else seems to matter; it is a time of highly focused concentration resulting in the individual's complete absorption in his or her particular task. During these times of peak performance, people feel completely in control without exerting any particular effort. They forget themselves as they are immersed in the moment, and often report that time seems to pass much more quickly than usual. The related phenomena of flow and optimal experience have generated such interest that researchers around the world collected more than eight thousand interviews and a quarter million questionnaires examining this state during the thirty years of research leading up to the year 2000.

Several conditions make the experience of flow most likely. First is clarity of goals. People who achieve flow (as when playing a musical instrument or engaging in an athletic event) generally know, moment by moment, what they need to do next. Ongoing momentary goals keep the action going. Another necessary condition is immediate feedback. To maintain focused concentration, it is essential to know how well one is doing. Finally, there must be an optimal balance between the level of challenge of the activity and one's level of skills. Optimal flow is usually reported when individuals are functioning above their mean or typical levels of both challenge and skill.

PSYCHOLOGICAL CONTRIBUTORS TO PHYSICAL HEALTH

An intriguing area of study in positive psychology has to do with psychological contributors to physical health. Psychologists have long posited that optimism, a sense of personal control, and the ability to give meaning to life are associated with mental health. Such qualities represent important reserves that provide resilience and a buffer to individuals in the midst of difficult life events. A subsequent line of research suggests that these sorts of qualities may provide benefits to physical health as well. For example, a series of such studies conducted at UCLA deal with men infected with acquired immunodeficiency syndrome (AIDS) and human immunodeficiency virus (HIV). Among other findings, it appears that the patient's ability to find meaning in this life-threatening illness is associated with a less rapid progression of the disease. In addition, those who remain optimistic, even unrealistically so, appear to gain health protective benefits from their "positive illusions." Optimistic thinking is clearly linked to good physical health in other research as well, but two important prerequisites must also be in place. First, the optimistic thinking must lead people to active, sustained behaviors based on their optimism. Second, the active behaviors sustained by optimism must have some real association with health.

To summarize the general thrust of other research in this area, positive emotional states are believed to be associated with healthier functioning in the cardiovascular and immune systems, while negative emotional states are associated with unhealthy functioning in these systems (for example, the association between chronic anger and cardiovascular distress). Research targeting the interface of positive psychological states and physiological functioning represents an important and growing focus in the positive psychology movement.

SOURCES FOR FURTHER STUDY

Argyle, Michael. *The Psychology of Happiness.* 2d ed. Philadelphia: Routledge, 2001. A readable and comprehensive account of happiness (subjective well-being) research by an eminent social psychologist. This second edition deals with the standard areas of the relationship of happiness to attachments, positive emotions, and individual personality traits, but also adds some less common material on cultural differences, humor, and the role of religion in happiness.

Csikszentmihalyi, Mihaly. *Finding Flow.* New York: Basic Books, 1997. A practical book that applies the insights gained from this author's thirty years of research. Helpful in teaching the reader how to achieve the gratifying "flow" state of full immersion in the task of the moment.

Diener, Ed, Eunkook M. Suk, Richard E. Lucas, and Heidi L. Smith. "Subjective Well-Being: Three Decades of Progress." *Psychological Bulletin* 125, no. 2 (1999): 276-302. A thorough but relatively succinct thirty-year review of the progression of theory and knowledge in the field of subjective well-being. Support is generally found for early work that greater happiness is found among married, religious, extroverted, optimistic persons, but adds material regarding the causes of subjective well-being and future research directions.

Fredrickson, Barbara L. "The Role of Positive Emotions in Positive Psychology." *American Psychologist* 56, no. 3 (2001): 218-226. The author, a psychologist and professor at the University of Michigan, describes her "broaden-and-build" theory of positive emotions. Positive emotions such as joy, interest, contentment, pride, and love are posited to broaden the individual's repertoire of thoughts and actions. For example, joy is seen to "broaden" by creating urges to play, push limits, and be creative. Positive emotions are discussed as a strength critical to human flourishing.

Gilham, Jane E., ed. *The Science of Optimism and Hope.* Philadelphia: Templeton Foundation Press, 2000.

An edited volume of research essays in honor of Martin E. P. Seligman, known for his seminal contributions and research over a thirty-five-year period in such areas as overcoming adversity, resisting illness and depression, and developing optimism. The chapters represent edited versions of presentations by thirty scholars given at a 1998 symposium of the same name, sponsored by the Templeton Foundation. The contents provide an overview of theory and research in the scientific study of optimism and hope.

Seligman, Martin E. P., and Mihaly Csikszentmihalyi, eds. "Special Issue on Happiness, Excellence, and Optimal Human Functioning." *American Psychologist* 55, no. 1 (January, 2000). This is the official journal of the American Psychological Association, which devoted its millennial issue to sixteen articles sampling the variety of topics encompassed by positive psychology. This is a helpful overview of the field, written in accessible language by specialists in their content areas.

Seligman, Martin E. P., Karen Reivich, Lisa Jaycox, and Jane Gillham. *The Optimistic Child.* New York: HarperPerennial, 1995. A substantive parenting book written in a popular style by a leader in the field of positive psychology. It teaches parents how to apply well-documented research findings to build optimism in their children, thereby providing the additional benefits of reducing the risk of depression, improving school performance and self-esteem, and supporting long-term personal resiliency.

David W. Brokaw

SEE ALSO: Altruism, cooperation, and empathy; Attitude formation and change; Biofeedback and relaxation; Health psychology; Humanism; Meditation and relaxation; Psychology: Historical approaches; Self-esteem.

Postpartum depression

TYPE OF PSYCHOLOGY: Psychopathology
FIELDS OF STUDY: Depression

Postpartum depression is a type of mood disorder that some women acquire days or weeks after giving birth. This disorder is characterized by emotional instability, fatigue, anxiety, and guilt. The treatment for postpartum depression includes therapy and, in some cases, antidepressant medications.

KEY CONCEPTS
- estrogen
- maternity blues
- postpartum psychosis
- progesterone

INTRODUCTION

Postpartum depression (PPD) has become a focus of research since 1970. Approximately 12 to 15 percent of mothers suffer from PPD. The disorder is defined as the onset of depression occurring within days or weeks after childbirth. Symptoms include sadness, irritability, fatigue, hopelessness, feelings of guilt, anxiety, and poor sleep. PPD can arise days, weeks, or even months after childbirth. The most common onset is within a few days of delivery, perhaps due to the hormonal changes that the body experiences. Some women acquire PPD two to six weeks postpartum due to neuroendocrine changes and lifestyle changes that accompany caring for the infant. No one theory accounts for all cases of PPD, but almost all researchers in this area agree on the importance of biological and psychosocial factors in the development of PPD.

POSTPARTUM EMOTIONAL DISORDERS

In addition to PPD, there are other forms of psychiatric illness that can arise postpartum. Maternity "blues" affects 50-80 percent of mothers after delivery. The symptoms, which begin on the second or third day postpartum, include anxiety, mood swings from joyfulness to tearfulness, irritability, and sleep difficulties, all of which typically remit within four weeks. However, 25 percent of these women will go on to suffer a major depression. Postpartum psychosis is a serious psychiatric disorder that occurs two to four weeks postpartum and requires immediate professional attention. Symptoms of this disorder include hallucinations (such as hearing voices), delusions (bizarre false beliefs) and mania (hyperactivity, increased energy levels, rapid speech, and destructive impulsive behavior). A small number of women will experience obsessions having to do with harming their babies. In this instance, a differential diagnosis is important to assess the risk of harm to the child. If the woman experiences voices commanding her to harm herself and/or her child—a psychotic reaction—measures must be taken to protect the mother and baby. However, if the woman is not psychotic but is distressed over alarming, intrusive thoughts (not voices) that she might harm her child, the risk of harming the child is greatly reduced in comparison to command hallucinations.

WHO SUFFERS?

Researchers are interested in identifying women at risk for PPD to increase understanding of its causes, and to alert the physician that preventative treatment may be required for a specific patient.

The strongest predictor of PPD is depression during pregnancy, but any history of mood disorders elevates the risk of PPD. In addition, a lack of social support, mixed feelings about the pregnancy, marital problems, and giving birth to a temperamentally difficult child all increase the chances of PPD. Furthermore, pregnant adolescents have a 30 percent chance of developing PPD. The majority of PPD patients have a family history of mood or anxiety disorders. In general, events that occur during pregnancy or delivery that are experienced by the mother as stressful (such as cesarian deliveries or premature births) increase the risk factors.

CAUSES OF PPD

Theories about the causes of PPD stress the importance of biological and psychological influences, although no single agreed-upon theory has emerged. One biological theory of the cause of PPD is that hormonal changes in the woman's body after childbirth affect her mood. Three days after childbirth, the hormones estrogen and progesterone show a sharp drop from their previously high levels during pregnancy, and these changes influence brain chemistry.

Some psychosocial factors (such as ambivalence about the pregnancy or low social support) can serve to increase stress and undermine coping resources. The fact that a family history of mood disorders is predictive of PPD might suggest that certain women are biologically vulnerable, and the addition of negative psychosocial factors interacts with this vulnerability to produce PPD.

TREATMENT OPTIONS

There are several treatment options for PPD and its variations. Most women who suffer from postpartum "blues" are advised simply to let the disorder run its course, with support from their spouse, family, and doctors. However, since 25 percent of these women will develop PPD, physicians monitor those patients with maternal "blues" to see whether the condition becomes more serious. If the symptoms persist for an extended period of time, usually more than five weeks postpartum, women are generally encouraged to seek psychotherapy or marital counseling. Through therapy, the patients can explore their thoughts and feelings, receive help for interpersonal problems, and learn strategies for coping with stress. Oftentimes the therapy continues after the PPD is no longer present. With severe cases of postpartum depression, an antidepressant is often used to complement psychotherapy. If the person experiences a psychotic reaction, then an antipsychotic medication is almost always warranted.

DSM-IV-TR Criteria for Postpartum Depression

POSTPARTUM ONSET SPECIFIER FOR MOOD DISORDERS
Specify with Postpartum Onset

Can be applied to current or most recent of the following:
• Major Depressive, Manic, or Mixed Episode in Major Depressive Disorder
• Major Depressive, Manic, or Mixed Episode in Bipolar I Disorder
• Major Depressive, Manic, or Mixed Episode Bipolar II Disorder
• Brief Psychotic Disorder

Onset of episode within four weeks postpartum

SOURCES FOR FURTHER STUDY

Dunnewold, Ann, and Diane G. Sanford. *Postpartum Survival Guide*. Oakland, Calif.: New Harbinger, 1994. This is an excellent source for the description, assessment, and treatment of postpartum depression. Written for the general public, this book includes a risk profile questionnaire, case studies, and a chapter for partners of women who are experiencing PPD. Provides numerous references for additional study.

Steiner, Meir, Kimberly A. Yonkers, and E. Eriksson, eds. *Mood Disorders in Women.* Malden, Mass.: Blackwell Science, 2000. This textbook includes a wealth of information about women and depression, including neuroanatomical sex differences; major depression in women; seasonal affective disorder; postpartum depression and other postpartum psychiatric disorders; and sex differences in the treatment of depression. Chapter content is uneven in that some sections require no previous knowledge of the topic, while other sections require training in biology and the diagnosis of psychological disorders. Hundreds of references to scientific studies are provided.

Lindsey L. Henninger and Laurence Grimm

SEE ALSO: Clinical depression; Depression; Endocrine system; Hallucinations; Hormones and behavior.

Post-traumatic stress disorder

TYPE OF PSYCHOLOGY: Psychopathology
FIELDS OF STUDY: Anxiety disorders

After an extreme psychological trauma, people tend to respond with stress symptoms that include reexperiencing the trauma through nightmares or unwanted thoughts, avoiding reminders of the traumatic event, loss of interest in daily life, and increased arousal; these symptoms can range from mild and temporary to very severe, chronic, and psychologically disabling.

KEY CONCEPTS
- flashback
- hyperarousal
- reexperience
- traumatic event

INTRODUCTION

It is common knowledge that there are psychological aftereffects from experiencing an intense psychological trauma. This discussion of post-traumatic stress symptoms will be organized around post-traumatic stress disorder (PTSD), one of the diagnostic categories of anxiety disorders recognized by the American Psychiatric Association. It should be real-ized at the outset, however, that it is normal for people to experience at least some of these symptoms after suffering a psychological trauma. The first step in understanding PTSD is to know its symptoms.

The first criterion for PTSD is that one has suffered a trauma. The American Psychiatric Association's definition of PTSD states that the trauma must be something that "is outside the range of usual human experience and that would be markedly distressing to almost anyone." It is not so much the objective event as one's perception of it that determines the psychological response. For example, the death of one's parents is not "outside the range of usual human experience," but it can result in some of the symptoms described later. Some of the traumatic experiences deemed sufficient to cause PTSD include threat to one's own life or the life of a close relative or friend, sudden destruction of one's home or community, seeing another person violently injured or killed, or being the victim of a violent crime. Specific experiences that often cause PTSD include combat, natural or man-made disasters, automobile accidents, airplane crashes, rape, child abuse, and physical assault. In general, the more traumatic the event, the worse the post-traumatic symptoms. Symptoms of stress are often more severe when the trauma is sudden and unexpected. Also, when the trauma is the result of intentional human action (for example, combat, rape, or assault), stress symptoms are worse than when the trauma is a natural disaster (flood or earthquake) or an accident (automobile crash). It has been found that combat veterans who commit or witness atrocities are more likely than their comrades to suffer later from PTSD.

The central symptom of post-traumatic stress disorder is that the person reexperiences the trauma. This can occur in a number of ways. One can have unwanted, intrusive, and disturbing thoughts of the event or nightmares about the trauma. The most dramatic means of reexperiencing is through a flashback, in which the person acts, thinks, and feels as if he or she were reliving the event. Another way in which experiencing might be manifested is intense distress when confronted with situations that serve as reminders of the trauma. Vietnam veterans with combat-related PTSD will often become very upset at motion pictures about the war, hot and humid junglelike weather, or even the smell of Asian cooking. A person with PTSD often will attempt to avoid thoughts, feelings, activities, or events that serve as unwanted reminders of the trauma.

Another symptom that is common in people with PTSD is numbing of general responsiveness. This might include the loss of interest in hobbies or activities that were enjoyed before the trauma, losing the feeling of closeness to other people, an inability to experience strong emotions, or a lack of interest in the future. A final set of PTSD symptoms involves increased arousal. This can include problems with sleeping or concentrating, irritability, or angry outbursts. A person with PTSD may be oversensitive to the environment, always on the alert, and prone to startle at the slightest noise.

The paragraphs above summarize the symptoms that psychologists and psychiatrists use to diagnose PTSD; however, there are other features that are often found in trauma survivors but are not part of the diagnosis. Anxiety and depression are common in people who have experienced a trauma. Guilt is common in people who have survived a trauma in which others have died. People will sometimes use alcohol or tranquilizers to cope with sleep problems, disturbing nightmares, or distressing, intrusive recollections of a trauma, and they may then develop dependence on the drugs.

Post-traumatic stress disorder is relatively common in people who suffer serious trauma. In the late 1980's, the most extensive survey on PTSD ever done was undertaken on Vietnam combat veterans. It found that more than half of all veterans who served in the Vietnam theater of operations had experienced serious post-traumatic stress at some point in their lives after the war. This represents about 1.7 million veterans. Even more compelling was the fact that more than one-third of the veterans who saw heavy combat were still suffering from PTSD when the survey was done—about fifteen years after the fall of Saigon. Surveys of crime victims are also sobering. One study found that 75 percent of adult females had been the victim of a crime, and more than one in four of these victims developed PTSD after the crime. Crime victims were even more likely

Post-traumatic stress disorder is common in combat veterans; it was called "shell shock" during World War I and "battle fatigue" during World War II. (Digital Stock)

to develop PTSD if they were raped, were injured during the crime, or believed that their lives were in danger during the crime.

Symptoms of post-traumatic stress are common after a trauma, but they often decrease or disappear over time. A diagnosis of PTSD is not made unless the symptoms last for at least one month. Sometimes a person will have no symptoms until long after the event, when memories of the trauma are triggered by another negative life event. For example, a combat veteran might cope well with civilian life for many years until, after a divorce, he begins to have nightmares about his combat experiences.

FROM WAR TO EVERYDAY LIFE

Most of the theory and research regarding PTSD have been done on combat veterans, particularly veterans of the Vietnam War. One of the most exciting developments in this area, however, is that the theory and research are also being applied to victims of other sorts of trauma. This has a number of important implications. First, it helps extend the findings about PTSD beyond the combat-veteran population, which is mostly young and male. Second, information gathered from combat veterans can be used to assist in the assessment and treatment of anyone who has experienced a serious trauma. Because a large proportion of the general population experiences severe psychological trauma at some time, understanding PTSD is important to those providing mental health services.

An extended example will illustrate the application of theory and research findings on PTSD to a case of extreme psychological trauma. The case involves a woman who was attacked and raped at knifepoint one night while walking from her car to her apartment. Because of injuries suffered in the attack, she went to an emergency room for treatment. Knowledge about PTSD can help in understanding this woman's experience and could aid her in recovery.

First, research has shown that this woman's experience—involving rape, life threat, and physical injury—puts her at high risk for symptoms of post-traumatic stress. Risk is so great, in fact, that researchers have proposed that psychological counseling be recommended to all people who are the victims of this sort of episode. This suggestion is being implemented in many rape-recovery and crime-victim programs around the United States.

Knowing what symptoms are common following a traumatic event can help professionals counsel a

---

DSM-IV-TR Criteria for Post-traumatic Stress Disorder (DSM code 309.81)

Person has been exposed to a traumatic event in which both of the following were present:
- person experienced, witnessed, or was confronted with event or events involving actual or threatened death or serious injury, or threat to physical integrity of self or others
- person's response involved intense fear, helplessness, or horror; in children, may be expressed instead by disorganized or agitated behavior

Traumatic event persistently reexperienced in one or more of the following ways:
- recurrent and intrusive distressing recollections of event, including images, thoughts, or perceptions; in young children, repetitive play may express themes or aspects of trauma
- recurrent distressing dreams of event; in children, frightening dreams without recognizable content may occur
- acting or feeling as if traumatic event were recurring (includes a sense of reliving the experience, illusions, hallucinations, and dissociative flashback episodes, including those occurring on awakening or when intoxicated); in young children, trauma-specific reenactment may occur
- intense psychological distress at exposure to internal or external cues that symbolize or resemble an aspect of traumatic event
- physiological reactivity on exposure to internal or external cues that symbolize or resemble an aspect of traumatic event

Persistent avoidance of stimuli associated with trauma and numbing of general responsiveness (not present before trauma), as indicated by three or more of the following:
- efforts to avoid thoughts, feelings, or conversations associated with trauma
- efforts to avoid activities, places, or people arousing recollections of trauma
- inability to recall an important aspect of trauma
- markedly diminished interest or participation in significant activities
- feeling of detachment or estrangement from others
- restricted range of affect (such as inability to have loving feelings)
- sense of a foreshortened future (such as not expecting to have career, marriage, children, or normal life span)

Persistent symptoms of increased arousal (not present before trauma), as indicated by two or more of the following:
- difficulty falling or staying asleep
- irritability or outbursts of anger
- difficulty concentrating
- hypervigilance
- exaggerated startle response

Duration of more than one month

Disturbance causes clinically significant distress or impairment in social, occupational, or other important areas of functioning

Specify Acute (duration less than three months) or Chronic (duration three months or more)

Specify if with Delayed Onset (onset at least six months after stressor)

victim about what to expect. This woman can expect feelings of anxiety and depression, nightmares and unwanted thoughts about the event, irritability, and difficulties in sleeping and concentrating. Telling a victim that these are normal responses and that there is a likelihood that the problems will lessen with time is often reassuring. Since research has shown that many people with these symptoms cope by using drugs and alcohol, it may also help to warn the victim about this possibility and caution that this is harmful in the long run.

One symptom of PTSD, psychological distress in situations that resemble the traumatic event, suggests why combat veterans who experience their trauma in a far-off land often fare better than those whose trauma occurs closer to home. Women who are raped in their home or neighborhood may begin to feel unsafe in previously secure places. Some cope by moving to a different house, a new neighborhood, or even a new city—often leaving valued jobs and friends. If an attack occurred after dark, a person may no longer feel safe going out after dark and may begin living a restricted social life. Frequently, women who are raped generalize their fear to all men and especially to sexual relations, seriously damaging their interpersonal relationships. Given the problems that these post-traumatic symptoms can cause in so many areas of one's life, it may not be surprising that one study found that nearly one in every five rape victims attempted suicide.

The main symptoms of post-traumatic stress are phobia-like fear and avoidance of trauma-related situations, thoughts, and feelings, and the most effective treatment for PTSD is the same as for a phobia. Systematic desensitization and flooding, which involve confronting the thoughts and feelings surrounding the traumatic event, are the treatments that appear to be most effective. It may seem paradoxical that a disorder whose symptoms include unwanted thoughts and dreams of a traumatic event could be treated by purposefully thinking and talking about the event; however, Mardi Horowitz, one of the leading theorists in traumatic stress, believes that symptoms alternate between unwanted, intrusive thoughts of the event and efforts to avoid these thoughts. Because intrusive thoughts always provoke efforts at avoidance, the event is never fully integrated into memory; it therefore retains its power. Systematic desensitization and flooding, which in-

volve repeatedly thinking about the event without avoidance, allow time for the event to become integrated into the person's life experiences so that the memory loses much of its pain.

Another effective way to reduce the impact of a traumatic event is through social support. People who have a close network of friends and family appear to suffer less from symptoms of trauma. After a traumatic experience, people should be encouraged to maintain and even increase their supportive social contacts, rather than withdrawing from people, as often happens. Support groups of people who have had similar experiences, such as Vietnam veteran groups or child-abuse support groups, also provide needed social support. These groups have the added benefit of encouraging people to talk about their experiences, which provides another way to think about and integrate the traumatic event.

Psychotherapy can help trauma victims in many ways. One way is to help the patient explore and cope with the way the trauma changes one's view of the world. For example, the rape victim may come to believe that "the world is dangerous" or that "men can't be trusted." Therapy can help this person learn to take reasonable precautions without shutting herself off from the world and relationships. Finally, symptoms of overarousal are common with PTSD. A therapist can address these symptoms by teaching methods of deep relaxation and stress reduction. Sometimes mild tranquilizers are prescribed when trauma victims are acutely aroused or anxious.

HISTORY

The concept of post-traumatic stress is very old and is closely tied to the history of human warfare. The symptoms of PTSD have been known variously as "soldier's heart," "combat neurosis," and "battle fatigue." Stephen Crane's novel *The Red Badge of Courage*, first published in 1895, describes post-traumatic symptoms in a Civil War soldier. It was the postwar experiences of the Vietnam combat veteran, however, studied and described by scholars such as Charles Figley, that brought great attention to issues of post-traumatic stress. It was not until 1980 that the American Psychiatric Association recognized "post-traumatic stress disorder" in its manual of psychiatric disorders. Since then there has been an explosion of published research and books on PTSD, the creation of the Society for Traumatic Stress

Studies in 1985, and the initiation of the quarterly *Journal of Traumatic Stress* in 1988. Since these developments, attention has also been directed toward post-traumatic symptoms in victims of natural disasters, violent crime, sexual and child abuse; Holocaust survivors; and many other populations. Surveys have found that more than 80 percent of college students have suffered at least one trauma potentially sufficient to cause PTSD, and many people seeking psychological counseling have post-traumatic stress symptoms. Thus, it is fair to say that the attention garnered by Vietnam veteran readjustment problems and by the recognition of PTSD as a disorder by the American Psychiatric Association has prompted the examination of many important issues related to post-traumatic stress.

Because research in this area is relatively new, there are many important questions that remain unanswered. One mystery is that two people can have exactly the same traumatic experience, yet one will have extreme post-traumatic stress and one will have no problems. Some factors are known to be important; for example, young children and the elderly are more likely to suffer from psychological symptoms after a trauma. Much research is needed, however, to determine what individual differences will predict who fares well and who fares poorly after a trauma.

A second area of future development is in the assessment of PTSD. For the most part, it is diagnosed through a self-report of trauma and post-traumatic symptoms. This creates difficulty, however, when the person reporting the symptoms stands to gain compensation for the trauma suffered. Interesting physiological and cognitive methods for assessing PTSD are being explored. For example, researchers have found that Vietnam veterans with PTSD show high levels of physiological arousal when they hear combat-related sounds or imagine their combat experiences. Finally, the future will see more bridges built between post-traumatic stress and the more general area of stress and coping.

SOURCES FOR FURTHER STUDY

Crane, Stephen. *The Red Badge of Courage.* Reprint. New York: W. W. Norton, 1982. This classic novel vividly portrays post-traumatic symptoms in Civil War soldiers, particularly the main character, young Henry Fleming; first published in 1895, the book has been called the first modern war novel. Many fiction and nonfiction accounts have also been written about American servicemen's experiences during and after the Vietnam War, and many provide firsthand descriptions of post-traumatic stress.

Figley, Charles R., ed. *Trauma and Its Wake: The Study and Treatment of Post-traumatic Stress Disorder.* New York: Brunner/Mazel, 1985. This edited book is one of the most often cited references in the field of PTSD and contains some of the most influential papers written on the subject. It is divided into sections on theory, research, and treatment; a second volume with the same title was published in 1986. It is part of the Brunner/Mazel Psychosocial Stress Series, the first volume of which was published in 1978; through 1990, this valuable series had published twenty-one volumes on many aspects of stress and trauma.

Figley, Charles R., and Seymour Leventman, eds. *Strangers at Home: Vietnam Veterans Since the War.* 1980. Reprint. New York: Brunner/Mazel, 1990. This edited book, containing chapters by psychologists, sociologists, political activists, historians, political scientists, and economists, presents a look at the experience of the Vietnam veteran from many different perspectives. Many of the authors were Vietnam veterans themselves, so the book gives a very personal, sometimes stirring view of its subject.

Grinker, Roy Richard, and John P. Spiegal. *Men Under Stress.* Philadelphia: Blakiston, 1945. Long before the term "post-traumatic stress disorder" was coined, this classic book described the stress response to combat in Air Force flyers. It is written in jargon-free language by men who had unusual access to the flight crews.

Horowitz, Mardi Jon. *Stress Response Syndromes.* New York: Jason Aronson, 1976. Horowitz is one of the leading psychodynamic theorists in the area of post-traumatic stress. In this readable book, he describes his theory and his approach to treatment.

Kulka, Richard A. *Trauma and the Vietnam War Generation.* New York: Brunner/Mazel, 1990. Presents the results of the federally funded National Vietnam Veterans Readjustment Study. In contrast to *Strangers at Home*, which is a subjective view of the Vietnam veteran's plight, this book is very factual. It contains dozens of tables and figures filled with statistics about the mental and physical health of Vietnam veterans. The same authors published *The National Vietnam Veterans Readjustment Study: Tables of Findings and Technical Appendices* in 1990. This companion volume contains hundreds of tables of detailed results from this comprehensive study.

Scott R. Vrana

SEE ALSO: Anxiety disorders; Aversion, implosion, and systematic desensitization; Coping: Social support; Phobias; Stress: Behavioral and psychological responses; Support groups.

Prejudice

TYPE OF PSYCHOLOGY: Social psychology
FIELDS OF STUDY: Attitudes and behavior; prejudice and discrimination

Prejudice, the expression of negative attitudes toward certain groups and members of groups, genders, races, and religions, is a worldwide concern. Among the effects of prejudice are discrimination, low self-esteem, demoralization, racial self-hatred, helplessness and lack of control, social ostracism, social avoidance, lack of opportunities, and political underrepresentation.

KEY CONCEPTS
- attitudes
- bias
- discrimination
- in-group/out-group distinction
- multicultural education
- prejudice
- realistic conflict theory
- reverse discrimination

INTRODUCTION

Prejudice can be defined as a global view or attitude about a group of people; prejudicial views are characterized by their inflexibility, and they are usually considered to be negative and directed toward minority or out-groups. The effects of prejudice in American society, and throughout the world, are generally considered devastating, not only to the individuals who suffer injustice, humiliation, and

violence as a result of discrimination based on prejudice but also to the integrity of society as a whole. Groups such as the Ku Klux Klan and other white supremacist groups attempt to promote segregation, prejudice, and discrimination, at least partly as a way of promoting a dominant status for the white race. Most people realize that this is both unconstitutional and unfair. Since people have no choice over the race, ethnicity, religion, or gender into which they are born, it is unjust to judge persons solely on the basis of biological givens such as skin color, hair color, facial structure, gender, or other such characteristics. Almost everyone has experienced some prejudice or discrimination and can understand its negative effects on self-esteem and self-image.

A classic book on prejudice that came from the field of social psychology is Gordon Allport's *The Nature of Prejudice*, published in 1954. His approach to prejudice is still considered contemporary because of his emphasis on cognitive factors such as categorization and normal cognitive bias. There are two broad categories of prejudice: personal prejudice and group prejudice. Allport's model involves in-group and out-group distinctions. In an extension of Allport's theory, Thomas Pettigrew proposed the "ultimate attribution error" in an article he published in 1979. Pettigrew suggests that people tend to favor the actions of people in their in-group (those whom they perceive as being "like them") and attribute negative motives to the same actions by out-group members. If an in-group member observes a negative act by an out-group member, the in-group member is likely to attribute the action to genetics or some other concrete factor. On the other hand, if an in-group member observes a positive act by an out-group member, he or she may attribute the act to luck, an exception to the rule, high motivation and effort, or the particular situational context in which the behavior occurred.

A study published in 1947 by Kenneth Clark and Mamie Clark on color preference of dolls in preschool children showed that even very young children preferred the "white" dolls to those representing their respective race or skin color. In the 1970's, Jane Elliott conducted an experiment with elementary school children in which she instructed the brown-eyed children to sit in the back of the room and told them they could not use the drinking fountain. Blue-eyed children were given special privileges such as extra recess time and extra lunch helpings. The two groups of children were told not to interact with each other. Elliott belittled and berated the brown-eyed children, and their academic performance faltered. The favored blue-eyed group became even more belittling to the brown-eyed children than the teacher was. After several days, roles were reversed, and the negative effects of prejudice were repeated. Eventually all the children disliked one another, demonstrating the destructive effects of status inequalities based on something as superficial as eye color.

THEORIZING PREJUDICIAL INFLUENCES

Donn Byrne, a social psychologist, has written about theories on the conditions under which prejudice may develop. Byrne and others believe that periods of economic hardship and scarce resources characterized by lack of availability of food and jobs can contribute to the occurrence and intensity of various types of prejudice. In the field of social psychology, this premise is part of what is known as "realistic conflict theory." Indeed, throughout history, in periods of resource scarcity and political unrest, the unfair effects of prejudice have flourished. From the mid-fifteenth and sixteenth centuries until the present, racial and religious prejudice leading to discrimination has resulted in violence against different ethnic and religious groups in what has been a worldwide phenomenon. From the United States to the various republics that, until 1992, made up the Soviet Union, and from Northern Ireland to South Africa, these problems have been significant. Efforts made by countries to achieve internal peace and stability have been difficult, at best, given climates of religious or ethnic intolerance and economic hardship.

Class status is one factor that has been found to have a profound effect on influencing prejudicial beliefs and expectations. In the 1940's, an epidemiological study of psychopathology, or mental illness, called the Midtown Study was initiated in Manhattan in New York City, and results were published in the 1960's. A number of stereotypes about lower-class patients which suggested they were incapable of achieving insight into their prob-

Prejudice toward the disabled may take the form of lack of empathy, avoidance of social interaction, lack of eye contact, and lack of respect. Those who are physically disabled, however, often display strong self-concepts and good social interaction skills that help combat such attitudes. (National Easter Seal Society)

lems, unable to ask for psychological help, and unable to examine their motives or moods were disputed by this research. In fact, the research showed that lower-class patients did want to achieve psychodynamic understanding and insight into their problems. The research also showed that patients of lower socioeconomic status had less access to treatment facilities than their higher-class counterparts.

Racial and ethnic bias has been found to exist even among mental health professionals, a group of professionals who should, by definition, be objective and neutral in their work; however, very little research has been published in this area. Some investigators found no evidence of racial bias upon diagnoses assigned by clinicians who were of different racial backgrounds. Others found that white, middle-class psychiatrists who recorded fewer symptoms for black patients as compared to white patients nevertheless concentrated on the more unusual or bizarre symptoms of the blacks. This practice resulted in the psychopathology of black patients appearing more severe than the psychopathology of white patients. Researchers and clinicians have noted that white patients have more often been given the label "neurotic" and black or Puerto Rican patients given the label "schizophrenic" for similar behaviors. Social psychologist Leonard Derogatis and others caution that race and social class designation are the most prominent indicators that affect psychological assessment and symptom presentation.

PREJUDICE AS AN "ISM"

Prejudice that has become widespread takes forms that are sometimes referred to as "isms": racism, classism, sexism, ageism, heterosexism, able-bodiedism, and so on. The prejudicial attitudes held regarding the disabled, of which there were more than 36 million in the United States in 1986, have been found to be one of the most insidious forms of misunderstanding. In American society, those with emotional or learning disabilities (the invisible disabilities) often suffer the worst misunderstanding and discrimination caused by ignorance, perpetuation of myths, social ostracism, and avoidance of contact. It is known that nondisabled persons have demonstrated lack of empathy, avoidance of social interaction, lack of eye contact, and lack of respect for the disabled. Research has shown that even disabled persons hold negative attitudes toward other disabled persons if the others have a disability different from their own. In reality, those who are physically disabled have been found to have strong self-concepts and good social interaction skills and have often been more able to provide support to others than the other way around.

INVESTIGATING TECHNIQUES

Psychologists have developed various techniques for investigating and measuring social attitudes such as prejudice. Various scales exist for this purpose, from the Thurstone scale to the more frequently used Likert format. The Thurstone method of paired comparisons is thought to provide a method for the selection of items on an attitude test. In the Likert format, attitudes are measured according to approval rankings on positive and negative dimensions, with variations in between two opposite rankings as possible selection points. For example, the choices for the question "What do you think of homosexuals holding public office?" would be "strongly approve," "approve," "undecided," "disapprove," and "strongly disapprove."

Respondents are asked to rank the intensity and direction of their attitudes by choosing one of the five available choices for a number of similar items. The semantic differential, another popular technique in social-attitude research, presents a concept or set of concepts, such as "Democrat," "God," or "Puerto Rican." The respondent is asked to rate the concept on a set of seven-point scales in which the endpoints are certain adjectives, such as "strong" and "weak," or "active" and "passive." The semantic differential has been criticized for difficulty with interpretations derived from it, but it remains popular for its ease of use. Public opinion surveys are also used to measure attitudes either for or against certain candidates, social issues, or legislation. These surveys, although useful, can be plagued with problems such as interviewer bias, subject selection bias, and question bias if not carefully designed.

EFFECTS

Many practical applications have developed from a knowledge of prejudice and its effects that go beyond surveys and attitude measurement instruments. Women, both Caucasians and minorities, who have been able to gain access to higher education and obtain advanced degrees have found that they are still paid less than men with the same credentials. Moreover, the phenomenon referred to as the "glass ceiling" suggests that there is only so far a woman can go in terms of advancement through corporate and institutional structures. It is true that very few top corporate positions or top government posts are filled by women. Some people believe that these few positions represent tokenism, or positive actions toward a few women to make it look as though the employer is playing fair. As a result of this glass ceiling, some women have filed discrimination suits and won. Others have taken a different path and have written extensively on the effect of gender bias on women. A 1991 book by Susan Faludi titled *Backlash: The Undeclared War Against American Women* describes the insidious price that the author believes has been paid for the small progress made by women in American society.

Different people respond in different ways to the effects of prejudice. Active or effective responses are ones that empower people to confront and correct bias and injustice. In contrast, passive or ineffective responses may lead to a self-fulfilling prophecy, low self-esteem, and racial self-hatred in reaction to the negative stereotyping effects of prejudice. Minority group members' angry reactions to racial prejudice have been found ultimately to be a healthy response or a way to "fight back" against being oppressed. This anger, even rage, can evolve into what has been termed cultural paranoia, which is described as a defense mechanism that has allowed blacks and other minority groups to live in a society that is filled with racism. Martin Luther King, Jr., used this mechanism in a positive way to confront and try to change racial oppression in American society.

Social and Eductional Responses

Active, effective responses have been most notable in what might be called empowerment movements. Grass-roots support groups formed for women's rights, civil rights, gay and lesbian rights, and patients' rights resulted in various institutions and organizations being formalized by these movements. These movements and their resulting institutions represent active responses to the effects of prejudice. More recently, an advocacy group for AIDS victims called ACT UP (an acronym for AIDS Coalition to Unleash Power) was formed to take dramatic measures for calling national attention to the epidemic of AIDS.

In the educational arena, efforts have taken the form of the development of prejudice-reduction programs and workshops and an intensive effort to develop a multicultural curriculum at all levels of education. A multicultural approach to education stresses educational innovations that challenge the majority culture's views on historical and social issues and strives for inclusivity and fairness in noting the contributions of all cultures, genders, and races to society. The book *Teaching a Psychology of People: Resources for Gender and Sociocultural Awareness* (1988), edited by Phyllis A. Bronstein and Kathryn Quina, is an excellent resource on a multicultural approach to psychology.

Historic Prejudice

In the 1960's, with the inception of the Civil Rights movement, the social psychology research literature began to focus in earnest on the concepts of prejudice and discrimination. In the period of time from 1954 to 1964, conflict, organized protest, civil rights marches, demonstrations, riots and acts of violence, and social injustice brought the social problems to the forefront. Researchers were drawn to investigate the complex phenomena and mechanisms of prejudice and discrimination. In 1964, an expanded Civil Rights Act was passed; this made the research all the more urgent. It has been noted, however, that during this period the broader focus of research on culture and diversity was sacrificed.

The history of prejudice is a long one. The fifteenth and sixteenth centuries ushered in a particularly dark period of mass persecution of women who practiced self-healing methods and midwifery. During the medieval period, women had also been victims of religious persecution, including some who simply were homeless or had a "sharp tongue" as well as some who were probably mentally ill. All told, this period of religious persecution, led by religious male patriarchs of the time (mostly representatives of the church), resulted in hundreds of thousands of people being tortured and put to death. A key impulse underlying this massive prejudice and persecution was the Roman Catholic church's opposition to women's sexuality. Sexuality was seen to be insatiable in women, and lust in both genders was thought to be uncontrollable. This prejudice was so strong that everything from bad crops to miscarriages was blamed on women identified as witches.

The persecution and death of six million Jewish people by the Nazis is yet another—and probably the most frightening—example of the possible outcomes of extreme prejudice and discrimination. Indeed, any form of genocide is the ultimate end product of severe prejudice.

Impact of Social Movements

The women's movement (originating in the 1900's), the gay and lesbian liberation movement, the patients' rights movement, and the Civil Rights movement have all had major impacts on mitigating the effects of prejudice. As these organized political groups have gained more support, each has been instrumental in consciousness-raising; reducing prejudice, social inequity, and social injustice; and increasing political, educational, and economic opportunity for their members. Affirmative action programs continue, although they have met with criticism that they go beyond the goal of correcting inequity in hiring practices. Some people believe that these policies have led to a social phenomenon referred to as reverse discrimination (the idea that certain methods intended to reduce discrimination, such as hiring quotas, have backfired and actually lead to discrimination against members of a majority group who may be more qualified than others who are hired); however, others believe that certain groups, such as Latinos, African Americans, and Native Americans, have suffered long-term damaging effects from discrimination and therefore need the help of affirmative action programs. The language differences between English-speaking and Spanish-speaking children in the United States from a very early age begin to limit the educational and work opportunities for these children's futures. Bilingual education is one possible avenue to maximize educational opportunities and future economic opportunities.

SOCIAL CLASS AND CULTURAL DISTINCTIONS

Social class and cultural distinctions also continue to bring opportunity to some people while eliminating opportunity for those of lower socioeconomic status. Many black children and other minorities have been locked into a cycle of poverty and hopelessness that impairs educational progress and motivation at a very early age. Although some progress has been made with the funding opportunities for offspring of low-income families (such as Head Start programs), designed to pave the way for success in higher education, many programs are cut in times of economic hardship, when people need them the most. This perpetuates a cycle of poverty, with prejudice leading to economic hardship for affected groups. The term "feminization of poverty" has been used to describe the economic impact of low-wage, menial jobs on women in the United States, Puerto Rico, and other nations. Newspapers and television news frequently report acts inspired by prejudice, such as "hate crimes" against minorities. Violations of the civil rights of minorities still occur, leading to public outcries for examination and correction of the racial inequalities in American institutions and society. Much more progress is clearly needed in studying ways to reduce prejudice and its devastating effects.

SOURCES FOR FURTHER STUDY

Allport, Gordon W. *The Nature of Prejudice*. Reading, Mass.: Addison-Wesley, 1954. This classic social psychology book on prejudice emphasizes cognitive factors such as categorization and normal cognitive bias, an approach that is still contemporary by today's standards.

Baron, Robert A., and Donn Byrne. *Social Psychology: Understanding Human Interaction*. 9th ed. Boston: Allyn & Bacon, 1999. This popular undergraduate social psychology text contains an excellent chapter titled "Prejudice and Discrimination: The Costs of Hating Without Cause." Explores social categorization, intergroup conflict, cognitive sources of bias, stereotypes, and much more.

Freeman, Howard E., and Norman R. Kurtz, eds. *America's Troubles: A Casebook on Social Conflict*. Englewood Cliffs, N.J.: Prentice-Hall, 1969. This well-written book explores many issues of prejudice in American society and presents many first-person essays that bring home to the reader the significant impact of bias on individuals, groups, and society.

Jones, Melinda. *Social Psychology of Prejudice*. Englewood Cliffs, N.J.: Prentice Hall, 2001. Covers racism, sexism, and antigay prejudice; values; stereotyping and categorization; individual differences in prejudice; intergroup relations; and stigma and identity.

Lips, Hilary. *Sex and Gender: An Introduction*. 3d ed. Mountain View, Calif.: Mayfield, 1996. Presents a thorough review of myths, theories, and research regarding sex and gender. In addition, the author explores behavior and experiences of males and females, comparing similarities and differences. Sex and gender are examined in social relationships, political life, and the workplace.

Morgan, Robin. *The Demon Lover: On the Sexuality of Terrorism*. New York: W. W. Norton, 1989. A feminist perspective on the influence of certain myths about masculinity and power that pervade cultural manifestations of violence and result in victims of prejudice becoming targets of violence.

Young-Bruehl, Elisabeth. *The Anatomy of Prejudices*. Cambridge, Mass.: Harvard University Press, 1998. Examines the sources and context of prejudices—arguing, in particular, for regarding prejudices in the plural rather than the singular.

Karen Wolford

Prejudice reduction

TYPE OF PSYCHOLOGY: Social psychology
FIELDS OF STUDY: Prejudice and discrimination

Several approaches to the reduction of prejudice have been studied over the years. Intergroup contact, the introduction of a common enemy, the crossing of social categories, and the presentation of information in the media are all strategies that have been considered in the effort to reduce prejudice. Evidence regarding the effectiveness of these strategies is mixed, and research has been directed toward examining the specific mechanisms underlying prejudice reduction.

KEY CONCEPTS
- belief congruence intervention
- common-enemy strategy
- cooperative team intervention
- cross-categorization
- intergroup contact
- interpersonal contact
- prejudice
- subtyping

INTRODUCTION

Gordon Allport defined prejudice as an attitude toward the members of an out-group in which the evaluative tendencies are predominantly negative. It seems self-evident that the reduction and elimination of prejudice are among the most pressing real-world problems confronting psychology. Several different approaches to the reduction of prejudice have been examined.

Each of these approaches to prejudice reduction is derived from one or more of the suspected root causes of prejudice. Numerous explanations have been offered in attempts to account for prejudice. For example, some people believe that individuals develop negative attitudes toward other groups that are perceived as competing with their own group. Alternatively, it is possible that differences in familiarity with one's own group versus other groups can lead to differential perceptions and evaluations of the two groups. Prejudice might also develop as people grow up and learn from others about the features of different groups, especially if the features depict negative characteristics for certain groups. Finally, social thinking might inherently involve categorization processes that often lead people to divide the world into "us" and "them." The different strategies designed to reduce prejudice generally focus upon one of these concerns and try to reduce that specific concern in the hope of reducing prejudice.

CONTACT HYPOTHESIS

One of the most obvious and most heavily researched techniques for reducing prejudice is exemplified by what is called the "contact hypothesis": that association with persons from a disliked group will lead to a growth of liking and respect for that group. Scholarly considerations of this basic idea can be traced back at least to the 1940's; for example, it can be found in Robin Williams's 1947 book, *The Reduction of Intergroup Tensions*. It is the seminal work of Gordon Allport, however, that is generally credited with being the classic formulation of the contact hypothesis. In *The Nature of Prejudice* (1954) Allport developed a taxonomy of relevant factors necessary for contact to be successful in reducing prejudice. These factors emphasized the nature of the contact experience, and they included the frequency and duration of contact, the relative status of the two groups, and the social atmosphere of the contact experience. Extensive reviews of the research examining the contact hypothesis have been published by Yehuda Amir in 1976 and Miles Hewstone and Rupert Brown in 1986. Some studies have demonstrated a reduction of prejudice toward the out-group, whereas other studies have shown contact actually to increase prejudice among members of the majority group along with causing a decrease in self-esteem and an increased sense of isolation among members of the minority group. Part of the difficulty may stem from the differences between intended contact and actual levels of contact. For example, Donald Taylor and his colleagues have argued that intergroup contact is often avoided. One study showed that black and white students in a desegregated school "resegregated" themselves into ethnic groups during classroom activities and recess. Thus, the general emphasis has shifted from "whether the contact hypothesis is valid" to "under what conditions, and in what domains, is the contact hypothesis valid."

A variant of the contact hypothesis in the context of desegregated schools is the cooperative team intervention. In this type of intervention, small groups of schoolchildren, including children of two ethnic groups, are assigned to complete a task in which they need to cooperate in order to succeed. Sometimes these small groups are later put into competition with other similar groups. Norman Miller and Gaye Davidson-Podgorny, in a study published in 1987, have shown that this type of cooperative team intervention is generally effective in reducing prejudice, at least in terms of attitudes toward outgroup classmates.

BELIEF CONGRUENCE INTERVENTION

An alternative approach is known as the belief congruence intervention. According to this strategy, prejudice and intergroup hostility are driven by the assumption that members of the out-group hold beliefs that are different from those held by the ingroup. Therefore, if it can be learned that members of the out-group are actually more similar to the ingroup, then members of the out-group might be liked more and prejudice will be diminished. This approach is illustrated by Rachel Dubois's 1950 "neighborhood festival," in which members of different ethnic groups talked about nostalgic memories of childhood, holidays, and so on. The goal was for participants to recognize that group experiences, customs, and meanings are in fact remarkably alike and that different ethnic groups actually share membership in a broader commonality. While this intervention sounds very appealing, its success rests upon a problematic assumption: The perceived differences between groups are illusory, and learning about intergroup similarities in beliefs will bring people to a more enlightened enjoyment of one another. If there are fundamental differences between the central beliefs of two groups (for example, as between Catholics and Protestants in Northern Ireland, or between Arabs and Jews in the Middle East), then the belief congruence approach is unlikely to be successful.

Finally, the role of the media in maintaining or reducing prejudice should be considered. Research has shown that ethnic minority groups are sometimes portrayed in negative ways in the news media and popular entertainment. While little research has examined the prejudice-reducing effects of the media, it is reasonable to speculate that more positive portrayals of ethnic minorities in the media might make a substantial contribution in the future to the reduction of prejudice. In line with this possibility, research by Fletcher Blanchard and his colleagues has found that exposure to the normative influence of other people expressing antiracist views can increase an individual's expression of antiracist views.

DESEGREGATION AND OTHER APPLICATIONS

There are several specific settings in which the contact hypothesis may be seen to operate. The most vivid example is desegregation in classroom settings. A considerable amount of research has examined this particular contact setting and, as indicated above, the results are mixed. As summarized by Janet Schofield in 1986, school desegregation in the United States may have had a less positive effect than one might have hoped because the problems that have characterized race relations in the United States have limited both the extent and the nature of intergroup contact in desegregated schools. Fortunately, there are several other contexts in which intergroup contact can be fostered. Unfortunately, the evidence regarding the effectiveness of these other contact interventions is also mixed. For example, in 1985 Yehuda Amir and Rachel Ben-Ari reported that tourists visiting a foreign country did not evidence decreased prejudice toward the (outgroup) members of that country. Similarly, in 1966 Otto Klineberg showed that the attitudes of foreign exchange students toward the local people were on the whole friendly on arrival, but became slightly less so on the average after a period of residence in that foreign country. Alternatively, in 1986 Ulrich Wagner and Uwe Macleit reported that increased contact with *Gästarbeiter* ("guest workers," the majority of whom are Turkish) in the Federal Republic of Germany was associated with reduced prejudice toward these foreign workers.

As delineated by Hewstone and Brown, there is a large dilemma plaguing research on the contact hypothesis involving the nature of the contact itself. On one hand, the contact could be strictly interpersonal, where members of the two opposing groups interact with one another as individuals. This approach is emphasized in the work of Norman Miller and Marilynn Brewer published in 1984. On the other hand, the contact could be strictly intergroup, where members of the two opposing groups interact with one another as group members. This approach is emphasized in the work of Hewstone and Brown. It is unclear which of these two types of contact is more effective. A related problem is the generalization of positive attitudes that might be stimulated by contact. The contact with specific individuals from another ethnic or national group might lead to more positive attitudes about those specific individuals, but this does not guarantee that those more positive attitudes will generalize to the rest of that ethnic or national group as a whole.

Recategorization

This sets the stage for the fundamental paradox of the contact hypothesis. As discussed by Jennifer Crocker in 1984, information about a single exceptionally positive out-group member may engage a "subtyping" mechanism: The exceptionally positive member may be functionally subtyped into a separate category, leaving the overall out-group category intact. As illustrated in a discussion by John Pryor and Thomas Ostrom in 1987, the professor who holds the stereotype that "athletes are unintelligent" will create a separate subtype of "smart athletes" in response to meeting a smart athlete, rather than changing the overall stereotype for athletes. The general form of the paradox can be stated as follows: In order to have the potential to change the negative evaluation of the out-group, the exceptional member of the out-group must be uniquely positive. If, however, the exceptional member of the out-group is uniquely positive, then he or she is likely to be subtyped into a class of his or her own, thereby leaving the overall negative evaluation of the out-group intact.

As the belief congruence approach shows, one concept of the reduction of prejudice is concerned with the idea that members of two groups can be led to redefine the boundaries between the groups. This idea is more directly illustrated in Willem Doise's research on cross-categorization. This refers to a situation in which one categorization that splits people into two groups (such as black-white) is crossed with a second categorization (such as liberal-conservative), so that people are split into four groups (white liberals, white conservatives, black liberals, and black conservatives). Doise has

found that this cross-categorization reduces discrimination between the two original groups. Presumably, learning that some of "them" are really like "us" helps to mitigate the prejudice against "them."

An extreme version of a recategorization strategy is illustrated in an intervention which might be called the common-enemy strategy. This approach was illustrated in Muzafer Sherif and colleagues' 1961 "Robbers Cave" study. In this study, eleven-year-old boys in a summer-camp setting were divided into two groups. The two groups engaged in a series of competitions, which resulted in both verbal and physical signs of prejudice toward the other group. When the two groups were combined to compete against a team from another camp, however, the negative attitudes toward the (former) out-group diminished.

The basic assumption underlying the common-enemy strategy is that a common enemy should cause the two (initially conflicting) groups to set aside their differences to overcome the external threat represented by the "common enemy." While there is little research evidence that directly examines this strategy (Sherif's study is the notable exception), ample anecdotal evidence illustrates the all-too-often-employed strategy of drawing disparate and disagreeing members of a political unit together by casting them as a cohesive unit in the face of some threat posed by an external out-group.

There are two problems with this approach that should be recognized: First, the strategy is likely to be effective only in the short term. As discussed by Muzafer and Carolyn Sherif, the introduction of a common enemy in the Robbers Cave study did draw the two conflicting groups together in an effort to defeat the new opposing out-group. As soon as the opposing out-group left the scene, however, the old conflicts between the two original groups of campers reemerged. A similar affect was seen in the eruption of ethnic conflict in Eastern Europe after the fall of the Soviet Union. Second, this strategy does not really reduce overall levels of prejudice and conflict; it simply redirects it. In other words, although groups A and B are no longer in conflict, these two groups have now joined in conflict against group C. This intervention carries with it moral concerns about the justification for selecting group C as a target for prejudice in an effort to reduce the original prejudice that group A held toward group B.

SOCIAL PSYCHOLOGY

Understanding prejudice and developing strategies to reduce it have long been major concerns of social psychologists. Techniques used for studying prejudice, however, have changed over the years. Earlier research relied heavily on observing the outward behavior of one group's members toward another group's members and analyzing people's responses on surveys. The development of computers and other sophisticated experimental techniques has enabled researchers to probe more deeply into the specific cognitive workings that may result in prejudice. This has helped illuminate a number of intriguing features about prejudice.

For example, Patricia Devine, in a study published in 1989, showed that what distinguishes unprejudiced people from prejudiced people is not that unprejudiced people automatically respond in nonprejudiced, egalitarian ways. Rather, both prejudiced people and unprejudiced people may engage in automatic, learned responses of negative evaluation toward stereotyped out-groups. The unprejudiced people, however, are able to engage controlled cognitive processes that thwart the expression of these undesirable prejudiced responses. Viewed in this way, Devine suggests, prejudices may be likened to bad habits, and the replacement of prejudiced responses with nonprejudiced responses can be likened to the breaking of such habits.

The work by Devine illustrates a key ingredient in all efforts to reduce prejudice. The way people learn and process information about groups may inherently lead to differential perceptions and evaluations of these groups. Because of a need to simplify and organize information, these differential perceptions and evaluations may be incorporated into stereotypes, which may be negative for some groups. As discussed by Brian Mullen in 1991, in order for a technique for reducing prejudice to be successful, it must take this cognitive processing of information about different groups into consideration. There does not seem to be any magic solution to the problem of prejudice. It seems apparent, however, that people need to be aware at some level of the cognitive biases that can develop. Consistent with Devine's findings, becoming consciously aware of the biases in thinking about certain groups may be an important first step in the effort to reduce prejudice.

SOURCES FOR FURTHER STUDY

Allport, Gordon W. *The Nature of Prejudice.* 1954. Reprint. New York: Perseus Books, 1988. This is the classic statement of prejudice and the contact hypothesis. Written for a scholarly audience, it still reads well—and is still timely—today.

Hewstone, Miles, and Rupert Brown, eds. *Contact and Conflict in Intergroup Encounters.* Oxford, England: Basil Blackwell, 1986. This edited volume brings together scholars from around the world who describe the results of specific contact experiences between particular groups in a wide variety of settings, including Northern Ireland, Israel, Germany, Quebec, and South Africa.

Jones, James M. *Prejudice and Racism.* 2d ed. New York: WCB/McGraw-Hill, 1996. This provocative and accessible monograph provides an excellent historical overview of prejudice and racism and an insightful discussion into the effectiveness and ineffectiveness of various strategies for addressing the problems of prejudice and racism.

Miller, Norman, and Marilynn Brewer, eds. *Groups in Contact: The Psychology of Desegregation.* Orlando, Fla.: Academic Press, 1984. This well-written edited volume considers theory and research on the effects of desegregation, particularly in schools in the United States.

Mullen, Brian. "Group Composition, Salience, and Cognitive Representations: The Phenomenology of Being in a Group." *Journal of Experimental Social Psychology* 27, no. 4 (1991): 297-323. This scholarly paper discusses a model of the cognitive mechanisms that seem to drive and maintain stereotyping and prejudice.

Oskamp, Stuart, ed. *Reducing Prejudice and Discrimination.* Hillsdale, N.J.: Lawrence Erlbaum, 2000. A collection of papers from a symposium on prejudice.

Craig Johnson and Brian Mullen

SEE ALSO: Ageism; Cooperative learning; Intergroup relations; Prejudice; Racism; Sexism; Social identity theory.

Prenatal physical development

TYPE OF PSYCHOLOGY: Biological bases of behavior; developmental psychology
FIELDS OF STUDY: Infancy and childhood

Prenatal development usually progresses in a predictable fashion, but can be disrupted by both environmental and genetic factors. Prenatal disruptions can create both physical and neurological abnormalities that range from fetal death, mental retardation, and severe physical deformities to language deficits and attention disorders. Prenatal diagnostic tests may detect some of the more adverse outcomes.

KEY CONCEPTS
- amniocentesis
- amnion
- chromosome
- embryo period
- fetal period
- placenta
- teratogen
- zygote period

INTRODUCTION

Pregnancy encompasses the development of a single-celled fertilized egg into a trillion-celled baby. The many changes that transform the fertilized egg into a newborn infant over nine months of human pregnancy constitute prenatal development. Prenatal development is comprised of three stages (the zygote, embryo, and fetal periods) and is also commonly categorized into three trimesters, each lasting three months. Although prenatal development typically follows a predictable course, development can be disrupted by both genetic and environmental factors. This disruption may result in a range of outcomes, from fetal death and severe abnormalities such as deformed or missing limbs, to minor abnormalities such as low birth weight and neurological dysfunction such as learning disabilities or Attention-deficit hyperactivity disorder (ADHD).

The fourth century B.C.E. Greek philosopher Aristotle is regarded as the first in Western civilization to study prenatal development. Since then, others have superficially investigated the topic. However, it was not until the beginning of the twentieth century that researchers intensified their study of prenatal development. In the early 1900's, researchers were significantly influenced by the evolutionary theories of Charles Darwin (1809-1882) and believed that all aspects of prenatal development were genetically determined. Josef Warkany, a pioneering American scientist, engendered a shift in the thinking of the scientific community during the 1940's. Warkany

documented that environmental factors, called teratogens, could adversely affect prenatal development and cause malformations at birth. About a decade later, the notion that environmental factors could harm prenatal development became mainstream after the 1950's thalidomide tragedy. Thalidomide was a drug given to pregnant women to combat symptoms of nausea. When taken in the first trimester of pregnancy, the drug produced severe physical deformities in infants, including missing arms and stunted limbs, and its use was subsequently banned. Following this tragedy and the resulting acceleration in understanding of the importance of intrauterine life, diagnostic tests have become routinely used to monitor the course of prenatal development.

STAGES OF PRENATAL DEVELOPMENT

Prenatal development begins when a sperm successfully fertilizes an egg (ovum) and usually lasts an average of thirty-eight weeks (nine months). The American College of Obstetrics and Gynecology has standardized the terminology used to describe the three stages of prenatal development. The first stage, the zygote (or germinal) stage, begins at fertilization and ends two weeks later, shortly after implantation of the zygote in the uterine wall. The second stage, the embryo stage (weeks 3 to 8), is the most vulnerable to teratogenic (environmental) insult. The fetal stage (weeks 9 to 38) represents the final and longest stage of prenatal development.

THE ZYGOTE STAGE (CONCEPTION TO WEEK 2)

Fertilization of an egg by a sperm creates a zygote. The two-week period of the zygote ends with its implantation into the uterine wall. During these two weeks, the zygote grows rapidly and is carried by currents in one of the Fallopian tubes toward the uterus. The movement through the Fallopian tube usually takes five days. The zygote divides from a single cell into a mass of approximately one hundred cells. Approximately one week after fertilization, the zygote is ready to attach itself to the uterine wall. Many potential pregnancies terminate at this point as a result of implantation failure. Implantation takes approximately one week to complete, connects the zygote with the woman's blood supply, and triggers hormonal changes that prevent menstruation. At this stage, the implanted zygote is less than a millimeter in diameter but is beginning to

Stages of Prenatal Development

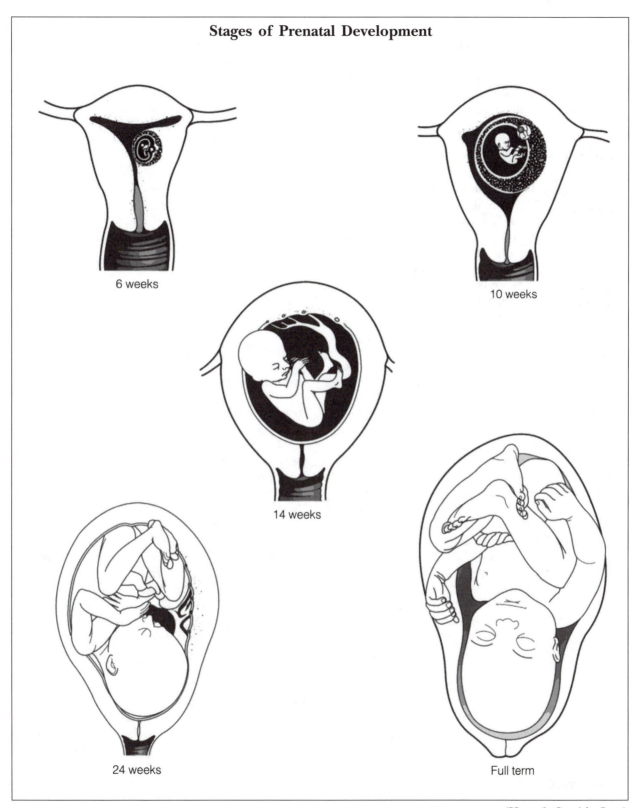

6 weeks

10 weeks

14 weeks

24 weeks

Full term

(Hans & Cassidy, Inc.)

differentiate into two structures: the germinal disc and the placenta. The germinal disc eventually develops into the baby, while the remaining cells transform into the placenta. The placenta is the structure through which nutrients and waste are exchanged between the mother and the developing child. Successful implantation and differentiation into the placenta and germinal disc mark the end of the period of the zygote.

THE EMBRYO STAGE (WEEKS 3 TO 8)

Upon successful implantation in the uterine wall, the zygote is called an embryo and pregnancy enters its second stage. The embryo stage typically begins three weeks after conception (fertilization) and lasts through the eighth week of pregnancy. At the beginning of the embryo stage, the embryo is only two millimeters long and less than an ounce in weight. The embryo is enclosed in a protective sac called the amnion, which is filled with amniotic fluid that cushions and maintains a constant temperature for the embryo. The embryo's cells form into three layers: The outer layer (ectoderm) becomes the hair, the outer layer of skin, and the nervous system; the middle layer (mesoderm) forms muscles, bones, and the circulatory system; and the inner layer (endoderm) forms the digestive system and lungs. At the beginning of this stage, the embryo looks more like a lizard than a human being, as a result of the shape of its body and head. By the end of the eighth week of pregnancy, the embryo manifests distinguishable human characteristics (eyes, arms, legs) and contains in rudimentary form all of its organs and body structures. Despite these significant changes, the embryo remains too small to be detected by the mother.

THE FETAL PERIOD (WEEKS 9 TO 38)

The longest and final phase of prenatal development is known as the fetal period. The fetal period represents a time when the finishing touches are put on the structures of the fetus. This period begins at nine weeks and ends with the birth of the baby. During this stage of pregnancy, the growth and development of the fetus is astounding. The fetus will increase in mass from less than one ounce at week 9, to eight ounces at four months, and to nearly eight pounds at birth. Around the start of the fetal period, the fetus begins to differentiate sex characteristics. At twelve weeks, the circulatory

system becomes functional. At sixteen weeks, the mother can detect fetal movements known as quickening. By twenty weeks, a fine layer of hair (called lanugo) begins to grow over most of the fetus's body. Sucking and swallowing reflexes are present by twenty-four weeks of gestation. Brain specialization becomes particularly acute by about twenty-eight weeks. At thirty-two weeks of gestation (seven months), the fetus is viable outside the mother's womb. By this time, most systems function well enough that a fetus born at this age has a chance to survive. Despite the potential to survive, premature birth predisposes a baby to myriad additional developmental problems (health problems, learning disabilities, and cognitive deficits). By thirty-two weeks of prenatal development, the fetus has regular periods of physical activity, and the eyes and ears begin to function. By thirty-six weeks of gestation, the fetus experiences rapid weight gain, and development consists largely of an increase in weight and length. At approximately thirty-eight weeks of gestation, birth will occur. The average newborn baby weighs between seven and eight pounds.

DISRUPTIONS IN PRENATAL DEVELOPMENT

Although most of prenatal development progresses in a healthy and predictable fashion, numerous factors can disrupt the course of prenatal development. It is customary to divide the possible cause of these malformations into genetic factors (chromosomal abnormalities) and environmental factors (such as those due to drugs or viral infections). There is often an interaction between environmental conditions and genetic factors such that the environment can either exacerbate or mitigate any potential adverse outcomes. The impact of both genetic and environmental factors may result in abnormalities that range from fetal death and severe structural defects to subtle neurological malformations that may not manifest themselves until several years after birth (as with learning disabilities or ADHD).

GENERAL RISK FACTORS

Parental age can have an impact on prenatal development. Women over the age of thirty-five are at greater risk of giving birth to children with birth defects such as Down syndrome and other chromosomal abnormalities. Recent research suggests that older men also have an increased risk of fathering children with birth defects as a result of the presence of damaged sperm that may fertilize the egg. Teenage girls are also at greater risk for giving birth to children with birth defects as a result of poor maternal health and inadequate prenatal care. When prenatal nourishment and care are lacking, the baby is more likely to be born prematurely, have a lower birth weight, and be at greater risk for learning difficulties and a host of behavioral and emotional problems. Recent research has also implicated maternal stress during pregnancy as a general risk factor. Roy Martin, a professor at the University of Georgia, indicates that maternal stress during pregnancy may be associated with a higher level of child temperamental difficulties, including irritability and excessive inhibition. Although this line of research is preliminary, it is hypothesized that these outcomes may be due to maternal stress hormones that disturb fetal neurological development.

GENETIC AND CHROMOSOMAL RISK FACTORS

Thousands of genetic and chromosomal anomalies can potentially disturb normal prenatal development. While many of the causes of genetic and chromosomal abnormalities are unknown, some may be attributable to exposure to teratogens that damage the chromosomes during prenatal development. Research emerging out of the Human Genome Project is continuously documenting additional chromosomal abnormalities that may have an impact on prenatal development. A chromosome is a microscopic component of a cell that carries its genetic makeup. One of the most common chromosomal disorders is Down syndrome. Individuals with Down syndrome have slanted eyes; thick, fissured tongues; and a flat, broad face. They are often mentally retarded and have significant language impairments. Other chromosomal and genetic disorders include Turner syndrome, Klinefelter syndrome, fragile X syndrome, muscular dystrophy, and neural tube defects that result in spina bifida. Many of these conditions produce mental retardation and physical anomalies such as brain damage, unusual appearance; and malformed limbs.

PRENATAL DIAGNOSTIC TESTS

Prenatal tests, such as amniocentesis, can detect the presence of many chromosomal and genetic abnormalities. Amniocentesis involves the insertion of a hollow needle through the mother's abdomen into the amniotic sac and the withdrawal of fluid containing fetal cells. Amniocentesis can detect chromosomal abnormalities such as Down syndrome, but it is not usually performed until the fifteenth week of pregnancy. Chorionic villus sampling (CVS) provides the same information as amniocentesis, but at a much earlier gestational period (seven weeks). In CVS, fetal cells are obtained from the placenta by means of a tube inserted through the vagina. There is greater risk of infection and miscarriage with CVS. Fetoscopy is a surgical procedure involving the insertion of an instrument that permits actual viewing of the fetus and the obtaining of fetal tissue. This procedure is more precise, than CVS and amniocentesis but carries a higher risk of miscarriage.

Ultrasound involves the use of sound waves that provide a computer-enhanced image of the fetus. It is a noninvasive, painless, and low-risk procedure that provides an actual image of the fetal shape and movement. It is useful for detecting normal and abnormal fetal development and for determining fetal position and age. Preimplantation diagnosis is an experimental, highly technical genetic examination of cells prior to their implantation in the uterine wall. It typically follows in vitro fertilization and permits the detection of specific genetic disorders. In the future, it may be useful for correcting genetic disorders as well.

Through prenatal diagnostic tests, researchers are now able to detect genetic weaknesses (and strengths) from the earliest moments of life. Researchers have also begun to experiment with ways of altering genetic messages, the results of which may lead to corrections of genetic abnormalities in the near future.

ENVIRONMENTAL RISK FACTORS

A teratogen is an environmental agent such as alcohol, cocaine, or infectious organism that has an adverse impact on prenatal development following maternal exposure. The word has Greek origins and literally means "monster-forming." Certain stages of prenatal development are more vulnerable to teratogens than others. Exposure during the period of the zygote usually results in spontaneous abortion of the fertilized egg, while exposure during the embryo stage can lead to major defects in bodily structure and quite possibly death. Exposure during the fetal period usually produces minor structural defects, such as wide-set eyes, and neurological impairment, such as mental retardation or learning problems. Some of the more commonly implicated teratogens include infectious agents such as cytomegalovirus, varicella virus, and human parvovirus B19 and drugs such as alcohol, cocaine, and nicotine.

The fetus is most vulnerable to the effects of teratogens during the first trimester. These effects are severe and may result in structural deformities and death. Sarnoff Mednick and others at the University of Southern California reported on a more subtle form of prenatal disturbance following second trimester exposure. Mednick reported preliminary data that linked second trimester viral infections to later psychological outcomes such as depression and schizophrenia. Research in this area, however, should be interpreted with caution and considered too inconclusive to warrant significant public concern.

There are additional environmental agents that can potentially disrupt the normal course of prenatal development. Studies have investigated the impact of caffeine. Although the results are equivocal, exposure to moderate amounts of caffeine may result in lower birth weight and decreased fetal muscle tone. Excessive caffeine use during pregnancy should, therefore, be avoided. The impact of alcohol during pregnancy is well documented. Chronic alcohol use produces fetal alcohol syndrome and associated cognitive deficits and physical deficits such as heart problems, retarded growth, and misshapen faces. Maternal alcohol use during prenatal development is the most common cause of mental retardation. Since even moderate daily alcohol use (two ounces of alcohol) has been associated with some of these outcomes, it is recommended that alcohol use during pregnancy be avoided. Nicotine exposure from cigarette smoking is another well-established teratogen. Research indicates that prenatal cigarette exposure increases the risk for low birth weight, cognitive deficits, learning problems, behavior problems, and even fetal death as a result of nicotine-induced placental and neurological defects.

Overall, the critical prenatal period for exposure to teratogens is during the first trimester of pregnancy. Within the first trimester, certain periods are even more sensitive to teratogens than others. For example, the first six weeks of pregnancy is a particularly sensitive period in the development of the central nervous system, while the eyes are vulnerable during weeks 5 through 8. It is commonly ac-

cepted that exposure to teratogens during the first eight weeks of pregnancy may induce major structural abnormalities. Exposure during the remainder of prenatal development, depending upon the type of teratogen and intensity and duration of exposure, may lead to minor structural abnormalities (wide eyes, webbed hands) as well as cognitive, behavioral, and psychological difficulties. While central nervous system development and brain growth are most vulnerable to disruptions during the first trimester of pregnancy, these structures continue to develop throughout the prenatal period. Thus, exposure to any environmental risk factor should be minimized if at all possible.

SOURCES FOR FURTHER STUDY

Kail, Robert V., and John C. Cavanaugh. *Human Development: A Lifespan View.* Belmont, Calif.: Wadsworth/Thomson Learning, 2000. Provides a comprehensive, yet highly readable, account of not only prenatal development but also human development across the life span. Illustrations and charts facilitate comprehension of material. Appropriate for the layperson and undergraduate student.

Lefrancois, Guy R. *The Lifespan.* Belmont, Calif.: Wadsworth, 1999. A comprehensive and scholarly text on life span development that is accessible to the layperson and the undergraduate student. Text includes a chapter on prenatal development and covers research and trends in the field.

Martin, Roy P., Jennifer Noyes, Joseph Wisenbaker, and Matti O. Huttunen. "Prediction of Early Childhood Negative Emotionality and Inhibition from Maternal Distress During Pregnancy." *Merrill-Palmer Quarterly* 45, no. 3 (1999): 370-391. Research article that investigates the link between maternal stress during pregnancy and later temperamental difficulties. This paper uses some statistical analyses; however, the conclusions are understandable.

Moore, Keith L., and T. V. N. Persaud. *Before We are Born.* Philadelphia: W. B. Saunders, 1993. A detailed, comprehensive, and accessible text on the topic of prenatal development and teratology. Although several years old, the text remains an excellent resource on the subject and was written by two of the leading scholars on prenatal development. Appropriate for a more advanced understanding of prenatal development and teratology.

Santrock, John W. *Life-Span Development.* New York: McGraw-Hill, 2002. A comprehensive text on human growth and development. An entire chapter has been devoted to the topic of prenatal development. Very accessible overview with colored illustrations and diagrams throughout the chapter. Appropriate for the layperson and undergraduate student.

Shepard, Thomas H., R. L. Brent, J. M. Friedman, K. L. Jones, R. K. Miller, C. A. Moore, and J. E. Polifka. "Update on New Developments in the Study of Human Teratogens." *Teratology* 65, no. 4 (2002): 153-161. This article reviews new and significant information on factors that may disrupt prenatal development. Some of the topics reviewed include recent research on the effects of binge drinking, cigarette smoking, and the ingestion of drugs prescribed for depression during pregnancy.

Warkany, Josef. *Congenital Malformations.* Chicago: Year Book, 1971. A classic treatise on teratology and one of the few books that provides a historical overview of the subject. Numerous illustrations of congenital malformations. Warkany has been recognized as a world authority and pioneer in the field of teratology.

Watson, Jennifer B., Sarnoff A. Mednick, Matti O. Huttunen, and Xueyi Wang. "Prenatal Teratogens and the Development of Adult Mental Illness." *Development and Psychopathology* 11, no. 3 (1999): 457-466. This article investigates the possible association between prenatal exposure to teratogens and later mental health outcomes. Drs. Mednick and Huttunen are among the leaders in this area of research.

Stefan C. Dombrowski
updated by Denise S. St. Cyr

See also: Birth: Effects on physical development; Development; Developmental disabilities; Down syndrome; Imprinting; Mental retardation; Motor development; Nervous system; Reflexes in newborns.

Preparedness

Type of psychology: Learning
Fields of study: Biological influences on learning

Preparedness, a biologically determined predisposition to acquire certain associations among stimuli, responses, and reinforcers more readily than others, imposes constraints on learning. An issue of central importance to behaviorism, preparedness has also provided insight into practical matters, especially the origin and character of phobias.

Key concepts
- acquisition
- arbitrariness
- classical conditioning
- conditioned taste aversion
- equipotentiality
- ethology
- extinction
- natural selection
- operant conditioning
- phobia

INTRODUCTION

Traditional learning theorists, such as Ivan Pavlov and B. F. Skinner, hold that the same basic, highly general laws of learning apply to all species. To uphold this view, they assert that a principle of equipotentiality pervades all learning. According to the equipotentiality principle, all associations between stimuli (in classical conditioning) and between responses and reinforcements (in operant conditioning) are acquired with equal ease. If these assumptions are true, laboratory demonstrations of rats learning responses that are arbitrary—a stimulus, response, or situation that is chosen at the convenience of the experimenter—such as pressing a bar to get food pellets, have great utility because they reveal general learning processes that broadly apply to all species. If not, then such studies only reveal how rats learn to press bars for food pellets in the artificial, controlled conditions of the laboratory. The large question is whether it is valid to apply principles based on the learning of rats to human learning and clinical practice.

In 1970, in a widely cited paper, Martin E. P. Seligman evaluated the premises of equipotentiality and the generality of the laws of learning and found them untenable. As an alternative, Seligman proposed a "continuum of preparedness," according to which animals placed in laboratory settings bring with them predispositions to learn specific tasks. These predispositions reflect an animal's evolutionary history. As a result, they may be highly prepared to learn whatever a particular experiment demands. Alternately, they may be contraprepared; that is, by virtue of their specialized evolutionary history, they may experience great difficulty in learning the association that a particular experiment demands. Finally, their position on the continuum may be intermediate: They may be unprepared. According to Seligman, this status typifies laboratory animals in most learning studies; consequently, the "general" laws of learning are really special cases that apply to unprepared situations.

The preparedness continuum imposes constraints on classical and operant conditioning as well as on more complex learning modes. Classical conditioning is the associative learning process whereby a reflex naturally produced by a biologically significant or unconditioned stimulus (US) comes to be elicited by an originally neutral or conditioned stimulus (CS) through repeated CS-US pairings. Operant conditioning is the process whereby animals come to link distinct consequences with distinct behavioral responses. The struggle for survival over evolutionary time within particular species has organized their learning capacities so that some CS-US and response-consequence connections form more or less readily than others.

Conditioned Taste Aversion

Genetic preparedness for specific CS-US connections was strongly suggested by a series of experiments by John Garcia and his collaborators on conditioned taste aversion. In the first and most widely cited of these studies, thirsty rats had access to two different water spouts. One spout delivered saccharine-sweetened ("tasty") water; the other gave unflavored water, but with each lick accompanied by both a flashing light and a clicking noise ("bright-noisy water"). Both tasty and bright-noisy water were potential conditioned stimuli. Afterward, some rats got electric shocks, some got heavy X-ray doses sufficient to induce nausea, and others were poisoned with lithium chloride. Two days later, the experimenters measured consumption of bright-noisy and tasty water. Rats that were sickened by either lithium chloride or X radiation avoided the tasty water but not the bright-noisy water, while those that were shocked displayed exactly opposite preferences. Later studies by Garcia and his coworkers obtained similar results, even when they stretched the

elapsed time between drinking flavored water (CS) and malaise (US) to twenty-four hours, a delay vastly longer than the seconds-long CS-US intervals usually required to demonstrate classical conditioning in the laboratory.

Conditioned taste aversion studies suggest that rats are highly prepared to associate a distinct taste with systemic illness. By contrast, they are relatively unprepared, or even contraprepared, to associate lights and sounds with nausea or taste with shock. These findings are consistent with their natural history. Rats are opportunists that readily exploit novel food sources. Given this predilection, survival is enhanced by the capacity to associate distinctive tastes with illness.

Avoidance and Reward Learning

Preparedness applies equally well to operant conditioning. Here, however, biological constraints influence the formation of response-consequence connections. A comparison of avoidance learning and reward learning in pigeons illustrates this. A study by Paul Brown and Herbert Jenkins published in 1968 demonstrated that pigeons quickly learn to peck lighted keys to obtain food rewards. Meanwhile, Philip Hineline and Howard Rachlin in 1969 showed that training pigeons to peck a key to avoid shock requires an enormous effort. Even then, one out of three pigeons does not learn the behavior. When wing flapping becomes the appropriate response, however, pigeons quickly learn to flap their wings to escape shock but not to get a food reward. Pigeons are prepared to associate pecking with a food reward and wing flapping with escape from shock. They are contraprepared to associate pecking with escape and flapping with feeding.

According to analyses published in 1970 by Robert Bolles and others, these findings accord well with the natural behavior of wild pigeons, but not with the principle of equipotentiality. Since pecking is an essential part of their feeding behavior, pigeons have no trouble associating it with feeding. Similarly, since flying away is their built-in defense against enemies, pigeons readily associate wing flapping with escape. Pecking to escape and flapping for food, however, are foreign to the intrinsic behavioral organization of pigeons. They are, accordingly, difficult for pigeons to learn.

Preparedness is by no means limited to the well-studied paradigms of operant and classical conditioning or to rats and pigeons. It is pervasive, applying to many forms of learning and many different species, including humans. Humans, like rats, also acquire conditioned taste aversions with great ease despite long CS-US intervals. More important, humans are highly prepared to use vocal sounds as the basis of a complex, grammatical language. Consequently, with minimal formal instruction, preschool children acquire language. By contrast, parents find preschoolers much less prepared to share or to sit still.

CONTRIBUTIONS TO PHOBIA STUDIES

The concept of preparedness has advanced both theory and practice in psychology. It has led to the wide acceptance of the principle that the evolutionary adaptation of species shapes their learning capacities. This insight is invaluable in animal training; it allows trainers to match particular species to particular learning tasks. The most influential application of preparedness, however, has been its use in understanding phobias—uncontrollable, debilitating fears of specific objects or situations.

In 1971, Seligman, inspired by Garcia's studies of conditioned taste aversion, advanced the thesis that phobias are special cases of prepared classical conditioning. As prepared fears, phobias would be rapidly acquired, resistant to extinction, irrational or insensitive to cognitive factors, and highly selective. Seligman observed that people acquire a disproportionate number of phobias to natural objects and situations, such as snakes, heights, and strangers, that threatened pretechnological people and their ancestors. In contrast, many truly hazardous modern innovations, such as power tools, motor vehicles, and electric outlets, seldom serve as phobic objects. Since the former class of objects do present some danger (but substantially less than the violent inventions of industry), Seligman argued that, over millions of years, natural selection—a major force of evolution, the process by which differential survival and reproductive success change the frequency of genes in a population—favored individuals who quickly learned to fear and avoid these natural dangers. Humans seem prepared to learn to fear some things but unprepared to fear other, more dangerous things. The nonarbitrary character of phobic associations accounts for other properties that Seligman ascribed to them: irrationality, ease of acquisition (the process by which an association is

formed in classical and operant conditioning), and resistance to extinction—persistence despite absence of reinforcement.

Beginning in the 1970's, Arne Öhman and others at the University of Uppsala systematically investigated the major dimensions of prepared fear conditioning and so developed a laboratory model of phobia for human subjects. Their typical experiment used electric shock as the US. They compared autonomic nervous system responses such as heart rate and skin conductance (a subtle indicator of fearful sweating) after conditioning either to pictures of fear-induced (snakes and spiders) or fear-irrelevant (triangles and flowers) conditioned stimuli. Preparedness theory holds that the classical conditioned responses to fear-relevant stimuli should share characteristics with phobias, such as ease of acquisition, irrationality, and resistance to extinction.

In one study, for example, in keeping with Seligman's notion that one-trial learning typifies phobias, Öhman and his colleagues successfully conditioned the skin-conductance response after only a single pairing of shock with spiders and snakes. In contrast, four or five such pairings were required to condition the fear-irrelevant stimuli. Similarly, the Uppsala group addressed the irrationality issue. They began by conditioning their subjects to either fear-relevant stimuli (snakes and spiders) or fear-irrelevant stimuli (houses). Next, the electrodes were removed and the subjects were told that they would get no more shocks. Skin-conductance responses to fear-irrelevant stimuli soon faded away, but those to fear-irrelevant stimuli persisted. Since positive information that the fear stimulus had been rendered harmless failed to reassure, persistent, autonomic fear reactions were interpreted as irrational and reminiscent of phobias. Finally, the Uppsala studies addressed resistance to extinction. Under normal laboratory conditions with unprepared conditioned stimuli, fear dissipates quickly when the CS is presented without reinforcement from the US. In more than a dozen studies by Öhman and his associates, conditioned fear responses to fear-relevant stimuli extinguished more slowly than those conditioned to fear-irrelevant stimuli. This finding is consistent with the clinical observation that phobias persist and often require special therapeutic procedures to become extinguished.

CRITICISMS AND REASSESSMENT

In 1987, Richard McNally published a comprehensive, critical review of preparedness studies. Although he conceded the central point of preparedness theory—that fears of evolutionary significance are overrepresented in clinical phobias—his survey also showed that attempts to replicate the findings of the Uppsala group regularly failed. Enhanced resistance to extinction of responses conditioned to fear-relevant stimuli emerged as the most consistently replicated finding. Many laboratories failed to confirm observations on ease of acquisition and irrationality. McNally attributed some of these difficulties to the fact that ethical considerations limited the intensity of unconditioned stimuli to non-painful levels. As a result, subjects may have been minimally fearful; the experimental situations may have lacked phobic terror.

Possibly in anticipation of such criticisms, Öhman, Ulf Dimberg, and Lars-Göran Öst refined the preparedness theory of phobias in 1985. They held that phobias could not be understood completely within the general framework of fear learning; in so doing, they moved the preparedness theory of phobia even further from general laws of learning than Seligman's formulation. Instead, they held that phobias must be understood as embedded within behavioral systems which provided the context for the evolution of specific prepared fears. A major feature of this revision was to treat animal and social phobias as different entities with contrasting ontogenic (developmental) and evolutionary histories. Thus, phobias for animals show links to predator avoidance, and social phobias (such as of public speaking) to social dominance hierarchies. As such, these phobias have contrasting developmental histories. For example, in keeping with the young mammal's vulnerability to predation, the onset of animal phobias appears early, typically before seven years. In contrast, social phobias usually emerge after puberty, when status becomes a pressing issue for socially living primates. Similarly, Öhman and his coauthors characterized animal phobias as an "avoidance package," while relating social phobias to submissiveness and communication of fear without the urge to avoid.

The many studies inspired by preparedness theory have promoted understanding of phobias and their development. They offer valuable insights into how typical clinical treatments work. They also suggest how phobias may be prevented in order to spare people the burden of a life dominated by fear.

PREPAREDNESS VERSUS EQUIPOTENTIALITY

The issue of preparedness versus equipotentiality and the generality of the laws of learning can be viewed as a skirmish within a long-standing philosophical dispute: the debate between the empiricists and the nativists. The empiricist position, articulated in the seventeenth century by John Locke, holds that human behavior, cognition, personality—indeed, humankind's entire psychological being—derives from experience. Locke likened the human infant to a blank tablet, a *tabula rasa*, upon which experience impressed its marks to form the individual's character. Nativists, exemplified by eighteenth century philosopher Immanuel Kant, made different claims. Kant argued that experience, although vital, could not totally account for a person's psychological being. Instead, he maintained that the human mind has inherent structures to which experience must accommodate.

An empiricist bias pervades psychology in general and behaviorism and learning theory in particular. Indeed, in the first decades of the twentieth century, nativist ideas in psychology ebbed so low that the founder of behaviorism, John B. Watson, would claim in 1925 that, if given a batch of healthy babies and total control of the environment, he could make them into anything he so chose—doctor, lawyer, beggar, thief.

INFLUENCE OF ETHOLOGY

The emergence of ethology (a branch of zoology devoted to the study of behavior under natural conditions) in the middle of the twentieth century, with its emphasis on instinct, tilted the balance in the direction of the nativists. At the same time, psychologists began to report compelling data that simply fell outside the framework of the empiricist, behavioral tradition. For example, Keller and Marian Breland discussed the occasional failure of operant conditioning procedures in animal training in an influential paper, "The Misbehavior of Organisms" (1961). They noted that such failures occurred when the operant behavior they were trying to shape interfered with innate responses related to food consumption. From such observations arose the biological boundaries of the learning movement of the

1970's, of which preparedness was an integral part. The 1980's and 1990's continued to witness an infusion of nativist, ethological views into the mainstream of learning psychology. The emergence of the concept of learning as an adaptive mechanism shaped by natural selection has led to continuing collaborative efforts between ethologists and psychologists.

SOURCES FOR FURTHER STUDY

Bolles, Robert C., and Michael D. Beecher, eds. *Evolution and Learning*. Hillsdale, N.J.: Lawrence Erlbaum, 1988. Presents a dozen essays describing how learning capacities and processes reflect an organism's evolutionary history. An essay by Bolles on the nativist-empiricist issue provides a philosophical context. This readable volume illustrates how concern with biological constraints on learning has developed into a productive interchange of ideas between the long-separated traditions of learning theory and ethology.

Klein, Stephen B., and Robert R. Mowrer, eds. *Contemporary Learning Theories: Instrumental Conditioning Theory and the Impact of Biological Constraints on Learning*. Hillsdale, N.J.: Lawrence Erlbaum, 1989. Contains a number of relevant essays dealing with issues such as phobias and taste aversion. Includes some unusual applications of the preparedness concept.

McNally, Richard. "Preparedness and Phobias: A Review." *Psychological Bulletin* 101, no. 2 (1987): 283-303. Summarizes and skeptically evaluates the evidence for the preparedness theory of phobia. Although difficult to read at points, the general reader should still be able to identify McNally's major points. The bibliography is extensive, if not definitive.

Öhman, Arne, Ulf Dimberg, and Lars-Göran Öst. "Animal and Social Phobias: Biological Constraints on Learned Fear Responses." In *Theoretical Issues in Behavior Therapy*, edited by Steven Reiss and Richard R. Bootzin. Orlando, Fla.: Academic Press, 1985. A summary and refinement of the position that phobias are examples of prepared conditioning. Clearly summarizes dozens of published studies, many of which are difficult to read in their original form.

Seligman, Martin E. P. "On the Generality of the Laws of Learning." *Psychological Review* 77 (September, 1970): 406-418. A well-written and exceptionally clear presentation of the concept of preparedness. Seligman's critique of general process learning theory remains a classic. In addition to its topical coverage, it provides a good example of a creative psychological synthesis.

Seligman, Martin E. P., and Joanne L. Hager, eds. *Biological Boundaries of Learning*. New York: Appleton-Century-Crofts, 1972. The single most important source of preparedness, this book collects all the important early literature under one cover. Includes the taste-aversion studies by John Garcia; classic experiments by Paul Brown and Herbert Jenkins, Philip Hineline and Howard Rachlin, Robert Bolles, and many others on preparedness and operant conditioning; Keller and Marian Breland's "The Misbehavior of Organisms"; and Seligman's "Phobias and Preparedness." Although some of the thirty-five papers are technical, many are well within the reach of general readers. Since the editors summarize and critique the technical reports, this collection is convenient to use.

Roy Fontaine

SEE ALSO: Behaviorism; Conditioning; Defense reactions: Species-specific; Ethology; Learning; Misbehavior; Pavlovian conditioning; Phobias; Radical behaviorism: B. F. Skinner; Skinner, B. F.; Taste aversion; Watson, John B.

Problem-solving stages

TYPE OF PSYCHOLOGY: Cognition
FIELDS OF STUDY: Problem solving

Problem-solving stages are the steps through which successful solutions to problems are obtained. Since problems are an inevitable and pervasive part of life, being successful at problem solving is an important asset.

KEY CONCEPTS
• algorithms
• evaluation
• heuristics
• implementation
• potential solutions
• problem

INTRODUCTION

Every person must solve problems every day. They solve problems as simple as deciding which television show to watch and as complex as deciding on a marriage partner. In either case, through effective thinking, a satisfactory answer can usually be found. Psychologists believe that there are a number of discrete stages in problem solving. Although they disagree over the exact number of stages required, as well as their exact descriptions and names, the following four stages are often described.

The first stage in problem solving is often called the information-gathering stage. During this stage, considerable information is collected, including the facts surrounding the problem, the goal or outcome desired, the major obstacles preventing a solution, and what information (knowledge) is needed to move toward the solution stage. One key factor in the information-gathering stage is the ability to separate relevant from irrelevant facts. Another key factor is assessing the problem accurately. A clear understanding of the problem is essential to problem solving.

In the second stage of problem solving, potential solutions are generated. Under normal situations, the more solutions generated, the better the chance of solving the problem, since a large number of potential solutions provides a wide choice of alternatives from which to draw. One method utilized in generating solutions is called trial and error. Here the would-be problem solver tries one approach and then another and perhaps arrives, by chance, at a solution. Although time consuming, exhaustive procedures such as trial and error do eventually result in a solution. Psychologists call any method that guarantees a solution to a problem an algorithm.

Once one or more possible solutions have been generated, it is necessary to choose a specific course of action. The third stage of problem solving, the implementation stage, begins with making a decision. In some problem-solving situations, a number of solutions may be appropriate or suitable. Yet, in comparison, some solutions may be better than others. Some solutions may involve less time and may be easier or more efficient to implement.

The implementation stage involves carrying out the specific plan of action. For many people, this stage of problem solving is difficult. Especially with difficult or complex problems, people are often reluctant to follow through on courses of action. Commitment to follow through is, in many ways, the turning point of problem solving. Intentions and plans of action become meaningless unless there is the commitment to carry them out.

The fourth and final stage of problem solving, in this model, is the evaluation stage. Once the solution or plan of action has been implemented, the person needs to consider whether it has met the original goal (the intended outcome). If not, the person needs to consider other plans of action. In some situations the person may need to retrace his or her steps—beginning again with stage two, the potential solutions stage. Eventually, with perseverance and commitment, workable solutions are usually found.

Another stage of problem solving worth consideration is incubation. Even though it is considered optional (occurring at some times and not others), incubation can be an important part of problem solving. Incubation refers to a period of time when the person stops thinking about the problem and focuses his or her attention on some other activity. During this time the solution may suddenly appear; it is often said to come "out of the blue."

Many people have experienced this sudden insight, and history is filled with reports of people who have made remarkable discoveries this way. Such reports point to the fact that it may be advisable to take time off from an unsolved problem. To continue to work ceaselessly on an unsolved problem may only create frustration.

TECHNIQUES FOR PROBLEM SOLVING

Heuristics are general strategies for problem solving that lessen the time and mental strain necessary for solving problems. Although much faster than algorithms—problem-solving methods that guarantee a solution—heuristics do not guarantee solutions as algorithms do. They work most of the time, but not always. A number of heuristic approaches exist. In "hill climbing," the person moves continually closer to the final goal without ever going backward. In subgoal analysis, a problem is broken down into smaller, more manageable steps.

One often-used heuristic technique combines hill climbing and subgoals. Means-end analysis compares a person's current position with the desired end (the goal). The idea is to reduce the distance to the goal. By dividing the problem into a number of smaller, more manageable subproblems, a solution may be reached. Another heuristic strategy is called working backward. With this strategy, the search for a solution begins at the goal, or end point, and moves backward to the person's current position.

Brainstorming is another popular problem-solving technique. Here people are asked to consider all possible solutions while, at the same time, not considering (judging) their immediate value or worth. The advantage of brainstorming is that it increases the diversity of solutions and promotes creative problem solving. So far, in stage two, various methods have been mentioned to generate potential solutions. Yet in real life, problem solving often bogs down, and solutions to problems (especially difficult or complex problems) are hard to find. The importance of perseverance in problem solving cannot be overemphasized.

Another method utilized in problem solving is called information retrieval. Here the would-be problem solver simply retrieves information from memory that appears to have solved similar problems in the past; however, information retrieval is limited. Many problems do not fit neatly into patterns of the past. Moreover, memory is not always reliable or accurate.

TYPES OF PROBLEMS

In a review of problem-solving research published in 1978, J. G. Greeno classified problems into three basic types: problems involving arrangement, problems that involve inducing structure, and problems of transformation.

Arrangement problems require the problem solver to arrange objects in a way that solves the problem. An example is arranging the letters *t, g, l, h* and *i* to spell "light." Solving such problems often involves much trial and error.

A second type of problem requires a person to discover a pattern or structure that will relate elements of the problems to one another. For example, in solving the problem, "2 is to 4 as 5 is to _____," the problem solver discovers that 4 is twice as large as 2. Thus, the number needed to solve the problem may be twice as large as 5; that number is 10. Another possible solution is 7, because both the difference between 2 and 4 and that between 5 and 7 is 2.

The third type of problem is one of transformation. Transformation problems differ from the other two types by providing the goal rather than requiring solvers to produce it. Word problems that give the answer and require a person to find the means to the solution are one example.

EXAMPLES OF PROBLEM SOLVING

Typically, progress through problem-solving stages is done in a relatively short time. Other situations require more time. Days, weeks, or months may be needed. The following hypothetical examples show how the stages of problem solving can be applied to real-life situations.

Jim has a problem. A friend of his, Bob, recently returned from a year of studying in France. Upon meeting Jim, Bob was cold and distant; he was not like the person Jim once knew, who was jovial, warm, and happy. Moreover, Bob did not want to associate with Jim. Jim is surprised, hurt, and confused; he does not know what he should do.

First, Jim needs to gather all the information he can. This represents the first stage of problem solving. Jim talks with Bob's parents, other family members, and students who were with him in France. After collecting this information and separating the relevant facts from the irrelevant ones, Jim notes that his friend's disposition changed dramatically after his breakup with a girlfriend after a six-month relationship. Jim notes that the presenting problem (Bob being cold and distant) is, under close scrutiny, not the "real" problem. Bob's present behavior is only a symptom (a consequence) of the real problem, which centers on the breakup of the relationship.

Jim wishes to help his friend. He talks with Bob's family about what can be done. Together they produce three possible solutions. After comparing the solutions, they decide that the best solution would be for Bob to seek personal counseling. Together they encourage Bob to make an appointment at the local mental health center. If Bob implements this plan of action, he may get the help he needs. If this does not work, the family and Jim will need to reevaluate the situation and try another plan of action.

Susan's assignment is to write a history paper; however, history has been a difficult subject for her in the past. She needs to do well on this paper to keep her grade-point average high. Susan needs to gather as much information as she can on her topic. She then needs to separate the relevant information from the more trivial or irrelevant. Next she needs to consider potential solutions to ensure a quality paper. She breaks down the paper-writing process into separate tasks (subgoals): preparing an outline, writing the first draft, editing, and rewriting. She executes the plan, doing one task at a time. After the final draft, she asks a classmate to read her paper and make comments and suggestions. Finally, with a few modifications (revisions), Susan's paper is ready to be submitted.

Ellen is a high school senior. Her goal is to become a lawyer, but she is unsure of what steps she must take to accomplish this goal. Her first step is to gather all the information she can on how to become a lawyer. She begins by surveying the literature on lawyers in her public library. She also checks with her high school counselor. The counselor gives her some of the specifics: the number of years required for college and law school; the best courses to take as an undergraduate student; the admissions tests necessary for college and law school; the cost of college and law school (including sources of financial aid).

Her next two steps are to devise a plan of action and to implement this plan. She begins by taking a college entrance examination and applying to the college of her choice. After being accepted, she plans her course of studies, keeping in mind the educational requirements of law school. Early in the fall semester of her senior year, she takes the law school admission test and then applies to law school. If she is accepted to law school, her goal of becoming a lawyer is within reach. If she is not accepted, she needs to revise her plan of action or even her goal. She may need to apply to another law school, retake the law school admission test if her score was low, or consider another option—perhaps becoming a paralegal or law assistant, or changing fields entirely.

Steve's car breaks down, and he has it towed to the garage. The mechanic on duty, whether he realizes it or not, applies various stages of problem solving. First of all, he gathers information by asking Steve what happened. Steve states that he was driving down Main Street and suddenly the motor stopped. The mechanic thus focuses on things which can cause the motor to stop suddenly (the potential solutions stage). The most obvious is a problem with the electrical system. After checking various electrical components (the implementation stage), the mechanic notes that the ignition coil is dead. After replacing the coil, the mechanic attempts to start the car (the evaluation stage). The car starts.

EVOLUTION OF PROBLEM-SOLVING RESEARCH

Various writers have attempted to analyze the stages in problem solving. One of the first attempts was that of John Dewey in 1910. Dewey's five stages utilized the "scientific method" to solve problems systematically through the reasoning process. The five stages are becoming aware of the difficulty; identifying the problem; assembling and classifying data and formulating hypotheses; accepting or rejecting the tentative hypotheses; and formulating conclusions and evaluating them.

Another attempt to analyze the stages of problem solving was that of Graham Wallas in 1926. He proposed that problem solving consisted of the following four steps: preparation, incubation, illumination, and verification. Gyrgy Plya, in 1957, also considered problem solving as involving four stages: understanding the problem, devising a plan, carrying out the plan, and checking the results. In *The IDEAL Problem Solver* (1984), John Bransford and Barry Stein outline a method of problem solving based on the letters IDEAL: *I*dentify the problem; *D*efine the problem; *E*xplore possible strategies; *A*ct on the strategies; and *L*ook at the effects of one's efforts.

One of the most famous scientific studies of the stages in problem solving was that of Karl Duncker in 1945. In his study, subjects were given a problem and asked to report aloud how their thinking processes were working. After examining the subject's responses, Duncker found that problem solving did indeed involve a sequence of stages. Presently, computers are used to solve problems. One of the early attempts to use computers in this way was called the general problem solver (GPS), devised by Allen Newell, J. C. Shaw, and Herbert Simon. Historically, problem solving has not been an area of wide research or interest; however, with increasing interest in cognitive psychology and its emphasis on thinking processes, the study of problem solving seems to have a secure future. Considering the number and scope of the problems that face people from day to day, it seems reasonable to continue—and even expand—the study of problem solving.

SOURCES FOR FURTHER STUDY

Andriole, Stephen J. *Handbook of Problem Solving.* Princeton, N.J.: Petrocelli Books, 1983. This book is designed to reach people of all disciplines who are interested in strengthening their problem-solving skills. It contains methods and techniques which can be used to solve problems of all kinds.

Benjamin, Ludy T., J. Roy Hopkins, and Jack R. Nation. *Psychology*. 3d ed. New York: Macmillan, 1994. In a section on problem solving, describes in detail the stages involved. The authors also list many of the procedures used to find solutions. A discussion on hindrances or obstacles to problem solving follows the section.

Bransford, John, and Barry S. Stein. *The IDEAL Problem Solver.* 2d ed. New York: W. H. Freeman, 1993. Chapter 2 presents a simple but powerful approach to problem solving based on the five components that make up the IDEAL approach. This book is easy to read, abundant in examples, clear, and concise. Excellent for anyone who needs help in solving problems.

Hayes, John R. *The Complete Problem Solver.* 2d ed. Hillsdale, N.J.: Lawrence Erlbaum, 1989. Attempts to teach general problem-solving skills. This book is written for the general public and offers help to anyone interested in solving problems.

Huffman, Karen, et al. *Psychology in Action.* 6th ed. New York: John Wiley & Sons, 2001. In a section on problem solving, the authors describe the stages as well as the barriers in problem solving. Examples are given; key words are explained. A good source for high school seniors and college freshmen.

Ted Eilders

See also: Artificial intelligence; Computer models of cognition; Concept formation; Decision making; Logic and reasoning; Problem-solving strategies; Thought: Inferential.

Problem-solving strategies

Type of psychology: Cognition
Fields of study: Cognitive processes; problem solving

Problem solving is one of the most basic tasks of life; psychologists have studied various obstacles to solving problems and have identified many of the strategies used in solving different types of problems.

Key concepts
- artificial intelligence
- computer simulation
- difference reduction
- functional fixedness
- means-ends analysis
- mental set effect
- problem solving by analogy
- working backward

Introduction

Problem solving is a complex process that involves the use of cognitive skill, prior experiences and their memories, and general knowledge about how the world works. In other words, people use logical thinking and reasoning, memory, and common sense when trying to solve any problem. When psychologists study problem solving, the process is typically divided into three steps: forming a representation of the problem, using a strategy to plan an approach to the problem, and executing the strategy and checking the results. This basic sequence is repeated each time one encounters a problem. First, one must understand the nature of the problem. Second, one thinks of different ways that the problem could be solved, relying on one's reasoning skills, memory for similar problems, and/or common sense. Third, one attempts to solve the problem with whatever strategy was formed and, if unsuccessful, forms another strategy and tries again. For example, when a sports team plays a game, first the players study the other team, looking for strengths and weaknesses. Then a game plan is formed and executed. The process can fail at any step: The team members might not really understand their opponents, a bad game plan may be formed, or the implementation of the plan may fail. The inability to complete any step in the process results in an obstacle to solving the problem, whatever that may be.

An old story describes the problem-solving ability of a college student taking a physics examination. One question on the exam asked how a barometer could be used to measure the height of a building (a barometer is a device sensitive to changes in atmospheric pressure). The student responded that a string could be tied to the barometer and lowered from the roof of the building, and then the string could be measured. The professor found this solution unacceptable, since it did not rely on a principle from physics. The student's second solution was to drop the barometer from the roof and measure the time it took to hit the ground, then calculate the height of the building using a formula involving gravity. Since this was not the solution for which the professor was looking, the student next suggested that the barometer be placed near the building on a sunny day and the height of the barometer as well as the length of the shadows from the barometer and building be measured. Then the student could develop two ratios and solve for the unknown quantity. While the professor was impressed, the student had not provided the desired solution, and the professor gave the student one more chance. If the student could think of one more method of using the barometer to discover the height of the building, the professor would give full credit. The student finally suggested that they find the owner of the building and say, "If you tell me how tall the building is, I will give you this barometer."

THREE TYPES OF STRATEGIES

Three different types of problem-solving strategies emerge when the issue is studied systematically: means-ends analysis, working backward, and problem solving by analogy. In means-ends analysis, the person examines and compares the solutions desired (sometimes called the goal state) with the methods (the means) available. When making this comparison of where one is to where one wants to be, subgoals are usually generated in such a way that when all the subgoals are completed, the problem is solved. For example, while the ultimate goal in planning a wedding is for two people to be married, there are also several subgoals to be considered, such as a marriage license, a minister, a place to be married, and what to wear. A person using means-ends analysis might develop subgoals to accomplish over time, keeping the ultimate goal in mind. This procedure of identifying the difference between the current state and the ultimate goal state and working to reduce the differences by using subgoals is called difference reduction, a particular form of means-ends analysis.

A second problem-solving strategy is to work backward. When one knows what the solution should be, often one can then work backward from the solution to fill in the means to the end. In solving a maze, for example, one may start working on the maze by beginning at the end line and working backward to the start line. After misplacing some-

thing, one often retraces one's steps, working backward to try to find the item. Another example is the person who wants to have a set amount of money left after paying all the bills. Working the problem in the forward direction (that is, paying the bills and seeing what is left over) may not result in the desired goal; starting with the goal first, however, can achieve the overall desired solution.

It should be noted that the working-backward strategy works only when the solution (or goal state) is known or believed to be known. When it is unknown, working backward cannot work. That is the case with a mechanic who is trying to fix a car when the exact cause of the malfunction is unknown. Although the desired solution is known (a working car), tracing the path backward does not work. In this type of situation, the mechanic is likely to try a means-ends strategy (for example, testing each major system of the car) or to use the next strategy, problem solving by analogy.

Solving problems by using analogies relies on the use of memories from prior problem-solving situations and the application of this information in solving a new problem. Often the initial representation of the problem may trigger memories for similar problems solved in the past. At other times, a person may actively search in memory for analogous or similar situations, then retrieve and apply such information.

The American educational system is largely based on the strategy of problem solving by analogy. Children are taught the facts, figures, and skills that are analogous to the facts, figures, and skills necessary in later life. Education is meant to be the prior experience, to be used in solving later problems. Homework is based on the idea of problem solving by analogy—providing early experiences that may be applicable to later problems (such as on a test).

FUNCTIONAL FIXEDNESS

The three general steps in the problem-solving process are problem representation, strategy formation, and execution of the strategy. Many obstacles in solving everyday problems are particularly sensitive to the role of problem representation. Two examples of common obstacles in problem solving are functional fixedness and mental set effects.

Functional fixedness is the idea that people often focus on the given function of an object while neglecting other potentially novel uses. Norman R. F.

Maier in 1931 demonstrated functional fixedness in his now-classic two-string problem. In this problem, two strings hang from the ceiling of a room, too far apart for a person to reach both at once. Yet the strings are long enough to reach one another and be tied. The problem is to tie the strings together. The only objects available to the person are a chair, some paper, and a pair of pliers. Maier found that most people he tested exhibited functional fixedness (that is, they did not use the items in the room in novel ways to solve the problem). Those that did solve the problem realized they needed to attach a weight (the pliers) to one string and swing the string like a pendulum to tie the strings together, thus avoiding functional fixedness.

Another classic example of functional fixedness can be found in Karl Duncker's 1945 candle-and-box problem. In this problem, people are presented with a candle, a box of tacks, and a book of matches; the problem is to attach the candle to the wall so that the candle can burn in its upright, proper position. People who possess functional fixedness are unable to see the box holding the tacks as a candle holder, emptied and attached to the wall, with the candle attached to the top of the box. Whenever one uses a knife or a dime as a screwdriver, one is showing a lack of functional fixedness—one is using an object in a manner for which it was not intended.

MENTAL SET EFFECTS

A second general obstacle in problem solving is called a mental set. A mental set is a conceptual block that prevents the appearance of an appropriate problem solution. Set effects most often occur because of sheer repetition of information (therefore, one does not search for alternative solutions) or because of a preconceived notion about the problem. One example of the mental set effect comes from Abraham Luchins's water-jug problem. In this problem, people were given three water jugs—A, B, and C—and the task was to manipulate the water in the jugs to obtain a desired quantity. For example, jug A holds 21 cups of water, jug B holds 127 cups, and jug C holds 3 cups; the desired amount is exactly 100 cups. The desired amount can be reached by filling B once, pouring once into jug A, then pouring twice into jug C. This answer can be expressed as "B – A – 2C" (or "127 – 21 – 3 – 3 = 100"). Luchins gave people a series of problems, all which could be

solved by this formula; however, he would occasionally include a problem that could also be solved by a simpler formula, such as A – C. People continued to use the more complex formula. Luchins thought that people get into a rut or mental set, and when the set yields positive results, they do not bother to exert effort to change (even when a simpler method exists).

NINE-DOT PROBLEM

A different example of the importance of problem representation is found with the "nine-dot problem." In the nine-dot problem, three rows of three dots each must be connected by four straight lines, with the restriction that the pen or pencil cannot be lifted from the page. The natural box shape that the dots form presents an obstacle similar to mental set—people cannot solve the problem until they realize that the lines must go outside the perceived square before the problem can be solved.

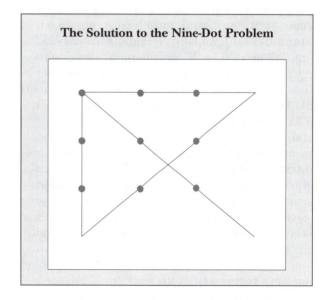

The Solution to the Nine-Dot Problem

IMPLICATIONS FOR PSYCHOLOGICAL STUDY

The formal study of problem solving is almost as old as the field of psychology itself. As early as 1898, Edward L. Thorndike studied the problem-solving ability of cats trying to escape from a puzzle box. This box was designed with levers, pulleys, and latches so that when the cat made a particular response inside, the door to the box would open and the cat could escape. Thorndike found that the cats could remember the escape sequence and that each time the cat was placed in the box, it escaped more quickly. He considered problem-solving ability as evidence of learning and called it the stamping in of behavior. Wolfgang Köhler in 1925 studied chimpanzees and found that they could experience a flash of insight (sometimes called the "aha!" phenomenon) in solving a problem, just as humans do. In the 1930's and 1940's, Edward Tolman studied the problem-solving abilities of rats in different types of mazes and found them to be very good at navigating a maze.

Problem solving is an exciting area in psychology because it is a basic, universal characteristic of all humans. Everyone faces a number of problems each day. To understand how people solve problems is, to a large degree, to understand basic human behavior, the goal of every psychologist. The importance of problem-solving strategies and obstacles lie at the foundation of understanding humankind.

The future is bright for those interested in the study of problem solving. The increasing use of computer technology has advanced the field considerably. Computer simulations are used in an attempt to emulate (mimic) how humans solve problems. In this approach, the human is most important. In other words, computer simulations are valuable in helping to understand why people do the things they do. Artificial intelligence, on the other hand, uses computer technology to seek the best possible and most efficient solutions to problems—not necessarily mimicking the processes of humans. In the study of artificial intelligence, the problem is the most important aspect. Regardless of the specific area of study, the various strategies and obstacles observed by psychologists make intriguing work, and they lie at the very heart of what humans continually do—solve problems.

SOURCES FOR FURTHER STUDY

Anderson, John R. *Cognitive Psychology and Its Implications.* 5th ed. New York: W. H. Freeman, 1999. This text is a long-standing classic in the field of cognitive psychology. Containing a chapter on problem solving, it is both scholarly and thorough. Much of the emphasis in the problem-solving chapter is on computer applications and their importance in the problem-solving field.

Eysenck, Michael W., and Mark T. Keane. *Cognitive Psychology: A Student's Handbook.* 4th ed. New York: Psychology Press, 2000. A textbook that covers the full range of topics in cognitive psychol-

ogy. The chapter on problem solving and reasoning is particularly good, and it is presented in a format unlike that of other textbooks.

Kalat, J. W. *Introduction to Psychology.* 6th ed. Belmont, Calif.: Wadsworth, 2001. This general psychology textbook presents an excellent introduction to problem solving in the cognition chapter, as well as related topics in other chapters (such as learning, memory, and intelligence). This text is easy to read, with good examples. Includes a comprehensive reference section if the reader desires more information.

Mayer, R. E. *Thinking, Problem Solving, Cognition.* 2nd ed. New York: W. H. Freeman, 1992. A book primarily dedicated to the topic of problem solving, which is unusual. The format of the text is interesting and creative, covering the historical perspective of problem solving, basic thinking tasks, an information-processing analysis, and implications and applications.

R. Eric Landrum

SEE ALSO: Concept formation; Creativity and intelligence; Decision making; Group decision making; Learning; Logic and reasoning; Problem-solving stages; Thought: Inferential.

Profiling

DATE: The nineteenth century forward
TYPE OF PSYCHOLOGY: Motivation; personality; social psychology
FIELDS OF STUDY: Aggression; attitudes and behavior; intelligence assessment; interpersonal relations; models of abnormality; personality assessment

Profiling is a psychological methodology which is used to collect information about known or unidentified individuals or groups to assess their psychological characteristics and how they relate to perpetuating a crime, participating in a behavior, or being victimized.

KEY CONCEPTS
- behavioral patterns
- forensic psychology
- intuition

- investigation
- motivations
- personality

INTRODUCTION

Profiling originated in the nineteenth century, when anthropologists hypothesized that criminals' psychological and physical traits could be correlated. Early efforts revealed that evaluating criminals' behavioral patterns during a police investigation aided in understanding their motivations and predicting future crimes they might commit and victims they might choose. Such techniques encouraged law enforcement personnel reliant on traditional criminology methods to comprehend and pursue elusive, anonymous perpetrators.

Edgar Allan Poe's fictional detective C. August Dupin foreshadowed behavioral profiling in the 1841 short story "The Murders in the Rue Morgue." Factual profiling received public attention in the late 1880's in London, when police surgeon Dr. Thomas Bond profiled the serial killer Jack the Ripper by reconstructing crime scenes to study behaviors during the murders, such as covering victims' faces with a sheet and the repetition of wound patterns. Although Bond speculated about the age, demeanor, and appearance of Jack the Ripper, no suspects were ever convicted.

During World War II, the Office of Strategic Services (OSS), the predecessor of the Central Intelligence Agency (CIA), profiled Adolf Hitler's personality characteristics. Psychiatrist Walter Langer evaluated Hitler's behavior in order to help military authorities develop a strategy to interrogate Hitler if he were captured. Langer accurately speculated that Hitler would commit suicide instead of surrendering. In later conflicts, the U.S. military utilized expert profiling of other enemy leaders such as Saddam Hussein and Osama bin Laden in an attempt to develop military plans to capture them and prevent terrorist actions they sponsored.

In the mid-twentieth century, psychiatrist James Brussels successfully profiled a serial bomber who terrorized New York City. Police were startled that profile details such as the bomber wearing a buttoned, double-breasted suit proved accurate when the criminal was apprehended.

MODERN PROFILING

The foundation of modern profiling is the realization that behavior reflects personality and that criminal actions satisfy the perpetrators' psychological or physical needs. Profilers attempt to think like both criminals and victims to comprehend why and how a crime occurred, and the role played in the crime by both perpetrators and victims. Behavioral scientists recognize that although every crime is unique, human behavior matches patterns.

Affiliated with law enforcement officers who share evidence, profilers use scientific methods supplemented with their instincts about aberrant behavior to create a psychological profile for each murderer. The serial nature of crimes such as kidnaping, rape, molestation, and arson provide profilers with patterns to examine for behavioral consistencies and deviations. Isolated incidents, such as theft, carjacking, and vandalism, are not as successfully profiled.

Computer databases have proven less reliable than profilers' intuition about specific individuals because of the variability of factors among criminals. Profiling is constantly developing to meet law enforcement needs. Cyberprofiling seeks to identify people who commit electronic crimes, such as hacking, based on behavior associated with that activity. Profilers choose techniques from several methods that they consider most useful.

THE FEDERAL BUREAU OF INVESTIGATION

In the 1960's, Howard Teten, a California police officer became a U.S. Federal Bureau of Investigation (FBI) special agent and collaborated with Pat Mullany, a specialist in abnormal psychological, to teach how crime scene evidence revealed behavioral clues. Teten initiated a course on applied criminology at the FBI Academy in 1970. In the late twentieth century, the FBI's Behavioral Science Unit (BSU) professionalized profiling as a form of forensic psychology. After Teten retired in 1978, director John Douglas and his colleague Robert Ressler emphasized organized (premeditated)/disorganized (impulsive) methodology to evaluate how criminals behaved at crime scenes.

From 1979 to 1983, BSU personnel interviewed prisoners concerning biographical information, their criminal actions, and choice of victims and sites. The BSU agents also collected court, police, and psychiatric records to compile a database useful for future profiling. The FBI's National Center for the Analysis of Violent Crime (NCAVC), established in

1984, helped law enforcement efforts to detect similar criminal activity in various jurisdictions.

PROFILING "ANONYMOUS"

The FBI's Crime Classification Manual outlines how psychological profiles should be compiled and evaluated. Offender profiling focuses on the behavior of criminals and how they commit crimes, comparing these profiles with established personality types and mental disorders. Investigative profiling studies evidence from crime scenes.

Profiling is a powerful forensic tool to solve seemingly unsolvable cases. When suspects are unknown, profilers can find psychological clues in the choices the culprit made, such as selection and number of victims, crime site, weapons, and alteration of the crime scene by destroying items, displaying bodies, or taking souvenirs.

The first investigation stage involves profiling the victim and noting any associations with the assailant or what the victim might have symbolized to the attacker. Profilers hypothesize how the criminal behaved with the victim and the motivation for the crime, specifically whether it was a planned or impulsive act and if it was based on anger and the need for power or because of a mental disorder or stimulant abuse. The assailant's behavior before and after the crime is also explored.

The use of weapons and restraints is evaluated and offers insight to the assailant's social skills, intellectual abilities, demographic description of race and age, and socioeconomic, marital, and employment status. Profilers speculate about the relationship the criminal has with family members and neighbors and any possible military service. Specific traits such as cowardice and feelings of inadequacy are identified in profiles.

Also, profilers assess any messages left by the criminal for law enforcement officers, media, or victims' family members. They integrate police and autopsy reports and interview survivors and witnesses to consider their perspectives about the assailant's personalities. Profiles provide a psychological identity to guide law enforcement personnel to find suspects who match specific behavioral patterns.

If they are aware of profiling, some criminals may purposefully alter their behavior to avoid apprehension, although some psychological traits are difficult to hide. Profilers look for any efforts at deception and focus on how offenders' signatures, which are behaviors not essential to the crime but which satisfy the offender, are present at crime scenes. If a suspect is captured, the profile is essential to the interrogation process.

INVESTIGATIVE PSYCHOLOGY

In 1985, Scotland Yard requested David Canter help incorporate psychological concepts into investigation methods. Although dubious, Canter successfully utilized environmental psychology methods to identify John Duffy as the so-called Railway Rapist. Canter's work established investigative psychology (IP) in the United Kingdom. Like the FBI, Canter used statistical information concerning criminal offenders and offenses. His five-factor IP model focuses on how criminals and victims interact.

First, interpersonal coherence examines how criminals act with victims and is based on the assumption that they treat people similarly in both criminal and noncriminal interactions. This factor suggests that victims represent significant people to assailants, such as former spouses or parents, toward whom the criminal is expressing symbolic rage. Second, Canter states that the time and place of crimes is significant to determine facts about the criminal's lifestyle. Third, criminal characteristics are assessed, although Canter disagrees with the FBI, saying that organized and disorganized classifications of criminals are misleading because a criminal might display both behaviors.

Fourth, Canter says profilers should consider whether assailants have previously been criminally active, and, if so, what crimes they have committed and for what duration they have engaged in a criminal career. Such experiences might have resulted in skills or behaviors demonstrated during the crime which would reduce the number of possible suspects. The final factor is forensic awareness, which assesses whether culprits are knowledgeable enough of investigation procedures for gathering evidence to wear gloves or remove incriminating items from scenes. In addition, Canter's offender behavior model, the circle theory, describes a marauder model, in which criminals operate from a base, and a commuter model, in which assailants travel to commit crimes.

BEHAVIORAL EVIDENCE ANALYSIS

Brent Turvey, a California forensic scientist, developed behavioral evidence analysis (BEA). Unlike other profiling methods, BEA reconstructs criminal events rather than psychologically interpreting an offender's behavior. By examining police, autopsy, and court records, Turvey recognizes how criminals can appear charming and gregarious but lie. His BEA profiling technique stresses that criminals frequently distort descriptions of their actions, which can influence reconstruction of their criminal behavior.

Four investigative steps occur in two phases. First, equivocal forensic analysis studies evidence to determine its most probable meaning. Second is victimology, in which the role of the victim is analyzed. The third step begins with crime scene characteristics, investigating why that location was chosen and its possible meanings to the criminal. Profilers decide if the site is a primary or secondary crime scene and if victims were moved. The final step focuses on offender characteristics, to assess the criminal's personality based on the previous three steps.

The investigative phase of BEA occurs when profilers develop a description of an unknown criminal type who is likely to have committed a known crime to provide investigators with leads. The trial phase evaluates evidence when a suspected culprit for a specific crime is known to assist investigators in conducting interrogations.

PUBLIC REACTION

Profiling success rates range from 50 to 85 percent. Profilers must objectively examine criminals' perceptions and how their behavior reveals their motivations without interjecting their moral values. Misrepresentations of profilers, often romanticizing them as being psychic, abound in films, television, fiction, and true-crime books. As a result, many law enforcement officers ignore or dismiss profiling. Others rely on imprecise profiles. A 1993 profile of the Unabomber based on his victims, which suggested he was highly educated in science and held antitechnology views, was discarded in favor of a profile which said the Unabomber was a blue-collar aviation worker. As a result, the apprehension of mathematician Theodore Kaczynski was delayed because of the focus on invalid suspects.

Critics express concern that innocent people might be falsely arrested, convicted, and imprisoned based on profiles which they consider to be individuals' hunches instead of evidence. Such profiling opponents cite errors by leading profilers, including

Douglas, who stresses that profiling can be fallible and should not replace a comprehensive investigation. Some people believe local investigators rather than FBI agents should profile suspects. Legal authorities note that, occasionally, organized offenders can leave a disorganized crime scene if they are committing crimes spurred by retaliation, drugs, or domestic violence. Such crime scenes might mislead profilers to describe incorrectly a perpetrator's behavior.

Many legal courts do not permit profiles to be submitted as evidence during trials because they do not prove an individual committed a specific crime, only that the person fits the profile of someone who could have been the perpetrator.

NONFORENSIC PSYCHOLOGICAL PROFILES

Noncriminal psychological profiling applications gauge personality characteristics compatible with professional, leisure, and consumer interests. Profiles can alert potential employers about possibly hazardous workers. They can also highlight employees who have the potential to be successful at various tasks. Psychological profiling can be incorporated into therapies to help patients understand their career and entertainment interests and modify their behavior.

Because of increased school violence, some schools are using psychological profiling to identify students who might pose safety risks. This intervention process is considered controversial because it relies on speculation and can unjustly accuse students, because no standard profile for violent students exists and children displaying identified behaviors exhibit them in varying degrees of intensity.

Some psychological profiling is unable to pinpoint assailants because of the diversity of people who exhibit shared psychological characteristics such as road rage. Racial profiling, often heightened after violent acts committed by members of a specific ethnic group, has been disputed as an ineffective way to identify possible culprits.

SOURCES FOR FURTHER STUDY

Canter, David V. *Criminal Shadows: Inside the Mind of the Serial Killer.* New York: HarperCollins, 1995. Discussion by leading British authority concerning the use of environmental psychology for behavioral profiling.

Douglas, John E., with Mark Olshaker. *Mindhunter: Inside the FBI's Elite Serial Crime Unit.* New York: Charles Scribner's Sons, 1995. Autobiography by pioneer FBI profiler explaining the development and application of investigative profiling methodology.

Holmes, Ronald M., and Stephen T. Holmes. *Profiling Violent Crimes: An Investigative Tool.* 2d ed. Thousand Oaks, Calif.: Sage Publications, 1996. Provides case studies as examples of successful psychological profiling.

Ressler, Robert K., and Tom Shachtman. *I Have Lived in the Monster.* New York: St. Martin's Press, 1997. Interviews, by a leading FBI profiler, with serial killers and commentary how such profiles aid criminal investigations.

Towl, Graham J., and David A. Crighton. *The Handbook of Psychology for Forensic Practitioners.* New York: Routledge, 1996. Guide for law enforcement personnel using psychological methods.

Turvey, Brent E. *Criminal Profiling: An Introduction to Behavioral Evidence Analysis.* San Diego, Calif.: Academic Press, 1999. Comprehensive account of how psychological profiles developed by reconstructing offenders' behavior based on crime scene evidence can help criminal investigators identify and capture culprits.

Wrightsman, Lawrence S. *Forensic Psychology.* Belmont, Calif.: Wadsworth Thomson Learning, 2001. Describes how profiling can supplement traditional investigative techniques.

Zonderman, Jon. *Beyond the Crime Lab: The New Science of Investigation.* Rev. ed. New York: John Wiley & Sons, 1999. Includes information about electronic psychological profiling.

Elizabeth D. Schafer

SEE ALSO: Forensic psychology; Law and psychology; Personality theory.

Projection

TYPE OF PSYCHOLOGY: Personality
FIELDS OF STUDY: Personality assessment

Projective personality traits are often assessed by tests which present ambiguous material to the person being tested; all behavior is included under the definition of personality, and responses to unstructured tests will reveal an individual's needs, wishes, and attitudes. It is assumed that the person will give responses that cannot or will not be given otherwise.

KEY CONCEPTS
• defense mechanisms
• projective method
• psychopathology

INTRODUCTION

The concept of projection goes back to Sigmund Freud (1858-1939), who introduced this term to describe certain psychopathological processes. It was described as a defense which permits one to be "unaware of undesirable aspects of one's personality by attributing aggressive and or sexual feelings to others or to the outside world." In that way, one can avoid being aware of those feelings in oneself. Projection is usually described as a defense mechanism whose purpose is to avoid feeling guilty or neurotically anxious. Freud's theory suggested that it was easier to tolerate punishment from the outside than to accept impulses inconsistent with one's self-concept and moral principles. Thus, it is simpler to accuse someone else of hating oneself than it is to admit hating the other person. Defense mechanisms are unconscious processes; one is not likely to admit consciously that one hates someone if one is neurotically anxious. In its extreme forms, Freud noted, distortion of reality can be of such major proportions that perception of the judgment of others takes the form of paranoia.

Freud later extended the use of the term "projection" to include times when there is no conflict. He believed that as one goes through life, memories of past events influence the way one sees the present. Early life experiences shape the future so that, for example, the kind of experiences one had with a brother when growing up influences how one sees "brothers" relate to their families. This leads to the basic assumption that all present responses to one's environment are based, as Albert Rabin put it, on personal needs, motivations, and unique tendencies. All of these are actually based on past experiences. Sheldon Korchin suggested that the weakening of the boundaries between self and others also occurs in empathy, which has been viewed as the opposite of projection. In empathy, one figuratively puts oneself in another person's shoes by accepting and experiencing the feelings of another person. Empathy, therefore, is an important part of establishing close and meaningful relationships with others and is an important aspect of personality.

Leopold Bellak saw projection as the term one uses to describe a greater degree of overall distortion. This is consistent with Freud's original use of the term. He differentiated this pathological and unconscious type of projection, which he called inverted projection, from simple projection. Simple projection occurs all the time and is not of great clinical significance.

For example, a woman wants to borrow her friend's hedge trimmer. As she walks down the block to her friend's house, she thinks about how she is going to ask for the hedge trimmer, since she knows that her friend is not overly enthusiastic about lending his garden tools. She begins to think that her friend might say that it took her a long time to return the trimmer the last time she borrowed it and perhaps that it needed maintenance after she used it. She answers this imagined comment by saying that it rained soon after she started and that she could not finish the job for three days.

She then imagines that her friend will say that she should have returned the trimmer and asked for it again later. She imagines answering that criticism by stating that she knew her friend had gone out of town and would not be back until later in the week. This imaginary conversation might continue until she arrives at her neighbor's house. Her neighbor is on the porch, and he greets her in a friendly manner. Nevertheless, she responds angrily by telling him that she would never want to borrow his old hedge trimmer anyway. Bellak would explain this incident by noting that the woman wants something from her neighbor but can recall his hesitancy to lend tools: He may turn her request down, which makes her angry. She then assumes that her friend is angry with her. Her response is to be angry with him because he is angry with her.

PROJECTIVE HYPOTHESIS AND TECHNIQUES

The projective hypothesis on which projective tests are based states that when one is confronted by an ambiguous stimulus, responses will reflect personal needs, wishes, and overall attitudes toward the outside world. This assumes that all of one's behavior, even the least significant aspects, is an expression of personality. As Anneliese Korner asserted, individuals who are presented with ambiguous material give responses that they cannot or will not give otherwise. The person who responds to projective techniques does not know what the presenter expects. The resistance to disclosing personal material (including wishes, fears, and aspirations) is diminished. In addition, Korner suggested that what is disclosed in response to projective techniques is not a chance event but is determined by previous life experiences.

Among the most widely known tests that use projective techniques are the Rorschach inkblot test and Henry Murray's Thematic Apperception Test (TAT). The Rorschach technique consists of ten standard inkblots to which a participant is asked to respond by telling the examiner what the blots look like. The TAT consists of twenty pictures designed to elicit stories which can give important clues to a person's life and personality. The set is sufficiently clear to permit one to tell stories without great difficulty, yet the pictures are ambiguous (unstructured) enough so that individuals will differ in the kinds of stories they will tell.

PROJECTION TESTS AND INTERPRETATIONS

John Exner raised the issue as to whether all responses to a projective technique such as the Rorschach test are necessarily aspects of projection. Is it true, he asked, that more ambiguous stimulus material produces more projection than does less ambiguous material? A simple example may be helpful. An individual might be shown a glass container with sand flowing from one portion of the glass to the other and asked to give this object a name. Most people will call it an egg timer. If, however, a thirty-five-year-old individual embellishes the description of the egg timer by stating that it represents the sands of time and is an indication that life is drawing to a close, that kind of response, in an individual of good health at that age, would seem to be an example of projection. Clearly, however, based on one response, it would be premature to build firm conclusions about this individual's attitudes toward life and death. Similarly, on the Rorschach test, one response descriptive of aggression may not be particularly diagnostic, but there is evidence that those who give higher frequencies of aggression responses show more aggressive verbal and nonverbal behaviors than those who do not.

Exner, in reporting on other studies, points out that Rorschach interpretations can also be useful with children. He noted that children change over time in their responses to the inkblots and that younger children change more than older children. Further, as children move into mid- and late adolescence, more overall stability is noted in the responses. Finally, he pointed out that perceptual accuracy stabilizes early.

A third study asked whether patients in a hospital setting who have experienced a major loss differ from patients who have not suffered such a loss. Mary Cerney defined three categories of major loss: death or serious injury to individuals close to the patient (including parents, close relatives, or friends); loss as a function of physical or sexual abuse such as incest, torture, or rape; and the observation of violence to other individuals. Cerney found differences in the responses between individual patients who had experienced such loss and patients who had not. She concluded that in this study, patients who had experienced early trauma had distinguishing Rorschach profiles. She further noted, however, that one needed further investigations to determine whether factors other than traumatic loss could contribute to this profile difference.

In a study designed to measure change in defense mechanisms following intensive psychotherapy, researchers compared two groups of individuals who were being treated in a small, long-term treatment facility with a psychoanalytic orientation. One group of patients was judged in advance to be composed of prime users of such defense mechanisms as repression and denial, while the other group was judged to comprise people who make much more use of projection. This categorization was based on a through evaluation six weeks after admission to the treatment center. After about fifteen months of intensive treatment, patients were evaluated again in a comprehensive manner. The use of defense mechanisms was established on the basis of responses to the TAT. Results indicated that all patients showed a reduction in the total use of defense mechanisms; this was associated with a reduction in psychiatric symptoms. Interestingly, the patients who made use of projection as a defense showed a greater decline in the use of that defense mechanism after treatment. Along with the decrease in psychiatric symptoms, both groups also showed, as one might expect, improved relationships with others from both a qualitative and a quantitative perspective.

APPLICATION TO PERSONALITY TRAITS

Freud also applied the concept of projection to everyday personality traits such as jealousy. He differentiated between normal jealousy, projected jealousy, and delusional jealousy. From a psychoanalytic view, he had little to say about normal jealousy; however, projected jealousy, he stated, came from two sources, either from actual unfaithfulness or from impulses toward unfaithfulness which have been pushed into one's unconscious. He speculated that married individuals are frequently tempted to be unfaithful. In view of that temptation, it is likely that one's conscience can be soothed by attributing unfaithfulness to one's partner. Jealousy arising from such a projection can be so strong as to take on the quality of a delusion. Many people are aware of individuals who incorrectly suspect their committed partner to be unfaithful. Freud would argue that these inaccurate expectations are unconscious fantasies of one's own infidelities and can be so analyzed in psychoanalytic therapy.

EVOLUTION OF RESEARCH

The term "projection" was introduced by Freud in 1894. Initially Freud viewed it as a defensive process, but by 1913 the concept was broadened to refer to a process that may occur even if there is no conflict. Exner believed that Freud's description of projection is most applicable in the context of projective tests. Exner also suggested that Freud's concept of projection fits in well with Henry Murray's discussion of the TAT. Murray's broadened explanation of projection included the idea that the ambiguity of responding to a social situation (the test materials) provides clues to that individual's personality makeup and its expression through responses to projective methods. Projective method refers to any task that provides an open-ended response that may reveal aspects of one's personality; tasks or tests commonly include standard stimuli that are ambiguous in nature. Lawrence Frank further emphasized the connection between projective tests and the unique expression of an individual's personality by stating the projective hypothesis.

Applied psychology has been heavily involved with the study of intelligence and the development of tests to evaluate achievement, memory, motor skills, and other cognitive aspects of human functioning. The study of personality was more heavily focused on individual traits, such as extroversion versus introversion. Emphasis on test construction focused on group norms, and comparisons of individual scores on tests were based on their relationships to group data. According to Exner, early Rorschach research also attempted to focus on group norms. To some extent, the focus on determining the meaning of individual responses was probably a reaction to the more "scientific" behavioral and statistically based methods commonly used.

As Exner noted, initial work with the Rorschach inkblots emphasized attempts to quantify personality characteristics; there was relatively little interest in the actual content of the responses. As interest in psychoanalysis swept the country, clinical psychologists began to focus on individual responses to tests, in contrast to their prior emphasis on group comparisons. Projective tests were very controversial, however, and a dichotomy developed between projective tests and the so-called objective tests. The latter tests were ones that could be scored reliably and for which group norms existed. Concurrently, numerous scoring systems were developed for the Rorschach test as well as for other projective measures.

In the late 1970's, Exner developed a comprehensive scoring system for the Rorschach which incorporated many of the features of the existing systems and integrated them into one overall method. In addition, he collected normative data on children, adolescents, and adults that provide opportunities for group comparisons. His comprehensive system is now widely taught in colleges and universities and has provided a measure of unity to the Rorschach test, which is still the personality instrument most widely used by clinicians. The assessment of personality traits will probably continue to flourish, and there will probably be an increasing emphasis on both subjective and objective responses in order to assess personality. Furthermore, computerized scoring of responses is common for objective personality tests and is beginning to be used with projective personality measures; this is likely to influence the future of personality tests.

SOURCES FOR FURTHER STUDY

Aiken, Lewis R. *Assessment of Adult Personality.* New York: Springer, 1997. This text-book is designed to introduce the reader to concepts, methods, and instruments important in personality assessment. It provides a straightforward discussion of psychodynamic theory in the context of projective testing and provides constructive criticisms.

Cronbach, Lee J. *Essentials of Psychological Testing.* 5th ed. New York: Harper & Row, 1990. The measurement of personality traits by projective tests is discussed in chapter 16. Discussion questions are included to assist the reader to understand why projective measures encourage both positive and negative evaluations. This chapter can be understood by high school and college students.

Leiter, E. "The Role of Projective Testing." In *Clinical and Experimental Psychiatry,* edited by Scott Wetzler and Martin M. Katz. New York: Brunner/Mazel, 1989. Leiter discusses projective testing and includes major changes in psychiatry as related to projective techniques. He focuses on changes in current diagnosis and relates them to projective measures.

Nathanson, S. "Denial, Projection, and the Empathic Wall." In *Denial: A Clarification of Concepts and Research,* edited by E. L. Edelstein, Donald L. Nathanson, and Andrew M. Stone. New York: Plenum, 1989. Discusses denial and projection and gives clinical illustrations. The author integrates concepts with other theories and provides relevant examples of research with infants. There is also a discussion of empathy and its relationship to substance abuse.

Walsh, W. Bruce, and Nancy E. Betz. *Tests and Assessments.* Englewood Cliffs, N.J.: Prentice-Hall, 1985. Of particular interest is the discussion on projective and behavioral assessment, which reviews the concepts behind projective testing and discusses types of projective techniques with specific examples.

Norman Abeles

SEE ALSO: Abnormality: Psychological models; Clinical interviewing, testing, and observation; Ego defense mechanisms; Personality interviewing strategies; Personology: Henry A. Murray; Psychoanalytic psychology and personality: Sigmund Freud; Rorschach inkblots; Thematic Apperception Test (TAT).

Psychoanalysis

DATE: The 1880's forward
TYPE OF PSYCHOLOGY: Developmental psychology; psychological methodologies; psychotherapy

FIELDS OF STUDY: Classic analytic themes and issues; general constructs and issues; humanistic-phenomenological models; humanistic therapies; models of abnormality; motivation theory; personality theory; psychodynamic and neoanalytic models; psychodynamic therapies; thought

Psychoanalysis is a form of intensive psychotherapy to treat emotional suffering, based on the concept that people are often unaware of what determines their emotions and behavior. By talking freely, while in an intensive relationship with the psychoanalyst, a person is able to overcome worries that may have limited his or her choices in life. Psychoanalysis is also a comprehensive theory of the mind and a method for understanding everyday behavior.

KEY CONCEPTS
- anxiety
- certification
- countertransference
- depression
- free association
- inhibitions
- psychoanalyst
- psychoanalytic institutes
- psychoanalytic psychotherapy
- psychotherapy
- symptoms
- transference
- unconscious

INTRODUCTION

Psychoanalysis began as a method for treating emotional suffering. Sigmund Freud (1856-1939), the founder of psychoanalysis, working at the beginning of the twentieth century, made many discoveries by studying patients with symptoms such as excessive anxiety (fear that is not realistic) or paralysis for which no physical cause could be found. He became the first psychoanalyst (often called analyst) when he developed the method of free association, in which he encouraged his patients to say whatever came to mind about their symptoms and their lives. He found that by talking in this way, his patients discovered feelings and thoughts they had not known they had. When they became aware of these unconscious thoughts and feelings, their symptoms lessened or disappeared.

Psychoanalysis as a form of psychotherapy continues to be an effective method for treating certain forms of emotional suffering, such as anxieties and inhibitions (inner constraints) that interfere with success in school, work, or relationships. It is based on the understanding that each individual is unique, that the past shapes the present, and that factors outside people's awareness influence their thoughts, feelings, and actions. As a comprehensive treatment, it has the potential to change many areas of a person's functioning. Although modern psychoanalysis is different in many ways from what was practiced in Freud's era, talking and listening remain important. Psychoanalytic psychotherapy is a modified form of psychoanalysis, usually with less frequent meetings and more modest goals.

From the beginning, psychoanalysis was more than just a treatment. It was, and continues to be, a method for investigating the mind and a theory to explain both everyday adult behavior as well as child development. Many of Freud's insights, which seemed so revolutionary at the beginning of the twentieth century, are now widely accepted by various schools of psychological thought and form the basis for several theories of psychological motivation, most theories of child development, and all forms of psychodynamic psychotherapy. Some of Freud's ideas, such as his theories about women, turned out to be wrong and were revised by other psychoanalysts during the 1970's and 1980's. Other ideas, such as those about the nature of dreams, although rejected by some scientists during the 1980's and 1990's, were returned to by other scientists by the beginning of the twenty-first century. Psychoanalytic ideas and concepts are used in communities to solve problems such as bullying in schools and can be applied in many other fields of study.

In the early years of psychoanalysis, Freud trained most psychoanalysts. Later, different schools of psychoanalytic thought branched out from this original source. Groups of psychoanalysts joined together in organizations, and each organization developed its own standards for training psychoanalysts. There were no nationally accepted standards for psychoanalytic training in the United States until the beginning of the twenty-first century, when several of these groups joined together to establish an Accreditation Council of Psychoanalytic Education. This council agreed to core standards for psychoanalytic institutes (schools that train psychoanalysts). Psychoanalytic psychotherapy, while practiced by trained psychoanalysts, is also practiced by psychotherapists who are not trained as psychoanalysts.

PSYCHOANALYTIC TREATMENT

Psychoanalysis is a method for helping people with symptoms that result from emotional conflict. Common symptoms in the modern era include anxiety (fear that is not realistic), depression (excessive sadness that is not due to a current loss), frequent unhealthy choices in relationships, and trouble getting along well with peers or family members. For example, some people may feel continuously insecure and worried about doing well in school or work despite getting good grades or reviews. Other people may be attracted to sexual and emotional partners who treat them poorly. Others may experience loneliness and isolation because of fears about close relationships. Others may sabotage their success by always changing direction before reaching their goals. Children may have tantrums beyond the age when these are normal, or be afraid of going to sleep every night, or feel unhappy with their maleness or femaleness.

The same symptom can have several different causes, an etiology Freud termed overdetermination. For example, depression may be due to inner emotional constraints that prevent success, to biological vulnerability, or to upsetting events (such as the death of a loved one), or it may result from a combination of these. Therefore, most psychoanalysts believe in meeting with a person several times before deciding upon the best treatment. Psychoanalysis is not for everyone who has a symptom. Sometimes psychoanalysis is not needed because the problems can be easily helped by other, less intensive forms of therapy. Sometimes biological problems or early childhood experiences leave a person too vulnerable to undertake the hard work of psychoanalysis. When psychoanalysis is not necessary, or not the best treatment for a particular person, a psychoanalyst may recommend psychoanalytic psychotherapy, a treatment that is based on the same principles as psychoanalysis but with less ambitious goals and, usually, less frequent sessions.

Psychoanalysis can treat specific emotional disorders, as described in the *Diagnostic and Statistical Manual of Mental Disorders: DSM-IV-TR* (rev. 4th ed., 2000), but can also help with multiple sets of problematic symptoms, behaviors, and personality traits (such as being too perfectionistic or rigid). Since psychoanalysis affects the whole person rather than just treating symptoms, it has the potential to promote personal growth and development. For adults, this can mean better relationships or marriages, jobs that feel more satisfying, or the ability to enjoy free time when this was difficult before. Children may do better in school after fears about competition and success diminish, or they may have more friends and get along better with parents after they begin to feel better about themselves.

Because psychoanalysis is a very individual treatment, the best way to determine whether it would be beneficial for an individual is through consulting an experienced psychoanalyst. In general, people who benefit from psychoanalysis have some emotional sturdiness. They tend to be capable of understanding themselves and learning how to help themselves. Usually, they have had important accomplishments in one or more areas of their lives before seeking psychoanalytic treatment. Often, they have tried other forms of treatment that may have been helpful but have not been sufficient to deal with all their difficulties. Sometimes they are people who work with others (therapists, rabbis, teachers) whose emotions have been interfering with their ability to do their jobs as well as possible. Whatever the problems, psychoanalysts understand them in the context of each individual's strengths, vulnerabilities, and life situation.

METHOD OF TREATMENT IN PSYCHOANALYSIS

A person who goes to a psychoanalyst for consultation usually meets with the analyst at least three times face-to-face before the analyst recommends psychoanalysis. Sometimes the patient and analyst meet for several weeks, months, or years in psychoanalytic psychotherapy; they decide upon psychoanalysis if they identify problems that are unlikely to be solved by less intensive treatment.

Once they begin psychoanalysis, the analyst and patient usually meet four or five times per week for fifty-minute sessions, as this creates the intensive personal relationship that plays an important role in the therapeutic process. The frequent sessions do not mean that the patient is very sick; they are necessary to help the patient reach deeper levels of awareness. (People with the severest forms of mental illness, such as schizophrenia, are not usually treated with psychoanalysis.) Often the adult patient lies on a couch, as this may make it easier to speak freely. The couch is not essential, and some patients feel more comfortable sitting up.

By working together to diminish obstacles to free expression in the treatment sessions, the analyst and patient come to understand the patient's worries and learn how the patient's mind works. The patient learns about thoughts and feelings he or she has kept out of awareness or isolated from each other. Through the intensity that comes from frequent meetings with the analyst, the patient often experiences the analyst as if the analyst were a parent or other important person from the past. This is called transference. Eventually, the patient has a chance to see these feelings from a more mature point of view. Although the patient may experience intense emotions within the analytic sessions, the anxieties and behaviors that brought him or her to treatment gradually diminish and feel more under control. The patient feels freer and less restricted by worries and patterns that belong to the past.

For example, a patient may be very fearful of angry feelings and avoid telling the analyst about them, expecting punishment or rejection. As a result, the patient may turn the anger on himself or herself in a form of self-sabotage. Often this is the way the patient dealt with angry feelings toward significant people while growing up. Over time, as the patient and analyst understand this behavior, the patient feels freer to express angry feelings directly and eventually feels less need to sabotage or self-punish.

Gradually, in the course of the intensive analytic relationship, the patient learns more about his or her maladaptive ways of dealing with distressing thoughts and feelings that have developed during childhood. By understanding them in adulthood or (for a child) at a later age, the patient gains a different perspective and is able to react in a more adaptive way. Rigid personality traits that had been used to keep the childhood feelings at a distance are no longer necessary, and the patient is able to react to people and situations in a more flexible way.

During the course of the treatment, the analyst will often have strong feelings toward the patient, called countertransference. Well-trained analysts are required to undergo psychoanalysis themselves before treating patients. In their own analysis, they learn how to cope with their countertransference feelings in ways that will not hurt the patient. For example, they learn not to take the patient's expressions of anger personally but to help the patient express the emotion more fully and understand where it originates.

Children and adolescents can be treated with psychoanalysis or psychoanalytic psychotherapy by using methods suitable for their ages. Most children play with toys, draw, or explore the room, in addition to talking, during their sessions with the analyst, and these activities provide ways to explore inner thoughts and feelings. The analyst meets with the parents before the treatment starts and continues to do so regularly during the course of the child's therapy or analysis. Adolescents usually sit face-to-face or draw and/or write about their feelings and worries. Occasionally, older adolescents want to lie on the couch. Adolescents often prefer that the analyst not meet with the parents on a regular basis. Instead, the analyst and adolescent usually develop some way to keep the parents informed about what they might need to know about the treatment.

PSYCHOANALYTIC PSYCHOTHERAPY

Psychoanalytic psychotherapy is more varied than psychoanalysis. It may be very intensive, or it may be focused on a specific problem, such as a recent loss or trouble deciding about a job. In psychoanalytic psychotherapy, the patient and therapist usually sit face-to-face and approach the patient's problems, whatever they are, in a more interactive way. Most often, patient and therapist meet twice per week in fifty-minute sessions. Once per week is also common but not considered to be as helpful. More frequent meetings (three to five times per week) may be necessary if the patient is in crisis or has chronic problems that are not treatable with psychoanalysis.

Although psychoanalysts are well trained to practice psychoanalytic psychotherapy, this treatment is also practiced by psychotherapists who are not psychoanalysts. Some of these therapists have taken courses at psychoanalytic institutes.

MEDICATION AND CONFIDENTIALITY ISSUES

In the early days of psychoanalysis, analysts believed that treatment with medication would interfere with psychoanalysis. Most modern psychoanalysts believe that, although medicine can sometimes interfere, there are times when it can be used in a helpful way in combination with psychoanalytic psychotherapy or even with psychoanalysis.

"Confidentiality" is the term used to describe the privacy necessary for individuals to be able to speak freely about all their thoughts and feelings. Responsible psychoanalysts and psychotherapists agree to keep private everything about their patients, including the fact that the patient has come for treatment, unless the patient gives permission to release some specific information. One exception is when patients are at risk for hurting themselves or someone else. In *Jaffe v. Redmond*, an important case decided by the U.S. Supreme Court in 1995, the Supreme Court confirmed that confidentiality is necessary for the patient to speak freely in psychotherapy.

TRAINING AND QUALIFICATIONS FOR PSYCHOANALYSTS

The International Psychoanalytic Association (IPA), formed during Freud's lifetime, is a worldwide organization of psychoanalysts that remained in place throughout the twentieth century. The American Psychoanalytic Association (APsA) was founded in 1911 and grew to three thousand members during the course of the twentieth century. All its members also belonged to the IPA. Many schools for psychoanalysts, or psychoanalytic institutes, were accredited (examined and found to meet a set of standards) by APsA over the years. APsA also developed an examination called certification to test graduate psychoanalysts.

Because the first psychoanalysts in the United States believed that psychoanalysis would be more highly valued if connected with the medical profession, the APsA initially only accepted psychiatrists (who are medical doctors) as members. Exceptions were made for professionals who applied to train as researchers. This contrasted with the practice in Europe, where many nonmedical psychoanalysts became members of the IPA. Nonmedical professionals, such as psychologists and social workers, who wanted to become psychoanalysts in the United States often trained in psychoanalytic institutes not recognized by the APsA. Some were recognized by the IPA and later banded together under the name of the International Psychoanalytic Societies (IPS). Other institutes developed outside both organiza-

tions, sometimes creating their own standards for training. By the last quarter of the twentieth century, nonmedical mental health professionals (such as psychologists and social workers) were accepted as members of APsA and grew in numbers, becoming a large proportion of the membership.

Because the title "psychoanalyst" was not protected by federal or state law in the twentieth century, anyone, even untrained persons, could call themselves a psychoanalyst in the United States. Many institutes developed in large cities, such as New York and Los Angeles, that were not connected with APsA or IPS and admitted trainees with varying backgrounds and qualifications. Some of these defined psychoanalysis in their own way, so that arguments developed about the dividing line between psychoanalysis and psychoanalytic psychotherapy. The American Psychological Association eventually developed its own examination to qualify a psychologist as a psychoanalyst.

TRAINING IN THE TWENTY-FIRST CENTURY

Since, by the beginning of the twenty-first century, no laws were yet in place in the United States to define who could practice psychoanalysis, it remained difficult for the public to tell who was qualified. In the late 1990's, several national organizations of the core mental health disciplines came together in a coalition called the Consortium for Psychoanalysis. By the turn of the century, they had agreed upon baseline standards that would be used to develop a national organization to accredit psychoanalytic institutes. These organizations were the American Psychoanalytic Association, the division of psychoanalysis of the American Psychological Association, the National Membership Committee on Psychoanalysis in Clinical Social Work, and the American Academy of Psychoanalysis.

Trained psychoanalysts in the twenty-first century who meet these standards already have a mental health degree, except in unusual cases, before becoming psychoanalysts. Once accepted for training at a psychoanalytic institute, these mental health professionals study many more years to become qualified psychoanalysts. They take courses and treat patients while supervised by experienced psychoanalysts. In addition, they are required to undergo psychoanalysis themselves in order to gain enough self-knowledge to keep their own problems from interfering with the treatment of patients.

PSYCHOANALYSIS AS A THEORY

All psychoanalytic theories are based on the idea that people are motivated by thoughts and feelings outside their awareness, that the past influences the present, and that each individual is unique. Because so much change and growth has occurred since Freud's era, psychoanalysis is no longer a single theory but encompasses many different theories. All psychoanalytic theories are theories of motivation (what makes people do what they do), theories of development (how people get to be the way they are), and theories of change (how psychoanalytic treatment works). Psychoanalytic theories are usually also theories of personality development (who people are) and personality disturbance.

Most theories emphasize the complexity of each person's symptoms and behavior and take into account many different influences. For example, the psychoanalytic theory called ego psychology describes development as a complex interaction of biology (inborn factors) and experience over time. Early childhood experiences are especially important because they influence the way a person's ability to cope with the world (ego functioning) develops. Each person adapts to the environment in a unique way that gradually becomes more consistent by the time the person grows to adulthood.

Psychoanalytic theories are comprehensive theories of mental functioning and disorder. For this reason, they originally formed the basis for the diagnosis and classification of mental disorders in America—DSM-I in 1952 and DSM-II in 1968. Many changes and developments took place in psychoanalytic theory during the second half of the twentieth century. The greatest change took place in theories about psychotic illness, female psychology, homosexuality, and the nature of the patient/analyst relationship. By the turn of the century, it was unusual to find, in real life, the silent analysts who were still sometimes created in films and cartoons.

Because of their complexity, psychoanalytic theories are more difficult to study and test than other theories. For example, Freud believed that dreams have meaning and are based on the fulfillment of unconscious wishes. Neuroscientists dismissed this theory for many years because it could not be demonstrated. Behavioral psychologists, who based their theories on observable behavior, did not consider thoughts and feelings outside a person's awareness to be important. Because of the emphasis on experi-

mental testing and the increasing public expectation for quick cures during the last quarter of the twentieth century, psychoanalytic theories became less popular. The DSM-III, the third edition of the diagnostic manual for mental disorders which came out in 1980, was based on categories of symptoms and behaviors, without any reference to underlying theory. The categories of mental disturbance in DSM-III (and later, in 1994's DSM-IV) were described in a way that would be easy to test in controlled experiments. People, and particularly insurance companies, became more interested in medicines and short-term treatments for symptoms and were less willing to pay for treatments like psychoanalysis that address the whole person.

Toward the end of the twentieth century and the beginning of the twenty-first, cognitive scientists (scientists who study the way people think) and neuroscientists (scientists who study the way the brain works) began to make discoveries that proved psychoanalytic theory to be correct in some important areas. For example, cognitive scientists proved that much of mental functioning goes on outside a person's awareness. Mark Solms, a neuroscientist, proved that dreams are formed in the part of the brain that deals with motivation and emotional meaning. Psychoanalysts began a dialogue with neuroscientists and cognitive scientists. Although some psychoanalysts thought psychoanalysis could not be studied experimentally in the same way as shorter-term therapies, others began to publicize studies demonstrating the effectiveness of psychoanalysis and psychoanalytic psychotherapy. Others began to develop further ways to study psychoanalytic theory and treatment.

PSYCHOANALYTIC THEORY APPLICATIONS

Psychoanalytic ideas have been applied in many fields of study. For example, psychoanalytic theories about loss and mourning have been used to help inner-city children cope with their reactions to losses in mourning groups. Psychoanalytic ideas about power and helplessness have been used in schools to decrease violence by changing the atmosphere in which bullies can thrive. Psychoanalytic ideas led to the concept of social and emotional learning whereby educators have demonstrated that intelligence is not just based on the ability to think but includes emotions and social abilities. Psychoanalytic ideas have been used in the study of literature to understand characters such as Hamlet or Othello. They have been used in the study of culture to understand terrorists and the cultures that support them. Psychoanalysts apply psychoanalytic theories in the help they offer to day care centers, businesses, diplomats, police officers, firefighters, rabbis, priests and others.

SOURCES FOR FURTHER STUDY

Brenner, Charles. *An Elementary Textbook of Psychoanalysis.* New York: Columbia University Press, 1955. This book introduces interested readers to the fundamentals of psychoanalysis, explaining core psychoanalytic concepts in clear language. Although written in 1955 (so it does not deal with some modern developments), it remains a good resource for understanding the basics from the point of view of ego psychology.

Gabbard Glenn. *Psychodynamic Psychiatry in Clinical Practice, DSM-IV Edition.* Washington, D.C.: American Psychiatric Press, 1994. This is a textbook that approaches DSM-IV from a psychoanalytic point of view. It includes an introductory section describing psychodynamic principles and then sections describing Axis I and Axis II disorders from a psychodynamic perspective.

Gay, Peter. *Freud: A Life for Our Times.* New York: W. W. Norton, 1988. This is a biography of Sigmund Freud written by his physician. It describes the history of psychoanalysis during Freud's lifetime.

Vaughan, Susan. *The Talking Cure: The Science Behind Psychotherapy.* New York: Henry Holt, 1998. This book is written for people who may want to visit a psychoanalyst or who want to learn about models of mind and brain that integrate psychoanalytic theories with other scientific theories. It includes several descriptions of what happens when patients visit psychoanalysts.

Wallerstein, R. S. *The Talking Cures: The Psychoanalyses and the Psychotherapies.* New Haven, Conn.: Yale University Press, 1995. This book provides a comprehensive history of psychoanalytic thought, including a detailed view of trends and developments in psychoanalysis from the 1940's onward. It describes conflicting and compatible psychoanalytic theories and the debate about the dividing line between psychoanalysis and psychotherapy.

Judith M. Chertoff

SEE ALSO: American Psychiatric Association; American Psychological Association; Analytic psychology: Jacques Lacan; Analytical psychology: Carl G. Jung; Analytical psychotherapy; Brief therapy; Confidentiality; Ego psychology: Erik Erikson; Freud, Sigmund; Individual psychology: Alfred Adler; Personality theory; Psychoanalytic psychology; Psychoanalytic psychology and personality: Sigmund Freud; Psychotherapy: Historical approaches; Social psychological models: Erich Fromm; Social psychological models: Karen Horney; Women's psychology: Sigmund Freud.

Psychoanalytic psychology

TYPE OF PSYCHOLOGY: Origin and definition of psychology
FIELDS OF STUDY: Psychodynamic and neoanalytic models; psychodynamic therapies

Psychoanalytic and neoanalytic schools of thought provide explanations of human and neurotic behavior. Each of these models contributes to the understanding of personality development and psychological conflict by presenting unique theoretical conceptualizations, assessment techniques, research methodologies, and psychotherapeutic strategies for personality change.

KEY CONCEPTS
- analytic psychology
- dynamic cultural schools of psychoanalysis
- individual psychology
- neoanalytic psychology
- psychoanalytic psychology
- psychosocial theory

INTRODUCTION

One grand theory in psychology that dramatically revolutionized the way in which personality and its formation were viewed is psychoanalysis. Orthodox psychoanalysis and later versions of this model offer several unique perspectives of personality development, assessment, and change.

The genius of Sigmund Freud (1856-1939), the founder of psychoanalysis, is revealed in the magnitude of his achievements and the monumental scope of his works. Over the course of his lifetime,

Freud developed a theory of personality and psychopathology (disorders of psychological functioning that include major as well as minor mental disorders and behavior disorders), a method for probing the realm of the unconscious mind, and a therapy for dealing with personality disorders. He posited that an individual is motivated by unconscious forces that are instinctual in nature. The two major instinctual forces are the life instincts, or eros, and the death instinct, or thanatos. Their source is biological tension whose aim is tension reduction through a variety of objects. Freud viewed personality as a closed system composed of three structures: the id, ego, and superego. The irrational id consists of the biological drives and libido, or psychic energy. It operates according to the pleasure principle, which seeks the immediate gratification of needs. The rational ego serves as the executive component of personality and the mediator between the demands of the id, superego, and environment. Governed by the reality principle, it seeks to postpone the gratification of needs. The superego, or moral arm of personality, consists of the conscience (internalized values) and ego ideal (that which the person aspires to be).

According to Freud, the origins of personality are embedded in the first seven years of life. Personality develops through a sequence of psychosexual stages which each focus upon an area of the body (erogenous zone) that gives pleasure to the individual; they are the oral, anal, phallic, latency, and genital stages. The frustration or overindulgence of needs contributes to a fixation, or arrest in development at a particular stage.

Freud also developed a therapy for treating individuals experiencing personality disturbances. Psychoanalysis has shown how physical disorders have psychological roots, how unbearable anxiety generates conflict, and how problems in adulthood result from early childhood experiences. In therapy, Freud surmounted his challenge to reveal the hidden nature of the unconscious by exposing the resistances and transferences of his patients. His method for probing a patient's unconscious thoughts, motives, and feelings was based upon the use of many clinical techniques. Free association, dream interpretation, analyses of slips of the tongue, misplaced objects, and humor enabled him to discover the contents of an individual's unconscious mind and open the doors to a new and grand psychology of personality.

RESPONSES TO FREUDIAN THEORY

The theory of psychosocial development of Erik Erikson (1902-1994) occupies a position between orthodox psychoanalysis and neoanalytic schools of thought. His theory builds upon the basic concepts and tenets of Freudian psychology by illustrating the influential role of social and cultural forces in personality development. Erikson's observations of infants and investigations of the parent-child relationship in various societies contributed to his development of the model of the eight stages of human development. He proposes that personality unfolds over the entire life cycle according to a predetermined plan. As an individual moves through this series of stages, he or she encounters periods of vulnerability that require him or her to resolve crises of a social nature and develop new abilities and patterns of behavior. Erikson's eight psychosocial stages not only parallel Freud's psychosexual ones but, more important, have contributed immensely to contemporary thought in developmental psychology.

Several other schools of thought arose in opposition to Freudian orthodoxy. Among the proponents of these new psychoanalytic models were Carl Gustav Jung (1875-1961), Alfred Adler (1870-1937), Karen Horney (1885-1952), and Harry Stack Sullivan (1892-1949). These theorists advocated revised versions of Freud's psychoanalytic model and became known as the neoanalysts.

JUNG'S APPROACH

Carl Jung's analytical psychology stresses the complex interaction of opposing forces within the total personality (psyche) and the manner in which these inner conflicts influence development. Personality is driven by general life process energy, called libido. It operates according to the principle of opposites, for example, a contrast between conscious and unconscious. An individual's behavior is seen as a means to some end, whose goal is to create a balance between these polar opposites through a process of self-realization. Personality is composed of several regions, including the ego (a unifying force at the center of consciousness), the personal unconscious (experiences blocked from consciousness), and the collective unconscious (inherited predispositions of ancestral experiences). The major focus of Jung's theory is the collective unconscious, with its archetypes (primordial thoughts and images), persona (public self), anima/animus (feminine and masculine components), shadow (repulsive side of the personality), and self (an archetype reflecting a person's striving for personality integration). Jung further proposed two psychological attitudes that the personality could use in relating to the world: introversion and extroversion. He also identified four functions of thought: sensing, thinking, feeling, and intuiting. Eight different personality types emerge when one combines these attitudes and functions. Like Freud, Jung proposed developmental stages: childhood, young adulthood, and middle age. Through the process of individuation, a person seeks to create an inner harmony that results in self-realization. In conjunction with dream analysis, Jung used painting therapy and a word association test to disclose underlying conflicts in patients. Therapy helped patients to reconcile the conflicting sides of their personalities and experience self-realization.

ADLER'S APPROACH

The individual psychology of Alfred Adler illustrates the significance of social variables in personality development and the uniqueness of the individual. Adler proposed that an individual seeks to compensate for inborn feelings of inferiority by striving for superiority. It is lifestyle that helps a person achieve future goals, ideals, and superiority. Adler extended this theme of perfection to society by using the concept of social interest to depict the human tendency to create a productive society. He maintained that early childhood experiences play a crucial role in the development of a person's unique lifestyle. An individual lacking in social interest develops a mistaken lifestyle (for example, an inferiority complex). Physical inferiority as well as spoiling or pampering and neglecting children contributes to the development of faulty lifestyles. Adler examined dreams, birth order, and first memories to trace the origins of lifestyle and goals. These data were used in psychotherapy to help the person create a new lifestyle oriented toward social interest.

HORNEY'S APPROACH

Karen Horney's social and cultural psychoanalysis considers the influence of social and cultural forces upon the development and maintenance of neurosis. Her theory focuses upon disturbed human relationships, especially between parents and children. She discussed several negative factors, such as parental indifference, erratic behavior, and un-

kept promises, which contributed to basic anxiety in children. This basic anxiety led to certain defenses or neurotic needs. Horney proposed ten neurotic needs that are used to reestablish safety. She further summarized these needs into three categories that depicted the individual's adjustment to others: moving toward people (compliant person), moving against people (aggressive person), and moving away from people (detached person). Horney believed that neurosis occurs when an individual lives according to his or her ideal rather than real self. She also wrote a number of articles on feminine psychology that stressed the importance of cultural rather than biological factors in personality formation. Like Freud, she used the techniques of transference, dream analysis, and free association in her psychotherapy; however, the goal of therapy was to help an individual overcome his or her idealized neurotic self and become more real as he or she experienced self-realization.

SULLIVAN'S APPROACH

Harry Stack Sullivan's interpersonal theory examines personality from the perspective of the interpersonal relationships that have influenced it, especially the mother-infant relationship. Sullivan believed that this relationship contributed to an individual's development of a "good me," "bad me," or "not me" personification of self. He also proposed six stages of development: infancy, childhood, juvenile epoch, preadolescence, early adolescence, and late adolescence. These stages illustrate an individual's experiences and need for intimacy with significant others. Overall, his theory emphasizes the importance of interpersonal relations, the appraisals of others toward an individual, and the need to achieve interpersonal security and avoid anxiety.

USE OF CASE STUDIES

Psychoanalytic psychology and its later versions have been used to explain normal and abnormal personality development. Regardless of their perspectives, psychologists in all these schools have relied upon the case study method to communicate their theoretical insights and discoveries.

The theoretical roots of orthodox psychoanalysis may be traced to the famous case of "Anna O.," a patient under the care of Josef Breuer, Freud's friend and colleague. Fascinated with the hysterical symptoms of this young girl and with Breuer's success in using catharsis (the talking cure) with her, Freud asked Breuer to collaborate on a work entitled *Studien über Hysterie* (1895; *Studies in Hysteria*, 1950) and discuss his findings. It was the world's first book on psychoanalysis, containing information on the unconscious, defenses, sexual cause of neurosis, resistance, and transference. Freud's own self-analysis and analyses of family members and other patients further contributed to the changing nature of his theory. Among his great case histories are "Dora" (hysteria), "Little Hans" (phobia), the "Rat Man" (obsessional neurosis), the "Schreiber" case (paranoia), and the "Wolf Man" (infantile neurosis). His method of treatment, psychoanalysis, is also well documented in contemporary cases, such as the treatment for multiple personality described in the book *Sybil* (1974).

In his classic work *Childhood and Society* (1950), Erikson discussed the applicability of the clinical method of psychoanalysis and the case-history technique to normal development in children. His case analyses of the Sioux and Yurok Indians and his observations of children led to the creation of a psychosocial theory of development that emphasized the significant role played by one's culture. Moreover, Erikson's psychohistorical accounts, *Young Man Luther: A Study in Psychoanalysis and History* (1958) and *Gandhi's Truth on the Origins of Militant Nonviolence* (1969), illustrated the applications of clinical analyses to historical and biographical research so prominent today.

The founders of other psychoanalytic schools of thought have similarly shown that their theories can best be understood in the context of the therapeutic situations and in the writings of case histories. Harold Greenwald's *Great Cases in Psychoanalysis* (1959) is an excellent source of original case histories written by Freud, Jung, Adler, Horney, and Sullivan. Jung's case of "The Anxious Young Woman and the Retired Business Man" clarifies the differences and similarities between his theory and Freud's psychoanalytic model. In "The Drive for Superiority," Adler uses material from several cases to illustrate the themes of lifestyle, feelings of inferiority, and striving for superiority. Horney's case of "The Ever Tired Editor" portrays her use of the character analysis method; that is, she concentrates upon the way in which a patient characteristically functions. Sullivan's case of "The Inefficient Wife" sheds some light on the manner in which professional advice may be given to another (student) practitioner. In retrospect, all these prominent theorists have exposed their independent schools of though through case histories. Even today, this method continues to be used to explain human behavior and to enhance understanding of personality functioning.

EVOLUTION OF STUDY

Historically, the evolution of psychoanalytic psychology originated with Freud's clinical observations of the work conducted by the famous French neurologist Jean-Martin Charcot and his collaborations on the treatment of hysteria neurosis with Breuer. The publication of *Studies in Hysteria* marked the birth of psychoanalysis since it illustrated a theory of hysteria, a therapy of catharsis, and an analysis of unconscious motivation. Between 1900 and 1920, Freud made innumerable contributions to the field. His major clinical discoveries were contained in the publications *Die Traumdeutung* (1900; *The Interpretation of Dreams*, 1913) and *Drei Abhandlungen zur Sexualtheorie* (1905; *Three Contributions to the Sexual Theory*, 1910; also translated as *Three Essays on the Theory of Sexuality*, 1949) as well as in various papers on therapy, case histories, and applications to everyday life. During this time, Freud began his international correspondence with people such as Jung. He also invited a select group of individuals to his home for evening discussions; these meetings were known as the psychological Wednesday society. Eventually, these meetings led to the establishment of the Vienna Psychoanalytical Society, with Adler as its president, and the First International Psychoanalytical Congress, with Jung as its president. In 1909, Freud, Jung, and others were invited by President G. Stanley Hall of Clark University to come to the United States to deliver a series of introductory lectures on psychoanalysis. This momentous occasion acknowledged Freud's achievements and gave him international recognition. In subsequent years, Freud reformulated his theory and demonstrated how psychoanalysis could be applied to larger social issues.

Trained in psychoanalysis by Anna Freud, Erikson followed in Sigmund Freud's footsteps by supporting and extending his psychosexual theory of development with eight stages of psychosocial identity. Among the members of the original psychoanalytic group, Adler was the first to defect from the Freudian school, in 1911. Protesting Freud's theory for the Oedipus complex, Adler founded his own individual psychology. Two years later, in 1913, Jung parted company with Freud to establish analytical psychology; he objected to Freud's belief that all human behavior stems from sex. With Horney's publications *New Ways in Psychoanalysis* (1939) and *Our Inner Conflicts: A Constructive Theory of Neurosis* (1945), it became quite clear that her ideas only remotely resembled Freud's. Objecting to a number of Freud's major tenets, she attributed the development of neurosis and the psychology of being feminine to social, cultural, and interpersonal influences. Similarly, Sullivan extended psychoanalytic psychology to interpersonal phenomena, arguing that the foundations of human nature and development are not biological but rather cultural and social.

ACCOMPLISHMENTS AND INFLUENCE

The accomplishments of Freud and his followers are truly remarkable. The creative genius of each theorist spans a lifetime of effort and work. The magnitude of their achievements is shown in their efforts to provide new perspectives on personality development and psychopathology, theories of motivation, psychotherapeutic methods of treatment, and methods for describing the nature of human behavior. Clearly, these independent schools of thought have had a profound influence not only upon the field of psychology but also upon art, religion, anthropology, sociology, and literature. Undoubtedly, they will continue to serve as the cornerstone of personality theory and provide the foundation for new and challenging theories of tomorrow—theories that seek to discover the true nature of what it means to be human.

SOURCES FOR FURTHER STUDY

Adler, Alfred. *Social Interest: A Challenge to Mankind.* New York: Capricorn Books, 1964. An excellent summary of Adler's theories of human nature and social education, incorporating his ideas on lifestyle, inferiority/superiority complex, neurosis, childhood memories, and social feelings. Also contains a chapter on the consultant and patient relationship, and a questionnaire for understanding and treating difficult children.

Erikson, Erik Homburger. *Identity, Youth, and Crisis.* New York: W. W. Norton, 1968. An impressive summation of Erikson's theories of human nature and development and the importance of societal forces. Erikson discusses his clinical observations, the life cycle and the formation of identity, and case histories to illustrate identity confusion and other relevant issues. This book carries forward concepts expressed in *Childhood and Society* (1963).

Freud, Sigmund. *A General Introduction to Psychoanalysis.* New York: W. W. Norton, 1977. An easy-to-read account of Freud's complete theory of psychoanalysis. Freud presents twenty-eight lectures to reveal major aspects of his theory, essential details in his method of psychoanalysis, and the results of his work. He also examines the psychology of errors, dream analysis technique, and general theory of neurosis.

Greenwald, Harold, ed. *Great Cases in Psychoanalysis.* New York: Ballantine, 1959. An outstanding source of case histories written by the theorists themselves. Greenwald uses these case histories to portray the historical context of the psychoanalytic movement. These original case studies provide insight into therapeutic methods used by these great analysts as well as their assessments. Included are Sigmund Freud, Alfred Adler, Carl Jung, Karen Horney, and Harry Stack Sullivan.

Horney, Karen. *The Neurotic Personality of Our Time.* New York: W. W. Norton, 1937. This classic work contains Horney's portrayal of the neurotic personality and the relevance of cultural forces in the etiology of psychological disturbances. This post-Freudian document examines Horney's theoretical conceptualizations, including basic anxiety, neurotic trends, methods of adjustment, and the role played by culture.

Mitchell, Stephen A. *Freud and Beyond: A History of Modern Psychoanalytic Thought.* New York: Basic Books, 1996. A short overview of psychoanalysis, with chapters devoted to Sigmund Freud, Harry Stack Sullivan, Melanie Klein, and other important thinkers.

Sullivan, Harry Stack. *The Interpersonal Theory of Psychiatry.* New York: W. W. Norton, 1953. A classic work on human development from an interpersonal perspective. Sullivan provides a comprehensive overview of his theory by describing his key concepts and developmental stages. He further illustrates the application of his theory by focusing upon inappropriate interpersonal relationships.

Joan Bartczak Cannon

SEE ALSO: Analytical psychology: Carl G. Jung; Case-study methodologies; Dreams; Ego defense mechanisms; Ego psychology: Erik Erikson; Individual psychology: Alfred Adler; Psychoanalysis; Psychoanalytic psychology and personality: Sigmund Freud; Psychosexual development; Psychotherapy: Effectiveness; Social psychological models: Erich Fromm; Social psychological models: Karen Horney; Women's psychology: Karen Horney; Women's psychology: Sigmund Freud.

Psychoanalytic psychology and personality

Sigmund Freud

TYPE OF PSYCHOLOGY: Personality
FIELDS OF STUDY: Classic analytic themes and issues; personality theory; psychodynamic and neoanalytic models

Sigmund Freud's theory of personality, emphasizing unconscious motivation, sexual instincts, and psychological conflict, is one of the most profound and unique contributions in psychology. Freud described both the normal and abnormal personality, and he proposed a therapy for the treatment of mental problems.

KEY CONCEPTS
- anal stage
- ego
- genital stage
- id
- instincts
- latency
- Oedipal conflict
- oral stage
- phallic stage
- superego

INTRODUCTION

Sigmund Freud (1856-1939) saw people as engaged in a personal struggle between their instinctual urges and the requirements of society. This conflict often takes place outside one's awareness, in the un-conscious, and affects all aspects of people's lives. The instinctual energy which fuels the mind has its source in the unconscious. It is highly mobile, and once engaged must achieve expression, however disguised the expression might be.

Freud likened the mind to an iceberg in that most of the mind is below the level of awareness—in the unconscious—as most of the mass of an iceberg is below the surface of the water. The id, the most primitive structure in the mind, is in the unconscious. The id is composed of the instincts (psychological representations of biological needs, they are the source of all psychological energy), including the sexual and other life instincts and the aggressive and other death instincts. For Freud, the sexual instincts were particularly important. They take a long time to develop, and society has a large investment in their regulation.

The instincts press for gratification, but the id itself cannot satisfy them, because it has no contact with reality. Therefore, the ego, which contacts the id in the unconscious but also is partly conscious, develops. The ego can perceive reality and direct behavior to satisfy the id's urges. To the extent that the ego can satisfy the id's instincts, it gains strength, which it can then use to energize its own processes, perceiving and thinking. It is important that the ego can also use its energy to restrict or delay the expression of the id. The ego uses psychological defense mechanisms to protect the individual from awareness of threatening events and to regulate the expression of the instincts. For example, a strong ego can use the defense mechanism of sublimation to direct some sexual energy into productive work rather than sexual activity itself.

In the course of development, the superego develops from the ego. The ego attaches energy to the significant people in the child's world—the caregivers—and their values are then adopted as the child's own ideal and conscience. This process becomes particularly significant during the phallic stage, between the ages of four and six. At that time, the child becomes sexually attracted to the opposite-sex parent. In giving up that passion, the child adopts the characteristics of the same-sex parent; this process shapes the child's superego. The superego is mostly unconscious, and it strives for perfection. Throughout life, the id will strive for instinctual gratification, and the superego will strive for perfection. It is the task of the ego to mediate between the two, when necessary, and to chart a realistic life course.

IMPORTANCE OF CHILDHOOD YEARS

Freud considered the childhood years particularly significant, not only because during these years the ego and superego develop from energy captured from the id but also because during this time the sexual instincts manifest themselves in a variety of forms. The sexual instincts become focused on particular erogenous zones of the child's body in a set order. This produces a series of psychosexual stages, each characterized by instinctual urges, societal response, conflict, and resolution. During the course of this process, lasting personality traits and defenses develop. At first, the sexual energy is focused on the mouth. In this, the oral stage, conflicts may surround feeding. At approximately age two, the anal stage begins. The sexual instincts focus on the anus, and conflicts may occur around toilet training. The

Sigmund Freud, the founder of psychoanalysis. (Library of Congress)

phallic stage, in which the child is attracted to the opposite-sex parent, follows. According to Freud, for boys this Oedipal conflict can be severe, as they fear castration from their father in retribution for their attraction to their mother. For girls, the conflict is somewhat less severe; in Freudian psychology, this less severe conflict means that in adulthood women will have less mature personalities than men. At approximately age six, the sexual instincts go into abeyance, and the child enters a period of latency. In adolescence, the sexual instincts again come to the fore, in the genital stage, and the adolescent has the task of integrating the impulses from all the erogenous zones into mature genital sexuality.

Psychological problems occur when the psychosexual stages have left the instinctual urges strongly overgratified or undergratified, when the instincts are overly strong, when the superego is overly tyrannical, or when the ego has dealt with childhood traumas by severe repression of its experiences into the unconscious. Undergratification or overgratification of the instincts during childhood can result in fixations, incomplete resolutions of childhood conflicts. For example, a person who is severely toilet trained can develop an "anal character," becoming either excessively neat, miserly, or otherwise "holding things inside." If the id urges are too strong, they may overwhelm the ego, resulting in psychosis. An overly strong superego can lead to excessive guilt. If the ego represses childhood trauma, relegating it to the unconscious, that trauma will persist, outside awareness, in affecting a person's thoughts and behaviors.

Freud believed that no one could escape the conflicts inherent in the mind but that one could gain greater familiarity with one's unconscious and learn to direct instinctual energies in socially appropriate ways. This was the task of psychoanalysis, a form of therapy in which a client's unconscious conflicts are explored to allow the individual to develop better ways of coping.

IMPACT ON WESTERN SOCIETY

Freud's theory has had a dramatic impact on Western society, strongly influencing the ways people view themselves and their interactions with others. Terms such as "Freudian slip," "Oedipus complex," and "unconscious" are a part of everyday language. Emotions may be seen as "buried deep," and emotional expression may be called therapeutic. Assumptions about the unconscious influence both popular and professional conceptions of mental life.

The assumption that the expression of emotion is healthy and the repression of emotion is unhealthy may be traced to Freud. To some extent, this idea has received support from research which suggests that unresolved anger may contribute to physical health problems. Unfortunately, the release of anger in verbal or physical aggression may cause those aggressive behaviors to increase rather than decrease. The vicarious experience of aggression via watching television or films may also teach aggression rather than reduce the urge to act aggressively.

ROLE OF DREAMS

Freud believed that dreams were one vehicle of unconscious expression. He viewed dreams as expressing the fulfillment of a wish, generally of a sexual nature. During sleep, the ego relaxes its restrictions on the id; instinctual wishes from the id, or repressed material from the unconscious, may be manifested in a dream. The bizarre sense of time and the confusing combinations of people and odd incidents in dreams reflect that the unconscious is without a sense of time, logic, or morality.

In dreams, the ego transforms material from the id to make it less threatening. Once one awakens, the ego disguises the true meaning of the dream further. Important points will be repressed and forgotten, and distortions will occur as the dream is remembered or told. For this reason, it is virtually impossible, according to Freud, to interpret one's own dreams accurately. A psychoanalyst interprets dreams by asking a patient to free associate—to say whatever comes to mind—about the dream content. In this fashion, the censoring of the ego may be relaxed, and the true meaning will be revealed to the therapist.

Revealing unconscious material is at the center of Freudian psychotherapy. Since Freud, many have viewed psychological problems as the result of childhood conflicts or traumas. Once the source is revealed, the patient is expected to improve. The nature of treatment is considerably more complicated than this might suggest, because the patient's ego may actively defend against acknowledging painful unconscious material. One of the few cases that Freud reported in detail was that of "Dora." Dora was referred to Freud because of a persistent cough that was assumed to be of psychological origin. According to Freud, such physical symptoms often are the result of childhood sexual conflict. Dora's cough and other psychosomatic complaints were found to be rooted in her sexual attraction to her father and to other men who were seen as resembling him—including a family friend, and even Freud himself. Her attraction was accompanied by jealousy of her mother and the family friend's wife. The situation was complicated, because Dora's father was having an affair with the family friend's wife, to whom Dora was also attracted, and the family friend had expressed his attraction for Dora.

All this and more is revealed in two dreams of Dora's that Freud analyzes in detail. The first is a dream of being awakened by her father, dressing quickly, and escaping a house that is on fire. The dream does its work by equating her father with the family friend, who once really was beside her bed as she awoke from a nap. This caused her to decide to "dress quickly" in the mornings, lest the friend come upon her unclothed. Her unconscious attraction for the friend, however, is belied by the symbol of fire, which might be likened to consuming passion. In her second dream, Dora dreamed that her father was dead and that a man said "Two and a half hours more." The dream symbolizes both Dora's turning away from her father as an object of her sexual interest and her intention (not evident to Freud at the time) of leaving therapy after two more sessions.

If Dora had not stopped therapy prematurely, Freud would have continued to bring his interpretation of her unconscious conflicts to the fore. In particular, he would have used her transference of childhood emotions to Freud himself as a vehicle for making the material revealed by her dreams, free associations, and behaviors evident to consciousness. The use of such transference is a key element of psychoanalysis. While this would not have completely resolved Dora's strong instinctual urges, it would have allowed her to come to terms with them in more mature ways, perhaps by choosing an appropriate marriage partner. Indeed, Freud reveals at the end of his report of this case that Dora married a young man she mentioned near the end of her time in therapy.

IMPACT AND CRITICISMS

Freud was a unique, seminal thinker. His theory was controversial from its inception; at the same time, however, it is such a powerful theory that, while many have criticized it, no subsequent personality theorist has been able to ignore the ideas Freud advanced. Psychoanalytic theory has also provided an interpretive framework for literary critics, historians, philosophers, and others.

Freud's theory was a product of his personal history, his training in science and medicine, and the Viennese culture in which he lived. Freud's early training was as a neurologist. As he turned from neurology to psychology, he continued to apply the skills of careful observation to this new discipline and to assume that the human mind followed natural laws that could be discovered. Viennese society at the time of Freud was one of restrictive social attitudes, particularly for women, and of covert practices that fell far short of public ideals. Thus it was relatively easy to see the psychological problems of the middle-class Viennese women who often were Freud's patients as being attributable to sexual conflicts.

Although Freud himself was dedicated to developing a science of mental life, his methods are open to criticism on scientific grounds. His theory is based upon his experiences as a therapist and his own self-analysis. His conclusions may therefore be restricted to the particular people or time his work encompassed. He did not seek to corroborate what his patients told him by checking with others outside the therapy room. Freud was not interested in the external "truth" of a report as much as its inner psychological meaning. He did not make details of his cases available to scrutiny, perhaps because of confidentiality. Although he wrote extensively about his theory, only five case histories were published. In all, these difficulties make the assessment of Freudian theory in terms of traditional scientific criteria problematic.

Freud's theory has had strong adherents as well as critics. Although theorists such as Alfred Adler and Carl Jung eventually broke with Freud, arguing against the primacy of the sexual instincts, his influence can be seen in their theories. Similarly, the important work of Erik Erikson describing human development through the life span has its roots in psychoanalytic theory. Many contemporary psychoanalytic theorists place a greater emphasis on the ego than did Freud, seeing it as commanding its own source of energy, independent of and equal to the id. Much contemporary literature and social criticism also possess a Freudian flavor.

SOURCES FOR FURTHER STUDY

Freud, Sigmund. *General Psychological Theory: Papers on Metapsychology.* New York: Macmillan, 1997. A collection of Freud's papers about the practice of psychoanalysis.

_____. *An Outline of Psychoanalysis.* Translated by James Strachey. New York: W. W. Norton, 1949. A brief introduction to Freudian theory. Beginning students of Freud may find the tone too didactic and the treatment too abbreviated; however, it is valuable when read in conjunction with a good summary of Freud from a secondary source.

Gay, Peter. *Freud: A Life for Our Time.* 1988. Reprint. New York: W. W. Norton, 1998. A very well-written biography of Freud. Places Freud's work in historical and psychological context. Accessible to the reader who may only have a passing familiarity with Freudian theory.

_____, ed. *The Freud Reader.* Reprint. New York: W. W. Norton, 1995. A well-edited volume of selections of Freud's work. *The Interpretation of Dreams, Fragment of an Analysis of a Case of Hysteria ("Dora"),* and *Three Essays on the Theory of Sexuality* are particularly important in defining the basics of Freud's theory.

Hall, Calvin Springer, and Gardner Lindzey. "Freud's Classical Psychoanalytical Theory." In *Theories of Personality.* 4th ed. New York: John Wiley & Sons, 1997. This chapter is the classic textbook summary of Freud's theory. Very readable, thorough, and accurate. Also presents a brief discussion of psychoanalytic research methods and criticisms of the theory.

Jones, Ernest. *The Life and Work of Sigmund Freud.* Edited and abridged by Lionel Trilling and Steven Marcus. New York: Basic Books, 1961. This is an abridged edition of Jones's three-volume biography of Freud. Jones was a confidant of Freud, and his official biographer. Interesting as an insider's account of Freud's life.

Kardiner, Abram. *My Analysis with Freud.* New York: W. W. Norton, 1977. Kardiner is a well-known analyst. This brief volume is a personal account of his own analysis, with Freud as the therapist. A fascinating insider's account of Freudian analysis and the forces that shaped the psychoanalytic movement.

Susan E. Beers

SEE ALSO: Abnormality: Psychological models; Dreams; Ego defense mechanisms; Ego, superego, and id; Freud, Sigmund; Oedipus complex; Penis envy; Psychoanalysis; Psychoanalytic psychology; Psychosexual development; Psychotherapy: Children; Psychotherapy: Effectiveness; Psychotherapy: Goals and techniques; Psychotherapy: Historical approaches; Women's psychology: Sigmund Freud; Women's psychology: Karen Horney.

Psychobiology

TYPE OF PSYCHOLOGY: Biological bases of behavior; cognition; language; learning; memory; sensation and perception

FIELDS OF STUDY: Auditory, chemical, cutaneous, and body senses; biological influences on learning; organic disorders; thought; vision

Psychobiology is the study of the relationship between the body and human experience, including sensation and perception, emotions, memory, language, movement, thinking, and learning.

KEY CONCEPTS
- anterograde amnesia
- Broca's aphasia
- hemi-inattention
- neurons
- neurotransmitters
- prefrontal lobotomy
- synapses
- visual agnosia
- Wernicke's aphasia

INTRODUCTION

For centuries, philosophers and scientists have addressed the question of the relationship between the brain and the mind. In the 1600's, the French philosopher René Descartes proposed the dualistic theory, which is the belief that the mind and the body are different entities and work independently of each other, but somehow interact. Descartes had problems, however, explaining how the invisible mind could influence a physical brain. He suggested that the mind and brain interact in the pineal gland, which is a small structure in the brain that releases the hormone melatonin.

Nearly all philosophers and neuroscientists today reject dualism. Their objection is that if the mind influences the brain, the mind must itself be composed of matter or energy. The alternative description of the relationship between the brain and the mind is monism, which is the belief that the universe consists of only one kind of existence.

The identity position is a popular version of monism that most philosophers and scientists support. This view suggests that mental processes and brain processes are the same thing but are described in different terms. For example, if a man sees a speeding truck approaching him as he is crossing a street, fear might be his mental experience and running across the street to avoid the truck is his behavioral response. However, another description of the same experience could include how his brain records and interprets the threatening visual scene and then triggers other physical reactions, such as increases in heart rate and blood pressure and the release of stress hormones. These physical reactions then send a message back to the brain, which instructs the muscles to move, enabling the man to run.

Currently, with the help of brain imaging technology, such as magnetic resonance imaging (MRI) and positron emission tomography (PET), much more is known about how the brain and human experience relate to each other. An MRI is a method of imaging the living brain by using a magnetic field and a radio frequency field to make certain atoms rotate in the same direction, and then removing those fields and measuring the energy that the atoms release. The MRI allows neuroscientists to see the structure of the brain without damaging it. PET is a method of mapping the activity of a living brain by recording the emission of radioactivity from injected chemicals. This allows neuroscientists to see what parts of the brain are active as the person is performing a particular task, such as solving math problems.

The human brain—composed of the hindbrain, the midbrain, and the forebrain—is an amazing structure. It is the only bodily organ with the ability to be aware of itself. This two- to three-pound, gelatinous mass makes it possible for human beings to recognize and interpret sensory information, to use the complex system of language, to store and recall an infinite amount of factual information and a lifetime of experiences, and to create new ideas and imagine the unseen.

HINDBRAIN AND MIDBRAIN

The hindbrain is the most primitive part of the brain and includes the medulla, the pons, the reticular formation, and the cerebellum. The medulla is just above the spinal cord and controls vital reflexes, such as breathing, heart rate, vomiting, salivation, coughing, and sneezing. The pons and the reticular formation (a set of pathways) mediate alertness and arousal, increasing and decreasing the brain's readiness to respond to stimuli. The cerebellum (from a Latin word meaning "little brain") is a large hindbrain structure that helps with balance and the coordination of motor movement. People who have a damaged cerebellum stagger when they walk and often lose their balance.

The midbrain in adult mammals is small and surrounded by the forebrain. In lower animals, such as birds, reptiles, and fish, it is larger and more prominent. The midbrain includes part of the reticular formation as well as other pathways and provides a route for important sensory information to reach the forebrain quickly.

FOREBRAIN

The forebrain consists of the limbic system, the thalamus, and the cerebral cortex. The limbic system includes several structures that mediate emotions and primary motivations, such as hunger, thirst, sex drive, and memory. These structures include the amygdala, the hypothalamus, and the hippocampus.

The amygdala plays an important role in the experience of fear and anxiety. Both fear and anxiety are "escape emotions," in that reacting to the emotion, as in fleeing from a threatening stimulus such as a poisonous snake, causes the intensity of the emotion to diminish.

The hypothalamus is a pea-sized structure located near the base of the brain. It contains a number of distinct parts, some of which regulate the release of certain hormones. The hypothalamus also forms the biological basis of motivating behaviors that are crucial for survival, such as feeding, drinking, temperature regulation, sexual behavior, and the fight-or-flight response.

The hippocampus (from a Latin word meaning "sea horse," because of its shape) is a large structure in the limbic system that is important in the creation of new memories. Memories are not stored in the hippocampus. Instead, the hippocampus is like a factory that creates new memories and then sends

them to other areas of the brain for storage. A famous case study of a man known as HM illustrates the function of the hippocampus. HM had severe seizures which originated in the hippocampus and could not be controlled by medication. The surgical removal of HM's hippocampus served as a drastic attempt to eliminate his debilitating seizures. As a result, HM developed anterograde amnesia, which is the inability to form new memories. All the memories that had been stored in his brain before the surgery were unharmed. HM was essentially stuck in a perpetual present. He could read the same newspaper repeatedly, having no memory of ever reading it before. He could be introduced to a stranger and have a normal conversation, but when the person left the room and later returned, he would have no recollection of meeting the person or having the conversation.

The thalamus is also part of the forebrain. It looks like two small footballs in the center of the brain. The thalamus is a relay center for sensory information. Sensory receptors, such as those located in the retina of the eye or in the eardrum, absorb physical stimuli from the environment, such as light or sound waves. The sensory systems send the information to the thalamus, which relays it on to the cerebral cortex for further processing. One exception is the olfactory system (the sense of smell), which has a direct connection to the cortex.

CEREBRAL CORTEX

The cerebral cortex (from a Latin word meaning "bark" or "covering") is the outer part of the brain, which is most developed in humans. The cortex consists of two hemispheres, one on the left and one on the right. The corpus callosum connects the two hemispheres, allowing communication between them. Each hemisphere of the cortex is composed of four lobes: the occipital, parietal, temporal, and frontal lobes.

The occipital lobes, which are located in the back of the brain, process visual information. The receptor cells in the retina of the eye absorb light and then send the information along the optic nerve to the thalamus, which then relays it to the occipital lobes. Visual perception, which is the process of recognizing and interpreting sensory information, occurs in the occipital lobes. If certain parts of the occipital lobes are damaged, it may result in visual agnosia, which is the inability to interpret visual information. Neurologist Oliver Sacks, in his book *The Man Who Mistook His Wife for a Hat* (1985), describes a music teacher, Dr. P, who had a visual agnosia. Dr. P first noticed that something was amiss when he became unable to recognize his students. However, he could recognize them when they spoke, since his auditory perception was intact. Sacks describes an interview with Dr. P in which he showed him a glove and asked him to identify it. Dr. P examined the glove carefully and described it as some sort of container with five pouches that could be used to carry coins of different sizes. He was able to describe the different features of the object, indicating that he was not blind, but was unable to recognize the object as a glove.

The parietal lobes lie between the occipital lobes and the central sulcus, which is one of the deepest grooves in the surface of the cortex. The parietal lobes are important for processing tactile information (the sense of touch), as well as body position and location. The lobe of each hemisphere records and interprets tactile stimulation from the opposite side of the body. A quarter placed in a person's right hand will be recognized by the agency of the left parietal lobe, for instance. The parietal lobes also play an important role in proprioception, a sensory system that gives the brain information about the position and movement of the body without relying on vision.

People who experience damage to the right parietal lobe sometimes show a fascinating condition called hemi-inattention. When this occurs, the person is unable to attend to the left side of the body and the world. A person with hemi-inattention may shave or apply makeup only to the right side of the face. While dressing, he or she may put a shirt on the right arm but leave the left side of the shirt hanging behind the body. The person may eat from only the right side of the plate, not noticing the food on the left side. This condition is not due to visual problems or the loss of sensation on the left side of the body, but is a deficit in the ability to direct attention to the left side of the body and the world.

The temporal lobes of the cortex are located on each side of the head, near the temples. The temporal lobes play an important role in recognizing and interpreting auditory information. The temporal lobes enable a person to identify familiar sounds, such as a police siren or a crying baby. Wernicke's area (named after Karl Wernicke, the neurolo-

gist who discovered its function), located in the left temporal lobe, mediates the ability to understand spoken language. When this area of the temporal lobe is damaged, the person may exhibit Wernicke's aphasia, a condition marked by poor language comprehension and difficulty remembering the names of objects.

The frontal lobes, located just behind the forehead, are specialized to control motor movements, spoken language, and higher-level thinking skills. The decision to scratch one's head or turn the page of a book is transmitted by the frontal lobes through the spinal cord to the muscles needed to perform the task. Like tactile sensation in the parietal lobes, each frontal lobe controls the opposite side of the body.

Broca's area (named after Paul Broca, the neurologist who discovered its function) is located in the frontal lobe, close to the motor area that controls facial and tongue movements. Most people who experience damage to this area in the left frontal lobe exhibit Broca's aphasia, which is an impairment of expressive language. People with Broca's aphasia may speak only nouns and verbs, omitting other parts of speech such as prepositions, conjunctions, adjectives, adverbs, helping verbs, and word endings that indicate number or tense. They have particular trouble applying grammar rules for word order, although their pronunciation may be adequate. People with Broca's aphasia who are deaf and use sign language also show such difficulties, even though they are able to use their hands well in other ways.

The frontal lobes are also important in planning, initiating, and inhibiting behavior. They help people adapt to changes in the environment, including developing strategies to solve problems, monitoring the progress of such strategies, and being able to switch tactics when necessary.

In 1848, Phineas Gage, a railroad worker, suffered a severe accident in which an explosion caused an iron rod to pierce his cheek, slice through his frontal cortex, and emerge through the top of his head, where it lodged. Miraculously, Gage survived, but he experienced a dramatic personality change. He went from being a gentle, competent worker to being aggressive, emotionally volatile, and incapable of functioning normally. This case is considered the first known natural prefrontal lobotomy. The prefrontal lobotomy, in which the prefrontal cortex is surgically damaged or the connections between the prefrontal cortex and the rest of the cortex are cut, later became a drastic treatment for certain mental disorders.

In the United States, Walter Freeman and James Watts, professors of neurology and neurosurgery, published a report in 1942 entitled "Psychosurgery in the Treatment of Mental Disorders and Intractable Pain." In the late 1940's and the early 1950's, about forty thousand prefrontal lobotomies were performed in the United States. The therapeutic goal of such psychosurgeries was to make difficult, aggressive patients calmer without damaging their sensory or motor abilities. Dr. Freeman often employed crude methods in these surgical procedures, sometimes using electric drills or metal picks. He performed many of these operations in his office rather than in a hospital, often carrying his equipment, which he called his "lobotomobile," around with him. Prefrontal lobotomies were performed on a wide range of people thought to be mentally disordered, with common results including apathy, loss of the ability to plan and take initiative, generally blunted emotions, and the loss of facial expression. Patients also became unable to inhibit socially unacceptable behaviors and tended to act impulsively, without the ability to predict the consequences of their behavior. In the mid-1950's, when effective drug therapies became available to treat many mental disorders, the use of lobotomies declined drastically. Dr. Freeman eventually lost his privilege to practice in most hospitals, and other neuroscientists denounced his practices after that time.

Damage to the frontal lobes due to strokes or other trauma often impairs a person's ability to initiate and organize behavior, as well as the ability to inhibit socially unacceptable behavior. After frontal lobe damage, a person who was once a model of social grace may become emotionally volatile, behaviorally explosive, and rude. Such people may use crude and profane language that they would never have uttered before the trauma.

LEARNING AND NEURONAL CONNECTIONS

Learning results in three different types of memory: declarative, procedural, and episodic memories. Declarative memories involve encoding and storing factual information, such as the name of one's first-grade teacher. Learning to type at a keyboard is an example of procedural memory. When asked to recall the location of the "L" key, most people find themselves moving the third finger on their right hand. Recalling letters in the sequence in which they appear on a keyboard, without using the fingers to mimic the required movement, is a task that most people find quite difficult. This is because the memory is encoded and stored in the brain as a sequence of motor movements rather than as factual information. Memories of life experiences, or episodic memories, are represented in the brain as visual scenes that can be relived through imagination.

How is it that, no matter how old a person becomes, there is always room in the brain to store new information and experiences? How can something as simple as learning a new word, which may take seconds to occur, form a memory in the brain that can potentially last a lifetime? The answer to these questions lies in the examination of the brain at the cellular level.

Neurons are specialized cells that have the ability to communicate with one another electrochemically. Most neurons do not physically touch each other, but are separated by small gaps called synapses. When a neuron receives a message from another neuron, it triggers an electrical impulse, which travels from the receiving end of the neuron to the transmitting end. When the electrical impulse reaches the end of the neuron, it causes chemicals, known as neurotransmitters, to be released into the synaptic gap. The neurotransmitters then flood across this gap, triggering another electrical impulse in the next neuron, and the sequence continues. Since there are billions of neurons in the human brain, and any one neuron can form synaptic connections with hundreds of other neurons, the potential for forming unique patterns of neuronal connections is virtually infinite. When learning a new word, a memory forms as a unique pattern of neuronal connections in the brain. Hearing the word only once, never recalling or using again, will likely result in the fading away of the new pattern of neuronal connections. However, recalling a word and using it repeatedly will likely cause its unique pattern of neuronal connections to become more durable, with the potential of lasting a lifetime. Thus, the neural representations of everything a person learns and remembers are unique patterns of neuronal connections in the brain.

SOURCES FOR FURTHER STUDY

Calvin, William H., and George A. Ojemann. *Conversations with Neil's Brain: The Neural Nature of Thought and Language*. Reading, Mass.: Perseus

Books, 1994. This is a story of a young man who was facing the surgical removal of a part of his temporal lobe to treat his severe seizure disorder. The book is composed of a very readable series of conversations among Neil, his neurosurgeon, and a neuroscientist.

Czerner, Thomas B. *What Makes You Tick? The Brain in Plain English.* New York: John Wiley and Sons, 2001. This book is a very accessible introduction to breakthroughs in brain research.

Kalat, James W. *Biological Psychology.* 7th ed. Belmont, Calif.: Wadsworth, 2001. This is a well-known, popular textbook used in college-level biological psychology classes. Key terms are clearly defined. "Stop and Check Questions" are included at various points in the text, with answers located at the end of each module. This text also includes relevant websites.

Marshall, Louise H., and Horace W. Magoun. *Discoveries in The Human Brain: Neuroscience Prehistory, Brain Structure, and Function.* Totowa, N.J.: Humana Press, 1998. This book chronicles significant people and events that have lead up to today's understanding of brain anatomy and physiology. It is an excellent source of information about landmark discoveries and contains many historical illustrations.

Sacks, Oliver. *The Man Who Mistook His Wife for a Hat and Other Clinical Tales.* New York: Summit Books, 1985. This is a beautifully written series of case studies of people with often strange neurological impairments.

Cathy J. Bogart

SEE ALSO: Brain damage; Brain specialization; Brain structure; Forgetting and forgetfulness; Kinesthetic memory; Memory; Memory: Animal research; Memory: Empirical studies; Memory: Sensory; Memory storage; Thought: Study and measurement.

Psychology
Definition

TYPE OF PSYCHOLOGY: Origin and definition of psychology

FIELDS OF STUDY: Classic analytic themes and issues; methodological issues

The term "psychology" first appeared in written form during the early sixteenth century and meant the systematic study of the soul and mind. The meaning of the concept changed gradually during the next three centuries, until psychology emerged in the 1880's as a separate field of study. Defined as the scientific study of mind and consciousness, the discipline was by the 1920's redefined as the scientific study of behavior and mental processes, creating some significant problems. In spite of definitional ambiguities, contemporary psychology is a vigorous and broad field of study.

KEY CONCEPTS
- act psychology
- behaviorism
- functionalism
- psychological domain
- structuralism

INTRODUCTION
The term "psyche," while personified by the ancient Greeks as a goddess, essentially means "breath," which was equated with soul or mind. The suffix "ology" means "science" or "study of." Psychology, as originally defined, then, means the scientific study of soul or mind. The term "scientific," as used here, means systematic; scientific fields of study did not emerge until the seventeenth century.

Apparently, the concept of psychology was not formulated until the early to middle sixteenth century, appearing first in 1530 as part of the title of a series of academic lectures given by Philipp Melanchthon, a German scholar. The first book with the Latin word *psychologia* (psychological) as part of the title was published in 1594. When used by philosophers and theologians during the next three centuries, the term had a gradually changing meaning, with the focus being much more on the study of mind and consciousness than on the soul.

Psychology, as a separate field of study, came into being in Germany in 1879 and, during the 1880's, in many other European countries and the United States. The field was defined as the scientific or systematic study of mind and consciousness and was largely modeled after physics and chemistry. Wilhelm Wundt (1832-1920), the acknowledged founder of the new discipline, believed that psychologists should be concerned primarily with investigating the structure of mind and consciousness using rigorous introspective techniques. Psychology was, according to Wundt, to focus on identifying the properties of simple mental elements and the laws by which these elements combined to form the more complex structures of mind and consciousness, for example, percepts and ideas. This approach, and a derivative of it developed in the United States by Edward Titchener, became known as structuralism. Animal research, the study of infants and children, the study of people with psychological problems, and concern with individual differences were not seen as central to psychology.

Some of Wundt's European contemporaries, however, such as Franz Brentano and Oswald Külpe, argued that psychology should focus on processes associated with mind and consciousness, such as perceiving, thinking, and intending, rather than attempting to divide the mental domain into simple elements. Brentano's approach became known as act psychology, in contrast to Wundt's mental-content psychology, and the two perspectives generated some interesting controversies. They did agree, though, that psychology should be concerned primarily with the study of mind and consciousness in normal adult human beings; animals, children, and people with mental and emotional problems were not of particular interest to them as subjects of research.

Also emphasizing conceptions of mind and consciousness as process rather than content were prominent early American psychologists such as William James, John Dewey, James Rowland Angell, and Harvey Carr. In contrast to Brentano and Külpe, however, these psychologists were primarily interested in the functions served by the processes. It was generally assumed that each of these capabilities evolved to help humans survive and that it was the job of psychologists to determine how seeing, hearing, feeling, thinking, willing, planning, and so forth contributed to individuals' survival. Since not everyone adapts equally well to the challenges of life, this approach to psychology, which became known as functionalism, emphasized the study of individuals differences in intelligence, personality, social skills, and so forth, as well as applied psychology and animal research. Psychology, however, was still defined as the systematic study of mind and

consciousness. Functionalism has its foundations in Charles Darwin's theory of evolution and in late nineteenth century British psychology and applied statistics.

With the introduction of animal research into psychology and continuing controversies over the meanings of the concepts of mind, consciousness, and terms referring to the varying aspects of private experience, some psychologists increasingly believed that a scientific psychology could only be created if research centered on behavior (responses) and environmental features (stimuli), both of which are observable. Therefore, when American psychologist John B. Watson proclaimed, in 1913, that psychology should abandon attempts to study mind and consciousness introspectively and redefine itself as the scientific study of behavior, many of his peers were ready to follow his call; behaviorism had its formal beginning.

The behavioral orientation had its greatest influence on American psychology from about the 1920's until the early 1970's, undergoing a number of transformations. During that time, most textbooks defined psychology as the scientific study of behavior, or of behavior and mental and affective processes. Even as the limits of behavioral psychology, in its various forms, became apparent by the late 1960's, definitions of psychology changed very little. According to most contemporary psychologists in the United States and in many other countries, psychology is primarily the study of behavior, and only secondarily—and sometimes grudgingly—the study of such difficult-to-define mental and affective states and processes as thoughts, percepts, images, and feelings. Nevertheless, even the concepts of mind and consciousness, the original concerns of psychology, have somewhat reluctantly been readmitted to the field as necessary research concerns.

DEFINITIONAL PROBLEMS

There are a number of serious problems associated with defining psychology as the scientific study of behavior and mental and affective states. Not only is the definition imprecise, but also it has apparently made it very difficult to generate an integrated body of psychological knowledge. While impressive research on the behavior of animals and humans has been conducted, and some progress has been made in understanding mental and affective processes and states, the knowledge generated is fragmented and therefore of limited value.

One could argue, in fact, that psychology is not the study of behavior at all but is rather the study of the information each person or animal has available that makes behavior—that is, directed and controlled actions—possible. While this information has traditionally been referred to as mind and consciousness, there might be some virtue in calling it "the psychological domain" in order to avoid long-standing arguments. Behavior is a methodological concept because it refers to something researchers must study in order to make inferences about the psychological domain. On the other hand, researchers can also investigate the products of human actions, such as the languages people develop, the buildings they construct, and the art and music they share, to the same end. Some psychologists perform research on the physiological processes associated with seeing, hearing, feeling, and thinking. Definitions of psychology should include the terms "culture" and "physiological and biochemical correlates" as well as the concept of behavior.

A better approach might be to define psychology as the systematic study of the psychological domain, this domain being the personal information that makes it possible for individual human beings and other life-forms to move with direction and control. To go beyond this definition is to describe how psychologists do research rather than what the field is about.

Another problem associated with standard definitions of psychology is the assumption that there is general agreement concerning the meaning of the concept of behavior. As has been pointed out by many analysts, that is not the case. The term has been used to refer to sensory responses, cognitive and affective processes, muscle movements, glandular secretions, activity taking place in various parts of the nervous system, and the outcomes or consequences of particular complex actions. Behavior, in other words, is an ambiguous concept. In a strict sense, the only actions or changes relevant to the psychological level of analysis are those that are self-initiated and unique to the total-life-form level of organization in nature, because it is these changes that depend on the psychological domain. Changes in the individual cells or subsystems of life-forms, on the other hand, do not constitute behavior in the psychological sense.

THE DEVELOPMENT OF A FIELD

Even though a clear and generally agreed-upon definition of psychology has not emerged, psychology today is a vigorous and broad scholarly field and profession, extending from biological subdisciplines and animal research laboratories to the study of humans in social, political, economic, industrial, educational, clinical, and religious contexts. It is not surprising, therefore, that psychologists have made contributions in a wide variety of areas; among the most notable are those having to do with cognitive and emotional development, child rearing, formulating new ways to view and treat psychological problems, devising ways to deal with the crises of life associated with each stage of human experience from infancy to old age, consumer research and marketing, group dynamics, and the development of tests and educational procedures.

Psychology is one of the most popular majors in American colleges, and the discipline has experienced dramatic growth since the 1940's. There were about 4,000 psychologists in the United States during the 1940's; by the early 1990's, there were approximately 100,000. Since the mid-1970's, the number of women majoring in psychology has held steady, while the number of men has decreased significantly; as a consequence, by the late 1980's, more women than men were earning Ph.D.'s in psychology.

One of the most challenging new areas of study is health psychology, which emerged during the 1980's in response to the health care crisis, brought about by increasing costs associated with an aging population, expensive high-technology medical techniques, the acquired immuno deficiency syndrome (AIDS) epidemic, economic restructuring and stagnation, and a variety of other factors. Pressures have also been emerging for people to reexamine their values and roles and, in a sense, their personal and national identities; these pressures derive from such powerful forces and dynamics as the feminist and multicultural movements, the emergence of nontraditional social and child-rearing arrangements, and the change from a production to a service society. A mass identity crisis may, in fact, provide the psychologists of the twenty-first century with their major challenge.

SOURCES FOR FURTHER STUDY

Carr, Harvey A. *Psychology: A Study of Mental Activity.* New York: Longmans, Green, 1925. Presents a clear picture of the functionalist view of psychology. Carr was one of the American psychologists who formalized functionalism.

Gilgen, Albert R. *American Psychology Since World War II: A Profile of the Discipline.* Westport, Conn.: Greenwood, 1982. Presents an overview of the major developments and trends in American psychology during World War II, which ended in 1945, and from the postwar period through the 1970's.

_____. "The Psychological Level of Organization in Nature and Interdependencies Among Major Psychological Concepts." In *Annals of Theoretical Psychology.* Vol. 5, edited by Arthur W. Staats and Leendert P. Mos. New York: Plenum, 1987. Presents a detailed rationale for defining psychology as the systematic study of the information available to each person that allows each individual to move with direction and control.

Lapointe, Franois H. "Who Originated the Term 'Psychology'?" *Journal of the History of the Behavioral Sciences* 8, no. 3 (1972): 328-335. The most thorough analysis of the origination of the term "psychology." An essential reference for anyone interested in the history of the concept.

Murray, David J. *A History of Western Psychology.* 2d ed. Englewood Cliffs, N.J.: Prentice-Hall, 1988. Includes clear discussions of the origins of the term "psychology" and the meaning of the concept for the act psychologists, the structuralists, the functionalists, and the behaviorists.

Porter, Roy. *Madness: A Brief History.* New York: Oxford University Press, 2002. A history of Western ideas about mental illness by one of the most respected historians of medicine. Changing ideas about "madness" help trace the evolution of the definition of psychology.

Titchener, Edward Bradford. *A Primer of Psychology.* Rev. ed. New York: Macmillan, 1913. Presents a clear and detailed analysis of psychology from the structuralist perspective, and in the process identifies many of the challenges involved in attempting to decipher the structure of mind and consciousness.

Albert R. Gilgen

SEE ALSO: Behaviorism; Cognitive psychology; Humanism; Psychoanalytic psychology; Psychology: Fields of specialization; Scientific methods; Structuralism and functionalism.

Psychology
Fields of specialization

TYPE OF PSYCHOLOGY: Origin and definition of psychology

FIELDS OF STUDY: Behavioral therapies; cognitive development; experimental methodologies; general constructs and issues; psychodynamic and neoanalytic models

Psychology is both a theoretical and an applied science. Psychologists use observational and experimental methods to reach a greater understanding of the human mind and human behavior. They then use this knowledge in a variety of settings to help people in their daily lives.

KEY CONCEPTS
- behaviorism
- cognitive psychology
- Gestalt psychology
- social psychology
- structuralism

INTRODUCTION

Because the fields of specialization within psychology are so numerous, one must first examine the science as an entity unto itself. This involves defining psychology, exploring the reasons for its existence, reviewing its history, and surveying the diverse specialists who assist various populations. Although the semantics of defining psychology differ from text to text, the actual explanation remains constant: It is the science of human behavior as it relates to the functions of the mind. More specifically, it provides evidence for why people experience a gamut of emotions, think rationally or irrationally, and act either predictably or unpredictably.

The discipline's very existence justifies humankind's need to plumb the depths of its interior to search for the self, to process conflict, to solve problems, and to think critically as well as act pragmatically. Its challenge is to assist people in understanding themselves. Humans have a natural curiosity; it moves them to try to determine their relationship to the world in which they live. With this comes the inclination to observe and compare other people: their ideas, behavior patterns, and abilities. These analyses and comparisons, which people cannot help but make, involve the self as well as others. People may be either overly harsh or selectively blind when examining themselves; both these situations can be a handicap and both can be helped by psychology.

At times, one's anxiety level may peak uncontrollably. Through the science of the mind, one seeks to temper one's agitation by becoming familiar with and acknowledging vague fears and uncomfortable feelings. Thus, one learns about the source of one's tension. From this, experts learn how behavior originates. They assist an individual in learning to cope with change; the person discovers how to make adequate adjustments in daily living. The fast pace that humans in industrialized society keep requires them now, more than ever before, to have a working knowledge of people—their thought processes and behavior patterns. From all of this, experts are able to arrive at reasonable predictions and logical conclusions about humankind's future behavior.

HISTORY AND SYSTEMS OF PSYCHOLOGY

Psychology did not become accepted as a formal discipline until the late nineteenth century. Prior to that time, even back to antiquity, questions were directed to philosophers, the wise men of the time. Though they were versed in reasoning, logic, and scholarship, only a few of these thinkers could deal with the complexities of the human mind. Their answers were profound and lengthy, but these scholars frequently left their audiences bewildered and without the solutions they sought. Some of these logicians used the Socratic method of reasoning; they

---

Degree Fields of Psychology Ph.D.'s

Arranged in descending order by number of degrees awarded in 1999:
- Clinical
- Counseling
- Developmental
- All other subfields (such as community psychology, sport psychology)
- Experimental/Physiological
- General
- Social and Personality
- Industrial/Organizational
- Cognitive
- School
- Educational

---

often frustrated those who questioned them and expected realistic replies. Inquires were redirected to the questioner, whose burden it was to arrive at his or her own solutions.

Gustav Fechner, a nineteenth century philosopher and physicist, postulated that the scientific method should be applied to the study of mental processes. It was his contention that experimentation and mathematical procedures should be used to study the human mind. From the mid-nineteenth century onward, many disciplines contributed to what was to become the science of psychology. Wilhelm Wundt and Edward Titchener were the leaders of the structuralist school, which identified the elements and principles of consciousness.

Other early giants of the field included William James and John Dewey. They inaugurated the study of functionalism, which taught that psychological knowledge should be applied to practical knowledge in fields such as education, business law, and daily living. A champion of behaviorism, John B. Watson, advocated that the study of psychology should concentrate on observable behavior; he urged that objective methods be adopted. The Gestalt movement was originated by Max Wertheimer. In concert with Kurt Koffka and Wolfgang Köhler, he embraced the premise that the whole may be different from its parts studied in isolation.

Psychoanalysis was developed by Sigmund Freud. He studied the unconscious using techniques of free association, hypnosis, and body language. The neobehaviorist model, in contrast, defended the behaviorist position that complicated phenomena such as mental and emotional activities cannot be observed. Love, stress, empathy, trust, and personality cannot be observed in and of themselves. Their effects, however, are readily apparent.

Carl Rogers and Abraham Maslow pioneered the area known as humanism in the 1950's and 1960's. Areas of interest to humanistic psychologists are self-actualization, creativity and transcendence, the search for meaning, and social change. Its goals are to expand and to enrich human lives through service to others and an increased understanding of the complexity of people, as individuals, in groups, organizations, and communities.

In the mid-twentieth century, with the development of cognitive psychology, mental processes such as attention, memory, and reasoning became the focus of direct study. This approach to understanding human thought analyzes cognitive processes into a sequence of ordered stages; each stage reflects an important step in the processing of information. In the 1980's and 1990's, the fields of cognitive science and cognitive neuroscience emerged. Psychologists began working with computer scientists, linguists, neurobiologists, and others to develop detailed models of brain and mind relationships.

MAJOR FIELDS IN PSYCHOLOGY

Psychology is both a theoretical and an applied science with over a dozen major fields. In 2002, the American Psychological Association listed fifty-three divisions, representing psychologists working in settings as diverse as community mental health clinics and large corporations and with interests ranging from the adult development and aging to the study of peace, conflict, and violence. Academic and research psychologists use observational and experimental methods to reach a greater understanding of the human mind and human behavior. Psychologists in the clinical specialties then use this knowledge to help people in their daily lives.

For example, children who are abused or neglected, or who suffer as a result of being members of dysfunctional families, require the services of child psychologists, who evaluate, diagnose, and treat youngsters; this usually occurs in a clinical setting. Thus, child psychologist are considered clinical practitioners. More than one-half of the Ph.D.s awarded in 1999 were in either clinical or counseling psychology.

Many psychologists also work in the area of education. Educational psychologists develop and analyze materials and strategies for effective educational curricula. School psychologists design instructive programs, consult with teachers, and assist students with problems.

Genetic psychologists study the activities of the human organism in relation to the hereditary and evolutionary factors involved; functions and origin play a central role. Physiological psychologists examine the biological bases of behavior. They are often interested in the biochemical reactions underlying memory and learning. Engineering psychologists design and evaluate equipment, training devices, and systems. The goal is to facilitate the re-

lationship between people and their environment. Industrial and organizational (I-O) psychologists research and develop programs that promote on-the-job efficiency, effectiveness, challenge, and positive disposition. They study ability and personality factors, special training and experience, and work and environment variables, as well as organizational changes.

Personality psychologists study the many ways in which people differ from one another; they are instrumental in analyzing how those differences may be assessed and what their impact is. Criminal psychologists study the complexities of a perpetrator's thought process. They are keenly interested in a criminal's habits, idiosyncrasies, and possible motives. Developmental psychologists study changes in people as they age and mature. Their work may be protracted over the span of an individual's life; their theories may be advanced several years after they were first conceived.

Social psychologists study how people influence one another. They may be interested, for example, in the concept of leaders and followers. Environmental psychologists monitor the physical and social effects of the environment on behavior. They are interested in how elements such as heat, noise, health, and activity affect the human condition. Their contributions are in the areas of urban planning, architecture, and transportation.

Consumer psychologists determine factors that influence consumer decisions, exploring such issues as the effect of advertising on purchasing decisions, brand loyalty, and the rejection or acceptance of new products. Experimental psychologists design and conduct basic and applied research in a variety of areas, including learning, sensation, attention and memory, language, motivation, and the physiological and neural bases of behavior. Comparative psychologists study the behavior, cognition, perception, and social relationships of diverse animal species. Their research can be descriptive as well as experimental and is conducted in the field or with animals in captivity.

TESTS AND MEASURES OF INDIVIDUAL DIFFERENCES

The scope of psychology's fields of specialization is great. The professionals who work in these areas strive to help humans know, understand, and help themselves. To accomplish this, psychologists use numerous tests to help them ascertain specific information about an individual, a group of people, or a particular population. Ability tests measure multiple aptitudes, creativity, achievement, and intelligence levels. Psychologists may perform occupational and clinical assessments. Also included in the area of assessment are personality tests, which encompass self-report inventories, measures of interests, attitudes and values, projective techniques, and performance and situational evaluations.

An example of a multiple-aptitude test is the Differential Aptitude Test (DAT), first published in 1947, then revised in 1963, 1973, and 1991. Its primary purpose is to counsel students in grades eight through twelve in educational and vocational matters. Creativity tests have received much attention from researchers and practitioners alike. The Aptitudes Research Project (ARP) was developed by the University of Southern California. It is a structure-of-intellect (SI) model, which encompasses all intellectual functions. Though its initial platform was reasoning, creativity, and problem solving, its base was expanded to divergent production. Until the ARP, research resources in this area were very limited.

Achievement tests, which differ from aptitude tests, measure the effects of specific instruction or training. Some of the most respected tests are the California Achievement Tests, the Iowa Tests of Basic Skills, the Metropolitan Achievement Test, and the Stanford Achievement Test. Their significance lies in reporting what the individual can do at the time of test administration. Aptitude instruments, on the other hand, make recommendations about future skills. Intelligence tests speak their own language; it is unfortunate, though, that so much importance is placed upon the results they yield. One should always remember that the scores identified in the Stanford-Binet test and in the various Wechsler intelligence scales are only part of a big picture about any given human being and should be evaluated accordingly.

Personality tests measure the emotional, motivational, interpersonal, and attitudinal characteristics of an individual. The Kuder Interest Inventories list occupations according to a person's interest area. The Rorschach Inkblot Projective Technique investigates the personality as a whole. The Thematic Apperception Test (TAT) researches personality and attitude. The Myers-Briggs Type Indicator is a widely used measure of personality dispositions and interests based on Carl G. Jung's theory of types.

PSYCHOLOGY AND SOCIETY

Psychology as a formal discipline is still relatively new; of its many specializations, some have found their way to maturity, while others are still in their early stages. The development of diverse fields has been justified by the changing nature of social and psychological problems as well as by changing perceptions as to how best to approach those problems. For example, because more people live closer together than ever before, they must interact with one another to a greater degree; finding ways to deal with issues such as aggression, racism, and prejudice therefore becomes crucial. Several divisions of the American Psychological Association reflect the diverse groups that interest psychologists: the Society of Pediatric Psychology, the Society for the Psychological Study of Ethnic Minority Issues, and the Society for the Psychological Study of Lesbian, Gay, and Bisexual Issues.

Economic conditions require most parents to work—whether they are single parents or parents in a two-parent family—thus depriving children of time with their parents. This has created a need for day-care centers; the care and nurturing of young people is being transferred, to a significant degree, to external agents. Moreover, older children may be expected to assume adult responsibilities before they are ready. All these issues point to an increasing need for family counseling. Educational institutions demand achievement from students; this can daunt students who have emotional or family problems that interfere with their ability to learn. The availability of school counselors or psychologists can make a difference in whether such children succeed or fail. Businesses and organizations use psychologists and psychological testing to avoid hiring employees who would be ineffective or incompatible with the organization's approach and to maximize employee productivity on the job.

The specialized fields of psychology have played both a facilitative and a reflective role. Therapists and counselors, for example, have enabled individuals to look at what they have previously accomplished, to assess the present, and to come to terms with themselves and the realities of the future. The future of psychology itself will hold further developments both in the refining of specializations that already exist and in the development of new ones as inevitable societal changes require them.

SOURCES FOR FURTHER STUDY

Butler, Gillian, and Freda McManus. *Psychology: A Very Short Introduction.* New York: Oxford University Press, 2000. Butler and McManus provide an understanding of some of psychology's leading ideas and their practical relevance. The authors answer some of the most frequently asked questions about psychology: What is psychology? How do humans use what is in the mind? How does psychology work? How do people influence each other? What can a psychologist do to help?

Colman, Andrew M. *What Is Psychology?* 2d ed. New York: Routledge, 1999. Extensively revised and updated, this introduction to psychology as a discipline assumes no prior knowledge of the subject. Examples are used throughout to illustrate fundamental ideas, with a self-assessment quiz focusing readers on a number of intriguing psychological problems. The book explains the differences between psychology, psychiatry, and psychoanalysis, and offers an exploration of the professions and careers associated with psychology.

Koch, Sigmund, and David E. Leary, eds. *A Century of Psychology as Science.* Washington, D.C.: APA Books, 1992. This reissued edition, originally published in 1985, comprehensively accesses the accomplishments, status, and prospects of psychology at the end of its first century as a science, while offering a new postscript. The forty-three contributors are among psychology's foremost authorities. Among the fields addressed are sensory processes and perception, learning, motivation, emotion, cognition, development, personality, and social psychology.

Rieber, Robert W., and Kurt Salzinger, eds. *Psychology: Theoretical-Historical Perspectives.* 2d ed. Washington, D.C.: APA Books, 1998. The approach to theory and history adapted by the contributors is to focus on some of the central figures in the development of the discipline. Within this approach, the authors offer analyses of three major theoretical currents in psychology: psychoanalysis, behaviorism, and the Geneva school. Other chapters focus on psychophysics (the oldest incarnation of experimental psychology) and on Gestalt, cognitive, and evolutionary psychology. Provides the reader with a broad overview of the development of a continually evolving field.

Simonton, Dean Keith. *Great Psychologists and Their Times: Scientific Insights into Psychology's History.* Washington, D.C.: APA Books, 2002. The book integrates relevant research on the psychology of eminent psychologists, from the pioneering work of Francis Galton to work published in the twenty-first century. Of particular interest are chapters exploring what aspects of the sociocultural context are most conducive to the emergence of illustrious psychologists and how these sociocultural conditions—including political events, economic disturbances, or cultural values—affect not only the magnitude of achievement but also the nature of that achievement.

Denise S. St. Cyr;
updated by Allyson Washburn

SEE ALSO: Behaviorism; Cognitive psychology; Development; Disaster psychology; Educational psychology; Existential psychology; Experimental psychology; Humanism; Industrial and organizational psychology; Media psychology; Mental health practitioners; Neuropsychology; Psychoanalytic psychology; Psychology: Definition.

Psychology

History

TYPE OF PSYCHOLOGY: Origin and definition of psychology

FIELDS OF STUDY: General constructs and issues

Psychological inquiry and psychology as a field have a varied history going back thousands of years.

KEY CONCEPTS
- behaviorism
- clinical psychology
- cognitive psychology
- connectionism
- empiricism
- functionalism
- introspection
- positivism

- psychoanalysis
- ratrionalism
- scientific method
- self psychology
- structuralism

INTRODUCTION

Psychology can be assessed from points of view that regard it as a folk, cultural, or religious process; as a philosophical approach; a scientific method; an academic discipline; or a set of postmodern assumptions.

From the folk process point of view, peoples have formed their own cultures and religions from the beginning of human history. These different cultures and religions have their own unique values and norms within which the human person is considered and evaluated. Out of these norms come the everyday beliefs and expectations that members of the group will hold about themselves, other people, and the world. Thus in every culture there is an implicit theory of psychology. Since this process is always operative, it has always been a factor in how specific thinkers such as philosophers, scientists, and psychologists, as well as laypeople, have been able to think about the human person. The folk process remains an especially important factor in some areas of psychology, such as humanistic psychology and clinical psychology.

Philosophy began to emerge about the year 600 B.C.E. At that time, Thales (c. 624-545 B.C.E.), a Greek thinker, began to consider systematically the nature of the world. His view that the world's basic element is water demanded that the philosopher give up the folk process, or "common sense," and argue for a conclusion based on rational premises. This new way of thinking and arguing led to a much broader set of possibilities in the understanding of the world and the human being. In terms of psychology, philosophers would concentrate on topics such as the relationship between the mind and the body and the process of acquiring knowledge, especially about what is outside the body. In the last decade of the twentieth century, cognitive psychology was strongly influenced by philosophic thinking.

By the end of the Middle Ages and the beginning of the Renaissance, another way of thinking and solving problems began to emerge. As a result of dissatisfaction with both religious and philosophic answers to understanding the world and its place in the cosmos, as well as knowledge about the nature of the human being, a process of systematic and repeated observation and rigorous thinking began to emerge. This new process, which has been labeled as a part of modern thinking, has become the scientific method, and required another separation from the folk process. For instance, when the Polish astronomer Nicolaus Copernicus (1473-1543) and the Italian mathematician and astronomer Galileo Galilei (1564-1642) argued from their observations that the earth revolved around the Sun rather than the opposite, "commonsense" view, they offended both religious authorities and philosophers, but they opened the door to a new way of solving problems and understanding the world and human beings. This new way was named science.

Thanks to both philosophy and science, by the middle to end of the nineteenth century various scholarly areas had emerged, each with a unique use of methodology and subject matter. One of these disciplines was psychology. In 1879, Wilhelm Maximilian Wundt (1832-1920), a German philosopher and physiologist, set up what is generally considered the first laboratory in experimental psychology. From that point, psychology began to be recognized as a discipline by scholars in the Western world.

Through an interaction with disciplines such as anthropology and linguistics, which were thriving on relativistic assumptions, and a philosophy of language that limited meaning to the particular and situational case, a psychological point of view developed in the mid- to late twentieth century called social constructionism. Although promoted by those who identify with the discipline of psychology, social constructionism is at odds with the assumptions of the modern period, including many of those that go with science, and is, therefore, labeled postmodern. Such an approach seeks only to describe and interpret rather than to explain, as is the aim in science. Parallel developments such as deconstruction in the field of literary criticism were taking place at the same time.

THE PHILOSOPHERS

Over the years, philosophers asked questions about the world and how humans come to have knowledge of it; provided assumptions that would limit or promote certain kinds of explanations; and attempted to summarize the knowledge that was available to an educated person.

Those thinkers who considered the nature of reality and the world between the years c. 624 to 370 B.C.E. were called pre-Socratics. One of them, Heraclitus (c. 540-480 B.C.E.), opposed Thales's idea of water as the basic element with his idea that fire was the basic element, and therefore the world and everything in it was in a state of flux and constant change. Empedocles (c. 495-435 B.C.E.) went a step further to propose that there were four basic elements: earth, air, fire, and water. This scheme, when applied by physicians such as the Greek Hippocrates (c. 460-377 B.C.E.) and the Greco-Roman Galen (c. 130-200 C.E.) led to the notion of the four humors and a prototheory of personality which has been influential for almost two thousand years.

From his understanding of the thinking of Socrates (469-399 B.C.E.) and Pythagoras (c. 580-500 B.C.E.), Plato (427-347 B.C.E.) constructed a systematic view of the human as a dualistic creature having a body that is material and a soul that is spiritual. This doctrine had significant consequences for religion, for philosophy, and for psychology. Plato also saw knowledge as acquired by the soul through the process of recollection of the form, which exists in an ideal and abstract state. Plato's student Aristotle (384-322 B.C.E.) systematized the study of logic, promoted the use of observation as a means of acquiring knowledge, and presented a different view of the human as one whose senses were reliable sources of information and whose soul, while capable of reasoning, was the form which kept the body (and the person) in existence.

The philosophers who came during the medieval period generally split into two camps: those who followed Plato and those who followed Aristotle. Just prior to the medieval period, Saint Augustine (354-430 C.E.), bishop of Hippo (now part of Algeria), had combined Neoplatonism, Christianity, and Stoicism (to the extent of believing that following the natural law was virtuous). The Neoaristotelian tradition was typified by Thomas Aquinas (1225-1274), an Italian Dominican priest, who integrated Aristotelian thought with Christianity and who promoted the use of reason in the obtaining of knowledge. Although not anticipated by Thomas, this Aquinas point of view would ease the way for what would become scientific thinking.

René Descartes (1596-1650), a French Renaissance philosopher, created a dualistic system called interactionism, where the soul, which was spiritual, interacted with the body, which was material. Both the notion of interaction and its site, the pineal gland, were so open to debate that the theory led to two different traditions: a rationalist tradition and an empiricist tradition. The rationalist tradition was led by German thinkers such as Gottfried Wilhelm Leibniz (1646-1716), who was also an inventor of the calculus; Immanuel Kant (1724-1804) who taught that the mind had an innate categorizing ability; and Johann Friedrich Herbart (1776-1841) who held that, if expressed in mathematical terms, psychology could become a science. All the rationalists opted for the notion of "an active mind," and Herbart's thinking was very influential for those, like Wundt, who would view psychology as a scientific discipline. The empiricist tradition was stronger in France and England. Several decisive representatives of empiricism were the Englishmen John Locke (1632-1704), David Hume (1711-1776), and John Stuart Mill (1806-1873). Empiricism postulated that all knowledge came through the senses and that the ideas that made up the mind were structured on the percepts of the senses. Eventually, in Mill's thinking, the ideas of the mind were held together through the laws of association.

Another tradition that was developed past the midpoint of this period was positivism. Positivism, as developed by the Frenchman August Compte (1798-1857), argued that the only knowledge that one can be sure of is information that is publicly observable. This would strongly influence both the subject matter and the methodology of science in general and psychology in particular.

In the beginning of the twentieth century, the Englishman Bertrand Russell (1872-1970) introduced symbolic logic, and his student Ludwig Wittgenstein (1889-1951) created a philosophy of language. Both of these developments were necessary precursors of the late twentieth century interest in the nature of mind, in which many disciplines came together to form cognitive science. Wittgenstein's work would open the door for social constructionism.

THE SCIENTISTS

The development of the scientific method was only one of the factors that was associated with the change from the Middle Ages to the Renaissance. Developments in anatomy, physiology, astronomy, and other fields from the middle of the sixteenth century to the beginning of the twentieth century have had a major impact on the understanding of science and have paved the way for psychology as a science. The work of Copernicus and Galileo, in freeing astronomy from folk and religious belief was a start. In the field of anatomy the Flemish scientist Andreas Vesalius (1514-1564) published in 1543 the first accurate woodcuts showing the anatomy of the human body. This was a decisive break with the tradition of Galen. By 1628, the Englishman William Harvey (1578-1657) had described accurately the circulation of blood.

In the meanwhile, the Englishman Francis Bacon (1561-1621), a contemporary of Galileo, offered a view of science that favored inductive reasoning on the basis of a series of observations. This was another break with the tradition of relying on the classical authorities. In 1687, the *Principia* was published by the Englishman Isaac Newton (1643-1727), who laid the foundation for the calculus, enhanced the understanding of color and light, grasped the notion of universal gravitation, and produced laws (natural law) of planetary motion.

Soon Swiss mathematicians, members of the Bernoulli family, and Leonhard Euler (1707-1783), were refining the differential and integral calculus that was invented independently of Newton by the philosopher Gottfried Leibniz (1646-1716).

In 1751, a Scot, Robert Whytt (1714-1766), working on frogs, noted the importance of the spinal cord for reflex action. Localization of function in the nervous system was beginning.

By 1754 the Swedish botanist Carolus Linnaeus (1707-1778) had produced a system of classification for plants, animals, and minerals that made observation and discussion in science simpler.

German anatomist Franz Joseph Gall (1758-1828) maintained that "faculties" of the brain were discernable by observing the contours of the skull: Phrenology was another step in localization but a false one that violated scientific axioms. It spread rapidly especially in the United States as a form of folk psychology and diagnosis.

In 1795, an assistant at the Royal Observatory in Greenwich, England, was found to be recording times of stellar transit consistently later than his supervisor. The German astronomer Friedrich Wilhelm Bessel (1784-1846) recognized that this was involuntary and might be calibrated as a personal equation. This recognition of reaction time foreshadowed many studies in the laboratories of psychology.

Italian physician and physicist Luigi Galvani (1737-1798) in 1791 stimulated movement in a frog's leg with electricity, demonstrating that electrical stimulation had a role in neural research. Englishman Charles Bell (1774-1842), in 1811, and Frenchman François Magendi (1783-1855), in 1822, demonstrated differential functions of the dorsal (sensory) and ventral (motor) roots of the spinal cord. Again, localization of function was promoted. In 1824-1825, Pierre Flourens (1794-1867) introduced the technique of ablation studies for brain tissue.

The field of physiology came together in the *Handbuch der Physiologie des Menschen für Vorlesungen* (1833-1840; manual of physiology), published by German Johannes Müller (1801-1858). Müller's law of specific nerve energies, which claimed that there was a specific pathway and type of signal for each kind of sensation, was a significant contribution.

The German Ernst Weber (1795-1878) expanded the study of touch and kinesthesis and created the Weber fraction and the two-point threshold. Gustav Theodor Fechner (1801-1887) expanded Weber's work into Weber's Law and provided a rationale and methodology for early psychology with his development of psychophysical methods.

The Frenchman Paul Broca (1824-1880) made use of the clinical method of studying brain lesions. With this methodology the language area was localized in the third frontal convolution of the cortex.

German Hermann von Helmholtz (1821-1894), a student of Johannes Müller who argued against his teacher's support for vitalism, applied the law of conservation of energy to living creatures, measured rate of nerve conduction, and wrote esteemed handbooks on the physics and physiology of vision and audition. An opposing theorist, German Ewald Hering (1834-1918), a nativist, created the opponent color process theory of color vision.

In 1870, Germans Gustav Fritsch (1838-1927) and Eduard Hitzig (1838-1907) introduced electrical stimulation of the brain demonstrating the motor areas of the brain.

From the middle to the latter part of the nineteenth century, Englishman Francis Galton (1822-1911), a cousin of Charles Darwin who was also interested in evolution, promoted mental testing and the study of individual differences. He also stimulated the work of the English mathematician Karl Pearson (1857-1936), who invented the statistics to support such studies and much of psychology.

By 1902, an American, Shepard Ivory Franz (1874-1933), combined the ablation technique with training procedures to investigate the function of the frontal lobes in cats. His work led to the work of the great American neuropsychologist Karl Spencer Lashley (1890-1958), who led the quest to find the neural basis for memory in his 1950 work *In Search of the Engram*. Two of Lashley's students, the Canadian Donald Olding Hebb (1904-1985), with his work on cell assemblies and phase sequences, and the American Roger Wolcott Sperry (1913-1994), with his work on split-brain preparations in the 1960's, would do much to promote neuropsychology and prepare for cognitive science.

BEGINNING OF PSYCHOLOGY AS A DISCIPLINE
In 1879, Wilhelm Wundt, a student of Helmholtz, brought together his two disciplines of physiology and philosophy by creating a laboratory for experimental psychology at the University of Leipzig in Germany. His laboratory attracted many of the individuals who would become leaders in the new science of psychology. Among these were the German Oswald Külpe (1862-1915), the Englishman Edward Bradford Titchener (1867-1927), and the American James McKeen Cattell (1860-1944).

Meanwhile, in the United States, William James (1842-1910), a scientist and philosopher who was familiar with European scholarly trends, published the defining American work on psychology, *The Principles of Psychology* (1890). This became the dominant text in the English-speaking world and attracted many more Americans to the study of psychology. Both Wundt and James were instrumental in separating psychology from other disciplines both in methodology and in subject matter. Both saw psychology as an introspective science which was to study adult human consciousness. Introspection required that the investigator focus on her or his own experience or awareness, that is, what the individual is thinking and feeling at any one moment.

THE SCHOOLS OF PSYCHOLOGY
There were very quickly a number of individuals who either agreed partly or disagreed wholly with Wundt and James. Some of these individuals argued their points persuasively and a number of schools or points of view coalesced around them during the

last decade of the nineteenth century and the first several decades of the twentieth century.

Coming from the German rationalist tradition of philosophy, Wundt took as his goal the understanding of consciousness using the method of introspection. Wundt's point of view has become known as voluntarism. Wundt stressed the role of will, choice, and purpose, all of which he saw present in attention and volition.

Wundt's student Titchener created a somewhat similar school of thought when, in 1892, he came to Cornell University in Ithaca, New York. Titchener also wanted to study consciousness using the introspective method. He differed from Wundt in that his preferred philosophy was English empiricism, and this led him to a different understanding of consciousness. His approach was to discover the elements of consciousness, and this approach was called structuralism. His successful program led to a strong interest in experimentation, especially on sensation and perception, in American psychology. He trained a large number of Americans in the almost four decades that he taught at Cornell.

American psychologists were not wholly devoted to either Wundt's or Titchener's approach to psychology even if they had received their Ph.D.'s with them. Instead, they often were motivated by their appreciation for the work of Charles Darwin, who had published his theory of evolution in his famous *On the Origin of Species by Means of Natural Selection* (1859). Darwin's writing had been popularized in the English-speaking world by the English writer and speaker Herbert Spencer (1820-1903), who promoted the idea of social Darwinism, that is, that processes of competition among groups of humans would weed out the unfit and thus help to perfect the human race. Following Spencer, many psychologists in America saw adaptation as a fundamental concern for their academic field. Among these was philosopher and psychologist John Dewey (1859-1952), whose 1896 article "The Reflex Arc Concept in Psychology" was seen as the formal beginning of the school of functionalism.

One student of both Wundt and James who was very influential in early functionalism was Granville Stanley Hall (1844-1924), who founded the *American Journal of Psychology* in 1887 and who founded Clark University and its psychology department in 1888. He was a leading proponent for developmental psychology, the founder of the American Psychological Association (in 1892), and an untiring organizer.

Also very influential in the promotion of applied psychology was a Prussian student of Wundt's who had followed James in the laboratories of Harvard University, Hugo Münsterberg (1863-1916), who arrived at Harvard University in 1892.

Two major branches of the school of functionalism were associated with the University of Chicago and Columbia University. There were three leaders at the University of Chicago. Dewey served from 1894 to 1904, when he moved to Teacher's College at Columbia University. He was succeeded by James Rowland Angell (1869-1949), who served for twenty-five years and who was followed by his student Harvey Carr (1873-1954), who specialized in the adaptive acts of learning and perception.

At Columbia University, the first significant leader was James McKeen Cattell, who accepted a professorship in 1891 and who stayed for twenty-six years. Also very influential was a student of Cattell's, Robert Sessions Woodworth (1869-1962). Woodworth wrote extensively on many topics in psychology, including physiological psychology, the history of psychology, motivation, and experimental psychology. He wrote the influential *Experimental Psychology* in 1938. The third major influence at Columbia was the very productive Edward L. Thorndike (1874-1949). Thorndike was active at Columbia from 1899 until 1940. He wrote on animal learning, developing a theory called connectionism that accounted for learning in an animal or human on the basis of a strengthening of a connection between a stimulus and a response. Besides learning theory, Thorndike also wrote on verbal behavior, educational practices, intelligence testing, and the measurement of other types of psychological and sociological phenomena. As a school of thought, functionalism came to represent the interests of a great number of American psychologists who were involved in areas that called for practical intervention such as testing, clinical, social, and developmental psychology.

The reaction to Wundtian psychology took a different direction in Europe. Influenced by a group of teachers who adopted a more holistic view of human functioning, a system known as Gestalt psychology started in Germany in 1910. Among the teachers was Franz Clemens Brentano (1838-1917). Brentano, trained in Aristotelian philosophy, promoted an "act psychology" which stated that the study of the mind had to do with mental acts (such as willing or perceiving), not the study of consciousness divisible into elements. One of Brentano's students at the University of Vienna was the Austrian Christian von Ehrenfels (1859-1932), who was himself licensed to teach at Vienna in 1888. Ehrenfels wrote a paper, "Über Gestaltqualitäten" (1890; on Gestalt qualities), that would be the formative document in the thinking of all future Gestalt psychologists. This paper asserted that the significant aspect in any perception was the pattern created by the individual elements and not the individual elements themselves, as with the melody rather than the individual notes of the melody. Foremost among the Gestalt psychologists was the Czech-born Max Wertheimer, who received his Ph.D. in 1904 from the University of Würzbürg. In 1910, Wertheimer involved the two other founders of Gestalt psychology in a study of apparent movement which became known as the phi phenomenon. These two were the German Kurt Koffka (1886-1941) and the Estonian Wolfgang Köhler (1887-1967). Both had just received their Ph.D.'s at the University of Berlin under the direction of the German Carl Stumpf (1848-1936), who was himself a student of Brentano and whose lifework was devoted to the study of music, space perception, and audition. His work would lead to the phenomenological approach that was common to Gestalt psychology. In the 1930's, with the coming to power of National Socialism in Germany, the three main Gestalt psychologists Wertheimer, Koffka, and Köhler emigrated to the United States, where they found behaviorism's associationism and elementism as unacceptable as it was in both Wundtian psychology and psychoanalysis.

William McDougall (1871-1938) was born in England, educated in England and at the University of Göttingen in Germany, and began his teaching at Oxford University in England. In 1920, he came to the United States, where he developed his brand of psychology called hormic psychology (from the Greek word *horme*, which means "urge"). He called himself a behaviorist, but one who viewed behavior as instinctually directed and at the same time as purposeful. McDougall was widely admired but seemed out of step with the dominant behaviorism of his time. His views are much more congenial with the cognitive psychology of the late twentieth century.

Basing part of his rationale on the work of the Russian reflexologist Ivan Petrovich Pavlov (1849-1936), who discovered the principles of conditioning while doing work on the digestive system of dogs, the American John Broadus Watson (1878-1958) promoted a radical behaviorism that rejected introspection as a method and suggested that the study of animal behavior was the equivalent of the study of human behavior. His lectures at Columbia University, which were published in the *Psychological Review* in 1913 under the title "Psychology as the Behaviorist Views It," are seen as the beginning of behaviorism. They certainly separated behaviorism from both structuralism and functionalism.

In 1900, Mary Whiton Calkins (1863-1930), an American student of William James, began her defense of a self psychology. Despite the functionalist interest in adaptation and the behaviorist rejection of introspection, Calkins would continue to assert that the self was an existential reality, that is, it was knowable in one's own awareness. After her death in 1930, the self came to be considered a conceptualization. Gordon Willard Allport (1897-1967), an American who studied extensively in Europe, became the leading self psychologist for another thirty years. In Allport's later years, clinicians such as Carl Ransom Rogers (1902-1987), who developed "client-centered therapy," would keep the idea of self and its centrality alive in psychology until the cognitive revolution of the 1960's and 1970's allowed the self to become a popular integrating construct again.

The Austrian physician Sigmund Freud (1856-1939) published *Studien über Hysterie* (1895; *Studies in Hysteria*, 1950) and began the school of therapy known as psychoanalysis. Psychoanalysis soon became a general theory of personality. Freud's possessiveness about the theory led to the ouster from his inner circle of two theorists who would go on to create their own approaches to psychoanalysis. The first was the Austrian Alfred Adler (1870-1937) in 1911. Adler's point of view would become known as individual psychology. The second, in 1913, was the Swiss Carl Gustav Jung (1875-1961), who questioned the sexual basis of the motivating energy proposed by Freud. Jung's point of view has become known as analytical psychology. By the 1930's, Freud's classic psychology of the unconscious had shifted to a greater appreciation of the conscious. Thus, Freud's daughter, Anna Freud (1895-1982), following the

interests of her father, published *Das Ich und die Abwehrmechanismen* (1936; *The Ego and the Mechanisms of Defense*, 1937). Classic psychoanalysis had changed into ego psychology. The best-known representative of the new ego psychology was the child analyst and writer Erik Homburger Erikson (1902-1994). Erikson, who was born in Germany and who had been analyzed by Anna Freud, came to the United States in 1933. His *Childhood and Society* (1950) made connections to and enriched developmental psychology, especially in terms of his reworking of Freud's five developmental stages into the "eight ages of man."

APPLIED PSYCHOLOGY

The Frenchman Alfred Binet (1857-1911) published the first individual test of intelligence in 1905. Lewis Madison Terman (1877-1956), an American student of G. Stanley Hall, published his revision of Binet's test, called the Stanford Binet, in the United States in 1912. An industry was born. The test was reissued in 1916, 1937, and 1960. Group tests of intelligence were developed for the military during both World War I and World War II. The needs of the military also promoted another applied psychology: clinical psychology. In World War II, short-term psychotherapy was found to be useful in returning combatants to active service. Many academic psychologists were pressed into training programs to become psychotherapists. By the time the war ended, a number of psychologists viewed themselves as clinicians and returned to redirect graduate programs in psychology toward clinical psychology. By the late 1940's testing, diagnosis, and clinical practice were well established.

NEOBEHAVIORISM

In 1924, a group of philosophers in Vienna, Austria, known as the Vienna Circle, revised and refined positivism into logical positivism, and in 1927, Percy Williams Bridgman (1892-1961), an American physicist, proposed operationism, in which every theoretical construct would be defined by the operations that were used to measure it. These developments allowed experimenters to deal positivistically with abstract variables and led to a more sophisticated behaviorism labeled neobehaviorism. Americans Edward Chace Tolman (1886-1959), Clark Leonard Hull (1884-1952), and Burrhus Frederic Skinner (1904-1990) were notable representatives of neobehaviorism, which specialized in the study of learning and motivation, mostly with nonhuman species. Skinner differed from the others in that he favored induction and description as the basis for his studies. Neobehaviorism was superseded by changes that brought about the cognitive revolution in the 1960's and 1970's. Its heritage remains in psychology in the area of methodology.

Also by the 1950's, a rift that had begun in the days of Titchener between those who saw themselves as pure scientific psychologists as opposed to those who practiced an applied psychology was reconceptualized as a conflict between the academic psychologists who maintained a behavioristic approach and the clinicians who were heavily influenced by psychoanalysis and were beginning to appreciate Rogers's client-centered approach. This struggle was exacerbated by the growing number of practitioners, who began to outnumber the academic psychologists. One result of this disciplinary conflict was the foundation of a separate organization for the academics, the American Psychological Society, formed in 1988.

THE 1960'S AND 1970'S

The emergence of the computer both as a tool and as a model of the human mind had a major effect on psychology. Neuroscience, philosophy, anthropology, linguistics, artificial intelligence, and psychology came together in the 1960's to form the basis for a new discipline: cognitive science. The new technology and the opportunity to work with people and ideas from other disciplines freed psychology to reinvestigate questions of mental functioning and consciousness.

In 1954, the American Abraham Maslow (1908-1970) published the influential *Motivation and Personality*, which began humanistic psychology, a movement seen by Maslow as an antidote to the dehumanizing assumptions of both behaviorism and psychoanalysis. By 1961 there was a *Journal of Humanistic Psychology* and by 1962 an American Association of Humanistic Psychologists. Carl Rogers, with his client-centered therapy, added to the attractiveness of the movement for American psychologists. Its emphasis on admitting the whole person to psychology gained more general acceptance, and together with the cognitive revolution promoted a more humanistic and cognitively oriented general psychology.

THE 1980'S AND 1990'S

Developmental psychology, building on the work of the Swiss Jean Piaget (1896-1980) from the 1920's through the 1960's, and cognitive psychology, stimulated by the early 1960's work of the Americans George Armitage Miller (b. 1920) and Jerome Seymour Bruner (b. 1915), began once again to study consciousness and its development, but this time from infancy through adulthood. A student of Miller, the German-born Ulric Neisser (b. 1928) built on this and his own earlier work *Cognitive Psychology* (1967) to bring to the 1980's and 1990's an integrative approach to consciousness, concept formation, perception, and selfhood. In general, the period was one of eclecticism and was labeled neofunctionalism by one historian.

SOCIAL CONSTRUCTIONISM

Another trend that impacted psychology was postmodern thought. Although present in philosophy and anthropology through the twentieth century, it became obvious in psychology only in the 1970's, where it was known as social constructionism. Since the 1970's, it has made its presence obvious in the subfield called cultural psychology and in social psychology. When applied to personality development, the concept of narrative as an inborn mechanism has become a focus for those who wish to describe the process of self development.

SOURCES FOR FURTHER STUDY

Gardner, Howard. *The Mind's New Science: A History of the Cognitive Revolution*. New York: Basic Books, 1987. The author shows the transforming effect the field of cognitive science had on psychology.

Hergenhahn, B. R. *An Introduction to the History of Psychology*. 4th ed. Belmont, Calif.: Wadsworth/ Thompson Learning, 2001. A very readable and thorough history of psychology from the pre-Socratics to the present.

Hilgard, Ernest R. *Psychology in America: A Historical Survey*. New York: Harcourt Brace Jovanovich, 1987. Hilgard knew many of the significant psychologists in twentieth century America. From a starting point in the colonial period, he recaps much of what went on in psychology in America (and sometimes Europe) until 1987. After dealing with the early schools of psychology, he looks at the development of the different subject areas in psychology.

Hunt, Morton. *The Story of Psychology*. New York: Doubleday, 1993. A narrative history of psychology written by a popular author who strives for the "big picture."

Koch, Sigmund, and David Leary, eds. *A Century of Psychology as a Science*. New York: McGraw-Hill, 1992. Many perspectives on how psychology and its subfields have changed over the hundred years that psychology has existed as a discipline are presented by late twentieth century experts.

Russell, Bertrand. *A History of Western Philosophy*. New York: Simon & Schuster, 1945. This remains one of the best and most readable introductions to the history of philosophy. It integrates the philosophers with the social and political circumstances in which they wrote.

Stevenson, Leslie, and David L. Haberman. *Ten Theories of Human Nature*. 3d ed. New York: Oxford University Press, 1998. A survey of different folk and religious theories, philosophical positions, and theories from scientific psychological work. It gives a broad perspective to the history of psychology.

Everett J. Delahanty, Jr.

SEE ALSO: Adler, Alfred; Adlerian psychotherapy; Allport, Gordon; Analytic psychology: Jacques Lacan; Analytical psychology: Carl G. Jung; Analytical psychotherapy; Behaviorism; Cognitive psychology; Community psychology; Constructivist psychology; Disaster psychology; Ego psychology: Erik Erikson; Erikson, Erik; Ethology; Evolutionary psychology; Existential psychology; Feminist psychotherapy; Forensic psychology; Freud, Anna; Freud, Sigmund; Gestalt therapy; Group therapy; Health psychology; Humanism; Individual psychology: Alfred Adler; Industrial and organizational psychology; Internet psychology; Jung, Carl G.; Media psychology; Neuropsychology; Pavlov, Ivan; Personology: Henry A. Murray; Piaget, Jean; Positive psychology; Psychoanalysis; Psychoanalytic psychology; Psychoanalytic psychology and personality: Sigmund Freud; Psychology: Definition; Psychology: Fields of specialization; Psychosurgery; Psychotherapy: Historical approaches; Radical behaviorism: B. F. Skinner; Religion and psychology; Rogers, Carl R.; Skinner, B. F.; Structuralism and functionalism; Thorndike, Edward L.; Transactional analysis; Watson, John B.; Women's psychology: Carol Gilligan; Women's psychology: Karen Horney; Women's psychology: Sigmund Freud.

Psychopathology

TYPE OF PSYCHOLOGY: Psychopathology

FIELDS OF STUDY: Behavioral therapies; general constructs and issues; models of abnormality; organic disorders; personality disorders

As a field of study, psychopathology has as its focus the description and causes of abnormal behavior, and of psychological and emotional problems. Several models or approaches to psychopathology differ with respect to the assumed causes of psychological problems. Many clinicians integrate different models to understand the basis of a client's problems, and combine different treatment approaches to maximize effectiveness.

KEY CONCEPTS

- behavior therapy
- biological approach
- biopsychosocial approach
- cognitive approach
- cognitive therapy
- culture and psychopathology
- learning approach
- mental illness
- somatic therapy

INTRODUCTION

Psychopathology refers to psychological dysfunctions that either create distress for the person, or interfere with day-to-day functioning in relationships, work, or leisure. Psychological disorders, abnormal behavior, mental illness, and behavior and emotional disorders are terms often used in place of psychopathology.

As a topic of interest, psychopathology does not have an identifiable, historical beginning. From the writings of ancient Egyptians, Hebrews, and Greeks it is clear, however, that ancient societies believed that abnormal behavior had its roots in supernatural phenomena, such as the vengeance of God and evil spirits. Although modern scientists have opposed that view, in the twenty-first century, many people who hold fundamentalist religious beliefs or live in isolated societies still maintain that abnormal behavior can be caused by the possession of spirits.

The Greek physician Hippocrates (460-377 B.C.E.) rejected demoniac possession and believed that psychological disorders had many natural causes, including heredity, head trauma, brain disease, and even family stress. Hippocrates was wrong when it came to specific details, but it is remarkable how accurate he was in identifying broad categories of factors that do influence the development of psychopathology. The Roman physician Galen (c. 129-198 C.E.) adopted the ideas of Hippocrates and expanded upon them. His school of thought held that diseases, including psychological disorders, were due to an imbalance of four bodily fluids, which he called humors: blood, black bile, yellow bile, and phlegm. For example, too much black bile, called melancholer, was believed to cause depression. Galen's beliefs have been discredited, but many of the terms he used have lived on. For instance, a specific subtype of depression is named after Galen's melancholer: Major Depression with Melancholic Features.

A major figure in the history of psychopathology is the German psychiatrist Emil Kraepelin (1856-1926). He claimed that mental illnesses, like physical illnesses, could be classified into distinct disorders, each having its own biological causes. Each disorder could be recognized by a cluster of symptoms, called a syndrome. The way in which he classified mental disorders continues to exert a strong influence on approaches to categorizing mental illnesses. The official classification system in the United States is the *Diagnostic and Statistical Manual of Mental Disorders: DSM-IV-TR* (rev. 4th ed., 2000). Many features of this manual can be traced directly to the writings of Kraepelin in the early years of the twentieth century.

EXAMPLES OF PSYCHOPATHOLOGY

There is a very broad range of psychological disorders. The DSM-IV-TR lists more than two hundred psychological disorders that differ in symptoms and the degree to which they affect a person's ability to function.

It is normal for someone to feel anxious on occasion. Generalized anxiety disorder is diagnosed when a person engages in excessive worry about all sorts of things, and feels anxious and tense much of the time. Most people who have this disorder function quite well. They can do well at work, have good relationships, and be good parents. It is the fact that they suffer so much from their anxiety that leads to a diagnosis. In contrast, schizophrenia can be completely debilitating. Many people with schizophre-

nia cannot hold a job, are hospitalized frequently, have difficulty in relationships, and are incapable of good parenting. Common symptoms of schizophrenia include delusions (a system of false beliefs, such as believing there is a vast conspiracy among extraterritorial aliens to control the government); hallucinations (seeing things that are not there or hearing voices that other people cannot hear); incoherence (talking in a way that no one can understand); or emotions that are expressed out of context (laughing when telling a sad story). The symptoms of schizophrenia make it difficult or impossible for the person to function normally and the fact that symptoms interfere with functioning is more important than the distress that the person feels.

Many disorders are marked by both subjective distress and impaired functioning. One such disorder is obsessive-compulsive disorder (OCD). An obsession is a recurrent, usually unpleasant thought, image, or impulse that intrudes into a person's awareness. Some common examples are thinking that every bump hit in the road while driving could have been a person struck by the car, believing that one is contaminated by germs, or picturing oneself stabbing one's children. Obsessions cause a great deal of distress. Obsessions typically lead to the development of compulsions. A compulsion is a repetitive act that is used by the person to stop the obsession and decrease the anxiety caused by the obsession. People who believe they have been contaminated may wash themselves for hours on end; those who believe that they have hit another person while driving may not be able to resist the urge to stop and look for someone injured. Behavioral compulsions can sometimes occupy so much time that the person cannot meet the demands of everyday life.

CAUSES OF PSYCHOPATHOLOGY

The most important goal of researchers in the field of psychopathology is to discover the causes (etiology) of each disorder. If the causes for disorders were known, then psychologists could design effective treatments and, it would be hoped, be able to prevent the development of many disorders. Unfortunately, theories of psychological disorders are in their infancy, and there are many more questions than there are answers. There is no general agreement among psychologists as to where to look for answers to the question of etiology. Consequently, some researchers stress the importance of biological causes, other researchers focus on psychological processes in the development of disorders, while still others emphasize the crucial role of learning experiences in the development of behavior disorders. All these approaches are important and each supplies a piece of the puzzle of psychopathology, but all approaches have their limitations.

THE LEARNING APPROACH. Psychologists who work within this model of psychopathology believe that abnormal behavior is learned through past experiences. The same principles that are used to explain the development of normal behavior are used to explain the development of abnormal behavior. For example, a child can learn to be a conscientious student by observing role models who are conscientious in their work. Another child may learn to break the rules of society by watching a parent break the same rules. In each case, observational learning is at work, but the outcome is very different. Using another example of a learning principle, a person who is hungry and hears someone preparing food in the kitchen may begin to salivate because the sounds of food preparation have, in the past, preceded eating food and food makes the person salivate. Those sounds from the kitchen are stimuli that have become conditioned so that the person learns to have the same reaction to the sounds as to food (salivation). This learning process is called classical conditioning. Experiencing pain and having one's life threatened causes fear. A person who is attacked and bitten by a dog might well develop a fear response to all dogs that is severe enough to lead to a diagnosis of a phobia. Just as the sounds in the kitchen elicit salivation, the sight of a dog elicits an emotional response. The same underlying principle of classical conditioning can account for the development of normal behavior as well as a disorder. There are many other principles of learning besides observational learning and classical conditioning. Together, psychologists use them to account for forms of psychopathology more complex than are exemplified here. Nonetheless, there are many disorders in which a learning approach to etiology seems farfetched. For example, no one believes that mental retardation, childhood autism, or schizophrenia can be explained by learning principles alone.

THE PSYCHOLOGICAL APPROACH. This model, sometimes called the cognitive approach, holds that many forms of psychopathology are best understood by studying the mind. Some psychologists within this tradition believe that the most important aspect of the mind is the unconscious. The Austrian psychoanalyst Sigmund Freud (1856-1939) believed that many forms of psychopathology are due to intense conflicts of which the person is unaware but which, nevertheless, produce symptoms of disorders.

Many psychological disorders are associated with obvious problems in thinking. Schizophrenics, people with attention-deficit hyperactivity disorder (ADHD), and those who suffer from depression all show difficulties in concentration. Memory problems are central in people who develop amnesia in response to psychological trauma. People who are paranoid show abnormalities in the way they interpret the behavior of others. Indeed, it is difficult to find examples of psychopathology in which thinking is not disordered in some way, be it mild or severe. Within the cognitive approach, depression is one of the disorders that receives the most attention. People who are depressed often show problems in emotion (feeling sad), behavior (withdrawing from people), and thinking. The cognitive formulation assumes that thinking is central, specifically the way depressed people think about the world, themselves, and the future. Dysfunctional thinking is believed to give rise to the other aspects of depression. Most of the research in the field of psychopathology derives from the cognitive perspective. One of the major challenges to this approach is determining whether thinking patterns cause disorders, or whether they are aspects of disorders that, themselves, are caused by nonpsychological factors. For example, depressed people have a pessimistic view of their futures. Does pessimism figure into the cause of the depression, or might depression be caused by biological factors and pessimism is just one of the symptoms of depression?

THE BIOLOGICAL APPROACH. The biological (biogenic) approach assumes that many forms of psychopathology are caused by abnormalities of the body, usually the brain. These abnormalities can be inherited, or can happen for other reasons. What these "other reasons" are is unclear, but they may include birth complications, environmental toxins, or illness of the mother during pregnancy.

Schizophrenia is one disorder that receives much attention among those researchers who follow the biogenic approach. A great deal of research has been conducted on the importance of neurotransmitters. Nerve cells in the brain are not connected; there is a small space between them. A nerve impulse travels this space by the release of chemicals in one nerve cell, called neurotransmitters, which carry the impulse to the receptors of the next cell. There are a large number of neurotransmitters, and new ones are discovered periodically. Early research on the relationship between neurotransmitters and psychopathology tended to view the problem as "too much" or "too little" of the amount of neurotransmitters. It is now known that the situation is much more complicated. In schizophrenia, the neurotransmitter dopamine has received most of the attention, with many studies suggesting that excessive amounts of dopamine cause some of the symptoms of schizophrenia. In fact, drugs that reduce the availability of dopamine to the cells are successful in alleviating some symptoms of the disorder. However, not all people with schizophrenia are helped by these drugs, and some people are helped by drugs that one would not expect if all there is to schizophrenia is too much dopamine. Researchers are finding that the way in which dopamine and another neurotransmitter, serotonin, work together may lead to a better biological theory of schizophrenia than the excessive dopamine hypothesis.

The biological approach is a highly technical field, and it relies heavily on advances in technologies for studying the brain. Powerful new tools for studying the brain are invented at a rapid pace. For example, researchers are now able to use neuroimaging techniques to watch how the brain responds and changes from second to second.

Heredity appears to be important in understanding who develops what kind of psychological disorder, but it is often unknown exactly what is inherited that causes the disorder. The fact that schizophrenia runs in families does not reveal what is being passed on from generation to generation. The fact that inheritance works at the level of gene transmission places hereditary research squarely within the biological approach.

One method for addressing the question of whether a disorder can be inherited is by studying twins. Some twins are identical; each twin has the same genes as the other. Other twins share only half of their genes; these are fraternal twins, and one could be male and the other female. If one identical twin has schizophrenia and the disorder is entirely inherited, the other twin should also develop schizophrenia. Among identical twins, if one twin is schizophrenic, the other twin has a 48 percent chance of having the same disorder, not a 100 percent chance. For fraternal twins, if one is schizophrenic, there is a 17 percent chance that the other twin will have the disorder. If neither twin has schizophrenia, and no one else in the immediate family has the disorder, there is only a 1 percent chance of developing this form of psychopathology.

Two important points can be made. First, genes matter in the transmission of schizophrenia. Second, the disorder is not entirely due to heredity. Researchers who focus on heredity have found that some other disorders seem to have a genetic component, but no mental illness has been found to be entirely due to heredity. Clearly, there are other factors operating, and the biological approach must be integrated with other approaches to gain a full picture of the etiology of psychopathology.

THE BIOPSYCHOSOCIAL APPROACH. As its name suggests, the biopsychosocial approach seeks to understand psychopathology by examining the interactive influences of biology, cognitive processes, and learning. This is the most popular model of psychopathology and, in its most basic form, is also referred to as the diathesis-stress model. A diathesis is a predisposing factor, and the diathesis may be biological or psychological. When discussing biological diatheses, most theories assume that the diathesis is present at birth. A problem with the regulation of neurotransmitters, which may lead to schizophrenia or depression, is one example. An example of a psychological diathesis is when a person's style of thinking predisposes him or her to a disorder. For instance, pessimism, minimizing good things that happen and maximizing negative events, attributing failures to personal defects, may predispose a person to depression. The stress aspect of the diathesis-stress model refers to the negative life experiences of the person. An early, chaotic family environment, child abuse, and being raised or living in a high-crime neighborhood are examples of stressful environments. From this perspective, a person will develop a disorder who has a predisposition for the disorder, in combination with certain life experiences that trigger the disorder.

Because the biological, learning, and psychological approaches have all contributed to the understanding of psychopathology, it is no surprise that most psychologists want to combine the best of each approach—hence, the biopsychosocial model. Given the present state of knowledge, each model represents more of an assumption about how psychopathology develops rather than a single theory with widespread scientific support. For virtually every psychological disorder, psychologists debate the causes of the disorder.

CULTURE AND PSYCHOPATHOLOGY

The importance of understanding the cultural context of psychopathology cannot be overstated. To be sure, some disorders that span cultures—depression, mental retardation, and schizophrenia are examples—but a culture not only defines what should be considered abnormal behavior but also determines how psychopathology is expressed. "Cultural relativism" refers to the fact that abnormality is relative to its cultural context; the same behavior or set of beliefs can be viewed as abnormal in one culture and perfectly familiar and normal in another culture. When viewed from an American perspective, the remedies, rituals, and beliefs of a witch doctor may seem to reflect some disorder within the witch doctor rather than a valued and culturally sanctioned means of treatment within that culture. No doubt members of a tribal culture in South America may regard the behavior of North American adolescents on prom night as grossly abnormal.

Some disorders only exist in certain cultures. A disorder known as *pibloktoq* occurs in Eskimo communities. The symptoms include tearing off one's clothes, shouting obscenities, breaking furniture, and performing other irrational and dangerous acts. The afflicted individual often follows this brief period of excited behavior by having a seizure, falling into a coma for twelve hours, and, upon awakening, having no memory of his or her behavior.

Some disorders may be very similar across two cultures but contain a cultural twist. For instance, in the United States, the essential feature of social anxiety disorder is a fear of performance situations that could lead to embarrassment and disapproval. In Japan and Korea, the main concern of people with this disorder is the fear that one's blushing, eye contact, or body odor will be offensive to others.

There are numerous examples of culturally based psychopathologies; the DSM-IV-TR lists twenty-five of them in an appendix. Moreover, throughout the manual, a brief statement accompanies the description of most disorders on the role of ethnic and cultural factors that are relevant for the given disorder, which can help the clinician arrive at an accurate diagnosis.

TREATMENT

The major forms of treatment for psychological disorders can be grouped according to the most popular models of psychopathology. Thus, there exists behavior therapy (learning approach), cognitive therapy and psychoanalysis (psychological approach), and somatic treatment, such as the use of medications (biological approach). Consistent with the biopsychosocial model, many therapists practice cognitive behavior therapy while their clients are taking medication for their disorders. These treatments, as well as the models from which they derive, represent common and popular viewpoints, but the list is not exhaustive (for instance, family systems is a model of disorders and the treatment is family therapy). The link between models of psychopathology and treatment is not as strong as it appears. Therapists tend to adopt the treatment belief of "whatever works," despite the fact that all therapists would prefer to know why the person is suffering from a disorder and why a specific treatment is helpful. In addition, even if the therapist is sure that the problem is a consequence of learning, he or she might have the client take medication for symptom relief during therapy. In other words, psychologists who are aligned with a specific model of psychopathology will still employ an array of treatment techniques, some of which are more closely associated with other models.

BEHAVIOR THERAPY. Based on learning theory, behavior therapy attempts to provide new learning experiences for the client. Problems that are fear based, such as phobias, will benefit from gradual exposure to the feared situation. If social anxiety is determined to be caused by a deficit in social skills, a behavior therapist can help the person learn new ways of relating to others. If the disorder is one of excess, as in substance abuse, the behavior therapist will provide training in self-control strategies. The parents of children who show conduct disorders will be taught behavior modification techniques that they could use in the home. Behavior therapy focuses on the client's present and future. Little time is spent discussing childhood experiences, except as they clearly and directly bear on the client's presenting problem. The therapist adopts a problem-solving approach and sessions are focused on a learning-theory-based conceptualization of the client's problems and discussions of strategies for change. Homework assignments are common, which leads behavior therapists to believe that therapy takes place between sessions.

COGNITIVE THERAPY. The basic tenet of cognitive therapy is that psychological problems stem from the way people view and think about the events that happen to them. Consequently, therapy focuses on helping clients change their viewpoints. For example, with a client who becomes depressed after the breakup of a relationship, the cognitive therapist will assess the meaning that the breakup has for the person. Perhaps he or she holds irrational beliefs such as, "If my partner does not want me, no one will," or "I am a complete failure for losing this relationship." The assumption is that the client's extreme, negative thinking is contributing to the depression. The therapist will challenge these beliefs and help the client substitute a more rational perspective; for example, "Just because one person left me does not mean that the next person will," and "Even if I failed at this relationship, it does not mean that I am a failure in everything I do."

Cognitive therapy has some similarity to behavior therapy. There is a focus on the present, history-taking is selective and related to the presenting problem, and homework assignments are routine. Indeed, because the two approaches share many things in common, many therapists use both forms of treatment, and refer to themselves as cognitive-behavioral therapists.

SOMATIC THERAPY. Somatic therapy is the domain of physicians (psychiatrists) because this form of treatment requires medical training. By far the most common example of somatic therapy is the use of psychotropic medications, medicine that will relieve psychological symptoms. Less common examples are electroconvulsive shock treatment, in which the client is tranquilized and administered a brief electric current to the brain to induce a convulsion, and brain surgery, such as leucotomy and lobotomy (rarely practiced).

The use of medications for psychological disorders has become enormously popular since 1970. Three main reasons are that the biological approach to understanding psychopathology is becoming more prominent; new drugs are being re-leased each year that have fewer side effects; and a great deal of research is being conducted to show that an ever-increasing number of disorders are helped by medication. The use of medication for psychological disorders is not viewed as a cure. Sometimes drugs are used to help a person through a difficult period. At other times they are an important adjunct to psychotherapy. Only in the most severe forms of psychopathology would a person be medicated for the rest of his or her life.

WHICH THERAPY IS BEST?

Researchers approach the question of which therapy is best in the context of specific disorders. No one therapy is recommended for every disorder. For instance, behavior therapy has proven to be highly successful with phobias, cognitive therapy shows good results with depression, and a trial of medication is essential for schizophrenia and bipolar disorder.

No matter what the presumed cause is of a specific disorder, a common practice is to provide medication for symptom relief, along with some form of psychotherapy to improve the person's condition over the long run.

SOURCES FOR FURTHER STUDY

American Psychiatric Association. *Diagnostic and Statistical Manual of Mental Disorders: DSM-IV-TR.* Rev. 4th ed. Washington, D.C.: Author, 2000. The manual is the official listing of psychological disorders and their diagnostic criteria. If one book defines the field of psychopathology, this is it. Some of the technical words are not defined, theories are not discussed, and treatment is ignored. Nonetheless, the reader can gain a great deal of knowledge about the different forms of psychopathology and how therapists arrive at diagnoses.

Barlow, David H., and Vincent M. Durand. *Abnormal Psychology.* 3d ed. Belmont, Calif.: Wadsworth, 2002. This undergraduate textbook is written for an audience with little or no background in psychology. The book covers a broad range of psychological disorders and is the best beginning text to learn about the biopsychosocial model of psychopathology. Hundreds of references are provided for further study in the field.

Kanfer, Frederick, H., and Arnold P. Goldstein, eds. *Helping People Change: A Textbook of Methods.* New York: Pergamon General Psychology, 1991. This is a classic in the field of clinical psychology. It covers many cognitive-behavioral techniques that are used for an array of psychological disorders. The target audience is undergraduate and graduate students in psychology, as well as practitioners who want to learn about this treatment modality. Each chapter is easy to understand and assumes only a basic knowledge of therapy and psychopathology.

Millon, Theodore, Paul H. Blaney, and Roger D. Davis, eds. *Oxford Textbook of Psychopathology.* New York: Oxford University Press, 1999. An advanced textbook for readers who have, at least, a college background in psychology and basic knowledge of the field of psychopathology. Twenty-seven chapters span almost seven hundred pages, and experts in the field author each chapter. Theory and assessment of disorders is emphasized.

Laurence Grimm and Lindsey L. Henninger

SEE ALSO: Abnormality: Biomedical models; Abnormality: Psychological models; Behavior therapy; Brief therapy; Cognitive behavior therapy; Cognitive therapy; Couples therapy; Drug therapies; Gestalt therapy; Group therapy; Observational learning and modeling therapies; Person-centered therapy; Play therapy; Psychotherapy: Children; Psychotherapy: Effectiveness; Psychotherapy: Goals and techniques; Psychotherapy: Historical approaches; Rational-emotive therapy; Reality therapy; Shock therapy.

Psychosexual development

TYPE OF PSYCHOLOGY: Personality
FIELDS OF STUDY: Classic analytic themes and issues

Psychosexual development proceeds along five distinct stages, named for the primary body parts from which individuals derive pleasure during a given period of their lives; they are the oral, anal, phallic, latency, and genital stages. According to Sigmund Freud, passing through these stages successfully is critical to the healthy development of human beings.

KEY CONCEPTS
- developmental stages
- ego
- fixation

- gratification
- id
- libido
- psychopathology
- regression
- superego

INTRODUCTION

Psychosexual development is a major developmental theory, proposed by Sigmund Freud (1856-1939), which suggests that humans behave as they do because they are constantly seeking pleasure. During different periods, or stages, of life, the types of pleasure a person seeks will change. Each change in body location from which the person finds pleasure represents one stage in psychosexual development. There are a total of five stages; four of them are named for the primary body part from which a person derives pleasure during a given time in life.

PSYCHOSEXUAL STAGES

The first stage is the oral stage, which begins at birth and ends around one year of age. Pleasure is gained from activities of the mouth, such as sucking at a mother's nipple to obtain nourishment. The purpose of this behavior is to secure physical survival, as the infant depends upon parents for food. The infant is entirely dependent, seeks immediate gratification of needs, and does not consider other people's needs or wishes or even recognize others as separate human beings. The selfish energy that drives the infant at this age is called libido and is attributed to the child's id, the pleasure-seeking part of a person.

The second stage is the anal stage, named for the child's preoccupation with feces and urine, as this is generally the time of toilet training. This stage begins around age one and ends around age three. The child now sees herself or himself as separate from other people and begins to assert wishes. The child becomes more demanding and controlling and often refuses parents' wishes, but the child also learns to delay gratification and put up with frustration. For example, the child will learn to hold in a bowel movement until a time convenient for the caregiver, rather than eliminate it as soon as pressure is felt on the sphincter. Learning to be assertive and autonomous, as well as to delay gratification, are the two most important advances for the child that occur during this stage of development. They make up an important part of a child's ego, the part of the psyche that defines who a person is and what a person wants from life.

Between age three and age six, the child passes through the phallic stage of psychosexual development. The child now knows who she or he is and who her or his parents are, and the child begins to have a sense of rules and regulations. Behavior becomes more moral, and the opinions of others begin to gain importance. The child begins to love others and wants to be loved by them. To ensure that others will continue to love and cherish her or him, the child learns to suppress pleasure derived from the genitalia because of social pressures against behaviors such as masturbation. According to Freud, children at this age fall in love with their parent of the opposite sex and envy their same-sex parent. This pattern is called the Oedipus complex in boys and the Electra complex in girls. The Oedipus complex results in the fear that the boy may be hated by his father for loving his mother. To prevent being punished (the feared punishment being castration), the boy begins to identify with and behave like his father and slowly learns to distance himself from his mother. Through this process of modeling and imitating the father, the boy learns rules and becomes a moral being. In the Electra complex, the girl feels that, because she has no penis, she has already received the ultimate punishment of castration. To compensate for the resultant feelings of envy of the male's penis, she decides that pregnancy will be important one day, as this is something not obtainable by the male. The girl's desire to bear a child begins. As she knows that only women bear children, she begins to identify and model after her mother and begins to distance herself from her father. The most important change in this stage of development is the child's acquisition of a superego, an internal sense of what is right and what is wrong that guides behavior and inhibits illegal or immoral acts.

The distancing from the same-sex parent in the phallic stage of development, which occurs around age five or six, is seen as ushering in the latency stage. At this time, children withdraw from the opposite sex and no longer seek pleasure from their own bodies. Instead, they reorient their behavior toward skill acquisition and learning, as well as peer interaction. This makes them ready for school and play with their peer group. Not until approxi-

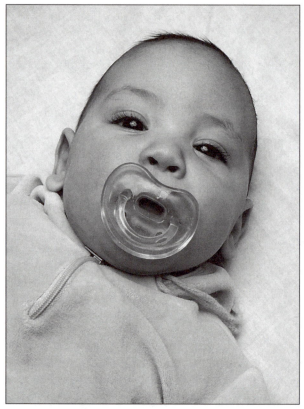

A pacifier or thumb may fulfill an infant's strong need for sucking during the early months of life, corresponding to the oral stage of psychosexual development. (PhotoDisc)

mately age thirteen will the desire for pleasure reawaken.

At around age thirteen, the adolescent enters the final stage of psychosexual development, the genital stage. At this time, the person has matured enough to be able to love others in an unselfish and altruistic manner and should be willing to put the welfare of others ahead of her or his own. Empathy and caring for humans begins, and the libido, which was selfishly directed in infancy, is now directed toward giving pleasure to others. The desire awakens to be intimately involved with a person of the opposite sex, according to Freud. This desire, however, is aim-inhibited, is complemented by feelings of affection, and does not find expression until the person has matured beyond adolescence. Mature sexuality develops as an activity that is pleasuring for both people involved, is the result of mature love, and serves procreation. Such maturity is the final goal of this stage of development.

DEVELOPMENT OF EGO AND SUPEREGO

The two most important outcomes of psychosexual development are the development of the ego and superego and the development of psychopathology (emotional or mental illnesses or problems of sufficient severity to warrant treatment by a psychologist or psychotherapist) if the stages are not successfully mastered. The anal and phallic stages are particularly critical in the development of the ego and superego. During the anal stage, ego development progresses rapidly as the child learns what he or she likes and what distinguishes him or her from other people. In the phallic stage, the development of the superego occurs as a result of the Oedipus and Electra complexes.

Only if the child accepts the rules of society—that is, falls out of love with the opposite-sex parent and identifies with the same-sex parent—is she or he able to feel free of fear of punishment. Thus, the child learns to live by rules and regulations out of fear of punishment. The internalized sense of rules is represented by the child's superego. The superego serves to counteract the selfish and pleasure-seeking actions of the id, which is present at birth and remains with all human beings throughout the life span. Often, the superego and id will come into conflict because a selfish desire expressed by the id is being opposed by the superego. The ego will then mediate between the two and will attempt to come up with a compromise solution. For example, a college student who has to study for an exam sometimes is overcome by the desire to attend a party instead. This desire is driven by the id. The superego then admonishes the student to stay home and continue to study without any breaks. The ego may finally step in and mediate, and the student may decide to study for two more hours, take a break for pleasure for an hour, and return to study some more.

DEVELOPMENT OF PSYCHOPATHOLOGY

The development of psychopathology is closely related to psychosexual development. First, pathology is seen as a possible consequence of fixation—that is, the child's failure to resolve a given stage and advance beyond it. Second, psychopathology may be caused by regression—the return to an earlier stage of development because of conflicts or problems. Adults with oral pathology, those who either did not move beyond or regressed to the oral stage, are said to be dependent and afraid to be alone, or else very hostile, evidencing verbal biting sarcasm to prevent getting too close to people. People with anal pathology can be either very retentive—that is, miserly, tense, orderly, and constricted—or expulsive—impulsive, disorganized, free-spending, and venting. Both types of pathology are severe and were considered by Freud to be not treatable through psychoanalysis. Only pathology arising from the phallic stage lends itself well to treatment. It is referred to as neurosis and implies that the person has significant conflicts between id wishes and superego restrictions that cannot be successfully mediated by the ego.

Neurotic pathology is seen as a result of a boy's failure to pass through the Oedipus complex or a girl's failure to pass through the Electra complex. In both cases, the child may fail to withdraw attachment to the same-sex parent and/or may fail to identify with the same-sex parent. Thus, healthy development is hampered and stopped. The child will live with the conflict of having a superego that is not completely developed and the awareness that the id's wish to possess the opposite-sex parent is inappropriate. The superego chastises the person yet is unable to stop the ego. Conflict is ever-present in the person, as the wishes of the id cannot be controlled by the incomplete superego but certainly can be recognized by the superego as inappropriate. This pathology sometimes leads the person to regress to earlier stages of development and develop an oral or anal personality. If there is no regression, only fixation at the phallic stage, the person will show traits of neurosis, such as being focused on gaining pleasure for the self in general, being centered on seduction, developing symptoms of hysteria, or developing physical complaints.

Pathology does not arise from the latency or genital stages, as progression to the latency stage implies successful resolution of the Oedipus and Electra complexes: The person has matured psychosexually beyond a point of development at which neurotic pathology develops. This is true because the child is considered to have developed all necessary structures of the self, or psyche, by the end of the phallic phase. The personality structure and characteristics evidenced by the child at that time are deemed lifelong traits and are not prone to significant future change.

Psychosexual development is critical from Freud's perspective primarily because it is responsible for the development of a healthy self-structure that consists of an id, an ego, and a superego. Further, it is the most important factor in the development of the psychopathology of human beings. Mastery or failure in the realm of psychosexual development has extremely important implications for a person's functioning and mental health.

HISTORIC CONTEXT

The Freudian stages through which psychosexual development progresses must be considered within the historical framework present at the time that Sigmund Freud conceptualized them—that is, from the perspective of the late 1800's and early 1900's. The spirit of the times was much different from that of today, particularly with regard to how freely people were allowed to express themselves in general and with regard to sexuality in particular. It was a time in which morals and ethics forbade many normal human urges and resulted in people having to deny large parts or aspects of themselves.

This atmosphere of self-denial resulted in many different symptoms, especially among women, who were expected to follow even stricter codes of behavior than men were. For example, sometimes people were observed to have paralysis of a hand that could not be explained by any actual neurological damage. Freud was one of the first physicians to recognize that this paralysis had psychological rather than physical causes. He hypothesized that the strong moral restrictions placed upon the individual were directly contrary to what the person wanted to do (perhaps masturbate, a definite transgression of permissible behavior). He believed that this person had a very strong id without a sufficiently strong superego to control it. The person's unconscious mind had to devise some other strategy to keep the id controlled—hence the paralysis of the hand. The idea that the individual has an unconscious mind was a crucial development in psychology and has been maintained to date by many types of psychologists, though not by all. It is directly related to the theory of psychosexual development.

IMPACT ON PSYCHOLOGY

Psychosexual development was proposed by Freud strictly to explain why certain symptoms developed in individuals. His ideas had an extremely strong impact on the future of psychology, as they were complex and explained human behavior in an understandable manner (given the spirit of the times in which they were formulated). Many followers applied Freud's theories to the treatment of psychopathology, and the profession of psychoanalysis was born. Psychoanalysts specialized in the treatment of persons with neuroses; they did so through daily sessions that lasted fifty minutes. Treatment often continued for many years. Only through this approach, psychoanalysts believed, could they effect changes in a person's psychic structure—that is, in the person's ego and the relationship between the id and superego. The profession of psychoanalysis is still a prominent one, but many changes have been made. Few psychoanalysts today follow a strictly Freudian approach to the development of a person's psyche; new ways of understanding human development and behavior have been developed. Psychoanalysis and psychosexual development, however, remain important features of psychology's history. They were important milestones in the discipline of clinical psychology, the branch of psychology concerned with the treatment of mental illness.

SOURCES FOR FURTHER STUDY

Freud, Sigmund. *Civilization and Its Discontents*. New York: W. W. Norton, 1961. Provides a good, brief overview of the psychosexual stages and places them in the larger context of general living. Written only ten years before Freud's death, this book contains his later ideas. The writing style is excellent.

_____. *Dora: An Analysis of a Case of Hysteria*. New York: Collier Books, 1963. Provides the case history of a woman who suffered from a neurosis. The treatment description of this case provides an excellent practical application of the theory of psychosexual development and its implications for psychopathology and personality development. Very readable; targets the layperson.

_____. *A General Introduction to Psychoanalysis*. New York: Garden City Books, 1952. Provides a thorough but very readable overview of the theories and thoughts Freud developed that support his notion of psychosexual development. A good and relatively brief primer for the layperson.

_____. *Three Case Histories*. New York: Collier Books, 1963. Provides three applied examples of psychopathology as an outgrowth of fixation at or regression to early psychosexual stages. Written for the layperson; presented in an interesting manner.

Rychlak, Joseph F. "The Beginnings of Psychoanalysis: Sigmund Freud." In *Introduction to Personality and Psychotherapy*. 2d ed. Boston: Houghton Mifflin, 1981. This chapter is part of a textbook and therefore somewhat technical, but it is an outstanding account of psychosexual development. It deals with the topic thoroughly, places it in a historical context, and discusses its implications for more recent psychology. An excellent overview that can be read by the layperson who is willing to spend some time rereading the material to understand it thoroughly.

Christiane Brems

SEE ALSO: Abnormality: Psychological models; Analytical psychotherapy; Dreams; Ego defense mechanisms; Oedipus complex; Penis envy; Psychoanalysis; Psychoanalytic psychology; Psychoanalytic psychology and personality: Sigmund Freud; Psychotherapy: Children; Social psychological models: Karen Horney.

Psychosomatic disorders

TYPE OF PSYCHOLOGY: Psychopathology
FIELDS OF STUDY: Cognitive processes; organic disorders; stress and illness

Psychosomatic disorders are physical disorders produced by psychological factors such as stress, mental states, or personality characteristics. A variety of psychological or psychotherapeutic interventions have been developed to alter the individual's ability to cope with stressful situations and to change the personality or behavior of the individual.

KEY CONCEPTS
- behavior modification
- biogenic
- biopsychosocial
- cognitive
- locus of control
- psychogenic

- psychological factors affecting physical condition
- psychosomatic disorders
- self-efficacy
- Type A behavior pattern

INTRODUCTION

The term "psychosomatic" was introduced by physician Flanders Dunbar in the early 1940's, shortly after Hans Selye presented the concept of "stress." Psychosomatic disorders are physical disorders which are caused by, or exacerbated by, psychological factors. These psychological factors fall into three major groups: stress resulting from encounters with the environment, personality characteristics, and psychological states. It should be noted that psychosomatic disorders are different from two other conditions with which they are often confused. Psychosomatic disorders are real—that is, they are actual physical illnesses that have underlying psychological causes or that are made worse by psychological factors. In somatoform disorders (such as hypochondriasis), by contrast, there is no physiological cause; another condition, malingering, is the faking of an illness.

Psychosomatic disorders can affect any of the organ systems of the body. Certainly, not all physical disorders or illnesses are psychosomatic disorders; in many cases, an illness or physical disorder is caused entirely by biogenic factors. In many other cases, however, there is no question about the importance of psychogenic factors. The American College of Family Physicians has estimated that 90 percent of the workload of doctors is the result of psychogenic factors.

Many familiar and common psychosomatic disorders that can affect the body's various organ systems. Included among them are skin disorders, such as acne, hives, and rashes; musculoskeletal disorders, such as backaches, rheumatoid arthritis, and tension headaches; respiratory disorders, such as asthma and hiccups; and cardiovascular disorders, such as hypertension, heart attacks, strokes, and migraine headaches. Other disorders have also been related to psychological factors, including anemia, weakening of the immune system, ulcers, and constipation. Genitourinary disorders such as menstrual problems, vaginismus, male erectile disorder, and premature ejaculation are included among psychosomatic disorders, as are certain endocrine and neurological problems.

The relationship between the mind and the body has long been the subject of debate. Early societies saw a clear link between the mind and the body. Early Greek and Roman physicians believed that body fluids determined personality types and that people with certain personality types were prone to certain types of diseases. Beginning during the Renaissance, the dominant line of thought held that there was little or no connection between the mind and the body. Illness was seen as the result of organic, cellular pathology. Destruction of body tissue and invasion by "germs," rather than personality type, were seen as the causes of illness.

Sigmund Freud's work with patients suffering from conversion hysteria began to demonstrate both the importance of psychological factors in the production of physical symptoms of illness and the value of psychological therapy in changing the functioning of the body. Research conducted in the 1930's and 1940's suggested that personality factors play a role in the production of a variety of specific illnesses, including ulcers, hypertension, and asthma.

THE ROLE OF STRESS

Even though Freud demonstrated the role of psychological factors in illness, the medical field has still focused upon the biological roots of illness and has still largely rejected or ignored the role of emotions and personality. Nevertheless, the ascending line of thought can be described as a biopsychosocial view of illness, which begins with the basic assumption that health and illness result from an interplay of biological, psychological, and social factors. This view provides a conceptual framework for incorporating human elements into the scientific paradigm. A man who suffers a heart attack at age thirty-five is not conceptualized simply as a person who is experiencing the effects of cellular damage caused by purely biological processes that are best treated by surgery or the administration of drugs. The victim, instead, is viewed as a person who also has engaged in practices that adversely affected his health. In addition to drugs and surgery, therefore, treatment for this man might include changing his views on the relative value of work and family

A therapist tries to help a toddler who suffers from psychosomatic problems through an experimental dolphin program for treating neurological disorders. (AP/Wide World Photos)

as well as emphasizing the importance of daily exercise and diet. If he smokes, he will be encouraged to quit smoking. He might receive training in stress management and relaxation techniques.

Few people today would argue with the proposition that stress is a fact of life. Most have far more experience with stressors—those events that humans find stressful—than they would willingly choose for themselves. Stress is one of the major causes of psychosomatic disorders. Stressors are often assumed to be external events, probably because stressful external events are so easily identified and recognized. Many stressors, however, come from within oneself. For example, an individual alone often sets strict standards for himself or herself and, in failing to meet those standards, often makes harsher personal judgments than anyone else would make. Especially since the late 1970's and early 1980's, cognitive psychologists have focused attention on the internal thinking processes, thoughts, values, beliefs, and expectations that lead people to put unnecessary pressure on themselves that results in the subjective sense of stress.

Another contribution made by cognitive psychologists was the realization that a situation can be a stressor only if the individual interprets it as stressful. Any event that people perceive as something with which they can cope will be perceived as less stressful than an event that taxes or exceeds their resources, regardless of the objective seriousness of the two events. In other words, it is the cognitive appraisal of the event, coupled with one's cognitive appraisal of one's ability to deal with the event, rather than the objective reality of the event, that determines the degree to which one subjectively experiences stress.

PERSONALITY TYPES

Continuing the tradition of the early Greek and Roman physicians, modern personality theorists have often noted that certain personality characteristics seem to be associated with a propensity to develop

---

DSM-IV-TR Criteria for [Specified Psychological Factor] Affecting [General Medical Condition] (DSM code 316)

General medical condition (coded on Axis III) present

Psychological factors adversely affect general medical condition in one of the following ways:
- factors have influenced the course of general medical condition as shown by close temporal association between psychological factors and the development or exacerbation of, or delayed recovery from, general medical condition
- factors interfere with treatment of general medical condition
- factors constitute additional health risks for individual
- stress-related physiological responses precipitate or exacerbate symptoms of general medical condition

Name based on nature of psychological factors (the most prominent, if more than one factor present):
- Mental Disorder Affecting [General Medical Condition]
- Psychological Symptoms Affecting [General Medical Condition]
- Personality Traits or Coping Style Affecting [General Medical Condition]
- Maladaptive Health Behaviors Affecting [General Medical Condition]
- Physiological Response Affecting [General Medical Condition]
- Other or Unspecified Psychological Factors Affecting [General Medical Condition]

---

illness, or even specific illnesses. Other personality characteristics appear to reduce vulnerability to illness. One of the best-known examples of a case in which personality characteristics affect health is that of the Type A behavior pattern (or Type A personality). The person identified as a Type A personality typically displays a pattern of behaviors which include's easily aroused hostility, excessive competitiveness, and a pronounced sense of time urgency. Research suggests that hostility is the most damaging of these behaviors. Type A personalities typically display hyperreactivity to stressful situations, with a corresponding slow return to the baseline of arousal. The hostile Type A personality, is particularly prone to coronary heart disease. By contrast, the less driven Type B personality does not display the hostility, competitiveness, and time urgency of the Type A personality, and is about half as likely to develop coronary heart disease.

Studies conducted in the 1970's and 1980's led to the suggestion that there is a Type C, or cancer-prone, personality. Although the role of personality characteristics is heavily debated in terms of the development of cancer, various characteristics related to stress have been found to suppress the immune system, thereby making an individual more vulnerable to some cancers. Personality characteristics have therefore also been found to be somewhat influential in the course of the disease. It is well known that many natural and artificial substances produce cancer, but many researchers have also noted that people with certain personality characteristics are more likely to develop cancer, are more likely to develop fast-growing cancers, and are less likely to survive their cancers, whatever the cause. These personality characteristics include repression of strong negative emotions, acquiescence in the face of stressful life situations, inhibition, depression, and hopelessness. Encounters with uncontrollable stressful events appear to be particularly related to the development or course of cancer. In addition, some research suggests that not having strong social support systems may contribute to the development or affect the outcome of cancer.

Research has begun to focus on the possible interaction among risk factors for cancer. For example, depressed smokers are many more times likely to develop smoking-related cancers than are either nondepressed smokers or depressed nonsmokers. One theory suggests that the smoking provides exposure to the carcinogenic substance that initiates the cancer, and depression promotes its development.

It has been suggested that hardiness is a broad, positive personality variable that affects one's propensity for developing stress-related illness. Hardiness is made up of three more specific characteristics: commitment (becoming involved in things that are going on around oneself), challenge (accepting the need for change and seeing new opportunities for growth in what others see as problems), and control (believing that one's actions determine what happens in life and that one can have an effect on the environment). It has been hypothesized that people who possess these characteristics are less likely to develop stress-related disorders because they view stressful situations more favorably than do other people. Commitment and control seem to be more influential in promoting health. Locus of control is a related concept which has received much attention.

CONTROL AND HELPLESSNESS

Locus of control refers to the location where one believes control over life events originates. An external locus of control is outside oneself; an internal locus of control is within oneself. The individual who perceives that life events are the result of luck, or are determined by others, is assuming an external locus of control. The belief that one's efforts and actions control one's own destiny reflects an internal locus of control. Internalizers are thought to be more likely to assume responsibility for initiating necessary lifestyle changes, to employ more direct coping mechanisms when confronted with stressful situations, and to be more optimistic about the possibility of successfully instituting changes that are needed. This last characteristic is sometimes called self-efficacy. Self-efficacy refers to the belief that one is able to do what is needed and attain the intended effect.

The concept of learned helplessness, on the other hand, produces feelings of complete lack of control and a fatalistic acceptance of events. Martin E. P. Seligman began to investigate this phenomenon in 1964. He found that when people are faced with a situation which they can do nothing to prevent or escape, they learn the attitude of helplessness. Seligman and colleagues later investigated the question of why some people do not adopt this attitude. They concluded that people who adopt a pessimistic explanatory style become helpless when adversity is encountered, but that an optimistic explanatory style prevents the development of learned helplessness.

Seligman has described the chain of events by which the pessimistic explanatory style may lead to illness. Beginning with unfortunate experiences such as a serious loss, defeat, or failure, the person with a pessimistic explanatory style becomes depressed. The depression leads to depletion of a neurotransmitter substance called catecholamine, and the body increases the secretion of endorphins—the body's own naturally produced form of morphine. When receptors in the immune system detect the increased presence of the endorphins, the immune system begins to turn itself down. Any disease agents that are encountered while the immune system is weakened have a much greater likelihood of overwhelming the remaining defenses of the immune system. This process is very similar to the situation faced by the individual who contracts the human immunodeficiency virus (HIV) and develops acquired immunodeficiency syndrome (AIDS). When the immune system of the person with AIDS is unable to function effectively, opportunistic infections against which the body could normally defend itself are able to take over. It is those opportunistic infections that kill, rather than the HIV itself.

INTERVENTIONS

Since the hyperreactivity of the Type A behavior pattern is thought to be at least partially genetically based, there are probably some limits on what can be done to reduce the incidence of coronary heart disease resulting from physiological hyperreactivity. There is, however, much that can be done in other areas. Persons who are prone to such disorders can be taught to exercise properly, eliminate unhealthy dietary practices, and reduce or quit smoking. Of particular interest to psychologists is the opportunity to help these individuals by teaching effective coping strategies, stress management, values training, behavior modification to control Type A behaviors, and cognitive control of depression and other negative emotions.

Studies by psychologists have demonstrated a wide range of interventions that can be helpful in reducing the danger of cardiovascular disease in Type A personalities. Exercise produces positive effects on physiological functioning, appears to improve general psychological functioning, and reduces Type A behaviors. Cognitive behavioral stress management techniques have been shown to reduce behavioral reactivity. Values training focusing on changing the person's perceptions of the importance of occupational success and competitiveness has enabled the individual to concentrate on more beneficial behaviors. Behavior modification techniques have been used to alter the kinds of behavior that appear to be most dangerous for the Type A person, substituting other behavioral responses in place of explosive speech and hostility. Cognitive control of emotions produces more rapid physiological recovery after stress.

Efforts by psychologists to help the Type C personality might focus on assertiveness training and altering the person's belief that it is not appropriate to display strong negative emotions, such as anger or frustration. Teaching the Type C person to fight back against stressful life situations, rather than acquiescing to them, might also be of benefit. Imag-

ery therapy appears to be beneficial to some cancer patients, perhaps for that reason, but also because it promotes the development of learned optimism in place of learned pessimism. Promoting the development of effective social support systems is another means for psychologists to have a positive impact in the fight against cancer.

PSYCHOSOMATICS AND THE FUTURE

It is important that a distinction be made between psychosomatic disorders and three other conditions listed in the *Diagnostic and Statistical Manual of Mental Disorders: DSM-IV-TR* (rev. 4th ed., 2000), which is the official classification system for mental disorders published by the American Psychiatric Association. Psychosomatic disorders, which are covered by the category Psychological Factors Affecting Physical Conditions, are not themselves considered mental disorders. While the psychological factors that cause the physical illness are unhealthy or abnormal from a psychiatric or psychological perspective, the psychosomatic disorder is a real, physical illness or condition controlled by real, physical processes.

Somatoform disorders, on the other hand, are mental disorders which manifest themselves through real or imagined physical symptoms for which no physical cause exists. These symptoms are not intentionally produced by the client. Conversion disorder is one of the somatoform disorders that laypeople often confuse with psychosomatic disorders. Unlike the case with psychosomatic disorders, there is no organic or physiological pathology that would account for the presence of the physical symptoms displayed by the person suffering from a conversion disorder. Hypochondriasis is the second somatoform disorder that is often confusing for laypeople. The person suffering from hypochondriasis fears or believes that he or she has the symptoms of a serious disease, but the imagined "symptoms" are actually normal sensations or body reactions which are misinterpreted as symptoms of disease.

Malingering is the third condition which is sometimes confused with psychosomatic disorders. The person who is malingering is faking illness and is reporting symptoms that either do not exist at all or are grossly exaggerated. The malingering is motivated by external goals or incentives.

By eliminating many of the diseases that used to be epidemic, especially those which killed people early in life, medical science has increased the average life expectancy of Americans by about thirty years since the beginning of the twentieth century. Eliminating the psychological factors that cause psychosomatic disorders holds promise for another increase in average life expectancy in the next few decades. Heart disease, cancer, and strokes are the top three killer diseases in the United States, and each has a powerful psychosomatic component. The reduction in human suffering and the economic benefits that can be gained by controlling nonfatal psychosomatic disorders are equally promising.

Cognitive and health psychologists have, particularly since the 1970's, tried to determine the degree to which cognitive psychotherapy interventions can boost immune system functioning in cancer patients. They have also used behavioral and cognitive therapy approaches to alter the attitudes and behaviors of people who are prone to heart disease and strokes with considerable success. In the near future, they can be expected to focus their efforts on two major fronts. The first will involve further attempts to identify the psychological factors which might increase people's propensity to develop psychosomatic disorders. The second will involve continuing efforts to develop and refine the therapeutic interventions intended to reduce the damage done by psychosomatic disorders, and possibly to prevent them entirely.

SOURCES FOR FURTHER STUDY

Chopra, Deepak. *Creating Health.* Boston: Houghton Mifflin, 1987. Chopra is a proponent of meditation, an approach that many American psychologists do not necessarily feel comfortable advocating. Nevertheless, this book is written by a practicing physician for the layperson. He covers a wide variety of psychosomatic disorders, suggests a variety of healthy habits, and presents the viewpoint that "health is our natural state."

Pert, Candace B. *Molecules of Emotion.* New York: Simon & Schuster, 1997. This is a highly accessible book written in an engaging style with wit and humor. Pert discusses her research on the scientific bases of mind-body medicine and the difficulties in integrating these concepts into Western medicine. The book contains appendices with a list of resources and practitioners, an extensive glossary, and recommended readings.

Seligman, Martin E. P. *Learned Optimism.* New York: Alfred A. Knopf, 1991. Chapter 2 provides an especially interesting account of how two young upstart graduate students can blow a hole in one of the most basic assumptions of a well-entrenched viewpoint and promote the development of a new way of looking at things. Chapter 10 describes how explanatory styles might affect health and the mechanism by which this is thought to occur. A test developed to measure explanatory styles is included in chapter 3, and the last chapters focus on how to develop an optimistic orientation. A very readable book which examines a most interesting concept.

Simonton, O. Carl, Stephanie Matthews-Simonton, and James L. Creighton. *Getting Well Again.* New York: Bantam Books, 1980. Cancer researchers and therapists examine the mind-body connection, effects of beliefs, causes of cancer, effects of stress and personality, and effects of expectations on the development and progress of cancer. They describe a holistic approach to treatment, emphasizing relaxation and visual imagery, that is reported to produce cancer survival rates that are twice the national norm. A very readable book which is readily available in paperback.

Taylor, Shelley E. *Health Psychology.* 3d ed. New York: McGraw-Hill, 1995. A moderately high-level college textbook that comprehensively covers the general field of health psychology. As could be expected, many research studies are presented, and not all of them corroborate one another. The general reader should have no particular difficulty handling this material; the writing is reader-friendly.

Wedding, Danny, ed. *Behavior and Medicine.* 2d ed. St. Louis: Mosby Year Book, 2001. This large volume covers an extensive area of behavior and medicine, which include stress and various behaviors which may affect physiological health. The articles cover such behavioral issues as substance abuse, stress management, pain, placebos, AIDS, cardiovascular risk, and adherence to medical regimens. Other behavioral issues are covered which relate to love and work, as well as developmental issues from infancy to death, dying and grief. The book is very readable, and includes illustrations, relevant poetry, bibliographies, summaries, and study questions at the end of each article.

John W. Nichols;
updated by Martha Oehmke Loustaunau

SEE ALSO: Cognitive behavior therapy; Cognitive therapy; Emotions; Endocrine system; Health psychology; Hypochondriasis, conversion, somatization disorder, and somatoform pain; Learned helplessness; Stress: Physiological responses; Stress-related diseases.

Psychosurgery

DATE: The 1930's forward
TYPE OF PSYCHOLOGY: Psychological methodologies
FIELDS OF STUDY: Anxiety disorders; biological treatments; depression; endocrine system; schizophrenias

Psychosurgery is brain surgery where brain parts are disconnected or removed to do away with psychiatric problems such as aggression, anxiety, and psychoses. It was used most from 1935 to 1965, until psychoactive drugs began to replace it. Psychosurgery is not carried out to relieve psychiatric symptoms due to structural brain disease such as brain tumors.

KEY CONCEPTS
- electroconvulsive therapy
- psychopharmaceuticals
- psychosurgery techniques
- somatic theory of insanity

INTRODUCTION

In the early twentieth century, the treatment of mental disease was limited to psychotherapy for neurotics and long-term care of psychotics in asylums. In the 1930's, these methods were supplemented by physical approaches using electroconvulsive therapy (ECT) and brain operations. The operations, psychosurgery, were in vogue from the mid-1930's to the mid to late 1960's. They became, and still are, hugely controversial, although their use had drastically declined by the last quarter of the twentieth century. Controversy arose because, for its first twenty-five years of existence, crude psychosurgery was too often carried out on inappropriate patients.

ECT developed after the 1935 discovery that schizophrenia could be treated by convulsions induced through camphor injection. Soon, convulsion production was accomplished by passage of electric current through the brain, as described in 1938 by Italian physicians Ugo Cerletti and Lucio Bini. ECT was most successful in alleviating depression and is still used for that purpose. In contrast, classic psychosurgery by bilateral prefrontal leucotomy (lobotomy) is no longer done because of its bad effects on the physical and mental health of many subjects. These effects included epilepsy and unwanted personality changes such as apathy, passivity, and low emotional responses. It should be remembered, however, that psychosurgery was first planned to quiet chronically tense, delusional, agitated, or violent psychotics.

HISTORY AND CONTEXT OF PSYCHOSURGERY

Psychosurgery is believed to have originated with the observation by early medical practitioners that severe head injuries could produce extreme changes in behavior patterns. In addition, physicians of the thirteenth to sixteenth centuries reported that sword and knife wounds that penetrated the skull could change normal behavior patterns. Regardless, from the mid-1930's to the mid-1960's, reputable physicians performed psychosurgery on both indigent patients in public institutions and on the wealthy at expensive private hospitals and universities.

Psychosurgery was imperfect and could cause adverse reactions, but it was performed because of the arguments advanced by powerful physician proponents of the method; the imperfect state of knowledge of the brain at the time; the enthusiasm of the popular press, which lauded the method; and many problems at overcrowded mental hospitals. The last reason is thought to have been the most compelling, as asylums for the incurably insane were hellish places. Patients were beaten and choked by attendants, incarcerated in dark, dank, padded cells, and subjected to many other indignities. At the same time, little could be done to cure them.

EGAS MONIZ INVENTS LEUCOTOMY

The two main figures in psychosurgery were António Egas Moniz, the Portuguese neurologist who invented lobotomy, and the well-known American neuropathologist and neuropsychiatrist Walter Freeman, who roamed the world convincing others to carry out the operations. The imperfect state of knowledge of the brain in relation to insanity was expressed in two theories of mental illness. A somatic (organic) theory of insanity proposed it to be of biological origin. In contrast, a functional theory supposed life experiences to cause the problems.

The somatic theory was shaped most by Emil Kraepelin, foremost authority on psychiatry in the first half of the twentieth century. Kraepelin distinguished twenty types of mental disorder, including dementia praecox (schizophrenia) and manic-depressive (bipolar) disorder. Kraepelin and his colleagues viewed these diseases as genetically determined, and practitioners of psychiatry developed complex physical diagnostic schema that identified people with various types of psychoses. In contrast, Sigmund Freud was the main proponent of the functional theory. Attempts to help mental patients included ECT, as well as surgical removal of tonsils, sex organs, and parts of the digestive system. All these methods had widely varied success rates that were often subjective and differed depending on which surgeon used them. By the 1930's, the most widely effective curative procedures were several types of ECT and lobotomy (psychosurgery).

The first lobotomy was carried out on November 12, 1935, at a hospital in Lisbon, Portugal. There, Pedro A. Lima, Egas Moniz's neurosurgeon collaborator, drilled two holes into the skull of a female mental patient and injected ethyl alcohol directly into the frontal lobes of her brain to destroy nerve cells. After several such operations, the tissue-killing procedure was altered to use an instrument called a leucotome. After its insertion into the brain, the knifelike instrument, designed by Egas Moniz, was rotated like an apple corer to destroy chosen lobe areas.

Egas Moniz—already a famous neurologist—named the procedure prefrontal leucotomy. He won a Nobel Prize in Physiology or Medicine in 1949 for his invention of the procedure. Within a year of his first leucotomy, psychosurgery (another term invented by Egas Moniz) spread through Europe. Justification for its wide use was the absence of any other effective somatic treatment and the emerging concept that the cerebral frontal lobes were the site of intellectual activity and mental problems. The selection of leucotomy target sites was based on two considerations using the position in the frontal lobes where nerve fibers—not nerve cells—were most concentrated and avoiding damage to large blood vessels. Thus, Egas Moniz targeted the frontal lobe's centrum ovale, which contains few blood vessels.

After eight operations—50 percent performed on schizophrenics—Egas Moniz and Lima stated that their cure rates were good. Several other psychiatric physicians disagreed strongly. After twenty operations, it became fairly clear that psychosurgery worked best on patients suffering from anxiety and depression, while schizophrenics did not benefit very much. The main effect of the surgery was to calm patients and make them docile. Retrospectively, it is believed that Egas Moniz's evidence for serious improvement in many cases was very sketchy. However, many psychiatric and neurological practitioners were impressed and the stage was set for wide dissemination of psychosurgery.

LOBOTOMY PROCEDURES

The second great proponent of leucotomy—the physician who renamed it lobotomy and greatly modified the methodology used—was Freeman, professor of neuropathology at George Washington University Medical School in Washington, D.C. In 1936, he tested the procedure on preserved brains from the medical school morgue and repeated Egas Moniz's efforts. After six lobotomies, Freeman and his associate James W. Watts became optimistic that the method was useful to treat patients exhibiting apprehension, anxiety, insomnia, and nervous tension, while pointing out that it would be impossible to determine whether the procedure had effected the recovery or cure of mental problems until a five-year period had passed.

As Freeman and Watts continued to operate, they noticed problems, including relapses to the original abnormal state, a need for repeated surgery, a lack of ability on the part of patients to resume jobs requiring the use of reason, and death due to postsurgical hemorrhage. This led them to develop a more precise technique, using the landmarks on the skull to identify where to drill entry holes, cannulation to assure that lobe penetration depth was not dangerous to patients, and use of a knifelike spatula to make lobotomy cuts. The extent of surgery also varied, depending upon whether the patient involved was suffering from an affective disorder or from schizophrenia. Their method, the "routine Freeman-Watts lobotomy procedure," became popular throughout the world.

Another method used for prefrontal lobotomy was designed by J. G. Lyerly in 1937. He opened the brain so that psychosurgeons could see exactly what was being done to the frontal lobes. This technique also became popular and was used throughout the United States. Near the same time, in Japan, Mizuho Nakata of Nigata Medical College began to remove from the brain parts of one or both frontal lobes. However, the Freeman-Watts method was most popular as the result of a "do-it-yourself manual" for psychosurgery that they published in 1942. Watts's book theorized that the brain pathways between cerebral frontal lobes and the thalamus regulate intensity of emotions in ideas, and acceptance of this theory led to better scientific justification of psychosurgery.

Another lobotomy procedure that was fairly widespread was Freeman's transorbital method, designed not only to correct shortcomings in his routine method but also in an attempt to aid many

more schizophrenics. The simple, rapid, but frightening procedure drove an ice-picklike transorbital leukotome through the eye socket, above the eyeball, and into the frontal lobe. Subjects were rendered unconscious with ECT and the procedure was done before they woke up. Use of this method gained many converts and, gruesome as it sounds, the method caused less brain damage than other psychosurgery procedures. It was widely used at state hospitals for the insane and was lauded by the press as making previously hopeless cases normal immediately.

Subsequently developed tereotaxic surgical techniques, such as stereotactic cingulatory, enabled psychosurgeons to create much smaller lesions by means of probes inserted into accurately located brain regions, followed by nerve destruction through the use of radioactive implants or by cryogenics. Currently, psychosurgery is claimed to be an effective treatment for patients with intractable depression, anxiety, or obsessional problems and a method that improves the behavior of very aggressive patients. Opponents say that these therapeutic effects can be attained by means of antipsychotic and antidepressant drugs. The consensus is that psychosurgery can play a small part in psychiatric treatment when long-term use of other treatments is unsuccessful and patients are tormented by mental problems.

MODE OF ACTION OF PSYCHOSURGERY

Collectively, the brain's limbic system is composed of the hippocampus, amygdala, hippocampal and cingulate gyri, limen insulae, and posterior orbital regions of cerebral frontal lobes. This system, its components linked by nerve pathways, controls emotional expression, seizure activity, and memory storage and recall. Moreover, cerebral lobe limbic system connections from the dorsal convexity of a frontal lobe comprise two pathways running to the cingulate gyrus and hippocampus and the hypothalamus and midbrain. The frontal lobe orbital surface also projects to the septal area of the hypothalamus. The limbic brain architecture therefore yields two neurotransport circuits in a frontolimbic-hypothalamic-midbrain axis. These are a medial frontal, cingulate, hippocampus circuit (MFCHC) and an orbital frontal, temporal, amygdala circuit (OFTAC), which control hypothalamic autonomic and endocrine action. The MFCHC and OFTAC connect in

Contemporary psychosurgery was founded in 1935 by the Portuguese neurosurgeon António Egas Moniz, who was awarded the Nobel Prize in Physiology or Medicine for his work. (© The Nobel Foundation)

the septa, preoptic area, midbrain, and hypothalamus.

The original Egas Moniz lobotomy divided the frontolimbic structures, and its bad effects were due to the disabling impairment of frontal lobe function. Psychosurgery on the anterior cingulate gyrus and on the thalamofrontal bundle (bimedial leucotomy) divided different parts of the same main circuit. Orbital undercutting severs red nerve tracts running from the posterior orbital cortex to the limbic system. Although psychosurgery is currently an uncommon procedure, when it is performed, the methods used are lower medial quadrant leucotomy, making lesions just before the fourth ventricle; stereotactic-subcaudate-tractotomy, making lesions with rear halves in the subcaudate area; removal of the anterior two inches of the cingulate gyrus; and stereotactic limbic leucotomy, lesioning the lower medial frontal lobe quadrant. These operations cause varied endocrine and autonomic disconnections, and are thus chosen to suit the mental condition being treated.

DIAGNOSIS AND TREATMENT

Diagnosis of a need for psychosurgery is based on observation of symptoms supporting abnormal psychological behavior. Examples are extremes of aggression, anxiety, obsession, or compulsiveness, as well as psychoses other than schizophrenia. The exclusion of schizophrenics, except for those having marked anxiety and tension, is based on data supporting poor responses by schizophrenics to lobotomy and other leucotomies. Surveys have shown that good surgical outcomes were only obtained in 18 percent of schizophrenics who underwent lobotomy, as compared with 50 percent of depressives.

Psychosurgery's unfavorable record between 1935 and 1965, and its postoperative irreversibility, speak to the need for careful study before suggesting such brain surgery. In addition, many members of the medical community believe that the choice of psychosurgery should be based on the long-term nature of symptoms untreatable by other means, as well as a severe risk of suicide. Before psychosurgery is attempted, other methods must be exhausted, such as repeated ECT, prolonged psychoanalysis, and aggressive pharmaceutical treatments with antipsychotic drugs. Some sources suggest, as criteria for choosing psychosurgery, the persistence of symptoms for more than ten years of treatment under

conditions where all possible nonsurgical methodology has been exhausted after its aggressive use. Others believe it inhumane to require a decade of illness before allowing the possibility of a cure.

Symptom severity is another hugely important criterion for psychosurgery. Examples of this are the complete inability to work at a job or carry out household chores, as well as long-term and severe endogenous depression. It is also suggested that patients who have strong psychological support from their families and stable environments are the best candidates. Careful assessment of patient symptoms, handicaps, and problems should always be carried out. Formal rating scales, personality assessment via school and work records, and information coming from close relatives or friends are also viewed as crucial.

The use of psychosurgery is limited to a very small number of patients not helped by existing chemotherapeutic or psychoanalytical methodology. It is fortunate that a wide variety of new techniques have made psychosurgery capable of destroying smaller and smaller targets. As knowledge of the brain and its functioning increases, it appears possible that modern psychosurgery may yet prove to be useful where other methods fail.

SOURCES FOR FURTHER STUDY

Feigenbaum, Ernes. *Stereotactic Cingulotomy as a Means of Psychosurgery.* Rockville, Md.: U.S. Department of Health and Human Services, Public Health Service, 1985. A useful description of one of the newer psychosurgical methods.

Fulton, John F. *Frontal Lobotomy and Affective Behavior: A Neuropsychological Analysis.* New York: W. W. Norton, 1951. Here, a prominent member of the American medical profession of the time describes António Egas Moniz and Pedro A. Lima and discusses human and animal lobotomy. Fulton is strongly for lobotomy and lauds its achievements and prospects. The book has good references and illustrations.

Lader, Malcolm H., and Reginald Herrington. *Biological Treatments in Psychiatry.* 2d ed. New York: Oxford University Press, 1996. Covers the human brain, mental illness, principles of its treatment, neuropharmacology, psychosurgery, and ECT. Good bibliography.

Rodgers, Joann Ellison. *Psychosurgery: Damaging the Brain to Save the Mind.* New York: HarperCollins,

1992. Covers psychosurgery in healing the chronically insane; describes methods which destroy only a few brain cells and their efficacy compared to drugs; and examines moral and medical pros and cons.

Turner, Eric A. *Surgery of the Mind.* Birmingham, England: Carmen Press, 1982. Answers questions regarding the ethics of carrying out psychosurgery, its consequences, and its justifications. Topics include the brain, its function and operation, selection and management of lobotomy patients, various types of psychosurgery, and follow-up of five hundred psychosurgeries.

Valenstein, Elliot S. *Great and Desperate Cures: The Rise and Decline of Psychosurgery and Other Radical Treatments for Mental Illness.* New York: Basic Books, 1986. Well-thought-out history of psychosurgery. Includes theories of mentation leading to psychosurgery, methodology of its great proponents, and reasons for its replacement and contemporary limited use. Illustrated.

_____, ed. *The Psychosurgery Debate: Scientific, Legal, and Ethical Perspectives.* New York: W. F. Freeman, 1980. Includes an overview of the history, rationale for, and extent of psychosurgery; patient selection; evaluation of methods used; description of legal and ethical issues; and an extensive bibliography.

Sanford S. Singer

SEE ALSO: Anxiety disorders; Bipolar disorder; Brain structure; Depression; Madness: Historical approaches; Psychotic disorders; Schizophrenia: Background, types, and symptoms; Schizophrenia: Theoretical explanations; Shock therapy.

Psychotherapy
Children

TYPE OF PSYCHOLOGY: Psychotherapy
FIELDS OF STUDY: Behavioral therapies; cognitive therapies; group and family therapies; psychodynamic therapies

Psychotherapy with children involves the use of psychological techniques in the treatment of children with behavioral, cognitive, or emotional disorders.

The specific focus of treatment varies and may involve children only, parents only, or a combination of these individuals.

KEY CONCEPTS
- behavior therapy
- behavioral parent training
- cognitive-behavioral therapy
- cognitive therapy
- externalizing disorders
- family therapy
- internalizing disorders
- interpretation
- learning theory
- play therapy
- working through

INTRODUCTION
Various psychological techniques designed to treat children's behavioral, cognitive, or emotional problems are used in psychotherapy with children. The number of children with psychological disorders underscores the need for effective child psychotherapy: It is estimated that between 7 and 14 million, or between 5 and 15 percent, of children in the United States suffer from psychological disorders. It is believed that only one-fourth to one-third of all children who have psychological problems receive psychotherapeutic services.

Children, like adults, may experience many different kinds of psychological disorders. For example, in the *Diagnostic and Statistical Manual of Mental Disorders: DSM-IV-TR* (rev. 4th ed., 2000), published by the American Psychiatric Association, nearly forty separate disorders are listed which primarily affect children. This number does not include many disorders, such as major depressive disorder, which primarily affect adults but may also affect children. In general terms, children's disorders can be divided into two major categories: externalizing and internalizing disorders.

EXTERNALIZING AND INTERNALIZING DISORDERS
Externalizing disorders are those in which children engage in activities that are physically disruptive or are harmful to themselves or others. An example of this type of disorder is conduct disorder. Conduct disorder is characterized by children's involvement in a continued pattern of behavior that demonstrates a fundamental disregard for the safety or

property of others. In contrast to externalizing disorders, internalizing disorders create greater emotional distress for the children themselves than for others around them. An example of an internalizing disorder is generalized anxiety disorder, in which the child experiences persistent, unrealistic anxiety regarding numerous situations and events, such as peer acceptance or school grades.

TYPES OF TREATMENT

PSYCHOANALYTIC THERAPY. In response to the prevalence and variety of childhood disorders, many different treatments have been developed to address children's psychological problems. Historically, the earliest interventions for addressing these problems were based on psychoanalytic theory, developed by Sigmund Freud. Psychoanalysis is a type of psychotherapy based on the idea that individuals' unconscious processes, derived from early childhood experiences, are responsible for the psychological problems they experience as adults. One of the first therapists to adapt Freud's psychoanalysis to the treatment of children was Anna Freud, his daughter.

Psychoanalysis had to be modified for the treatment of children because of its heavy reliance on individuals' verbalizing their unconscious thoughts and feelings. Anna Freud realized that children would not be able to verbalize regarding their experiences to the extent necessary for effective treatment. Therefore, beginning in the 1920's, she created play therapy, a system of psychotherapy in which children's responses during play provided information regarding their hidden thoughts and feelings. Although play therapy had its roots in Sigmund Freud's psychoanalysis, this type of therapy came to be associated with other systems of psychotherapy. For example, Virginia Axline demonstrates her version of play therapy in the 1964 book *Dibs: In Search of Self;* her approach is based on Carl Rogers's person-centered therapy.

BEHAVIOR THERAPY. Also in the 1920's, Mary Cover Jones was applying the principles of behavior therapy developed by John B. Watson and others to the treatment of children's fears. Behavior therapy rests on the notion that all behavior, whether adaptive or maladaptive, is learned and thus can be unlearned. Jones's treatment involved reconditioning, a procedure in which the object of which the child is afraid is gradually associated with a pleasurable activity. By regularly associating the feared object with a pleasurable activity, Jones was able to eliminate children's fears.

FAMILY THERAPY. Although early child analysts and behaviorally oriented psychologists attributed many children's problems to difficulties within their family environments, these treatment providers' primary focus was on treating the children, not their parents. In the early 1940's, however, Nathan Ackerman, a psychiatrist trained in the psychoanalytic tradition, began to treat children in conjunction with their families. His justification for seeing all family members in treatment was that families, like individuals, possess hidden conflicts that prevent them from engaging in healthy psychological functioning. Therefore, the role of the family therapist was to uncover these family conflicts, thus creating the possibility that the conflicts could be addressed in more adaptive ways. Once these family conflicts were properly handled, the causes of the child's psychological problems were removed. Ackerman's approach marked the beginning of the use of family therapy for the treatment of children's problems.

PARENT TRAINING. Another historical movement within child psychotherapy is behavioral parent training (BPT). BPT evolved from the recognition that parents are important in shaping their children's behavior and that they can be trained to eliminate many of their children's problems. Beginning in the late 1960's, researchers such as Gerald Patterson and Rex Forehand began to develop programs designed to target parents as the principal persons responsible for change in their children's maladaptive behavior. In this system of psychotherapy, parents were taught ways to assess and to intervene in order to correct their children's misbehavior. The role of the child was deemphasized to the point that the child might not even be seen by the therapist during the treatment process.

COGNITIVE AND COGNITIVE-BEHAVIORAL THERAPIES. In the 1970's, some psychologists, including Donald Meichenbaum, began to apply the principles of behavior therapy to not only overt, but also covert, behaviors (that is, thoughts). Thus, the cognitive tradition was begun. Cognitive therapies are based on the mediational model, a model based on the belief that cognitive activity affects behavior. The goal of cognitive therapy is to institute behavioral changes via modifications in thoughts, especially maladaptive ones. Many child therapies actually use both cognitive and behavioral approaches in combination: cognitive-behavioral therapy. The cognitive-behavioral approach can be conceptualizeid as a two-pronged approach addressing both thoughts and behaviors while emphasizing their reciprocal relationship (thought affects behavior and behavior affects thought).

TREATMENT FORMATS

It is estimated that more than two hundred different types of child psychotherapy exist; however, these specific types of therapy can be roughly divided into three larger categories of treatment based on the primary focus of their interventions. These three categories are children only, parents only, or children and parents combined.

CHILD-ONLY FORMAT. Individual child psychotherapy, the first category of psychotherapy with children, focuses on the child alone because of the belief that the greatest amount of improvement can result when the child is given primary attention in treatment. An example of individual child treatment is psychodynamic play therapy. Originating from the work of Anna Freud, psychodynamic play therapy has as its basic goal providing the child with insight into the internal conflicts that have caused his or her psychological disorder. Once the child has gained sufficient insight, he or she is guided in handling these conflicts in more adaptive ways. Play therapy can be divided into three basic phases: initial, interpretative, and working-through phases.

In the initial phase of play therapy, the major goal is to establish a cooperative relationship between the child and the therapist. The attainment of this goal may require considerable time for several potential reasons. These reasons include a child's unwillingness to participate in therapy, lack of understanding regarding the therapy process, and lack of a previous trusting relationship with an adult. The participation in play activities provides an opportunity for the therapist to interact with the child in a relaxed and interesting manner. The specific kinds of play utilized differ from therapist to therapist but may include competitive games (such as checkers), imaginative games involving different figures (hand puppets, for example), or cooperative games (playing catch).

Once a sufficient level of cooperation is established, the therapist can begin to make interpretations to the child regarding the play. These interpretations consist of the therapist identifying themes in the content or style of a child's play that may relate to a psychological problem. For example, in playing with hand puppets, a child referred because of aggressive behavior may regularly enact stories in which a larger puppet "beats up" a smaller puppet. The child's therapist may interpret this story as meaning that the child is aggressive toward others because he or she feels inadequate.

Once the child gains insight into the internal conflict that has caused his or her problematic behavior, the child is guided by the therapist to develop a more adaptive way of handling this conflict. This final process of therapy is called working through. The working-through phase may be the most difficult part of treatment, because it involves the child abandoning a repetitive and maladaptive manner of handling a conflict in favor of a new approach. In comparison to most other psychotherapies, this treatment process is lengthy, ranging from months to years.

PARENT-ONLY FORMAT. The second category of child psychotherapy, parent training, focuses intervention on the parents, because they are viewed as potentially the most effective persons available to alleviate the child's problems. This assumption is based on several factors, including the great amount of time parents spend with their children, the parents' control over the child's access to desired reinforcers, and the parents' understanding of the child's behavior because of their past relationship with the child. Behavioral parent training (BPT) is the most common type of parent training program. In BPT, parents are taught ways to modify their children's environment in order to improve behavior.

The initial phase of this treatment process involves instructing parents in the basics of learning theory. They are taught that all behavior, adaptive or maladaptive, is maintained because it is reinforced. The application of learning theory to the correction of children's misbehavior involves three principles. First, positive reinforcement should be withdrawn from children's maladaptive behavior. For example, a father who meets the demands of his screaming preschooler who throws a temper tantrum in the checkout line of the grocery store because she wants a piece of candy is unwittingly reinforcing the child's screaming behavior. Second, appropriate behavior that is incompatible with the maladaptive behavior should be positively reinforced. In the case of the screaming preschooler, this would involve rewarding her for acting correctly. Third, aversive consequences should be applied when the problem behavior recurs. That is, when the child engages in the misbehavior, he or she should consistently experience negative costs. For example, the preschooler who has a temper tantrum in the checkout line should not be allowed money to purchase gum, which she had previously selected as a potential reward for good store behavior, as the cost for her tantrum. In order to produce the greatest effect, positive reinforcement and negative consequences should be administered as close as possible to the occurrence of the appropriate or inappropriate behavior.

FAMILY FORMAT. The final category of child psychotherapy, family therapy, focuses intervention on both the child and the child's family. Family therapy rests on the assumption that the child's psychological problems were created and are maintained by interactions among different family members. In this model, attention is shifted away from the individual child's problems toward the functioning of the entire family. For example, in structural family therapy, a widely practiced type of family therapy, the boundaries between different family members are closely examined. Family boundaries represent the degree of separation between different family members or subsets of members (for example, the parent-versus-child subset). According to Salvador Minuchin, the originator of structural family therapy, families in which there is little separation between parents and children may cause certain children to misbehave as a way to gain increased emotional distance from their parents. On the other hand, families characterized by too much separation between parents and children may cause certain children to become depressed because of the lack of a confiding relationship with a parental figure. Regardless of the child's specific disorder, all family members, not the child or parents alone, are the focus of treatment.

EFFICACY OF PSYCHOTHERAPY

The two large questions that can be asked regarding psychotherapy for children are whether it is effective and whether one type of treatment is more effective than others. The answer to the first question

is very clear; psychotherapy is effective in treating the majority of children's psychological disorders. Two major studies in the 1980's reviewed the existing research examining the effects of child psychotherapy. The first of these studies was conducted by Rita Casey and Jeffrey Berman in 1985, and the second was conducted by John Weisz, Bahr Weiss, Mark Alicke, and M. L. Klotz in 1987. Both these studies found that children who received psychotherapy were better off than approximately 75 percent of the children who did not receive psychotherapy. Interestingly, Weisz and colleagues found that younger children (ages four to twelve) appeared to obtain more benefit from psychotherapy than older children (ages thirteen to eighteen). In addition, Casey and Berman found that girls tend to receive more benefit from psychotherapy than do boys.

As one might expect, some controversy exists in attempting to answer the second question, regarding which treatment is the most effective. Casey and Berman concluded that all treatments were equally effective; however, Weisz and colleagues found that behavioral treatments were more effective than nonbehavioral treatments. Disagreement regarding which type of psychotherapy is most effective should not be allowed to obscure the general conclusion that psychotherapy for children is clearly beneficial. Many investigators would suggest that the characteristics shared by all types of child psychotherapy are responsible for the relatively equivalent improvement produced by different treatments. For example, one of these common characteristics may be the therapist's and child's expectations that therapy will result in a reduction in the child's psychological problems. In spite of the treatments' apparent differences in rationale and method, it may be that this component, as well as other common elements, accounts for much of the similarity in treatment outcomes.

The number of psychotherapeutic approaches available to treat children's psychological disorders has exploded since their introduction in the 1920's. Recent research has clearly demonstrated the effectiveness of psychotherapy for children. Controversy still remains, however, regarding which treatment approach is the most effective; continued research is needed to address this issue. Of greater urgency is the need to provide psychotherapy to the approximately 5 to 10 million children with psychological disorders who are not being served. Perhaps even more cost effective, in terms of both alleviating human suffering and reducing costs, would be the development of programs to prevent children's psychological disorders.

SOURCES FOR FURTHER STUDY

Ammerman, R. T., M. Hersen, and C. Last, eds. *Handbook of Prescriptive Treatments for Children and Adolescents*. Boston: Allyn & Bacon, 1999. Edited book in which leading scholars present current empirically derived information on the treatment of various psychological and behavioral disorders in children and adolescents. A prescriptive approach to treatment, current research on the various disorders and problems, case descriptions, and discussion of potential problems in treatment implementation are also provided.

Axline, Virginia. *Dibs: In Search of Self*. New York: Ballantine Books, 1964. This book, written for a general audience, presents Axline's play therapy, illustrated by the presentation of a clinical case. The two-year treatment process with Dibs, a seriously disturbed child, is described in detail. The book provides an excellent example of child-centered play therapy.

Brems, C. *A Comprehensive Guide to Child Psychotherapy*. Boston: Allyn & Bacon, 2001. Discusses the basic principles of child therapy. Topics covered include intake and assessment, treatment planning, therapeutic process, cross-cultural issues, and termination.

Briesmeister, J. M., and C. E. Schaefer, eds. *Handbook of Parent Training: Parents as Cotherapists for Children's Behavior Problems*. New York: John Wiley & Sons, 1997. Aimed at professions who advise parents, this book presents a prescriptive approach to dealing with common childhood behavioral problems such as bed-wetting, noncompliance, and sleep difficulties, while involving parents as cotherapists.

Gordon, T. *Parent Effectiveness Training: The Proven Program for Raising Responsible Children*. New York: Three Rivers Press, 2000. A book aimed at teaching parents effective means of solving common parent-child conflicts such as communication difficulties and teenage rebellion.

Kendall, P. C., ed. *Child and Adolescent Therapy*. New York: Guilford Press, 2000. Edited volume in which child therapy experts discuss recent developments in and applications of cognitive-behavioral theory. Specific applications address a variety of psychological, behavioral, and medical disorders including attention-deficit hyperactivity disorder (ADHD), depression, anxiety, aggression, and chronic health conditions.

Minuchin, Salvador. *Families and Family Therapy*. Cambridge, Mass.: Harvard University Press, 1974. This book, largely intended for professionals, is widely cited by family therapy experts as one of the most pivotal works in the field. Minuchin outlines his views regarding the functioning of healthy and unhealthy families. Specifically, he addresses the maladaptive interactions among family members that create psychological disorders such as anorexia nervosa in children.

Monte, Christopher. "Anna Freud: The Psychoanalytic Heritage and Developments in Ego Psychology." In *Beneath the Mask: An Introduction to Theories of Personality*. 4th ed. Fort Worth, Tex.: Holt, Rinehart and Winston, 1991. In this textbook chapter, Monte describes Anna Freud's contributions to the field of child psychotherapy. The chapter traces Freud's adaptation of her father's psychoanalytic therapy to her work with children. This is a valuable work because it describes Freud's therapy in understandable terms which is difficult, given the complexity of child psychoanalysis.

Nemiroff, Marc A., and Jane Annunziata. *A Child's First Book About Play Therapy*. Washington, D.C.: American Psychological Association, 1990. Children ages four to seven who are entering play therapy are the intended audience of this book. The book uses frequent illustrations and simple words to communicate to children the purpose and process of children's play therapy. An excellent resource for parents.

Reinecke, M. A., F. M. Dattilio, and A. Freeman, eds. *Cognitive Therapy with Children and Adolescents*. New York: Guilford, 1995. Authors present cognitive-behavioral therapy techniques commonly used in the treatment of child and adolescent disorders. Chapters include reviews of empirical literature, case studies, and specific cognitive-behavioral techniques for use with specific childhood and adolescent disorders.

R. Christopher Qualls;
updated by Ellen C. Flannery-Schroeder

Psychotherapy

Effectiveness

TYPE OF PSYCHOLOGY: Psychotherapy
FIELDS OF STUDY: Evaluating psychotherapy

Psychotherapy is a rapidly expanding field; it has been estimated that there are more than four hundred psychotherapeutic approaches. Research evaluating the effectiveness of psychotherapy serves a primary role in the development and validation of therapeutic approaches. Studies have examined the effectiveness of psychotherapy on thousands of patients. Although such studies often produce contradictory and perhaps even disappointing findings, there is clear evidence that psychotherapy is effective.

KEY CONCEPTS
- case study
- empathy
- meta-analysis
- neurotic disorders
- placebo
- randomization
- relapse
- spontaneous remission

INTRODUCTION

Although the roots of psychotherapy can be traced back to ancient times, the birth of modern psychotherapy is frequently targeted with the famous case of "Anna O." in 1882. Physician Josef Breuer, who was a colleague of Sigmund Freud, described Anna O. as a twenty-one-year-old patient with multiple

symptoms including paralysis and loss of sensitivity in her limbs, lapses in awareness, problems in vision and speech, headaches, and dual personality. During treatment, Breuer found that if Anna discussed every occurrence of a symptom until she described its origin and vividly recalled its first appearance, the symptom would disappear. Hypnosis was also employed to help Anna O. eliminate the symptoms more rapidly. (Eventually, Breuer stopped working with this patient because of numerous difficulties, including his jealous wife and his patient's tendency to become hysterical.) Anna O., whose real name was Bertha Pappenheim, later became well known throughout Germany for her work with children, prostitutes, and Jewish relief organizations.

The case of Anna O. is not only important as perhaps representing the birth of modern psychotherapy but also characteristic of a method of investigation referred to as the case study or case report. A case report attempts to highlight descriptions of a specific patient and treatment approach, typically as reported by the therapist. Given the fact that most patients treated in psychotherapy are seen individually by a single therapist, it is not surprising that some of the most influential literature in the history of psychotherapy is based on case reports. Unfortunately, the majority of case reports are inherently problematic in terms of scientific merit and methodological rigor. Moreover, it is difficult to determine which factors are most effective in the treatment of any particular patient. Thus, whereas case reports are common in the history of psychotherapy research, their value is generally limited.

EARLY STUDIES

The earliest psychotherapy outcome studies were conducted from the 1930's to the 1960's. These initial investigations were concerned with one primary question: Does psychotherapy demonstrate positive effects? Unfortunately, the research methodology employed in these studies was typically flawed, and interpretations proved ambiguous. The most common area of disagreement in the early investigations was the concept of spontaneous remission. Psychotherapy was evaluated in comparison to the rates of improvement seen among patients who were not currently receiving treatment.

For example, British psychologist Hans Eysenck created a furor in the early 1950's, one which continued to trouble psychologists and mental health

DSM-IV-TR Criteria for Some Psychotic Disorders

DELUSIONAL DISORDER (DSM CODE 297.1)

Nonbizarre delusions (involving situations occurring in real life, such as being followed, poisoned, infected, loved at a distance, or deceived by spouse or lover, or having a disease) of at least one month's duration

Symptoms for schizophrenia not met; tactile and olfactory hallucinations may be present if related to delusional theme

Apart from impact of delusion(s) or its ramifications, functioning not markedly impaired and behavior not obviously odd or bizarre

If mood episodes have occurred concurrently with delusions, their total duration has been brief relative to duration of delusional periods

Disturbance not due to direct physiological effects of a substance or general medical condition

Type based on predominant delusional theme:
- Erotomanic Type: Delusions that another person, usually of higher status, is in love with individual
- Grandiose Type: Delusions of inflated worth, power, knowledge, identity, or special relationship to deity or famous person
- Jealous Type: Delusions that individual's sexual partner is unfaithful
- Persecutory Type: Delusions that person (or someone to whom person is close) is being malevolently treated in some way
- Somatic Type: Delusions that person has some physical defect or general medical condition
- Mixed Type: Delusions characteristic of more than one of above types but no one theme predominates
- Unspecified Type

BRIEF PSYCHOTIC DISORDER (DSM CODE 298.8)

Presence of one or more of the following symptoms:
- delusions
- hallucinations
- disorganized speech (such as frequent derailment or incoherence)
- grossly disorganized or catatonic behavior

Symptom not included if culturally sanctioned response pattern

Duration of episode of disturbance at least one day but less than one month, with eventual full return to premorbid level of functioning

Disturbance not better accounted for by Mood Disorder with Psychotic Features, Schizoaffective Disorder, or Schizophrenia and not due to direct physiological effects of a substance or general medical condition

Specify:
- With Marked Stressor(s) (brief reactive psychosis): Symptoms occur shortly after and apparently in response to events that, singly or together, would be markedly stressful to almost anyone in similar circumstances in person's culture
- Without Marked Stressor(s): Psychotic symptoms do not occur shortly after, or are not apparently in response to events that, singly or together, would be markedly stressful to almost anyone in similar circumstances in person's culture
- With Postpartum Onset: Onset within four weeks postpartum

SHARED PSYCHOTIC DISORDER (DSM CODE 297.3)

Delusion develops in individual in context of close relationship with another person(s) who has already-established delusion

Delusion similar in content to that of person with already-established delusion

Disturbance not better accounted for by another psychotic disorder (such as Schizophrenia) or a Mood Disorder with Psychotic Features and not due to direct physiological effects of a substance or general medical condition

PSYCHOTIC DISORDER NOT OTHERWISE SPECIFIED (DSM CODE 298.9)

---

workers for several decades. Eysenck concluded, on the basis of his review of twenty-four studies, that psychotherapy produced no greater changes in individuals than did naturally occurring life events. Specifically, he argued that two-thirds of people with neurotic disorders improve over a two-year period with or without psychotherapy. Two particular problems with his review warrant comment, however.

First, the studies that were included in his review rarely employed randomization, which raises significant concerns about subsequent interpretations. Second, later analyses of the same data set demonstrated that Eysenck's original estimates of improvements in the absence of treatment were inflated.

The manner in which research investigations were conducted (the research methodology) became more sophisticated in the 1970's. In particular, research designs included appropriate control groups to account for spontaneous improvements, randomly assigned experimental conditions, well-specified treatment protocols administered by well-trained therapists, and improved instruments and procedures to measure effectiveness. As a result, it became increasingly clear that many psychotherapies demonstrate statistically significant and clinically meaningful effects on patients. Not all patients reveal improvement, however, and many patients relapse following successful treatment.

In 1977, researchers Mary Smith and Gene Glass presented a review of 375 psychotherapy outcome studies carried out by means of a newly devised methodology called "meta-analysis." Meta-analysis literally means "analysis of analyses" and represents a statistical procedure used to summarize collections of research data. Meta-analysis is frequently regarded as more objective and more sophisticated than traditional review procedures such as those employed by Eysenck. Smith and Glass revealed that most patients who entered outpatient psychotherapy showed noticeable improvement. In addition, the average therapy patient improved more than did 75 percent of comparable control patients.

The results reported by Smith and Glass were controversial, and they stimulated much productive debate. In particular, the authors were criticized for certain procedural steps (for example, excluding particular studies and including others). In response to such criticism, many researchers conducted additional meta-analytic investigations to examine the empirical effectiveness of psychotherapy. Of particular importance is the large follow-up investigation that was conducted by Smith, Glass, and Thomas Miller in 1980. The authors presented many detailed analyses of their results and expanded the data set from 375 studies to 475 studies involving approximately twenty-five thousand patients treated by seventy-eight therapies over an average of sixteen sessions. Smith, Glass, and Miller revealed that the average therapy patient was better off than 80 percent of the control group.

To date, numerous studies have provided evidence for the general effectiveness of psychotherapy to produce positive changes in targeted problem areas; however, psychotherapy is not a unitary procedure applied to a unitary problem. Moreover, many of the nearly four hundred psychotherapeutic

approaches have yet to be systematically evaluated. Thus, it is important to understand the empirical evidence for specific treatment approaches with specific patient populations. It is similarly important to note that each therapist is a unique individual who provides his or her own unique perspective and experience to the psychotherapeutic process. Fortunately, positive effects are generally common among psychotherapy patients, and negative (deterioration) effects, which are also observed regularly, often appear related to a poor match of therapist, technique, and patient factors.

PATIENT IMPROVEMENT AND TREATMENT EVALUATION

Recent research has focused on some of the factors associated with patient improvement, and several specific methods have been used to evaluate different treatments. Common research designs include contrasting an established treatment with a new treatment approach (for example, systematic desensitization versus eye-movement desensitization for anxiety) or therapeutic format (group depression treatment versus individual depression treatment), separating the components of an effective treatment package (such as cognitive behavioral treatment of anxiety) to examine the relative effectiveness of the modules, and analyzing the interactions between therapist and patient during psychotherapy (process research).

The results from studies employing these designs are generally mixed and reveal limited differences between specific therapeutic approaches. For example, in the largest meta-analytic studies, some analyses revealed that behavioral and cognitive therapies were found to have larger positive changes when compared to other types of psychotherapy (psychodynamic and humanistic), while other analyses did not. Similarly, several large comparative studies revealed considerable patient improvement regardless of treatment approach. Such results must be carefully evaluated, however, because there are numerous reasons for failing to find differences between treatments.

All psychotherapy research is flawed; there are no perfect studies. Thus, studies should be evaluated along several dimensions, including rigor of methodology and adequacy of statistical procedures. Psychotherapy is both an art and a science, and it involves the complex interaction between a socially sanctioned helper (a therapist) and a distressed patient or client. The complexity of this interaction raises some significant obstacles to designing psychotherapy research. Thus, methodological problems can be diverse and extensive, and they may account for the failure to find significant differences between alternative psychotherapeutic approaches. Some researchers have argued that the combination of methodological problems and statistical limitations (such as research samples that are too small to detect differences between groups or inconsistency with regard to patient characteristics) plagued many of the studies completed in the 1980's.

Still, the search for effective components of psychotherapy remains a primary research question focused on several key areas, including patient characteristics, therapist characteristics, treatment techniques, common factors across different psychotherapies, and the various interactions among these variables. As highlighted in Sol Garfield and Allen Bergin's edited book entitled *Handbook of Psychotherapy and Behavior Change* (1986), some evidence reveals that patient characteristics (such as amount of self-exploration and ability to solve problems and express emotions constructively) are of primary importance in positive outcomes. Therapist characteristics such as empathy, interpersonal warmth, acceptance toward patients, and genuineness also appear to play a major role in successful therapy. Treatment techniques seem generally less important than the ability of the therapist and patient to form a therapeutic relationship.

Additional studies have asked patients at the conclusion of psychotherapy to identify the most important factors in their successful treatment. Patients have generally described such factors as gradually facing their problems in a supportive setting, talking to an understanding person, and the personality of their therapist as helpful factors. Moreover, patients frequently conclude that their success in treatment is related to their therapist's support, encouragement, sensitivity, honesty, sense of humor, and ability to share insights. In contrast, other research has examined negative outcomes of psychotherapy in order to illuminate factors predictive of poor outcomes. These factors include the failure of the therapist to structure sessions and address primary concerns presented by the patient, poorly timed interventions, and negative therapist attitudes toward the patient.

COMMON FACTORS

Taken as a whole, psychotherapy research reveals some consistent results about many patient and therapist characteristics associated with positive and negative outcomes. Yet remarkably few differences have been found among the different types of treatment. This pattern of evidence has led many researchers to conclude that factors which are common across different forms of psychotherapy may account for the apparent equality among many treatment approaches. At the forefront of this position is psychiatrist and psychologist Jerome D. Frank.

In various books and journal articles, Frank has argued that all psychotherapeutic approaches share common ingredients that are simply variations of age-old procedures of psychological healing such as confession, encouragement, modeling, positive reinforcement, and punishment. Because patients seeking treatment are typically demoralized, distressed, and feeling helpless, all psychotherapies aim to restore morale by offering support, reassurance, feedback, guidance, hope, and mutual understanding of the problems and proposed solutions. Among the common factors most frequently studied since the 1960's, the key ingredients outlined by the client-centered school are most widely regarded as central to the development of a successful therapeutic relationship. These ingredients are empathy, positive regard, warmth, and genuineness.

Various factors should be considered when one chooses a therapist. To begin with, it may be wise to consider first one's objectives and motivations for entering treatment. A thoughtful appraisal of one's own goals can serve as a map through the maze of alternative treatments, therapy agencies, and diverse professionals providing psychotherapeutic services. In addition, one should learn about the professionals in one's area by speaking with a family physician, a religious adviser, or friends who have previously sought psychotherapeutic services. It is also important to locate a licensed professional with whom one feels comfortable, because the primary ingredients for success are patient and therapist characteristics. All therapists and patients are unique individuals who provide their own distinctive perspectives and contributions to the therapy process. Therefore, the most important factor in psychotherapeutic outcome may be the match between patient and therapist.

RESULTS OF META-ANALYSIS

Although the roots of psychotherapy can be traced back to antiquity, psychotherapy research is a recent development in the field of psychology. Early evidence for the effectiveness of psychotherapy was limited and consisted of case studies and investigations with significant methodological flaws. Considerable furor among therapists followed psychologist Hans Eysenck's claims that psychotherapy is no more effective than naturally occurring life events are. Other disagreements followed the rapid development of many alternative and competing forms of psychotherapy in the 1960's and 1970's. Claims that one particular approach was better than another were rarely confirmed by empirical research. Still, psychotherapy research is a primary method in the development, refinement, and validation of treatments for diverse patient groups. Advancements in research methodology and statistical applications have provided answers to many important questions in psychotherapy research.

Rather than examining the question of whether psychotherapy works, researchers are designing sophisticated research programs to evaluate the effectiveness of specific treatment components on particular groups of patients with carefully diagnosed mental disorders. Researchers continue to identify specific variables and processes among patients and therapists that shape positive outcomes. The quality of interactions between patient and therapist appear to hold particular promise in understanding psychotherapy outcome.

To address the complexity of psychotherapy, research must aim to address at least two important dimensions: process (How and why does this form of therapy work?) and outcome (To what degree is this specific treatment effective for this particular client in this setting at this time?). In addition, empirical comparisons between psychotherapy and medications in terms of effectiveness, side effects, compliance, and long-term outcome will continue to shape clinical practice for many years to come. As one example, the National Institute of Mental Health (NIMH) sponsored a large comparative psychotherapy and drug treatment study of depression. In that investigation, the effectiveness of individual interpersonal psychotherapy, individual cognitive therapy, antidepressant medication, and placebo conditions were tested. While findings from initial analyses revealed no significant differences between any of the

treatment conditions, secondary analyses suggested that severity of depression was an important variable. For the less severely depressed, there was no evidence for the specific effectiveness of active-versus-placebo treatment conditions. The more severely depressed patients, however, responded best to antidepressant medications and interpersonal therapy. Future reports from the NIMH team of researchers may reveal additional results which could further shape the ways in which depressed patients are treated.

SOURCES FOR FURTHER STUDY

Beutler, Larry E., and Marjorie Crago, eds. *Psychotherapy Research: An International Review of Programmatic Studies.* Washington, D.C.: American Psychological Association, 1991. Reviews a variety of large-scale and small-scale research programs in North America and Europe. Presents a summary of research findings from studies investigating various aspects of psychotherapy including prevention of marital distress, process variables in psychotherapy, treatment of difficult patients, and inpatient hospitalization approaches.

Frank, Jerome David. *Persuasion and Healing.* 3d ed. Baltimore: The Johns Hopkins University Press, 1993. Provides an overview of Frank's position on psychotherapy. The significance of common treatment components shared by all forms of healing, including psychotherapy, continues to be an important consideration in treatment outcome work.

Garfield, Sol L., and Allen E. Bergin, eds. *Handbook of Psychotherapy and Behavior Change.* 4th ed. New York: John Wiley & Sons, 1993. Provides a historical overview and synopsis of research studies concerned with the evaluation of psychotherapy. Patient and therapist variables are highlighted in terms of their importance in successful intervention. Additional topics include training therapeutic skills, medications and psychotherapy, and the effectiveness of treatment approaches with children, couples, families, and groups.

Kazdin, Alan E. *Single-Case Research Designs: Methods for Clinical and Applied Settings.* New York: Oxford University Press, 1982. Provides an overview of various research methods used in psychotherapy research. In particular, this book presents information about case studies and single-case research designs. Single-case research has become increasingly common in psychotherapy research as an alternative approach to group designs.

Smith, Mary Lee, and Gene V. Glass. "Meta-Analysis of Psychotherapy Outcome Studies." *American Psychologist* 32, no. 9 (1977): 752-760. A classic in the field of psychotherapy research, this journal article represents a significant step in the manner in which knowledge is distilled from the scientific literature. This controversial article concluded that psychotherapy was effective.

Smith, Mary Lee, Gene V. Glass, and Thomas I. Miller. *Benefits of Psychotherapy.* Baltimore: The Johns Hopkins University Press, 1980. Presents many detailed analyses from 475 psychotherapy research studies that were systematically analyzed via meta-analysis. Provides a follow-up to many of the criticisms that were expressed about Smith and Glass's initial psychotherapy meta-analysis.

Gregory L. Wilson

SEE ALSO: Adlerian psychotherapy; Behavioral family therapy; Clinical depression; Cognitive behavior therapy; Gestalt therapy; Group therapy; Obsessive-compulsive disorder; Phobias; Psychoanalytic psychology and personality: Sigmund Freud; Psychotherapy: Goals and techniques; Psychotherapy: Historical approaches.

Psychotherapy

Goals and techniques

TYPE OF PSYCHOLOGY: Psychotherapy
FIELDS OF STUDY: Evaluating psychotherapy

The goals to be reached in the meetings between a psychotherapist and a client, or patient, and the techniques employed to accomplish them vary according to the needs of the client and the theoretical orientation of the therapist.

KEY CONCEPTS
- behavioral therapy
- corrective emotional experience
- desensitization
- eclectic therapy
- humanistic therapy
- interpretation
- psychodynamic therapy
- resistance
- shaping
- therapeutic alliance

INTRODUCTION

Psychotherapy is an interpersonal relationship in which clients present themselves to a psychotherapist in order to gain some relief from distress in their lives. It should be noted that although people who seek psychological help are referred to as "clients" by a wide range of psychotherapists, this term is used interchangeably with the term "patients," which is traditionally used more often by psychodynamically and medically trained practitioners. In all forms of psychotherapy, patients or clients must tell the psychotherapist about their distress and reveal intimate information in order for the psychotherapist to be helpful. The psychotherapist must aid clients in the difficult task of admitting difficulties and revealing themselves, since a client's desire to be liked and to be seen as competent can stand in the way of this work. The client also wants to find relief from distress at the least possible cost in terms of the effort and personal changes to be made, and, therefore, clients often prevent themselves from making the very changes in which they are interested. This is termed resistance, and much of the work of the psychotherapist involves dealing with such resistance.

The goals of the client are determined by the type of life problems that are being experienced. Traditionally, psychotherapists make a diagnosis of the psychiatric disorder from which the client suffers, with different disorders presenting certain symptoms to be removed in order for the client to gain relief. The vast majority of clients suffer from some form of anxiety or depression, or from certain failures in personality development, which produce deviant behaviors and rigid patterns of relating to others called personality disorders. Relatively few clients suffer from severe disorders, called psychoses, which are characterized by some degree of loss of contact with reality. Depending on the particular symptoms involved in the client's disorder, psychotherapeutic goals will be set, although the client may not be aware of the necessity of these changes at first. In addition, the diagnosis allows the psychotherapist to anticipate the kinds of goals that would be difficult for the client to attain. Psychotherapists also consider the length of time they will likely work with the client. Therefore, psychotherapeutic goals depend on the client's wishes, the type of psychiatric disorder from which the client suffers, and the limitations of time under which the psychotherapy proceeds.

Another factor that plays a major role in determining psychotherapeutic goals is the psychotherapist's theoretical model for treatment. This model is based on a personality theory that explains people's motivations, how people develop psychologically, and how people differ from one another. It suggests what occurred in life to create the person's problems and what must be achieved to correct these problems. Associated with each theory is a group of techniques that can be applied to accomplish the goals considered to be crucial within the theory utilized. There are three main models of personality and treatment: psychodynamic therapies, behavioral therapies, and humanistic therapies. Psychodynamic therapists seek to make clients aware of motives for their actions of which they were previously unconscious or unaware. By becoming aware of their motives, clients can better control the balance between desires for pleasure and the need to obey one's conscience. Behavioral therapists attempt to increase the frequency of certain behaviors and decrease the frequency of others by reducing anxiety associated with certain behavior, teaching new behavior, and rewarding and punishing certain behaviors. Humanistic therapists try to free clients to use their innate abilities by developing relationships with clients in which clients can be assured of acceptance, making the clients more accepting of themselves and more confident in making decisions and expressing themselves.

Most psychotherapists use a combination of theories, and therefore of goals and techniques, in their practice. These "eclectic" therapists base their decisions about goals and techniques upon the combined theory they have evolved or upon a choice among other theories given what applies best to a client or diagnosis. It also appears that this eclectic approach has become popular because virtually all psychotherapy cases demand attention to certain common goals associated with the various stages of treatment, and different types of therapy are well suited to certain goals and related techniques at particular stages.

THERAPEUTIC RELATIONSHIPS

When clients first come to a psychotherapist, they have in mind some things about their lives that need to be changed. The psychotherapist recognizes that before this can be accomplished, a trusting relationship must be established with clients. This has been termed the "therapeutic alliance" or a "collaborative relationship." Establishing this relationship becomes the first goal of therapy. Clients must learn that the therapist understands them and can be trusted with the secrets of their lives. They must also learn about the limits of the therapeutic relationship: that the psychotherapist is to be paid for the service, that the relationship will focus on the clients' concerns and life experiences rather than the psychotherapist's, that the psychotherapist is available to clients during the scheduled sessions and emergencies only, and that this relationship will end when the psychotherapeutic goals are met.

The therapist looks early for certain recurring patterns in what the client thinks, feels, and does. These patterns may occur in the therapy sessions, and the client reports about the way these patterns have occurred in the past and how they continue. These patterns become the focal theme for the therapy and are seen as a basic reason for the client's troubles. For example, some clients may complain that they have never had the confidence to think for themselves. They report that their parents always told them what to do without explanation. In their current marriage, they find themselves unable to feel comfortable with any decisions, and they always look to their spouse for the final say. This pattern of dependence may not be as clear to the clients as to psychotherapists, who look specifically for similarities across past and present relationships. Furthermore, clients will probably approach the psychotherapist in a similar fashion. For example, clients might ask for the psychotherapist's advice, stating that they do not know what to do. When the psychotherapist points out the pattern in the clients' behavior, or suggests that it may have developed from the way their parents interacted with them, the psychotherapist is using the technique of interpretation. This technique originated in the psychodynamic models of psychotherapy.

When clients are confronted with having such patterns or focal themes, they may protest that they are not doing this, find it difficult to do anything different, or cannot imagine that there may be a different way of living. These tendencies to protest and to find change to be difficult are called "resistance." Much of the work of psychotherapy involves overcoming this resistance and achieving the understanding of self called insight.

One of the techniques the psychotherapist uses to deal with resistance is the continued development of the therapeutic relationship in order to demonstrate that the psychotherapist understands and accepts the client's point of view and that these interpretations of patterns of living are done in the interest of the achievement of therapeutic goals by the client. Humanistic psychotherapists have emphasized this aspect of psychotherapeutic technique. The psychotherapist also responds differently to the client from the way others have in the past, so that when the client demonstrates the focal theme in the psychotherapy session, this different outcome to the pattern encourages a new approach to the difficulty. This is called the corrective emotional experience, a psychotherapeutic technique that originated in psychodynamic psychotherapy and is emphasized in humanistic therapies as well. For example, when the client asks the psychotherapist for advice, the psychotherapist might respond that they could work together on a solution, building on valuable information and ideas that both may have. In this way, the psychotherapist has avoided keeping the client dependent in the relationship with the psychotherapist as the client has been in relationships with parents, a spouse, or others. This is experienced by the client emotionally, in that it may produce an increase in self-confidence or trust rather than resentment, since the psychotherapist did not dominate. With the repetition of these responses by the psychotherapist, the client's ways of relating are corrected. Such a repetition is often called working through, another term originating in psychodynamic models of therapy.

Psychotherapists have recognized that many clients have difficulty with changing their patterns of living because of anxiety or lack of skill and experience in behaving differently. Behavioral therapy techniques are especially useful in such cases. In cases of anxiety, the client can be taught to relax through relaxation training exercises. The client gradually imagines performing new, difficult behaviors while relaxing. Eventually, the client learns to stay relaxed while performing these behaviors with the psychotherapist and other people. This process

is called desensitization, and it was originally developed to treat persons with extreme fears of particular objects or situations, termed phobias. New behavior is sometimes taught through modeling techniques in which examples of the behavior are first demonstrated by others. Behavioral psychotherapists have also shown the importance of rewarding small approximations to the new behavior that is the goal. This shaping technique might be used with the dependent client by praising confident, assertive, or independent behavior reported by the client or shown in the psychotherapy session, no matter how minor it may be initially.

ALLEVIATING DISTRESS

The goals and techniques of psychotherapy were first discussed by the psychodynamic theorists who originated the modern practice of psychotherapy. Sigmund Freud and Josef Breuer are generally credited with describing the first modern case treated with psychotherapy, and Freud went on to develop the basis for psychodynamic psychotherapy in his writings between 1895 and his death in 1939. Freud sat behind his clients while they lay upon a couch so that they could concentrate on saying anything that came to mind in order to reveal themselves to the psychotherapist. This also prevented the clients from seeing the psychotherapist's reaction, in case they expected the psychotherapist to react to them as their parents had reacted. This transference relationship provided Freud with information about the client's relationship with parents, which Freud considered to be the root of the problems that his clients had. Later psychodynamic psychotherapists sat facing their clients and conversing with them in a more conventional fashion, but they still attended to the transference.

Carl Rogers is usually described as the first humanistic psychotherapist, and he published descriptions of his techniques in 1942 and 1951. Rogers concentrated on establishing a warm, accepting, honest relationship with his clients. Rogers established this relationship by attempting to understand the client from the client's point of view. By communicating this "accurate empathy," clients would feel accepted and therefore would accept themselves and be more confident in living according to their wishes without fear.

Behavioral psychotherapists began to play a major role in this field after Joseph Wolpe developed systematic desensitization in the 1950's. In the 1960's and 1970's, Albert Bandura applied his findings on how children learn to be aggressive through observation to the development of modeling techniques for reducing fears and teaching new behaviors. Bandura focused on how people attend to, remember, and decide to perform behavior they observe in others. These thought processes, or "cognitions," came to be addressed in cognitive psychotherapy by Aaron T. Beck and others in the 1970's and 1980's. Cognitive behavioral therapy became a popular hybrid that included emphasis on how thinking and behavior influence each other.

In surveys of practicing psychotherapists beginning in the late 1970's, Sol Garfield showed that the majority of therapists practice some hybrid therapy or eclectic approach. As it became apparent that no one model produced the desired effects in a variety of clients, psychotherapists utilized techniques from various approaches. An example is Arnold Lazarus's multimodal behavior therapy, introduced in 1971. It appears that such trends will continue and that, in addition to combining existing psychotherapeutic techniques, new eclectic models will produce additional ways of understanding psychotherapy as well as different techniques for practice.

SOURCES FOR FURTHER STUDY

Garfield, Sol L. *Psychotherapy: An Eclectic Approach.* New York: John Wiley & Sons, 1980. Focuses on the client, the therapist, and their interaction within an eclectic framework. Written for the beginning student of psychotherapy and relatively free of jargon.

Goldfried, Marvin R., and Gerald C. Davison. *Clinical Behavior Therapy.* New York: Holt, Rinehart and Winston, 1976. An elementary, concise description of basic behavioral techniques. Includes clear examples of how these techniques are implemented.

Goldman, George D., and Donald S. Milman, eds. *Psychoanalytic Psychotherapy.* Reading, Mass.: Addison-Wesley, 1978. A very clear, concise treatment of complicated psychodynamic techniques. Explains difficult concepts in language accessible to the layperson.

Phares, E. Jerry. *Clinical Psychology: Concepts, Methods, and Profession.* 3d ed. Chicago: Dorsey Press, 1988. An overview of clinical psychology that includes excellent chapters summarizing psycho-dynamic, behavioral, humanistic, and other models of psychotherapy. Written as a college-level text.

Rogers, Carl Ransom. *Client-Centered Therapy.* Boston: Houghton Mifflin, 1951. A classic description of the author's humanistic psychotherapy that is still useful as a strong statement of the value of the therapeutic relationship. Written for a professional audience, though quite readable.

Teyber, Edward. *Interpersonal Process in Psychotherapy: A Guide to Clinical Training.* Chicago: Dorsey Press, 1988. An extremely clear and readable guide to modern eclectic therapy. Full of practical examples and written as a training manual for beginning psychotherapy students.

Wolpe, Joseph. *The Practice of Behavior Therapy.* 4th ed. Elmsford, N.Y.: Pergamon, 1990. Written by the originator of behavioral psychotherapy. Introduces basic principles, examples of behavioral interventions, and many references to research. Initial chapters are elementary, but later ones tend to be complicated.

Richard G. Tedeschi

SEE ALSO: Aversion, implosion, and systematic desensitization; Behavioral family therapy; Cognitive therapy; Drug therapies; Existential psychology; Feminist psychotherapy; Group therapy; Music, dance, and theater therapy; Psychoanalysis; Psychoanalytic psychology; Psychotherapy: Effectiveness.

Psychotherapy
Historical approaches

TYPE OF PSYCHOLOGY: Psychotherapy
FIELDS OF STUDY: Classic analytic themes and issues; psychodynamic and neoanalytic models

Psychotherapy as a socially recognized process and profession emerged in Europe during the late nineteenth century. Although discussions of psychological or "mental healing" can be found dating back to antiquity, a cultural role for the secular psychological healer has become established only in modern times.

Key concepts

- catharsis
- functional disorders
- mental healing
- mesmerism
- nonspecific treatment factors
- suggestion
- transference

Introduction

The term "psychotherapy" (originally "psycho-therapy") came into use during the late nineteenth century to describe various treatments that were believed to act on the psychic or mental aspects of a patient rather than on physical conditions. It was contrasted with physical therapies such as medications, baths, surgery, diets, rest, or mild electrical currents, which, while producing some mental relief, did so through physical means. The origins of psychotherapy have been variously traced. Some authors call attention to the practices of primitive witch doctors, to the exorcism rites of the Catholic Church, to the rhetorical methods of Greco-Roman speakers, to the naturalistic healing practices of Hippocrates, and to the Christian practice of public (and later, private) confession.

One of the best argued and supported views claims a direct line of development from the practice of casting out demons all the way to psychoanalysis, the most widely recognized form of psychotherapy. The casting out of demons may be seen as leading to exorcism, which in turn led to the eighteenth century mesmeric technique (named for Franz Mesmer) based on the alleged phenomenon of "animal magnetism." This led to the practice of hypnosis as a psychological rather than a physiological phenomenon and finally to the work of Sigmund Freud, a late nineteenth century Viennese neurologist who, in his treatment of functional disorders (signs and symptoms for which no organic or physiological basis can be found), slowly moved from the practice of hypnosis to the development of psychoanalysis.

Therapist as "Healer"

There are two histories to be sought in the early forms of treatment by psychotherapy: One is an account of the relationship between a patient and a psychological healer; the other is the story of the specific techniques that the healer employs and the

reasons that he or she gives to rationalize them. The latter began as religious or spiritual techniques and became naturalized as psychological or physiological methods. The prominence of spiritual revival during the mid- to late nineteenth century in the United States led to the rise of spiritual or mental healing movements (the healing of a disorder, functional or physical, through suggestion or persuasion), as demonstrated by the Christian Science movement. Religious healing, mental healing, and psychotherapy were often intertwined in the 1890's, especially in Boston, where many of the leading spokespersons for each perspective resided.

The distinction among these viewpoints was the explanation of the cure—naturalistic versus spiritualistic—and to a lesser degree, the role or relationship between the practitioner and the patient. A psychotherapist in the United States or Europe, whether spiritualistic or naturalistic in orientation, was an authority (of whatever special techniques) who could offer the suffering patient relief through a relationship in which the patient shared his or her deepest feelings and most secret thoughts on a regular basis. The relationship bore a resemblance to that which a priest, rabbi, or minister might have with a member of the congregation. The psychotherapeutic relationship was also a commercial one, however, since private payment for services was usually the case. Freud came to believe that transference, the projection of emotional reactions from childhood onto the therapist, was a critical aspect of the relationship.

Evolution of Practice

Initially, and well into the early part of the twentieth century, psychotherapists treated patients with physical as well as functional (mental) disorders, but by the 1920's, psychotherapy had largely become a procedure addressed to mental or psychological problems. In the United States, its use rested almost exclusively with the medical profession. Psychiatrists would provide therapy, clinical psychologists would provide testing and assessment of the patient, and social workers would provide ancillary services related to the patient's family or societal and governmental programs. Following World War II, all three of these professions began to offer psychotherapy as one of their services.

One could chart the development of psychotherapy in a simplified, time-line approach, beginning with the early use of the term by Daniel H. Tuke in *Illustrations of the Influence of the Mind upon the Body in Health and Disease* in 1872, followed by the first use of the term at an international conference in 1889 and the publication of Sigmund Freud and Josef Breuer's cathartic method in *Studien über Hysterie* (1895; *Studies in Hysteria*, 1950). Pierre Janet lectured on "The Chief Methods of Psychotherapeutics" in St. Louis in 1904, and psychotherapy was introduced as a heading in the index to medical literature (the *Index Medicus*) in 1906; at about the same time, private schools of psychotherapy began to be established. In 1909, Freud lectured on psychoanalysis at Clark University. That same year, Hugo Münsterberg published *Psychotherapy*. James Walsh published his *Psychotherapy* in 1912. During the 1920's, the widespread introduction and medicalization of psychoanalysis in the United States occurred. Client-centered therapy was introduced by Carl Rogers in 1942, and behavior-oriented therapy was developed by Joseph Wolpe and B. F. Skinner in the early 1950's.

HISTORIC TREATMENT OF ABNORMAL BEHAVIOR

Whatever form psychotherapy may take, it nearly always is applied to the least severe forms of maladjustment and abnormal behavior—to those behaviors and feelings that are least disturbing to others. When the patient has suffered a break with reality and experiences hallucinations, delusions, paranoia, or other behaviors that are socially disruptive, physical forms of treatment are often utilized. The earliest examples include "trephining," a Stone Age practice in which a circular hole was cut into the brain cavity, perhaps to allow the escape of evil spirits. The best-known of the Greek theories of abnormal behavior were naturalistic and physicalistic, based on the belief that deviations in levels of bile caused mental derangement. The solution was bleeding, a practice that continued until the early nineteenth century. Rest, special diets, exercise, and other undertakings that would increase or decrease the relevant bile level were also practiced.

Banishment from public places was recommended by Plato. Initially, people were restricted to their own homes. Later, religious sanctuaries took in the mentally ill, and finally private for-profit and public asylums were developed. Institutions that specialized in the housing of the mentally ill began opening during the sixteenth century. Among the best-known institutions were Bethlehem in London, (which came to be known as "Bedlam"), Salpetriere in Paris, and later St. Elizabeth's in Washington, D.C. Beyond confinement, treatments at these institutions included "whirling" chairs in which the patient would be strapped; the "tranquilizing" chair for restraining difficult patients; the straitjacket, which constrained only the arms; rest and diet therapies; and hot and cold water treatments.

By the 1930's, electroconvulsive therapy (shock therapy) was invented; it used an electric charge that induced a grand mal seizure. During the same period, the earliest lobotomy procedures were performed. These surgeries severed the connections between the brain's frontal lobes and lower centers of emotional functioning. What separates all these and other procedures from psychotherapy is the employment of physical and chemical means for changing behavior and emotions, rather than persuasion and social influence processes.

Periodic reforms were undertaken to improve the care of patients. Philippe Pinel, in the late eighteenth century, freed many mental patients in Paris from being chained in their rooms. He provided daily exercise and frequent cleaning of their quarters. In the United States, Dorothea Lynde Dix in the mid-1800's led a campaign of reform that resulted in vast improvement in state mental hospitals. In the 1960's and 1970's, some states placed restrictions on the use of electroconvulsive therapy and lobotomies, and the federal government funded many community mental health centers in an attempt to provide treatment that would keep the patient in his or her community. Since the 1950's, many effective medications have been developed for treating depressions, anxieties, compulsions, panic attacks, and a wide variety of other disorders.

FREUD'S PSYCHOANALYTIC CONTRIBUTIONS

Modern textbooks of psychotherapy may describe dozens of approaches and hundreds of specific psychotherapeutic techniques. What they have in common is the attempt of a person in the role of healer or teacher to assist another person in the role of patient or client with emotionally disturbing feelings, awkward behavior, or troubling thoughts. Many contemporary therapies are derivative of Sigmund Freud's psychoanalysis. When Freud opened his practice for the treatment of functional disorders in

Vienna in the spring of 1886, he initially employed the physical therapies common to his day. These included hydrotherapy, electrotherapy, a mild form of electrical stimulation, massage, rest, and a limited set of pharmaceutical agents. He was disappointed with the results, however, and reported feeling helpless.

He turned to the newly emerging procedure of hypnosis that was being developed by French physicians. Soon he was merely urging his patients to recall traumatic episodes from childhood rather than expecting them to recall such memories under hypnosis. In what he called his "pressure technique," Freud would place his hand firmly on a patient's forehead, apply pressure, and say, "you will recall." Shortly, this became the famous method of free association, wherein the patient would recline on a couch with the instruction to say whatever came to mind. The psychoanalytic situation that Freud invented, with its feature of one person speaking freely to a passive but attentive audience about the most private and intimate aspects of his or her life, was unique in the history of Western civilization.

OTHER HISTORIC CONTRIBUTIONS

Psychoanalysis was not the only method of psychotherapy to emerge near the end of the nineteenth century, as an examination of a textbook published shortly after the turn of the century reveals. James Walsh, then dean and professor of functional disorders at Fordham University, published his eight-hundred-page textbook on psychotherapy in 1912. Only two pages were devoted to the new practice of psychoanalysis. For Walsh, psychotherapy was the use of mental influence to treat disease. His formulation, and that of many practitioners of his time, would encompass what today would be termed behavioral medicine. Thus, the chapters in his book are devoted to the different bodily systems, the digestive tract, cardiotherapy, gynecological psychotherapy, and skin diseases, as well as to the functional disorders.

The techniques that Walsh describes are wide ranging. They include physical recommendations for rest and exercise, the value of hobbies as diversion, the need for regimentation, and varied baths, but it is the suggestion and treatment of the patient rather than the disease (that is, the establishment of a relationship with detailed knowledge of the patient's life and situation) that are the principal

means for the cure and relief of symptoms. A concluding chapter in Walsh's book compares psychotherapy with religion, with the view that considering religion simply as a curative agent lessens its meaning and worth.

BEHAVIOR THERAPY

In the mid-twentieth century, two new psychotherapies appeared that significantly altered the field, although one of them rejected the term, preferring to call itself behavior therapy in order to distinguish its method from the merely verbal or "talk" therapies. The first was found in the work of psychologist Carl Rogers. Rogers made three significant contributions to the development of psychotherapy. He originated nondirective or client-centered therapy, he phonographically recorded and transcribed therapy sessions, and he studied the process of therapy based upon the transcripts. The development of an alternative to psychoanalysis was perhaps his most significant contribution. In the United States, psychoanalysis had become a medical specialty, practiced only by psychiatrists with advanced training. Rogers, a psychologist, created a role for psychologists and social workers as therapists. Thus, he expanded the range of professionals who could legitimately undertake the treatment of disorders through psychotherapy. The title of his most important work, *Counseling and Psychotherapy: Newer Concepts in Practice* (1942), suggests how other professions were to be included. In the preface to his book, Rogers indicated that he regarded these terms as synonymous. If psychologists and social workers could not practice therapy, they could counsel.

Behavior therapy describes a set of specific procedures, such as systematic desensitization and contingency management, that began to appear in the early 1950's, based on the work of Joseph Wolpe, a South African psychiatrist, Hans Eysenck, a British psychologist, and the American experimental psychologist and radical behaviorist B. F. Skinner. Wolpe's *Psychotherapy by Reciprocal Inhibition* appeared in 1958 and argued that states of relaxation and self-assertion would inhibit anxiety, since the patient could not be relaxed and anxious at the same time. It was argued that these were specific techniques based upon the principles of learning and behavior; hence, therapeutic benefits did not depend upon the nonspecific effects of mere suggestion or placebo. Behavior therapy was regarded by its developers as the first scientific therapy.

PSYCHOTHERAPY PERSPECTIVES AND CRITICISMS

In all of its forms, the rise of psychotherapy may be explained in a variety of ways. The cultural role hypothesis argues that psychotherapists are essentially a controlling agency for the state and society. Their function is to help maintain the cultural norms and values by directly influencing persons at the individual level. This view holds that whatever psychotherapists might say, they occupy a position in the culture similar to that of authorities in educational and religious institutions. A related view argues that psychotherapy arose in Western culture to meet a deficiency in the culture itself. Such a view holds that if the culture were truly meeting the needs of its members, no therapeutic procedures would be required.

Psychotherapy has been explained as a scientific discovery, although exactly what was discovered depends on one's viewpoint. For example, behavior therapists might hold that the fundamental principles of behavior and learning were discovered, as was their applicability to emotional and mental problems. Others might hold that nonspecific or placebo effects were discovered, or at least placed in a naturalistic context. Another explanation follows the historical work of Henri Ellenberger and views psychotherapy as a naturalization of early religious practices: exorcism transformed to hypnotism, transformed to psychoanalysis. The religious demons became mental demons and, with the rise of modern psychopharmacology in the 1950's, molecular demons.

More cynical explanations view psychotherapy as a mistaken metaphor. Recalling that the word was originally written with a hyphen, they argue that it is not possible to perform therapy, a physical practice, on a mental or spiritual object. Thus, psychotherapy is a kind of hoax perpetuated by its practitioners because of a mistaken formulation. Others suggest that the correct metaphor is that of healing and hold that psychotherapy is the history of mental healing, or healing through faith, suggestion, persuasion, and other rhetorical means. Whatever one's opinion of psychotherapy, it is both a cultural phenomenon and a specific set of practices that did not exist prior to the nineteenth century and that have had enormous influence on all aspects of American culture.

SOURCES FOR FURTHER STUDY

Corsini, Raymond J., comp. *Current Psychotherapies.* 6th ed. Itasca, Ill.: Peacock, 2000. An excellent survey of more than a dozen approaches to psychotherapy, with a brief historical description of the origin of each.

Cushman, Philip. *Constructing the Self, Constructing America: A Cultural History of Psychotherapy.* Cambridge, Mass.: Perseus, 1997. Charts the change over time of the American conception of "self," along with changing conceptions of psychotherapy and its uses.

Ellenberger, Henri F. *The Discovery of the Unconscious: The History and Evolution of Dynamic Psychiatry.* New York: Basic Books, 1970. A comprehensive and scholarly history of nonmedical psychiatry. Traces the development of psychotherapy from exorcism to hypnosis to suggestion to the methods of Sigmund Freud and Carl G. Jung.

Freedheim, Donald, Jane Kessler, and Donald Peterson, eds. *History of Psychotherapy: A Century of Change.* Washington, D.C.: American Psychological Association, 1992. A collection of over sixty papers on the history of psychotherapy in the United States. Covers theoretical approaches, the biographies of leading figures, and the projects of current major research centers.

Janet, Pierre. *Psychological Healing: A Historical and Clinical Study.* 2 vols. New York: Macmillan, 1925. Reflects the biases of its author but provides detailed descriptions of nonmedical treatments from the middle of the nineteenth century to the early part of the twentieth century. Contains material that can be found nowhere else.

Masson, Jeffrey Moussaieff. *Against Therapy: Emotional Tyranny and the Myth of Psychological Healing.* New York: Atheneum, 1988. Attacks the very idea of psychotherapy by examining selected historical instances from the nineteenth century onward.

Pande, Sashi K. "The Mystique of 'Western' Psychotherapy: An Eastern Interpretation." In *About Human Nature: Journeys in Psychological Thought,* edited by Terry J. Knapp and Charles T. Rasmussen. Dubuque, Iowa: Kendall/Hunt, 1989. Argues that psychotherapy appears only in Western cultures and that it serves as an illustration of what these cultures lack.

Rogers, Carl. *Counseling and Psychotherapy: Newer Concepts in Practice.* Boston: Houghton Mifflin, 1942.

Introduces nondirective or client-centered therapy, and provides the first verbatim transcripts of all the therapy sessions for a single patient.

Torrey, Edwin Fuller. *The Mind Game: Witchdoctors and Psychiatrists.* New York: Bantam Books, 1973. A leading American psychiatrist argues that the cultural and social role of the psychological healer has its origins in the primitive practices of the witch doctor.

Valenstein, Elliot S. *Great and Desperate Cures: The Rise and Decline of Psychosurgery and Other Radical Treatments.* New York: Basic Books, 1986. This is a scholarly and readable account of the history of physical therapies for mental disorders. While it focuses on lobotomy, many other forms of treatment are also described.

Wolpe, Joseph. *Psychotherapy by Reciprocal Inhibition.* Stanford, Calif.: Stanford University Press, 1958. Introduces the techniques of behavior therapy; Wolpe argues for specific therapeutic techniques to reduce anxiety.

Terry J. Knapp

SEE ALSO: Abnormality: Psychological models; Analytical psychotherapy; Cognitive therapy; Conditioning; Madness: Historical concepts; Operant conditioning therapies; Psychoanalysis; Psychology: History; Psychosurgery; Shock therapy.

Psychotic disorders

TYPE OF PSYCHOLOGY: Psychopathology
FIELDS OF STUDY: Biological treatments; schizophrenias

Psychotic disorders are mental illnesses that are characterized by a breakdown in reality. Psychotic symptoms include delusions, hallucinations, and disorganized speech. Psychotic disorders, which may occur throughout the life span, vary in their etiology, onset, course, and treatment. Typically, psychotic disorders are treated with medication.

KEY CONCEPTS
- antipsychotic medication
- bipolar disorder
- delusion
- delusional disorder

- dementia
- dissociative identity disorder
- hallucination
- major depression
- schizoaffective disorder
- schizophrenia
- thought disorder

INTRODUCTION

Psychotic disorders are a group of mental illnesses that share psychosis as one of their clinical features. Psychosis involves a gross impairment in one's sense of reality, as evidenced by symptoms such as delusions, hallucinations, thought disorder, and bizarre behavior. These psychotic symptoms may be a primary component of illness or may be secondary to a mental or physical condition.

TYPES OF PSYCHOTIC SYMPTOMS

Delusions are false beliefs that are associated with misinterpretations of perceptions or experiences. There are different types of delusions. The most common are persecutory delusions and grandiose delusions. Persecutory delusions are delusions in which the person believes that he or she is being spied upon or plotted against. Grandiose delusions are delusions in which the person believes that he or she possesses special abilities or is related to a famous person or deity.

Hallucinations are false perceptions in the absence of any real stimulus. Hallucinations may involve any of the five senses. There are auditory hallucinations, such as hearing voices; visual hallucinations, such as seeing faces or flashes of light; tactile hallucinations, such as feeling a tingling, electrical, crawling, or burning sensation; and olfactory hallucinations, such as smelling something not perceived by others. Gustatory hallucinations, or false tastes, are very rare. Most hallucinations are auditory hallucinations.

Thought disorder is defined as a disturbance in the form or content of thought and speech. In psychosis, the person's speech may be incomprehensible or remotely related to the topic of conversation. Examples of formal thought disorder are neologisms, which are made-up words whose meaning is only known to the psychotic person, and loose associations, in which the person's ideas shift from one subject to another, loosely related topic, without the person seeming aware of the shift. Delusions are examples of disorders of thought content. Psychotic behavior is typically bizarre and/or grossly disorganized.

Psychotic symptoms can appear at any point during the life course, though it is difficult to diagnose psychotic symptoms in preverbal children (prior to age five or six). Psychotic disorders can appear for the first time in individuals over age sixty-five.

CONCEPTUALIZATIONS OF PSYCHOTIC DISORDERS

In 1896, the German clinical psychiatrist Emil Kraepelin proposed that there were two broad yet fundamental categories of psychotic disorder: manic-depressive illness, which is now referred to as bipolar disorder; and dementia praecox, which was labeled schizophrenia by the Swiss psychiatrist Eugen Bleuler in 1908. Kraepelin delineated dementia praecox on the basis of course and outcome, noting that it was associated with a deteriorating course and poor outcome. According to Kraepelin, manic-depressive illness was associated with a more episodic and less deteriorating course relative to dementia praecox.

Psychotic disorders are currently classified on the basis of presenting symptoms rather than on the basis of underlying etiological processes. Episodes of psychosis can be brief or chronic in duration, lasting from a few days to many years, and psychotic symptoms may be mild, moderate, or severe in form. Although the various types of psychotic disorders have some common symptoms, their onset, course, and development are often substantially different.

Ongoing research efforts to clarify the cognitive and physiological mechanisms associated with different psychotic illness will hopefully help to aid in future diagnosis. According to the *Diagnostic and Statistical Manual of Mental Disorders: DSM-IV-TR* (rev. 4th ed., 2000), published by the American Psychiatric Association, psychotic symptoms are a central feature of schizophrenia and other psychotic disorders. Schizophrenia, which is often a severe and debilitating mental illness, is found in approximately 1 percent of the general population and affects over 2.5 million Americans. Onset of the disorder is most likely to occur between the ages of eighteen and thirty-five, and females have a somewhat later age of onset than males. Schizophrenia can occur in childhood, although this is rare, and can also have a late onset after the age of forty-five. Rates of schizophrenia do not vary substantially in terms of race or eth-

nicity, but the disorder is more prevalent in urban than in rural areas.

The DSM-IV-TR outlines other psychotic disorders that differ from schizophrenia primarily in terms of illness duration and severity. Schizophreniform disorder is diagnosed when the individual shows symptoms of schizophrenia that last less than six months. As the term implies, the psychotic symptoms in schizophreniform disorder are identical in form to schizophrenia but they have a briefer duration. Some individuals with schizophreniform disorder will eventually develop schizophrenia. Schizoaffective disorder contains features of a mood disturbance, with manic and/or depressive episodes, as well as the symptoms of schizophrenia. Schizoaffective disorder is less common than schizophrenia and may be associated with better functional outcome. Brief psychotic disorder, which is diagnosed if psychotic symptoms last for more than one day but no longer than four weeks, may develop in response to severe environmental stress or psychological trauma. Delusional disorder is less common and less severe than schizophrenia. In delusional disorder, the person has one or more delusions for at least one month. Other than the delusions, the person does not share any of the other psychotic symptoms typically observed in people with schizophrenia. Shared psychotic disorder, also termed *folie à deux*, occurs when a person who is involved with a psychotic individual shares the ill person's delusional ideas.

Psychotic symptoms may also be present in bipolar disorder and major depression. Bipolar disorder is characterized by periods of elevated, expansive, or irritable mood that may alternate with periods of depressed mood. In 1990, Frederick K. Goodwin and Kay R. Jamison reported that approximately 58 percent of individuals with bipolar disorder have at least one psychotic symptom during their lifetimes, which is most likely to occur during a manic episode. Psychotic symptoms may also accompany major depression. Psychotic symptoms are most likely to be associated with severe episodes of affective disturbance and could be either mood congruent or mood incongruent. Mood congruent psychotic symptoms contain themes that are consistent with the current affective state, such as a depressed individual with delusional thoughts about death. Mood incongruent psychotic symptoms involve content that is inconsistent with the current mood state, such as a depressed individual with delusional ideas about possessing special powers.

Some psychotic disorders are the direct result of external or environmental factors. Psychotic symptoms that result from psychoactive substance use or toxin exposure are classified as a substance-induced psychotic disorder. For example, some people may appear at hospital emergency rooms because of amphetamine-induced psychosis or cocaine-induced psychosis. In these cases, psychotic symptoms appear to arise due to the ingestion of a psychoactive (psychomimetic) substance. However, it is not known whether the people who experience psychotic symptoms while using a drug were already prone to psychosis (diathesis) and the drug was the additional stressor, or whether the drug was the proximal causal agent in the development of the psychosis.

Psychotic symptoms can be present in other disorders but are not considered to be defining features of the illness. Psychotic symptoms, especially paranoid delusions, are observed in people with dementia. Dementia is any condition in which there is a progressive deterioration of one's memory, abstract thinking, and judgment and decision-making abilities. The most common types of dementia are Alzheimer's disease and vascular dementia. Psychotic symptoms may also accompany a disorder known as dissociative identity disorder. Dissociative identity disorder (formerly known as multiple personality disorder) is associated with a failure to integrate various aspects of identity, memory, and consciousness.

DIFFERENTIAL DIAGNOSIS

Because the symptoms found across psychotic disorders greatly overlap, differential diagnosis of these conditions is often challenging. If a patient presents with psychotic symptoms, each of the psychotic disorders is considered when making a differential diagnosis. When diagnosing a psychotic disorder, it is important for mental health professionals to first obtain a thorough personal and family history of the patient. Information about the onset and course of presenting symptoms should also be obtained. If necessary, a physical examination or laboratory tests may be required in order to rule out other causes of the symptoms, such as brain injury.

Often, other psychotic disorders, such as schizoaffective disorder or schizophreniform disorder, must be ruled out from schizophrenia. The duration of psychotic symptoms will help differentiate whether the disorder is schizophrenia, schizophreniform disorder, or brief psychotic disorder. The length of affective impairment as well as the overlap between mood and psychotic symptoms is often helpful when distinguishing between schizoaffective disorder and psychotic mood disorder. The presence of other conditions, such as dementia or amnesic episodes, along with psychotic symptoms may aid in differential diagnosis as well.

ETIOLOGICAL FACTORS

Diathesis-stress models have been proposed as a way to explain the onset and development of many of the psychotic disorders. In this view, the diathesis, or underlying predisposition to illness, remains latent and unexpressed until it interacts with a sufficient amount of environmental stress. Individuals may vary in terms of the amount of their underlying diathesis and the stress required to bring about disorder. If an individual has a large diathesis, less stress is required to bring about illness onset. Conversely, if an individual with a substantial genetic diathesis is in a relatively low-stress environment, he or she may be protected from developing the illness. Diathesis-stress models have formed the basis for research on the role of genetic and environmental factors in the development of schizophrenia and related psychotic disorders.

TREATMENT APPROACHES

Antipsychotic medications are considered an effective means of alleviating psychotic symptoms. Conventional (typical) antipsychotics were used to treat psychotic symptoms beginning in the 1950's. More recently, novel (atypical) antipsychotics, such as clozapine, risperidone, and olanzapine, have been introduced, which greatly reduce the severity of extrapyramidal side effects and are more effective at reducing negative or deficit symptoms relative to the typical antipsychotics. The optimal medication dose required is often obtained through a series of judgments made by the psychiatrist, who gradually increases or tapers the dosage based upon observed treatment response. Psychopharmacological treatment has been found to be very effective in reducing symptoms during acute psychotic episodes and in preventing future relapses.

Typically, the treatment of choice for individuals with mood disorders, such as bipolar disorder or major depression, is a mood stabilizer or antidepressant. If psychotic features are present, an anti-psychotic medication may be added to the treatment regimen.

Psychotherapy may also be helpful to individuals with psychotic disorders to assist them in medication compliance and other aspects of having a chronic mental illness. Psychosocial treatments, such as social skills training and family psychoeducation, can enhance the daily functioning and quality of life of individuals with psychotic disorders. By strengthening social support networks and teaching life skills, such interventions could improve social and vocational functioning, enhance one's ability to cope with life stressors, and potentially protect against illness exacerbation.

SOURCES FOR FURTHER STUDY

Goodwin, Frederick K., and Kay R. Jamison. *Manic Depressive Illness*. New York: Oxford University Press, 1990. This is a comprehensive book on bipolar disorder. It provides information on diagnosis, theories regarding the etiology of the disorder, and treatment options.

Gottesman, Irving I. *Schizophrenia Genesis: The Origins of Madness*. New York: W. H. Freeman, 1991. This highly readable book summarizes information about the genetic factors involved in schizophrenia. It provides a comprehensive overview of the theory, methods, and findings of behavioral genetics research.

Oltmanns, Thomas F., and Richard E. Emery. *Abnormal Psychology*. 3d ed. Englewood Cliffs, N.J.: Prentice Hall, 2001. This is a psychopathology textbook that has several in-depth chapters. It provides an up-to-date review of etiological theories as well as research findings regarding schizophrenia and other psychotic disorders.

Weiden, Peter J., Patricia L. Scheifler, Ronald J. Diamond, and Ruth Ross. *Breakthroughs in Antipsychotic Medications*. New York: W. W. Norton, 1999. This highly readable book is written for the general public, especially for mental health consumers and their family members. It provides introductory and technical information about various antipsychotic medications, as well as related issues such as when to change medications, paying for medications, and how to increase medication compliance.

Diane C. Gooding and Kathleen A. Tallent

SEE ALSO: Bipolar disorder; Dementia; Drug therapies; Hallucinations; Paranoia; Schizophrenia: Background, types, and symptoms; Schizophrenia: Theoretical explanations.

Q

Quasi-experimental designs

TYPE OF PSYCHOLOGY: Psychological methodologies
FIELDS OF STUDY: Experimental methodologies;
   methodological issues

The ideal psychological study is a true experiment that allows unequivocal causal judgments to be made about the variables being investigated; the goal is to have confidence in the validity of judgments made from the experimental data. Quasiexperimental designs are ways of collecting data that maximize confidence in causal conclusions when a true experiment cannot be done.

KEY CONCEPTS
- control group
- dependent variable
- external validity
- hypothesis
- independent variable
- internal validity
- plausible rival alternative hypothesis
- post-test
- pretest
- true experiment

INTRODUCTION

The feature that separates psychology from an area such as philosophy is its reliance on the empirical method for its truths. Instead of arguing deductively from premises to conclusions, psychology progresses by using inductive reasoning in which psychological propositions are formulated as experimental hypotheses that can be tested by experiments. The outcome of the experiment determines whether the hypothesis is accepted or rejected. Therefore, the best test of a hypothesis is one that can be interpreted unambiguously. True experiments are considered the best way to test hypotheses, because they are the best way to rule out plausible alternative explanations (confounds) to the experimental hypothesis. True experiments are studies in which the variable whose effect the experimenter wants to understand, the independent variable, is randomly assigned to the experimental unit (usually a person); the researcher observes the effect of the independent variable by responses on the outcome measure, the dependent variable.

For example, if one wanted to study the effects of sugar on hyperactivity in children, the experimenter might ask, "Does sugar cause hyperactive behavior?" Using a true experiment, one would randomly assign half the children in a group to be given a soft drink sweetened with sugar and the other half a soft drink sweetened with a sugar substitute. One could then measure each child's activity level; if the children who were assigned the sugar-sweetened drinks showed hyperactivity as compared to the children who received the other drinks, one could confidently conclude that sugar caused the children to show hyperactivity. A second type of study, called a correlational study, could be done if one had investigated this hypothesis by simply asking or observing which children selected sugar-sweetened drinks and then comparing their behavior to the children who selected the other drinks. The correlational study, however, would not have been able to show whether sugar actually caused hyperactivity. It would be equally plausible that children who are hyperactive simply prefer sugar-sweetened drinks. Such correlational studies have a major validity weakness in not controlling for plausible rival alternative hypotheses. This type of hypothesis is one that is different from the experimenter's preferred hypothesis and offers another reasonable explanation for experimental results. Quasi-experimental designs stand between true experiments and correlational studies in that they control for as many threats to validity as possible.

PLAUSIBLE ALTERNATIVE EXPLANATIONS

Experimental and Quasi-Experimental Designs for Research (1966), by Donald T. Campbell and Julian Stanley, describes the major threats to validity that need to be controlled for so that the independent variable can be correctly tested. Major plausible alternative explanations may need to be controlled when considering internal validity. ("Controlled" does not mean that the threat is not a problem; it means only that the investigator can judge how probable it is that the threat actually influenced the results.)

An external environmental event may occur between the beginning and end of the study, and this historical factor, rather than the treatment, may be the cause of any observed difference. For example, highway fatalities decreased in 1973 after an oil embargo led to the establishment of a speed limit of 55 miles per hour. Some people believed that the cause of the decreased fatalities was the 55-mile-per-hour limit. If the oil embargo caused people to drive less because they could not get gasoline or because it was higher priced, however, either of those events could be a plausible alternative explanation. The number of fatalities may have declined simply because people were driving less, not because of the speed-limit change.

Maturation occurs when natural changes within people cause differences between the beginning and end of the study. Even over short periods of time, for example, people become tired, hungry, or bored. It may be these changes rather than the treatment which causes observed changes. An investigation of a treatment for sprained ankles measured the amount of pain people had when they first arrived for treatment and then measured their pain again four weeks after treatment. Finding a reduction in reported pain, the investigator concluded that the treatment was effective. Since a sprained ankle will probably improve naturally within four weeks, however, maturation (in this case, the natural healing process) is a plausible alternative explanation.

Testing is a problem when the process of measurement itself leads to systematic changes in measured performance. A study was done on the effects of a preparatory course on performance on the American College Test (ACT)—a college entrance exam. Students were given the ACT, then given a course on improving their scores, then tested again; they achieved higher scores, on the average, the second time they took the test. The investigator attributed the improvement to the prep course, when actually it may have been simply the practice of taking the first test which led to improvement. This plausible alternative explanation suggests that even if the students had not taken the course, they would have improved their scores on the average upon retaking the ACT. The presence of a control group (a group assembled to provide a comparison to the treatment group results) would improve this study.

A change in the instruments used to measure the dependent variable will also cause problems. This is a problem particularly when human observers are rating behaviors directly. The observers may tire, or their standards may shift over the course of the study. For example, if observers are rating children's "hyperactivity," they may see later behavior as more hyperactive than earlier behavior not because the children's behavior has changed but because, through observing the children play, the observers' own standards have shifted. Objective measurement is crucial for controlling this threat.

Selection presents a problem when the results are caused by a bias in the choice of subjects for each group. For example, a study of two programs designed to stop cigarette smoking assigned smokers who had been addicted for ten years to program A and smokers who had been addicted for two years to program B. It was found that 50 percent of the program B people quit and 30 percent of the program A people quit. The investigators concluded that program B is more effective; however, it may be that people in program B were more successful simply because they were not as addicted to their habit as the program A participants.

Mortality, or attrition, is a problem when a differential dropout rate influences the results. For example, in the preceding cigarette study, it might be that of one hundred participants in program A, ninety of them sent back their post-test form at the end of the study; for program B, only sixty of the participants sent their forms back. It may be that people who did not send their forms back were more likely to have continued smoking, causing the apparent difference in results between programs A and B.

When subjects become aware that they are in a study, and awareness of being observed influences their reactions, reactivity has occurred. The famous Hawthorne studies on a wiring room at a Western Electric plant were influenced by this phenomenon. The investigators intended to do a study on the effects of lighting on work productivity, but they were puzzled by the fact that any change they made in lighting—increasing it or decreasing it—led to improved productivity. They finally decided it was the workers' awareness of being in an experiment that caused their reactions, not the lighting level.

Statistical regression is a problem that occurs when subjects are selected to be in a group on the basis of their extreme scores (either high or low) on a test. Their group can be predicted to move toward the average the next time they take the test, even if the treatment has had no effect. For example, if low-scoring students are assigned to tutoring because of the low scores they achieved on a pretest, they will score higher on the second test (a posttest), even if the tutoring is ineffective.

EXTERNAL THREATS TO VALIDITY

External threats to validity constitute the other major validity issue. Generally speaking, true experiments control for internal threats to validity by experimental design, but external threats may be a problem for true experiments as well as quasi-experiments. Since a scientific finding is one that should hold true in different circumstances, external validity (the extent to which the results of any particular study can be generalized to other settings, people, and times) is a very important issue.

An interaction between selection and treatment can cause an external validity problem. For example, since much of the medical research on the treatment of diseases has been performed by selecting only men as subjects, one might question whether those results can be generalized to women. The interaction between setting and treatment can be a problem when setting differ greatly. For example, can results obtained on a college campus be generalized to a factory? Can results from a factory be generalized to an office? The interaction of history and treatment can be a problem when the specific time the experiment is carried out influences people's reaction to the treatment. The effectiveness of an advertisement for gun control might be judged differently if measured shortly after an assassination or mass murder received extensive media coverage.

EXAMINING SOCIAL PHENOMENA AND PROGRAMS

Quasi-experimental designs have been most frequently used to examine the effects of social phenomena and social programs that cannot be or have not been investigated by experiments. For example, the effects of the public television show *Sesame Street* have been the subject of several quasi-experimental evaluations. One initial evaluation of *Sesame Street* concluded that it was ineffective in raising the academic abilities of poor children, but a reanalysis of the data suggested that statistical regression artifacts had contaminated the original evaluation and that *Sesame Street* had a more positive effect than was initially believed. This research showed the potential harm that can be done by reaching conclusions while not controlling for all the threats to validity. It also showed the value of doing true experiments whenever possible.

Many of the field-research studies carried out on the effects of violent television programming on children's aggressiveness have used quasi-experimental designs to estimate the effects of violent television. Other social-policy studies have included the effects of no-fault divorce laws on divorce rates, of crackdowns on drunken driving on the frequency of drunken driving, and of strict speed-law enforcement on speeding behavior and accidents. The study of the effects of speed-law enforcement represents excellent use of the "interrupted time series" quasi-experimental design. This design can be used when a series of pretest and post-test data points are available. In this case, the governor of Connecticut abruptly announced that people convicted of speeding would have their licenses suspended for a thirty-day period on the first offense, sixty days on a second offense, and longer for any further offenses. By comparing the number of motorists speeding, the number of accidents, and the number of fatalities during the period before the crackdown with the period after the crackdown, the investigators could judge how effective the crackdown actually was. The interrupted time series design provides control over many of the plausible rival alternative hypotheses and is thus a strong quasi-experimental design. The investigators concluded that it was probable that the crackdown did have a somewhat positive effect in reducing fatalities but that a regression artifact may also have influenced the results. The regression artifact in this study would be a decrease in fatalities simply because there was such a high rate of fatalities before the crackdown.

USE IN ORGANIZATIONAL PSYCHOLOGY

Organizational psychology has used quasi-experimental designs to study such issues as the effects of strategies to reduce absenteeism in businesses, union-labor cooperation on grievance rates, and the effects of different forms of employee ownership on job attitudes and organizational performance. The latter study compared three different conversions to employee ownership and found that employee ownership had positive effects on a company to the extent that it enhanced participative decision making and led to group work norms supportive of higher productivity. Quasi-experimental studies are particularly useful in those circumstances where it is impossible to carry out true experiments but policymakers still want to reach causal conclusions. A strong knowledge of quasi-experimental design principles helps prevent incorrect causal conclusions.

RESEARCH APPROACH

Psychology has progressed through the use of experiments to establish a base of facts that support psychological theories; however, there are many issues about which psychologists need to have expert knowledge that cannot be investigated by performing experiments. There are not too many social situations, outside a university laboratory, where a psychologist can randomly assign individuals to different treatments. For example, psychologists cannot dictate to parents what type of television programs they must assign their children to watch, they cannot tell the managers of a group of companies how to implement an employee stock option plan, and they cannot make a school superintendent randomly assign different classes to different instructional approaches. All these factors in the social environment vary, and quasi-experimental designs can be used to get the most available knowledge from the natural environment.

The philosophy of science associated with traditional experimental psychology argues that unless a true experiment is done it is impossible to reach any causal conclusion. The quasi-experimental view argues that a study is valid unless and until it is shown to be invalid. What is important in a study is the extent to which plausible alternative explanations can be ruled out. If there are no plausible alternative explanations to the results except for the experimenter's research hypothesis, then the experimenter's research hypothesis can be regarded as true.

EVOLUTION OF PRACTICE

The first generally circulated book that argued for a quasi-experimental approach to social decision making was William A. McCall's *How to Experiment in Education*, published in 1923. Education has been one of the areas where there has been an interest in and willingness to carry out quasi-experimental studies. Psychology was more influenced by the strictly experimental work of Ronald A. Fisher that was being published at around that time, and Fisher's ideas on true experiments dominated psychological methods through the mid-1950's.

The quasi-experimental view gained increasing popularity during the 1960's as psychology was challenged to become more socially relevant and make a contribution to understanding the larger society. At that time, the federal government was also engaged in many social programs, sometimes collectively called the War on Poverty, which included housing programs, welfare programs, and compensatory educational programs; they needed to be evaluated. Evaluation was needed so that what worked could be retained and what failed could be discontinued. There was an initial burst of enthusiasm for quasi-experimental studies, but the ambiguous results that they produced were discouraging, and this has led many leading methodologists to re-emphasize the value of true experiments.

Rather than hold up the university-based laboratory true experiment as a model, however, they called for implementing social programs and other evaluations using random assignment to treatments in such a way that stronger causal conclusions could be reached. The usefulness of true experiments and quasi-experiments was also seen to be much more dependent on psychological theory: The pattern of results obtained by many different types of studies became a key factor in the progress of psychological knowledge. The traditional laboratory experiment, upon which many psychological theories are based, was recognized as being very limited in external validity, and the value of true experiments—carried out in different settings, with different types of people, and replicated many times over—was emphasized. Since politicians, business managers, and other social policymakers have not yet appreciated the advantages in knowledge to be gained by adopting a true experiment approach to social innovation, quasi-experimental designs are still an important and valuable tool in understanding human behavior.

Sources for Further Study

Campbell, Donald Thomas, and Julian C. Stanley. *Experimental and Quasi-Experimental Designs for Research.* Chicago: Rand McNally, 1966. The clearest and most accessible presentation of the principles of quasi-experimental design, still in print. Includes many excellent examples and a description of sixteen experimental and quasi-experimental designs, each evaluated for twelve threats to validity. Many examples are from educational research. Includes illustrations of designs.

Cook, Thomas D., and Donald T. Campbell. *Quasi-Experimentation: Design and Analysis Issues for Field Settings.* Chicago: Rand McNally, 1979. A large book built on the foundations of Donald Campbell and Julian Stanley's 1966 work. It has a much more complete consideration of the philosophical analysis of cause and effect, a reorganized conception of validity issues, detailed statistical analysis methods for quasi-experiments, and a discussion on the conduct of randomized experiments in field settings. By recasting validity into statistical conclusion validity, construct validity, internal validity, and external validity, a more comprehensive view is presented.

Cronbach, Lee Joseph. *Designing Evaluations of Educational and Social Programs.* San Francisco: Jossey-Bass, 1982. Cronbach disagrees with the Campbell, Stanley, and Cook approach to quasi-experimentation in that he thinks they overemphasize internal validity and the importance of unequivocal causal conclusions. Cronbach argues that the major issue shaping any quasi-experimentation should be the application that the study is designed to inform. He develops a different typology of issues based on this criterion of value.

Trochim, William M. K., ed. *Advances in Quasi-Experimental Design and Analysis.* San Francisco: Jossey-Bass, 1986. A series of articles by various experts on quasi-experimental design. Some of the issues are rather technical, but most of the articles are understandable. Chapter 3, "Validity Typologies and the Logic and Practice of Quasi-Experimentation," by Melvin M. Mark, is an excellent overview, review, and discussion of different approaches to quasi-experimentation.

Don R. Osborn

SEE ALSO: Archival data; Complex experimental designs; Experimentation: Independent, dependent, and control variables; Field experimentation; Hypothesis development and testing; Psychotherapy: Effectiveness; Sampling; Scientific methods; Violence and sexuality in the media; Within-subject experimental designs.

R

Race and intelligence

TYPE OF PSYCHOLOGY: Biological bases of behavior; intelligence and intelligence testing

FIELDS OF STUDY: Biological influences on learning; general issues in intelligence; intelligence assessment

The relationship between race and intelligence has long been the subject of heated debate among social scientists. At issue is whether intelligence is an inherited trait or is primarily attributable to environmental influences.

KEY CONCEPTS
- intelligence quotient (IQ) tests
- nature versus nurture
- twin studies

INTRODUCTION

In 1969, educational psychologist Arthur Jensen published an article in the *Harvard Educational Review* entitled "How Much Can We Boost I.Q. and Scholastic Achievement?" He attempted to explain the consistent finding that whites, on the average, outperform blacks by about 15 points on intelligence quotient (IQ) tests. His major conclusion was that racial differences in intelligence are primarily attributable to heredity and that whites, as a racial group, are born with abilities superior to those of blacks.

Jensen, as well as William Shockley, presents the hereditarian hypothesis of intelligence. It argues that some people are born smarter than others and that this fact cannot be changed with training, education, or any alteration in the environment. Because they believe that African Americans as a group are not as smart as Caucasians, they suggest that special programs, such as Head Start, which are designed to help disadvantaged children improve in school achievement, are doomed to fail.

In contrast to the hereditarians, Urie Bronfenbrenner and Ashley Montagu can be described as environmentalists. They believe that although intelligence has some genetic component, as do all human characteristics, the expression of intelligent behavior is defined, determined, and developed within a specific cultural context. Therefore, what people choose to call intelligence is primarily caused by the interaction of genetics with environmental influences. Environmentalists believe that a person can improve in his or her intellectual functioning with sufficient changes in environment.

Richard Herrnstein and Charles Murray's *The Bell Curve* (1994) reopened the issue of heredity versus environment in the attainment of intelligence. The authors argue that Caucasians are inherently superior to African Americans in IQ levels, presenting a mass of statistical evidence to support their position. Critics of *The Bell Curve* attack it on a number of fronts. There is a failure to separate hereditary from genetic variables. The definition of race proves a difficult one. The IQ tests themselves come into the same culture bias category. The statistical tests hide more than they reveal. There is difficulty replicating Hernnstein and Murray's results. The defects mount up rather quickly.

Much of the hereditarian argument is based on two types of studies: those comparing IQ test performance of twins and those of adopted children. Because identical twins have the same genetic endowment, it is thought that any differences observed between them should be attributable to the effects of the environment. Hereditarians also suggest that one should observe more similarities in the IQs of parents and their biological children (because they share genes) than between parents and adopted children (who are biologically unrelated and therefore share no genes).

Statistical formulas are applied to comparisons between family members' IQs to determine the relative contributions of heredity and environment. Using this method, Sir Cyril Burt in 1958 reported a heritability estimate of .93. This means that 93 percent of the variability in intelligence could be explained genetically. People have also interpreted this to mean that 93 percent of the intelligence level is inherited. Jensen has more recently reported heritability estimates of .80 and .67, depending on what formula is used. Hereditarians have also pointed out that when they compare African Americans and Caucasians from similar environments (the same educational level, income level, or occupation), the reported IQ differences remain. This, they argue, supports their view that heredity is more important in determining intelligence. The same arguments have been made for the work of Hernnstein and Murray.

For environmentalists, it is not so much the reported IQ differences between different racial groups that are in question. Of more concern are the basic assumptions made by the hereditarians and the reasons they give for the reported differences. Not surprisingly, environmentalists challenge the hereditarian arguments on several levels. First, they point out that there is no evidence of the existence of an "intelligence" gene or set of genes. They say that scientists have been unsuccessful in distinguishing the genetic from the environmental contributions to intelligence.

Environmentalists also refute the assumption that IQ tests adequately measure intelligence. Although IQ has been noted to be a good predictor of success in school, it turns out to have little relationship to economic success in life. S. E. Luria reports an analysis that shows that the son of a Caucasian businessman with an IQ of 90 has a greater chance of success than an African American boy with an IQ of 120. This example calls into question what actually is being assessed. It is not at all clear that "intelligence" is being measured—especially since there is no generally accepted definition of intelligence among social scientists.

The definition of race is also problematic. Although most people may identify several racial groups (such as African, or black; Caucasian, or white; and so on), Ashley Montagu and many other social scientists agree that race is a pseudoscientific concept, used as a social or political category to assign social status and to subordinate nonwhite populations. Because of intermingling among different cultural groups, it is also difficult to identify strict biological boundaries for race, which in turn makes

genetic interpretations of racial comparisons of IQ differences much less meaningful.

In addition to questioning what IQ tests measure, many psychologists have criticized IQ tests as being biased against individuals who are culturally different from the mainstream group (Caucasians) and who have not assimilated the white, middle-class norms upon which the tests were based. Tests developed in one culture may not adequately measure the abilities and aptitude of people from another culture, especially if the two cultures emphasize different skills, ways of solving problems, and ways of understanding the world.

Environmentalists have also criticized the research and statistical techniques used by the hereditarians. It is now widely acknowledged that the data reported

Some psychologists believe that intelligence is defined, determined, and developed within a cultural context. Urie Bronfenbrenner, a child development expert, noted that children improved their performance on IQ tests in the presence of positive environmental changes. (AP/Wide World Photos)

by Burt, upon which Jensen heavily relied, were false. In many different studies, he came up with the same figures (to the third decimal point) for the similarities between IQ scores for twins. This is statistically impossible. He also did not take into account how other variables, such as age and gender, might have produced higher IQ values in the twins he studied. Rather, he assumed that they shared genes for intelligence.

It is also charged that the concept of heritability is misunderstood by the hereditarians. This is a statistic that applies to groups, not to individuals. If one states that the heritability estimate of a group of IQ scores is .80, that does not mean that 80 percent of each IQ score is attributable to genetics, but that 80 percent of the difference in the group of scores can be attributed to genetic variation. Therefore, according to the enviromentalists, it is incorrect for hereditarians to establish heritability within one group (such as Caucasian children) and then apply that figure to a different racial group (such as African American children).

CONSEQUENCES OF VARIOUS POSITIONS

Several examples may help clarify the relationships between heredity, environment, and characteristics such as IQ. The first example involves a highly heritable characteristic, height. A farmer has two fields, one rich in nutrients (field A) and the other barren (field B). The farmer takes seeds from a bag that has considerable genetic variety, plants them in the two fields, and cares for the two fields of crops equally well. After several weeks, the plants are measured. The farmer finds that within field A, some plants are taller than others in the same field. Since all these plants had the same growing environment, the variation could be attributed to the genetic differences in the seeds planted. The same would be the case with the plants in field B.

The farmer also finds differences between the two fields. The plants in field A are taller than the plants in field B, because of the richer soil in which they grew. The difference in the average heights of the plants is attributable to the quality of the growing environment, even though the genetic variation (heritability) within field A may be the same as that within field B. This same principle applies to IQ scores of different human groups.

Taking the example further, the farmer might call a chemist to test the soil. If the chemist was able

to determine all the essential missing nutrients, the farmer could add them to the soil in field B for the next season. The second batch of plants would grow larger, with the average height being similar to the average height of plants in field A. Similarly, if one is comparing African Americans and Caucasians, or any number of racial groups, on a characteristic such as IQ test scores, it is important to understand that unless the groups have equivalent growing environments (social, political, economic, educational, and so on), differences between the groups cannot be easily traced to heredity.

As another example, one might take a set of identical twins who were born in Chicago, separate them at birth, and place one of the twins in the !Kung desert community in Africa. The life experiences of the twin in Africa would differ significantly from those of his Chicago counterpart because of the differences in diet, climate, and other relevant factors required for existence and survival in the two environments. The twin in Africa would have a different language and number system; drawing and writing would likely not be an important part of daily life. Therefore, if one were to use existing IQ tests, one would have to translate them from English to the !Kung language so that they could be understood. The translation might not truly capture the meaning of all the questions and tasks, which might interfere with the !Kung twin's understanding of what was being asked of him. More problems would arise when the !Kung twin is asked to interpret drawings or to copy figures, since he would not be very familiar with these activities.

It is likely that the !Kung twin would perform poorly on the translated IQ test, because it does not reflect what is emphasized and valued in his society. Rather, it is based on the schooling in society in which the Chicago twin lives. This does not mean that the !Kung twin is less intelligent than his Chicago twin. Similarly, the Chicago twin would do poorly on a test developed from the experience of !Kung culture, because the !Kung test would emphasize skills such as building shelter, finding water, and other activities that are not important for survival in Chicago. In this case, the !Kung test would not adequately measure the ability of the Chicago twin.

Studies done by psychologist Sandra Scarr show that evidence for a genetic basis for racial differences in IQ is far from clear. She looked at the IQ scores of African American children who were born into working-class families but were adopted and reared by white middle-class families. The IQ scores of these children were close to the national average and were almost 10 to 20 points higher than would have been expected had they remained in their birth homes.

Change in children's environments seems to be a critical factor in enhancing their ability to perform on the IQ tests, as seen in the research done by Scarr. Bronfenbrenner found similar results. He examined a dozen studies that looked at early intervention in children's lives; he found that whenever it was possible to change the environment positively, children's scores on IQ tests increased.

HISTORICAL DEVELOPMENT OF RACIAL CONTEXT

The notion of inherited differences is an ancient one; however, the concept of racial classifications is more recent. According to psychologist Wade Nobles, the Western idea of race emerged during the sixteenth century as Europeans began to colonize other parts of the world. As they came into contact with people who looked different from them, many Europeans developed the notion that some races were superior to others. This belief often was given as a justification for slavery and other oppressive activities.

Charles Darwin's theory of evolution was critical in promoting the belief that human differences were a result of heredity and genetics. His notion of "the survival of the fittest" led psychologists to research racial differences in intelligence in order to understand the successes and failures of different human groups. Francis Galton, Darwin's cousin, was instrumental in furthering the hereditarian perspective in psychology. In his book *Hereditary Genius: An Inquiry into Its Laws and Consequences* (1869), he attempted to illustrate that genius and prominence follow family lines. He also began the eugenics movement, which supported the use of selective mating and forced sterilization to improve racial stock. *The Bell Curve* is simply a more recent argument along the same lines. Nothing really new is added to the argument. There is a bit more sociobiological jargon and a mass of statistics that do not hold up to careful scrutiny.

Following Galton's lead, many psychologists embraced the notions of inherited racial differences in intelligence. The pioneering work of anthropologist Franz Boas, in attacking the popular conception of race, fostered research to attack the myths attached to that concept, including the myth of inherent superiority or inferiority. G. Stanley Hall, the founder of the American Psychological Association, believed that African people were at a lower evolutionary stage than Caucasians. By the beginning of the 1900's, psychological testing was being widely used to support the view that intelligence was hereditary and was little influenced by the environment. More recently, Burt, Herrnstein, and Jensen have argued in favor of an overriding genetic factor in intelligence.

There were also early efforts to challenge the hereditarian perspective in psychology. During the 1920's and 1930's, Herman Canady and Howard Long, two of the first African Americans to receive graduate degrees in psychology, produced evidence showing the importance of environmental influences on IQ test performance. They were concerned about increasing scientific justifications for the inequality and injustice experienced by African Americans, Native Americans, and other groups. Fighting racism was a major reason Leon Kamin became involved in the debate about race and intelligence. He gathered the original information that had been reported by scientists and reexamined it; Kamin was responsible for discovering that Burt had reported false information. He also noted that many hereditarians misused and misinterpreted their statistics.

Hereditarians maintain that racial differences in IQ test scores are primarily caused by genetics and that these scores do reflect differences in intelligence; environmentalists say no. It has not been proved definitively that IQ tests measure intelligence; however, the evidence does suggest that performance on IQ tests is determined by the interaction between genetic and environmental influences. The quality of the environment will determine how well people will reach their potential. In a society where the history of certain groups includes oppression, discrimination, and exclusion from opportunity, it is difficult to explain differences in achievement as being primarily inherited. Instead, it would seem to be a more important goal to eliminate injustices and to change the conditions of life so that all people could do well.

SOURCES FOR FURTHER STUDY

Devlin, Bernie, et al., eds. *Intelligence, Genes, and Success: Scientists Respond to "The Bell Curve."* New York:

Springer, 1997. A number of psychologists and social scientists respond to the claims of Hernnstein and Murray.

Fancher, Raymond E. *The Intelligence Men: Makers of the IQ Controversy.* New York: W. W. Norton, 1985. Examines the historical contexts of the IQ controversy. The life experiences of the major hereditarians and environmentalists and how these experiences influenced their perspectives are emphasized. This book is easy to read and does an excellent job of making complex statistics understandable.

Goldsby, Richard. *Race and Races.* New York: Macmillan, 1971. Provides straightforward and accurate information about issues of race, racial differences, and racism. There is a balanced discussion of both the hereditarian and environmentalist perspectives of the IQ controversy. Enjoyable and easy to read for high school and college students alike.

Gould, Stephen Jay. *The Mismeasure of Man.* Revised and expanded ed. New York: Norton, 1997. Gould replies to the work of Hernnstein and Murray, questioning both their motives and their methods.

Guthrie, Robert V. *Even the Rat Was White.* New York: Harper & Row, 1976. Provides an excellent historical view of how psychology has dealt with race as an issue. The first section of the book focuses on methods of study, early psychological testing, and the development of racism in the profession of psychology.

Hernnstein, Richard, and Charles Murray. *The Bell Curve.* New York: Free Press, 1994. This book argues that differences in black and white IQ scores are genetically based.

Jensen, Arthur R. *Bias in Mental Testing.* New York: Free Press, 1980. An attempt to deal comprehensively with the issues of IQ testing and bias. Jensen challenges the criticisms against IQ tests and offers research to support his view that group differences in IQ test scores are not attributable to bias.

Kamin, Leon J. *The Science and Politics of IQ.* New York: Halstead Press, 1974. Discusses the political nature of the role psychologists have played in support of IQ testing. The role of psychologists in the eugenics movement and in education is discussed. Includes strong critiques of the work done by Burt and Jensen.

Montagu, Ashley, ed. *Race and IQ.* New York: Oxford University Press, 1975. Written to challenge the interpretations offered by the hereditarians. Most of the articles were previously published in professional journals or popular magazines. Some of the chapters contain very technical material; however, the authors generally do an effective job translating this into more understandable language.

Derise E. Tolliver;
updated by Frank A. Salamone

SEE ALSO: Ability tests; College entrance examinations; Intelligence; Intelligence quotient (IQ); Intelligence tests; Prejudice; Racism; Testing: Historical perspectives.

Racism

TYPE OF PSYCHOLOGY: Social psychology
FIELDS OF STUDY: Prejudice and discrimination

Students of racism examine the phenomenon of negative attitudes and behavior by members of the majority toward those who belong to racial and ethnic minorities. The topic of racism, which straddles the boundaries between social psychology and sociology, is connected with the study of intergroup relations, cognition, and attitudes in general.

KEY CONCEPTS
- attribution theory
- discrimination
- prejudice
- scapegoating
- social construction of race
- stereotypes

INTRODUCTION

The social and psychological study of prejudice and discrimination, including prejudice and discrimination against African Americans, has a long history; the term "racism," however, did not enter the language of social psychology until the publication of the Kerner Commission Report of 1968, which blamed all-pervasive "white racism" for widespread black rioting in American cities. While usually applied to black-white relations in the United States, the term is also sometimes used with regard to white Americans' relations with other minority groups, such as Asians or Latinos, or to black-white relations outside the United States, for example, in Britain, Canada, or South Africa. Most of the studies and research on racism have focused on white racism against blacks in the United States.

Racism is seen by many social psychologists not as mere hatred but as a deep-rooted habit that is hard to change; hence, subvarieties of racism are distinguished. Psychoanalyst Joel Kovel, in his book *White Racism: A Psychohistory* (1970), distinguishes between dominative racism, the desire to oppress blacks, and aversive racism, the desire to avoid contact with blacks. Aversive racism, Samuel L. Gaertner and John Dovidio find, exists among those whites who pride themselves on being unprejudiced. David O. Sears, looking at whites' voting behavior and their political opinions as expressed in survey responses, finds what he calls symbolic racism: a resentment of African Americans for making demands in the political realm that supposedly violate traditional American values. Social psychologist James M. Jones distinguishes three types of racism: individual racism, the prejudice and antiblack behavior deliberately manifested by individual whites; institutional racism, the social, economic, and political patterns that impersonally oppress blacks regardless of the prejudice or lack thereof of individuals; and cultural racism, the tendency of whites to ignore or denigrate the special characteristics of black culture.

Where Dovidio and Gaertner find aversive racism, Irwin Katz finds ambivalence. Many whites, he argues, simultaneously see African Americans as disadvantaged (which creates sympathy) and as deviating from mainstream social norms (which creates antipathy). Such ambivalence, Katz contends, leads to exaggeratedly negative reactions to negative behaviors by an African American, but also to exaggeratedly positive reactions to positive behaviors by an African American. He calls this phenomenon ambivalence-induced behavior amplification.

The reasons suggested for individual racism are many. John Dollard and others, in *Frustration and Aggression* (1939), see prejudice as the scapegoating of minorities in order to provide a release for aggression in the face of frustration; in this view, out-

bursts of bigotry are a natural response to hard economic times. Muzafer and Carolyn Sherif, in *Groups in Harmony and Tension* (1953) and later works, see prejudice of all sorts as the result of competition between groups. Theodor Adorno and others, in *The Authoritarian Personality* (1950), view prejudice, whether directed against blacks or against Jews, as reflective of a supposedly fascist type of personality produced by authoritarian child-rearing practices. In *Racially Separate or Together?* (1971), Thomas F. Pettigrew shows that discriminatory behavior toward blacks, and the verbal expression of prejudices against them, can sometimes flow simply from a white's desire to fit in with his or her social group. Finally, both prejudice and discrimination, many psychologists argue, are rooted in those human cognitive processes involved in the formation of stereotypes.

RACISM AND STEREOTYPES

Stereotypes are ideas, often rigidly held, concerning members of a group to which one does not belong. Social psychologists who follow the cognitive approach to the study of racism, such as David L. Hamilton, Walter G. Stephan, and Myron Rothbart, argue that racial stereotyping (the tendency of whites to see blacks in some roles and not in others) arises, like any other kind of stereotyping, from the need of every human being to create some sort of order out of his or her perceptions of the world. Although stereotypes are not entirely impervious to revision or even shattering in the face of disconfirming instances, information related to a stereotype is more efficiently retained than information unrelated to it. Whites, it has been found, tend to judge blacks to be more homogeneous than they really are, while being more aware of differences within their own group: This is called the out-group homogeneity hypothesis. Whites who are guided by stereotypes may act in such a way as to bring out worse behavior in blacks than would otherwise occur, thus creating a self-fulfilling prophecy.

Why is stereotypical thinking on the part of whites about African Americans so hard to eliminate? The history of race relations in the United States deserves some of the blame. Some mistakes in reasoning common to the tolerant and the intolerant alike—such as the tendency to remember spectacular events and to think of them as occurring more frequently than is really the case (the availability heuristic)—also occur in whites' judgments about members of minority groups. In addition, the social and occupational roles one fills may reinforce stereotypical thinking.

Thomas F. Pettigrew contends that attribution errors—mistakes in explaining the behavior of others—may have an important role to play in reinforcing racial stereotypes. The same behavioral act, Pettigrew argues, is interpreted differently by whites depending on the race of the actor. A positive act by a black might be ascribed to situational characteristics (for example, luck, affirmative action programs, or other circumstances beyond one's control) and thus discounted; a positive act by a white might be ascribed to personality characteristics. Similarly, a negative act might be ascribed to situational characteristics in the case of a white, but to personality characteristics in the case of a black. The tendency of whites to view the greater extent of poverty among blacks as solely the result of lack of motivation can be seen as a form of attribution error.

POLICY GUIDES

Institutional racism occurs when policies that are nonracial on their face have differential results for the two races. For example, a stiff educational requirement for a relatively unskilled job may effectively exclude blacks, whose educational preparation may be weaker, at least in part because of past racial discrimination. The policy of hiring friends and relatives of existing employees may also exclude blacks, if blacks have not historically worked in a particular business. In both cases, the effect is discriminatory even if the intent is not.

Somewhat connected with the concept of institutional racism is Pettigrew's notion of conformity-induced prejudice and discrimination. A classic example is that of the pre-Civil Rights era southern United States, where urban restaurant owners, regardless of their personal feelings about blacks, re-

---

Race and Biology

Most social and behavioral scientists are agreed that race is a social construct. Ethnicity is the better term. However, in the popular mind there appears little difference between the two terms. Certainly people react to race as if it were real. The wars of the late twentieth and early twenty-first centuries have been essentially racial wars, and the hatred evidenced in Bosnia, Rwanda, and Afghanistan were fueled by racial hatred. Efforts to promote multiculturalism and cultural diversity appear as academic exercises that have little impact outside the privileged and sheltered areas of academe.

Backlashes against affirmative action, the rise of "whiteness" studies, and the rediscovery of white ethnicity have all arisen against attempts to promote racial justice. Certainly, there have been advances in civil rights but much remains to be done. It has become increasing clear, however, that efforts to promote racial justice through advocating guilt tend to backfire. Better psychological and sociological foundations need be raised in the increasingly complex area of race relations.

America's increasing racial complexity, for example, has questioned the old dichotomous black/white categorization of race. No one is yet quite sure how to categorize biracial and multiracial people. Efforts to educate the public on the fact that there is only one human race do not appear to get very far. For some, there is advantage to be had in keeping the old racial categories, however biologically erroneous they may be.

Frank A. Salamone

---

fused them service out of deference to local norms. Another example is the case of the white factory worker who cooperates with black fellow workers on the job and in union activities but strenuously opposes blacks moving into his neighborhood; norms of tolerance are followed in one context, norms of discrimination in the other.

The concept of symbolic (sometimes called "modern") racism, a form of covert prejudice said to be characteristic of political conservatives, arose from a series of questions designed to predict whether white Californians would vote against black political candidates. It has been used to explain opposition to school busing to achieve integration and support for the 1978 California referendum proposition for limiting taxes. John B. McConahay shows that white experimental subjects who score high on the modern racism scale, when faced with hypothetical black and white job candidates with identical credentials, are more likely than low scorers to give a much poorer rating to the black candidate's resume.

Aversive racism cannot be detected by surveys. Since aversive racists wish to maintain a nonprejudiced self-image, they neither admit to being prejudiced nor discriminate against blacks when social norms clearly forbid it; when the norms are ambiguous, however, they do discriminate. In a New York City experiment, professed liberals and professed conservatives both got telephone calls from individuals identifiable from their speech patterns as either black or white. At first, the caller said he had the wrong number; if the recipient of the call did not hang up, the caller then asked for help regarding a disabled car. Conservatives were less likely to offer help to the black, but liberals were more likely to hang up when they were told by the black that a wrong number had been called. In another experiment, white college students proved just as willing to accept help from a black partner as from a white one when the help was offered. When the subjects had to take the initiative, however, discomfort with the reversal of traditional roles showed up: More asked for help from the white partner than from the black one.

Both symbolic and aversive, but not dominative, racists manifest ambivalence in their attitudes toward blacks. Katz's concept of ambivalence-induced behavior amplification has been tested in several experiments. In one experiment, white college student subjects were told to insult two individuals, one black and one white. After they had done so, they proved, when asked for assistance in a task later on, more willing to help the black they had insulted than the white person.

The effect of the availability heuristic in reinforcing stereotypes is seen in the case of a white who is mugged by a black criminal. If the victim knows no other blacks, he or she may well remember this one spectacular incident and forget the many blacks who are law-abiding. The effect of occupational roles in reinforcing stereotypes can be seen in the example of a white policeman who patrols a black slum neighborhood and jumps to the conclusion that all blacks are criminals.

Experiments on stereotyping indicate that white subjects remember the words or actions of a solo black in an otherwise all-white group better than they do the words or actions of one black in a group of several blacks. With a mixed group of speakers, some white and some black, white experimental subjects proved later to be more likely to confuse the identities of the black speakers than those of the white speakers, while remembering the race of the former. The self-fulfilling prophecy concept has been tested in experiments with white subjects interviewing supposed job candidates. The white subjects were more ill at ease and inarticulate interviewing a black candidate than in interviewing a white one; in turn, the black candidate was more ill at ease than the white one, and made more errors.

Since most such experiments use college students as subjects, there is inevitably some doubt about their generalizability to the outside world. Nevertheless, it seems likely that the evidence from social psychology experiments of just how deeply rooted racial bias is among white Americans has played at least some role in leading governments to adopt affirmative action policies to secure fairer treatment of blacks and other minorities in hiring procedures.

HISTORY AND DEVELOPMENTS

Although the study of racism per se began with the racial crisis of the 1960's, the study of prejudice in general goes back much further; as early as the 1920's, Emory Bogardus constructed a social distance scale measuring the degree of intimacy members of different racial and ethnic groups were willing to tolerate with one another. At first, psychologists tended to seek the roots of prejudice in the emotional makeup of the prejudiced individual rather than in the structure of society or the general patterns of human cognition. For many years, the study of antiblack prejudice was subsumed under the study of prejudice in general; those biased against blacks were thought to be biased against other groups, such as Jews, as well.

In the years immediately following World War II, American social psychologists were optimistic about the possibilities for reducing or even eliminating racial and ethnic prejudices. Adorno's *The Authoritarian Personality*, and *The Nature of Prejudice* (1954), by Gordon Allport, reflect the climate of opinion of the time. Allport, whose view of prejudice represented a mixture of the psychoanalytic and cognitive approaches, used the term "racism" to signify the doctrines preached by negrophobe political demagogues; he did not see it as a deeply ingrained bad habit pervading the entire society. Thomas F. Pettigrew, who wrote about antiblack prejudice from the late 1950's on, cast doubt on the notion that there was a specific type of personality or pattern of child rearing associated with prejudice. Nevertheless, he long remained in the optimistic tradition, arguing that changing white people's discriminatory behavior through the enactment of civil rights laws would ultimately change their prejudiced attitudes.

The more frequent use by social psychologists of the term "racism" from the late 1960's onward indicates a growing awareness that bias against blacks, a visible minority, might be harder to uproot than that directed against religious and ethnic minorities. Social psychologists studying racial prejudice shifted their research interest from the open and noisy bigotry most often found among political extremists (for example, the Ku Klux Klan) to the quiet, everyday prejudices of the average apolitical individual. Racial bias against blacks came to be seen as a central, rather than a peripheral, feature of American life.

Responses to surveys taken from the 1940's to the end of the 1970's indicated a steady decline in the percentage of white Americans willing to admit holding racist views. Yet in the 1970's, the sometimes violent white hostility to school busing for integration, and the continuing social and economic gap between black and white America, gave social psychologists reason to temper their earlier optimism. The contact hypothesis, the notion that contact between different racial groups would reduce prejudice, was subjected to greater skepticism and ever more careful qualification. Janet Ward Schofield, in her field study of a desegregated junior high school, detected a persistence of racial divisions among the pupils; reviewing a number of such studies, Walter Stephan similarly discerned a tendency toward increased interracial tension in schools following desegregation. The pessimism suggested by field studies among younger teenagers was confirmed by experiments conducted in the 1970's and 1980's on college students and adults; such studies demonstrated the existence even among supposedly nonprejudiced people of subtle racism and racial stereotyping.

Yet while social psychological experiments contribute to an understanding of the reasons for negative attitudes toward blacks by whites, and for discriminatory behavior toward blacks even by those whites who believe themselves to be tolerant, they do not by any means provide the complete answer to the riddle of racial prejudice and discrimination. Unlike many other topics in social psychology, racism has also been investigated by journalists, historians, economists, sociologists, political scientists, legal scholars, and even literary critics. The techniques of social psychology—surveys, controlled experiments, and field studies—provide only one window on this phenomenon.

SOURCES FOR FURTHER STUDY

Allport, Gordon W. *The Nature of Prejudice.* Cambridge, Mass.: Addison-Wesley, 1954. This detailed, beautifully written, and influential book, accessible to both the general reader and the scholar, devotes equal space to anti-Jewish and antiblack prejudice, with passing references to other types of prejudice. Contains one of the earliest expositions of the contact hypothesis, and one of the earliest treatments of the relationship between prejudice and stereotyping. Somewhat dated by both its optimistic meliorism and its references to extremist political movements of the 1940's.

Bell, Derrick. *Faces at the Bottom of the Well: The Permanence of Racism.* New York: Basic Books, 1992. This book gives a clear insight into racism in the United States.

Campbell, Duane. *Choosing Democracy: A Practical Guide to Multicultural Education.* Upper Saddle River, N.J.: Prentice Hall, 1998. A textbook for teachers and other educators on how to create a nonracist classroom.

Dovidio, John F., and Samuel L. Gaertner, eds. *Prejudice, Discrimination, and Racism.* Orlando, Fla.: Academic Press, 1986. This rich collection includes one essay apiece on aversive racism and racial ambivalence; three essays on racial stereotyping; a difficult but rewarding chapter by John D. McConahay on the formulation and testing of the symbolic racism concept; an essay by Janet Schofield on the persistence of aversive racism in a recently desegregated school; and a piece by James L. Jones on cultural racism.

Gilroy, Paul. *Against Race: Imaging Political Culture Beyond the Color Line.* Cambridge, Mass.: The Belknap Press of Harvard University Press, 2000. A controversial argument that focusing on racism as a social issue ironically reinforces a continuation of racist attitudes.

Katz, Irwin. *Stigma: A Social Psychological Analysis.* Hillsdale, N.J.: Lawrence Erlbaum, 1981. A slim but path-breaking study which reports on subjects' reactions to both blacks and the physically handicapped, and develops the notion of ambivalence-induced behavior amplification.

Katz, Phyllis A., and Dalmas A. Taylor, eds. *Eliminating Racism: Profiles in Controversy.* New York: Plenum, 1988. Contains an essay by Marilynn Brewer and Norman Miller on the contact hypothesis; several essays on school desegregation; an essay by James L. Jones on three types of racism and possible remedies for each; and a piece by David O. Sears on symbolic racism. Several essays compare and contrast antiblack racism with sexism and with bigotry against Mexican Americans, Japanese Americans, and American Indians. Includes introductory and concluding essays by the editors, chapter references, and author and subject indexes. For the general reader.

Pettigrew, Thomas F. "Prejudice." In *Prejudice,* by Thomas F. Pettigrew, George M. Frederickson, Dale T. Knobel, Nathan Glazer, and Reed Ueda. Cambridge, Mass.: The Belknap Press of Harvard University Press, 1982. Presents a concise and clearly written review of the social psychological literature on prejudice and racism up to 1980.

Steele, Shelby. *The Content of Our Character: A New Vision of Race in America.* New York: HarperCollins, 1990. Steele presents a conservative view of race relations.

Stephan, Walter G., and David Rosenfield. "Racial and Ethnic Stereotypes." In *In the Eye of the Beholder: Contemporary Issues in Stereotyping,* edited by Arthur G. Miller. New York: Praeger, 1982. A good critical review of the social psychological literature on whites' and blacks' stereotyping of each other.

West, Cornell. *Race Matters.* Boston: Beacon Press, 1993. A personalized analysis of the meaning of race in America.

Paul D. Mageli;
updated by Frank A. Salamone

SEE ALSO: Ageism; Attitude formation and change; Groups; Intergroup relations; Prejudice; Prejudice reduction; Race and intelligence; Sexism; Social identity theory.

Radical behaviorism
B. F. Skinner

TYPE OF PSYCHOLOGY: Personality
FIELDS OF STUDY: Behavioral and cognitive models; instrumental conditioning

Radical behaviorism describes the views of B. F. Skinner, an influential figure in American psychology since the 1930's. Skinner argued that most behavior is controlled by its consequences; he invented an apparatus for observing the effects of consequences, advocated a technology of behavior control, and believed that everyday views about the causes of behavior were an obstacle to its true understanding.

KEY CONCEPTS
• contingency of reinforcement
• discriminative stimulus
• experimental analysis of behavior
• mentalism
• operant
• private events
• rule-governed behavior
• shaping

INTRODUCTION

According to B. F. Skinner (1904-1990), the behavior of an organism is a product of current and past environmental consequences and genetic endowment. Since little can be done, at least by psychology, about genetic endowment, Skinner focused on those things that could be changed or controlled: the immediate consequences of behavior. By consequences, Skinner meant the results or effects that a particular behavior (a class of responses, or "operant") produces. There are many ways to open a door, for example, but since each one allows a person to walk to the next room, one would speak of a "door-opening" operant. The consequences not only define the class of responses but also determine how often members of the class are likely to occur in the future. This was termed the Law of Effect by early twentieth century American psychologist Edward L. Thorndike, whose work Skinner refined.

Skinner analyzed behavior by examining the antecedents and consequences which control any specific class of responses in the individual organism.

From this view, he elaborated a psychology that encompassed all aspects of animal and human behavior, including language. By the late 1970's, historians of psychology ranked Skinner's work as the second most significant development in psychology since World War II; the general growth of the field was ranked first. Three journals arose to publish work in the Skinnerian tradition: *Journal of the Experimental Analysis of Behavior, Journal of Applied Behavior Analysis,* and *Behaviorism.* Moreover, an international organization, the Association for Behavior Analysis, was formed, with its own journal.

CONTROLLING VARIABLES

Skinner theorized that there are several kinds of consequences, or effects. Events that follow behavior and produce an increase in the rate or frequency of the behavior are termed reinforcers. In ordinary language, they might be called rewards, but Skinner avoided this expression because he defined reinforcing events in terms of the effects they produced (their rate of occurrence) rather than the alleged feelings they induced (for example, pleasure). To attribute the increase in rate of response produced by reinforcement to feelings of pleasure would be regarded by Skinner as an instance of mentalism—the attribution of behavior to a feeling rather than an event occurring in the environment. Other consequences which follow a behavior produce a decrease in the rate of behavior. These are termed punishers. Skinner strongly objected to the use of punishment as a means to control behavior because it elicited aggression and produced dysfunctional emotional responses such as striking back and crying in a small child. Consequences (reinforcers and punishers) may be presented following a behavior (twenty dollars for building a doghouse, for example, or an electric shock for touching an exposed wire) or taken away (a fine for speeding, the end of a headache by taking aspirin). Consequences may be natural (tomatoes to eat after a season of careful planting and watering) or contrived (receiving a dollar for earning an A on a test).

Reinforcing and punishing consequences are one example of controlling variables. Events that precede behaviors are also controlling variables and determine under what circumstances certain behaviors are likely to appear. Events occurring before a response occurs are called discriminative stimuli because they come to discriminate in favor of a particular piece of behavior. They set the occasion for the behavior and make it more likely to occur. For example, persons trying to control their eating are told to keep away from the kitchen except at meal times. Being in the kitchen makes it more likely that the person will eat something, not simply because that is where the food is kept but also because being in the kitchen is one of the events which has preceded previous eating and therefore makes eating more likely to occur. This is true even when the person does not intend to eat but goes to the kitchen for other reasons. Being in the kitchen raises the probability of eating. It is a discriminative stimulus (any stimulus in the presence of which a response is reinforced) for eating, as are the table, the refrigerator, or a candy bar on the counter. Any event or stimulus which occurs immediately before a response is reinforced becomes reinforced with the response and makes the response more likely to occur again if the discriminative stimulus occurs again. The discriminative stimulus comes to gain some control over the behavior.

DISCRIMINATIVE AND REINFORCING STIMULI

Discriminative stimuli and reinforcing stimuli are the controlling variables Skinner used to analyze behavior. These events constitute a chain of behavior called a contingency of reinforcement. It is a contingency because reinforcement does not occur unless the response is made in the presence of the discriminative stimuli. Contingencies of reinforcement are encountered every day. For example, a soda drink is purchased from a machine. The machine is brightly colored to act as a discriminative stimulus for dropping coins in a slot, which in turn yields a can or bottle of soft drink. The machine comes to control a small portion of a person's behavior. If the machine malfunctions, a person may push the selector button several times repeatedly, perhaps even putting in more coins, and still later, strike the machine. By carefully scheduling how many times an organism must respond before reinforcement occurs, the rate of response can be controlled as is done in slot or video machines, or gambling devices in general. Responses are made several hundred or thousand times for very little reinforcement—a near win or a small payoff. Schedules of reinforcement are another important set of controlling variables which Skinner explored.

Contingencies are relationships among controlling variables. Some of the relationships become abstracted and formulized, that is, put in the form of rules. When behavior is under the control of a rule, it is termed rule-governed behavior, as opposed to contingency-shaped behavior. As a person first learns any skill, much of his or her behavior is rule governed, either through written instructions or by the person's repeating the rule to himself or herself. For example, a novice golfer might review the rules for a good swing, even repeating them aloud. Eventually, though, swing becomes automatic; it seems to become "natural." The verbal discriminative stimuli have shifted to the very subtle and covert stimuli associated with swing without the golfer's thinking about it, and the natural consequences of a successful swing take over.

Operant Chamber Experiments

The operant chamber is a small experimental space or cage that Skinner invented to observe the effects that consequences have on behavior. A food-deprived organism (Skinner first used rats and later switched to pigeons) is placed in the chamber containing a lever that, when depressed, releases a small piece of food into a cup from which the organism eats. The first bar-press response is produced through the process of shaping, or reinforcing approximations to bar pressing (for example, being near the bar, having a paw above the bar, resting a paw on the bar, nearly depressing the bar) until bar pressing is regularly occurring. Once the operant of bar pressing is established, an experimental analysis of the variables which influence it can be done. The schedule of reinforcement can be changed, for example, from one reinforcer for each response to five responses required for each reinforcer. Changes in the rate of response can be observed on a device Skinner invented, a cumulative record, which automatically displays the rate at which the operant is occurring. A discriminative stimulus can be introduced in the form of a small light mounted on the wall of the chamber. If bar presses are reinforced only when the light is turned on, the light will come to have some control over the operant. Turning the light on and off will literally turn bar pressing on and off in a food-deprived rat.

Skinner controlled his own behavior in the same fashion that he had learned to control the behavior of laboratory organisms. He arranged a "writing environment," a desk used only for that purpose; wrote at a set time each day; and would keep careful records of time spent writing. Other examples of self-management may be found in Skinner's novel of his research, *Walden Two* (1948). In this fictionalized account, children learn self-control through a set of exercises that teach ways to tolerate increasing delays of reinforcement.

Behavioral Analysis of Language

Skinner also performed a behavior analysis of language (*Verbal Behavior*, 1957). For example, a behavioral analysis of the word "want," "believe," or "love," an operational definition in Skinner's sense, would be all those circumstances and situations which control the use of the word, that is, the discriminative stimuli for the verbal response. Skinner tried to show in *Verbal Behavior* that speaking and writing could be explained with the same principle he had used to explain animal behavior. Many of Skinner's works, and much of his private notebooks, are taken up with the recording of how words are used. His purpose was to de-mentalize them, to show that what controls their use is some aspect of the environment or some behavioral practice on the part of the verbal community, rather than some internal or mental event. The earliest uses of the word "to know," for example, referred to action, something the individual could do, rather than something he or she possessed or had stored inside the mind.

Understanding Skinner's Contributions

So much has been written about Skinner, some of it misleading or false, that it is important to clarify what he did not do. He did not rear either of his daughters in a "Skinner box." His youngest daughter was reared during her infancy with the aid of an "aircrib," a special enclosed crib Skinner built that allowed control of air temperature and humidity, and in which the infant could sleep and play without the burden of clothes. "Aircribs" were later available commercially. Skinner did not limit his analysis of behavior only to publicly observable events, as did the methodological behaviorists. Part of what made Skinner's behaviorism radical was his insistence that a science of behavior should be able to account for those private events—events to which only the individual has access, such as the pain of a toothache—to which only the individual has access. He described how the community teaches its members to describe covert events such as toothaches and headaches. He did not regard such events as anything other than behavior. That is, he did not give them a special status by calling them "mental events."

Skinner did not argue that reinforcement explains everything. He allowed, especially in his later works, that genetic endowment plays a role in the determination of behavior, as do rules and antecedent events. He did not reject physiological explanations of behavior when actual physiology was involved. He did object to the use of physiological terms in psychological accounts, unless the physiological mechanisms were known. For Skinner, physiology was one subject matter and behavior was another. Finally, he did not ignore complex behavior. Many of his works, particularly *Verbal Behavior* and *The Technology of Teaching* (1968), offered behaviorist analyses of what in other psychologies would be termed cognitive phenomena, such as talking, reading, thinking, problem solving, and remembering.

Skinner made many contributions to twentieth century psychology. Among them was his invention of the operant chamber and its associated methodology. Operant equipment and procedures are employed by animal and human experimental psychologists in laboratories around the world. Most of these psychologists do not adhere to Skinner's radical behaviorism or to all the features of his science of behavior. They have, however, found the techniques that he developed to be productive in exploring a wide variety of problems, ranging from the fields of psychopharmacology to learning in children and adults to experimental economics. Skinner and his followers developed a technology of behavior that included techniques for working with the developmentally disabled, children in elementary classrooms, and persons with rehabilitation or health care problems; they also considered approaches to public safety, employee motivation and production, and any other field which involved the management of behavior. Although the technology developments never reached the vision described in *Walden Two*, the efforts are ongoing.

Skinner may have exhausted the Law of Effect. The idea that consequences influence behavior can be found in many forms in the literature of psychology and philosophy, especially since the middle of the nineteenth century, but it is only in the

work of B. F. Skinner that one sees how much of human and animal behavior can be brought within its purview. Because Skinner took behavior as his subject matter, he greatly expanded what could be regarded as being of interest to psychologists. Behavior was everywhere, in the classroom, at the office, in the factory. Nearly any aspect of human activity could become the legitimate object of study by a Skinnerian psychologist, a point well illustrated in Skinner's description of a utopian community which takes an experimental attitude toward its cultural practices and designs a culture based on a science of behavior (*Walden Two*). Finally, Skinner conceptualized an epistemology, a way of understanding what it means for humans to know something, that may be a lasting contribution to twentieth century philosophy.

RELATIONSHIP WITH DARWINISM AND PRAGMATISM

In placing the radical behaviorism of B. F. Skinner in historical context, two nineteenth century doctrines are often invoked. One view, shared by Skinner, is that operant psychology represents an extension of the principle of natural selection which Charles Darwin described at the level of the species. Natural selection explained the origin of species; contingencies of reinforcement and punishment explain the origin of classes of responses. The environment selects in both cases. In operant psychology, the role of the environment is to reinforce differentially and thereby select from among a pool of responses which the organism is making. The final effect is some one particular operant which has survival or adaptive value for the individual organism. Skinner has suggested that cultural evolution occurs in a similar fashion.

It is also observed that Skinner's psychology resembles nineteenth century pragmatism. The pragmatists held that beliefs are formed by their outcome, or practical effect. To explain why someone does something by reference to a belief would be regarded as mentalism by Skinner; he would substitute behavior for beliefs. Yet he comes to the same doctrine: one in which environmental consequences act in a Darwinian fashion. Finally, Skinner's philosophy shows the influence of the nineteenth century positivism of physicist Ernst Mach. Skinner desired a description of behavior and its causes, while avoiding mental states or other cognitive or personality entities that intervene between behavior and the environment.

SOURCES FOR FURTHER STUDY

Kazdin, Alan E. *Behavior Modification in Applied Settings.* 6th ed. Belmont, Calif.: Wadsworth, 2000. An introduction to behavior modification that can be understood by the high school or college student. Operant techniques are clearly described, with the emphasis on how they are applied in a wide range of settings. Excellent discussion of recent developments in the field.

Modgil, Sohan, and Celia Modgil, eds. *B. F. Skinner: Consensus and Controversy.* New York: Falmer Press, 1987. A collection of essays by psychologists and philosophers. Each topic has a pro and contrary opinion, with replies and rebuttals. Although written at a professional level, this is an excellent volume for a global view of Skinner's ideas and for the clearest understanding of what is "radical" about Skinner's behaviorism.

O'Donoghue, William, and Kyle Ferguson. *The Psychology of B. F. Skinner.* Thousand Oaks, Calif.: Sage Publications, 2001. An attempt to clarify Skinner's psychology through discussion of his life, contributions to psychology, and philosophy of science.

Skinner, B. F. *About Behaviorism.* New York: Alfred A. Knopf, 1974. In this work, Skinner argues for his radical behaviorism by contrasting it with methodological behaviorism and by illustrating how it treats topics such as perception, memory, verbal behavior, private events, and thinking.

_____. *Particulars of My Life.* New York: Alfred A. Knopf, 1976.

_____. *The Shaping of a Behaviorist.* New York: Alfred A. Knopf, 1979.

_____. *A Matter of Consequences.* New York: Alfred A. Knopf, 1983. Skinner published his autobiography in these three separate volumes. The first describes his life from birth, through his college years as an English major, to his entering Harvard University for graduate study in psychology. *The Shaping of a Behaviorist* presents his years at Harvard and his rise to national prominence. *A Matter of Consequences* begins with his return to Harvard as a professor in the late 1940's.

_____. *Science and Human Behavior.* New York: Macmillan, 1953. A fine introduction to Skinner's thought. The principles of operant psychol-

ogy are described, with numerous examples of the applicability to an individual's life and the major institutions of society. The chapter on private events illustrates one important way in which Skinner's radical behaviorism differs from methodological behaviorism.

_____. *Walden Two.* New York: Macmillan, 1948. A description of a fictional community based upon experimental practices and behavioral principles. The book was the source of inspiration for several communes and illustrates how all aspects of culture can be submitted to a behavioral analysis. Contains a lengthy criticism of democracy as a form of government.

Vargas, Julie S. "B. F. Skinner, Father, Grandfather, Behavior Modifier." In *About Human Nature: Journeys in Psychological Thought,* edited by Terry J. Knapp and Charles T. Rasmussen. Dubuque, Iowa: Kendall/Hunt, 1987. An intimate description of Skinner by his eldest daughter, who is herself a psychologist. Skinner's home, study, and the activities occurring over a Thanksgiving weekend are described.

Terry J. Knapp

SEE ALSO: Behavioral family therapy; Behaviorism; Cognitive behavior therapy; Conditioning; Learning; Operant conditioning therapies; Rule-governed behavior; Skinner, B. F.

Rape and sexual assault

TYPE OF PSYCHOLOGY: Psychopathology
FIELDS OF STUDY: Sexual disorders

The study of rape and sexual assault examines the relationship of sexually disordered persons and nonconsensual sexual activity with others. Rape is an assaultive behavior of one person upon another, where the assault involves sexual activity and the behavior involves one person fulfilling sexual desires by using a nonconsenting person.

KEY CONCEPTS
- rape
- rapist profiles
- sexual paraphilias
- stalking behavior

INTRODUCTION

Sexual assault is the threat or actual act of sexual physical endangerment of a nonconsensual person or legally defined minor child, regardless of consent. Rape is forced sexual intercourse upon a nonconsensual person or legally defined minor child, regardless of consent. Definitions of rape and sexual assault are further delineated by states' criminal codes. The *Crime Classification Manual* (1992) notes that "Definitions of what constitutes rape and sexual assault vary from state to state, resulting in marked differences in the reported frequencies of offense and behavior categories in different samples reported in the literature."

The United States Department of Justice reported in the Uniform Crime Report that 89,107 attempted or completed forcible rapes were reported to law enforcement agencies in 1999. This figure represents a victim ratio of 32 persons in every 100,000. However, it is significant to note that rape and sexual assault are the most underreported of the index crimes. Aggravated assault, robbery, and murder are commonly reported at near incidence level, but sex-related crimes are often not reported or are charged inaccurately.

Persons married or cohabiting may be victims of forced sexual activity but do not report the behavior of their partner, or if they do report the behavior, it is commonly considered domestic violence and the formal legal charge is reduced to simple assault and does not represent the true, sexual nature of the assault. The question as to whether a husband can rape his wife has been debated in many courtrooms. The cross-examination of the victim is often a humiliating experience, and consequently many victims choose not to press charges against the offender. Many women choose not to report forcible intercourse if they had previously been a consensual partner with the offender. It is also common that while children who are sexually molested by a parent are removed from the home under an order of child abuse, the offending parent is not charged with rape or sexual assault.

SEXUAL PARAPHILIAS

The American Psychiatric Association's *Diagnostic and Statistical Manual of Mental Disorders: DSM-IV-TR* (rev. 4th ed., 2000) recognizes a group of disorders known as sexual paraphilias. The essential features of a paraphilia are recurrent, intense, sexually arous-

ing fantasies, sexual urges, or behaviors, generally involving nonhuman objects or the suffering or humiliation of oneself or one's partner or children or other nonconsenting persons, that occur over a period of at least six months. For some individuals, paraphiliac fantasies or stimuli are obligatory for erotic arousal and are always included in the sexual activity.

It is significant to note that not all sexual paraphilias result in sexual assault or rape, and it is the preference of the individuals afflicted with these disorders to identify consensual adult partners. It is also significant to note that with the exception of sexual masochism, the sexual paraphilias are male-exclusive disorders. However, some of the paraphilias are specific to nonconsensual parties and children. Children, because of their age, by law cannot consent to sexual activity. There are half a dozen paraphilias that are commonly associated with nonconsensual partners.

EXHIBITIONISM. The DSM-IV-TR defines exhibitionism as "behaviors involving the exposure of one's genitals to an unsuspecting stranger." The nature of this paraphilia requires a nonconsensual relationship with a stranger; consequently, it must be considered a form of sexual assault.

FROTTEURISM. The DSM-IV-TR defines frotteurism as "touching and rubbing against a nonconsensual person." A frotteur (usually a man) rubs his genitals against his victim, often in a crowded public place, or fondles his victim. Like exhibitionism, the nature of this paraphilia requires a nonconsensual victim, and consequently must be considered a sexual assault.

VOYEURISM. The DSM-IV-TR defines voyeurism as "the act of observing unsuspecting individuals, usually strangers, who are naked, in the process of disrobing, or engaging in sexual activity." A voyeur (usually a man) is sexually excited by looking ("peeping"), sometimes masturbating to orgasm either in the process of peeping or later, while retrospectively reviewing what he has seen, but he does not seek actual sexual contact with his victims. As in the previous paraphilias, the nature of voyeurism requires a nonconsenting person, and consequently is considered a sexual assault.

PEDOPHILIA. The DSM-IV-TR defines pedophilia as "recurrent, intense sexually arousing fantasies, sexual urges, or behaviors involving sexual activity with a prepubescent child or children (generally age thirteen years or younger)." Pedophiliac behav-

A high school student fights off a police officer during a simulated attack as part of a RAD (rape, aggression, defense) class. Defense skills can increase a woman's confidence and may protect her from becoming the victim of a sexual assault. (AP/Wide World Photos)

ior is prohibited by law. State statutes define the minimum age at which a person may consent to sexual relations. Pedophilia is by definition a violation of law and consequently is a sexual assault.

SEXUAL SADISM. The DSM-IV-TR defines sexual sadism as "recurrent, intense, sexually arousing fantasies, sexual urges, or behaviors involving acts (real, not simulated) in which the psychological or physical suffering (including humiliation) of the victim is sexually exciting to the person." Persons afflicted with this sexual paraphilia are continuously looking for a consensual partner. The practice of sexual sadism is commonly comorbid with sexual masochism. The DSM-IV-TR defines sexual masochism as "recurrent, intense, sexually arousing fantasies, sexual urges, or behaviors involving the act (real, not simulated) of being humiliated, beaten, bound, or otherwise made to suffer."

Persons suffering from one or both of these sexual paraphilias frequent bars and social clubs where similarly afflicted persons congregate. They are able to establish consensual relationships and mutually satisfy their sexual urges. In the absence of a consensual partner, or when a masochistic party refuses to proceed as far as the sadist desires, the sadist will force compliance and a sexual assault takes place. Sexual assaults that occur because the masochist refuses to continue to participate are rarely reported. When there are no consensual partners available and the sadist is experiencing intense sexual arousal, he may forcibly rape a nonconsensual and stranger party.

RAPE

The concept of rape has a historical and common definition of a man forcing a nonconsenting woman to engage in sexual intercourse. The definition is no longer contemporary. Men and women engage in sexual intercourse with children under the legal age of consent and consequently meet the statutory definition of rape. Men and women also engage in same-sex relationships that may result in behaviors that may be, in fact, forcible sexual assault, or may be rape as defined by statute. Some hate-motivated crimes involve rape and sodomy. Consequently, the entire legal and philosophical concept of rape must be viewed from an expanded, inclusive definition.

The *Crime Classification Manual* includes a taxonomy of rape and sexual assault that includes numerous categories: criminal enterprise rape, felony rape, personal cause sexual assault, nuisance offenses, domestic sexual assault, entitlement rape, social acquaintance rape, subordinate rape, power-reassurance rape, exploitative rape, anger rape, sadistic rape, child/adolescent pornography, historical child/adolescent sex rings, multidimensional sex rings, abduction rape, formal gang sexual assault, and informal gang sexual assault. The manual also classifies rapists based upon motivations.

The taxonomic studies that describe the styles of convicted rapists focus on the interaction of sexual and aggressive motivations. Although all rape clearly includes both motivations, for some rapists the need to humiliate and injure through aggression is the most salient feature of the offense, whereas for others the need to achieve sexual dominance is the most salient feature of the offense. John Douglas and Robert Ressler, both retired Federal Bureau of Investigation (FBI) agents who were the initial founders of the FBI's Behavioral Sciences Unit, identified four primary subcategories of rapists.

POWER-REASSURANCE RAPIST. Also referred to as a compensatory rapist, this individual is commonly afflicted with one or more of the sexual paraphilias and these paraphilias are clearly demonstrated in the method in which the rape is preformed. These rapists are preoccupied with their particular sexual fantasies and commonly have a vision of their "perfect" victim. They are highly sexually aroused as they attempt to locate their "perfect" victim and may demonstrate voyeurism, exhibitionism, masturbation practices, and pedophilia. They are delusional, believing that their victim truly loves them in return. These individuals commonly cannot achieve and maintain normal, age-appropriate heterosexual or homosexual relationships, and compensate for their personal perception of inadequacy by stalking and assaulting a younger or older, and weaker, victim.

EXPLOITATIVE RAPIST. The exploitative rapist, also referred to as an impulsive rapist, commits the crime of rape as an afterthought while committing another crime. These rapes generally occur when a victim is found at the site of a burglary or armed robbery. There is no premeditation in this rape and the motivation is purely coincidental to the original intended criminal activity. It is not uncommon for persons to take hostages during an armed robbery or car-jacking and then impulsively rape the hostage.

ANGER RAPIST. The anger rapist, also referred to a displaced aggressive rapist, commits sexual assault because he is angry. He is commonly not angry at his victims, because they are usually strangers. Rather, the displaced aggressive rapist is angry at his boss, his wife, or just a set of circumstances. Unable to take out his anger at the source, he displaces his anger upon his victim. The rape is characterized by very violent behavior and the victim is commonly severely injured and may be killed.

SADISTIC RAPIST. The sadistic rapist, also referred to as a sexually aggressive rapist, possesses the sexual sadism paraphilia and cannot achieve sexual arousal or satisfaction unless he is inflicting pain on his victim. The rapist believes that his victim likes his or her sex rough, and consequently will demonstrate a variety of torturous behaviors during the rape. While the rape is violent, it does differ from the rape by the displaced aggression rapist. The sexually aggressive rapist will demonstrate behaviors that have sexual overtones, while the displaced aggressive rapist will demonstrate unrestrained violence, more violence than is necessary to subdue his victim.

OTHER RAPIST CLASSIFICATIONS. Other classifications of rapists include gang rapists motivated by retaliation, intimidation, or adolescent-like impulsivity. Persons who utilize rape drugs to incapacitate their victims are generally compensating for their inability to achieve normal sexual relations and are commonly personality disordered.

SOURCES FOR FURTHER STUDY

American Psychiatric Association. *Diagnostic and Statistical Manual of Mental Disorders: DSM-IV-TR*. Rev. 4th ed. Washington, D.C.: Author, 2000. The DSM-IV-TR is the most comprehensive and contemporary description of mental health, personality, and sexual disorders.

Bartol, Curt. *Criminal Behavior: A Psychosocial Approach*. Upper Saddle River, N.J.: Prentice Hall, 2002. The author summarizes the theories and practical aspects of sexual assault and rape.

Dobbert, Duane, ed. *Forensic Psychology.* Columbus, Ohio: McGraw Hill Primus, 1996. The editor compiles significant contributions from distinguished authors on a variety of topics pertaining to forensic psychology.

Douglas, John E., Ann W. Burgess, Allen G. Burgess, and Robert K. Ressler. *Crime Classification Manual.* San Francisco: Jossey-Bass, 1992. The most comprehensive taxonomy of criminal behavior.

Goode, Erich. *Deviant Behavior.* Upper Saddle River, N.J.: Prentice Hall, 1997. The author provides an excellent description of a variety of deviant behavior.

Duane L. Dobbert

SEE ALSO: Battered woman syndrome; Domestic violence; Juvenile delinquency; Law and psychology; Sexual variants and paraphilias; Violence by children and teenagers; Violence and sexuality in the media.

Rational-emotive therapy

TYPE OF PSYCHOLOGY: Psychotherapy
FIELDS OF STUDY: Cognitive therapies

Developed by psychologist Albert Ellis, rational-emotive therapy aims to minimize the client's self-defeating cognitive style by helping the client acquire a more rational and logical philosophy of life. It has been successfully applied to marital couples, family members, individual patients, and group clients across a host of psychological difficulties, including alcoholism, depression, anxiety disorders, and sexual dissatisfaction.

KEY CONCEPTS
- A-B-C theory of personality
- irrational beliefs
- long-range hedonism
- rational-emotive treatment
- scientific thinking

INTRODUCTION

Rational-emotive therapy (RET) was founded in 1955 by Albert Ellis following his disappointment

with traditional methods of psychoanalysis. From 1947 to 1953, Ellis had practiced classical analysis and analytically oriented psychotherapy, but he came to the conclusion that psychoanalysis was a superficial and unscientific form of treatment. Specifically, rational-emotive therapy was developed as a combined humanistic, cognitive, and behavioral form of therapy. Although Ellis initially used RET primarily in individual formats, group and workshop formats followed quickly. Ellis published approximately fifty books and more than five hundred articles on RET, and he presented more than fifteen hundred public workshops.

According to Ellis (in 1989), the philosophical origins of rational-emotive therapy include the Stoic philosophers Epictetus and Marcus Aurelius. In particular, Epictetus wrote that "people are disturbed not by things, but by the view which they take of them" during the first century C.E. in *The Encheiridion.* Ellis also gives much credit for the development of rational-emotive therapy to the theory of human disturbance highlighted by psychotherapist Alfred Adler. Specifically, Ellis was persuaded by Adler's conviction that a person's behavior originates from his or her ideas. As Ellis began writing about and describing RET in the 1950's and 1960's, clinical behavior therapy was conceptually distinct and distant from Ellis's ideas. The primary similarity was that Ellis employed a host of behavioral techniques in his approach.

As time passed, however, behavior therapy engaged in a controversial yet productive broadening of what was meant by "behavior" and started to include cognition as a form of behavior that could be learned, modified, and studied. Ellis's RET approach shares many similarities with other common cognitive-behavioral approaches to treatment. These include Donald Meichenbaum's cognitive-behavioral modification (focusing on self-instructional processes and adaptive coping statements), Maxie C. Maultsby, Jr.'s, rational behavior therapy (which is essentially RET with some adaptations, including written self-analysis techniques and rational-emotive imagery), and Aaron T. Beck's cognitive therapy. Cognitive therapy has many similarities to RET but was developed independently; it uses fewer "hardheaded approaches." For example, Beck advocates the use of collaborative empiricism and a focus on automatic thoughts and underlying cognitive schemas. RET strongly emphasizes irrational beliefs (unreasonable evaluations that sabotage an individual's goals and lead to increased likelihood of experiencing needless pain, suffering, and displeasure), especially "unconditional shoulds" and "absolutistic musts," as the root of emotional and behavioral disturbances.

PRINCIPAL PROPOSITIONS

There are six principal propositions of rational-emotive therapy as Ellis described them in 1989. First, people are born with rational and irrational tendencies. That is, individuals may be either self-helping or self-defeating, short-range hedonists or long-range hedonists; they may learn by mistakes or repeat the same mistakes, and they may actualize or avoid actualizing their potentials for growth. Second, cultural and family experiences may exacerbate irrational thinking. Third, individuals may seem to think, act, and feel simultaneously. Thinking, however, appears actually to precede actions and feelings. For example, the process of "appraising" a situation usually triggers feelings.

Fourth, RET therapists differ from person-centered therapists in that RET practitioners do not believe that a warm interpersonal relationship between therapist and patient is a sufficient or even necessary condition for effective change. RET therapists also do not believe that personal warmth is necessary in order to accept clients fully. In fact, it is important in RET treatment to criticize and point out the deficiencies in a person's behavior and thinking style. Moreover, Ellis argues that RET therapists often need to use "hard-headed methods" to convince clients to employ more self-discipline.

Fifth, rational-emotive therapists use a variety of strategies, including assertiveness training, desensitization, operant conditioning, support, and role-playing. The usual goal of RET is to help rid clients of symptoms and modify underlying thinking styles that create symptoms. Ellis further identifies two basic forms of RET: general RET, which is similar to other forms of cognitive behavior therapy; and preferential RET, which includes general RET but also emphasizes philosophic restructuring and teaches clients how to dispute irrational thoughts and inappropriate behaviors via rules of logic and the scientific method. Sixth, all emotional problems are caused by people's tendencies to interpret events unrealistically and are maintained by irrational beliefs about them.

CONNECTIONS WITH IRRATIONALITY

Thus, the basic underlying tenet of RET is that emotional disturbances are primarily the result of irrational thinking. Specifically, RET argues that people upset themselves with "evaluative irrational beliefs" (rather than with "nonevaluative" irrational beliefs). For example, in an essay published in 1987, Ellis described the following scenario:

> If you devoutly believe that your fairy godmother looks out for you and is always ready to help you, you may live happily and undistressedly with this highly questionable and unrealistic belief. But if you evaluate your fairy godmother's help as extremely desirable and go even further to insist that *because* it is desirable, you absolutely *must* at all times have her help, you will almost certainly make yourself anxious (whenever you realize that her magical help that you *must* have may actually be absent) and you will tend to make yourself extremely depressed (when you see that in your hour of need this help does not actually materialize).

Although many forms of irrationality exist, rational-emotive therapy focuses on a client's strong "desires" and "commands." Ellis has developed various lists of irrational beliefs that highlight the most common thinking difficulties of patients. These include such beliefs as "I must do well or very well"; "I am a bad or worthless person when I act weakly or stupidly"; "I need to be loved by someone who matters to me a lot"; "People must treat me fairly and give me what I need"; "People must live up to my expectations or it is terrible"; "My life must have few major hassles"; and "I can't stand it when life is unfair."

Ellis has refined his ideas about irrational thoughts to three primary beliefs. These are: "I *must* do well and be approved by *significant* others, and if I don't do as well as I *should* or *must*, there is something really rotten about me. It is terrible that I am this way and I am a pretty worthless, rotten person"; "You (other humans with whom I relate, my original family, my later family that I may have, my friends, relatives, and people with whom I work) *must, ought,* and *should* treat me considerately and fairly and even *specially* (considering what a doll I am)!"; and "Conditions under which I live—my environment, social conditions, economic conditions, political conditions—must be arranged so that I easily and immediately, with no real effort, have a free lunch and get what I command." In summary, Ellis defines the three primary irrationalities as "I *must* do well;

you *must* treat me beautifully; the world *must* be easy."

ORIGIN OF IRRATIONAL BELIEFS AND ACTIONS

Psychological disturbances are based on irrational thinking and behaving. The origin of irrational beliefs and actions stems from childhood. Irrational beliefs are shaped in part by significant others (parents, relatives, and teachers), as well as from misperceptions on the part of children (such as superstitions and over-interpretation). Rational-emotive therapy also maintains that individuals have tendencies, which are both biologically and environmentally determined, for growth and actualization of their potential. On the other hand, Ellis argues that people also have powerful innate tendencies to condemn themselves, others, and the world when they do not get what they "childishly need." This pattern of self-sabotage is argued by Ellis to be both inborn and acquired during childhood. Moreover, via repetitive self-talk and self-evaluative tendencies, false beliefs are continually reindoctrinated by the individual. From the RET perspective, self-blame and self-condemnation are the cornerstones of most emotional disturbances. By challenging self-blame and self-condemnation, via an analysis and refutation of irrational beliefs, a client can be helped.

ASSESSING MENTAL HEALTH

Ellis defines mental health as incorporating self-interest, social interests, self-direction, tolerance, acceptance of ambiguity and uncertainty, scientific thinking, commitment, risk taking, self-acceptance, long-range hedonism (the idea that well-adjusted people seek happiness and avoid pain today, tomorrow, and in the future), nonperfectionism, and self-responsibility for one's emotional disturbances. Three primary processes seem to be associated with mental functioning and mental disorders: self-talking, self-evaluating, and self-condemning. That is, individuals are constantly engaged in an internal dialogue (self-talk) with themselves, appraising and commenting upon events that occur in their lives. Individuals also are self-evaluating in that humans seek meaning and constantly evaluate events and themselves, frequently placing blame on themselves for events. Self-evaluating is thus often associated with self-condemnation. As Ellis pointed out in an essay published in 1989, this condemnation may start in response to evaluating oneself as doing poorly at work or in school, which in turn leads to feeling guilty. This vicious cycle then leads to condemning oneself for condemning oneself, condemning oneself for not being able to stop condemning oneself, and finally condemning oneself for entering psychotherapy and not getting better.

Emotional and behavioral difficulties often occur when simple preferences are chosen above thoughtful decisions. Ellis believes that individuals have inborn growth and actualization tendencies, although they may become sabotaged through self-defeating and self-condemning patterns. Based on the RET model, clients benefit from exposure to three primary insights. Insight number one is that a person's self-defeating behavior is related to antecedent and understandable causes. Specifically, an individual's beliefs are more important in understanding emotional upset than are past or present activating events. Insight two is that individuals actually make themselves emotionally disturbed by reindoctrinating themselves with irrational and unproductive kinds of beliefs. Insight three is that through hard work and practice, irrational beliefs can be corrected.

TREATMENT STEPS

As detailed by Gerald Corey in 1986, practitioners of rational-emotive therapy actively teach, persuade, and direct clients to alter irrational styles of thinking and behaving. RET can be defined as a process of reeducation in which clients learn to think differently and solve problems. The first step in treatment often focuses on distinguishing rational (or reasonable) thoughts from irrational (or unreasonable) beliefs. Educational approaches are employed to highlight for the client that he or she has acquired many irrational "shoulds, oughts, and musts." The second step in treatment emphasizes an awareness of how psychological disturbances are maintained through a client's repeated reindoctrination of illogical and unreasonable beliefs. During the third phase of treatment, therapists assist clients in modifying maladaptive thinking styles and abandoning irrational beliefs. Via a variety of cognitive, emotive, and behavioral approaches, self-condemnation and self-blame are replaced with more rational and logical views. Finally, the fourth step in RET involves developing a rational lifestyle and philosophy. Specifically, from internalizing rules of logic and scientific thinking, individuals may prevent future psychological disturbances and live more productive lives.

A-B-C Theories

The A-B-C theory of personality and the A-B-C (D-E) theory of emotional change are also central to RET approaches. "A" refers to an activating event. Activating events can include facts, events, behaviors, or perceived stimuli. "B" refers to beliefs triggered by the event or beliefs about the event. "C" refers to the consequential emotional (behavioral or cognitive) outcomes that proceed directly from beliefs. "D" is the application of methods to dispute or challenge irrational beliefs, and "E" refers to the effect of disputing beliefs on the emotional (behavioral or cognitive) reaction of the client.

Activating events are generally regarded as inherently neutral, and they have no particular emotional meaning in and of themselves. Thus, activating events do not directly cause emotions. Instead, beliefs about events primarily cause emotional reactions. For example, a woman who had been depressed for more than twelve months following the death of her husband from terminal cancer was participating in a hospice therapy group and had demonstrated little or no improvement over the last year. She reasoned that because her husband was dead, she would never feel happy again (nor "should" she feel happy again, since he was dead and she was "not entitled" to experience pleasure without him). She added, "He was the center of my life and I can never expect to feel happiness without him." Her resulting emotional reaction was severe depression, which accompanied her complicated grief and underlying anger.

In an effort to uncover and dispute her unreasonable beliefs, a variety of strategies were employed. First, group members provided feedback about her reasonable and unreasonable ideas following (and during) her husband's death. In particular, group members pointed out that she could expect to experience happiness again in her life since she had experienced pleasure on many occasions before she met her husband, while her husband was away during military service, and while they were married and she enjoyed activities in which he did not share. Next, her emotional reaction was examined and viewed as being caused not by her husband's death, but instead by the manner in which

she interpreted his death (as awful), her own ability to cope and change (as limited), and her future (as hopeless). A variety of behavioral and cognitive strategies were employed to challenge her irrational and self-condemning assumptions. Behavioral homework assignments included increasing activity levels and engaging in pleasurable activities to challenge the notion that she could never experience happiness again. Self-confidence and hope were fostered via strategies which highlighted her ability to cope with stress. This client also found cognitive homework assignments, wherein she listed her irrational beliefs on a daily log and then disputed those beliefs or replaced or modified them with more reasonable statements, to be helpful.

Limitations

Rational-emotive therapy and its various techniques have been evaluated in at least two hundred studies. Although many of these studies have been associated with various methodological flaws, the effectiveness of RET with a broad range of psychological disturbances is impressive. At the Evolution of Psychotherapy Conference in Phoenix, Arizona, in 1985, Ellis himself identified several limitations of RET (and other therapies). These included several key "irrationalities." Because individuals falsely believe that they are unchangeable, they fail to work to change themselves. Because individuals falsely believe that activating events cause emotional reactions, they blame the activating events and fail to change their beliefs about them. Individuals falsely believe that unpleasant emotional reactions must be good or useful and should be cherished instead of minimized. Individuals are often confused about emotional reactions (for example, concern and caution versus anxiety and panic) and experience difficulty surrendering the inappropriate negative feelings. Because some RET techniques require subtle and discriminative styles of thinking by clients, some clients are not capable of succeeding in therapy. RET is not particularly useful for young children or developmentally delayed individuals (typically RET requires a chronological age of at least eight years and average intelligence).

Criticisms

Albert Ellis is regarded by many psychologists as the most prominent theorist in the cognitive-behavioral school of psychotherapy. His insight and conceptualizations are evident in many of the various cognitive-behavioral psychotherapeutic approaches. Specifically, the A-B-C theory of personality is well regarded among cognitive behavioral therapists, and many of Ellis's treatment strategies are frequently used by clinicians across other schools of psychotherapy. On the other hand, Ellis's interpersonal style in treatment has been criticized by many authors. Specifically, a warm, confiding relationship between therapist and client is often deemphasized in Ellis's writings, and confrontational interactions may be commonly observed in videotapes of rational-emotive therapy. It also appears, however, that more attention is being paid to the quality of the interpersonal relationship between RET practitioner and client. Moreover, the strengths of the RET approach are not based on the style of any particular therapist, but instead are evident in its underlying theory and therapeutic strategies.

Undoubtedly, the influence of rational-emotive therapy in the field of psychotherapy will continue to be prominent. Ellis has written extensively on the application of RET principles to diverse psychological disturbances. The Institute for Rational-Emotive Therapy in New York continues to train hundreds of therapists and serves as a distribution center for most of the books and pamphlets developed by RET therapists.

SOURCES FOR FURTHER STUDY

Corey, Gerald. *Theory and Practice of Counseling and Psychotherapy*. 6th ed. Belmont, Calif.: Wadsworth, 2000. Corey reviews many of the primary schools of psychotherapy and specifically highlights the key concepts, therapeutic techniques, and research associated with RET. Also provides a brief critique of RET.

Ellis, Albert. *Better, Deeper, and More Enduring Brief Therapy: The Rational Emotive Behavior Therapy Approach*. New York: Brunner/Mazel, 1995. An overview of RET and description of its applications to group, marital and family, sex, and other specialized forms of therapy.

_____. *Overcoming Destructive Beliefs, Feelings, and Behaviors: New Directions for Rational Emotive Behavior Therapy*. Buffalo, N.Y.: Prometheus, 2001. A restatement of RET principles for the twenty-first century, with emphasis on the use of verbs (emphasizing action and change) rather than nouns in discussing problems.

Ellis, Albert, and Robert A. Harper. *A New Guide to Rational Living*. 3d rev. ed. North Hollywood, Calif.: Wilshire Book, 1998. A self-help book emphasizing RET approaches. A classic RET book in that therapists have suggested this book for their clients for many years. Presents a clear, straightforward approach to RET.

Gregory L. Wilson

SEE ALSO: Behavior therapy; Cognitive behavior therapy; Cognitive therapy; Couples therapy; Depression; Ellis, Albert; Group therapy; Person-centered therapy; Psychotherapy: Effectiveness; Psychotherapy: Goals and techniques; Self-actualization; Strategic family therapy.

Reactive attachment disorder

TYPE OF PSYCHOLOGY: Developmental psychology; psychopathology

FIELDS OF STUDY: Biology of stress; childhood and adolescent disorders; cognitive development; infancy and childhood

Reactive attachment disorder (RAD) is the most recent variant of a general condition of impoverished psychosocial and physical development found in infants and children deprived of appropriate caretaking. The symptoms of RAD are believed to remit in an improved environment with a responsive caregiver.

KEY CONCEPTS
- attachment theory
- attachment therapy
- developmental delays
- failure to thrive
- hospitalism
- psychosocial development

INTRODUCTION

Since the 1940's, a substantial body of literature has documented the adverse effects of deprivation and institutionalization on infants and young children. Physical, cognitive, and social developmental delays are often present in such children. In a classic study published in 1945, Rene Spitz examined a group of children in an orphanage and compared them with children reared in a more attentive foster home setting. His results revealed slowed physical, motor, and intellectual development and high mortality in the orphanage group compared with essentially normal development in the comparison children. A variety of terms have been used to describe the diverse clinical features of this condition, including failure to thrive, psychosocial dwarfism, maternal deprivation, anaclitic depression, and, most recently, reactive attachment disorder (RAD). This plethora of different terms probably reflects a deeper confusion regarding this syndrome's symptom picture and etiology.

DESCRIPTION

RAD was first included in the third edition of the *Diagnostic and Statistical Manual of Mental Disorders* (DSM-III), published in 1980. In subsequent editions, the criteria were altered to reflect an emphasis on psychosocial maladjustment rather than on disrupted physical development. The revised fourth edition, DSM-IV-TR (2000), describes the cardinal feature of RAD as disturbed and developmentally inappropriate social relations produced by persistent neglect or abuse on the part of the child's caregiver. There are two distinct manifestations of RAD, the "inhibited" and the "disinhibited" subtypes. Inhibited children are withdrawn and fail to initiate social relations. Disinhibited children are characterized by indiscriminate sociability and a lack of selectivity in seeking out attachment figures. The inhibited subtype is more common, although trustworthy estimates of the prevalence of RAD are difficult to come by. Nevertheless, there appears to be little evidence demonstrating that these two subtypes are manifestations of the same underlying condition. Some researchers estimate that RAD occurs in approximately 1 percent of the population, while DSM-IV-TR states only that it is "very uncommon."

The onset of RAD occurs before five years of age. Prior editions of the DSM required that RAD emerge before six months, but this criterion was altered in response to researchers' objections that selective attachments are not formed at such an early age. Nevertheless, the current criteria still allow clinicians to diagnose infants with RAD if they see fit.

Associated features of RAD include the physical signs of an impoverished rearing environment, such

---

DSM-IV-TR Criteria for Reactive Attachment Disorder

REACTIVE ATTACHMENT DISORDER OF INFANCY OR EARLY CHILDHOOD (DSM CODE 313.89)

Markedly disturbed and developmentally inappropriate social relatedness in most contexts, beginning before age five

Evidenced by either inhibition or disinhibition

INHIBITIONS

- Persistent failure to initiate or respond in a developmentally appropriate fashion to most social interactions
- Manifested by excessively inhibited, hypervigilant, or highly ambivalent and contradictory responses (for example, responding to caregivers with a mixture of approach, avoidance, and resistance to comforting, or exhibiting frozen watchfulness)

DISINHIBITIONS

- Diffuse attachments
- Manifested by indiscriminate sociability with marked inability to exhibit appropriate selective attachments (for example, excessive familiarity with relative strangers or lack of selectivity in choice of attachment figures)
- Disturbances not accounted for solely by developmental delay (as in mental retardation) and do not meet criteria for a pervasive developmental disorder

Pathogenic care as evidenced by at least one of the following:

- persistent disregard of the child's basic emotional needs for comfort, stimulation, and affection
- persistent disregard of the child's basic physical needs
- repeated changes of primary caregiver, preventing formation of stable attachments (such as frequent changes in foster care)

Presumption exists that pathogenic care is responsible for the disturbed behavior

Types: Inhibited Type (inhibitive behavior predominates) or Disinhibited Type (disinhibited behavior predominates)

as developmental delays, feeding disorders, growth delays (that is, failure to thrive), physical abuse, and malnutrition. With the provision of a supportive environment and adequate caretaking for the child, the behavioral difficulties associated with RAD should ostensibly remit.

Other disorders that emerge in childhood can be difficult to distinguish from RAD. Children with RAD may manifest subnormal intellectual functioning comparable to mental retardation, but RAD can be differentiated by the improvement that typically occurs with an enriched environment. Autistic children often exhibit impaired communication and repetitive patterns of movement, but RAD children are much more socially oriented. One must also distinguish the socially indiscriminate disinhibited type of RAD from the often impulsive behavior of attention-deficit hyperactivity disorder (ADHD, known earlier as childhood hyperactivity). Although adverse environmental conditions and pathogenic relationships in childhood may increase the risk for later antisocial behavior, no direct etiological links have been established between these behaviors and the characteristics of RAD.

CONTROVERSIES

Controversies abound concerning the conceptualization, diagnosis, and treatment of RAD. Foremost is the striking paucity of evidence for the validity of this diagnosis. For example, there is little controlled research examining the family history, course, and outcome, biological correlates, or laboratory performance of children with RAD. Such validity research will be essential to justify the continued inclusion of RAD in the diagnostic system.

With respect to the DSM-IV-TR criteria, some researchers, such as Fred Volkmar, object to the stipulation that RAD must be the product of adverse caretaking. This requirement renders it impossible to ascertain the prevalence of RAD among children not subjected to pathogenic care.

Another diagnostic controversy concerns the labeling of RAD as an attachment disorder. Some developmental psychologists suggest that RAD is best conceptualized as a developmental disorder or a maltreatment syndrome. As conceptualized in the developmental literature, the prominent feature of disordered attachment is a disturbance in the child's use of a primary caregiver as a base of safety and security. From this point of view, evidence of an at-

tachment disorder would require assessment of the child on a number of dimensions not included in the RAD criteria (such as comfort seeking, exploratory behavior, or affectionate responses). Moreover, findings in the child maltreatment literature suggest that although maltreated children often develop insecure or disorganized relational patterns to cope with the erratic care they receive, this is not necessarily synonymous with disordered attachment. Lastly, some developmental researchers note that the organic correlates of the conditions from which RAD derived (such as hospitalism or failure to thrive) have not been causally linked to attachment problems.

A third area of controversy surrounding RAD is the emergence of unvalidated and potentially dangerous "attachment therapies," which are sometimes used with disruptive children and adolescents believed to be traumatized by early adverse emotional experiences or adoption. Attachment therapies include rebirthing (a procedure in which several adults simulate the birth process by constricting children in blankets and pillows and pushing down the makeshift "birth canal"), holding therapy (in which the therapist forcefully restrains the child to achieve "rage reduction" and ostensibly correct aberrations in the "bonding cycle"), and therapeutic parenting (a strict regimen approved by attachment therapists by which parents exert their authority and impose rigid controls on the child). Rebirthing has been linked to several tragic incidents, including the 2000 death in Colorado of Candace Newmaker, a ten-year-old girl who suffocated during the process as her therapists ignored her cries for help. Despite the absence of well-controlled studies in peer-reviewed journals supporting the efficacy of attachment therapies, many proponents of these techniques claim that they are effective and safe. Responsible mental health professionals must take further steps to protect the public from the ever-growing industry of attachment therapies and similar unvalidated treatments.

SOURCES FOR FURTHER STUDY

Mercer, Jean. "'Attachment Therapy' Using Deliberate Restraint: An Object Lesson on the Identification of Unvalidated Treatments." *Journal of Child and Adolescent Psychiatric Nursing* 14, no. 2 (2001): 105-114. An informative look at the methods, controversies, and consequences of attachment therapy.

Money, John. *The Kaspar Hauser Syndrome of "Psychosocial Dwarfism": Deficient Statural, Intellectual, and Social Growth Induced by Child Abuse.* Amherst, N.Y.: Prometheus Books, 1992. A thorough review of the physical and behavioral symptoms of early deprivation The author adopts a unique historical perspective on the notorious nineteenth century case of Kaspar Hauser, a young man found at the gates of Nuremberg, Germany, after seventeen years of isolation in a dungeon.

Richters, Margot Moser, and Fred R. Volkmar. "Reactive Attachment Disorder of Infancy or Early Childhood." *Journal of American Academy of Child and Adolescent Psychiatry* 33, no. 3 (1994): 328-332. The authors examine the current diagnosis of RAD and discuss controversies regarding the validity of this diagnosis. This article also reviews objections raised by developmentalists regarding the labeling RAD of as an attachment disorder.

Spitz, Rene. "Hospitalism: An Inquiry into the Genesis of Psychiatric Conditions in Early Childhood." *Psychoanalytic Study of the Child* 1 (1945): 53-74. A classic in child maltreatment research. The author presents his observations of developmental and psychiatric problems in children subjected to extended periods of interpersonal neglect and minimal caregiving.

Volkmar, Fred R. "Reactive Attachment Disorder." In *DSM-IV Sourcebook*, edited by Thomas A. Widiger, Allen J. Frances, Harold Alan Pincus, Ruth Ross, Michael B. First, and Wendy Davis. Vol. 3. Washington, D.C.: American Psychological Association, 1997. Well-written overview of the status and evolution of RAD in DSM-III and subsequent revisions. The author outlines the history of RAD and recommends changes in its conceptualization.

Katherine A. Fowler and Scott O. Lilienfeld

SEE ALSO: Attachment and bonding in infancy and childhood; Developmental disorders; Family life: Children's issues; Mother-child relationship.

Reality therapy

TYPE OF PSYCHOLOGY: Psychotherapy
FIELDS OF STUDY: Cognitive therapies

Reality therapy is a system of counseling or psychotherapy which attempts to help clients accept responsibility for their behavior. Its aim is to teach clients more appropriate patterns of behavior. Its significance is that it helps clients meet their basic needs more effectively.

KEY CONCEPTS
- freedom
- morality of behavior
- responsibility
- success identity

INTRODUCTION

William Glasser, the founder of reality therapy, believes that people are motivated to fulfill five basic needs: belonging, power, freedom, fun, and survival. When these needs are not met, problems begin. Individuals lose touch with the objective reality of life (what is appropriate behavior and what is not) and often stray into patterns of behavior that are self-defeating or destructive. The reality therapist attempts to help such people by teaching them more appropriate patterns of behavior. This, in turn, will enable individuals to meet their basic needs more effectively.

Reality therapy differs from conventional theories of counseling or psychotherapy in six ways. Reality therapy rejects the concept of mental illness and the use of diagnostic labels; it works in the present, not the past; it rejects the concept of transference (the idea that clients relate to the therapist as an authority figure from their past); it does not consider the unconscious to be the basis of present behavior; the morality of behavior is emphasized; and finally, reality therapy teaches individuals better ways to fulfill their needs and more appropriate (and more successful) ways to deal with the world.

THERAPY PROCESS

In practice, reality therapy involves eight steps. First the therapist makes friends, or gains rapport and asks the client what he or she wants. Then the client is asked to focus on his or her current behavior. The client is helped to make a realistic evaluation of his or her behavior. Therapist and client make a plan for the client to do better, which consists of finding more appropriate (realistic) ways of behaving. The therapist gets a commitment from the client to follow the plan that has been worked out. The therapist accepts no excuses from the client if the plan is not followed. No form of punishment is utilized, however, if the client fails to follow through. Finally, the therapist must never give up on the client.

Paramount to the success of reality therapy is the planning stage, consisting of discovering ways to change the destructive or self-defeating behavior of the client into behavior oriented toward success. Success-oriented behavior leads to a success identity: the feeling that one is able to give and receive love, feel worthwhile, and meet one's needs appropriately. Glasser states that putting the plan into writing, in the form of a contract, is one way to help ensure that the client will follow through. The client, not the therapist, is then held accountable for the success or failure of follow-through. Commitment is, in many ways, the keystone of reality therapy. Resolutions and plans of action become meaningless unless there is a decision (and a commitment) to carry them out.

ROLE OF THERAPISTS

Reality therapists usually see their clients once weekly, for between forty-five minutes and one hour per visit. Therapists come from a variety of disciplines, including psychiatry, psychology, counseling, and social work. It is important in applying reality therapy that the therapist adopt no rigid rules. The therapist has a framework to follow, but within that framework he or she should be as free and creative as possible.

Like behavior therapists, reality therapists are basically active, directive, instructive, and oriented toward action. Reality therapists use a variety of techniques, including role-play, humor, question-and-answer sessions, and confrontation. They do not employ some commonly accepted therapeutic techniques, such as interpretation, insight, free association, analysis of transference and resistance, and dream analysis. In addition, reality therapists rarely recommend or promote the use of drugs or medications in treatment.

Confrontation is one technique of special consideration to reality therapy. Through confrontation, therapists force clients to evaluate their present behavior and to decide whether they will change it. Reality therapy maintains that the key to finding happiness and success is accepting responsibility. Thus the therapist neither accepts any excuses from the client for his or her self-defeating or destructive

behavior nor ignores the reality of the situation (the consequences of the client's present behavior). The client is solely responsible for his or her behavior. Conventional psychotherapy often avoids the issue of responsibility; the client (or "patient") is thought to be "sick" and thus not responsible for his or her behavior.

Throughout reality therapy, the criterion of what is "right" plays an important role in determining the appropriateness of behavior; however, the therapist does not attempt to state the morality of behavior. This is the task and responsibility of the client. Clients are to make these value judgments based on the reality of their situation. Is their current behavior getting them what they want? Does their current behavior lead to success or to failure? The basic philosophy of reality therapy is that people are ultimately self-determining and in charge of their lives. People are, in other words, free to choose how they act and what they will become.

STRENGTHS AND WEAKNESSES

The strengths of reality therapy are that it is relatively short-term therapy (not lasting for years, as classical psychoanalysis does), consists of simple and clear concepts that can be used by all types of helpers, focuses on present behavioral problems, consists of a plan of action, seeks a commitment from the client to follow through, stresses personal responsibility, can be applied to a diverse population of clients (including people in prison, people addicted to drugs and alcohol, and juvenile offenders), and accepts no excuses, blame, or rationalizations.

The weaknesses of reality therapy are that it fails to recognize the significance of the unconscious or of intrapsychic conflict, minimizes the importance of one's past in present behavior, appears overly simplistic (problems are rarely simplistic in nature), may give the therapist an inappropriate feeling of power or control, minimizes the existence of biological or biochemical factors in mental illness, and fails to recognize the significance of psychiatric drugs in the treatment of mental illness.

PRACTICAL APPLICATIONS

Reality therapy can be applied to individuals with many sorts of psychological problems, from mild to severe emotional disorders. It has been used in a variety of counseling situations, including individual and group counseling, marriage and family counseling, rehabilitation counseling, and crisis intervention. The principles of reality therapy have been applied to teaching, social work, business management, and community development. Reality therapy is a popular method of treatment in mental hospitals, correctional institutions, substance abuse centers, and facilities for delinquent youth.

Marriage therapy is often practiced by reality therapists; the number of sessions ranges from two to ten. Initially, it is important to clarify the couple's goals for marriage counseling: Are they seeking help in order to preserve the marriage, or have they already made the decision to end the relationship? In marriage counseling, Glasser recommends that the therapist be quite active, asking many questions while trying to understand the overall patterns of the marriage and of the interrelationship.

EVALUATION OF CURRENT BEHAVIOR

Reality therapists stress current behavior. The past is used only as a means of enlightening the present. The focus is on what a client is doing now. Through skillful questioning, clients are encouraged to evaluate current behavior and to consider its present consequences. Is their current behavior getting them what they want or need? If not, why? As this process of questioning and reflecting continues, clients begin to acknowledge the negative and detrimental aspects of their current behavior. Slowly, they begin to accept responsibility for these actions.

Once responsibility is accepted, much of the remaining work consists of helping clients identify specific and appropriate ways to fulfill their needs and wants. This is often considered the teaching stage, since the therapist may model or teach the client more effective behavioral patterns.

It is difficult to discuss the application of reality therapy to specific problems, since reality therapists do not look at people as objects to be classified according to diagnostic categories. Reality therapists, like others in the holistic health movement, believe that most ailments—whether physical or psychological—are manifestations of the way people choose to live their lives. William Glasser has stated:

It makes little difference to a reality therapist what the presenting complaint of the client is; that complaint is a part of the way the client is choosing now to deal with the world. . . . When the client begins to realize that instead of being the victim of some disease or diagnostic category he is a victim of his own ineffective behavior, then therapy begins and diagnosis becomes irrelevant.

CASE STUDY

The following example shows how the eight steps of reality therapy can be applied to a real-life situation. The client's name is Jim; he is thirty-five years old. For years, Jim has been unable to hold a job. He is twice divorced and is subject to angry outbursts. He has been arrested three times for disorderly conduct. Recently Jim has lost his driver's license because of alcohol intoxication; he has been referred by the court for counseling.

In step one, the therapist makes friends and asks the client what he or she wants. Here the reality therapist, David, will make himself available to Jim as a caring, warm individual but not as someone whom Jim can control or dominate. David will ask, "What is it that you want?" Jim says, "Well, what I want is a job." Once the client states what he or she wants, the therapist can move to step two, asking the client to focus on his or her current behavior. Together David and Jim talk about Jim's behavior—his tendency for angry outbursts, his arrests, and his problems with alcohol.

The third step attempts to get clients to evaluate their present behavior and to see whether what they are now doing is getting them what they want. David asks Jim whether getting in fights is helping him find a job. As this step unfolds, Jim begins to understand that what he is doing is not helping him to become employable. Paramount at this step is that the clients see that their current behavior is within their control: They "choose" to act this way.

Once clients begin to see that what they are doing is not working (not getting them what they want), then the next step (step four) is to help them make a plan to do better. Once Jim realizes that getting in fights and drinking is ineffective and self-defeating, then David will begin to talk with him about a plan to change his behavior and find more appropriate ways of behaving. They plan a course of action. To "cement" this plan, a contract is made. The contract might state that Jim will not get in fights, Jim will control his anger, and Jim will stay out of bars and refrain from alcohol. David may also advise Jim on how to get a job: where to look for work, whom to contact, even what to wear and say during a job interview. Throughout this job search, which may be long and frustrating, David needs to be encouraging and supportive.

Step five involves getting a commitment from the client to follow through. David now asks Jim, "Are you going to live up to the contract? Are you going to change your behavior?" David needs to stress that commitment is the key to making this plan a success. David also must accept only a yes or no answer from Jim. Reality therapy does not accept excuses or reasons why plans are not carried through; this is step six. David's response to excuses should be that he is not interested in why Jim cannot do it; he is interested in when Jim will do it.

Step seven holds that David needs to be "tough" with Jim, but must not punish him if he does not follow through. Instead of finding ways to punish Jim, David may ask instead, "What is it that will get you to follow through?" Reality therapy recognizes that punishment is, in the long run, rarely effective. Step eight is simply never giving up. For most people, change does not come naturally, nor is it easy. A good therapist, like a good friend, does not give up easily. David needs to persevere with Jim. Through perseverance, Jim's life can change.

CONTRIBUTIONS OF WILLIAM GLASSER

The tenets of reality therapy were formed in the 1950's and 1960's as a reaction to the dominant psychotherapeutic approaches of the times, which were closely based on Freudian psychoanalysis. William Glasser, the founder of reality therapy, was trained as a physician and psychoanalyst, but during his psychiatric training in the early 1950's, he became more and more dissatisfied with the psychoanalytic approach. What disturbed him was the insistence of psychoanalysis on viewing the patient as a victim of forces beyond his or her control. In other words, the person was not considered responsible for his or her current behavior.

In 1956, Glasser became a consultant to a school for delinquent female adolescents in Ventura, California, developing a new therapeutic approach that was in sharp opposition to classical psychoanalysis. In 1962, he spoke at a meeting of the National Association of Youth Training Schools and presented his new ideas. The response was phenomenal; evidently many people were frustrated with the current mode of treatment.

Initially Glasser was hesitant to state his dissatisfaction with the conventional approach to treatment, psychoanalysis; however, his faculty supervisor, G. L. Harrington, was supportive. This started a long relationship in which Harrington helped Glasser formulate many of the ideas that became reality therapy.

In 1965, Glasser put his principles of counseling into a book entitled *Reality Therapy: A New Approach to Psychiatry*. Since then, he has written extensively, including *Schools Without Failure* (1968), *The Identity Society* (1972), *Positive Addiction* (1976), *Stations of the Mind: New Directions for Reality Therapy* (1981), *Control Theory: A New Exploration of How We Control Our Lives* (1985), and *The Quality School* (1990). The Institute for Reality Therapy, in Canoga Park, California, offers programs designed to teach the concepts and practice of reality therapy. A journal, the *Journal of Reality Therapy*, publishes articles concerning the research, theory, and application of reality therapy. Reality therapy has seen remarkable success since its conception, and many consider it one of the important approaches to counseling and psychotherapy.

SOURCES FOR FURTHER STUDY

Corey, Gerald. *Theory and Practice of Counseling and Psychotherapy*. 6th ed. Belmont, Calif.: Wadsworth, 2000. An excellent source of information on the major theories of counseling and psychotherapy. In one chapter, Corey states the essentials of reality therapy. Also gives a detailed evaluation of the strengths and weaknesses of reality therapy.

Glasser, Naomi, ed. *What Are You Doing? How People Are Helped Through Reality Therapy*. New York: Harper & Row, 1986. Presents twenty-five successful cases of reality therapy. Each case, described in detail, shows how reality therapy is put into practice. The cases range from a patient in a mental hospital to teenage delinquents to problems of aging. An excellent teaching aid in the training of counselors.

Glasser, William. *Control Theory: A New Explanation of How We Control Our Lives*. New York: Harper & Row, 1985. Control theory explains how individuals function. It states that behavior originates from within the individual and is need satisfying. A significant book, easy to read and understand.

_____. *Quality School*. 3d ed. New York: HarperPerennial, 1998. Glasser applies the concepts of reality therapy to education, wedded to concepts of Total Quality Management. The aim is to create a friendly and noncoercive environment by emphasizing pride in producing high-quality work.

_____. *Reality Therapy: A New Approach to Psychiatry.* 1965. Reprint. New York: HarperCollins, 1989. Describes Glasser's basic concepts of reality therapy. Glasser also shows how the reality therapist gets involved with the client and how he or she teaches clients more responsible ways to live their lives. This book was a significant contribution to psychotherapy in that it offered an alternative to psychoanalytic therapy.

_____. *Reality Therapy in Action.* New York: HarperCollins, 2000. A collection of case histories chosen to illustrate Glasser's thesis that making better choices in life in the process of therapy alters brain chemistry for the better.

Ted Eilders

SEE ALSO: Abnormality: Psychological models; Behavioral family therapy; Cognitive behavior therapy; Cognitive therapy; Existential psychology; Psychoanalysis; Psychoanalytic psychology; Rational-emotive therapy.

Reflexes

TYPE OF PSYCHOLOGY: Biological bases of behavior
FIELDS OF STUDY: Nervous system

A reflex is one of the most basic types of behavior that can be elicited; over the years, psychologists and physiologists have studied the behavioral and biological processes associated with reflex production in the hope of understanding principles and processes involved in generating both simple behaviors and a variety of more complex behaviors such as learning, memory, and voluntary movement.

KEY CONCEPTS
- classical (Pavlovian) conditioning
- infantile reflexes
- monosynaptic reflex
- polysynaptic reflex
- spinal reflex

INTRODUCTION

The reflex is undoubtedly the simplest form of behavior that has been studied widely by psychologists and neuroscientists. Reflexes involve two separate yet highly related events: the occurrence of an eliciting stimulus and the production of a specific response. Most organisms are capable of displaying a variety of complex behaviors; however, because these behaviors are complex, it has been very difficult, if not impossible, to understand biological or psychological processes involved in generating or modifying the variety of complex behaviors that most organisms can display. In attempts to study these complex behaviors, a number of researchers have adopted a strategy of studying simpler behaviors, such as reflexes, that are thought to make up, contribute to, or serve as a model of the more complex behavior.

SPINAL REFLEX

A number of reflexes can be generated in the mammalian spinal cord even after it has been surgically isolated from the brain. The stretch reflex is an example of a spinal reflex. When a muscle is stretched, such as when a tendon is tapped or when an attempt is made to reach for an object, sensory "detectors" or receptors within the muscle are activated to signal the muscle stretch. These receptors are at the end of very long nerve fibers that travel from the muscle receptor to the spinal cord, where they activate spinal motor neurons. The motor neurons control the same muscle on which the stretch receptor that initiated the stretch signal is located. When activated, the spinal motor neurons signal the muscle, causing it to contract. In this manner, when a muscle stretch is detected, the stretch reflex ensures that a contraction is generated in the muscle to counteract and balance the stretch. This type of reflex is referred to as a "monosynaptic reflex" because it involves only one synapse: the synapse between the sensory receptor neuron and the motor neuron (where a synapse is the junction between two neurons).

Another example of a spinal reflex is the flexion or withdrawal reflex. Anyone who has accidentally touched a hot stove has encountered this reflex. Touching a hot stove or applying any aversive stimulus to the skin activates pain receptors in the skin. These receptors are at the end of long sensory fibers that project to neurons in the spinal cord. The spinal neurons that receive input from the sensory fibers are not motor neurons, as in the stretch reflex, but rather very small neurons called spinal interneurons. The interneurons make synaptic contact on other interneurons as well as on motor neurons that innervate flexor muscles. When activated, the flexor muscles typically cause limb withdrawal. The flexor reflex ensures that a relatively rapid withdrawal of one's hand from a hot stove will occur if it is accidentally touched. The flexor reflex is an example of a "polysynaptic reflex" because there are two or more synapses involved in the reflex (the presence of at least one synapse between a sensory neuron and an interneuron and a second synapse between the interneuron and a motor neuron).

One functional difference between monosynaptic and polysynaptic reflexes is the amount of information processing that can take place in the two reflex systems. The monosynaptic reflex is somewhat limited, because information flow involves only the synapse between the sensory and motor neurons. This type of reflex is ideal for quick adjustments that must be made in muscle tension. Conversely, polysynaptic reflexes typically involve a number of levels of interneurons. Hence, convergence and divergence of information can occur as information flows from sensory to motor elements. In essence, the polysynaptic system, in addition to having afferent and efferent components, has a "processor" of sorts between the sensory and motor elements. In intact organisms, the integration that takes place within the processor allows information to be shared by other regions of the nervous system. For example, some of the interneurons send information upward to the brain. When a hot stove is touched, the brain is informed. This sensory experience is likely to be evaluated and stored by the brain, therefore making it less likely that the hot stove will be touched a second time.

MUSCULATURE REFLEXES

Reflexes are not limited to the spinal cord. Responses involving the musculature of the face and neck can also be reflexive in nature. For example, a puff of air that strikes the cornea of the human eye elicits a brisk, short-latency eyelid closure. Like the polysynaptic spinal reflexes, this eyeblink reflex appears to involve three elements: a sensory nerve, called the trigeminal nerve, that carries information from receptors in the cornea of the eye to the trigeminal nucleus (a cranial nerve nucleus); interneurons that connect the trigeminal nucleus with several other brain-stem neurons; and a motor nerve that originates from brain-stem motor neurons and contracts the muscles surrounding the eye to produce the eyeblink. This reflex is defensive in nature because it ensures that the eyeball is protected from further stimulation if a stimulus strikes the cornea.

USE OF AUTONOMIC NERVOUS SYSTEM

Not all reflexes involve activation of skeletal muscles. For example, control of the urinary bladder involves a spinal reflex that activates smooth muscles. Also, temperature regulation is partially the product of a reflexive response to changes in external or internal environments. Many of these types of reflexes engage the autonomic nervous system, a division of the nervous system that is involved in regulating and maintaining the function of internal organs.

Not all reflexes involve simple, local, short-latency responses. The maintenance of posture when standing upright is a generally automatic, reflexive system that one does not think about. This system includes neurons in the spinal cord and brain stem. The body's equilibrium system (the vestibular or balance system) involves receptors in the middle ear, brain-stem structures, and spinal motor neurons, while locomotion requires the patterned activation of several reflex systems. Finally, a number of behavioral situations require a rapid response that integrates the motor system with one of the special senses (such as quickly applying the car brakes when a road hazard is seen). These are generally referred to as reaction-time situations and require considerable nervous system processing, including the involvement of the cerebral cortex, when engaged. Nevertheless, these responses are considered reflexive in nature because they involve an eliciting stimulus and a well-defined, consistent response.

ROLE IN LEARNING AND MEMORY

Reflexes have also been widely studied by psychologists and biologists interested in learning and memory. Russian physiologists Ivan Sechenov and Ivan Pavlov have generally been credited with the first attempts to study systematically how reflexes could be used to examine relationships between behavior and physiology. Pavlov in particular had a huge influence on the study of behavior. Most students are familiar with the story of Pavlov and his successful demonstration of conditioned salivation in dogs produced by pairing a bell with meat powder. Over the years, the Pavlovian conditioning procedure (also known as classical conditioning) has often been used to study the behavioral principles and neural substrates of learning. The conditioning of a variety of reflexes has been observed, including skeletal muscle responses such as forelimb flexion, hindlimb flexion, and eyelid closure, as well as autonomic responses such as respiration, heart rate, and sweat gland activity.

One of the most widely studied classical conditioning procedures is classical eyelid conditioning. This reflex conditioning procedure has been studied in a variety of species, including rabbits, rats, cats, dogs, and humans. Mostly because of the research efforts of Isadore Gormezano and his colleagues, which began in the early 1960's, much is known about behavioral aspects of classical eyelid conditioning in rabbits. In this paradigm, a mild electric shock or air puff is presented to elicit reliably a reflexive blink from the rabbit. The blink is typically measured by means of devices that are attached to the nictitating membrane, a third eyelid that is present in a variety of species, including the rabbit. During training sessions, a neutral stimulus such as a tone or light is delivered 0.3 to 1.0 second prior to the air puff. After about one hundred of these tone and air-puff pairings, the rabbit learns to blink when the tone or light is presented (the rabbit begins to use the tone to signal the impending air-puff presentation).

This preparation has yielded a wealth of data concerning the parameters of behavioral training that produce the fastest or slowest learning rates (such as stimuli intensities, time between stimuli, and number of trials per day). Furthermore, this simple reflexive learning situation has been used to study how the brain codes simple forms of learning and memory. A number of researchers (most notably Richard F. Thompson) have studied the activity of a variety of brain structures during learning and performance of the classically conditioned eyelid response. These studies have shown that discrete brain regions such as the cerebellum and hippocampus alter their activity to generate or modify the conditioned response. In brief, these researchers have used the conditioning of a very simple reflex to advance the understanding of how the brain might code more complex learning and memory processes.

INNATE REFLEXES

The study of reflexes has not been limited to learning and memory. Developmental psychologists have studied a variety of innate reflexes that are generated by newborn infants. Sucking is a very prominent reflex that is readily observed in newborns. Also related to feeding is the rooting reflex, which can be elicited when the cheek of an infant is stroked softly. The skin stimulation causes the infant to open his or her mouth and turn toward the point of stimulation. This reflex has obvious applications in helping the infant locate food. The infant's ability to hold on to objects is, in part, attributable to the presence of the grasp reflex. When an object touches the palm of a newborn's hand, the newborn's fist will close immediately around the object, thus allowing the infant to hold the object for a short period of time. The infantile reflexes disappear within a few months after birth and are replaced by voluntary responses. Most developmental researchers believe that the infantile reflexes are temporary substitutes for the voluntary responses. Apparently, the voluntary responses are not present during the first few months of life because various parts of the infant nervous system, including the cerebral cortex, have not matured sufficiently to support the behavior. Therefore, the disappearance of the infantile reflexes serves as an important marker of neural and behavioral development.

CONTRIBUTIONS TO PSYCHOLOGY

The study of reflexes has played a prominent role in shaping the field of psychology. During the late nineteenth century and early twentieth century, Sir Charles Sherrington, a British physiologist, conducted an extensive series of studies concerned with spinal reflexes. He showed that a number of skin stimulations, such as pinching or brushing, produced simple responses even when a spinal transection separated the spinal cord from the rest of the nervous system. From these experiments, he argued that the basic unit of movement was the reflex, which he defined as a highly stereotyped, unlearned response to external stimuli. This work created a flurry of activity among physiologists and psychologists, who tried to trace reflexes throughout the nervous system and assemble them into more complex behaviors.

Early in the twentieth century, many psychologists and physiologists, including Sherrington and Pavlov, adopted the reflex as the basic unit of behavior to study, in part because of the relative simplicity of the behavior and in part because of the ease with which the behavior could be reliably elicited by applying external stimuli. Based on his research, Sherrington believed that complex behaviors were produced by chaining together simple reflexes in some temporal order. This basic idea provided the framework for much of the physiological and behavioral work completed early in the twentieth century. Sechenov and Pavlov also believed that the concept of the reflex could explain more complex behaviors. Pavlov, for example, showed that not all reflexes were innate; rather, new reflexes could be established by associating a "neutral" stimulus (a stimulus that did not initially produce a reflex) with a stimulus that reliably elicited a reflex. As a result of this demonstration, Pavlov proposed an elaborate theory of reflex learning that involved forming associations between stimuli in the cerebral cortex.

In the latter half of the twentieth century, many psychologists interested in studying overt behavior and physiologists interested in studying nervous system function adopted the study of reflexes as a means of simplifying behavior or nervous system activity. Psychologists such as Gormezano, Robert Rescorla, and Allan Wagner, who have studied classical conditioning phenomena, hope to develop a comprehensive understanding of the learning process that occurs when simple paradigms such as classical conditioning are used. Behavioral neuroscientists and neurobiologists (such as Thompson and Eric Kandel) who study nervous system function have used reflexes as the basic unit of behavior in hope of catching a glimpse of nervous system function when a fairly simple behavioral response is being generated and modified by learning experiences. In both cases, a major reason for using the reflex as the unit of behavior is to simplify the experimental situation. Indeed, researchers are not likely to understand complex behavioral processes without first understanding how simpler behaviors and nervous system functions are generated, modified, and maintained. The study of reflexes, from both a behavioral and biological standpoint, has provided and should continue to provide a valuable approach for understanding human behavior as well as understanding how the nervous system generates activity to produce the behavior.

SOURCES FOR FURTHER STUDY

Carlson, Neil R. *Foundations of Physiological Psychology.* 5th ed. Boston: Allyn & Bacon, 2001. A very up-to-date textbook on the neuroscience of behavior.

Domjan, Michael, and Barbara Burkhard. *The Principles of Learning and Behavior.* 4th ed. Belmont, Calif.: Wadsworth, 1997. This text is widely used by students interested in learning and behavior. The sections on the history of the reflex and its use in the learning research field is particularly applicable to the present discussion.

Fancher, Raymond E. *Pioneers of Psychology.* 3d ed. New York: W. W. Norton, 1996. This book provides biographies of several prominent psychologists who have had an impact on the field. Included is a chapter detailing the experiments and theories of Ivan Pavlov. Valuable for understanding how the study of the reflex fits into the history of psychology.

Gleitman, Henry, Alan J. Fridlund, and Daniel Weisberg. *Psychology.* 5th ed. New York: W. W. Norton, 2000. This text provides broad coverage of the field of psychology. The chapters on development, learning, and memory should provide the reader with additional information concerning reflexes and other simple behaviors.

Joseph E. Steinmetz

SEE ALSO: Brain structure; Nervous system; Neurons; Pavlovian conditioning; Reflexes in newborns.

Reflexes in newborns

TYPE OF PSYCHOLOGY: Developmental psychology
FIELDS OF STUDY: Infancy and childhood

Healthy neonates are born with a repertoire of skills that help them to adapt to their new environment immediately after birth. By exploring the nature and bases of these early abilities, researchers have gained a better understanding of processes that govern development during the earliest periods of the human life cycle.

KEY CONCEPTS
- cortical brain centers
- homeostasis
- primitive reflex
- reflex
- subcortical brain centers
- sudden infant death syndrome (SIDS)
- survival reflex

INTRODUCTION

For many years, it was thought that newborns were completely helpless, fragile and hardly ready for survival in the relatively unprotected world into which they were born. Extensive research has now shown that the healthy neonate is born with a set of prepared reactions to the environment which aids its survival. These prepared reactions are referred to as reflexes. Reflexes make survival possible by taking charge of new surroundings. The newborn's surroundings were previously controlled and protected by the mother's biological system. Reflexes are inborn responses that help a newborn adapt to his or her new surroundings outside the womb from the moment of birth.

Immediate adjustment to a new environment is essential for the newborn. The extrauterine environment is very different from the environment from which the fetus emerged at birth. The newborn is faced with a variety of changes to which immediate adaption is necessary. Breathing must now be self-sufficient, requiring that the newborn's own lungs be used for the first time. Food must be actively approached, consumed, and digested. During the prenatal period, the fetus received nutrients passively from the mother, and waste was discharged into the mother's bloodstream. For the first time, digestion and waste elimination must be regulated by the newborn's own lungs, skin, kidneys, and gastrointestinal tract.

Finally, the newborn is much less protected in the extrauterine environment than he or she was when developing within the uterus. The developing fetus experienced a world of constancy because of the insulating effects of life in amniotic fluid. At birth, however, the infant will immediately experience perhaps its first fluctuations in temperature, light, and sound. The neonate will therefore need to be prepared to maintain a relatively constant body temperature and a degree of internal homeostasis—the tendency to maintain internal stability by

responding in a coordinated fashion to any changes in the external world—immediately after birth. Reflexes assume many of these functions automatically. From the moment of birth, reflexes are elicited by stimuli in the extrauterine environment. Reflex action is controlled largely by subcortical brain centers in the central nervous system.

ROLE OF CENTRAL NERVOUS SYSTEM

The human central nervous system (CNS) is organized hierarchically. Simple, uncoordinated actions are controlled by "lower," or subcortical, brain centers; progressively higher-order, coordinated activities are controlled by "higher," or cortical, brain centers. Reflexes are among the simplest patterns of action exhibited by humans and are controlled by lower brain centers. The lower brain centers are the most highly developed at birth, and they control the majority of human behavior until they are supplanted by higher cortical brain centers. As humans mature and their central nervous systems become more developed, the higher brain centers (cortical brain centers) assume control of the previously reflexive behaviors. That is, as humans develop voluntary control over their behavior, reflexes previously elicited automatically by stimulation no longer respond. This occurs rapidly over the first year of life and is evidenced by the disappearance of many reflexive behaviors.

EARLY SURVIVAL RESPONSES

The most fundamental reflexes exhibited in the newborn involve reactions to unpleasant or life-threatening stimuli. These reflexes protect the infant from further aversion or possible life-threatening situations. For example, several reflexes allow the newborn to maintain a clear airway for normal breathing. This is important because regular breathing rhythms are not firmly established in the newborn; normal, healthy newborns occasionally neglect to breathe for brief periods of time. When this occurs, carbon dioxide builds up in their bloodstream and the breathing reflex is triggered. This causes the neonates reflexively to start breathing again. Should neonates experience a clogged airway because of mucus or some other obstruction, a reflexive sneeze or cough may serve to remove the obstruction.

Similarly, neonates respond reflexively to the presence of food. At birth, a light stroking of the cheek of an infant will result in a rooting reflex. The

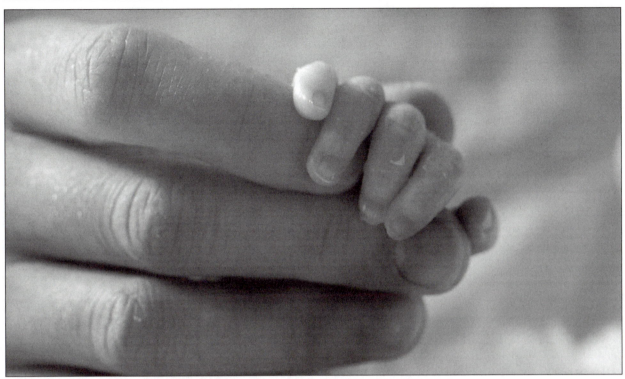

Newborns possess a grasping reflex that allows them to hold tightly to objects. (PhotoDisc)

rooting reflex is characterized as a head turn. This turn positions the baby for nutrient seeking. The sucking and swallowing reflexes enable neonates to consume nutrients, a process that is aided significantly by the activation of other parts of the human digestive tract.

Neonates respond reflexively to changes in temperature and touch. For example, heat causes a neonate's blood vessels to expand so that more heat can be dispersed through the skin. Conversely, cold causes a neonate's blood vessels to contract so that heat can be conserved inside the body. Neonates respond to painful physical stimulation such as a pin prick on the foot by reflexively withdrawing the limb. Similarly, neonates respond to loud noises or bright lights by turning away from the source of the aversive stimulus.

Perhaps one of the most general reflexes is the crying reflex. Crying is an important reflex which alerts caregivers that all is not well. Crying is especially important for maintaining homeostasis. Infants cry when they are overstimulated, understimulated, hungry, too cold or hot, in pain, or otherwise uncomfortable. Crying serves to communicate to

caregivers as well as to release energy, ward off danger, or possibly clear an air passage.

With the exception of the rooting reflex, which is replaced by more voluntarily controlled food-seeking behaviors, the reflexes discussed above remain with humans for their entire lives and are generally referred to as survival reflexes because they play a crucial role in survival across the entire life span.

PRIMITIVE REFLEXES

Newborns also exhibit a variety of reflexive actions that have no clear survival value. These nonadaptive reflexes are referred to as primitive reflexes. Primitive reflexes disappear early in the first year of life. Several of these primitive reflexes are interesting precursors of abilities that will be exhibited later in life. For example, neonates exhibit an early stepping reflex which closely resembles mature walking. This quickly disappears at about eight weeks of life and will reemerge at about twelve to fifteen months as infants take their first true steps. Similarly, newborns will reflexively swim if placed in a prone position on a water surface. Newborns also grasp when the palm is touched. Early versions of both swimming and grasping will disappear in the first three months, and, in the case of grasping, will give way first to slapping movements and then to progressive dexterity of gripping with palm and fingers at about six months.

Evolutionary accounts of the existence of primitive reflexes in humans suggest that they are remnants of survival reflexes present in humans' evolutionary ancestors. For example, the moro reflex is a startle reflex in which an infant, when placed in a supine position on his or her back, raises the arms and pulls them toward the center of the chest. The moro reflex serves as a very adaptive clinging response among primates (for example, chimpanzees) that require their infants to hold on to their mother as they travel. Again, this reflex is triggered by perceived loss of balance (falling, contact) with the caregiver. For humans, however, it is a primitive reflex with no apparent value. It disappears gradually during the first six months of life.

While having no apparent survival value, the pattern of appearance and disappearance of primitive reflexes is taken as an indication of normal neurological development. The pattern of reflex disappearance follows closely the maturity of the central nervous system. It is suggested that primitive reflexes are controlled primarily by lower subcortical brain centers which are gradually giving way to rapidly developing higher brain centers.

PRACTICAL APPLICATIONS

Reflex integrity is an important component of several newborn screening instruments. The Brazelton Neonatal Behavior Assessment Scale explores a newborn's responsiveness to several environmental stimuli as a function of neurological functioning. The Brazelton scale assesses the strength of twenty reflexes as well as a newborn's ability to respond to twenty-six situations such as orienting to and from a tester's voice. If an infant is extremely unresponsive, a low Brazelton score may indicate the existence of brain damage or other neurological dysfunction.

Lewis Lipsitt, a researcher studying newborn reflexes, found an important relationship between the integrity of a child's nervous system and the development of reflexes. Lipsitt conducted research on sudden infant death syndrome (SIDS), a complication in which apparently healthy infants suddenly stop breathing and die in their sleep. The cause of this disorder is unknown. It is most common in in-

fants from two to four months of age. In 1997, the National Institutes of Health estimated that between five thousand and six thousand infants in the United States die of this disorder each year. Lipsitt posited that these infants have a specific learning disability that keeps them from assuming voluntary control of previously involuntary survival reflexes; perhaps some damage to cortical brain centers prevents them from successfully learning the survival reflexes needed. For example, if a four-month-old infant's nasal passage is blocked, the infant may not struggle to clear the breathing passage because his or her survival reflexes have not been sufficiently controlled by cortical brain centers.

INFANCY DEVELOPMENT

The focus on reflexes in newborns has been more generally stimulated by interest in understanding the rapid development of humans during the period of infancy. Infancy is now understood as the period of most rapid development in a human's entire life span. During the first two years of life, an infant's brain will reach 75 percent of its eventual weight. Physical growth will accompany brain growth to enable an infant to display an array of complex motor and cognitive skills that emerge in rapid succession. Developmental psychologists have made considerable progress in understanding this period of development. This progress has been aided by advances in technology and research methods, primarily in the area of brain physiology and function.

Researchers now understand, in contrast to earlier thinking, that humans are born with a variety of skills which aid their survival during this particularly vulnerable developmental period. Previously, researchers, physicians, and parents had assumed that infants were fragile and helpless. Infants are indeed more prepared for life on earth than was reflected in previous attitudes. Today, it is known that all major sense organs are functioning at birth and that newborns are capable of learning and experiencing their world actively very shortly after birth.

Nineteenth century psychologist William James described infants as born into a blooming, buzzing confusion. This is clearly far from the truth. Reflexes play an important role in the realization of many early developing abilities. Researchers have used them as a window on the developing nervous system, and have understood significant variation in neurological development from the pattern of reflexes. Infants interact with the world reflexively until they have matured enough to engage in more active exploration of their world.

SOURCES FOR FURTHER STUDY

Harris, Judith Rich, and Robert M. Liebert. *The Child*. 3d ed. Englewood Cliffs, N.J.: Prentice-Hall, 1991. An excellent review of characteristics of the newborn. Provides a much more thorough view of the baby than other texts in the introductory developmental genre.

Lipsitt, Lewis. "Critical Conditions in Infancy: A Psychological Perspective." *American Psychologist* 34, no. 10 (1979): 973-980. Discusses SIDS in America. Lipsitt describes his model of sudden infant death syndrome.

Maurer, Daphne, and Charles Maurer. *The World of the Newborn*. New York: Basic Books, 1988. A good overview of the entire period of infancy. Describes in very readable detail the emerging competencies of infants as they mature.

Piper, Martha, and Johanna Darrah. *Motor Assessment of the Developing Infant*. Philadelphia: W. B. Saunders, 1994. Aimed at physical therapists assessing the motor development of infants from birth to eighteen months.

Shaffer, David Reed. *Developmental Psychology: Childhood and Adolescence*. 6th ed. Belmont, Calif.: Wadsworth, 2001. A well-written textbook on developmental psychology. The section on infant physical development provides a good source of extra reading about reflexes.

Richard J. Ricard

SEE ALSO: Birth: Effects on physical development; Motor development; Physical development: Environment versus genetics; Prenatal physical development; Sensation and perception.

Reinforcement

TYPE OF PSYCHOLOGY: Learning; memory; motivation

FIELDS OF STUDY: Aversive conditioning; behavioral and cognitive models; behavioral therapies; cognitive learning; general constructs and issues; instrumental conditioning; motivation theory; Pavlovian conditioning

Reinforcement is one of the most pervasive concepts in psychology, ranging from basic research to applications in psychotherapy. Modern usage of the term is limited to specific consequences of behavior that lead to increases in the future probability of that same behavior. A great deal of effort has been dedicated to discovering various types of reinforcers, the effects of varying delivery patterns, and what makes consequences effective reinforcers.

KEY CONCEPTS

- bliss point
- establishing operation
- intermittent reinforcement
- negative reinforcers
- positive reinforcers
- Premack principle
- primary reinforcers
- punishment
- secondary reinforcers
- social reinforcers

INTRODUCTION

The casual, everyday use of the word "reinforcement" generally refers to the granting of a reward for some behavior. While the use of this term by psychologists is more formal, a great deal of research has been dedicated to studying the effects of rewards on behavior. The most influential of the early studies were those done in the 1890's by American psychologist Edward Lee Thorndike (1874-1949). Thorndike created a problem box from which a hungry cat could escape by performing a specific action, such as pulling on a wire, stepping on a pedal, or some similar behavior, thereby gaining access to food. From these studies Thorndike proposed his famous Law of Effect. That is, actions that are followed by satisfying events are more likely to reoccur while actions that are followed by discomfort will become less likely. The more satisfying and/or the more discomfort, the greater the effect on subsequent behavior.

Not all psychologists have used the word "reinforcement" to describe the same processes. In research where he conditioned dogs to salivate to tones, the Russian physiologist Ivan Pavlov (1849-1936) called pairing a stimulus (food) that automatically elicits a response (salivation) to a new stimulus (a tone) reinforcing. That is, the food reinforced the ability of the tone to generate the same response. This process has come to be known as Pavlovian conditioning. Unlike Thorndike, who was referring to consequences after the organism emitted some specific behavior, Pavlov was describing an effect that occurred during the presentation of stimuli before the organism responded. Another difference was that Thorndike studied an animal's voluntary behavior while Pavlov studied a reflexive, glandular response.

Most psychologists followed Thorndike and reserved the term "reinforcer" for voluntary behavior and its consequences. For many, though, it meant any consequence to a behavior, whether it increased or decreased the behavior's future probability. In this usage, a reinforcer could mean any kind of motivation, whether it was to seek a pleasant or to avoid an unpleasant set of circumstances. To be sure, there were modifying words for these specific situations. Thus, if a behavior acquired some desired commodity (such as food), reducing a need or a drive state, it was said to be positive reinforcement. On the other hand, if the behavior caused an unpleasant situation to be terminated or avoided, it was called negative reinforcement. Both of these consequences would increase the rate of the behavior.

To make matters more confusing, some psychologists employed the term "reinforcement" even when the consequence reduced the likelihood of a specific behavior. In the 1960's, American psychologist Gregory A. Kimble described omission training as withholding a positive reinforcer when a specified response is emitted. Conversely, Kimble said that if a negative reinforcer is given when the response occurs, this is punishment.

MODERN DEFINITIONS

In order to maintain a reasonable degree of consistency, most psychologists use the term "reinforcement" exclusively for a process of using rewards to increase voluntary behavior. The field of study most associated with this technique is instrumental conditioning. In this context, the formal definition states that a reinforcer is any consequence to a behavior that is emitted in a specified situation that has the effect of increasing that behavior in the future. It must be emphasized that the behavior itself is not sufficient for the consequence to be delivered. The circumstances in which the behavior occurs are also important. Thus, standing and cheering at a basketball game will likely lead to approval (social rein-

forcement), whereas this same response is not likely to yield acceptance if it occurs at a funeral.

A punisher is likewise defined as any consequence that reduces the probability of a behavior, with the same qualifications as for reinforcers. A behavior that occurs in response to a specified situation may receive a consequence that reduces the likelihood that it will occur in that situation in the future, but the same behavior in another situation would not generate the same consequence. For example, drawing on the walls of a freshly painted room would usually result in an unpleasant consequence, whereas the same behavior (drawing) in one's coloring book would not.

The terms "positive" and "negative" are also much more tightly defined. Former use confused these with the emotional values of good or bad, thereby requiring the counterintuitive and confusing claim that a positive reinforcer is withheld or a negative reinforcer presented when there is clearly no reward, and, in fact, the intent is to reduce the probability of that response (such as by described Kimble). A better, less confusing definition is to consider "positive" and "negative" as arithmetic symbols, as for adding or subtracting. They therefore are the methods of supplying reinforcement (or punishment) rather than descriptions of the reinforcer itself. Thus, if a behavior occurs, and as a consequence something is given that will result in an increase in the rate of the behavior, this is positive reinforcement. Giving a dog a treat for executing a trick is a good example. One can also increase the rate of a behavior by removing something upon its production. This is called negative reinforcement. A good example might be when a child who eats his or her vegetables does not have to wash the dinner dishes. Another example is the annoying seatbelt buzzer in cars. Many people comply with the rules of safety simply to terminate that aversive sound.

The descriptors "positive" and "negative" can be applied to punishment as well. If something is added upon the performance of a behavior which results in the reduction of that behavior—positive punishment. On the other hand, if this behavior causes the removal of something that reduces the response rate—negative punishment. A dog collar that provides an electric shock when the dog strays too close to the property line is an example of a device that delivers positive punishment. Loss of television privileges for rudeness is an example of negative punishment.

TYPES OF REINFORCERS

The range of possible consequences that can function as reinforcers is enormous. In order to make sense of this assortment, psychologists tend to place them into two main categories: primary reinforcers and secondary reinforcers. Primary reinforcers are those that require little, if any, experience to be effective. Food, drink, and sex are common examples. While it is true that experience will influence what would be considered desirable for food, drink, or an appropriate sex partner, there is little argument that these items, themselves, are natural reinforcers. Another kind of reinforcer that does not require experience is called a social reinforcer. Examples are social contact and social approval. Even newborns show a desire for social reinforcers. Psychologists have discovered that newborns prefer to look at pictures of human faces more than practically any other stimulus pattern, and this preference is stronger if that face is smiling. Like the other primary reinforcers, experience will modify the type of social recognition that is desired. Still, it is clear that most people will go to great lengths to be noticed by others or to gain their acceptance and approval.

Though these reinforcers are likely to be effective, most human behavior is not motivated directly by primary reinforcers. Money, entertainment, clothes, cars, and computer games are all effective rewards, yet none of these would qualify as natural or primary reinforcers. Because they must be acquired, they are called secondary reinforcers. These become effective because they are paired with primary reinforcers. The famous American psychologist B. F. Skinner (1904-1990) found that the sound of food being delivered was sufficient to maintain a high rate of bar pressing in experienced rats. Obviously, under normal circumstances the sound of the food only occurred if food was truly being delivered.

How a secondary reinforcer becomes effective is called two-factor theory and is generally explained through a combination of instrumental and Pavlovian conditioning (hence the label "two-factor"). For example, when a rat receives food for pressing a bar (positive reinforcement), at that same time a neutral stimulus is also presented, the sound of the food dropping into the food dish. The sound is paired with a stimulus that naturally elicits a reflexive response; that is, food elicits satisfaction. Over many trials, the sound is paired consistently with food; thus, it will be conditioned via Pavlovian methods to elicit the same response as the food. Additionally, `this process occurred during the instrumental conditioning of bar pressing by using food as a reinforcer.

This same process works for most everyday activities. For most humans, money is an extremely powerful reinforcer. Money itself, though, is not very attractive. It does not taste good, does not reduce any biological drives, and does not, on its own, satisfy any needs. However, it is reliably paired with all of these things and therefore becomes as effective as these primary reinforcers. In a similar way, popular fashion in clothing, hair styles, and personal adornment, popular art or music, even behaving according to the moral values of one's family or church group (or one's gang) can all come to be effective reinforcers because they are reliably paired with an important primary reinforcer, namely, social approval. The person who will function most effectively as the approving agent changes throughout life. One's parents, friends, classmates, teachers, teammates, coaches, spouse, children, and colleagues at work all provide effective social approval opportunities.

WHY REINFORCERS WORK

Reinforcers (and punishers) are effective at influencing an organism's willingness to respond because they influence the way in which an organism acquires something that is desired, or avoids something that is not desired. For primary reinforcers, this concerns health and survival. Secondary reinforcers are learned through experience and do not directly affect one's health or survival, yet they are adaptive because they are relevant to those situations that are related to well-being and an improved quality of life. Certainly learning where food, drink, receptive sex partners, or social acceptance can be located is useful for an organism. Coming to enjoy being in such situations is very useful, too.

An American psychologist, David Premack, has argued that it is the opportunity to engage in activity, and not the reinforcer itself, that is important. That is, it is not the food, but the opportunity to eat that matters. For example, he has shown that rats will work very hard to gain access to a running wheel. The activity of running in the wheel is apparently reinforcing. Other researchers have demonstrated that monkeys will perform numerous boring, repetitive tasks in order to open a window just to see into another room. This phenomenon has come to be known as the Premack principle. Premack explains that any high-probability activity can be used to reinforce a lower-probability behavior. This approach works for secondary reinforcers, too. The opportunity to spend money may be the reinforcer, not the money itself. Access to an opportunity to eat, to be entertained, to be with others who are complimentary about one's taste are all highly probable behaviors; thus they reinforce work for which one may be paid.

According to Premack's position, a child might eat vegetables in order to gain access to apple pie, but not vice versa. Obviously, for most children getting apple pie is a far more effective reward than getting vegetables. Nonetheless, as unexpected as this is, such a reversal is possible. For this to work two conditions must be met: The child must truly enjoy eating the vegetables (though apple pie could still be preferred), and the child must have been deprived of these vegetables for a fair amount of time. This may make more sense when considering what happens to a child who overindulges in a favored treat. The happy child who is allowed to dive into a Halloween bag of candy, after having polished off a few pounds of sweets, would not find candy all that attractive.

A newer view of Premack's position that incorporates situations such as these is called the bliss point. That is, for each organism there is a particular level of each activity that is most desirable (that is, the bliss point). If one is below that level, that activity has become more probable and can be used as a reinforcer for other behaviors, even those that normally have a higher probability. Thus, if a child has not had vegetables in quite a while and has become tired of apple pie, the vegetables would be effective as reinforcers to increase pie eating, though only temporarily. Once the child has acquired the bliss point for vegetable eating (which is likely to be fairly quickly), its effectiveness is ended.

The bliss point idea addresses some of the confusion about positive and negative reinforcers as well. Intuitively, it seems that positive reinforcement should be the addition of a pleasant stimulus, and that negative reinforcement would be the removal of an unpleasant stimulus. However, as anyone who has overindulged in some favored activity knows, there are times when what is normally very pleasant becomes distinctly unpleasant. Thus, adding this stimulus would not be reinforcing, even though in general it seems that it should be. It is as if the organism conducts a cost-benefit analysis concerning its current state. If the consequence is preferable to the alternative, even one that is not particularly attractive, it will function as a reinforcer. Therefore, adding what would normally be an unpleasant stimulus is positively reinforcing if it is better than going without.

Another useful idea about what makes a particular situation reinforcing is called the establishing operation. This concept describes the process of creating a need for the particular stimulus. After a large meal, food is not an effective reinforcer, but after a period of not eating, it is. Denying an organism food establishes food as an effective reinforcer. The organism is below its bliss point. Secondary reinforcers can be explained by this concept as well. By pairing neutral stimuli with primary reinforcers, one is establishing their effectiveness. Finally, that different organisms find different situations or stimuli satisfying is no surprise. Ducks find the opportunity to swim satisfying; chickens do not. A species' natural history establishes what will be effective as well.

PATTERNS OF REINFORCER DELIVERY

It is not necessary to deliver a reinforcer on every occurrence of a behavior to have the desired effect. In fact, intermittent reinforcement has a stronger effect on the stability of the response rate than reinforcing every response. If the organism expects every response to be reinforced, suspending reinforcement will cause the response to disappear very quickly. If, however, the organism is familiar with occasions of responding without reinforcement, responding will continue for much longer upon the termination of reinforcers.

There are two basic patterns of intermittent reinforcement: ratio and interval. Ratio schedules are based on the number of responses required in order to receive the reinforcer. Interval schedules are based on the amount of time that must pass before a reinforcer is available. Both schedules have fixed and variable types. On fixed schedules, whatever the rule is, it stays that way. If five responses are required in order to earn a reinforcer (a fixed ratio 5, or FR 5), every fifth response is reinforced. A fixed interval ten seconds (FI 10) means that the first response after ten seconds has elapsed is reinforced, and this is true every time (responding during the interval is irrelevant). Variable schedules change the rule in unpredictable ways. A VR 5 (variable ratio 5) is one in which, on the average, the fifth response is reinforced, but it would vary over a series of trials. A variable interval ten seconds (VI 10) is similar. The required amount of time is an average of ten seconds, but on any given trial it could be different.

An example of an FR schedule is pay for a specific amount of work, such as stuffing envelopes. The pay is always the same; stuffing a certain number of envelopes always equals the same pay. An example of an FI is receiving the daily mail. Checking the mail box before the mail is delivered will not result in reinforcement. One must wait until the appropriate time. A VR example is a slot machine. The more attempts, the more times the player wins, but in an unpredictable pattern. A VI example would be telephoning a friend whose line is busy. Continued attempts will be unsuccessful until the friend hangs up the phone, but when this will happen is unknown.

Response rates for fixed schedules follow a fairly specific pattern. Fixed ratio schedules tend to have a steady rate until the reinforcer is delivered; then there is a short rest, followed by the same rate. A fixed interval is slightly different. The closer one gets to the required time, the faster the response rate. Upon receiving the reinforcer there will be a short rest, then a gradual return to responding, becoming quicker an quicker over time. This is called a "scalloped" pattern. (Though not strictly a FI schedule, it does have a temporal component, so it illustrates the phenomenon nicely.) Students are much more likely to study during the last few days before a test, and very little during the days immediately after the test. As time passes, study behavior gradually begins again, becoming more concentrated the closer the next exam date comes.

Sources for Further Study

Hilgard, Ernest R. *Psychology in America: A Historical Review.* San Diego, Calif.: Harcourt, Brace, Jovanovich, 1987. An excellent text describing the history and development of all facets of psychology. Chapters 3, 6, and portions of 10 are especially relevant to reinforcement.

Kimble, Gregory A. *Hilgard and Marquis' Conditioning and Learning.* 2d ed. New York: Appelton-Century-Crofts, 1961. Though somewhat dated and fairly advanced, this text gives an excellent and thorough review of the field of learning theory.

Kimble, Gregory A., Michael Wertheimer, and Charlotte L. White, eds. *Portraits of Pioneers in Psychology.* Washington, D.C.: America Psychological Association, 1991. This is an edited text with various authors describing the lives and contributions of the most important theorists from the early days of psychology. Most of the authors were personally familiar with their subjects, giving an interesting, personal view. Especially relevant are the essays on Ivan Pavlov and Edward L. Thorndike.

Lieberman, David A. *Learning: Behavior and Cognition.* 3d ed. Belmont, Calif.: Wadsworth, 2000. This is a college-level text for advanced psychology students, but it gives a very strong review of modern learning theory. Chapters 5-8 and 10 are especially relevant to reinforcement.

Salvador Macias III

See also: Aversion, implosion, and systematic desensitization; Behaviorism; Conditioning; Habituation and sensitization; Learned helplessness; Learning; Operant conditioning therapies; Pavlovian conditioning; Phobias; Reflexes.

Religion and psychology

Type of psychology: Cognition; developmental psychology; emotion; motivation; social psychology

Fields of study: Attitudes and behavior; coping; social perception and cognition; stress and illness

The relationship between religion and psychology usually involves the study of religious belief and behavior from a psychological perspective. The psychological study of religion includes a focus on both religious behavior and religious belief, uses various models of human nature, and utilizes many psychological concepts.

KEY CONCEPTS

- extrinsic religious orientation
- intrinsic religious orientation
- moral behavior
- quest religious orientation
- religion
- religious conversion
- spirituality

INTRODUCTION

Both religion and psychology are broad topics that encompass a vast array of human experience. The study of the psychology of religion is the effort to understand and predict the thoughts, feelings, and actions of persons as they act religiously. (The psychology of religion is different from the idea of psychology itself as a religion, which suggests that the field of psychology, with its own interpretation of the meaning of personal existence, be granted the status of an alternative worldview or a secular religion.) The psychology of religion is also distinct from religious psychology, which usually attempts to integrate the tenets of a faith system (such as Judaism, Islam, or Christianity) with the findings of psychological science.

The word "religion" is rooted in two Latin words: *legare* and *religio*. *Legare* denotes a process of rebinding or reconnecting. *Religio* means to restrain or hold back, which implies that one purpose of religion is to bridle human motives and impulses. Religion can be understood, then, as a force that reconnects human fragmentation to a sense of wholeness and restrains problematic drives and impulses. It should be noted that a supernatural deity is not mentioned or even implied in this definition. Thus, religion may involve a reconnection to God, nature, the self, some cosmic force, or almost anything else as one strives to be complete or whole.

Some research in the psychology of religion considers the function that religion serves for the individual. From this perspective, religion may be seen as a confirmation of hope, a conservation of values, a means by which to establish goals and measure personal development, a source of comfort, or a quest for the ideal relationship. Sigmund Freud, for example, considered religious experience to be a search for an external source of control to supersede the ambivalent feelings that individuals have toward their parents. Thus, Freud viewed God as nothing more, psychologically, than an exalted fa-

ther. He further maintained that the root of all religion is a longing for a father figure.

Another example of the perceived functional value of religion is in the study of religious conversions. A religious conversion may be understood as simply a transformation or a turning from one belief to another. Conversions may occur within religious contexts that are traditionally accepted by society (such as any major religious tradition) or may occur in cults or sects outside society's mainstream. Psychologists and other social scientists have often focused on the functional value of cultic conversions. One model, for example, suggests that the potential cultic convert must first experience enduring and strongly felt tensions that have not been met by traditional religious institutions. Once the cult movement is encountered, strong emotional bonds are established, and attachments to individuals outside the cult begin to diminish. Eventually, there is an intensive interaction between the new convert and the cult. Through these processes, the individual may believe that his or her needs are being met, while at the same time the control of the cult over the individual becomes substantially stronger. Thus, the religious practices of the cult serve a particular function both for the individual and for the group.

While some psychologists stress the functional aspects of religion, others view the study of religious experience more in terms of its substance by investigating such topics as different ways of being religious, whether religiousness is related to social compassion, participation in religious behaviors such as church attendance and prayer, the importance of religion, and believers' openness to doubt. For example, Gordon Allport wanted to investigate the characteristics of mature religion. He distinguished between those with an intrinsic religious orientation that is characterized by an inner, personal, and meaningful faith and those with an extrinsic religious orientation, in which faith is used for some other self-interest. In the mature intrinsic orientation, the person's faith is a "master motive" that will be given priority over other motives, especially those that may conflict (such as a particular economic or sexual motive). In the immature extrinsic religious orientation, religion provides some sort of payoff or gain outside the self, such as the protection of social or economic well-being.

Allport's notion of religious orientation has generated considerable interest among psychologists of

Spirituality and Religion

The sociologist of religion Wade Clark Roof studied the spiritual journeys of "baby boomers," a post-World War II generation, and titled his book *A Generation of Seekers* (1993). He found that 60 percent of this cohort abandoned organized religion as young adults, either temporarily or permanently. For example, if they returned at all, many Christians shifted their affiliations from mainline Protestant churches to other denominations. By the late 1960's, baby boomers were young adults exposed to an emerging counterculture. This was a time of tremendous social upheaval associated with the Vietnam War and a time of profound disillusionment with U.S. institutions, including organized religions. Consequently, many young adults who had rejected religion embraced a so-called New Age sensibility with respect to personal faith or spirituality. These disaffected seekers embarked upon an individualized search for union with the transcendent, however defined. The new spirituality embraced myriad phenomena, including practices based on Eastern religions, neopaganism, goddess worship, ecoreligion, and a bewildering variety of New Age ideas.

By privatizing the search for union with the divine (that is, by seeking personal wholeness outside traditional organizations) large numbers of people were actively seeking alternatives to traditional faith communities. Furthermore, Roof and others characterized their post-Enlightenment, secularized Western world as rational, technical, scientific, and therefore alienating. Depending on the degree of alienation, many Americans born after World War II were simply unwilling to search for spiritual wholeness in the church, synagogue, or mosque. In sum, there are two main forces contributing to the emergence of the new spirituality: the secularization (increasing worldliness) of modern Western society and the subsequent failure of religious organizations to meet personal, spiritual needs.

Even though all major religions are centered on a core spiritual awareness of the transcendent, the term "religion" in popular culture has taken on a negative connotation and is distinct from spirituality. Religion when perceived negatively is seen as impeding one's personal spiritual growth. On the other hand, the term "spirituality" has taken on a positive connotation since private seeking is perceived as promoting individual growth. Interestingly, the history of religion in America is rooted in an individualism that, in the case of Protestantism, is a result of the Reformation, which held a similar view of the impedimentary nature of the Catholic Church. Why, however, are churches seen by the disaffected as incapable of fostering personal, spiritual growth?

Sociologists offer an explanation. They have theorized that as society becomes increasingly secular, organized religion loses relevance or utility and is necessarily transformed. Since religious organizations such as churches accommodate the host culture, they mirror the prevailing worldview of rationality and are emptied of the supernatural and mystical. Thus, the shift in recent decades from organized religion to privatized spirituality is not entirely surprising.

At the end of the twentieth century, psychologists saw the conceptual polarization of religion and spirituality as a deterrent to the development of clinical applications and programs of research. In science, it is critical that researchers agree on what constructs mean. Kenneth I. Pargament, for example, points out that spirituality involves a search for life's meaning or significance in the experience of the sacred or divine, which is the central function of religion. While enthusiasm for spirituality divorced from religion is a well-documented trend, there are still people committed to religion whose spiritual needs are nurtured and sustained by the traditions, rituals, and scripture of formal religion. These are people who consider themselves both spiritual and religious.

Results from research point to considerable overlap in the meanings of the two terms. However, according to psychologist Peter C. Hill and his associates, there are two properties that distinguish between religion and spirituality: nonsacred goals and contact with groups. For example, some people ("extrinsics" in Gordon Allport's model) are committed to religion for nonsacred reasons. Their needs for status, power, and affiliation may be met in religious organizations. Also, identifiable groups in organizations validate certain behaviors, feelings, thoughts, and experiences. This is different for spiritual seekers not committed to a faith community: By virtue of the private nature of their search, there are no identifiable groups, nor are their goals unrelated to the sacred.

It remains to be seen whether or not social scientists will refine their constructs for spirituality and religion in light of the critique offered by Hill and his associates. However, theoretical consensus needs to be reached before researchers can move beyond the merely descriptive. In other words, current definitions and methods for studying spirituality as a fundamental human search for meaning are in the early stages of development.

Tanja Bekhuis

religion, and his theory has undergone some revision. It appears that intrinsic and extrinsic religiousness are not totally opposite. That is, some people may have both religious orientations, while others may have neither orientation. Furthermore, some psychologists have questioned whether the intrinsic orientation is really a mature religion. In part, this debate revolves around ways in which religious orientation is measured by means of self-reported responses to questions on a scale. The concern is that some people may respond a certain way to appear "good." An alternative religious orientation that has been proposed as a truly mature religion has been called the "quest" orientation. This orientation is characterized by an active searching for existential truth that may sometimes involve a certain degree of doubt or questioning. Defenders of Allport's notion of mature religion as an intrinsic orientation suggest that a quest orientation may be a necessary step in religious development but should not be understood as mature religion.

PSYCHOLOGICAL IMPLICATIONS OF RELIGION

While a psychological study of religion is of interest to many in its own right, others question the value of such research: Why bother with a psychological analysis of religious behavior?

One reason is that religion is apparently an important dimension in the life of many people. Religious conversions, for example, are very prevalent in Western society, and evidence indicates that during the 1980's Africa and many parts of Asia reported large numbers of religious conversions, particularly to Christianity, as well. Data from a 1996 Gallup Poll indicate that 39 percent of U.S. adults consider themselves to be "born-again" or evangelical Christians. The extent to which these percentages reflect genuine personal conversions is unclear; however, the indications are quite clear that religious conversion of some type, even if it means simply the confirmation of parental upbringing, occurs in the lives of many people.

Religion has other important psychological implications as well. Studies in the 1940's and 1950's showed repeatedly that religious people, as measured by frequency of church attendance, scored higher on measures of racial prejudice than did non-

religious people. This may be a disturbing finding to some, given that most religious teaching, regardless of tradition, stresses compassion, patience, and love for humanity. Yet there were also some notable exceptions to this general pattern. Allport decided to apply the intrinsic-extrinsic religious orientation concept to the study of prejudice. His reasoning was that "extrinsics" may be most likely to demonstrate prejudice, since their religious approach is one in which an individual seeks security and comfort, which are also by-products of prejudice (as when one sees oneself as superior to others). Hence, the person who attends church because it is psychologically comforting or because it increases his or her status in the community is more likely, for similar reasons, to have prejudicial attitudes. Research has generally supported Allport's reasoning. Extrinsically oriented individuals (identified as those with immature religion) demonstrate higher levels of prejudice than either intrinsics or nonreligious individuals. People who score indiscriminately high on both intrinsic and extrinsic measures of religion, however, demonstrate the highest prejudice levels of all. Evidence suggests that these people tend to see things in blanket categories (such as "all reli-

Many people seek out a priest, rabbi, minister, or other spiritual adviser in response to depression, anxiety, and other types of psychological distress. (St. Elizabeths Hospital Museum)

gion is good"). Since prejudice is a negative pre-judgment based on a stereotype, such people may also tend to see, for example, all minorities as bad.

The relationship between religion and prejudice is actually a part of a much broader question: Does religion have a positive effect on human behavior? Unfortunately, a simple, straightforward answer cannot be provided. One creative study at Princeton Theological Seminary was conducted to see if people with religion on their minds would be more likely to help someone in need. In the study, based upon the New Testament parable of the Good Samaritan, in which only the Samaritan, not the religiously minded priest or the Levite, helped a victim along a roadside, it was discovered that theological students were no more likely to help someone in need if they were about to give a talk on the Good Samaritan than if they were to give a talk on the job market for seminary graduates. Rather, the more crucial issue was how much time they had. Those who thought they were late were far less likely to help.

This one study certainly does not determine whether religion is a good predictor of moral behavior. In some cases, research has shown what some may think is intuitively obvious. Most studies indicate that religious individuals are less likely to engage in extramarital sexual behavior or use illicit drugs. Those with an intrinsic religious orientation, compared to extrinsics and the nonreligious, are less likely to cheat on an exam if given an opportunity to do so. Similarly, those who are highly committed to their faith are less likely blindly to obey an authority figure who orders them to hurt someone. It appears that religion can be an important predictor of some significant human behaviors.

Another common question involves religion and mental health. Religious symbolism is frequently found in the speech of those who are seriously disturbed, so this is a legitimate concern. Albert Ellis, an outspoken atheist and the creator of rational-emotive therapy (which suggests that irrational beliefs are at the heart of most psychological problems), considers religion harmful to one's well-being. The idea that one needs some supernatural power on which to rely, insists Ellis, is an irrational belief. Freud, who also saw religion as unhealthy, identified it as a neurosis of the masses. Certainly, the 1997 Heaven's Gate mass suicide in Rancho Santa Fe, California, as well as a number of other incidents, indicates that people may often engage in bizarre behavior in the name of religion. Yet research on a number of mental health variables, including fear of death, anxiety, loneliness, sense of well-being, dogmatism, and authoritarianism, generally indicates that religious people are neither better nor worse off than other persons.

Historical Background

Psychology and religion have had an intermittent relationship during the twentieth century. William James's classic book *The Varieties of Religious Experience: A Study in Human Nature* (1902) provided the early impetus for the psychology of religion. G. Stanley Hall, the first president of the American Psychological Association, wrote *Jesus, the Christ, in the Light of Psychology* (1917), which dealt with the underlying motivations of religious conversion. From 1920 to 1960, however, there was little interest in the field. Annual reviews on the subject in the *Psychology Bulletin* appeared less regularly from 1904 to 1920 and ceased altogether after 1933. Probably the greatest reason for the demise of the psychology of religion during this period was the idea that psychology should become an established science like the natural sciences. The study of religious experience, reasoned most experts, does not lend itself well to the scientific enterprise. Another reason that psychologists steered away from religion was the rise, during this period, of Freud's psychoanalytic theory, which many believed undermined the legitimacy of religious experience.

During the late 1950's and early 1960's, however, organizations such as the Christian Association for Psychological Studies and the Society for the Scientific Study of Religion were founded. The Catholic Psychological Association became Division 36 (Psychologists Interested in Religious Issues) of the American Psychological Association. At the same time, professional journals such as the *Journal for the Scientific Study of Religion* were established. In part, this about-face was caused by the changing religious patterns of society. Western culture has become increasingly religious since the 1950's. Also, psychology's infatuation with the prevailing view of science during the 1930's and subsequent decades has waned. No longer do many psychologists believe that psychology should (or can) become a science in the same way that physics, for example, is a science. This means that psychology is open to new methods and new areas of study, including religion.

An even more radical step since the 1970's has been the attempt by some psychologists to integrate theology with psychology. Though theology includes Judaism, Islam, Hinduism, and other major world religions, most of the effort at reconciliation has been directed toward Christian theology (particularly evangelical or conservative theology). Journals such as the *Journal of Psychology and Christianity* and the *Journal of Psychology and Theology* have been established as mechanisms of scholarly interchange on the relationship between psychological and theological understandings of the person. Even accredited graduate programs espousing an integrated study have opened and flourished.

Despite these dramatic changes by psychologists with regard to the study of religion, research has indicated that psychologists remain among the least religious of all scientists. Nevertheless, it is of interest to many to see whether these changes will affect the study of religious experience in the decades ahead.

SOURCES FOR FURTHER STUDY

Benner, David G., and Peter C. Hill, eds. *Baker Encyclopedia of Psychology and Counseling.* Grand Rapids, Mich.: Baker Book House, 1999. This encyclopedic reference has a special focus on religious issues and the integration of psychology with the Christian faith, but it includes most other psychological and some theological topics as well. Originally developed for ministers, it is thorough yet very understandable. An excellent resource.

Carter, John D., and Bruce Narramore. *The Integration of Psychology and Theology: An Introduction.* Grand Rapids, Mich.: Zondervan, 1979. This short paperback successfully accomplishes its mission of presenting a systematic framework by which the relationship between psychology and theology (particularly conservative Christian theology) can be understood. Reasons for the sometimes tense relationship between psychology and religion are also discussed.

Hill, Peter C., Kenneth I. Pargament, Ralph W. Hood Jr., Michael E. McCullough, James P. Swyers, David B. Larson, and Brian J. Zinnbauer. "Conceptualizing Religion and Spirituality: Points of Commonality, Points of Departure." *Journal for the Theory of Social Behavior* 30, no. 1 (2000): 51-77. The authors of this paper discuss the relevance of spirituality to psychology of religion and consider the overlap between religion and spirituality. They offer a careful analysis of the two concepts for future research.

Hood, Ralph W., Jr., Bernard Spilka, Bruce Hunsberger, and Richard Gorsuch. *The Psychology of Religion: An Empirical Approach.* 2d ed. New York: Guilford, 1996. This text, suitable for advanced undergraduates, is an especially good review of the field from an empirical perspective. Three of the four authors are past presidents of the Psychology of Religion division, American Psychological Association. New chapters on coping and socialization by families and school have been added for this edition.

Paloutzian, Raymond F. *Invitation to the Psychology of Religion.* 2d ed. Boston: Allyn & Bacon, 1996. This paperback textbook is truly an "invitation" to be introduced to the psychology of religion. The author is reasonably successful at reducing a large amount of material into a readable text. This book is a good place to begin one's study.

Pargament, Kenneth I. *The Psychology of Religion and Coping: Theory, Research, and Practice.* New York: Guilford, 1997. This book is a thoughtful and well-written work by a creative psychologist who studies how religion affects the way people cope with stress and how they turn to religion to find meaning in crisis. Highly recommended.

Peck, M. Scott. *The Road Less Traveled: A New Psychology of Love, Traditional Values, and Spiritual Growth.* New York: Simon & Schuster, 1978. An application-oriented book that takes the reader on a journey through confrontation and resolution of problems toward a higher level of self-understanding. Borrowing from humanistic psychology, this controversial book is surely thought-provoking.

Stern, E. Mark, ed. *The Other Side of the Couch: What Therapists Believe.* New York: Pilgrim Press, 1981. A fascinating exposé of the private religious beliefs of twenty-four therapists. Each briefly relates his or her own faith, sometimes admitting and other times vehemently denying its influence on his or her psychotherapy. The book can be appreciated by college readers.

Wulff, David M. *Psychology of Religion: Classic and Contemporary Views.* 2d ed. New York: John Wiley & Sons, 1997. A brilliant blend of various strains of thought and research that is destined to become a classic in the psychology of religion. The author deals evenhandedly with all major religious traditions, something not found in most other books in the psychology of religion. Designed for advanced readers at the undergraduate level.

Peter C. Hill;
updated by Tanja Bekhuis

SEE ALSO: Altruism, cooperation, and empathy; Attitude-behavior consistency; Attitude formation and change; Coping: Social support; Helping; Moral development; Religiosity: Measurement.

Religiosity

Measurement

TYPE OF PSYCHOLOGY: Cognition; developmental psychology; motivation; psychological methodologies; social psychology
FIELDS OF STUDY: Attitudes and behavior; coping; methodological issues; social motives; social perception and cognition; stress and illness

The study of religiosity (religious feelings, beliefs, and behaviors) by psychologists and other scholars involves a variety of quantitative and qualitative methods. The traditional measurement approach is psychometric and rests on substantive or functional scales of various aspects of religiosity.

KEY CONCEPTS
- denomination
- extrinsic religious orientation
- functional scales
- intrinsic religious orientation
- psychometric theory
- qualitative method
- quantitative method
- quest orientation
- religiosity
- substantive scales

INTRODUCTION
During the twentieth century, academic psychologists were concerned with developing an empirical science that would compare favorably with other natural sciences. Hence, the constructs in models of

human behavior were operationalized with the goal of yielding numeric data that could be analyzed statistically. Quantitative methods (experiments, quasi-experiments, surveys, correlational studies) superseded the earlier descriptive, qualitative methods (Oedipal interpretations, clinical and literary case studies, introspective reports) and required relatively objective measurement of psychological attributes or traits. A fundamental notion in psychometric theory is that measurements taken on people should at the very least allow ordering along some continuum or dimension, such as intelligence or anxiety. However, measurement also may connote appraisal or understanding. Thus, the early explorations of religious experience (such as those of Sigmund Freud, Carl Jung, or William James) may be very broadly considered as involving, in some sense, the "measure" of religious experience.

The development of models and methods in the study of religiosity (religious feelings, beliefs, and behaviors) parallels this general time line, although the emphasis on empiricism occurred in the latter half of the twentieth century. Since then, most psychologists of religion have been academic social psychologists who relied heavily on psychometric measures of religiosity, such as self-report questionnaires. However, since the 1980's, a resurgent interest in narrative or interpretive methods has competed with the psychometric tradition. Additionally, psychology of religion has become an international enterprise more open to qualitative methods. For example, Europeans are not averse to phenomenological interpretations of religious experience. The result of these diverging views is a broadening of the methodological base for testing models and theories of religion and an increasing sophistication with respect to measurement of religiosity. Many psychologists welcome this development, as they feel that more meaningful research is possible. For example, Kenneth I. Pargament, a renowned psychologist who studies coping behavior and religious beliefs, maintains that empirical methods must be balanced with phenomenological or interpretive methods, since religious experience is often private and symbolic and, therefore, not observable.

SOCIAL PSYCHOLOGY, ATTITUDES, AND SURVEYS
Mainstream social psychologists regard attitudes as learned habits for responding to social stimuli and attempt to identify the cognitive, affective (emo-

tional), and behavioral components of the attitude. Religiosity (also known as religiousness) is generally understood as a person's essential attitude toward religion. The word "religion" has a Latin root which implies binding and restraining. Religion is therefore a personal and social force which serves to bind people together in a community of worshipers, unite them in reverence with a spiritual dimension of existence, and restrain their inappropriate impulses via moral commandments.

The form of attitude surveying with which the average American would be most familiar is the national opinion poll as conducted by George Gallup, Louis Harris, a major newspaper or magazine, or a marketing research firm. For example, the Gallup Poll measures a person's overall religiosity by asking, "How important is religion in your life?" Nationally, more than half of the adults surveyed respond "very important," where importance tends to increase with age. Also, there are gender, ethnic, and church affiliation differences; for example, the subgroups comprising women, African Americans, or Protestants are most likely to say that religion is very important.

Pollsters usually break down religion into specific behavioral, cognitive, and affective components. An important behavioral component is affiliation with a particular denomination (a religious organization within the host culture usually referred to as a church). In 1999, about 90 percent of all adults in the United States claimed a religious affiliation (such as Protestant, Catholic, or Jewish), but only about 69 percent said they were actually members of a specific denomination. This figure is slightly lower for men, the young, or people living in the West. The largest single denomination in the United States in 1999 was Roman Catholic (27 percent), followed by Baptists (18 percent), then Methodists (9 percent). However, taken in the aggregate, 59 percent of the adults surveyed were Protestant.

Attending worship services is another behavior that may be measured. Forty percent of U.S. adults attended a service during the last seven days. Since 1939, this figure has been very stable. Other measurable religious activities include reading the Bible and praying: 47 percent of U.S. adults have read the Bible in the last week and 75 percent pray daily.

Another approach would be to measure people's level of acceptance or endorsement of specific church policies (or of government laws relating to religion). For example, 78 percent of American Catholics disagree with the official teachings of their church of not allowing divorced people to remarry in the church and 84 percent disagree with not permitting people to use artificial means of birth control. Polls have also discovered that about three-quarters of all Americans would accept teaching about world religions and the Bible (as literature and history) in the public schools.

Cognitive dimensions of religiousness include beliefs about God or a spiritual reality, as well as what people believe about religion. Ninety-five percent of U.S. adults believe in God or in a higher power. Seventy-two percent believe in heaven and 56 percent believe in hell. Sixty-five percent believe that religion, rather than being out of date, can answer most of today's problems; 42 percent believe that religion is increasing its influence on American life, while 52 percent believe it is losing influence. People have high confidence in organized religions or churches relative to other institutions, and clergy are ranked highly with respect to honesty and ethical standards when compared to other professions. (These statistics were, however, gathered prior to the exposures of sexual misconduct in the Roman Catholic church in the United States in 2002.)

The affective components of religiosity deal with emotions, priorities, values, and evaluations. For example, in evaluating the overall priority they give to religion in their lives, 60 percent of Americans state that religion is "very important," while only one in eight says it is "not very important." In evaluating how well their own church meets their personal and family needs, 67 percent say "good" or "excellent."

RELIGIOUS ORIENTATION SCALES

In the 1960's, a dominant theme in research on religiosity emerged in response to the work of Gordon Allport, who had developed a model of religious orientation characterized by intrinsic and extrinsic dimensions. The former type of religiosity is interiorized, private, devotional, and based on individual commitment. Some items purporting to measure intrinsic religiosity have dealt with personal piety, church attendance, and the importance of religion. Extrinsic religiosity is more institutional, public, and pragmatic. Some of the items on scales designed to measure the extrinsic dimension include seeing religion as a vehicle for social relationships, consolation of grief, maintenance of order, and adherence to tradition. Many psychometric scales have been developed to assess orientation, an aspect of religiosity. Some measure orientation with a single intrinsic/extrinsic, bipolar scale, others with two distinct subscales. In contrast, in 1991 C. Daniel Batson and P. Schoenrade developed the Quest Scale hto measure a third type. A quest orientation recognizes the positive value of doubt in the face of complex, existential questions regarding the meaning of life. What is particularly interesting is that Quest Scale scores tend to correlate negatively with prejudice measures.

OTHER MEASURES OF RELIGIOSITY

Peter C. Hill and Ralph W. Hood, Jr., edited a much-needed compendium of scales titled *Measures of Religiosity* (1999). There are 126 scales grouped in seventeen chapters, thematically arranged. For example, there are measures of beliefs, attitudes, orientation, development, commitment, experience, values, and coping. Scales are presented along with information about the measured variable or dimension; scoring; psychometric properties, including evidence for reliability and validity; characteristics of people studied during the test development phase (norming samples); documentation regarding where the measure appeared in the research literature; and references for follow-up study. By identifying measures of similar constructs with different names or, conversely, measures of dissimilar constructs with the same name, Hill and Hood hope to promote a better understanding of the constructs measured. Richard Gorsuch also has suggested that construct and convergent validity could be improved if different researchers would use the same measures in well-developed, theoretically driven programs of research.

It is rare for scales used in the measurement of religiosity to meet well-known criteria for psychological tests. For example, few researchers publish standardized norms or even basic descriptive statistics for the samples used, such as measures of central tendency (means or medians) and variability (standard deviations or ranges). While reliability may be good, information regarding validity is often inadequate. Validity is further compromised by the inherent sampling bias of many American religiosity scales, since most were developed using samples of convenience comprising U.S. Protestants. There-

fore, scales may be invalid for groups other than U.S. Protestants. Traditional criteria and standards for scales may be found in texts such as *Psychological Testing* (1997) by Anne Anastasi and Susana Urbina or in the *Standards for Educational and Psychological Testing* (1985).

Religiosity measures may be classified as substantive scales or functional scales. If the former, the focus is on content, and if the latter, the focus is on process. For example, measures of religious beliefs tend to be substantive and are about *what* is believed, whereas measures of religious orientation tend to be functional and are variants or departures from Allport and Ross's Religious Orientation Scale (1967).

Although social psychologists still dominate the field, developmental, cognitive, and evolutionary psychologists are contributing measures that correspond to their models of religious experience. While measures across these domains are primarily paper-and-pencil questionnaires, some are structured or semistructured interviews and some, as in the evolutionary approach, measure neurophysiological variables as indicators of religious or spiritual states.

HOW RELIGIOSITY MEASURES ARE USED

Numerous applications of the various measures of religiosity are possible. Researchers can correlate any of these to other attitudes, personality traits, or demographic variables. Questions such as whether religious people are more superstitious, how religiosity differs between Democrats and Republicans, and whether religion helps people cope with marital problems can be addressed. For example, depending upon how one decides to measure religion (and how one measures superstition), there is a slight tendency for more religious people to be a little less superstitious, but there are many people who are neither very religious nor very superstitious—and there are some who are both.

Using data from political polls, it can be verified that Jews, Catholics, and black Baptists tend to vote for Democrats, while most mainline white Protestant groups tend to vote for Republicans. Much of this correlation can be explained by historical and social-class features, however, in addition to the religious positions of the denominations.

Whether (and how) religion helps people cope with marital or other real-life problems is a difficult question to resolve. True experimentation, with random assignment of people to experimental and control conditions, would be necessary to confirm a cause-and-effect relationship. What seems to be apparent, however, is that religious people have a lower incidence of divorce and report slightly higher levels of marital satisfaction. This could be attributable to the fact that religious people feel more obligated to report that they have better marital relations, or it could be attributable to the fact that people who have problems in staying with a spouse also have problems in staying with their religion. When parents are asked whether religion has helped strengthen their family relationships, nearly four in five report that it has.

Clinical applications of the measurement of religiosity are also numerous. Very religiously committed individuals may have a problem with entering purely secular psychotherapy. The therapist may be seen as a nonbeliever who will challenge the patient's worldview. Depending on the denomination, patients' motivation for change may be tempered by the belief that their sufferings are a punishment inflicted by God.

From a more positive perspective, a patient's religion can both serve as a source of impulse control (for example, as a check on suicidal tendencies) and provide a wide range of formal and informal social supports. For all these reasons, it is necessary for clinicians to assess the religiosity of their patients. Tolerant therapists can then use the patient's worldview as a reference point. Therapists who cannot tolerate a given patient's religiosity can make an appropriate referral (to another therapist who can) before the therapist is frustrated and the psychotherapeutic relationship has been damaged.

Other applications are possible in social and applied psychology. By understanding the religiosity of their "target segment," for example, advertisers can tailor commercial and political messages in order to synchronize them with the values and worldviews of potential customers or voters.

HISTORICAL BACKGROUND

In the late nineteenth century, psychologists turned to the field of religion and speculated about its origins and importance. William James was one of the foremost scholars of this period. His approach was chiefly that of the case study. The strength of his qualitative and narrative approach was that religion was embedded within the broader context of human life. The weakness was that two different investigators could look at the same religious person or phenomenon and come to very different conclusions, for there were no quantitative data.

The psychoanalyst Erik Erikson also employed the case-study approach. For example, he wrote about the lives of Martin Luther and Mahatma Gandhi in terms of his eight-stage, epigenetic theory. Other theorists with a positive view of religion included neo-Freudians such as Carl Jung and Erich Fromm, and humanistic "third force" representatives such as Abraham Maslow. However, for these theorists, religion was secondary to their studies of personality and their work was, therefore, seen by academic psychologists of religion as more philosophical than scientific.

For these reasons, the quantitative approach of the pollsters and psychologists dominates academic psychology. Yet doubt may be cast upon the scientific status of this approach as well. A serious problem has to do with social desirability—people often respond in a way they think they should respond. Even though responses may be anonymous, people may (unconsciously or not) seek to portray themselves in a favorable light (in other words, as more religious than they really are). Another concern is the use of ambiguous terms in questions. Each denomination tends to define terms in its own way. What one denomination calls "services" might be called "worship" or "Mass" by another. The Lord's Supper is also known as Holy Communion and the Eucharist. Terms such as "God" and "personal commitment" may be so vague as to preclude construct validity.

The same item may have a different meaning for different people. For example, a person answering "rarely or never" to the question "How often do you ask God to forgive your sins?" may be an atheist who sees no purpose to the confession or a pious individual who rarely sins. Someone who disagrees with the statement "The word of God is revealed only in the Scriptures" may be an atheist or someone who believes in the possibility of present-day revelation. Certainly, national polls and measures of religiosity have ignored the importance of the context of the respondent's denomination. Religiosity, as measured by the same scale, may mean one thing for an Orthodox Jew and another for a Jehovah's Witness.

Many social scientists predicted the demise of religion during the twentieth century. Karl Marx believed that religion was the "opiate" of the people—a social institution used by the ruling classes to control and placate the exploited masses. After a proletarian revolution and the establishment of a just (Communist) social order, reasoned Marx, there would be no need for religion or, for that matter, the other instruments of state repression. Sigmund Freud contended that, as psychoanalysis became more prevalent, people would turn away from religion; society would be composed of self-restrained individuals in control of their sexual and aggressive drives. The behaviorist B. F. Skinner regarded religious behavior as the result of accidental reinforcement, a superstitious approach to life that would diminish as humanity developed better technology for controlling the contingencies of its own reinforcement.

Instead, religion remains in myriad forms. For example, many intellectuals have moved away from institutionalized religion toward secular humanism. This requires those who study religion to rethink certain definitions, such as whether secular humanism can be defined as a religion and whether its religiosity can be measured. A more relevant question is not whether religion will continue to exist, but whether qualitative methods can attain the precision that science demands and whether quantitative methods can ever adequately measure the richness of human religious experience.

SOURCES FOR FURTHER STUDY

Allport, Gordon Willard. *The Individual and His Religion: A Psychological Interpretation.* New York: Macmillan, 1950. This brief and readable book gives a sympathetic look at how religion can influence the many dimensions of a person's life. Allport lays out the theoretical foundation for his internal-external measurement of religiosity.

American Educational Research Association, American Psychological Association, and National Council on Measurement in Education. *Standards for Educational and Psychological Testing.* Washington, D.C.: American Psychological Association, 1985. The standards for evaluating and using tests reflect the consensus of professionals. Includes technical standards for design, development, and selection of tests with the layperson in mind.

Anastasi, Anne, and Susan Urbina. *Psychological Testing.* 7th ed. Upper Saddle River, N.J.: Prentice Hall, 1997. This is a classic introduction to psychometric theory and includes chapters on reliability and validity. The text is very readable.

Erikson, Erik Homburger. *Gandhi's Truth: On the Origin of Militant Nonviolence.* New York: W. W. Norton, 1969.

_____. *Young Man Luther: A Study in Psychoanalysis and History.* New York: W. W. Norton, 1962. These are sensitive and reverential treatments of great religious leaders, from the perspective of Erikson's eight-stage theory of development.

Gallup, George, Jr., and D. Michael Lindsay. *Surveying the Religious Landscape: Trends in U.S. Beliefs.* Harrisburg, Pa.: Morehouse, 1999. Brief book presents results from national polls of American beliefs, practices, feelings, and attitudes regarding religion. This book is easy to understand and includes an appendix describing how the surveys are designed.

Hill, Peter C., and Ralph W. Hood Jr., eds. *Measures of Religiosity.* Birmingham, Ala.: Religious Education Press, 1999. Compendium of scales of religiosity; excellent coverage of various measured aspects or dimensions. Each scale presented with brief history of its development and information regarding psychometric properties.

Hood Jr., Ralph W., Bernard Spilka, Bruce Hunsberger, and Richard Gorsuch. *The Psychology of Religion: An Empirical Approach.* 2d ed. New York: Guilford, 1996. This text, while more challenging than Meadow and Kahoe, is an especially good review of the field from an empirical perspective. Three of the four authors are past presidents of the Psychology of Religion division of the American Psychological Association. New chapters on coping and socialization by families and school have been added for this edition.

Meadow, Mary Jo, and R. D. Kahoe. *Psychology of Religion: Religion in Individual Lives.* New York: Harper & Row, 1984. This is one of the easiest-reading texts in the field. Nevertheless, its topical coverage is quite broad. The authors explore many different ways of measuring specific facets of religion. Their review of the intrinsic/extrinsic concept is one of the most comprehensive, and it is certainly one of the most balanced.

Wulff, David M. *The Psychology of Religion: Classic and Contemporary.* 2d ed. New York: John Wiley &

Sons, 1997. A thorough and balanced introduction to the scientific study of religion. Both quantitative and qualitative approaches are introduced.

T. L. Brink;
updated by Tanja Bekhuis

SEE ALSO: Archetypes and the collective unconscious; Attitude-behavior consistency; Attitude formation and change; Behavioral assessment and personality rating scales; Religion and psychology; Survey research: Questionnaires and interviews.

Research ethics

TYPE OF PSYCHOLOGY: All
FIELDS OF STUDY: General constructs and issues

Research ethics are part of a broader set of general principles operating in the field of psychology that focus on maintaining certain standards of behavior for psychologists who conduct or supervise research.

KEY CONCEPTS
- animal testing
- confidentiality
- consent
- control groups
- data
- deception
- release of information
- side effects

INTRODUCTION
In order to advance knowledge about human behavior, individuals in the field of psychology conduct research. Such endeavors involve both human and nonhuman participants. The use of nonhuman participants is usually understood to mean that there will be animal testing, or the use of animals, in the research. With either type of participant, lawful conduct and efforts to protect the welfare of the research participants are always of the utmost concern. The field of psychology, through the work of the American Psychological Association (APA), has devised a set of general ethical principles that apply to research to protect the participant and the data, or information, derived from such work.

In addition, ethical guidelines are designed to protect the interests of involved others, such as students and colleagues, who may be active in the research process as assistants and coinvestigators, rather than as research participants. Protections for these individuals come in the form of guidelines regarding professionalism, honesty among colleagues, proper supervision, vigilance against plagiarism, and the maintenance of appropriate professional boundaries.

Guidelines for ethical research exist to protect all involved in psychology research, the public at large, and the field of psychology as a whole.

PROTECTING ANIMAL PARTICIPANTS
The protection of research participants is a key element of research ethics in psychology. Separate guidelines for protections exist for nonhuman and human participants. Animal participants must be treated with respect and care. The research must be purposeful and have benefits clearly outweighing the cost of involving the animals. Nonanimal alternatives must have been explored. The type of animal selected must be best suited to answer the research question, based on the most current literature. The animals used must be treated in a humane way so as to reduce the risk of pain or suffering as much as possible. The animals must be properly monitored to ensure that they are free from pain and suffering and kept in good care. No work may be conducted on the animals until a research plan has been approved by an appropriate committee overseeing animal care.

In addition, any staff members assisting with animal research must be familiar with these guidelines, as well as with all the laws and regulations involved in the conduct of this work. They must be adequately trained and supervised in the conduct of such work, which includes having knowledge of any behavioral or other indicators that suggest that an animal might be distressed or in need of health care. Further, very strict guidelines exist regarding the quality of housing provided for the animals, how animals may or may not be selected for use, and the types of experimental procedures permitted. If animal studies are conducted outside the laboratory, in the animals' natural habitat, researchers must also follow guidelines designed to minimize disturbance of the animals and their environment.

PROTECTING HUMAN PARTICIPANTS

Human participants must be treated with respect, and all commitments to them must be honored. Their privacy and confidentiality must be maintained, meaning that their participation and the information that they reveal are kept secret, known only to the researchers and their staff, and protected in the way in which they are presented in written descriptions of the study. Human subjects must be exposed to as little risk as is necessary. Research procedures should be as minimally invasive as possible. Participants must be adequately informed about the purposes of the research and the relative risks and benefits of participating. They are formally asked to consent, or give permission, for their participation, a process known as informed consent. They must be free to withdraw from participation for any reason with no negative consequences to them.

Some special issues deserving discussion are the use of deception, limits to confidentiality, and use of control groups. Deception is the obscuring or withholding of information which is vital to the experiment but which may mislead participants to some degree. Psychologists are never to deceive participants about matters that might affect their willingness to serve as participants, such as physical risks, discomfort, or unpleasant emotional experiences. Psychologists also cannot use deception unless it is absolutely necessary to the study and judged to outweigh the costs of the manipulation. Finally, when deception is used, participants must be debriefed about the deception as soon as possible.

Limits to confidentiality are also important. While efforts are made to keep data and research findings separate from the identity of the research participants, in some cases confidentiality is limited, such as when the participant reports a plan of self-harm or harm to another person, especially a child, elder, or other vulnerable person. It is the duty of the psychologist to act upon such knowledge to protect the general good by reporting the information to the appropriate authorities or individuals. Therefore, as part of the consent process, researchers must explain these limits to potential participants.

Finally, control groups in research deserve a special mention. Control groups provide a special experimental condition in which research participants receive as little assessment and intervention as possible. These groups may be used to allow researchers to see experimentally the results of the simple passage of time or the simple effect of assessment on research participants. In research involving the treatment of mental health conditions, particularly where there are known effective treatments for the disorder in question, the use of a true control group is controversial and discouraged. Participation in research where random assignment to a control group might occur could be seen as a way of delaying or withholding treatment from someone who needs it. In such cases, researchers have had to resort to other means to establish experimental control. For instance, waiting-list controls might be used under the logic that it is typical for individuals to have to wait for treatment under normal circumstances, so doing so under an experimental paradigm does not constitute undue harm. Researchers have also employed minimal treatment controls, where a minimum level of treatment is provided to the control group. In such cases, participants might be allowed to receive the experimental treatment later if it were found to be more effective than the minimal treatment. Finally, in some cases, researchers must provide a full-fledged active treatment to participants, such as standard care, when trying to assess the utility of a new treatment strategy. In such cases, the negative consequences of receiving no care outweigh the benefits of comparing the new treatment to a no-care situation.

In addition to these issues, many provisions are related to the training of research staff and the maintenance and care of the data collected to support these general goals. Just as guidelines prohibit research on animals until the work plan has been reviewed, no research with humans should be conducted until the research plan is assessed by an institutional review board (IRB). This committee oversees the identification of risks and benefits of the research, the communication of this information to the participants, and the overall safety and ethical soundness of the research plan.

PROTECTING DATA

Once data have been collected, the information and any files related to it must receive special protections. This is primarily important for data from human participants because of confidentiality issues, but it can also be important for animal data because of procedural and other information that may be contained in the data records or research files.

A basic consideration is that the raw data, such as data collected from a human participant, must be kept in a secure location and in a manner that protects the identity of the participant. This requirement usually means that questionnaire and other data are identified by code numbers rather than by individual participant names. In addition, any links among code numbers and participant identities must be minimized and stored in a place separate from the data or any representation of them, such as electronic files.

Data should be retained for five years after the publication of any reports so that colleagues may examine the information to determine whether the conclusions were properly pursued and represented. This is done by the assigned owner of the data, a designation usually agreed upon by all senior investigators involved in the research planning. If the data are to be collected using monies from the federal government, however, the government may require a longer maintenance period, such as ten years after collection. Also, the government may require that the data be made public for any related request, rather than only collegial requests.

Finally, prior to their presentation in research reports, the data should be verified, meaning that errors should be processed out in order to avoid the presentation of misleading findings. Data on discrete research questions should not be published in duplicate form in order to avoid misrepresenting the findings or placing them out of context. Also, the presentation of data collected for research purposes should be limited to those purposes. A scientist may present the data for some other use, such as training or education, but, as with all presentations, care to protect the confidentiality and welfare of the research participants must take priority.

PROFESSIONALISM AND PUBLICATIONS

Another set of issues related to research ethics involves publications. For those serving as professional reviewers, ethical guidelines apply because new research reports are privileged information. Therefore, reviewers are bound to treat the information reviewed as highly confidential. In deciding to serve as a reviewer, a psychologist must acknowledge any conflicts of interest that might be present regarding relationship with the author, any companies connected to the research, or any other relationships that might affect the ability to be impar-

tial. When a conflict exists, the potential reviewer must resign from the process.

Similar disclosures of conflicts of interest are required of the authors of research reports. For example, when an individual receives money from a drug company or a health maintenance organization (HMO) to conduct a study that could affect how that drug or that HMO is perceived, it is important for the researcher to acknowledge that financial relationship, as well as any other influence that the company or HMO might have had on the findings and their presentation in the research report. This disclosure allows for fair review of the findings for readers.

In general, psychologists are advised to avoid taking multiple roles; this is true for those in research as well. For instance, a psychologist would not seek to enroll friends and family members in his or her own research and would be advised against becoming a stockholder in a drug company when conducting research on a drug made by that company. Such dual relationships might make it difficult to be impartial or to be seen as impartial by others in the reporting of any data collected.

A final issue regarding research ethics relates to publication credit: who is included as an author on papers and presentations, as well as the order of authorship. In general, persons who substantially contribute to the production of the research report in ways that directly apply to the intellectual content should be included as authors. Typically, authorship on papers is decided before the research is started as part of the research plan. This agreement allows each person to anticipate his or her contributions and to input effort to the process fairly. Additionally, it facilitates the ownership of responsibility for the authors to ensure that all ethical guidelines for research in the field were adhered to in the conduct of the study. Typically, assurances to this effect are required by many journals in order for the report to be accepted for publication.

NEW CHALLENGES

As the human population grows, so too do the complexities of human life and the potential for problems. The human community is no longer simply a local tribe but a global force composed of different peoples with different languages, cultural customs, histories, and resources. As communication among different peoples increases, the potential for miscommunication is likely to increase as well. Research in psychology will remain quite important as it—combined with knowledge from such fields as sociology, anthropology, and political science—will be key in the untangling of such miscommunications. Research ethics and guidelines will encourage proactive communications about research endeavors and their potential impact.

It is important to realize, however, that not all countries demand the same standard of ethics for research in general, or research in psychology more specifically, as do the legal and professional governing bodies in the United States. For the most part, the research ethics standards observed in the United States are among the highest worldwide. American researchers conducting research or collaborating in other countries may be permitted or even encouraged by local authorities to act in accord with somewhat different standards. The researchers will be encouraged to maintain the highest of standards while striving to understand and respond to the local standards. In such cases, consultation with senior colleagues is important to ensure that the issues at hand are thoroughly considered.

An example of an issue that might require consideration involves the use of incentives to encourage participation. For a study of health behavior, for instance, each participant might be offered $100 for five hours of participation. By American standards, this amount might not seem like much for that period of time. If the study were done in a very poor country, however, this incentive could be astronomical in relation to what most people earn in a year. Such an incentive could cause social unrest and other problems that the researcher might not anticipate without the review of a local IRB. In this example, a local IRB might recommend that they researchers pay only $1 as an incentive, which might seem absurdly low from an American perspective. It is in such circumstances that culture and research ethics and methods must continue to grow to allow work to advance without causing disruption.

Another complexity affecting contemporary psychological research is scientific knowledge in the field of genetics and the increasing use of personal medical records and data sharing for research purposes. For instance, one must ask what constitutes adequate consent to participate in a research project that includes genetic testing and the use of personal medical records. While the individual participant may weigh the costs and benefits of participating, what about the family members? Should they be asked to sign a release allowing the individual to give information to researchers? This question arises because such research may expose the participant's entire family to risks such as loss of insurability, unwanted information about health risks, and loss of privacy. The question becomes how extensive consent to participation should be. While provisions may be written into the management of the data collected in order to protect individual participants, side effects or unanticipated consequences may arise that have deleterious effects. A scenario involving genetic research may prompt conversations among family members about the information, including potential miscommunications. It also might lead to accidental loss of privacy, particularly if family members report information in a pedigree format, in which a family tree is described. In such cases, one family member may reveal information about other family members that those members do not want revealed and that could expose them to unanticipated risks. These examples provide food for thought regarding how research ethics in psychology and other areas of science will need to grow in the future in order to address the complexities brought about by modern human life.

SOURCES FOR FURTHER STUDY

American Psychological Association. *Publication Manual of the American Psychological Association.* 5th ed. Washington, D.C.: Author, 2001. Outlines the basic standards and guidelines for publishing in psychology, with sections devoted to ethical issues in the conduct and publication of psychological activities, including research.

American Psychological Association. Committee on Animal Research and Ethics (CARE). *Guidelines for Ethical Conduct in the Care and Use of Animals.* Washington, D.C.: Author, 2002. Guidelines for the proper care and use of animals in psychological research are presented in detail, along with information on how to report violations of such guidelines.

Carroll, Marilyn E., and J. Bruce Overmier, eds. *Animal Research and Human Welfare: Advancing Human Welfare Through Behavioral Science.* Washington, D.C.: American Psychological Association, 2001. Examines the use of animals in research related to human health. Describes health advances and the importance of laboratory models for understanding human health conditions.

Josselson, Ruthellen, ed. *Ethics and Process in the Narrative Study of Lives*. Thousand Oaks, Calif.: Sage Publications, 1996. Case examples of ethical issues that arose in the collection of stories and anecdotal descriptions from research participants are discussed.

Koocher, Gerald P., and Patricia Keith-Spiegel. *Ethics in Psychology: Professional Standards and Cases*. 2d ed. New York: Oxford University Press, 1998. The broad and basic ethical issues applying to psychologists are described, along with several key discussion points on research ethics.

Sales, Bruce D., and Susan Folkman, eds. *Ethics in Research with Human Participants, First Edition*. Washington, D.C.: American Psychological Association, 2000. Outlines basic ethical considerations for working with human participants. Highlights several areas of consideration that will likely become more important as psychology advances to studying more complex behavior in individuals and groups.

Street, Linda L., and Jason B. Luoma, eds. *Control Groups in Psychosocial Intervention Research: Ethical and Methodological Issues*. Hillsdale, N.J.: Lawrence Erlbaum, 2002. Explores the special ethical considerations that arise in the consideration of withholding treatment from research participants when effective treatment is known to be available.

Nancy A. Piotrowski

SEE ALSO: Animal experimentation; Archival data; Complex experimental designs; Confidentiality; Data description; Experimental psychology; Experimentation: Ethics and subject rights; Experimentation: Independent, dependent, and control variables; Field experimentation; Observational methods; Quasi-experimental designs; Scientific methods; Survey research: Questionnaires and interviews; Within-subject experimental designs.

Reticular formation

TYPE OF PSYCHOLOGY: Biological bases of behavior
FIELDS OF STUDY: Auditory, chemical, cutaneous, and body senses; nervous system; sleep

The reticular formation is a system of interneurons in the brain stem that receives and integrates sensory information from all parts of the body. It influences almost all functions of the nervous system but is especially known for its effects on attentiveness, waking, and sleeping.

KEY CONCEPTS
- afferent
- arousal
- brain stem
- efferent
- epilepsy
- integration
- interneuron
- nucleus
- reticular activating system
- sleep circuit

INTRODUCTION

The term "reticular formation" is used to refer to one of several so-called reticular structures of the central nervous system. A reticulum is a mesh or network, and reticular formation designates a specific grouping of more than ninety nuclei of interneurons that have common characteristics in the area of the brain stem. The nuclei are clusters of cell bodies of neurons that form a network of their dendritic and axonal cellular processes, those extensions that bring information into the cell and transmit information from the cell.

The mesh reaches throughout the brain stem, as well as to higher and lower regions of the central nervous system as far as the cerebral cortex and spinal cord, serving both sensory and integrative functions. Anatomically, the reticular formation is continuous from the medulla oblongata, the lowest part of the brain stem, through the pons to the midbrain. It connects with the intermediate gray region of the spinal cord and sends processes into the higher brain areas of the thalamus and hypothalamus.

Neurons of the reticular formation contain many dendritic processes, afferent cytoplasmic extensions that carry electrical stimuli toward the cell nucleus, arranged perpendicular to the central axis of the body. Each cell also contains a single long axon, with numerous collateral branches, that extends along the body's axis, going to the higher or lower regions of the central nervous system. The axon carries impulses away from the nucleus of the neuron toward the synapse, where it passes information on to the next neighboring cell. The axons and dendrites, present in large numbers, make up the mesh, or reticulum, that gives the reticular formation its name. The many aggregated processes make it extremely difficult to identify the clustered groups of neurons (nuclei) to which the individual cells belong.

INFORMATION AND AROUSAL

The reticular formation is a portion of an important informational loop in the brain that allows the modification and adjustment of behavior. This loop extends from the cerebral cortex to subcortical areas (lower brain regions), including the reticular formation, and then back to the cortex. The reticular formation makes connections with all the portions of the loop and plays an important role in exciting or inhibiting the functions of the lower motor neuron centers. This loop is important in practically all functions of the nervous system and behavior, particularly sleep/wakefulness, emotional stress, depression and distress, the induction of rapid eye movement (REM) sleep, and even sleepwalking.

The process of arousal appears to take place as the reticular formation sends impulses to an area of the thalamus occupied by the midline thalamic nuclei. These nuclei then pass the information on to the cortex, which is stimulated to become more aware that information is coming and more attentive to receiving the information. This is an oversimplification of the process, however, as other areas of the brain also seem to be involved in arousal. The neurotransmitters involved in the reticular formation's connection to the cortex are thought to include both cholinergic and monoamine systems in the arousal process, although these are still not well understood.

The basic functions of the reticular formation are twofold: to alert the higher centers, especially in the cortex, that sensory information is coming into the processing areas; and to screen incoming information being passed upward on sensory (afferent) pathways toward the higher centers of the brain, blocking the passage of irrelevant information and passing along the information that should be acted upon by the higher brain. All sensory information must be passed through the lower regions of the brain before reaching the associative regions of the

cerebral cortex. The cortex is unable to process incoming information unless it has been alerted and aroused and unless the information is channeled through the proper lower brain regions. Besides the reticular formation, the thalamus is also involved in this function, taking information from the reticular formation and passing it on to the cortex, where it is then processed and coordinated to produce motor behavior.

INFORMATION INHIBITION

Because the reticular formation has so many pathways from each cell leading to many other cells, it is very quickly inhibited by anesthetics that act by inhibiting the transfer of information between cells at the synapse. This inhibition of activity leads to unconsciousness from a general lack of sensation and loss of alertness and arousal as polysynaptic pathways are shut down. Under proper medical control, use of anesthesia to turn off the reticular formation can be lifesaving, allowing surgical procedures that could not be tolerated without it.

Lesions of the brain stem may damage the reticular formation, producing the uncontrolled unconsciousness of coma if they occur above the level of the pons on both sides. Coma that results from drug overdose or drug reaction occurs mainly as the result of depression of the reticular formation. Any lesion of the brain stem that affects the reticular formation directly will also have a secondary effect on other structures on the brain stem, causing disappearance of its reflex reactions. Damage to ascending efferent pathways from the reticular formation to the cortex sometimes can also cause coma. Because the reticular formation aids the brain stem in regulating critical visceral vital functions such as breathing and blood circulation, damage to this area may threaten life itself.

The actions of alcohol on behavior also are the result of its effects on the reticular formation. Alcohol blocks the actions of this area, allowing a temporary loss of control over other brain regions. This lack of behavioral inhibition from higher brain centers produces a feeling of excitement and well-being at first. Later effects of continued alcohol intake lead to depression of emotions and behavior, followed by depression of basic body functions that can produce unconsciousness.

The production of unconsciousness through sleep is also associated with the reticular formation, particularly the part that is in the pons and another center in the lower medulla. The lower medullary sleep/waking center seems to work with the basal forebrain to modulate the induction of sleep. Rapid eye movement sleep may be controlled, at least in part, by specific nuclei in the pontine reticular formation.

BEHAVIORAL EFFECTS

Stimulation of the reticular formation and other areas (the hippocampus and amygdala) improves memory retention (memory consolidation) if electrical current is applied directly to the reticular cells immediately after a training session. It is difficult to understand how this stimulation operates, however, since in some cases stimulating these same areas instead produces retrograde amnesia, causing the loss of memory retention. It is thought that the level of electrical stimulation may cause these different results. The highest and lowest stimulation levels reduce memory consolidation in some cases, and intermediate stimulation seems to be the most effective. The nature of the training process is also important in the results, as learning seems to be more difficult with high stimulation levels associated with aversive conditioning.

Another aspect of the reticular formation and its possible effects on behavior is the theory that many (or perhaps most) convulsive epileptic seizures originate there. Since this area can be stimulated by electrical impulses and by convulsive drugs to produce seizures, it is thought that the reticular formation may be the site from which stimulation of the cerebral cortex starts. It is difficult to establish the origins of epilepsy conclusively, since there are no adequate animal models for this disorder, but antiepileptic drugs are shown to depress neuron function in the reticular formation. The actual source of the convulsive behavior is thought to be the nonspecific reticular core of this formation.

RESEARCH AND EXPERIMENTATION

The reticular formation influences nearly all aspects of nervous system function, including sensory and motor activities and somatic and visceral functions. It is important in influencing the integrative processes of the central nervous system, acting upon the mind and behavior. Included in this influence are the stimulatory aspects of arousal, awakening,

and attentiveness, as well as the inhibitory aspects of drowsiness, sleep induction, and general disruption of the stimulatory functions. To understand how this region of the brain can be so important in such contradictory functions, it is important to consider the integration of excitatory and inhibitory inputs and the consolidation of their overall influences. Depending upon which type of stimulus has the greatest effect, the net result on behavior can be alertness or drowsiness, active function or the inactivity of sleep.

Research on anesthetized cats in the late 1940's produced an increased understanding of the activities of the reticular formation. It was shown that electrical stimulation of the brain stem caused changes in the cat's electroencephalograph (EEG) readings that were similar to changes occurring in humans when they were aroused from a drowsy state to alertness. From these observations and others, it has been concluded that the ascending reticular system of the brain stem acts as a nonspecific arousal system of the cerebral cortex.

In the 1950's, Donald Lindsley and his colleagues studied the reticular formation as the source of arousal. They showed that two discrete flashes of light shown to a monkey produced discrete electrical responses (evoked potentials) in the visual cortex. If the pulses were very close together, only one potential was evoked, showing that the cortex could not distinguish both within that time. If two electrical stimulations were applied directly to the reticular formation at the short interval, however, two discrete flashes were expressed in the cortex, showing the influence of the reticular formation on the threshold level of the cortex's response to stimuli. J. M. Fuster, one of Lindsley's coworkers, examined the behavioral responses that resulted from electrical stimulation of the reticular formation in monkeys trained to discriminate between two objects. Reducing the time of visual exposure to the objects also reduced the correct responses, but stimulation of the reticular formation at the same time as the visual exposure reduced the error level. This indicated that increased arousal and attentiveness to the visual stimuli were produced by electrical activation of the reticular formation.

J. M. Siegal and D. J. McGinty's work on stimulation of the reticular formation in cats in the 1970's showed that individual neurons seem to have a role in controlling various motor functions of the body.

Other studies show that various autonomic responses, such as vomiting, respiration, sneezing, and coughing, may also originate at least in part from the reticular formation.

It is thought that the period of sleep known as rapid eye movement (REM) sleep, or paradoxical sleep, is a time of memory consolidation. During this time, the reticular formation, the hippocampus, and the amygdala are stimulated to activate the higher brain centers, and arousal occurs. REM sleep is considered paradoxical because the brain waves produced during this time are similar to those produced during stimulation of the awake brain. Vincent Bloch and his colleagues have shown that laboratory animals and human subjects deprived of REM sleep display decreased memory consolidation. During this process, short-term memories are converted somehow into long-term memories, which withstand even disruptions of the electrical activities of the brain. The reticular formation is an important part of memory function, but much remains to be discovered about this and other reticular activities.

Sources for Further Study

Carlson, Neil R. *Physiology of Behavior.* 7th ed. Boston: Allyn & Bacon, 2000. This introduction to nervous system physiology, written for college psychology majors, covers the reticular formation in several chapters. Basic anatomy and connections to other parts of the brain are discussed in chapter 4. Chapter 8 touches on the formation's role in control of movement. Chapter 9 covers its role in arousal, sleep, and waking.

Fromm, Gerhard H., Carl L. Faingold, Ronald A. Browning, and W. M. Burnham, eds. *Epilepsy and the Reticular Formation: The Role of the Reticular Core in Convulsive Seizures.* New York: Liss, 1987. This collection of short articles supports the proposal of the first author that all epileptic convulsions are caused by the interaction of areas of the cerebral cortex with the reticular formation. The reticular core is thought to be the activating structure producing the electrical discharges of the cortex. Many references.

Hobson, J. Allan, and Mary A. B. Brazier, eds. *The Reticular Formation Revisited: Specifying Function for a Nonspecific System.* New York: Raven Press, 1980. A compilation of papers presented at an international symposium in 1978. Separate sections cover historical aspects, methods of study, arousal, motor control of the body from the brain stem, chemical regulatory processes and neurotransmitters, and mechanisms of behavioral state control, including sleep. References accompany each paper.

Klemm, W. R., and Robert P. Vertes, eds. *Brainstem Mechanisms of Behavior.* New York: John Wiley & Sons, 1990. Provides a modern synthesis of the knowledge of this area of psychology, the actions of the medulla, pons, and midbrain. Articles in the first part of the book cover general information on how the brain stem, including the reticular formation, is involved in behavior. The larger second section discusses special research topics. The last article covers brain-stem functions in sleep control. Numerous references.

Romero-Sierra, C. *Neuroanatomy: A Conceptual Approach.* New York: Churchill Livingstone, 1986. This review book for medical students discusses the reticular formation in several sections, with anatomical structure, motor function, and visceral control. Diagrams and lists of functions present the material in an easily understood format. Suggested readings are included.

Sadock, Benjamin J., and Virginia Sadock, eds. *Kaplan and Sadock's Comprehensive Textbook of Psychiatry.* 7th ed. Philadelphia: Lippincott, Williams & Wilkins, 2000. The functional neuroanatomy of the brain stem and reticular formation are covered in this text for medical students. A later portion of the chapter also covers the physiology of sleep.

Steriade, Mircea, and Robert W. McCarley. *Brainstem Control of Wakefulness and Sleep.* New York: Plenum, 1990. This comprehensive text provides a unity of viewpoint on the topic not found in edited collections. References to the different areas of the reticular formation are found throughout the book, in discussions of the sensory information entering the brain stem and the motor control carrying instructions to muscles, among others. Brain waves in sleep and waking are discussed as originating from the reticular area. Extensive references.

Jean S. Helgeson

See also: Attention; Brain structures; Consciousness; Dreams; Insomnia; Nervous system; Neurons; Sleep; Sleep apnea syndromes and narcolepsy.

Retirement

TYPE OF PSYCHOLOGY: Developmental psychology
FIELDS OF STUDY: Aging

With increased longevity and improved health, most Americans today are healthy and active at retirement age. An increasing number of retired individuals are embarking on a second or third career. Others only partially retire as they continue their previous work but at a reduced number of hours. Many find that volunteer work provides opportunities for social interaction and a positive identity. Longitudinal studies have explored a wide range of contextual factors that influence life satisfaction during retirement.

KEY CONCEPTS
- activity theory
- disengagement theory
- leisure
- longitudinal studies
- retired population
- role differentiation

INTRODUCTION

Retirement only became an accepted part of American life in the latter half of the twentieth century. The possibility of retirement was introduced into the American lifestyle with the Social Security Act in 1935. From 1900 to 2000, the percentage of men over sixty-five who continued to work declined as much as 70 percent. At the same time, the percentage of all adults over sixty-five who work at least part-time has steadily increased since 1960. Although the majority of older Americans do not choose to work after sixty-five, more than 11 percent of Americans do so after they reach retirement age. Frank Floyd and his colleagues, in their 1992 Retirement Satisfaction Inventory, found four primary reasons for retirement: job stress, pressure from employer, desire to pursue one's own interests, and circumstances such as health problems

"Retired population" is defined as all persons aged sixty-five and over. Traditionally, sixty-five has been the age at which persons could retire and receive full social security benefits in the United States, although a law is in place to gradually raise the retirement age to sixty-seven. Approximately 78 million people belong to the large cohort of baby boomers who will begin to reach the traditional age of retirement in 2010. In 1900, only about three million were retired at sixty-five, in 2000 the number increased to thirty-five million, and it is projected that by 2050, the number will be increased to sixty-seven million. If future projections are anywhere close to accurate, it can be assumed that it will take approximately four working Americans to provide for every retiree in 2050.

WORKING DURING RETIREMENT

Federal law allows individuals past the age of sixty-five to continue working. However, the decision to continue working in some form after retirement or to discontinue work altogether is a complex one. More people today feel that they have sufficient finances to comfortably exist without working if that is their preference. The primary determiner for most is their health status. Employer pension benefits were found to reduce the probability of future employment in some form, while part-time work was more likely for those who were limited to Social Security benefits. Spousal influence is often cited by the retiree as a major factor in deciding whether or not to choose future employment, although spouses report that they perceive themselves as having little influence on the decision. Specific training and the job opportunities that are available within a community are also important in determining postretirement work.

One survey reported that 80 percent of baby boomers expect to work during their retirement years. Over one-third wanted part-time work because they would personally find it interesting or enjoyable. A little under one-fourth planned to work for financial reasons. In another study, nearly 70 percent planned to work for pay during postretirement because they wanted to stay active and involved.

The probability of working after retirement has a positive correlation with educational attainment and being married to a working spouse. The primary characteristics associated with men who work in their seventies and eighties are good health, a strong psychological commitment to work, and a distaste for retirement.

RETIREES IN THE WORK FORCE

The Retirement History Study by the Social Security Administration identified four career job exits for postretirement employment: part-time employment in one's career job, part-time employment in a new job, full-time employment in a new job, and full-time retirement. The Age Discrimination Act of 1967 prohibited firing people because of their age before they retired and, in 1978, the mandatory retirement age was extended from sixty-five to seventy. Mandatory retirement was banned altogether in 1986, except for a few occupations where safety is at issue.

Studies have found older adults to be productive participants in the workforce. They have lower rates of absenteeism, show a high level of job satisfaction, and experience fewer accidents. There is a cyclic relationship between higher cognitive ability and complex jobs. Older adults who work in more complex job settings demonstrate higher cognitive ability, and those with a higher level of intellectual functioning are more likely to continue working as older adults. It is also important to note that ageist stereotypes of workers and their ability can encourage early retirement or have an adverse effect on the career opportunities given older adults.

ADJUSTMENT TO RETIREMENT

Retirement may represent "golden years" for some, but not necessarily for all. Certain factors have been found to have an impact on the degree of satisfaction retirees experience. Some of these factors are found within society and have an indirect influence on how life is experienced for those who retire. Other factors are directly related to specifics in the individual's life.

Data from longitudinal studies have identified factors that influence adjustment to retirement. (The longitudinal approach to research studies the same individuals over an extended period of time.) Those who adjust best are more likely to be healthy, active, better educated, satisfied with life prior to retirement, have an adequate level of financial resources, and have an extended social network of family and friends. Factors that contribute to a less positive adjustment to retirement are poor health, inadequate finances, and general or specific stress in various areas of life. Those who demonstrate flexibility function better in the retirement setting in which the structured environment of work is missing. Individuals who have cultivated interests and friends unrelated to work show greater adaptation to retirement.

A primary factor in adjustment is whether retirement was voluntary or involuntary. Forced retirement has been ranked as one of the top ten crisis situations which cause stress. When retirement is voluntary, adjustment is more positive. Those who do not voluntarily retire are more likely to be unhealthy and depressed.

In a 1968 study, Robert Peck identified a developmental task of role differentiation that older adults face as they experience retirement. Peck believed that older adults must redefine their feeling of worth in terms that differ from work roles. This means they should pursue valued activities in which they can invest the time that they previously spent in their work profession.

An important aspect of successful adjustment is preretirement planning. Those who are most satisfied with retirement are those who have been preparing for it for several years. Adults can begin preparing psychologically for retirement in middle age. Decisions need to be made relative to activities that will be used to stay active, socially involved, and mentally alert. Of most importance during this time is the task of finding constructive and fulfilling leisure activities that can be continued into retirement. Individuals who are already involved in a number of leisure activities will experience less stress when they make the transition from work to retirement.

During the middle of the twentieth century, disengagement theory was proposed as the approach older adults used to withdraw from obligations and social relationships. It was suggested that this would provide enhanced life satisfaction. Retirement was viewed as part of the disengagement process. Although this theory has not been considered acceptable for some time, it would be fair to say that it represented a prevailing belief about older adults during the first half of the twentieth century.

Researchers have since found support for the activity theory, which is the exact opposite of disengagement theory. The activity theory proposes that the more active and involved older adults are, the more likely they are to experience life satisfaction. Supporting research suggests that activity and productivity cause older adults to age more successfully and to be happier than those who disengage. The theory further suggests that greater life satisfaction can be expected if adults continue their middle-adulthood roles into late adulthood. For those who lose their middle-adulthood roles, it is important that they find substitute roles to keep them active.

MARRIAGE AND FAMILY RELATIONSHIPS

Retirement is often a time when adults have sufficient time to develop their social lives. In a study published in 2000, aging expert Lillian Troll found that older adults who are embedded in family relationships have less distress than those who are family deprived. There is a gender difference in the perspectives of older parents relative to the importance of support from family members. Women perceived support from children as most important whereas men considered spousal support as most important.

For married couples, retirement may bring changes for both spouses. The change in the husband's role as a provider can cause him to feel more dependent upon the marriage itself. The wife is less likely to be affected by her employment status, which seems to have little impact on her perception of being dependent. When retirement allows a spouse to leave a high-stress job, marital quality is improved.

In some ways, retirement may be harder on males than females. Men are more likely than women to experience retirement as a complete change in life habits and occupations. Even when women retire from outside employment, they may notice little difference in the amount of home chores they assume. Males are more likely to feel that they do not have enough to do, and the change is experienced more suddenly than it is for women. Richard V. Burkhauser and Joseph F. Quinn in 1989 found that nearly one-third of the men who take on a part-time job do so two years after retirement.

WORK, RETIREMENT, AND LEISURE

The perception of retirement is affected by work and leisure experiences during the preretirement years. Leisure refers to the activities and interests one chooses to engage in when free from work responsibilities. Many find it difficult to seek leisure activities during the height of their work careers because of the traditional American work ethic and the value placed on productivity. They may view leisure activities as boring and lacking challenge.

Midlife is the first opportunity many adults have to include leisure activities in their schedule. This can be an especially appropriate time if they are experiencing physical changes in strength and endurance as well as changes in family responsibilities.

Those who are able to find constructive and fulfilling leisure activities during this time are psychologically prepared from the middle adult years for retirement. Some developmentalists believe that middle adults tend to reassess priorities and that this becomes a time of questioning how their time should be spent.

Late adulthood, with its possibility of representing the years from sixty-five to over one hundred years, is the longest span of any period of human development. The improved understanding of the nature of life after sixty-five and the greater commitment on the part of medical/mental health personnel to the improvement of health conditions for the older adult are giving all retirees a better chance of being satisfied with the years beyond their work experience.

SOURCES FOR FURTHER STUDY

Bengtson, Vern L., and K. Warner Schaie. *Handbook of Theories of Aging.* New York: Springer, 1995. A well-researched handbook with renowned editors and contributors from the area of adult development. Especially good for the development of theory-building in aging. Well organized with good references.

Maddox, H. George L., Caleb E. Finch, Robert C. Atchley, and J. Grimley Evans, eds. *The Encyclopedia of Aging.* 2d ed. New York: Springer, 1995. Comprehensive and authoritative volume with over five hundred entries on various topics of interest to older persons. Atchley is well-known for his theory of stages in the retirement process.

Pipher, Mary Bray. *Another Country: Navigating the Emotional Terrain of Our Elders.* New York: Berkeley, 1999. Writing from the perspective of family relationships, Pipher provides another best-seller. This one emphasizes the need for relationships between generations with a specific focus upon family members in later adulthood. Pipher notes the need to nurture interdependency as a result of America's move from a communal to an individualistic culture.

Ryff, Carol D., and Victor W. Marshall, eds. *The Self and Society in Aging Processes.* New York: Springer, 1999. Although written for the serious reader in adult development, this source considers the important relationship between the concept of self and later life experiences. Has a chapter on the retirement process.

Vaillant, George E. *Aging Well: Surprising Guideposts to a Happier Life from the Landmark Harvard Study of Adult Development.* New York: Little, Brown, 2002. Results are shared from Harvard's long-running study of adult development. Vaillant concludes that individual lifestyle choices are more important than genetics, wealth, or other factors in determining how happy adults are in their later lives. Has a chapter on retirement, play, and creativity.

Lillian J. Breckenridge

SEE ALSO: Ageism; Aging: Cognitive changes; Aging: Physical changes; Aging: Theories; Coping: Social support; Death and dying; Ego psychology: Erik Erikson; Midlife crises.

Road rage

DATE: The 1980's forward
TYPE OF PSYCHOLOGY: Personality; sensation and perception; social psychology; stress
FIELDS OF STUDY: Aggression; attitudes and behavior

Road rage is a phrase indicating impulsive aggression by enraged operators of motor vehicles who lose emotional control and intentionally intimidate other drivers.

KEY CONCEPTS
- aggressive drivers
- antisocial
- driver violence
- frustration
- impulsiveness
- stress

INTRODUCTION

A global problem, road rage became a concern for social psychologists in the late 1980's, when the term first began to be used. Although incidents of driver violence had occurred in previous decades, they were considered isolated events based on factors unrelated to driving. By the 1980's, cases became more frequent and were directly tied to stimuli surrounding motorists. Violence intensified because more people carried weapons and used them impulsively. As aggressive drivers compromised public transportation safety, researchers sought to understand why some drivers become enraged, lose control, and commit hostile actions against strangers over disputed traffic behavior.

Although some psychologists describe road rage as a pathological condition related to an adjustment reaction disorder, the American Psychiatric Association's *Diagnostic and Statistical Manual of Mental Disorders DSM-IV-TR* (rev. 4th ed., 2000) does not include road rage as a mental illness. That organization considers road rage the result of a defective personality. Several authorities have said that the media exaggerate road casualty statistics to sensationalize coverage of driving behavior and that politicians, the U.S. Department of Transportation, and other groups rely on scientifically unsound studies, particularly an American Automobile Association (AAA) report cited as evidence of an overwhelming threat, to seek funding and publicity.

Admitting that road rage incidents happen, critics stress that vehicular injuries and fatalities actually decrease when alleged epidemics of road rage occur. Psychologists note that road rage is not confined to individuals suffering mental illnesses such as intermittent explosive disorder or displaying antisocial or narcissistic behaviors but can also be triggered by use of stimulants, exhaustion, physiological ailments, and weather.

DIAGNOSING ROAD RAGE

Degrees of road rage range from name-calling and obscene gesturing to physical confrontations and murder. Feeling empowered by the strength, anonymity, and speed of their cars, angry drivers committing road rage challenge other drivers for such perceived slights as driving too slowly or taking a parking space. Drivers often feel compelled to punish other motorists. Many drivers consider their cars as personal territory and can become temperamental and vengeful if they believe that that space has been violated.

Some out-of-control drivers cut others off in traffic, stare menacingly, throw things, honk, flash headlights, brake unexpectedly, or bump from behind to express anger. Other furious drivers chase their victims, forcing them to stop or crash, and then engage in screaming, punching, breaking windows, and even shooting other drivers. Road rage assailants mostly become angry with people they do not know.

ROAD RAGE PROFILES

E. Scott Gellar, a Virginia Polytechnic Institute and State University psychology professor, examined why drivers succumb to road rage. He explained that such people were destructive and mean because of their negativity. Gellar differentiated between aggressive driving—which constitutes risky behavior such as speeding, tailgating, and passing dangerously—and road rage—which is the lack of emotional control while driving and the development of aggression which can escalate into violence.

Defining road rage as a mental disorder that interferes with normal social behavior, Arnold Nerenberg, a Los Angeles traffic psychologist, specialized in road rage therapy. He explained that the human psyche seeks to release its aggression on anonymous people who it feels have purposefully interfered with it. Yale University psychiatrist John Larson ranked degrees of road rage, emphasizing that vigilante driving is the most extreme. He attributed some road rage cases to assumptions based on automobile types that drivers often associate with certain personalities.

Specific conditions often exacerbate road age because of physiological or psychological arousal. Rush-hour traffic and construction zones frustrate people already prone to emotional outbursts, who misdirect their anger at others. Societal pressures for speed push hurried drivers to reach destinations quickly and to become overwhelmed by delays. Some impatient drivers consider sitting in traffic because of road repairs or holiday congestion as a personal threat to their time and plans. Personal stress related to work and family security can cause feelings of powerlessness and intensify drivers' sense of entitlement to roads.

Drivers of all ages commit road rage, and women and men can be equally aggressive behind the wheel. Various studies identify a gender, ethnicity, or age group as being more likely to participate in road rage, but a specific profile cannot be compiled. Some people commit a single act of road rage, while others are perpetually hostile motorists. Some personality traits that enraged drivers might share include being emotionally immature, intolerant, disrespectful, self-righteous, and competitive.

TREATMENT OPTIONS

Few drivers feel regret after initiating acts of road rage. Most assert they were correct and rationalize their actions. They do not view road rage as problematic and blame other drivers for enraging them. Hostile drivers perceive themselves as more competent drivers than those who offend them and consider their anger to be an inborn personality trait that cannot be changed. Personalizing driving situations, they seek apologies from drivers who they believe have wronged them and become argumentative when denied such submissive responses.

In order to defend against road rage, psychologists advise drivers confronted by angry motorists to remain calm and ignore gestures to avoid being drawn into a confrontation. Most psychologists suggest that enraged drivers should admit they have a problem, assume responsibility, and try to alter their behavior and control their anger to avoid being provoked into road rage patterns.

University of Hawaii psychologist Leon James promotes supportive driving by acting courteously, yielding as necessary, and forgiving other drivers' mistakes. Nerenberg counsels his patients by riding in cars and mimicking their aggressive behavior. His therapy also involves visualization and relaxation techniques to overcome self-defeating behavioral patterns.

SOURCES FOR FURTHER STUDY

Fong, G., D. Frost, and S. Stansfeld. "Road Rage: A Psychiatric Phenomenon?" *Social Psychiatry and Psychiatric Epidemiology* 36 (2001): 277-286. Examines whether road rage is a mental disorder.

Fumento, Michael. "Road Rage Versus Reality." *Atlantic Monthly* 282 (August, 1998): 12-17. Explains how the media contributed to road rage hype.

James, Leon, and Diane Nahl. *Road Rage and Aggressive Driving: Steering Clear of Highway Warfare.* Amherst, N.Y.: Prometheus Books, 2000. Discussion with possible solutions to combat road rage.

Larson, John A., and Carol Rodriguez. *Road Rage to Road-Wise.* New York: Forge, 1999. Studies factors contributing to road rage and psychological strategies to resolve anger.

Michael, Mike. "The Invisible Car: The Cultural Purification of Road Rage." In *Car Cultures,* edited by Daniel Miller. New York: Berg, 2001. An anthropological analysis of road rage.

Elizabeth D. Schafer

SEE ALSO: Aggression; Aggression: Reduction and control; Anger; Impulse control disorders.

Rogers, Carl R.

BORN: January 8, 1902, in Oak Park, Illinois
DIED: February 4, 1987, in La Jolla, California
IDENTITY: American founder of client-centered
    therapy
TYPE OF PSYCHOLOGY: Psychotherapy
FIELDS OF STUDY: General constructs and issues;
    humanistic therapies

*Rogers is best known as the founder of client-centered
therapy.*

Carl Ransom Rogers was the fourth of six children.
His parents were living monuments to the Protestant
work ethic, which had a lifelong effect on Rogers's
character. Rogers proved to be a bright and able student in school, though he was given to daydreaming. Still, there was never any question in his family
that Rogers would attend college. He completed his
undergraduate work at the University of Wisconsin
and took his doctoral degree in clinical and educational psychology at Teachers College, Columbia
University.

Rogers held a number of important positions
during his professional career. After finishing graduate school, he worked in human services for the
state of New York. His first academic position was at
Ohio State University. He then became director of
the Guidance Center at the University of Chicago.
In 1957, he accepted a teaching position at the University of Wisconsin, where he served until he
moved to the Western Behavioral Science Institute
in California.

Rogers is best known as the founder of client-centered therapy. He outlined seven principles that
characterize the approach. The first is facilitation.
The client is responsible for his or her own healing.
The therapist is merely the facilitator, mirroring
back what the client says. The second principle is
problem. The client's personal problem is the focal
point around which therapy sessions are organized.
The client has to decide what is the correct course
of action for addressing his or her problem. The
third principle is realness. The therapist must set
aside any artificial guise that he or she may wear and
become a "real person." The client must follow suit
and drop any pretenses during the therapy sessions.
The fourth principle is prizing. The therapist must
express unconditional regard for the client. Each

person is of inherent worth. The fifth principle is
empathy. The therapist must become a nonjudg-
mental listener. He or she must come to view the
world through the client's eyes. The sixth principle
is trust. The therapist must trust the client's judgment. Whatever decision the client makes regarding
his or her problem, the therapist must support the
decision because it represents the "right" one for
the client at the time. The seventh principle is congruence. The process of psychotherapy is a two-
edged sword. Just as the therapist must express empathy, trust, and prizing for the client, so the client
must reciprocate and express the same qualities for
the therapist. When everything falls into place—all
seven principles are acted upon—real change can
take place in human character.

SOURCES FOR FURTHER STUDY

Nye, Robert D. *Three Psychologies: Perspectives from
    Freud, Skinner, and Rogers.* 6th ed. Pacific Grove,
    Calif.: Brooks/Cole, 2000. Compares the theoret-
    ical approaches of three very different psycholo-
    gists through overviews, real-life examples, and
    commentaries.
Rogers, Carl, and David E. Russell. *Carl Rogers—The
    Quiet Revolutionary: An Oral History.* Granite Bay,
    Calif.: Penmarin, 2002. An oral autobiography
    and memoir.
Thorne, Brian. *Carl Rogers.* Thousand Oaks, Calif.:
    Sage Publications, 1992. A biography and intro-
    duction to Rogers's work.

Stanley D. Ivie

SEE ALSO: Person-centered therapy; Psychotherapy:
Goals and techniques.

Rorschach, Hermann

BORN: November 8, 1884, in Zurich, Switzerland
DIED: April 2, 1922, in Herisau, Switzerland
IDENTITY: Swiss psychiatrist
TYPE OF PSYCHOLOGY: Personality; psychological
    methodologies; psychopathology
FIELDS OF STUDY: Personality assessment; personal-
    ity disorders; personality theory

Rorschach developed the inkblot personality test.

Hermann Rorschach's father was an art teacher. As a result, Hermann developed an avid interest in art. During his childhood, he was fascinated with inkblots. In school, he was often preoccupied drawing random inkblot designs, which earned him the nickname "Kleck," German for "inkblot."

Rorschach studied for five years at the University of Zurich, earning an undergraduate degree in 1907. While in school, he worked at the university hospital's psychiatric ward, taking a residency at a mental institution in Munsterlingen, Switzerland, in 1909. In 1912, Rorschach earned his doctorate in medicine from Zurich. In 1914, he took a job as a resident physician at the Waldau Mental Hospital in Bern. Two years later, he was hired at the Krombach Mental Hospital in Appenzell, Switzerland. He was elected as the vice president of the Swiss Psychoanalytic Society in 1919.

Between 1911 and 1921, Rorschach worked on inkblot experiments that would yield meaningful re-sults for understanding a subject's personality traits. He presented his inkblot method in his book *Psychodiagnostik* (1921). The book also contained his more general theories of human personality. Rorschach designed ten inkblot cards, each with a different symmetrical pattern. He argued that, by recording a subject's responses to this series of ink-blots, the amount of introversion and extroversion that a person possessed could be determined, as well as clues about intelligence, emotional stability, and mental abnormalities. In 1942, his book appeared in English translation as *Psychodiagnostics: A Diagnostic Test Based on Perception.*

Although Rorschach's inkblots do not depict any particular objects, they contain shapes that suggest physical items. Five of the cards are black and white, two are primarily black and white with some color, and three are in color. Subjects describe what they see in each inkblot. The responses are then analyzed in terms of what part of the picture was focused on, the content and originality of the response, and the subject's attention to details. Before he could make planned improvements to his ink-blot test, Rorschach died of appendicitis in 1922.

After Rorschach's death, colleagues applied his inkblot test to a number of subjects, and it rapidly gained popularity. The test is still considered as a valuable tool in the fields of psychology and psychiatry and is still used as a standard testing method for compiling a personality profile. However, it is no longer used as an absolute diagnosis, but only to provide indicators of potential psychiatric traits or problems.

Hermann Rorschach. (Library of Congress)

SOURCES FOR FURTHER STUDY

Dana, Richard Henry, ed. *Handbook of Cross-Cultural and Multicultural Personality Assessment.* Hillsdale, N.J.: Laurence Erlbaum, 2000. Discusses use of Rorschach's inkblot test for assessing personality traits in different ethnic groups and cultures.

Inman, Sally, Martin Buck, and Helena Burke, eds. *Assessing Personal and Social Development: Measuring the Unmeasurable.* London: Falmer, 1999. Addresses the use of the inkblot test in assessing child development.

Shrout, Patrick E., and Susan T. Fiske, eds. *Personality Research, Methods, and Theory.* Hillsdale, N.J.: Laurence Erlbaum, 1995. Insights on how the inkblot test is used in personality assessment.

Alvin K. Benson

SEE ALSO: Personality rating scales; Rorschach inkblots.

Rorschach inkblots

DATE: 1921 forward
TYPE OF PSYCHOLOGY: Personality
FIELDS OF STUDY: Personality assessment

The Rorschach inkblot test is widely used to assess various aspects of a person's personality. It consists of ten standardized inkblots, always given in the same order. The subject relates to the examiner what he or she sees in the blots as well as what it is about the blot that suggests that particular thing. Although several scoring systems have been developed, today most clinicians use the Exner Comprehensive System to score and interpret the Rorschach inkblot test.

KEY CONCEPTS
- ambiguous stimuli
- norms
- personality assessment
- projective techniques

INTRODUCTION

Personality assessment is the measurement of affective aspects of a person's behavior, such as emotional states, motivation, attitudes, interests, and interpersonal relations. One type of personality assessment measurement is the use of projective techniques. These techniques require that the client respond to a relatively unstructured task that permits a variety of possible responses. The fundamental assumption is that the individual's responses to the ambiguous stimuli will reflect significant and relatively enduring personality characteristics. The Rorschach inkblot test is one such technique.

The idea that associations with ambiguous visual stimuli provide a key to personality is an ancient one, going back to the classical period in early Greece. The use of inkblots as stimuli for imagination achieved popularity in Europe during the nineteenth century. A parlor game called Blotto required players to create responses to inkblots. Although the Swiss psychiatrist Hermann Rorschach

(1884-1922) was not the first to involve inkblots in the study of psychological processes, his work was qualitatively different in establishing the framework from which personality descriptions could be made. Rorschach's work became known with the publication of *Psychodiagnostik* (1921; *Psychodiagnostics*, 1942). Tragically, he died within a year, at the age of thirty-eight, of complications of appendicitis.

The test was adopted by five American psychologists of very different backgrounds. Each developed a scoring system based on his or her theoretical background, but all five saw the data as having perceptual-cognitive and symbolic components. In the early 1970's, the American psychologist John Exner developed the Comprehensive System to provide the Rorschach community with a common methodology, language, and literature base. Today the Exner Comprehensive System is the most widely used system to administer, score, and interpret the Rorschach. Doctoral-level psychologists require advanced training and supervision to administer, score, and interpret the Rorschach inkblot test.

ADMINISTRATION, SCORING, AND INTERPRETATION

The Rorschach utilizes ten cards, on one side of which is printed a bilaterally symmetrical inkblot. Five of the blots are in shades of gray and black only; two add additional touches of bright red; and the remaining three combine several pastel shades. The Rorschach inkblot test may be administered to preschool children through adults. The client is shown each card in a specific order and asked to relate what the blot could represent. The examiner keeps a verbatim record of what is said and done, including spontaneous remarks, position of the card, and expressions of emotion.

After all ten cards are presented, the examiner questions the client systemically regarding the location of the responses and aspects of the blot to which the associations were given. The examiner then scores the test, usually using the Exner Comprehensive System. Examples of variables scored include content (What did the client see?), location (In what part of the blot did he or see she it?), and quality of the response (Can it be seen easily by others?). The scores are then compared with norms which are the test performance of the standardization sample. Thus, an adult outpatient would be compared with a large group of other adult outpatients to discover where he or she falls on each variable in relation to the comparison group, and a nine-year-old child would be compared to other nine-year-olds. Each score would be examined to determine if it would be considered an average, below average, or above average score.

Finally, the psychologist interprets the test, focusing on those scores or combinations of scores that vary from the average performance of the standardization group. The interpretations focus on many aspects of personality, including affective features, capacity for control and stress tolerance, cognitive processes, interpersonal perception, self-perception, and situation-related stress. Information from other tests, interviews, and case history records is also utilized in formulating the interpretations. For example, if the Rorschach shows a high amount of situational stress, a clinical interview can determine what the situational stress is about. An alternative interpretative approach to the Rorschach is a clinical one. In this approach, the focus is on the interpretation of content rather than a strict analysis of scores. Most psychologists combine both approaches as a means of enhancing the interpretations.

A doctor administers a Rorschach inkblot in 1950 to a patient complaining of headaches. (Hulton Archive)

SOURCES FOR FURTHER STUDY

Anastasi, Anne. *Psychological Testing.* 6th ed. New York: Macmillan, 1988. An excellent overview on psychological testing by one of the pioneers in the field. Chapters cover basics in assessment, the origins of psychological testing and types of tests, and projective techniques. The section on the Rorschach inkblot test and related instruments gives a good basic overview of the use of ambiguous stimuli.

Erdberg, Philip. "Rorschach Assessment." In *Handbook of Psychological Assessment*, edited by Gerald Goldstein and Michel Hersen. 2d ed. New York: Pergamon Press, 1990. Written by a recognized Rorschach expert, this chapter gives a concise history of the use of inkblots in psychological testing and then focuses on practical questions (such as how the person prefers to cope with need states) to review the research literature on various elements of the Rorschach. This is an excellent summary of how the Rorschach is interpreted.

Exner, John E. *The Rorschach: A Comprehensive System Volume 1, Basic Foundations.* 3d ed. New York: John Wiley & Sons, 1993. This is the first volume of a three-volume set on Exner's Comprehensive System. While written primarily for psychologists who will administer, score, and interpret the Rorschach, part 1 of this volume on the history and nature of the Rorschach is both interesting and informative.

Karen D. Multon

SEE ALSO: Beck Depression Inventory (BDI); California Psychological Inventory (CPI); Children's Depression Inventory (CDI); Clinical interviewing, testing, and observation; Depression; Diagnosis; *Diagnostic and Statistical Manual of Mental Disorders*

(DSM); Minnesota Multiphasic Personality Inventory (MMPI); Personality: Psychophysiological measures; Personality interviewing strategies; Personality rating scales; State-Trait Anxiety Inventory; Thematic Apperception Test (TAT).

Rule-governed behavior

TYPE OF PSYCHOLOGY: Learning
FIELDS OF STUDY: Behavioral and cognitive models; instrumental conditioning

A rule (or instruction) is a verbal stimulus that describes a behavior and its consequences. Rules can establish even complicated behaviors quickly and effectively, but they may produce insensitivity to changing contingencies. The study of rules allows an operant analysis of processes which are often termed "cognitive."

KEY CONCEPTS
- contingency
- discriminative stimulus
- rule
- schedule of reinforcement
- shaping
- stimulus control

INTRODUCTION

Following the tradition of B. F. Skinner, the famous Harvard University psychologist who pioneered the study of operant conditioning, behavior analysts initially examined the behavior of rats and pigeons because nonhuman subjects could be studied under well-controlled conditions in the experimental laboratory. This made it possible for operant psychologists to discover a number of important behavioral principles and to demonstrate that much of the behavior of their experimental subjects was shaped and maintained by contingencies of reinforcement. "Contingencies" can be thought of as cause-effect relations between a context (in operant terms, a "discriminative stimulus"), an action ("response"), and the consequence ("reinforcement") it produces. For example, if pressing a bar is followed by food only when a light is on and never when it is off, a rat's behavior is gradually shaped by these contingencies until the rat presses the lever only when the light is on.

When operant researchers began to bring human subjects into the laboratory, however, the analysis went beyond behavior directly shaped by contingencies to include behavior under the control of instructions or rules. According to Skinner, a rule is a "contingency-specifying stimulus." It functions as a discriminative stimulus (SD), but it differs from other SDs in that it is a *description* of a behavior-outcome relation. Other SDs are stimuli in the environment that acquire control over behavior only through specific training; rules, in contrast, have an immediate effect on behavior because they make use of an already existing language repertoire. For example, through a history of careful shaping, a seeing-eye dog can be trained to stop at red lights and cross the street only when the light is green. A verbal child, however, can be taught the same discrimination simply by being told, "Go when the light is green; don't go when the light is red."

Proverbs, maxims, advice, instructions, commands, and so forth all function as rules when they control behavior. In complete form, rules specify an antecedent condition, an action, and its consequences, and take the form of if-then statements, as in "If you want to get to the other side safely, [then] cross the street only when the light is green." Most rules, however, are only partial statements of contingencies, specifying exclusively the antecedent (such as a male figure or the word "men" on a door), the behavior (a sign reading do not enter), or the consequence ("Lose twenty-five pounds in one month!"), and it is left to the individual to fill in the blanks.

Despite an abundance of rules in the human environment, many people are not reliable rule followers. Otherwise, through the mere presence of rules, drivers would respect speed limits, students would study, and telling people "Just say no" would solve the drug problem in American society. Control by rules is often deficient because rules only determine the topography, or form, of behavior, but they do not impart the motivation to act. Stated differently, rules tell people what to do (such as "Just say no"), but whether people actually do it depends on other circumstances.

ROLE OF CONTINGENCIES

For a rule to be followed, it must be part of an effective contingency: Either the outcome specified in the rule must function as a reinforcer, or the rule giver must be able to mediate aversive consequences for noncompliance. Psychologists Steven C. Hayes and Robert D. Zettle have drawn an important distinction between contingency-shaped and rule-governed behavior. They assert that contingency-shaped behavior is controlled by one set of contingencies, usually consisting of a situation, an action, and a consequence (such as being offered a cigarette, smoking, and feeling relaxed).

In contrast, rule-governed behavior involves two sets of contingencies. One of them is the behavior-outcome relation specified in the rule itself ("If you want to avoid addiction, just say no"). The second involves social consequences for rule following, such as praise or criticism from significant others or social pressure to comply with peer norms. As the following examples will show, at times both sets of contingencies support rule following, but sometimes they compete with each other. In one example, a man is lost and his wife insists that he ask for directions. He is told to "turn left at the light and then follow the signs to the interstate." The man is likely to follow these directions, because both sets of contingencies surrounding rule following are congruent: The natural consequences of finding the highway are indeed reinforcing to him, and the social consequences are reinforcing because following the directions will satisfy his wife and spare him criticism. In another example, however, a child is given a box of candy. Her mother says, "You may have only one piece of candy before dinner, or else you will spoil your appetite." The contingency specified in the rule may be ineffective, because eating only one piece of candy if there is more may never have been reinforcing to the child. Hence, if the child obeys, it is not for the contingency specified in the rule but for the parental consequences that would result from noncompliance.

Behavior under the control of a description of contingencies does not involve a new process, but is consistent with an operant framework postulating that the probability of behavior is controlled by its outcome. Rule governance results from an extensive history of reinforcement in which rule following has directly led to contact with the contingencies specified in the rule, to social consequences associated with compliance and noncompliance, or both.

ROLE IN LEARNING

Teaching people to follow rules is important for a number of reasons, which B. F. Skinner outlined in his book *About Behaviorism* (1974). Most important, many behaviors can be acquired much more quickly through rules than through shaping by the contingencies described in the rules. For example, it is easier to teach a boy the basics of a card game by explaining the rules to him than by playing with him until he gradually (if at all) figures out the rules for himself. Furthermore, there are cases when the contingencies are so complex or vague that most people would never contact them without the help of rules. Learning to type with ten fingers illustrates such a case. Without appropriate instruction, the immediate success accruing from a "hunt-and-peck" method will reinforce typing with two fingers, and the person will never learn to use ten fingers, even though in the long run this would have been much more efficient.

According to Roger L. Poppen in a 1989 essay, initially people learn rules from a multitude of external sources such as parents, peers, teachers, television, and books, and eventually they learn to extract rules from interacting with and observing environmental contingencies. Parents encourage the rehearsal and internalization of rules so that these self-instructions then help children guide their own behavior in similar circumstances.

BEHAVIOR-ANALYTIC THEORY

The effects of rules on behavior have been extensively studied within a behavior-analytic methodology. A summary of this research can be found in a chapter by Margaret Vaughan in the book *Rule-Governed Behavior: Cognitions, Contingencies, and Instructional Control*, edited by Steven C. Hayes (1989). Most of these human operant studies use a method in which subjects press a button that, according to some schedule of reinforcement (an arrangement that specifies which responses within an operant class will be reinforced), occasionally produces points exchangeable for money. Depending on the preparation, button pressing may be controlled by the contingency between pressing and point delivery; in this case, the behavior would be contingency-shaped. Button pressing may also be controlled by experimenter instructions, in which case the behavior would be rule governed.

A number of studies showed that experimenter-provided instructions quickly bring the behavior under stimulus control (behavior occasioned by a stimulus because the stimulus signals some consequence of responding) but also create insensitivity to the scheduled contingencies. For example, telling subjects that "the best way to earn points is to press the button fast" (a fixed-ratio contingency) immediately allows them to respond correctly and earn points. When the contingencies are then surreptitiously changed, however, subjects continue to follow the instructions for long periods of time although they have become obsolete and no longer produce points. In contrast, when subjects receive no instructions and their responses are shaped, sensitivity to changing contingencies develops; that is, when the schedule of reinforcement changes, subjects adjust their behavior to the new schedule and continue to earn points. This observation has led operant researchers to conclude that insensitivity to contingencies may be an inherent property of instructional control.

EFFECT OF "IRRATIONAL BELIEFS"

The insensitivity effect of rules has intriguing implications: Instructing people how to solve problems is immediately effective, but it may be counterproductive in the long run, because individuals may come to act in accordance with outdated rules. Their behavior may come to be guided by what cognitivists call "irrational beliefs" or "unrealistic expectations," which from an operant perspective would be considered inaccurate statements about contingencies resulting from broad overgeneralizations of old rules. The following example illustrates how an "irrational belief" may come to control behavior. A mother might tell her child, "Stop making noise! I don't love you when you are bad." This rule may quiet the child immediately, and because it is effective, the parent may use it in other situations. Over the course of her development, the child learns many instances of what her parent considers "bad" (perhaps disobeying instructions, perhaps asserting herself, showing anger, and so on). Gradually she internalizes a generalized rule, "I am only lovable when others approve of me," and evolves into an adult who tries to please everybody and feels unworthy at any sign of disapproval, however ineffective this behavior may be.

Humans live in a world in which rules abound, in the form of instructions, advice, warnings, cookbooks, self-help books, laws, and social norms. They are intended to provide guidelines for effective behavior. Even when no external rules are available,

most people can formulate their own plans of action. The greatest advantage of rules is that they can be extremely helpful and can establish effective behavior quickly. Their greatest disadvantages are that rules do not produce behavior unless other contingencies support rule following and (as Skinner has pointed out) that they may be troublesome rather than helpful when the contingencies change but the rules do not.

EVOLUTION OF STUDY

Operant research with human subjects emerged in the 1950's. Originally, behavioral researchers attempted to replicate findings from experimental work with rats and pigeons to demonstrate the generality of the principles of behavior discovered in the animal laboratory. It soon became apparent that people often showed response patterns not comparable to those of animal subjects on the same schedules of reinforcement. For example, a cumulative record of responding on a fixed-interval schedule for animals typically shows "scallops" (a pause after reinforcement, followed by a gradually accelerating response rate until delivery of the next reinforcer). In contrast, human subjects typically time the interval by counting; toward the end, they respond as few times as necessary to obtain the reinforcer.

Behavior analysts suspected that the differences between human and animal responding mainly stemmed from people's prior conditioning history and from instructions, both experimenter-provided and self-generated, with which they approached the experimental tasks. These assumptions began to focus the attention of operant researchers on the role of instructions. By the mid-1970's, instruction following became synonymous with rule-governed behavior and began to evolve into a field of study in its own right.

IMPORTANCE OF APPROACH

One importance of rule governance lies in the possibility of a rapprochement between behaviorist and cognitivist positions. Behaviorists have often been accused of disregarding or failing to acknowledge the importance of "higher mental processes." While such accusations are polemic and extremely misleading, it is true that it was not until the mid-1970's that operant psychologists began a systematic empirical analysis of cognitive-verbal processes. The study of rule-governed behavior marked the beginning of the experimental analysis of phenomena that until then pertained to the domain of cognitive psychology.

The analysis of rule-governed behavior is important for another reason. It provides some insights into causal mechanisms that may underlie current cognitive therapies. For example, in 1987 Roger Poppen presented an excellent theoretical analysis of a self-efficacy approach and of rational-emotive therapy, while in 1982, Zettle and Hayes presented a similar analysis of cognitive restructuring and cognitive therapy for depression. The common denominator of these diverse cognitive approaches is their assertion that people's reactions to their environment are mediated by covert verbal statements, which, when dysfunctional, are given labels such as irrational beliefs, low self-efficacy, and negative expectancies. From an operant perspective, such formal categorizations are considered not very useful because formally distinct verbal statements may all have the same function, while statements identical in form may have different functions (one person might say "I can't do it; I'm too dumb" to avoid an unpleasant task, while another person may say the same thing to request assistance).

Within a framework of rule-governed behavior, all these "dysfunctional cognitions" are considered partial statements of contingencies, and the behavior they produce is rule governed. Hence, findings from basic experimental research on rule-governed behavior could conceivably be brought to bear on clinical phenomena, which eventually might lead to a better understanding of psychological dysfunctions and to the development of more effective therapies.

SOURCES FOR FURTHER STUDY

Catania, A. Charles. *Learning.* Reissued ed. Englewood Cliffs, N.J.: Prentice-Hall, 1997. Chapter 9 of this book deals with an operant approach to language, including an excellent brief summary of rule-governed behavior.

Poppen, Roger L. "Some Clinical Implications of Rule-Governed Behavior." In *Rule-Governed Behavior: Cognitions, Contingencies, and Instructional Control,* edited by Steven C. Hayes. New York: Plenum, 1989. Contains a compelling analysis of clinical phenomena that until recently have been regarded as the exclusive domain of cognitive therapists. Poppen shows how rule-governed be-

havior may account for so-called maladaptive cognitions in terms of ineffective rules. He suggests ways to integrate behavioral and cognitive approaches to therapy.

Skinner, B. F. *About Behaviorism.* New York: Alfred A. Knopf, 1974. This book is highly recommended for anybody not familiar with behaviorism and an operant approach to psychology. It provides an in-depth introduction to behaviorism as a science of behavior and is very readable. Presents a compressed analysis of rule-governed behavior.

_____. "An Operant Analysis of Problem Solving." In *Problem-Solving: Research, Method, and Theory,* edited by Benjamin Kleinmuntz. New York: John Wiley & Sons, 1966. Although Skinner clearly differentiated between two types of operant behavior as early as 1947, when he gave the William James lectures at Harvard University, it was not until 1966 that he published a paper exclusively on this topic. Skinner's paper is recommended to familiarize the student with the original source of the topic.

Vaughan, Margaret. "Rule-Governed Behavior in Behavior Analysis: A Theoretical and Experimental History." In *Rule-Governed Behavior: Cognitions, Contingencies, and Instructional Control,* edited by Steven C. Hayes. New York: Plenum, 1989. Vaughan traces the study of rule-governed behavior from the 1950's to 1989 and presents a very accessible summary of relevant experimental research.

Zettle, Robert D., and Steven C. Hayes. "Rule-Governed Behavior: A Potential Theoretical Framework for Cognitive-Behavioral Therapy." In *Advances in Cognitive-Behavioral Research and Therapy,* edited by Philip C. Kendall. Vol. 1. New York: Academic Press, 1982. This chapter presents one of the most widely cited explanations of rule governance. The authors were the first to draw attention to the dual set of contingencies surrounding rules. The chapter also examines the role of self-rules and presents a compelling analysis of various cognitive therapies in terms of rule-governed behavior.

Edelgard Wulfert

SEE ALSO: Behavior therapy; Behavioral family therapy; Behaviorism; Cognitive behavior therapy; Conditioning; Radical behaviorism: B. F. Skinner.

S

S-R theory
Neal E. Miller and John Dollard

TYPE OF PSYCHOLOGY: Personality

FIELDS OF STUDY: Behavioral and cognitive models; models of abnormality; personality theory

Miller and Dollard developed a personality theory that was based on Clark Hull's stimulus-reponse learning theory. They used this theory and a number of psychoanalytic concepts to explain how neurosis developed. They also showed how psychotherapy could be conceptualized as a learning process by using an S-R model of higher mental processes.

KEY CONCEPTS
- conflict
- cue
- cue-producing response
- drive
- habit
- imitation
- reinforcement
- response
- response hierarchy
- secondary drive

INTRODUCTION

Much, if not most, human behavior is learned. How human beings learn is one of the central, and most controversial, topics in psychology. Neal E. Miller and John Dollard used principles of learning developed by Clark Hull, who studied how animals learn, and applied them to explain complex human behavior.

According to Miller and Dollard, human behavior occurs in response to cues. A red traffic light, for example, is a cue to stop, whereas green is a cue to go. A cue is simply any stimulus that is recognized as different from other stimuli. A cue may bring about a variety of responses, but some responses are more likely to occur than others. The response to a cue most likely to occur is called the dominant response. Responses to a cue are arranged in a response hierarchy, from the dominant response to the response least likely to occur. A person's response hierarchy can change. The hierarchy that a person has originally is called the initial hierarchy. If the initial hierarchy is inborn, it is known as the innate hierarchy. When a hierarchy changes, the result is known as the response hierarchy.

RESPONSE HIERARCHY AND LEARNING

Change in a response hierarchy occurs as a result of learning. There are four fundamental considerations in the explanation of how learning occurs: drive, cue, response, and reinforcement.

A drive is an intense stimulus, such as hunger, that motivates a response. The cue is the stimulus that elicits the response. If the dominant response in the hierarchy results in a reduction in the drive, then reinforcement will occur. Reinforcement means that the association, or connection, between the cue (stimulus) and response is strengthened; the next time the cue occurs, therefore, that response will be even more likely to occur. Reinforcement occurs when a person realizes that the response has led to a reward, although such awareness is not always necessary; reinforcement can also occur automatically. In other words, Miller and Dollard's theory states that for persons to learn, they must want something (drive), must do something (response) in the presence of a distinct stimulus (cue), and must get some reward for their actions (reinforcement).

If the dominant response does not result in a reward, the chance that the dominant response will occur again is gradually lessened. This process is called extinction. Eventually, the next response in the hierarchy will occur (in other words, the person will try something else). If that response results in reward, it will be reinforced and may become the dominant response in the hierarchy. In this way, according to Miller and Dollard, humans learn and change their behavior. According to this theory, connections between stimulus and response are learned; these are called habits. Theories that view learning in this way are called stimulus-response, or S-R, theories. The total collection of a person's habits make up his or her personality.

ROLE OF DRIVES

Drives, as previously noted, motivate and reinforce responses. Some drives, such as hunger, thirst, sex, and pain, are inborn and are known as primary drives. These drives are naturally aroused by certain physiological conditions; through learning, however, they may also be aroused by cues to which they are not innately connected. For example, one may feel hungry when one sees a favorite restaurant even though one has recently eaten. Drives aroused in this way (that is, by previously neutral cues) are called secondary, or learned, drives.

The natural reaction to an aversive stimulus is pain. Pain is a primary drive; it motivates a person to act, and any response which reduces pain will be reinforced. Neutral cues associated with pain may also produce a response related to pain called fear (or anxiety). Fear motivates a person to act; a response which reduces fear will be reinforced. Fear is therefore a drive; it is a drive which is especially important for understanding neurotic behavior, according to Miller and Dollard. For example, a fear of a harmless cue such as an elevator (an elevator phobia) will motivate a person to avoid elevators, and such avoidance will be reinforced by reduction of fear.

CUE RESPONSES

A response to one cue may also occur to cues which are physically similar to that cue; in other words, what one learns to do in one situation will occur in other, similar situations. This phenomenon is called stimulus generalization.

Many responses are instrumental responses; that is, they act on and change some aspect of the environment. Other responses are known as cue-producing responses; the cues from these reponses serve to bring about other responses. Words are especially important cue-producing responses; someone says a word and another person responds, or one thinks a word and this is a cue for another word. Thinking can be considered as chains of cue-producing responses—that is, as a sequence of asso-

ciated words; in this way Miller and Dollard sought to describe the higher mental processes such as thinking, reasoning, and planning.

SOCIAL ROLE OF LEARNING

In their book *Social Learning and Imitation* (1941), Miller and Dollard pointed out that to understand human behavior one must know not only the process of learning (as described above) but also the social conditions under which learning occurs. Human learning is social—that is, it occurs in a social context, which can range from the societal level to the interpersonal level. The process of imitation is one example of how what an individual learns to do depends on the social context.

Imitation involves matching, or copying, the behavior of another person. If the matching behavior is rewarded, it will be reinforced, and the individual will therefore continue to imitate. The cue that elicits the imitating response is the person being imitated (the model), so that the imitative behavior, in Miller and Dollard's analysis, is dependent on the presence of the model. In this way, Miller and Dollard used S-R theory to explain how individuals learn what to do from others and thereby learn how to conform to society.

PSYCHOANALYTIC APPROACH TO NEUROSIS

In their best-known work, *Personality and Psychotherapy: An Analysis in Terms of Learning, Thinking, and Culture* (1950), Dollard and Miller applied S-R theory to explain how neurosis is learned and how it can be treated using learning principles. They pointed out three central characteristics of neurosis that require explanation: misery, stupidity, and symptoms. The misery that neurotics experience is a result of conflict. Conflict exists when incompatible responses are elicited in an individual. An approach-approach conflict exists when a person has to choose between two desirable goals; once a choice is made, the conflict is easily resolved. An avoidance-avoidance conflict exists when an individual must choose between two undesirable goals. An approach-avoidance conflict exists when an individual is motivated both to approach and to avoid the same goal. The last two types of conflicts may be difficult to resolve and under certain conditions may result in a neurosis.

Dollard and Miller tried to explain some aspects of psychoanalytic theory in S-R terms; like Sigmund Freud, the founder of psychoanalysis, they emphasized the role of four critical childhood training situations in producing conflicts that can result in neurosis. These are the feeding situation, cleanliness training, sex training, and anger-anxiety conflicts. Unfortunate training experiences during these stages of childhood may result in emotional problems. Childhood conflicts arising from such problems may be repressed and may therefore operate unconsciously.

The "stupidity" of the neurotic is related to the fact that conflicts which produce misery are repressed and unconscious. Dollard and Miller explained the psychoanalytic concept of repression in terms of S-R theory in the following manner. Thinking about an experience involves the use of cue-producing responses (that is, the use of words) in thinking. If no words are available to label an experience, then a person is unable to think about it—that is, the experience is unconscious. Some experiences are unconscious because they were never labeled; early childhood experiences before the development of speech and experiences for which the culture and language do not provide adequate labels are examples of experiences which are unconscious because they are unlabeled. Labeled painful experiences may also become unconscious if a person stops thinking about them. Consciously deciding to stop thinking about an unpleasant topic is called suppression. Repression is similar to suppression except that it is automatic—that is, it occurs without one consciously planning to stop thinking. For Dollard and Miller, therefore, repression is the automatic response of stopping thinking about very painful thoughts; it is reinforced by drive reduction and eventually becomes a very strong habit.

The third characteristic of neuroses requiring explanation are symptoms. Phobias, compulsions, hysteria, and alcoholism are examples of symptoms. Symptoms arise when an individual is in a state of conflict-produced misery. This misery is a result of the intense fear, and other intense drives (for example, sexual drives), involved in conflict. Because the conflict is unconscious, the individual cannot learn that the fear is unrealistic. Some symptoms of neurosis are physiological; these are direct effects of the fear and other drives which produce the conflict. Other symptoms, such as avoidance in a phobia, are learned behaviors that reduce the fear and/or drives of the conflict. These symptoms are reinforced, therefore, by drive reduction.

THERAPEUTIC TECHNIQUES

Dollard and Miller's explanation of psychotherapy is largely a presentation of key features of psychoanalysis described in S-R terms. Therapy is viewed as a situation in which new learning can occur. Because neurotic conflict is unconscious, new learning is required to remove repression so that conflict can be resolved. One technique for doing this, taken directly from psychoanalysis, is free association; here, neurotic patients are instructed to say whatever comes to their consciousness. Because this can be a painful experience, patients may resist doing this, but, because the therapist rewards patients for free associating, they eventually continue. While free associating, patients become aware of emotions related to their unconscious conflicts and so develop a better understanding of themselves.

Another technique borrowed from psychoanalysis involves a phenomenon known as transference. Patients experience and express feelings about the therapist. Such feelings really represent, in S-R terms, emotional reactions to parents, teachers, and other important persons in the patient's past, which, through stimulus generalization, have been transferred to the therapist. The therapist helps the patient to recognize and label these feelings and to see that they are generalized from significant persons in the patient's past. The patient in this way learns how she or he really feels. The patient learns much about herself or himself that was previously unconscious and learns how to think more adaptively about everyday life. The patient's symptoms are thereby alleviated.

EXTENDING THE BEHAVIORIST APPROACH

The S-R theory used by Miller and Dollard had its intellectual roots in the thinking of the seventeenth century, when human beings were thought of as being complicated machines which were set in motion by external stimuli. At the beginning of the twentieth century, the stimulus-response model was adopted by John B. Watson, the founder of behaviorism. Watson used the S-R model to explain observable behavior, but he avoided applying it to mental processes because he believed that mental processes could not be studied scientifically.

Miller and Dollard extended the behaviorism of Watson to the explanation of mental events through their concept of the cue-producing response and its role in the higher mental processes. This was an S-R explanation: Mental processes were seen as arising from associations between words that represent external objects; the words are cues producing responses. Miller and Dollard's approach, therefore, represented a significant departure from the behaviorism of Watson. Miller and Dollard tried to explain mental events in their book *Personality and Psychotherapy*, in which they attempted to explain many psychoanalytic concepts in S-R terms. Since psychoanalysis is largely a theory of the mind, it would have been impossible for them not to have attempted to describe mental processes.

CONTRIBUTIONS TO MENTAL PROCESSES RESEARCH

The approach to explaining mental processes used by Miller and Dollard, though it represented a theoretical advance in the 1950's, was gradually replaced by other explanations beginning in the 1960's. The drive-reduction theory of learning that they advocated came under criticism, and the S-R view that humans passively react to external stimuli was criticized by many psychologists. As a result, new theories of learning emphasizing cognitive (mental) concepts were developed.

New ways of thinking about mental processes were also suggested by fields outside psychology; one of these was computer science. The computer and its program were seen as analogous to human mental processes, which, like computer programs, involve the input, storage, and retrieval of information. The computer and its program, therefore, suggested new ways of thinking about the human mind. Miller and Dollard's S-R theory has largely been replaced by concepts of contemporary cognitive science.

Miller and Dollard's theory still exercises an important influence on contemporary thinking in psychology. Their analysis of psychoanalysis in terms of learning theory made the important point that neuroses could be unlearned using the principles of learning. Behaviorally oriented treatments of emotional disorders owe a debt to the intellectual legacy of Miller and Dollard.

SOURCES FOR FURTHER STUDY

Dollard, John, et al. *Frustration and Aggression.* 1939. Reprint. Westport, Conn.: Greenwood Press, 1980. An early application of S-R theory to complex human behavior. The presentation of the hypothesis that aggression is inevitably caused by frustration is seen here.

Dollard, John, and Neal E. Miller. *Personality and Psychotherapy: An Analysis in Terms of Learning, Thinking, and Culture.* New York: McGraw-Hill, 1950. The best known of the works of Miller and Dollard. Presents a theory of personality and an S-R presentation of psychoanalytic theory and psychoanalytic therapy.

Hall, Calvin Springer, Gardner Lindzey, and John Campbell. *Theories of Personality.* 4th ed. New York: John Wiley & Sons, 1997. This book has a chapter on S-R theory and presents a detailed overview of the theory of Miller and Dollard.

Miller, Neal E. "Studies of Fear as an Acquirable Drive: I. Fear as a Motivator and Fear-Reduction as Reinforcement in the Learning of New Responses." *Journal of Experimental Psychology* 38 (1948): 89-101. A classic paper that served as the experimental basis for postulating that fear is a secondary drive.

Miller, Neal E., and John Dollard. *Social Learning and Imitation.* 1949. Reprint. Westport, Conn.: Greenwood Press, 1979. Presents an application of S-R theory to social motivation with a special emphasis on imitation.

Sanford Golin

SEE ALSO: Behaviorism; Conditioning; Drives; Learning; Miller, Neal E., and John Dollard; Observational learning; Social learning: Albert Bandura.

Sampling

TYPE OF PSYCHOLOGY: Psychological methodologies
FIELDS OF STUDY: Experimental methodologies; methodological issues

Probability sampling is a scientific method that uses random selection to generate representative samples from populations. It enables researchers to make relatively few observations and to generalize from those observations to a much wider population. Nonprobability sampling does not ensure the representativeness of selected samples.

KEY CONCEPTS
- element
- observation unit
- parameter

- population
- sample
- sampling error
- sampling frame
- sampling unit
- statistic
- validity

INTRODUCTION

A critical part of social research is the decision as to what will be observed and what will not. It is often impractical or even impossible to survey or observe every element of interest. Sampling methodology provides guidelines for choosing from a population some smaller group that represents the population's important characteristics. There are two general approaches to selecting samples: probability and nonprobability sampling.

Probability sampling techniques allow researchers to select relatively few elements and generalize from these sample elements to the much larger population. For example, in the 1984 United States presidential election, George Gallup's final pre-election poll correctly predicted that the popular vote would split 59 percent to 41 percent in favor of Ronald Reagan. This accurate prediction was based on the stated voting intentions of a tiny fraction—less than 0.01 percent—of the 92.5 million people who voted in the election. Accuracy was possible because Gallup used probability sampling techniques to choose a sample that was representative of the general population. A sample is representative of the population from which it is chosen if the aggregate characteristics of the sample closely approximate those same aggregate characteristics in the population. Samples, however, need not be representative in all respects; representativeness is limited to those characteristics that are relevant to the substantive interests of the study. The most widely used probability sampling methods are simple random sampling, systematic sampling with a random start, stratified sampling, and multistage cluster sampling.

Nonprobability sampling methods, such as purposive, convenience, and quota sampling, do not ensure a representative sample. These samples are not useful for drawing conclusions about the population because there is no way to measure the sampling error. Purposive and convenience sampling allow the researcher to choose samples that fit his or her particular interest or convenience; quota sampling aims to generate a representative sample by developing a complex sampling frame (a quota matrix) that divides the population into relevant subclasses. Aside from being cumbersome, however, the nonrandom selection of samples from each cell of the quota matrix decreases the likelihood of generating a representative sample.

Probability theory is based on random selection procedures and assumes three things: that each random sample drawn from a population provides an estimate of the true population parameter, that multiple random samples drawn from the same population will yield statistics that cluster around the true population value in a predictable way, and that it is possible to calculate the sampling error associated with any one sample. The magnitude of sampling error associated with any random sample is a function of two variables: the homogeneity of the population from which the random sample is drawn and the sample's size. A more homogeneous parent population will have a smaller sampling error associated with a given random sample. Moreover, sampling error declines as the size of one's random sample increases, since larger samples are more likely than smaller ones to capture a representative portion of the parent population. In fact, for small populations (less than fifty members), it is often best to collect on the entire population rather than use a sample because this often improves the reliability and credibility of the data.

FORMULATING THE SAMPLE

When sampling is necessary, it is essential that the researcher first consider the quality of the sampling frame. A sampling frame is the list or quasi list of elements from which a probability sample is selected. Often, sampling frames do not truly include all of the elements that their names might imply. For example, telephone directories are often taken to be a listing of a city's population. There are several defects in this reasoning, but the major one involves a social-class bias. Poor people are less likely to have telephones; therefore, a telephone directory sample is likely to have a middle- and upper-class bias. In order to generalize to the population composing the sampling frame, it is necessary for all of the elements to have equal representation in the frame. Elements that occur more than once will have a greater probability of selection, and the overall sample will overrepresent those elements.

Regardless of how carefully the researcher chooses a sampling frame and a representative sample from it, sample values are only approximations of population parameters. Probability theory enables the researcher to estimate how far the sample statistic is likely to diverge from population values, using two key indices called confidence levels and confidence intervals. Both of these are calculated by mathematical procedures that can be found in any basic statistics book.

A confidence level specifies how confident the researcher can be that the statistics are reliable estimates of population parameters, and a confidence interval stipulates how far the population parameters might be expected to deviate from sample values. For example, in the 1984 presidential election, *The Washington Post* polled a sample of 8,969 registered voters; based on their responses, the newspaper reported that 57 percent of the vote would go to Ronald Reagan and 39 percent would go to Walter Mondale. The poll in *The Washington Post* had a confidence level of 95 percent, and its confidence interval was plus or minus three percentage points. This means that pollsters could be 95 percent confident that Reagan's share of the 92.5 million popular votes would range between 54 percent and 60 percent, while Mondale's vote would vary between 36 percent and 42 percent. When reporting predictions based on probability sampling, the researcher should always report the confidence level and confidence interval associated with the sample.

SAMPLING TECHNIQUES
A basic principle of probability sampling is that a sample will be representative of the population from which it is selected if all members of the population have an equal chance of being selected in the sample. Flipping a coin is the most frequently cited example: The "selection" of a head or a tail is independent of previous selections of heads or tails. Instead of flipping a coin, however, researchers usually use a table of random numbers.

A simple random sample may be generated by assigning consecutive numbers to the elements in a sampling frame, generating a list of random numbers equal to one's desired sample size, and selecting from the sampling frame all elements having assigned numbers that correspond to one's list of random numbers. This is the basic sampling method assumed in survey statistical computations,

but it is seldom used in practice because it is often cumbersome and inefficient. For that reason, researchers usually prefer systematic sampling with a random start. This approach, under appropriate circumstances, can generate equally representative samples with relative ease.

A systematic sample with a random start is generated by selecting every element of a certain number (for example, every fifth element) listed in a sampling frame. Thus, a systematic sample of one hundred can be derived from a sampling frame containing one thousand elements by selecting every tenth element in the frame. To ensure against any possible human bias, the first element should be chosen at random. Although systematic sampling is relatively uncomplicated, it yields samples that are highly representative of the populations from which they are drawn. The researcher should be alert, however, to the potential systematic sampling problem called sampling frame periodicity, which does not affect simple random methods. If the sampling frame is arranged in a cyclical pattern that coincides with the sampling interval, a grossly biased sample may be drawn.

SAMPLING FRAME PERIODICITY
Earl Babbie has described a study of soldiers that illustrates how sampling frame periodicity can produce seriously unrepresentative systematic samples. He reports that the researchers used unit rosters as sampling frames and selected every tenth soldier for the study. The rosters, however, were arranged by squads containing ten members each, and squad members were listed by rank, with sergeants first, followed by corporals and privates. Because this cyclical arrangement coincided with the ten-element sampling interval, the resulting sample contained only sergeants.

Sampling frame periodicity, although a serious threat to sampling validity, can be avoided if researchers carefully study the sampling frame for evidence of periodicity. Periodicity can be corrected by randomizing the entire list before sampling from it or by drawing a simple random sample from within each cyclical portion of the frame.

The third method of probability sampling, stratified sampling, is not an alternative to systematic sampling or simple random sampling; rather, it represents a modified framework within which the two methods are used. Instead of sampling from a total population as simple and systematic methods do, stratified sampling organizes a population into homogeneous subsets and selects elements from each subset, using either systematic or simple random procedures. To generate a stratified sample, the researcher begins by specifying the population subgroups, or stratification variables, that are to be represented in a sample. After stipulating these variables, the researcher divides all sampling frame elements into homogeneous subsets representing a saturated mix of relevant stratification characteristics. Once the population has been stratified, a researcher uses either simple random sampling or systematic sampling with a random start to generate a representative sample from the elements falling within each subgroup. Stratified sampling methods can generate a highly useful sample of any well-defined population and may have a smaller sampling error than any other sampling method.

COMPREHENSIVE SAMPLING

Simple random sampling, systematic sampling, and stratified sampling are reasonably simple procedures for sampling from lists of elements. If one wishes to sample from a very large population, however, such as all university students in the United States, a comprehensive sampling frame may not be available. In this case, a modified sampling method, called multistage cluster sampling, is appropriate. It begins with the systematic or simple random selection of subgroups or clusters within a population, followed by a systematic or simple random selection of elements within each selected cluster. For example, if a researcher were interested in the population of all university students in the United States, it would be possible to create a list of all the universities, then sample them using either stratified or systematic sampling procedures. Next, the researcher could obtain lists of students from each of the sample universities; each of those lists would then be sampled to provide the final list of university students for study.

Multistage cluster sampling is an efficient method of sampling a very large population, but the price of that efficiency is a less accurate sample. While a simple random sample drawn from a population list is subject to a single sampling error, a two-stage cluster sample is subject to two sampling errors. The best way to avoid this problem is to maximize the number of clusters selected while decreasing the number of elements within each cluster.

STATISTICAL THEORY

As Raymond Jessen points out, the theory of sampling is probably one of the oldest branches of statistical theory. It has only been since the early twentieth century, however, that there has been much progress in applying that theory to, and developing a new theory for, statistical surveys. One of the earliest applications for sampling was in political polling, perhaps because this area provides researchers with the opportunity to discover the accuracy of their estimates fairly quickly. This area has also been useful in detecting errors in sampling methods. For example, in 1936, the *Literary Digest*, which had been accurate in predicting the winners of the United States presidential elections since 1920, inaccurately predicted that Republican contender Alfred Landon would win 57 percent of the vote over incumbent President Franklin D. Roosevelt's 43 percent. The *Literary Digest*'s mistake was an unrepresentative sampling frame consisting of telephone directories and automobile registration lists. This frame resulted in a disproportionately wealthy sample, excluding poor people who predominantly favored Roosevelt's New Deal recovery programs. This emphasized to researchers that a representative sampling frame was crucial if the sample were to be valid.

In the 1940's, the U.S. Bureau of the Census developed unequal probability sampling theory, and area-probability sampling methods became widely used and sophisticated in both theory and practice. The 1945 census of agriculture in the United States was collected in part on a sample, and the 1950 census of population made extensive use of built-in samples to increase its accuracy and reduce costs.

One of the most important advances for sampling techniques has been increasingly sophisticated computer technology. For example, once the sampling frame is entered into the computer, a simple random sample can be selected automatically. In the future, computer technology, coupled with increasingly efficient and accurate information-gathering technology, will enable researchers to select samples that more accurately represent the population.

Sampling techniques are essential for researchers in psychology. Without relying on sampling as the basis for collecting evaluative data, the risk and cost involved with adopting new methods of treatment would be difficult to justify. Evaluating the effectiveness of new programs would be prohibitive, and some populations are so large and dispersed that observing each element is impossible.

Probability sampling is the most effective method for the selection of study elements in the field of psychology for two reasons. First, it avoids conscious or unconscious biases in element selection on the part of the researcher. If all elements in the population have an equal chance of selection, there is an excellent chance that a sample so selected will closely represent the population of all elements. Second, probability sampling permits estimates of sampling error. Although no probability sample will be perfectly representative in all respects, controlled selection methods permit the researcher to estimate the degree of expected error in that regard.

SOURCES FOR FURTHER STUDY

Babbie, Earl R. *The Practice of Social Research.* 9th ed. Belmont, Calif.: Wadsworth, 2000. Written in clear, easy-to-understand language with many illustrations. Babbie discusses both the logic and the skills necessary to understand sampling and randomization. Contains appendices, a bibliography, an index, and an excellent glossary. One of the appendixes contains a table of random numbers.

Blalock, Hubert M., Jr. *Social Statistics.* 2d ed. New York: McGraw-Hill, 1979. Provides an extensive section on sampling that pays particular attention to random sampling, systematic sampling, stratified sampling, and cluster sampling. Although there are some formulas and computations, the majority of the discussion is not technical, and the explanations are clear.

Henry, Gary T. *Practical Sampling.* Newbury Park, Calif.: Sage Publications, 1990. Provides detailed examples of selecting alternatives in actual sampling practice. Not heavily theoretical or mathematical, although the material is based on the theoretical and mathematical sampling work that has preceded it. Provides references for those interested in proceeding deeper into the literature.

Jessen, Raymond James. *Statistical Survey Techniques.* New York: John Wiley & Sons, 1978. Provides a clear introduction to statistical sampling. The examples are clear and relevant, and they illustrate the points made on sampling technique. Although this book is not written for mathematicians, each chapter contains mathematical notes that demonstrate points made in the chapter.

Kish, Leslie. *Survey Sampling.* 1965. Reprint. New York: John Wiley & Sons, 1995. This book is the definitive work on sampling in social research; the coverage ranges from the simplest matters to the most complex and mathematical. Somewhat difficult reading, but Kish manages to be both highly theoretical and extremely practical.

Karen Anding Fontenot

SEE ALSO: Data description; Experimentation: Independent, dependent, and control variables; Hypothesis development and testing; Scientific methods; Statistical significance tests; Survey research: Questionnaires and interviews.

Schizophrenia
Background, types, and symptoms

TYPE OF PSYCHOLOGY: Psychopathology
FIELDS OF STUDY: Schizophrenias

Schizophrenia is a severe mental illness that interferes with a person's ability to think and communicate. Researchers have studied the illness for decades, and while genetic factors contribute to the illness, the specific genetic mechanisms and how they interact with environmental factors remain unknown.

KEY CONCEPTS
- affect
- antipsychotic medication
- delusions
- genetic factors
- hallucinations
- insight
- neuroleptics
- psychosis
- tardive dyskinesia

INTRODUCTION

Schizophrenia affects approximately one out of every hundred individuals. It is considered to be one of the most severe mental illnesses, because its symptoms can have a devastating impact on the lives of patients and their families. The patient's thought processes, communication abilities, and emotional expressions are disturbed. As a result, many patients with schizophrenia are dependent on others for assistance with daily life activities.

Schizophrenia is often confused, by the layperson, with multiple personality disorder. The latter is an illness which is defined as two or more distinct personalities existing within the person. The personalities tend to be intact, and each is associated with its own style of perceiving the world and relating to others. Schizophrenia, in contrast, does not involve the existence of two or more personalities; rather, it is the presence of psychotic symptoms and characteristic deficits in social interaction that define schizophrenia.

The diagnostic criteria for schizophrenia have changed over the years; however, certain key symptoms, including disturbances in thought, perception, and emotional experiences, have remained as defining features. The most widely used criteria for diagnosing schizophrenia are those listed in the *Diagnostic and Statistical Manual of Mental Disorders: DSM-IV-TR* (rev. 4th ed., 2000). This manual is published by the American Psychiatric Association and is periodically revised to incorporate changes in diagnostic criteria.

The DSM-IV-TR contains the following symptoms for diagnosing schizophrenia: delusions, hallucinations, disorganized thought, speech, or behavior, and flattened (less responsive) affect; symptoms must have been present for at least six months, and the individual must show marked impairment in a major area of functioning such as work or interpersonal relations. Further, the presence of other disorders, such as drug reactions or organic brain disorders associated with aging, must be ruled out. Thus, the diagnosis of schizophrenia typically involves a thorough physical and mental assessment. While no single individual symptom is necessary for a person to receive a diagnosis of schizophrenia, according to the DSM-IV-TR, the persistent and debilitating presence of bizarre hallucinations, a hallucinated voice commenting on the individual, or hallucinated conversations between two voices is a strong indication of schizophrenia. The presence of delusions or hallucinations and loss of contact with reality is referred to as psychosis and is often present in schizophrenia, but psychotic symptoms can be seen in other mental disorders (for example, bipolar disorder or substance-induced psychotic disorder), so the term "psychosis" is not synonymous with the diagnosis of schizophrenia.

Warning Signs for Schizophrenia

The following behaviors can be early warning signs:
- hearing or seeing something that is not there
- a constant feeling of being watched
- peculiar or nonsensical way of speaking or writing
- strange body positioning
- feeling indifferent to very important situations
- deterioration of academic or work performance
- a change in personal hygiene and appearance
- a change in personality
- increasing withdrawal from social situations
- irrational, angry, or fearful response to loved ones
- inability to sleep or concentrate
- inappropriate or bizarre behavior
- extreme preoccupation with religion or the occult

Source: National Mental Health Association (NMHA) factsheet "Schizophrenia: What You Need to Know."

While not emphasized by the DSM-IV-TR, international and cross-cultural study of the symptoms of schizophrenia has noted that the most frequently observed symptom in schizophrenia is patients' lack of insight. That is, despite sometimes overwhelming evidence of gross abnormalities in perception and behavior, patients with schizophrenia are likely to deny that those problems are symptomatic of a disorder.

Each of these symptoms can take a variety of forms. Delusions are defined as false beliefs based on incorrect inferences about external reality. Delusions are classified based on the nature of their content. For example, grandiose delusions involve false beliefs about one's importance, power, or knowledge. The patient might express the belief that he or she is the most intelligent person in the world but that these special intellectual powers have gone unrecognized. As another example, persecutory delusions involve beliefs of being persecuted or conspired against by others. The patient might claim, for example, that there is a government plot to poison him or her.

Hallucinations are sensory experiences that occur in the absence of a real stimulus. In the case of auditory hallucinations, the patient may hear voices calling or conversing when there is no one in physical proximity. Visual hallucinations may involve seeing people who are deceased or seeing inanimate objects move on their own accord. Olfactory (smell) and tactile (touch) hallucinations are also possible.

The term "affect" is used to refer to observable behaviors that are the expression of an emotion. Affect is predominantly displayed in facial expressions. "Flat" affect describes a severe reduction in the intensity of emotional expressions, both positive and negative. Patients with flat affect may show no observable sign of emotion, even when experiencing a very joyful or sad event.

Among the symptoms of schizophrenia, abnormalities in the expression of thoughts are a central feature. When speech is incoherent, it is difficult for the listener to comprehend because it is illogical or incomplete. As an example, in response to the question "Where do you live?" one patient replied, "Yes, live! I haven't had much time in this or that. It is an area. In the same area. Mrs. Smith! If the time comes for a temporary space now or whatever." The term "loose associations" is applied to speech in which ideas shift from one subject to another subject that is completely unrelated. If the loosening of associations is severe, speech may be incoherent. As an illustration of loose associations, a patient described the meaning of "A rolling stone gathers no moss" by saying, "Inside your head there's a brain and it's round like a stone and when it spins around it can't make connections the way moss has little filaments."

With regard to speech, a variety of other abnormalities are sometimes shown by patients. They may use "neologisms," which are new words invented by the patient to convey a special meaning. Some show "clang associations," which involve the use of rhyming words in conversation: "Live and let live, that's my motto. You live and give and live-give." Abnormalities in the intonation and pace of speech are also common.

DSM-IV-TR Criteria for Schizophrenia

Characterized by two or more of the following, each present for significant portion of time during one-month period (less if treated successfully):

- delusions
- hallucinations
- disorganized speech (such as frequent derailment or incoherence)
- grossly disorganized or catatonic behavior
- negative symptoms (affective flattening, alogia, or avolition)

Only one criterion symptom required if delusions are bizarre or hallucinations consist of a voice keeping running commentary on person's behavior or thoughts, or two or more voices conversing with each other

For a significant portion of time since onset, one or more major areas of functioning (work, interpersonal relations, self-care) markedly below level achieved prior to onset; when onset in childhood or adolescence, failure to achieve expected level of interpersonal, academic, or occupational achievement

Continuous signs of disturbance persist for at least six months, including at least one month of active-phase symptoms (less if treated successfully) and possibly including periods of prodromal or residual symptoms; during prodromal or residual periods, signs of disturbance may be manifested by only negative symptoms or two or more symptoms present in attenuated form (such as odd beliefs, unusual perceptual experiences)

Schizoaffective Disorder and Mood Disorder with Psychotic Features ruled out because either no Major Depressive, Manic, or Mixed Episodes have occurred concurrently with active-phase symptoms or mood episodes have occurred during active-phase symptoms, but their total duration brief relative to duration of active and residual periods

Disturbance not due to direct physiological effects of a substance or a general medical condition

If history of Autistic Disorder or another Pervasive Developmental Disorder present, additional diagnosis of Schizophrenia made only if prominent delusions or hallucinations are also present for at least one month (less if treated successfully)

Classification of longitudinal course (applied only after at least one year has elapsed since initial onset of active-phase symptoms):

- Episodic with Interepisode Residual Symptoms: Episodes defined by reemergence of prominent psychotic symptoms; also specify if with Prominent Negative Symptoms
- Episodic with No Interepisode Residual Symptoms
- Continuous: Prominent psychotic symptoms present throughout period of observation; also specify if with Prominent Negative Symptoms
- Single Episode in Partial Remission; also specify if with Prominent Negative Symptoms
- Single Episode in Full Remission
- Other or Unspecified Pattern

In addition to these symptoms, some patients manifest bizarre behaviors, such as odd, repetitive movements or unusual postures. Odd or inappropriate styles of dressing, such as wearing winter coats in the summer, may also occur in some patients. More deteriorated patients frequently show poor hygiene. In order to meet the diagnostic criteria for schizophrenia, the individual must show signs of disturbance for at least six months.

TYPES AND TREATMENT OF SCHIZOPHRENIA

Because no one symptom is sufficient for a diagnosis of schizophrenia, patients vary in the numbers and intensity of their symptoms. Four subtypes of schizophrenia are recognized; the differentiation among them is based upon the symptom profile, and the criteria are clearly described in DSM-IV-TR.

Catatonic schizophrenia is predominantly characterized by abnormal motor behavior. The patient may be in a "catatonic stupor," which means that he or she shows a marked reduction in movement and is sometimes mute. Other catatonic schizophrenic patients adopt a rigid posture (catatonic rigidity), which they will maintain despite efforts to move them. In disorganized schizophrenia, the primary symptoms are incoherence, catatonic behavior, and flat or inappropriate affect. In paranoid schizophrenia, the predominant symptom is a preoccupation with a systematized delusion, in the absence of incoherence, loose associations, or abnormal affect. The label undifferentiated schizophrenia is applied to cases that do not meet the specific criteria for catatonic, disorganized, or paranoid schizophrenia, but do show prominent delusions, hallucinations, incoherence, or disorganized behavior. Residual schizophrenia is a diagnosis used to refer to the presence of flattened affect or limited speech and less severe delusions or hallucinations in individuals with a prior history of schizophrenia.

In his writings, Eugen Bleuler often used the phrase "the group of schizophrenias," because he believed the disorder could be caused by a variety of factors. In other words, he believed that schizophrenia may not be a single disease entity. Today, some researchers and clinicians who work in the field take the same position. They believe that the differences among patients in symptom patterns and the course of the illness are attributable to differences in etiology. Despite the assumption that there may be different subtypes of schizophrenia, however, each with its own etiology, there is no definitive evidence to support this. In fact, the five subtypes listed in DSM-IV-TR show similar courses and receive the same medications and psychotherapeutic treatments. Thus the distinctions among them are purely descriptive at this point.

Because schizophrenic symptoms have such a devastating impact on the individual's ability to function, family members often respond to the onset of symptoms by seeking immediate treatment. Clinicians, in turn, often respond by recommending hospitalization so that tests can be conducted and an appropriate treatment can be determined. Consequently, almost all patients who are diagnosed with schizophrenia are hospitalized at least once in their lives. The majority experience several hospitalizations.

Research on the long-term outcome of schizophrenia indicates that the illness is highly variable in its course. A minority of patients have only one episode of illness, then go into remission and experience no further symptoms. Unfortunately, however, the majority of patients have recurring episodes that require periodic rehospitalizations. The most severely ill never experience remission, but instead show a chronic course of symptomatology. For these reasons, schizophrenia is viewed as having the poorest prognosis of all the major mental illnesses.

Prior to the 1950's, patients with schizophrenia were hospitalized for extended periods of time and frequently became "institutionalized." There were only a few available somatic treatments, and those proved to be of little efficacy. Included among them were insulin coma therapy (the administration of large doses of insulin in order to induce coma), electroconvulsive therapy (the application of electrical current to the temples in order to induce a seizure), and prefrontal lobotomy (a surgical procedure in which the tracts connecting the frontal lobes to other areas of the brain are severed).

In the 1950's, a class of drugs referred to as antipsychotic medications were discovered to be effective in treating schizophrenia. Antipsychotic drugs significantly reduce some of the symptoms of schizophrenia in many patients. The introduction of antipsychotic medications (also called neuroleptics) in combination with changes in public policy led to a dramatic decline in the number of patients in public mental hospitals. Antipsychotic medications have freed many patients from confinement in hospitals and have enhanced their chances for functioning in the community. Not all patients benefit from typical antipsychotic medications, and the discovery of new classes of medications has offered hope to patients and families. Despite the benefits of antipsychotic medications, they can also produce serious side effects, particularly tardive dyskinesia, a movement disorder associated in some patients with chronic use of typical antipsychotic medications.

The public policy that has contributed to the decline in the number of hospitalized patients with schizophrenia is the nationwide policy of deinstitutionalization. This policy, which has been adopted and promoted by most state governments in the years since 1970, emphasizes short-term hospitalizations, and it has involved the release of some patients who had been in institutions for many years. Unfortunately, the support services that were needed to facilitate the transition from hospital to community living were never put in place. Consequently, the number of homeless schizophrenic patients has increased dramatically. Some of these are patients whose family members have died or have simply lost touch with them. Other patients have withdrawn from contact with their families, despite efforts by concerned relatives to provide assistance. The plight of the homeless mentally ill is of great concern to mental health professionals.

History and Future Directions

Writing in the late 1800's, the eminent physician Emil Kraepelin was among the first to document the symptoms and course of this illness, referring to it as "dementia praecox" (dementia of early life). Subsequently, Eugen Bleuler applied the term "schizophrenia," meaning splitting of the mind, to the disorder. Both Kraepelin and Bleuler assumed that organic factors are involved in schizophrenia. Contemporary research has confirmed this assumption; brain scans reveal that a significant proportion of schizophrenia patients do have organic abnormalities. The precise nature and cause of these abnormalities remain unknown.

In the majority of cases, the onset of schizophrenic symptoms occurs in late adolescence or early adulthood. The major risk period is between twenty and twenty-five years of age, but the period of risk extends well into adult life. For some patients, there are no readily apparent abnormalities prior to the development of illness. For others, however, the onset of schizophrenia is preceded by impairments in social, academic, or occupational functioning. Some are described by their families as having had adjustment problems in childhood. Childhood schizophrenia is relatively rare. It is estimated to occur in about one out of every ten thousand children. When schizophrenia is diagnosed in childhood, the same diagnostic criteria and treatments are applied.

Schizophrenia shows no clear pattern in terms of its distribution in the population. It occurs in both males and females, although it tends to have a slightly earlier onset in males than in females. The illness strikes individuals of all social, economic, and ethnic backgrounds. Some patients manifest high levels of intelligence and are excellent students prior to becoming ill; others show poor academic performance and signs of learning disability. While the specific pathophysiology associated with schizophrenia remains obscure, the preponderance of evidence demonstrates a significant role for genetic factors in the risk for developing schizophrenia.

Schizophrenia is an illness that has been recognized by medicine for more than a hundred years. During this time, only modest progress has been made in research on its etiology. Some significant advances have been achieved in treatment, however, and the prognosis for schizophrenia is better now than ever before. Moreover, there is reason to believe that the availability of new technologies for studying the central nervous system will speed the pace of further discovery.

Sources for Further Study

Bleuler, Eugen. *Dementia Praecox: Or, The Group of Schizophrenias.* Translated by Joseph Zinkin. New York: International Universities Press, 1950. Original German first published in 1911. A classic book in the field, this provides excellent descriptions of the symptoms and very interesting discussions of possible causal factors.

Gottesman, Irving I. *Schizophrenia Genesis: The Origins of Madness.* New York: W. H. Freeman, 1991. An accessible overview for both general and professional readers; includes numerous first-person accounts of the experience of schizophrenia from the perspective of patients and family members.

Herz, Marvin I., Samuel J. Keith, and John P. Docherty. *Psychosocial Treatment of Schizophrenia.* New York: Elsevier, 1990. This book, volume 4 in the Handbook of Schizophrenia series, examines psychosocial causes of schizophrenia and psychosocial treatment approaches. Discusses early intervention. Behavior therapy and supportive living arrangements are covered; results of long-term outcome studies are also reviewed.

Hirsch, Steven R., and Daniel R. Weinberger. *Schizophrenia.* Oxford: Blackwell Science, 1995. A comprehensive review by two masters in the field.

Kraepelin, Emil. *Clinical Psychiatry.* Translated by A. Ross Diefendorf. Delmar, N.Y.: Scholars' Facsimiles & Reprints, 1981. A facsimile reprint of the seventh (1907) edition of Kraepelin's classic text. Reveals the origins of contemporary thinking about schizophrenia and other mental disorders.

Maj, Mario, and Norman Sartorius. *Schizophrenia.* New York: John Wiley & Sons, 1999. This book, part of a World Psychiatric Association series bringing evidence from empirical studies to clinical practitioners, is an integration of the worldwide research literature on schizophrenia.

Neale, John M., and Thomas F. Oltmanns. *Schizophrenia.* New York: John Wiley & Sons, 1980. This book provides a comprehensive overview of the illness and examines many of the research methods for exploring its causes.

Walker, Elaine F., ed. *Schizophrenia: A Life-Span Developmental Perspective.* San Diego, Calif.: Academic Press, 1991. The entire life-course of schizophrenic patients is addressed in this book, from early childhood precursors to geriatric outcome.

Elaine F. Walker;
updated by Loring J. Ingraham

SEE ALSO: Abnormality: Biomedical models; Abnormality: Psychological models; Diagnosis; *Diagnostic and Statistical Manual of Mental Disorders* (DSM); Drug therapies; Madness: Historical concepts; Psychosurgery; Schizophrenia: High-risk children; Schizophrenia: Theoretical explanations.

Schizophrenia
High-risk children

TYPE OF PSYCHOLOGY: Psychopathology
FIELDS OF STUDY: Schizophrenias

Researchers have been conducting studies of children whose parents suffer from schizophrenia in order to identify the indicators of risk for this psychiatric illness; preliminary findings indicate that it may someday be possible to prevent the onset of schizophrenia. Longitudinal studies of high-risk children may provide information regarding developmental precursors of adult schizophrenia.

KEY CONCEPTS
- etiology
- genetics
- longitudinal study
- premorbid
- schizophrenia

INTRODUCTION

The term "high-risk" has been applied to biological offspring of schizophrenic parents, because they are known to be at genetic risk for the same disorder shown by their parents. Numerous researchers are studying high-risk children in order to shed light on the origins of schizophrenia. This approach has many advantages over other research methods and has already yielded some important findings.

The importance of research on children at risk for schizophrenia stems from a need to understand the precursors of the illness. Over the years, researchers have studied schizophrenia from many different perspectives and with a variety of methods. Despite many decades of work, however, investigators have not yet been successful in identifying the causes or developing a cure. Some progress has been made in clarifying the nature and course of schizophrenia, and there have been considerable advances in the pharmacological treatment of symptoms; however, the precursors and the origins remain a mystery.

Because the onset of schizophrenia usually occurs in late adolescence or early adulthood, patients typically do not come to the attention of investigators until they have been experiencing symptoms for some period of time. At that point, researchers have to rely on the patient and other informants for information about the nature of the individual's adjustment prior to the onset of the illness. These retrospective accounts of the patient's functioning are often sketchy and can be biased in various ways. Yet it is well accepted that progress toward the ultimate goal—the prevention of schizophrenia—will not be achieved until researchers are able to identify individuals who are vulnerable to the disorder.

In response to this concern, several investigators emphasized the importance of studying the development of individuals known to be at heightened statistical risk for schizophrenia. Specifically, it was proposed that repeated assessments should be conducted so that data on all aspects of the development of at-risk children would be available by the time they enter the adult risk period for schizophrenia. In this way, it might be possible to identify precursors of the illness in subjects who had not yet received any treatment for the disorder. Another major advantage of studying subjects prior to the provision of treatment is that only then is it possible to differentiate true precursors of the illness from the consequences or side effects of treatment for the illness.

By the late 1950's, it was well established that schizophrenia tends to run in families. The general population rate for the disorder is about 1 percent. In contrast, it has been estimated that children who have one biological parent with schizophrenia have a 10 to 15 percent chance of developing the disorder. When both biological parents are diagnosed with schizophrenia, the risk rate is thought to be around 40 percent. It is apparent, therefore, that offspring of schizophrenic parents are indeed at heightened risk for developing the same disorder. Conducting longitudinal studies of these high-risk children is an efficient way of studying individuals who are most likely to develop schizophrenia.

In the sections that follow, the progress of these research programs will be reviewed. In particular, the various areas of abnormality that have been noted in children at high risk for schizophrenia will be discussed. Before reviewing the findings, however, some of the methodological issues involved in high-risk research will be described.

The first large-scale prospective longitudinal study of high-risk children was initiated in Denmark in the mid-1960's by Sarnoff Mednick and Fini Schulsinger. They followed a group of one hundred children who had at least one schizophrenic parent and two hundred comparison children whose parents had no psychiatric disorder. Since the Danish study was initiated, a number of other research groups have initiated similar high-risk research programs.

A second longitudinal study of particular note is the New York High-Risk Project, led by L. Erlenmeyer-Kimling. Erlenmeyer-Kimling and her associates followed two independent series of three groups of children: children with at least one schizophrenic parent, children with one or two parents with major affective disorder (typically depression), and children whose parents were psychiatrically normal. One notable feature of the New York High-Risk Project is that the investigators included an at-risk comparison group, consisting of offspring of other psychiatrically disturbed individuals. Comparisons between high-risk offspring (children with at least one schizophrenic parent) and offspring of mood-disordered parents is especially useful in identifying behavioral precursors that are specifically associated with the later development of schizophrenia, rather than an adult psychiatric outcome in general.

METHODOLOGICAL ISSUES

One of the major challenges in conducting high-risk research is locating the sample. As previously stated, schizophrenia is a relatively rare disorder in that it occurs in about 1 percent of the general population. Moreover, because most schizophrenic patients experience an onset of illness in late adolescence or early adulthood, they are less likely to marry or have children. This is especially true of schizophrenic patients who are men. Consequently, the majority of the subjects of high-risk research are offspring of schizophrenic mothers. Further, of the schizophrenic women who do have children, a substantial portion do not keep their children but instead place them for adoption. This further complicates the task of identifying samples of high-risk children. In order to be assured of identifying a sample of adequate size, researchers in this field establish formal arrangements with local treatment facilities in order to increase their chances of identifying all the high-risk children in their geographic area.

Another important issue confronted by high-risk researchers is the question of when in the child's life span the study should be initiated. Most investigators are interested in identifying the very earliest signs of vulnerability for schizophrenia. Therefore, it is desirable to initiate a high-risk study with subjects who are infants. In this way, investigators will be able to examine the entire premorbid life course of patients. If there are any markers of vulnerability apparent in infancy, they will be able to identify them. The investigator who initiates a study of infant subjects, however, must wait an extended period of time in order to gather any information about their adult psychiatric outcomes. In order to reduce the period between the initiation of the study and

Schizophrenia in Children

Early warning signs:
- trouble discerning dreams from reality
- seeing things and hearing voices that are not real
- confused thinking
- vivid and bizarre thoughts and ideas
- extreme moodiness
- peculiar behavior
- concept that people are "out to get them"
- behaving younger than chronological age
- severe anxiety and fearfulness
- confusing television or movies with reality
- severe problems in making and keeping friends

Source: National Mental Health Association (NMHA) factsheet "Children's Mental Health: Schizophrenia in Children," 1996.

the entry of the subjects into the major risk period for schizophrenia, most investigators have initiated high-risk projects on subjects who are in middle or late childhood.

The problem of attrition (loss of subjects) is another aspect of concern to high-risk researchers. As mentioned, the long-term goal is to compare those high-risk children who succumb to schizophrenia to those who do not. Consequently, the most crucial information will be provided only when the researchers are knowledgeable about the adult psychiatric outcome of the subjects. Because a sample of one hundred high-risk children may eventually yield only ten to fifteen schizophrenic patients, it is of critical importance to investigators that they maintain contact with all subjects so that they can determine their adult psychiatric outcomes.

Finally, the question of how to select an appropriate comparison group is salient to high-risk researchers. Again, one of the ultimate goals is to identify specific signs of vulnerability to schizophrenia. An important question is whether the signs identified by researchers are simply manifestations of vulnerability to any adult psychiatric disorder or signs of specific vulnerability to schizophrenia. In order to address this question, it is necessary to include groups of children whose parents have psychiatric disorders other than schizophrenia.

RESEARCH FINDINGS

The results from studies of high-risk children suggest that the predisposition for schizophrenia may

be detectable at an early age. Reports on the developmental characteristics of high-risk children have revealed some important differences between children of schizophrenic parents and children whose parents have no mental illness. The differences that have been found tend to fall into three general areas: motor functions, cognitive functions, and social adjustment. When compared to children of normal parents, high-risk subjects have been found to show a variety of impairments in motor development and motor abilities. Infant offspring of schizophrenic parents tend to show delays in the development of motor skills, such as crawling and walking. Similarly, studies of high-risk subjects in their middle childhood and early adolescent years reveal deficits in fine and gross motor skills and coordination. It is important to emphasize, however, that these deficiencies are not of such a severe magnitude that the child would be viewed as clinically impaired in motor skills. Yet the deficiencies are apparent when high-risk children, as a group, are compared to children of normal parents.

Numerous studies have found that children at high risk for schizophrenia also show impairments in cognitive functions. Although their scores on standardized tests of intelligence are within the normal range, they tend to be slightly below that of children of normal parents. With regard to specific abilities, investigators have found that high-risk children show deficiencies in their capacity to maintain and focus attention. These deficiencies are apparent as early as the preschool years and involve the processing of both auditory and visual information. Recall that the New York High-Risk Project included a comparison group of offspring of individuals with affective illnesses such as depression. The results of the project, which started in 1971 and has now followed the offspring from childhood to midadulthood, indicated that attention deviance, impairments in gross motor skills, and memory deficits were relatively unique to risk for schizophrenia. That is, these deficits were more prevalent in high-risk children (offspring of schizophrenic parents) than among offspring of affectively ill parents. Erlenmeyer-Kimling and associates have noted that among all the neurobehavioral predictors of later development of schizophrenia, attention deviance appears to be the most specifically related to genetic risk for schizophrenia. In the New York High-Risk Project, the offspring of schizophrenic parents showed more attention deviance than either the offspring of affectively ill parents or the offspring of normal parents. Because attentional deficits have been found so consistently in high-risk children, some researchers in the field have suggested that these deficits may be a key marker of risk for schizophrenia.

When compared to children of parents without psychiatric disorder, offspring of schizophrenic parents tend to manifest a higher rate of behavioral problems. These include a higher rate of aggressive behaviors, as well as an increased frequency of social withdrawal. In general, children of schizophrenic parents are perceived as less socially competent than comparison children. It is important to take into consideration, however, that children of parents with other psychiatric disorders are also found to show problems with social adjustment. Consequently, it is unlikely that behavioral adjustment problems are uniquely characteristic of risk for schizophrenia.

RESEARCH USES

The goal of high-risk research is to identify factors that can successfully predict those who are most likely to develop subsequent cases of schizophrenia or schizophrenia-related disorders. Only a subgroup—in fact, a minority—of high-risk children will eventually manifest schizophrenia. The most significant question, therefore, is not what differentiates high-risk children from a comparison group, but rather what differentiates high-risk children who develop schizophrenia from high-risk children who do not. Even those individuals who are predicted to be at heightened risk who do not eventually develop schizophrenia are interesting and potentially informative. The high-risk offspring who do not develop schizophrenia can inform investigators about resiliency factors that are likely to be important. Only a few high-risk research projects have followed their subjects all the way into adulthood. Only limited data are thus available regarding the childhood characteristics that predict adult psychiatric outcome. The findings from these studies confirm the predictions made by the researchers. Specifically, the high-risk children who eventually develop schizophrenia show more evidence of motor abnormalities, memory deficits, and attentional dysfunction in childhood than those who do not.

The findings of neurobehavioral abnormalities in preschizophrenic individuals during childhood are consistent with the etiologic hypotheses held by most researchers in the field. Specifically, such abnormalities would be expected in a disorder that is presumed to be attributable to a central nervous system impairment that is, at least in part, genetically determined. These findings are consistent with the hypothesis that an early brain insult may manifest itself in neurobehavioral abnormalities early on but can remain latent (unexpressed) as clinical symptoms for many years.

LIMITATIONS

Like all approaches to research, the high-risk method has some limitations. One limitation concerns whether the findings from these studies can be generalized to a wider population. Although it is true that schizophrenia tends to run in families, it is also true that the majority of schizophrenic patients do not have a schizophrenic parent. As a result, the subjects of high-risk research may represent a unique subgroup of schizophrenic patients. The fact that they have a parent with the illness may mean that they have a higher genetic loading for the disorder than do schizophrenic patients whose parents have no mental illness. Moreover, there are undoubtedly some environmental stresses associated with being reared by a schizophrenic parent. In sum, high-risk children who become schizophrenic patients may differ from other schizophrenic patients both in terms of genetic factors and in terms of environment. Some other problems with the method, mentioned above, include subject attrition and the extensive waiting period required before adult psychiatric outcome is determined.

Some investigators have attempted to address the issue of identifying markers of vulnerability with alternative methodologies. For example, it has been shown that children with behavioral problems are more likely to develop schizophrenia in adulthood than are children who manifest no significant behavioral difficulties. Thus, some researchers are conducting longitudinal studies of maladjusted children in order to identify precursors of schizophrenia. Taking a novel approach, one study has utilized childhood home movies of adult-onset schizophrenic patients as a database for identifying infant and early childhood precursors. Up to this point, the findings from these studies are consistent with those from high-risk research.

FUTURE DIRECTIONS

Based on the research findings, there is good reason to believe that individuals who succumb to schizophrenia in adulthood manifested signs of vulnerability long before the onset of the disorder, perhaps as early as infancy. These findings have some important implications. First, they provide some clues to etiology; they suggest that the neuropathological process underlying schizophrenia is one that begins long before the onset of the clinical symptoms that define the illness. Thus, the search for the biological bases of this illness must encompass the entire premorbid life course. Second, the findings suggest that it may eventually be possible to identify individuals who are at risk for schizophrenia so that preventive interventions can be provided. As time goes on, more of the high-risk children who have been the subjects of these investigations will pass through the adult risk period for schizophrenia. One can therefore anticipate that important new findings from high-risk research will be forthcoming.

SOURCES FOR FURTHER STUDY

Erlenmeyer-Kimling, L., et al. "Attention, Memory, and Motor Skills as Childhood Predictors of Schizophrenia-Related Psychoses: The New York High-Risk Project." *American Journal of Psychiatry* 157 (2000): 1416-1422. This paper provides results from the New York High-Risk Project and places them in the context of the overall goals of prediction and detection of schizophrenia.

Gooding, Diane C., and William C. Iacono. "Schizophrenia Through the Lens of a Developmental Psychopathology Perspective." In *Risk, Disorder, and Adaptation.* Vol. 2 in *Manual of Developmental Psychopathology*, edited by D. Cicchetti and D. J. Cohen. New York: John Wiley & Sons, 1995. This book chapter provides a detailed discussion of research findings from studies of high-risk children as well as a discussion of alternative research strategies.

Gottesman, Irving I. *Schizophrenia Genesis: The Origins of Madness.* New York. W. H. Freeman, 1991. Provides a comprehensive overview of the genetic determinants of schizophrenia, written by the foremost authority in the field. Very readable; explains the theory and methods of behavioral genetics research and presents a detailed description of the findings.

Mednick, Sarnoff A., and Thomas F. McNeil. "Current Methodology in Research on the Etiology of Schizophrenia: Serious Difficulties Which Suggest the Use of the High-Risk Group Method." *Psychological Bulletin* 70, no. 6 (1968): 681-693. This classic paper served to introduce the idea of the high-risk method to researchers in the field of psychopathology. It clearly lays out the rationale behind the approach.

Walker, Elaine F., ed. *Schizophrenia: A Life-Course Developmental Perspective.* San Diego, Calif.: Academic Press, 1991. This book provides an overview of knowledge in the life course of schizophrenia. Chapters are written by experts in the field.

Walker, Elaine F., and Richard J. Lewine. "Prediction of Adult-Onset Schizophrenia from Childhood Home Movies of the Patient." *American Journal of Psychiatry* 147, no. 8 (1990): 1052-1056. Preliminary results from a novel study of the precursors of schizophrenia are presented in this paper. This approach complements the high-risk method in that it holds promise for validating the findings of high-risk research.

Watt, Norman F., et al., eds. *Children at Risk for Schizophrenia.* New York: Cambridge University Press, 1984. This edited volume summarizes the major high-risk projects under way throughout the world at the time it was written. It demonstrates the importance of this work in furthering understanding of the origins of schizophrenia.

Elaine F. Walker;
updated by Diane C. Gooding

SEE ALSO: Abnormality: Biomedical models; Abnormality: Psychological models; Diagnosis; *Diagnostic and Statistical Manual of Mental Disorders* (DSM); Drug therapies; Madness: Historical concepts; Psychosurgery; Schizophrenia: Background, types, and symptoms; Schizophrenia: Theoretical explanations.

Schizophrenia
Theoretical explanations

TYPE OF PSYCHOLOGY: Psychopathology
FIELDS OF STUDY: Models of abnormality; schizophrenias

Schizophrenia is one of the most severe and potentially devastating of all psychological disorders. Over the years, a variety of theoretical explanations, sometimes poorly supported by direct experimental evidence, have been proposed. Current empirical research supports the operation of genetic factors in schizophrenia and suggests that such factors may act in concert with environmental factors during early development to elevate the risk for subsequent illness.

KEY CONCEPTS
- environment
- genetic factors
- interaction
- neurodevelopment
- neurotransmitter
- organic
- schizophrenia spectrum
- schizotypal

INTRODUCTION

Schizophrenia, an illness that strikes 1 percent of adults, involves changes in all aspects of psychological functioning. Thinking disorders, perceptual distortions and hallucinations, delusions, and emotional changes are the most prominent of such changes. Although some people recover completely, in many others the illness is chronic and deteriorative. For many years, because the causes of schizophrenia were poorly understood, a wide range of theories were proposed to account for the development of schizophrenia. These early theories about schizophrenia can be classified into four types: psychodynamic, family interaction, learning/attention, and organic. Current theories of schizophrenia focus primarily on genetic factors and their interaction with environmental conditions, particularly the environment experienced before birth and during early development.

PSYCHODYNAMIC THEORIES

Psychodynamic theories originated with Sigmund Freud, who believed that schizophrenia results when a child fails to develop an attachment to his or her parent of the opposite sex. This causes a powerful conflict (called an Oedipal conflict in males) in which unconscious homosexual desires threaten to overwhelm the conscious self. To prevent these desires from generating thoughts and feelings that cause painful guilt or behaviors that would be punished, the ego defends itself by regressing to a state in which awareness of the self as a distinct entity is

lost. Thus, the person's behavior becomes socially inappropriate; the person mistakes fantasies for reality and experiences hallucinations and delusions.

Harry Stack Sullivan, a follower of Freud, believed that failure of maternal attachment creates excessive anxiety and sets the pattern for all future relationships. Unable to cope in a world seen as socially dangerous, the individual retreats into fantasy. Having done so, the individual cannot grow socially or develop a sense of trust in or belonging with others. By late adolescence or early adulthood, the person's situation has become so hopeless that all pretense of normality collapses and he or she withdraws totally and finally into a world of fantasy and delusion.

FAMILY AND LEARNING THEORIES

Family interaction theories dwell even more intensely on parent-child, especially mother-child, relationships. Theodore Lidz and coworkers, after conducting studies on families with a schizophrenic member, concluded that one or both parents of a future

Swiss psychiatrist Eugen Bleuler, who first named the disease "schizophrenia" in a 1908 paper. His discoveries challenged the traditional view of its causes and treatment.

schizophrenic are likely to be nearly, if not overtly, psychotic. They proposed that the psychotogenic influence of these parents on a psychologically vulnerable child is most likely the cause of schizophrenia.

Gregory Bateson and colleagues proposed a family interaction theory called the double-bind theory. Bateson suggested that schizophrenia results when parents expose a child to a family atmosphere in which they never effectively communicate their expectations, and therefore the child is unable to discover which behaviors will win approval. Scolded for disobeying, for example, the child changes his or her behavior only to be scolded for being "too obedient." Subjected to such no-win situations constantly, the child cannot develop an attachment to the family, and this failure generalizes to all subsequent relationships.

Learning theories propose that failure of operant conditioning causes the bizarre behavior of schizophrenia. In one version, conditioning fails because mechanisms in the brain that support operant learning, such as reinforcement and attention, are faulty, thus preventing the learning of appropriate, adaptive behaviors.

For example, a person who is unable to focus attention on relevant stimuli would be unable to learn the stimulus associations and discriminations necessary for successful day-to-day behavior. Such an individual's behavior would eventually become chaotic. This learning/attention theory proposes a defect in perceptual filtering, a function of the brain's reticular formation. This system filters out the innumerable stimuli that impinge upon one's senses every moment but are unimportant. In schizophrenia, the theory proposes, this filtering system fails, and the individual is overwhelmed by a welter of trivial stimuli. Unable to cope with this confusing overstimulation, the person withdraws, becomes preoccupied with sorting out his or her thoughts, and becomes unable to distinguish internally generated stimuli from external ones.

ORGANIC THEORIES

Organic theories of schizophrenia are influenced by the knowledge that conditions known to have organic causes (that is, causes stemming from biological abnormalities) often produce psychological symptoms that mimic the psychotic symptoms of schizophrenia. Among these are vitamin-deficiency diseases, viral encephalitis, temporal-lobe epilepsy,

and neurodegenerative disease such as Huntington's disease and Wilson's disease. In contradistinction to historical theories of schizophrenia that have little empirical support, considerable research supports the operation of genetic factors in schizophrenia; such factors are most often assumed to influence the development of the brain and its resilience to a variety of physiological and psychological stressors. In the diathesis-stress model, such a genetic defect is necessary for the development of chronic schizophrenia but is not sufficient to produce it. Stressful life events must also be present. The genetic abnormality then leaves the person unable to cope with life stresses, the result being psychosis. Research demonstrating the operation of genetic factors in schizophrenia in no way implies the absence of environmental factors which operate to influence the course of the disorder.

Many brain abnormalities have been proposed as causes of schizophrenia. One suggestion is that schizophrenia results from generalized brain pathology. For example, some researchers suggest that widespread brain deterioration caused by either environmental poisoning or infection by a virus causes schizophrenia.

Alternatively, some biochemical abnormality may be at fault. The endogenous psychotogen theory proposes that abnormal production of a chemical substance either inside or outside the brain produces psychotic symptoms by affecting the brain in a druglike fashion. Substances similar to the hallucinogenic drugs lysergic acid diethylamide (LSD) and mescaline are popular candidates for the endogenous psychotogen. The dopamine theory, however, proposes that schizophrenia results when a chemical neurotransmitter system in the brain called the dopamine system becomes abnormally overactive or when dopamine receptors in the brain become abnormally sensitive to normal amounts of dopamine. In addition to dopamine, other neurotransmitters have been proposed as important in the development and maintenance of schizophrenia.

NEUROLOGICAL AND GENETIC STUDIES

Theories of schizophrenia are instrumental in generating experiments that provide definite knowledge of the condition. Experimental support for psychodynamic theories of the development and progression of schizophrenia has not been forthcoming. Therefore, most empirical researchers regard psychodynamic theories of schizophrenia as having little scientific merit. Family interaction theories also have not been supported by subsequent experiments. Although studies have found disturbed family relationships, the evidence suggests that these are most likely the result of, not the cause of, having a schizophrenic individual in the family. Family interaction has, however, been shown to be influential in modifying the course of illness and the risk of relapse. Studies consistently fail to find that parent-child interactions are psychotogenic, and the once-popular notion of the schizophrenogenic parent has been discarded. Only learning/attention and organic theories are strongly supported by experimental evidence. The evidence for attentional or learning deficits resulting from a fault in the reticular formation is strong, and it stems from electrophysiological and behavioral studies.

The electroencephalogram (EEG) is often found to be abnormal in schizophrenic patients, showing excessive activation that indicates overarousal. Furthermore, studies of evoked potentials, electrical events recorded from the cortex of the brain in response to specific sensory stimuli, often find abnormalities. Significantly, these occur late in the evoked potential, indicating abnormality in the brain's interpretation of sensory stimuli rather than in initial reception and conduction.

Behavioral studies show that schizophrenic patients often overreact to low-intensity stimuli, which corresponds to their complaints that lights are too bright or sounds are too loud. In addition, patients are often unusually distractible—unable to focus attention on the most relevant stimuli. Orienting responses to novel stimuli are deficient in about half of schizophrenic patients. Patient self-reports also indicate that, subjectively, the individual feels overwhelmed by sensory stimulation.

Thus, considerable evidence suggests that, at least in many patients, there is an abnormality in the sensory/perceptual functioning in the brain, perhaps in the perceptual filtering mechanism of the reticular formation.

Franz J. Kallmann's twin studies of the 1940's provided convincing evidence of a genetic factor in schizophrenia. He found that genetically identical monozygotic twins are much more likely to be concordant for schizophrenia (that is, both twins are much more likely to be psychotic) than are dizygotic twins, who are not genetically identical. Stud-

ies using genealogical techniques also showed that schizophrenia runs in families.

The criticism of these studies was that twins not only are genetically similar but also are exposed to the same family environment, and therefore genetic and environmental factors were confounded. Seymour Kety and colleagues, working with adoption records in Scandinavia, effectively answered this criticism by showing that adoptees with schizophrenia are more likely to have biological relatives with schizophrenia or related illnesses than the biological relatives of unaffected adoptees. These studies showed that schizophrenia is more closely associated with genetic relatedness than with family environment. In addition, these studies showed that the genetic liability is not a liability to psychopathology in general (that is, relatives of individuals with schizophrenia are not at elevated risk for all forms of mental disorder) but that there is a range of severity of illness observed in the relatives of individuals with schizophrenia. The range of less severe schizophrenia-like conditions observed is called the schizophrenia spectrum of illness; schizotypal personality is the most frequently studied form. Schizotypal personality disorder occurs more frequently than schizophrenia itself among the relatives of individuals with schizophrenia.

Presumably, this genetic predisposition works by producing some organic change. Studies using advanced brain-imaging techniques indicate that, in many patients, there is nonlocalized brain degeneration, which is revealed by the increased size of the ventricles, fluid-filled spaces within the brain. What causes this degeneration is unknown, but some researchers suggest that it is caused by a virus and that a genetic factor increases susceptibility to infection and the subsequent damaging effects of a viral disease. Although direct evidence of a virus has been found in a minority of patients, the viral theory is still considered speculative and unproved. There is no evidence that schizophrenia is contagious.

BIOCHEMICAL STUDIES

Experimental evidence of biochemical abnormalities in the brain's dopamine neurotransmitter systems is, however, impressive. Antipsychotic drugs are effective in relieving the symptoms of schizophrenia, especially positive symptoms such as hallucinations and delusions. These drugs block dopamine receptors in the brain. Furthermore, the more powerfully the drugs bind to and block dopamine receptors, the smaller the effective dose that is necessary to produce a therapeutic result.

Further evidence comes from a condition called amphetamine psychosis, which occurs in people who abuse amphetamine and similar stimulants such as cocaine. Amphetamine psychosis so closely mimics some forms of schizophrenia that misdiagnoses have been common. Furthermore, amphetamine psychosis is not an artifact of disturbed personality; experiments show that normal control subjects will develop the condition if they are given high doses of amphetamines every few hours for several days. Amphetamine psychosis, which is believed to result from the overactivation of dopamine systems in the brain, is treated with antipsychotic drugs such as chlorpromazine.

Direct evidence of abnormality in the dopamine systems comes from studies using advanced techniques such as positron emission tomography (PET) scanning. These studies show that the brains of schizophrenic patients, even those who have never been treated with antipsychotic medications, may have abnormally large numbers of dopamine receptors in an area called the limbic system, which is responsible for emotional regulation.

Dopamine-blocking drugs, however, help only a subset of patients. Studies show that those most likely to benefit from medication are patients who display primarily positive symptoms. Patients who show negative symptoms—such as withdrawal, thought blocking, and catatonia—are less likely to be helped by medication.

HISTORY OF THE CONCEPT OF SCHIZOPHRENIA

The disorders that are now called schizophrenia were first characterized in the nineteenth century. Emil Kraepelin first grouped these disorders, referring to them by the collective name dementia praecox, in 1893.

Many early neurologists and psychiatrists thought these dementias were organic conditions. This view changed, however, after Swiss psychiatrist Eugen Bleuler published his classic work on the disorder in 1911. Bleuler proposed that the primary characteristic of the condition was a splitting of intellect from emotions. He introduced the term "schizophrenia" (literally, "split mind"). Bleuler, influenced by the psychodynamic theories of Freud, believed that the bizarre content of schizophrenic thoughts and perceptions

represented a breaking away from an external reality that was too painful or frightening. His ideas became especially influential in the United States.

Attempts to treat schizophrenia with traditional psychotherapies were, however, unsuccessful. Success rates rarely surpassed the rate of spontaneous recovery, the rate at which patients recover without treatment. Because medical interventions such as lobotomy, insulin shock therapy, and electroconvulsive therapy were also ineffective, psychiatric hospitals were filled with patients for whom little could be done.

The discovery of antipsychotic drugs and changing public policy about institutionalization in the 1950's changed things dramatically. Hospital populations declined. The surprising effectiveness of these medications, in concert with the discovery of amphetamine psychosis in the 1930's and the genetic studies of the 1940's, renewed the belief that schizophrenia is an organic condition.

Two problems impeded further understanding. First, techniques available for investigating the brain were primitive compared with modern techniques. Therefore, reports of organic changes in schizophrenia, although common, were difficult to confirm. Second, since the routinely administered medications powerfully influenced brain functioning, it became a problem to distinguish organic changes that were important in causing the disorder from those that were merely secondary to the action of antipsychotic drugs in the brain.

Indeed, it became "common wisdom" among many psychologists that organic factors identified by researchers were not primary to the disorder but were, rather, side effects of medication. Soft neurological signs such as eye-movement dysfunctions, abnormal orienting responses, and unusual movements were considered drug related even though Kraepelin and others had described them decades before the drugs were discovered. The drugs came to be called "major tranquilizers," implying that medication allowed patients to function more effectively by relieving the overwhelming anxiety that accompanied the disorder but that the drugs did not influence the schizophrenic process itself.

The fact that antipsychotic drugs have little usefulness as antianxiety agents in nonschizophrenics did not shake this opinion. Neither did the discovery of more powerful antianxiety agents such as Librium (chlordiazepoxide) and Valium (diazepam), even after they were shown to be almost useless in treating schizophrenia.

The next dramatic change in understanding schizophrenia came in the 1960's with the discovery of monoamine neurotransmitters, including dopamine, and the discovery that these chemical systems in the brain are strongly affected in opposite ways by psychotogenic drugs, such as cocaine and amphetamine, and antipsychotic drugs, such as chlorpromazine. Carefully conducted twin and adoption studies confirmed the role of genetic factors in schizophrenia and encouraged the search for the mechanism by which genes influenced the risk for developing schizophrenia. In the following decades, evidence that prenatal and perinatal factors are instrumental in the development of schizophrenia has led to the emerging consensus that schizophrenia should be considered from a neurodevelopmental perspective.

SOURCES FOR FURTHER STUDY

Bowers, Malcolm B. *Retreat from Sanity: The Structure of Emerging Psychosis*. New York: Human Sciences Press, 1974. A fascinating description, often in the words of patients, of the experiences many people have in the very early stages of psychosis. Especially interesting are descriptions of "peak" and "psychedelic" experiences resulting from sensory alterations during the onset of the disorder.

Gottesman, Irving I. *Schizophrenia Genesis: The Origins of Madness*. New York: W. H. Freeman, 1991. An excellent, well-written book that is easily accessible to the general reader. Highly recommended.

Gottesman, Irving I., James Shields, and Daniel R. Hanson. *Schizophrenia: The Epigenetic Puzzle*. Cambridge, England: Cambridge University Press, 1982. More technical than *Schizophrenia Genesis* but still accessible to anyone with a solid background in genetics of the type obtained in a good general biology course. Concentrates on genetic studies and gives complete references to original technical articles.

Hirsch, Steven R., and Daniel R. Weinberger. *Schizophrenia*. Malden, Mass.: Blackwell Science, 1995. A comprehensive review by two masters in the field.

Maj, Mario, and Norman Sartorius. *Schizophrenia*. New York: John Wiley & Sons, 1999. This book, part of a World Psychiatric Association series bringing evidence from empirical studies to clinical practitioners, is an integration of the worldwide research literature on schizophrenia.

Myslobodsky, Michael S., and Ina Weiner. *Contemporary Issues in Modeling Psychopathology*. Boston: Kluwer Academic Publishers, 2000. Presents several alternative theories of schizophrenic psychopathology and empirical approaches to and evidence from tests of those theories.

Raine, Adrian, Todd Lencz, and Sarnoff A. Mednick. *Schizotypal Personality*. New York: Cambridge University Press, 1995. An overview of the less severe schizophrenia-like disorder seen in some relatives of patients with schizophrenia. Discusses links (and differences) between schizotypal personality and schizophrenia.

Snyder, Solomon H. *Madness and the Brain*. New York: McGraw-Hill, 1974. Written in a lively, breezy style, this short volume deals with biomedical factors in many psychological disorders, including schizophrenia. Especially interesting is Snyder's discussion of drug effects, neurotransmitters, and schizophrenia.

Torrey, Edwin Fuller. *Surviving Schizophrenia: A Family Manual*. Rev. ed. New York: Perennial Library, 1988. One of the best books available for the general reader on schizophrenia. Intended primarily for members of families that have a schizophrenic family member, this book should be read by everyone who is interested in the disorder, including every mental health worker. Torrey writes wonderfully and pulls no punches when dealing with outmoded theories and poorly done experiments. Many libraries have only the first edition; read the revised edition if possible.

William B. King;
updated by Loring J. Ingraham

SEE ALSO: Abnormality: Biomedical models; Abnormality: Psychological models; Diagnosis; *Diagnostic and Statistical Manual of Mental Disorders* (DSM); Drug therapies; Madness: Historical concepts; Psychosurgery; Schizophrenia: Background, types, and symptoms; Schizophrenia: High-risk children.

Scientific methods

TYPE OF PSYCHOLOGY: Psychological methodologies
FIELDS OF STUDY: Descriptive methodologies; experimental methodologies

Scientific methods refer to the techniques psychologists use to study psychological and behavioral processes in humans and animals. Although there are many variations to each, there are generally five scientific methods on which psychologists rely. These include the experiment, correlation, survey, naturalistic observation, and case study. Each of the five approaches has special features, along with limitations, that help psychologists make inferences about the phenomenon under study.

KEY CONCEPTS

- between- and within-subjects designs
- conditions or levels of the independent variable
- confounding or extraneous variable
- dependent variable
- experimental and control groups
- experimental design
- independent variable
- operational definitions
- placebo effect
- population
- positive and negative correlations
- sample
- subject selectivity

INTRODUCTION

Since its inception as an identifiable discipline in the 1870's, psychology has relied on scientific methods for studying psychological and behavioral processes in both humans and animals. Embracing such an approach represented a significant landmark in the history of psychology. The use of these methods helped identify psychology as a separate and distinct discipline, allowing it to break away from its roots in philosophy.

Historians have credited the German physician and psychophysiologist Wilhelm Wundt (1832-1920) as being the first to employ scientific methods in the study of psychological processes. For doing so, Wundt is often known as the "father of psychology." Although his methods were crude by modern-day standards, Wundt examined how perceptions were formed in the mind by simply asking subjects to look within themselves and reflect on what they were thinking when he exposed them to a variety of sensory stimuli such as different intensities of light or sound. This approach, known as "introspection," in the end proved to be too unreliable in characterizing psychological processes and was eventually abandoned. Despite its failure as a scientific method, the use of introspection by Wundt represented the first attempt at studying mental events objectively and laid the foundation for the scientific methods used by psychologists today.

Since the time of Wundt, psychologists have developed a variety of methodological approaches. Although variations exist, generally there are five scientific methods on which psychologists rely. They are experiment, correlation, survey, naturalistic observation, and case study. The selection of an appropriate method will depend on a number of issues such as the nature, intensity, and duration of the phenomena under investigation, the species, gender, age, weight, and other variables associated with the individuals being studied, the number of individuals available for study, the sensitivity, reliability, and validity of the measures and devices used to study the phenomenon, and ethical and/or legal concerns that might limit or alter the specific methodological procedures and tactics employed.

GENERAL ISSUES

Regardless of the particular method used, the researcher must be concerned about a variety of general issues before conducting the investigation. Paramount among them is the identification of the population of interest, selecting a sample from the population, ethical guidelines in conducting the research, and statistical analysis of the research data.

The population is the entire universe of individuals about whom the researcher wishes to identify some law of nature or relationship. The researcher should be clear as to exactly which individuals constitute the population. Because it is almost always impossible to study every individual in the population, the researcher is left with the next best thing: selecting a subgroup from the population, called a sample, to study. The individuals selected for the sample are called subjects. Subjects are almost always selected in a nonbiased, random fashion that ensures that each individual in the population has an equal chance of being included in the sample. Researchers must be certain that the sample represents accurately the characteristics of the population so that the data collected can be confidently applied to the population at large.

As researchers conduct their investigations, they must follow a number of ethical guidelines that ensure that subjects are protected from risk or harm.

Many professional organizations, such as the American Psychological Association and the Society for Neuroscience, have published guidelines that help researchers meet the ethical standards of using human and animal subjects. In addition, researchers must conform to many federal and state laws and peer-review institutional committees (such as the Institutional Review Board and Institutional Animal Care and Use Committee) that regulate and oversee research activities and ensure the protection of research subjects. Once the data are collected, the researcher must summarize and analyze the results with statistical tests and procedures to help determine whether relationships or trends exist and to draw conclusions from the study.

EXPERIMENT

The experiment is the one of the most frequently used techniques for studying psychological and behavioral processes. It is the only method of the five techniques discussed that allows for the determination of cause-effect relationships. Its rationale lies in the active manipulation by the experimenter of a variable called the independent variable and the effects of it on an outcome measure called the dependent variable. Also crucial to the experimental method is the control of other variables, called confounding or extraneous variables. Confounding or extraneous variables are those that are not intentionally manipulated by the experimenter but somehow influence the results. The entire plan for the experiment, including techniques for controlling or eliminating confounding variables, is referred to as the experimental design. Well-conceived experimental designs are crucial for allowing the experimenter to make clear and concise conclusions from the data that are collected in the experiment. In fact, constructing the experimental design is the most crucial aspect of the experiment. Once a well-designed experiment is conceived, it is only a matter of following the "game plan."

A simple experimental design illustrates the nuances that are involved in the conception of the experimental design: A researcher wants to determine whether a new drug, "Drug A," improves memory. The experimenter would have some subjects in the experiment ingest or be injected with the drug shortly before learning some task on which a test of retention would be given at a later time. Because Drug A is the variable that is being actively manipu-

lated by the experimenter to determine its effects on memory, it is referred to as the independent variable, and those individuals exposed to it are collectively referred to as the experimental group.

However, by definition, a variable is something that exists in more than one form. In order to compare the effects of the drug on memory, the experimenter needs to include another group of participants who are not exposed to the drug. This latter group of subjects are collectively referred to as the control group, since their performance on the memory test will provide a baseline measurement of how well individuals who are not given the drug remember the information. Comparing the performance of the experimental subjects with those in the control group is the only way to assess the effect of Drug A on memory. Without the inclusion of the control subjects there would be no way to determine whether the drug had any beneficial (or deleterious) effects on memory.

The inference of causality in the experiment relies on the fact that the experimental and control subjects should differ only on the independent variable. That is, in order to infer that the drug improves or worsens memory it is necessary that the only variable that can account for effects on memory is the drug itself. The possibility of any other variable accounting for differences among the performance of the two groups on the test of retention represents a confounding variable. A closer examination of the experimental design described above, however, does reveal the presence of a confounding variable. The control subjects were simply not given any "drug," while the experimental subjects received an active dose of the drug. It is a real possibility that the performance of the experimental subjects might have been affected simply by the fact that they received something and that they expected that their performance would be altered in some way. This is referred to as the placebo effect—the effect of psychological expectation on performance.

In order to eliminate or control for the influence of a placebo effect it is crucial that the control subjects also receive a "drug," but that the substance that they receive contain an inactive substance. In fact, in order to assess whether the active dose of the drug does indeed affect memory and what role, if any, a placebo effect has, it might be wise also to include a control group of subjects that do not receive anything. Thus, three groups of participants would constitute the experimental design, with one group receiving the active dose of the drug, another receiving a placebo, and a third group receiving nothing at all. If all three groups of subjects were included, then the experimental design would have one independent variable (Drug A) with three different variations of it. The different variations of the independent variable are referred to as the conditions or levels of the independent variable.

Confounding variables can take many forms and must be carefully evaluated when constructing any experimental design. Other factors, such as gender, body weight, general intelligence, age of the subjects, ambient temperature, humidity, lighting, distracting sounds in the testing room, and purity and consistency of the drug might represent possible sources of confounding variables in this experiment. In order to ensure that confounding variables are not affecting the outcome measure, the general rule of thumb is to ensure that the subjects in the experiment are the same or similar with regard to all variables except the independent variable. It is only when this rule is met that inferences of causality can be made with any degree of certainty.

COMPLEX DESIGNS

Conducting experiments is time-consuming and costly. Therefore, it is prudent that the experimental design be constructed in such a way as to maximize the information gained from the enterprise. In this regard, researchers often will study more than one independent variable in an experiment. In the experimental design already described, the researchers might wish to determine whether the time of drug administration has any effect on the drug's ability to influence memory processes. The experimental design would then necessitate the inclusion of other groups of subjects, some of whom would be given the drug, placebo, or nothing at all during the morning while others would be given the drug, placebo, or nothing at all in the afternoon. If this were the design, then six, rather than three, groups of participants would be needed and "time of administration" would be another independent variable with two levels (morning versus afternoon). In this case, since each level of each independent variable is combined with each level of the other independent variable to form six groups of subjects, the experimental design would represent a factorial design as opposed to a single-variable design. The number of levels of each independent variable is used when identifying factorial designs. Thus, this study with three levels of Drug A and two levels of time of administration would be described as a "3 × 2" design (said "three by two").

Adding more independent variables to the experimental design does have its drawbacks. In addition to increasing the complexity of the experimental design and the time required to complete the study, it also requires the recruitment of additional subjects. In the above 3 × 2 study, six groups of subjects would be required. If there were twelve subjects in each of the six groups (the number of subjects in a group usually ranges from eight to twelve) then seventy-two subjects in total would be needed, with both independent variables being between-subjects variables. (A between-subjects variable is in effect when subjects serve in one and only one level of the independent variable.) Since both variables in this case are between-subjects variables, then the experimental design is identified as a "3 × 2 between-subjects design."

However, there exists another way of assigning subjects to the six groups. It is possible that each subject could be tested under the influence of the drug, placebo, and nothing at all both in the morning and in the afternoon on separate days. In this case all participants would serve as subjects in all six groups, thus requiring only twelve subjects in total. In this instance, each of the two independent variables would be described as within-subjects variables and the design referred to as a "3 × 2 within-subjects design." (A within-subjects variable is in effect when subjects serve in more than one level of the independent variable. "Repeated measures" is often used as a synonymous term.)

Within-subjects designs, although having the advantage of requiring fewer subjects, do have their disadvantages. Chief among them is the fact that subjects are exposed to the test situation multiple times, thus making their performance on subsequent tests potentially tainted by the virtue of being exposed earlier to other conditions, a confounding variable referred to as "order effect." To help minimize order effects in within-subjects designs, it is prudent to expose subjects to the various conditions in different sequences. This will help to prevent the introduction of any specific order effects on the dependent variable and thus allow for a more reliable inference of causality.

Another confounding variable associated with within-subjects designs is called the "carry-over effect." This confounding variable is related to the possibility that treatments made to the subjects under earlier conditions might still exist and affect performance under later conditions of the independent variable. In the experiment described above, for example, the drug may still be physiologically active in the body at the time when subjects are tested in the placebo or nothing-at-all conditions, and thus might influence performance under those conditions. Elimination of this confounding variable, often by waiting a sufficient amount of time before the next condition is tested, is critical to any design in which exposure to one level of the independent variable might influence performance when subjects are exposed to other levels of the independent variable.

A compromise between within- and between-subjects designs is the mixed design. Mixed designs have at least one between- and one within-subjects variable. In the example being discussed, independent groups of subjects might serve in the drug, placebo, and nothing-at-all groups, but all subjects would be administered their respective treatments both in the morning and in the afternoon on different days. Fewer subjects, therefore, are needed, while at the same time avoiding or at least minimizing some of the confounding variables associated with repeatedly testing subjects. In the present example, thirty-six subjects would be recruited, with twelve individuals serving in each of the three levels of the drug, and all subjects receiving their respective treatments both in the morning and in the afternoon on separate days. The design would thus be described as a "3 × 2 mixed design with repeated measures on the last variable."

Another important aspect of experimental designs is accurately and precisely defining the phenomenon under study in terms of how it is measured—what is known as creating operational definitions. Regardless of the phenomenon under study, experimenters must precisely communicate to others in the scientific community how they measured the phenomenon. For example, memory might be measured by counting the number of words recalled from a list of words learned previously. It can also be measured in many other ways. Selecting the exact way in which the phenomenon is measured (that is, selecting the dependent variable) is entirely up to the experimenter, but the method must meet generally accepted criteria in the field and must be described in detail sufficient to enable other competent researchers to use the same method.

CORRELATION

In addition to the experiment, psychologists also frequently use the correlation method. Unlike the experiment, the correlation method does not allow for conclusions of causality. It does, however, allow researchers to identify relationships among variables. More specifically, the correlation approach allows the researcher to determine whether variables change in some consistent manner over time.

Although many variables can be simultaneously examined using the method of correlation (multiple regression), the simplest correlation method examines two variables and thus is called bivariate correlation. In bivariate correlation, subjects are studied with regard to their performance on two variables, designated the X and Y variables. Thus, each subject provides two scores, and the scores from all the subjects in the study are then statistically analyzed to determine whether a relationship between the two variables exists. A statistical technique used to analyze bivariate data is the Pearson Product Moment Correlation Coefficient, better known as Pearson r. Pearson r yields a coefficient value that lies between −1.00 and +1.00. The absolute value of Pearson r indicates the magnitude of the relationship, with values close to or equal to the absolute value of 1.00 indicating a strong relationship, and values close to or equal to zero indicating little or no relationship. The sign of Pearson r, on the other hand, indicates whether the change in the two variables occurs in the same (positive values) or opposite (negative values) directions.

Bivariate data are often graphically presented in a scatter plot. A scatter plot is a graph with X and Y axes, on which each subject's X and Y scores are plotted. Consider a set of students' scores on an exam and the number of hours students studied for the exam (figure 1) along with the scatter plot that graphs the relationship between these two variables (figure 2). As can be seen in the scatter plot, there is a positive relationship (positive correlation) between the number of hours studied and the student's exam score. Generally speaking, as the number of hours increases so do exam scores. In fact, the value for the Pearson r coefficient for these data is +0.92.

	Hours Studied (X variable)	Exam Score (Y variable)
Student #1	2	56
Student #2	7	77
Student #3	8	98
Student #4	5	73
Student #5	1	23
Student #6	10	94
Student #7	6	88
Student #8	3	62
Student #9	9	91
Student #10	0	40

Figure 1: Hours studied and exam score data.

	Number of Alcoholic Drinks	Number of Words Remembered
Subject #1	3	14
Subject #2	7	4
Subject #3	1	24
Subject #4	9	5
Subject #5	5	12
Subject #6	2	22
Subject #7	0	25
Subject #8	4	17
Subject #9	6	10
Subject #10	7	9

Figure 3: Number of drinks and words remembered data.

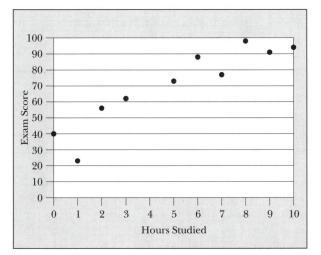

Figure 2: Correlation between hours studied and exam score.

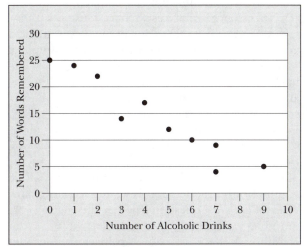

Figure 4: Correlation between number of alcoholic drinks and number of words remembered.

Now consider another set of data that correlates the number of alcoholic drinks and the number of words remembered from a list of twenty-five words (figure 3) and its associated scatter plot (figure 4). These data also indicate a strong bivariate relationship with the value of the Pearson r coefficient = −0.96. However, the direction of the relationship is negative (as reflected in the value of Pearson r), indicating that as the number of alcoholic drinks increases, the number of words remembered decreases—an example of a negative correlation.

Correlations can be helpful to researchers in a number of ways. First, they may provide suggestions for variables that ought to be studied using experi-ments, since the experiment is the only method that can establish cause-effect relationships. Correlations are also useful when active manipulation of a variable cannot be performed because of ethical, le-gal, or practical limitations (such as exposure to lead paint in children, exposure to environmental radiation, or exposure to job stress). Finally, correlations are used to identify trends in large groups of individuals in the population suggestive of interest-ing or potentially dangerous social or medical phe-nomena (such as the relationship between smoking cigarettes and the development of cancer, or expo-sure to sources of drinking water and development of bacterial illness).

SURVEY

The survey method relies on questionnaires administered to a fairly large number of subjects in order to determine their opinions, reactions, and views. The most critical aspect of survey research is developing the questions that will be asked of subjects. Constructing the questions ought to be done in a manner that does not increase the likelihood of biased responses. Thus, the researcher must always be aware of how each question is phrased. The questions should not contain language that would make the respondents more or less likely to answer in a particular manner. Another critical aspect of survey research is the recruitment of subjects. The manner in which subjects are recruited, such as by telephone, in a shopping mall, or in a classroom, might affect the type of individual participating in the survey. In essence, what researchers must ask themselves is, "Who is participating in my survey and why are they participating in my survey?" For example, if surveys are administered over the telephone, who is more likely to take the time to answer questions, and might individuals who do participate have a special interest in the survey and/or have a vested in the survey's outcome? As discussed above, all research methods use samples, and the subjects who form the sample should be representative of the population at large. Therefore, if only a specialized segment of the population is willing to participate, researchers must question whether they have a confounding variable called subject selectivity.

Although there are many ways in which questions can be asked, the most frequently used ways of constructing questionnaires involve closed-ended questions, open-ended questions, or Likert scale responses. Closed-ended questions limit the responses subjects can make to discrete categories, such as "agree," "disagree," "no opinion," "yes," or "no." The advantage of closed-ended questions is that the data collected are much more amenable to categorizing and statistical analysis. The disadvantage, however, is that subjects' responses are limited to predetermined discrete categories.

Open-ended questions, on the other hand, allow subjects more freedom in expanding or qualifying their responses. For example, a subject may respond "yes" to a question, but that response may only apply to certain conditions. For example, subjects may qualify a response to the question "Are you in favor of abortion?" by saying, "Only in the case of rape or incest." This flexibility does come with a price; open-ended questions often make responses difficult to categorize and analyze statistically. It is therefore crucial that the researcher decide ahead of time on operational definitions that set clear criteria for categorizing responses.

Likert scale responses involve asking subjects to rate their response intensities on a scale typically from 0 to 7 or 10, with low values indicating a small degree of intensity or agreement and greater values indicating a large degree of intensity or agreement. For example, the item, "On a scale of 0 to 10, rate your feeling toward abortion, with 10 indicating total support" might yield a score of 4 if the subject is against abortion except in cases of rape or incest. In this manner, subjects are allowed somewhat more freedom to qualify their responses but still need to stay within the confines of a limited number of response categories. This objectification of the data facilitates scoring and categorizing responses, making the data more amenable to statistical analysis.

NATURALISTIC OBSERVATION

Although the experiment, survey, and correlation methods are useful, they do suffer from the problem that subjects are aware that they are being studied and thus their behavior or responses might be altered in some manner. Observing the behavior of subjects in their natural environment, such as observing ape behavior in the wild, is an attempt to minimize this confounding variable. Moreover, it has been argued that results derived from naturalistic observations are more reliable since they are obtained outside the artificial environment of the laboratory.

The general rule of thumb with naturalistic observations is that the researcher must be an unobserved observer. If subjects are consciously aware that they are being observed, then the entire rationale for using this method is undermined. Although naturalistic observation has the advantage of allowing a wider range of behaviors to be exhibited, it does require special attention to operation definitions. As with other methods, researchers must clearly construct operational definitions and scoring systems that will guide their observations and will allow other competent researchers to confirm their findings. Similarly, the data collected from naturalistic observational studies are organized and analyzed with statistics in order for trends to be identified and conclusions to be drawn.

CASE STUDY

Sometimes individuals exhibit rare disorders or behaviors that are notable or illustrate some special feature of a disease. In this instance, psychologists might employ the case-study method to characterize and describe this individual to the research community. Case studies necessitate providing an intense and highly descriptive profile of the individual being studied. The major drawback of the case-study method is that only one rare individual from the population is studied, thus limiting the degree to which the findings can be generalized to the larger population. However, case studies are informative especially in the field of clinical psychology, where previously known disorders or diseases of the brain or the mind can be further characterized, or new disorders or diseases can be identified.

SOURCES FOR FURTHER STUDY

Allen, Mary J. *Introduction to Psychological Research.* Itasca, Ill.: F. E. Peacock, 1995. This book provides a simple and highly accessible overview on research methods.

Crawford, Helen J., and Larry B. Christensen. *Developing Research Skills: A Laboratory Manual.* 3d ed. Needham Heights, Mass.: Allyn & Bacon, 1995. This workbook contains several exercises that help students hone their research skills.

Heiman, Gary W. *Basic Statistics for the Behavioral Sciences.* 3d ed. Boston: Houghton Mifflin, 2000. A very good introduction to the various statistical procedures used in research.

Kirk, Roger E. *Experimental Design: Procedures for the Behavioral Sciences.* Belmont, Calif.: Brooks/Cole, 1965. Although old, this book has remained the standard guide for researchers in the field. It is recommended only to seasoned researchers.

Smith, Randolph A., and Stephen F. Davis. *The Psychologist as Detective: An Introduction to Conducting Research in Psychology.* 2d ed. Upper Saddle River, N.J.: Prentice Hall, 2001. A very good undergraduate textbook providing broad coverage of psychological methods and related statistical issues.

Anthony C. Santucci

SEE ALSO: Animal experimentation; Archival data; Case-study methods; Complex experimental designs; Data description; Experimental psychology; Experimentation: Ethics and subject rights; Experimentation: Independent, dependent, and control variables; Field experimentation; Hypothesis development and testing; Observational methods; Quasi-experimental designs; Sampling; Statistical significance tests; Survey research: Questionnaires and interviews; Within-subject experimental designs.

Seasonal affective disorder

TYPE OF PSYCHOLOGY: Personality; psychopathology
FIELDS OF STUDY: Depression; personality disorders

Seasonal affective disorder (SAD) is a form of major depressive disorder believed to exhibit two forms: winter depression, beginning in late fall or winter, and spring-onset, which continues through summer and fall.

KEY CONCEPTS
- double-blind study
- hypersomnia
- libido
- lux
- placebo

INTRODUCTION

Seasonal affective disorder (SAD) became the focus of systematic scientific research in the early 1980's. Research originally focused on seasonal changes in mood that coincided with the onset of winter and became known as winter depression. Symptoms consistently identified by Norman Rosenthal and others as indicative of winter depression included hypersomnia, overeating, carbohydrate craving, and weight gain. Michael Garvey and others found the same primary symptoms and the following secondary ones: decreased libido, irritability, fatigue, anxiety, problems concentrating, and premenstrual sadness. Several researchers have found that winter depression is more of a problem at higher latitudes. Thomas Wehr and Norman Rosenthal report on a description of winter depression by Frederick Cook during an expedition to Antarctica in 1898. While winter depression was the form of seasonal affective disorder that received the most initial attention, there is another variation that changes with the seasons.

Summer depression affects some people in the same way that winter depression affects others. Both are examples of seasonal affective disorder. According to Wehr and Rosenthal, symptoms of summer depression include agitation, loss of appetite, insomnia, and loss of weight. Many people with summer depression also have histories of chronic anxiety. As can be seen, the person with a summer depression experiences symptoms which are almost the opposite of the primary symptoms of winter depression.

In order to diagnose a seasonal affective disorder, there must be evidence that the symptoms vary according to a seasonal pattern. If seasonality is not present, the diagnosis of SAD cannot be made. In the Northern Hemisphere, the seasonal pattern for winter depression is for it to begin in November and continue unabated through March. Summer depression usually begins in May and continues through September. Siegfried Kasper and others reported that people suffering from winter depression outnumber those suffering from summer depression by 4.5 to 1. Wehr and Rosenthal reported that as people come out of their seasonal depression they experience feelings of euphoria, increased energy, less depression, hypomania, and possibly mania.

Philip Boyce and Gordon Parker investigated seasonal affective disorder in Australia. Their interest was in determining whether seasonal affective disorder occurs in the Southern Hemisphere and, if so, whether it manifests the same symptoms and temporal relationships with seasons as noted in the Northern Hemisphere. Their results confirmed the existence of seasonal affective disorder with an onset coinciding with winter and remission coinciding with summer. Their study also provided evidence that seasonal affective disorder occurs independently of important holidays and celebrations, such as Christmas. There is also a subsyndromal form of seasonal affective disorder. This is usually seen in winter depression and represents a milder form of the disorder. It interferes with the person's life, although to a lesser degree than the full syndrome, and it is responsive to the primary treatment for seasonal affective disorder.

HYPOTHESES OF ETIOLOGY

Three hypotheses are being tested to explain seasonal affective disorder: the melatonin hypothesis, the circadian rhythm phase shift hypothesis, and the circadian rhythm amplitude hypothesis.

The melatonin hypothesis is based upon animal studies and focuses on a chemical signal for darkness. During darkness, the hormone melatonin is produced in greater quantities; during periods of light, it is produced in lesser quantities. Increases in melatonin level occur at the onset of seasonal affective disorder (winter depression) and are thought to be causally related to the development of the depression.

The circadian rhythm phase shift hypothesis contends that the delay in the arrival of dawn disrupts the person's circadian rhythm by postponing it for a few hours. This disruption of the circadian rhythm is thought to be integral in the development of winter depression. Disruptions in the circadian rhythm are also related to secretion of melatonin.

The third hypothesis is the circadian rhythm amplitude hypothesis. A major tenet of this hypothesis is that the amplitude of the circadian rhythm is directly related to winter depression. Lower amplitudes are associated with depression, and higher ones with normal mood states. The presence or absence of light has been an important determinant in the amplitude of circadian rhythms.

The melatonin hypothesis is falling out of favor. Rosenthal and others administered to volunteers in a double-blind study a drug known to suppress melatonin secretion and a placebo. Despite melatonin suppression, there was no difference in the degree of depression experienced by the two groups (drug and placebo). In addition, no difference was observed in melatonin rhythms when persons with SAD were compared with those not suffering from the disorder.

Nevertheless, scientists have continued to investigate the role played by neurological chemicals in the etiology of the disorder. Some of these studies have focused on the possible role of neurotransmitters such as serotonin, dopamine, and norepinephrine. It is known that these chemicals may play a role in some forms of depression. For example, low levels of serotonin have been linked with some disorders; similar depressed levels have been observed in SAD patients during the winter months. If at least some forms of SAD are linked to reduction in serotonin production or uptake, this would explain the craving for carbohydrates observed in some patients.

Association of SAD with reduced pharmacological agents does not exclude other possible causes. It is certainly possible that diagnosis of SAD encompasses a variety of disorders associated with several causes. Evidence for a genetic predisposition is also undergoing investigation and cannot be eliminated as a contributing factor. At least one study utilizing adult twins has suggested that nearly 30 percent of SAD cases may have a genetic basis.

DIAGNOSIS OF SAD

Diagnosis is based upon the description of the disorder as updated in the *Diagnostic and Statistical Manual of Mental Disorders: DSM-IV-TR* (rev. 4th ed., 2000). According to the manual, the presence of five specific symptoms typical of depression constitutes the criteria for diagnosis; these symptoms must have been present during a two week interval prior to diagnosis. Symptoms include general daily depression, loss of interest in normal activities, significant loss of appetite, fatigue, insomnia, decreased ability in thinking or reasoning, and/or thoughts of suicide or death. In order to be diagnosed with SAD, the patient must exhibit among the symptoms either depression or loss of interest in normal activities. In order to differentiate SAD from other forms of depression, these symptoms must exhibit a seasonal pattern which has been experienced over a period of at least three years, with at least two of these periods occurring consecutively. Two forms of SAD have been described. The more common type, affecting approximately 15 percent of the population at some period within their lifetime, is referred to as fall-onset or winter depression. Generally this form appears in late fall and lasts until the following spring. A less common form of SAD is typically a spring-onset form of depression. This form generally lasts throughout the summer into the following season.

Regardless of the form of SAD, for diagnostic purposes the depressed person must experience the beginning and ending of the depression during the sixty-day window of time at both the beginning and ending of the seasons. The patient must not have been diagnosed with other forms of depression, though the incidence of SAD appears highest among patients with a history of mood disorders.

TREATMENT

Historically, light or phototherapy has been the principal method of treatment for SAD. Studies have repeatedly shown that exposure of patients to bright light, at least 2,500 lux, has had some success in relieving the depression associated with the disorder. Such phototherapy sessions have generally consisted of two to four hours of exposure per day; similar results have been observed if the light intensity is increased to 10,000 lux, using treatment sessions as short as thirty minutes.

The major advantage of phototherapy is that it represents a nonpharmacological approach to treatment of the problem. However, as many as one-third of the patients exhibiting SAD do not respond to light therapy. Frequently, those patients who responded least well were those suffering from the highest degree of depression. The inclusion of negative air ionization in conjunction with light therapy has resulted in some degree of success with such patients.

A variety of pharmacological agents have been developed for treatment of SAD patients who show no response to conventional treatments. These include serotonin reuptake inhibitors (SSRIs) such as fluoxetine, paroxetine and sertraline. Trials have been most successful when using these agents in combination with phototherapy, rather than either treatment alone.

DSM-IV-TR Criteria for Seasonal Affective Disorder

SEASONAL PATTERN SPECIFIER FOR MOOD DISORDERS

Specify with Seasonal Pattern

Can be applied to pattern of Major Depressive Episodes in the following:
- Bipolar I Disorder
- Bipolar II Disorder
- Major Depressive Disorder, Recurrent

Regular temporal relationship between the onset of Major Depressive Episodes in Bipolar I or Bipolar II Disorder or Major Depressive Disorder, Recurrent, and a particular time of the year (such as regular appearance of Major Depressive Episode in fall or winter)

Cases excluded involving an obvious effect of seasonal-related psychosocial stressors (such as regularly being unemployed every winter)

Full remissions (or change from depression to mania or hypomania) also occur at a characteristic time of the year (for example, depression disappears in spring)

In the last two years, two Major Depressive Episodes have occurred demonstrating temporal seasonal relationships and no nonseasonal Major Depressive Episodes have occurred

Seasonal Major Depressive Episodes substantially outnumber nonseasonal Major Depressive Episodes that may have occurred over individual's lifetime

EPIDEMIOLOGY OF SAD

Philip Boyce and Gordon Parker, two Australian scientists, studied SAD in the Southern Hemisphere. Since the Southern Hemisphere has weather patterns reversed from those in the Northern Hemisphere, and since holidays occurring during the winter in the Northern Hemisphere occur during the summer in the Southern Hemisphere, these researchers were able to reproduce Northern Hemisphere studies systematically while eliminating the possible influence of holidays, such as Christmas. Their findings support those of their colleagues in the Northern Hemisphere. There is a dependable pattern of depression beginning during autumn and early winter and ending in the late spring and early summer. The incidence of SAD is significantly greater in North America than in Europe, suggesting a possible genetic or climate influence on appearance of the disorder.

It is important to study the prevalence of SAD in order to understand how many people are affected by it. Siegfried Kasper and others investigated the prevalence of SAD in Montgomery County, Maryland, a suburb of Washington, D.C. The results of their study suggested that between 4.3 percent and 10 percent of the general population is affected to some extent. Mary Blehar and Norman Rosenthal report data from research in New York City that between 4 percent and 6 percent of a clinical sample met the criteria for SAD. More significantly, between 31 percent and 50 percent of people responding to a survey reported changes to their life which were similar to those reported by SAD patients. There are strong indications that the overall prevalence rate for SAD is between 5 percent and 10 percent of the general population. As much as 50 percent of the population may experience symptoms similar to but less intense than those of SAD patients.

Prevalence studies have found that the female-male ratio for SAD is approximately 4 to 1. The age of onset is about twenty-two. The primary symptoms of SAD overlap with other diagnoses which have a relatively high female-to-male ratio. For example, people diagnosed with winter depression frequently crave carbohydrate-loaded foods. In addition to carbohydrate-craving obesity, there is another serious disorder, bulimia nervosa, which involves binging on high-carbohydrate foods and has a depressive component. Bulimia nervosa is much more common in females than it is in males.

While most of the research has focused on SAD in adults, it has also been found in children. Children affected with SAD seem to experience a significant decrease in their energy level as their primary symptom rather than the symptoms seen in adults. This is not unusual; in many disorders, children and adults experience different symptoms.

The winter variant of SAD is much more common than the summer variant. It appears that winter depression is precipitated by the reduction in light that accompanies the onset of winter. As a result, it is also quite responsive to phototherapy. Summer depression, the summer variant of SAD, is precipitated by increases in humidity and temperature associated with the summer months. This suggests a different (and currently unknown) mechanism of action for the two variations.

The importance of light in the development and treatment of the winter variant of SAD has been demonstrated in a variety of studies worldwide. The general finding is that people living in the higher latitudes are increasingly susceptible to SAD in the winter.

EARLY HISTORY OF SAD

The observation that seasons affect people's moods is not new. Hippocrates, writing in 400 B.C.E., noted in section 3 of his "Aphorisms" that, "Of natures (*temperaments?*), some are well- or ill-adapted for summer, and some for winter." What Hippocrates noticed (and many others since have noticed) is that there are differences in the way people experience the various seasons. Summer and winter are the most extreme seasons in terms of both light and temperature and, not surprisingly, are the seasons in which most people have problems coping.

As noted above, a physician, Frederick Cook, on an expedition to Antarctica in 1898, noted that the crew experienced symptoms of depression as the days grew shorter. This same report (mentioned by Wehr and Rosenthal) revealed that "bright artificial lights relieve this to some extent." Emil Kraepelin reported in 1921 that approximately 5 percent of his patients with manic-depressive illness also had a seasonal pattern to their depressions. The data from antiquity to the present strongly favor the existence of a form of mood disturbance associated with seasonal variation. Just as the observation of seasonal variations in mood and behavior dates back to antiquity, so does the use of light as a treatment. Wehr and Rosenthal report that light was used as a treatment nearly two thousand years ago. Not only was light used but also it was specified that the light was to be directed to the eyes.

In summary, seasonal affective disorder seems to have some degree of relationship to carbohydrate-craving obesity, bulimia nervosa, bipolar disorder (formerly known as manic-depressive illness), and premenstrual syndrome. It affects women more often than men and is more frequently seen covarying with winter than with summer. The winter variant is probably caused by changes in light; it is more severe in the higher latitudes. The summer variant seems to be attributable to intolerance of heat and humidity and would be more prevalent in the lower latitudes. Whether the cause is related to variation in circadian rhythms, abnormal levels of neurotransmitters, genetics, or combinations of these, reduced exposure to sunlight appears to be a major contributor.

SOURCES FOR FURTHER STUDY

Boyce, Philip, and Gordon Parker. "Seasonal Affective Disorder in the Southern Hemisphere." *American Journal of Psychiatry* 145, no. 1 (1988): 96-99. This study surveyed an Australian sample to determine the extent to which the people experienced symptoms of seasonal affective disorder and to see if the pattern was similar to that of people in the Northern Hemisphere. The results are presented as percentages and are easily understood. Addresses the issue of separating holidays from climatic changes and presents a table of symptoms for seasonal affective disorder.

Kasper, Siegfried, Susan L. Rogers, Angela Yancey, Patricia M. Schulz, Robert A. Skwerer, and Norman E. Rosenthal. "Phototherapy in Individuals with and Without Subsyndromal Seasonal Affective Disorder." *Archives of General Psychiatry* 46, no. 9 (1989): 837-844. This study extends research into seasonal variants of affective disorder to people who have less intense forms. Addresses issues of the difficulty of establishing adequate experimental control and practical implications for people with these disorders.

Kasper, Siegfried, Thomas A. Wehr, John J. Bartko, Paul A. Gaist, and Norman E. Rosenthal. "Epidemiological Findings of Seasonal Changes in Mood and Behavior." *Archives of General Psychiatry* 46, no. 9 (1989): 823-833. A thorough description of the major prevalence study on seasonal affective disorder. The statistics are fairly advanced, but the authors' use of figures and tables makes the results understandable. An extensive reference list is provided.

Lam, R. W. "An Open Trial of Light Therapy for Women with Seasonal Affective Disorder and Comorbid Bulimia Nervosa." *Journal of Clinical Psychiatry* 62, no. 3 (2001): 164-168. A discussion of the use of light therapy in the treatment of two of the more common psychiatric/mood disorders.

Partonen, Timo, ed. *Seasonal Affective Disorder: Practice and Research.* New York: Oxford University Press, 2001. Emphasis is on the clinical disorder of SAD. The first portion of the book deals primarily with presentation of the illness in a clinical situation; the second half of the text addresses research into SAD, including evidence for its physiological basis.

Rosenthal, Norman E. *Winter Blues: Seasonal Affective Disorder—What It Is and How to Overcome It.* New York: Guilford, 1998. A thorough description of SAD by an expert in the field. The author describes the clinical patterns associated with various degrees of the disorder.

Singer, Ethan. "Seasonal Affective Disorder: Autumn Onset, Winter Gloom." *Clinician Reviews,* November, 2001. The author provides an updated overview of the condition. In addition to epidemiological references, various physiological explanations for the disorder are discussed, as well as alternative treatments.

Wileman, S., et al. "Light Therapy for Seasonal Affective Disorder in Primary Care." *British Journal of Psychiatry* 178 (2001): 311-316. A clinical description of the disorder which includes a summary of the most popular method of treatment, as well as a discussion of the efficacy of light therapy.

Wurtman, Richard J., and Judith J. Wurtman. "Carbohydrates and Depression." *Scientific American* 260 (January, 1989): 68-75. The authors provide a good review of seasonal affective disorder and the relationships that may exist between it and maladaptive behaviors. They also review the more important theories about the cause and treatment of seasonal affective disorder.

James T. Trent;
updated by Richard Adler

SEE ALSO: Abnormality: Biomedical models; Bipolar disorder; Circadian rhythms; Clinical depression; Depression.

Self

TYPE OF PSYCHOLOGY: Personality; developmental psychology; social psychology; consciousness
FIELDS OF STUDY: Attitudes and behavior; general constructs and issues; personality theory; social perception and cognition

The self is a term that is widely used and variously defined. It has been examined by personality theorists as a central structure. Social cognitive psychology has explored the individual and interpersonal processes that influence such dimensions as self-systems, self-concept, self-consciousness, and self-efficacy. Recent research has challenged psychology to rethink its concept of the self.

KEY CONCEPTS

- being-in-the-world
- identity
- identity crisis
- narrative
- self-awareness
- self-concept
- self-efficacy
- self-in-relation
- self-system
- subjectivity

INTRODUCTION

The concept of the self was invoked in Western thought long before the advent of the discipline of psychology. During the Renaissance and Enlightenment, scholars often depicted humans as having a soul, spirit, or metaphysical essence. The famous argument by French Renaissance philosopher René Descartes (1596-1650), "I think, therefore I am," placed its fundamental confidence in the assumption that the "I"—an active, unique identity—could be directly experienced through introspection and therefore trusted to exist. Descartes's dualistic formulation of the mind-body relation set the stage for a number of assumptions about the self: that the self is an active, unitary, core structure of the person which belongs to and is consciously accessible to the individual.

During the Enlightenment, empiricist and associationist philosophers retained the mind-body distinction but emphasized the material, objectively observable behaviors of the body, with more stress on observable information, as seen in the rephrasing

of Descartes by Scottish philosopher David Hume (1711-1776): "I sense, therefore I am." William James (1842-1930), philosopher and founder of American scientific psychology, recognized that the personal experience of one's own stream of consciousness—the sense of "I" or subjectivity—is fleeting and fluid, and less measurable than the objective "me" with its body, relationships, and belongings. However, he considered the self to be made up of both subjective and objective components, a perspective reflected in the various theories of the self present in contemporary psychology.

Many psychologists believe that there is an internal self *in potentia* that takes shape and grows as long as an adequate environment is provided. Others emphasize a social component, suggesting that the self develops directly out of interpersonal interactions.

PSYCHOANALYTIC AND PSYCHODYNAMIC THEORIES

Sigmund Freud (1856-1939), Austrian founder of psychoanalysis at the turn of the twentieth century, had little use in his tripartite theory of the psyche for the idea of self as one's central identity. He conceptualized the ego as an important but secondary structure that mediates between the instincts of the id and the strictures of the superego. However, other psychodynamic theorists of the first half of the twentieth century returned to the idea of a center of personality. Carl Jung (1875-1961), a Swiss psychiatrist, thought of the self as an important archetype—an energized symbol in the collective unconscious—that organizes and balances the contradictory influences of other archetypes and in fact transcends opposing forces within the psyche. The archetype itself is an inborn potential, while its actual development is informed by personal experiences. Karen Horney (1885-1952), a German psychiatrist, believed that each individual is born with a real self, containing healthy intrinsic potentials and capabilities. However, because of basic anxiety and a belief that one is unlovable, some individuals become alienated from their real selves and pursue an unrealistic idealized self. Margaret Mahler (1897-1985), Hungarian-born pediatrician and psychoanalyst, described the separation-individuation process of the first three years of life, by which a child achieves individual personhood through psychologically separating from other people.

In contrast, Harry Stack Sullivan (1892-1949), an American psychiatrist, believed that personality and self can never be fully disconnected from interpersonal relations. His concept of the self-system is thus a set of enduring patterns of relating to others that avoids anxiety by striving for others' approval (the "good-me"), avoiding their disapproval (the "bad-me"), and dissociating from whatever causes their revulsion (the "not-me"). Heinz Kohut (1931-1981), Austrian founder of self psychology, also stressed that healthy selfhood is only attained through satisfying, empathically attuned interactions between infants and caregivers. Caregivers initially provide the self with a sense of goodness and strength and are therefore termed self-objects. The healthy self then develops its own ambitions, ideals, and skills, while deprivation from self-objects results in an injured self.

DEVELOPMENTAL THEORIES

While these psychodynamic theorists focused on the emotional and relational dimensions of early development, others, such as German-born Erik Erikson (1902-1994), who trained in psychoanalysis with Anna Freud, also emphasized cognitive and identity development over the entire life span. Erikson's theory, in which the ego confronts a series of psychosocial crises, recognized such childhood stages as autonomy versus shame and doubt, initiative versus guilt, and industry versus inferiority as important to ego development. However, it was his conceptualization of the identity crisis during adolescence that has been highly influential on contemporary research on self-concept and self-esteem. By searching out and eventually choosing life strategies, values, and goals, the adolescent establishes a sense of inner assuredness and self-definition, which serve to promote healthy intimacy, productivity, and integration later in life. James Marcia, an American developmental psychologist, demonstrated in the 1960's, 1970's, and 1980's that adolescents who actively explore the question "Who am I?" and achieve their own sense of identity are more likely to have positive outcomes, including high self-esteem, self-direction, and mature relationships. Erikson, Marcia, and other developmental scholars recognize that the task of establishing identity can be facilitated or hampered by the values and traditions presented in families and social structures.

HUMANISTIC AND EXISTENTIAL/
PHENOMENOLOGICAL PERSPECTIVES

Since the 1920's, humanistic and existential traditions have focused on the human being as a whole,

and division into parts or structures is resisted insofar as it leads to dehumanizing the person. Thus, the self as such is often renamed or deemphasized in these theories. Gordon Allport (1897-1967), an American psychologist, used the concept of "proprium" to describe the unique, holistic organization of personality and awareness that develops over the life span, culminating in ownership of one's own consciousness in adulthood. American psychologist Carl Rogers (1902-1987) also deemphasized the role of self, which he thought was merely one differentiated aspect of one's phenomenological, conscious experience. Rogers's self-image was a complex representation of the total organism as perceived through self-reflection. Abraham Maslow (1908-1970), another American psychologist, proposed that one of the most advanced human needs was the pull to be true to one's own nature. While he called this pull "self-actualization," he did not theorize the self to be a central structure, but a unique range of capacities, talents, and activities. American existentialist psychologist Rollo May (1909-1994) suggested that instead of thinking of a person as having a central, internal self that is separated from the world, a person should be considered to be a being-in-the-world (*Dasein* in German), who is in all ways related to the physical and especially the social environment.

THE SELF AS A REGULATOR OF INDIVIDUAL
PROCESSES

Beginning in the 1950's and accelerating through the turn of the twenty-first century, much research on personality has moved away from extensive personality theories toward empirically testable hypotheses. Models of the self focus on describing and observing the mental mechanisms by which individuals moderate and control their internal processes and their interactions with the world within specific social traditions and expectations.

Albert Bandura, the American founder of social cognitive psychology, conceptualizes the person as part of an interactive triad consisting of individual, behavior, and environment. Like radical behaviorism, social cognitive theory assumes that all human behavior is ultimately caused by the external environment. However, Bandura also describes individuals as having cognitions with which they regulate their own behavior, through the establishment of guiding performance standards. His idea of the self-system consists of internal motivations, emotions, plans, and beliefs which are organized into three processes: self-observation, judgmental processes, and self-reaction. In self-observation, the individual consciously monitors his or her own behavior and describes it. Through judgmental processes, values are placed on the observations, according to personal standards internalized from past experience and comparisons to others. The self-reaction is the self-system's way of punishing, rewarding, changing, or continuing with renewed motivation the behavior that has been self-observed.

Bandura's concept of self-observation has been further refined in research on self-awareness, self-consciousness, and self-monitoring. American social psychologists such as Robert Wicklund, Arnold Buss, Mark Davis, and Stephen Franzoi have defined self-awareness as a state of focusing attention on oneself, while self-consciousness is defined as a traitlike tendency to spend time in the state of such self-awareness. Most such research distinguishes between private self-awareness or self-consciousness, in which a person attends to internal aspects of self such as thoughts and emotions, and public self-awareness or self-consciousness, in which a person attends to external aspects of self that can be observed by others, such as appearance, physical movements, and spoken words. Private self-awareness and self-consciousness have been associated with intense emotional responses, clear self-knowledge, and actions that are consistent with one's own attitudes and values. Self-monitoring is related primarily to public self-consciousness and is described by American psychologist Mark Snyder as the tendency to engage in attempts to control how one is perceived in social interactions. Snyder's research suggests that high self-monitors use current situations to guide their reactions more than do low self-monitors, which can lead to the relationships of high self-monitors being dependent on situations or activities.

Social cognitive theory has also directed research on self-efficacy, the belief that one will be capable of using one's own behavior, knowledge, and skills to master a situation or overcome an obstacle. For example, Bandura showed in 1986 that people in recovery from a heart attack were more likely to follow an exercise regimen when they learned to see themselves as having physical efficacy. Perceived self-efficacy was demonstrated throughout the 1980's and 1990's as contributing to a wide range of be-

haviors, from weight loss to maternal competence to managerial decision making.

A final theme coming to prominence since the 1970's relates to identity and self-concept. Self-concept has been defined by American psychologist Roy Baumeister as one's personal beliefs about oneself, including one's attributes and traits and one's self-esteem, which is based on self-evaluations. American developmental psychologists such as Jerome Kagan, Michael Lewis, and Jeanne Brooks-Gunn found that by their second year, children become capable of recognizing and cognitively representing as their own their actions, intentions, states, and competencies. With further development, people appear to form not one unitary self-concept, but a collection of self-schemas or ideas about themselves in relation to specific domains such as school or work. American psychologist Hazel Markus has also found time to be a relevant dimension of self-concept, in that persons develop possible selves: detailed concepts of who they hope and fear to become in the future.

Identity is defined as who a person is, including not only the personal ideas in the self-concept but also the public perceptions of a person in his or her social context (for instance, birth name or roles in cultural institutions). Identity consists of two major features: continuity or sameness of the person over time, and differentiation of the person as unique compared to others and groups of others. As mentioned with regard to Erikson's theory and Marcia's research, adolescence has been demonstrated to be a primary stage for exploring the values, beliefs, and group memberships that constitute identity. However, identity continues to evolve during adulthood with changes in roles (such as student versus parent) and activities (work versus retirement).

NEUROPSYCHOLOGICAL PERSPECTIVES

From a neuropsychological perspective, brain functions underlie all dimensions and activities of the self. Yet an important question is how the functioning of biophysical structures such as the brain and nervous system can give rise to the self, which can be consciously experienced, either directly or through its activity. This question relies on the same mind-body problem that first arose with Descartes. One solution to this mental-physical divide proposed by such neuroscientists as Australian Sir John Eccles and Hungarian-born Michael Polanyi is the concept of emergent systems, or marginal control of lower systems by the organizational rules of higher systems. As the nervous system evolved into a complex set of structures, neural circuitry gained a concomitant complexity of organized functioning such that a new property, consciousness, emerged. This emergent property has capabilities and activities (such as the experience of mental images) that are a result of the organization of neural patterns but are not reducible to its component neural parts, much as water molecules have different qualities from those of hydrogen and oxygen atoms alone. Yet consciousness and thus experience of the self are necessarily embodied in and constrained by these patterned brain and biological processes.

Thus, the sense of self as having continuity relies on the capacity of several structures of the brain (such as the hippocampus and specialized areas of the association cortex) for forming, storing, and retrieving personal memories, as well as representations of background bodily and emotional states. A specific self-concept, as explored in social cognitive research, can only be developed through the organizational capacity of the prefrontal cortex to self-observe and construct cognitive schemas. The prefrontal cortex is also involved in carrying out many actions attributed to the self, such as the planned action of self-efficacy, and the techniques of presenting the self in a particular light, as in self-monitoring. Research such as that by Antonio Damasio, an American neurologist, indicates that when normal functioning of specific neural circuits is disturbed, deficits also occur in these experiences of self as knower and owner of mental and physical states. For example, with anasagnosia, damage to the right somatosensory cortices impairs a person's ability to be aware of damage to the body or associated problems in the functioning of the self. The body itself may become completely disowned by the person, and the unified sense of "me" is fractured.

CULTURE AND GENDER DIFFERENCES IN THE EXPERIENCE OF SELF

Empirical and theoretical scholarship since the 1970's has presented alternatives to the universality of the self across culture and gender, and has challenged the utility of the construct as heretofore defined. Humans' experiences of self have been found to vary substantially across cultures and gender, especially regarding the importance of independence

and separation versus interdependence and relationship. For example, American psychologist Hazel Markus, Japanese psychologist Shinobu Kitayama, and their colleagues found in their 1991 and 1997 studies that the concept of an individualized self as uniquely differentiated from others is descriptive of Americans' psychological experience. In contrast, Japanese personal experience is often more consistent with collective, relational roles, a conclusion that has been replicated with other collectivist cultures.

Feminist psychologists working at the Stone Center in Massachusetts have drawn on the developmental psychological work of Americans Nancy Chodorow and Carol Gilligan, observing that many women find the notion of a discrete and individualized self places too much emphasis on separation between people. This research group proposed the concept of self-in-relation to capture the extent to which one's core sense of being is defined by one's relationships with and commitments to other individuals. Likewise, as American developmental psychologist Mary Field Belenky and her colleagues interviewed women about their learning processes, they found that the sense of self as an individual, separate knower and speaker is only one stage of development. The individualist stage is often followed by respect for the ways one's subjectivity is informed by empathy and intimacy with others. These empirical observations suggest that theories of the self should attend more carefully to the interplay of individual and interpersonal or social experience.

POSTMODERN, DIALOGICAL, AND NARRATIVE THEORIES

The advancement since the 1970's of postmodernism has led many psychologists to recognize that persons construct their own realities through social rules, roles, and structures. Kenneth Gergen, an American social psychologist, proposes that the self gains its unity and identity from the consistency of the social roles a person plays. He points out that the more a person's roles multiply and conflict, as is common in fast-paced technological societies, the less cohesive and the more obsolete the concept of self becomes.

New Zealand-born cognitive psychologist Rom Harré and American psychologists Edward Sampson and Frank Richardson have each advanced alternative theories in which the concept of self is still viable, but which emphasize the necessity of recognizing the multiplicity of perspectives within a self. Drawing on the sociological traditions of symbolic interactionism, especially the "looking-glass self" of American sociologists George Herbert Mead and Charles Cooley, these theorists see the self as constructed only through intimate involvement in interpersonal interaction and especially language, which allow one to reflect on oneself and create the social bonds that define one as a self. The unique and specific manner with which one articulates oneself appears to reflect one's culture and social audience, but also one's beliefs and commitments about identity.

American developmental psychologist Dan McAdams has led research on the narratives persons tell to describe and explain their lives to themselves and others, concluding that the linguistic construction of the self is a continuous and central task of the entire life span. Jerome Bruner, an American cognitive psychologist, suggests that through narrative, the various dimensions of self—public and private, structure and activity—become interrelated in meaningful stories and serve to promote both the growth of the individual and the survival of human culture.

SOURCES FOR FURTHER STUDY

Bandura, Albert. "The Self-System in Reciprocal Determinism." *American Psychologist* 33 (1978): 344-358. Lays out major concepts of social cognitive theory with respect to the role of the self-system. Theory and research are well elaborated and accessible to nonprofessionals.

Damasio, Antonio R. *Descartes' Error: Emotion, Reason, and the Human Brain.* New York: Avon Books, 1994. Provides a review of neural circuitry and an overview of contemporary neurological research on personality and the self, especially regarding the role of the body and emotions in reasonable, planful action. The content is complex but presented in an engaging and straightforward style.

Derlega, Valerian J., Barbara A. Winstead, and Warren H. Jones. *Personality: Contemporary Theory and Research.* Chicago: Nelson-Hall, 1999. Provides clear overviews of contemporary research in self-concept, identity, self-awareness, and self-consciousness.

Gergen, Kenneth J. *The Saturated Self.* New York: Basic Books, 1991. This influential text is written for nonprofessionals to describe how contemporary society has undermined traditional concepts of the self. The author's nontechnical, entertaining style makes this a good introduction to postmodernism and its new theories of self.

Hall, Calvin S., Gardner Lindzey, and John B. Campbell. *Theories of Personality.* New York: John Wiley & Sons, 1998. A popular text used in undergraduate and graduate courses, explaining the major theories' tenets about the self and personality.

Kitayama, Shinobu, Hazel Rose Markus, Hisaya Matsumoto, and Vinai Norasakkunkit. "Individual and Collective Processes in the Construction of the Self: Self-Enhancement in the United States and Self-Criticism in Japan." *Journal of Personality and Social Psychology* 72, no. 6 (1997): 1245-1267. Explores the role of culture in persons' experience of and formulation of self, and describes cross-cultural differences in the maintenance of the self.

Lewis, Michael, and Jeanne Brooks-Gunn. *Social Cognition and the Acquisition of Self.* New York: Plenum, 1979. Describes the authors' classic series of studies on development of self-recognition and other aspects of self-concept, and places the empirical work in the context of self theories and philosophy of science.

Snodgrass, Joan Gay, and Robert L. Thompson, eds. *The Self Across Psychology.* New York: New York Academy of Sciences, 1997. This text is written at a fairly high level of professional conceptualization, yet provides a diverse representation of empirical and theoretical approaches to studying the self.

Stevens, Richard. *Understanding the Self.* Thousand Oaks, Calif.: Sage Publications, 1996. An undergraduate text integrating various perspectives on the self into other topics of psychology, such as phenomenology and biopsychology.

Mary L. Wandrei

SEE ALSO: Analytic psychology: Jacques Lacan; Analytical psychology: Carl G. Jung; Attitude-behavior consistency; Cognitive psychology; Consciousness; Crowd behavior; Death and dying; Ego psychology: Erik Erickson; Ego, superego, and id; Gender-identity formation; Identity crises; Intimacy; Introverts and extroverts; Multiple personality; Personality theory; Projection; Psychoanalytic psychology and personality: Sigmund Freud; Self-actualization; Self-disclosure; Self-esteem; Self-perception theory; Self-presentation; Social identity theory; Social psychological models: Erich Fromm; Social psychological models: Karen Horney; Thought: Study and measurement.

Self-actualization

TYPE OF PSYCHOLOGY: Personality
FIELDS OF STUDY: Humanistic-phenomenological
    models; personality theory

*Self-actualization, a constructive process of function-
ing optimally and fulfilling one's potentials, is perhaps the central concept and most influential model
within humanistic psychology. The self-actualization
theory and model have had important applications
in the fields of counseling, education, and business,
and hold significant implications for basic conceptions of humankind and for society.*

KEY CONCEPTS
- actualizing tendency
- existentialism
- humanistic psychology
- organismic theory
- phenomenology
- self
- synergy

INTRODUCTION

Self-actualization, as a concept, a theory, and a
model, has extended the domain and impact of psychology. Humanistic psychology—a branch of psychology that emphasizes growth and fulfillment,
autonomy, choice, responsibility, and ultimate values such as truth, love, and justice—has become
an important paradigm for understanding personality, psychopathology, and therapy. Applications
have been extensive in education, counseling, religion, and business. Suggesting action and implying consequences, self-actualization holds clear
and significant implications regarding the dimensions of psychology, the basic conception of humankind, and the functions and organization of
society.

Self-actualization is often defined as a process of
growing and fulfilling one's potential, of being self-
directed and integrated, and of moving toward full
humanness. The most complete description of the
self-actualizing person has been provided by the psychologist Abraham Maslow (1908-1970), who devoted much of his professional life to the study of
exceptional individuals. Maslow abstracted several
ways in which self-actualizing people could be characterized.

CHARACTERIZING SELF-ACTUALIZERS

Compared to ordinary or average persons, self-actualizing persons, as Maslow describes them, may be
characterized as follows. They show a more efficient
and accurate perception of reality, seeing things as
they really are rather than as distortions based on
wishes or neurotic needs. They accept themselves,
others, and nature as they are. They are spontaneous both in behavior and in thinking, and they focus on problems outside themselves rather than being self-centered. Self-actualizing persons enjoy and
need solitude and privacy; are autonomous, with
the ability to transcend culture and environment;
have a freshness of appreciation, taking pleasure
and finding wonder in the everyday world; and have
peak experiences or ecstatic, mystic feelings that
provide special meaning to everyday life. They show
social interest, which is a deep feeling of empathy,
sympathy, identification, and compassionate affection for humankind in general, and have deep interpersonal relationships with others. They carry a
democratic character structure that includes humil-
ity, respect for everyone, and emphasis on common
bonds rather than differences; they distinguish between means and ends, and they possess a clear
sense of ethics. Self-actualizers have a philosophical
and unhostile sense of humor, and they are creative
and inventive in an everyday sense. They are resistant to enculturation, with a degree of detachment
and autonomy greater than that found in people
who are motivated simply to adjust to and go along
with their own in-groups or society. Their value system results from their great acceptance of self and
others and easily resolves or transcends many dichotomies (such as work/pleasure, selfish/unselfish,
good/bad) that others view as absolute opposites.

Carl Rogers (1902-1987), another influential humanistic psychologist, characterized the fully functioning person in ways that parallel Maslow's description. Rogers's theory holds that people have an
actualizing tendency, which is an inherent striving
to actualize, maintain, and enhance the organism.
When people function according to valuing processes based within them and are therefore following their actualizing tendency, experiences can be
accurately symbolized into awareness and efficiently
communicated. Thus, according to Rogers, full humanness involves openness to experiences of all
kinds without distorting them. People thus open to
experience will show a flexible, existential kind of

living that allows change, adaptability, and a sense of flow. These people trust their own internal feelings of what is right, and they use the self as their basis for and guide to behavior. Rogers, like Maslow, holds that such people do not necessarily adjust or conform to cultural prescriptions, but nevertheless they do live constructively.

Rogers, Maslow, and most self-actualization theorists present an optimistic and favorable view of human nature. Unlike Sigmund Freud and classical psychoanalysts, who believed humans to be basically irrational and human impulses to require control through socialization and other societal constraints, self-actualization theorists regard human nature as constructive, trustworthy, positive, forward moving, rational, and possessing an inherent capacity to realize or actualize itself.

POSITIVE AND NEGATIVE REACTION

Although Maslow approached his study of growing individuals from a somewhat more absolute, rational theoretical perspective than Rogers, who came from a more relativistic, phenomenological, and clinical direction, the theorizing and empirical observations of both psychologists converge upon a similar description of a self-actualizing or fully functioning person who makes full use of capacities and potentialities. Such descriptions have aroused much positive as well as negative reaction. One reason is the implicit suggestion that humankind can or should be self-actualizing. The values of actualizing one's self, of fulfilling one's potentials and possessing the characteristics described by Maslow and Rogers, are always implied. Thus, self-actualization is more than a psychological construct; it becomes a possible ethic. Many humanistic proponents have viewed values as necessary in their theorizing; Maslow made an impassioned plea that values, crucial to the development of humanistic psychology, be integrated into science.

Critics of self-actualization theory have argued that it reflects the theorists' own values and individualist ideology; that it neglects sociohistorical and cultural changes by being rooted in unchanging biology; that there may be social-class or cultural bias in the descriptions; that the concept may be misused and encourage the creation of a cultural aristocracy of "superior" people; and that many people may well choose an ideal self that does not match Maslow's characterization. In addition, critics have misunderstood the concept by erroneously thinking

that self-actualizing is synonymous with selfishness and self-indulgence or is consistent with asocial or antisocial behavior. In fact, Maslow and Rogers described self-actualizers as not being overly concerned with themselves, but as typically engaged in larger issues and problems such as poverty, bigotry, warfare, and environmental concerns; as having a highly ethical nature; and as having relationships with others that have a positive and even therapeutic quality.

The various criticisms and arguments surrounding self-actualization have led to clarifications and improvements in understanding the concept, and they attest to the vitality of this major, provocative, and influential psychological construct.

A POSITIVE GROWTH MODEL

Self-actualization presents a growth model that can be and has been used in diverse areas such as counseling, education, and business. In addition, there are implications for people's way of conceptualizing humankind and for structuring institutions and organizing society.

As a model for therapists and counselors and their clients, self-actualization is an alternative to the medical or illness model, which implies that the person coming to the therapist is beset by disease and requires a cure, often from some external source or authority. The self-actualization model represents a positive process, a fostering of strengths; it is concerned with growth choices, self-knowledge, being fully human, and realizing one's potential; yet it also encompasses an understanding of anxiety, defenses, and obstacles to growth. Psychological education, facilitation of growth, self-help and self-learning, and counseling to deal with problems of living and with dysfunctional defenses all are implied in the self-actualization model for human fulfillment and actualization of potentials. This model also avoids problems associated with an adjustment model, in which therapists may socialize conformity or adjustment to a particular status quo or societal mainstream.

Carl Rogers employed the model in his nondirective, client-centered counseling, later called the person-centered approach. Grounded in trust and emphasizing the therapist's unconditional positive regard, empathy, and genuineness, this therapy system allows the client's natural and healthy growth tendencies and organismic valuing processes to determine choices and behaviors. Much research has supported the importance of these therapist characteristics and has documented the increased congruence and process of growth of clients, beginning with Rogers's own empirical research explorations. Rogers's approach to counseling has become one of the most influential in the psychotherapy field.

USE IN WORKPLACE MANAGEMENT

Maslow's application of self-actualization theory to management represents another very influential contribution. Douglas McGregor described a humanistic theory of management (theory Y) that respects human rights and treats workers as individuals. This theory was contrasted with theory X, a managerial view that holds that people dislike work and must therefore be controlled, coerced, conditioned, or externally reinforced in order to obtain high work productivity. Maslow's own book on management assumes the existence of higher needs in all workers that, if met in the world of work, would demonstrate the inherent creativity and responsibility of workers and result in greater satisfaction, increased self-direction, and also greater work productivity. Many influential management theorists, including McGregor, Rensis Likert, and Chris Argyris, have acknowledged Maslow's influence on them. Many field and research studies have supported the value of the self-actualization model as applied to management. Maslow contended that such enlightened management policies are necessary for interacting with a growing, actualizing population; in the world of work, as elsewhere, the highest levels of efficiency can be obtained only by taking full account of the need for self-actualization that is present in everyone.

EXAMINING SYNERGIC SOCIETIES

One of the major conclusions and implications stemming from the self-actualization model is that a synergic society can evolve naturally from the present social system; such a society would be one in which every person may reach a high level of fulfillment.

Ruth Benedict tried to account for differences in societies that related to the overall human fulfillment they could afford their citizens. She prepared brief descriptions of four pairs of cultures. One of each pair was an insecure society, described as nasty, surly, and anxious, with low levels of moral behavior and high levels of hatred and aggression. The contrasting culture was a secure one, described as comfortable, showing affection and niceness. The concept of synergy differentiated these two groups. In high-synergy societies, social arrangements allowed for mutually reinforcing acts that would benefit both individual people and the group; these societies were characterized by nonaggression and cooperation. In low-synergy societies, the social structure provided for mutually opposed and counteractive acts, whereby one individual could or must benefit at the expense of others; these were the cultures in which aggression, insecurity, and rivalry were conspicuous.

Roderic Gorney described how the absolute amount of wealth in a society did not determine the degree of synergy or quality of life in that society. More crucial, he found, were the economic arrangements within the society—whether the resources were concentrated among a "have" group (low synergy) or were dispersed widely to all (high synergy). Gorney argued that low-synergy arrangements in societies promoted higher levels of aggression and mental disorder. Thus, to minimize aggression and mental disorder and to promote self-development and zestful investment in living and learning, Gorney specified that a society should increase the degree of synergy fostered by its institutions.

Thus, the self-actualization model and theory have clear implications for societies and their political and economic structures. The model suggests action and implies consequences. It stresses a particular type of relationship between the society and the individual as a social being. The commingling of individual and social concerns and involvements translates self-actualization theory into practical consequences and is precisely what Maslow described as characterizing his self-actualizers. Self-actualizing people easily resolve superficial dichotomies, and choices are not inevitably seen as "either/or." Work and play, lust and love, self-love and love for others need not be opposites. Maslow described the individual-societal holism by noting that self-actualizing people were not only the best experiencers but also the most compassionate people, the great reformers of society, and the most effective workers against injustice, inequality, and other social ills.

Thus, what self-actualization theory suggests is an integration of self-improvement and social zeal; Maslow held that both can occur simultaneously.

INFLUENCES AND CONTRIBUTORS

The development of the self-actualization concept was influenced by many sources. Carl G. Jung, Otto Rank, and Alfred Adler, departing from Freud's classical psychoanalytic formulations, emphasized the importance of individuality and social dimensions. Jung, credited with being the first to use the term "self-actualization," developed the concept of the self as a goal of life; self-actualization meant a complete differentiation and harmonious blending of the many aspects of personality. Rank emphasized the necessity of expressing one's individuality to be creative. Adler described self-actualization motives with the concept of striving for superiority or perfection; this innate striving, or great upward drive, was a prepotent dynamic principle of human development. Adler also believed that a constructive working toward perfection (of self and society) would result from a loving, trustworthy early social environment.

Kurt Goldstein, the first psychologist who explicitly used self-actualization as the master motive or most basic sovereign drive, was a leading exponent of organismic theory; this approach emphasized unity, consistency, coherence, and integrity of normal personality. Goldstein held self-actualization to be a universal phenomenon; all organisms tend to actualize their individual capacities and inner natures as much as possible. Prescott Lecky also propounded the achievement of a unified and self-consistent organization as the one developmental goal; his concepts of self-consistency and unified personality have much in common with organismic theory. Later, Gordon Allport stressed methods for studying the unique and undivided personality; he described motivation for normal adults as functionally autonomous, and in the individual's conscious awareness. Fritz Perls's Gestalt therapy emphasized here-and-now awareness and integrated personality.

Sociology and cultural anthropology influenced other theorists. Karen Horney spoke of the real self and its realization; Erich Fromm wrote of the "productive orientation," combining productive work and productive love; and David Riesman described the autonomous person and theorized about inner- and other-directed personalities. Arthur Combs and Donald Snygg, influenced by the phenomenological approach, emphasized the maintenance and enhancement of the self as the inclusive human need motivating all behavior. Their description of the adequate self is quite similar to the contemporary description of self-actualization.

Existentialist views, emphasizing the present, free will, values and ultimate concerns, and subjective experience as a sufficient criterion of truth, influenced conceptualizing about self-actualization. Rollo May's description of existential being is important in this respect.

From all these sources came the backdrop for the modern description of self-actualization—the emphasis on the uniqueness of the individual; a holistic, organismic, and phenomenological approach to human experience and conduct; and the need to discover a real self and to express, develop, and actualize that self.

SOURCES FOR FURTHER STUDY

Goble, Frank G. *The Third Force: The Psychology of Abraham Maslow.* New York: Grossman, 1970. An accessible, highly readable book. Summarizes in brief, succinct chapters the major concepts and ideas of Maslow, such as basic needs, human potential, psychological growth, values, and synergy. Concludes with a survey of applications in education, mental health, and business and industry.

Jones, Alvin, and Rick Crandall, eds. "Handbook of Self-Actualization." *Journal of Social Behavior and Personality,* no. 5 (1991). A special issue. A collection of papers on self-actualization and optimal functioning, including theoretical and analytical papers, empirical studies, and examination of issues in assessing self-actualization. The papers, variable in quality and sophistication, cover the field broadly, present interesting implications, and point to future directions.

Maslow, Abraham Harold. *Motivation and Personality.* 3d ed. New York: Harper & Row, 1987. Presents Maslow's classic paper describing self-actualizing people and includes major sections on his motivation theory, on normality and abnormality, and on methodology in psychology. Slightly revised by editors, this third edition is more readable than earlier ones. Two additional chapters succinctly describe Maslow's tremendous influence and impact. Includes chronological bibliography of his writings.

_____. *Toward a Psychology of Being.* 3d ed. New York: John Wiley & Sons, 1998. A second major book of Maslow's psychological writings, with significant sections on growth and motivation, self-actualizing cognition, creativeness, and values. The style is rather pedantic.

Rogers, Carl. *A Way of Being.* Reprint. Boston: Mariner, 1995. A clear presentation of experiences and ideas personally and professionally important to Rogers. Personal chapters deal with experiences in communication, origins of his philosophy, views on reality and his career, and feelings on aging. Other chapters describe foundations, applications, and implications of his person-centered approach, including education, community building, and empathy as a way of life. Includes chronological bibliography of Rogers's works.

Edward R. Whitson

SEE ALSO: Abnormality: Psychological models; Existential psychology; Gestalt therapy; Humanism; Humanistic trait models: Gordon Allport; Person-centered therapy; Self-esteem.

Self-disclosure

TYPE OF PSYCHOLOGY: Social psychology
FIELDS OF STUDY: Interpersonal relations

Self-disclosure is the process of revealing personal information during communication with others. Progress in self-disclosure depends on personal skills and interpersonal intimacy; appropriate self-disclosure is important in communicating effectively and maintaining healthy close relationships.

KEY CONCEPTS
- interdependence
- intimacy
- loneliness
- reciprocity
- social penetration

INTRODUCTION

Self-disclosure is the process of communicating personal information to another individual. It involves a willingness to reveal intimate thoughts and feelings rather than superficial or obvious characteristics. Scientists studying personal relationships have found that, as two people become acquainted and interact over time, they reveal more of themselves to each other. For example, when two people first know each other, their conversation may be limited to the weather, mutual interests, and similarly "safe" topics. The topics they discuss are neutral, and the feelings they express are matters of public knowledge. As their relationship develops, they feel com-

fortable disclosing more intimate feelings and experiences. Later in their friendship, their conversation may be entirely about their feelings, personal problems, and other experiences that are not public knowledge. Self-disclosure is the process by which communication in a relationship becomes more private and intimate.

The term "self-disclosure" was introduced by psychologist Sidney Jourard in his 1964 book *The Transparent Self: Self-Disclosure and Well-Being*. Early work by therapists and researchers speculated that self-disclosure is essential for the health and growth of personal relationships; however, not all self-disclosures serve to promote relationships. Disclosures can be distinguished as either appropriate or inappropriate. Healthy intimacy is promoted when one's self-disclosure suits the time and place as well as the relationship. When two people are close friends, for example, it is appropriate for them to reveal personal information or feelings to each other.

In contrast, confessing intimate feelings or confiding personal experiences to a stranger or mild acquaintance is inappropriate. Personal revelations are too intimate for those interactions. Such inappropriate self-disclosure elicits withdrawal or rejection by others. Self-disclosure can also be inappropriate because it is not intimate enough. For example, if two long-time friends converse about their lives and one refuses to tell the other about a problem because it is somewhat personal, the other may feel rejected or slighted. Because of their history as friends, personal confidences are appropriate, while nondisclosure is not.

LEVELS OF COMMUNICATION

The quality of self-disclosure was considered in the 1973 book *Social Penetration: The Development of Interpersonal Relationships*, by Irwin Altman and Dalmas Taylor. Altman and Taylor argue that, as a relationship develops, communication between partners increases in two qualities or dimensions: breadth and depth. Breadth increases before depth. Communication becomes broader as partners add more topic areas to their conversation. Eventually the two people's communication also deepens: Their interaction becomes less superficial and more intimate. For example, two people whose early friendship is based on a common interest in music will discover other things in common (greater breadth) as they communicate. Eventually, they not only talk about what they mutually enjoy but also confide in each other and help each other solve problems (greater depth).

Altman and Taylor argue that most relationships develop in a more satisfactory way when self-disclosure proceeds (breadth before depth) over time; however, not all individuals conform to this ideal. For example, some persons are "low revealers," unable to proceed to more personal levels of communication over time. Others are "high revealers," indiscriminately disclosing too much to others, irrespective of the exact relationships or interactions between them. Disclosing too little prevents a relationship from becoming more intimate and may result in its termination. Disclosing too much signals intrusiveness rather than intimacy, and it usually causes others to withdraw rather than to respond with equal intimacy.

Healthy self-disclosure adheres to a "norm of reciprocity"—the expectation that partners will exchange disclosures, taking turns revealing similar levels of intimacy. For example, if one partner confides to the other, "I am worried that I might not succeed in reaching this goal," the other can reciprocate by admitting similar feelings or understanding the fear of failure. It would not be reciprocal to change the subject or offer superficial reassurance such as, "I know you will do just fine." Self-disclosure is risky, because it makes the revealer more vulnerable to the confidant's rejection or ridicule. Reciprocal self-disclosure establishes trust, since partners are confiding on similar levels and their knowledge of each other is balanced.

As relationships develop, Altman has argued, immediate reciprocity is unnecessary, because trust has already been established. Thus, long-time friends can have nonreciprocal conversations without threatening their level of intimacy. In a particular interaction, one partner may confide while the other listens without reciprocating. They both know that their roles can be reversed in some future conversation.

Disclosure depends on the style as well as the content of communication. An individual may wish to discuss a personal problem or concern with a friend but not know how to express himself or herself effectively. The complaint, "Sometimes things can be very hard for a person to deal with," is more vague and less disclosing than the statement, "I feel very frustrated and need help solving a problem." In this example, the former disclosure is closed and impersonal while the latter is more open and per-

sonal. To be open and personal, self-disclosing statements should be relevant to the immediate situation, expressed in personal terms ("I feel . . ." rather than "People say . . ."), specifically addressed to the listener, clearly explanatory rather than vague or hinting, and specific rather than general.

ROLE IN RELATIONSHIPS

Differences in patterns of self-disclosure can account for differences in relationship development, conflict, personal distress, and loneliness. Individual differences in self-disclosure—the fact that some people are high revealers and others low revealers—help explain why some relationships become more intimate while others never progress. For example, a low revealer may feel unable to reciprocate when a new friend confides a secret or problem. The nondiscloser may be unsure of the other's response to a personal revelation, fearful of rejection, or unable to express himself or herself. The friend who has confided in the nondiscloser is left feeling unsatisfied or mistrustful by the lack of response and may discourage future interactions.

In contrast, a high revealer's indiscriminate disclosures can offend others. Overdisclosing to a stranger can cause him or her to withdraw and terminate any further interaction. Even friends can be disturbed by a high revealer's willingness to confide inappropriately to others besides themselves. Their own confidences in the overdiscloser may also seem to be at risk. Differences in people's willingness and ability to engage in self-disclosure can affect the success and development of their relationships.

Research and theory on self-disclosure contribute to a larger body of work on communication in close relationships. The study of relationships combines the observations and perspectives of social psychology, sociology, counseling, and communication studies. Early work in this multidisciplinary field focused on how relationships begin, including motivations for affiliation and factors in interpersonal attraction. Researchers have since turned their attention to relationship development and maintenance, processes dependent on the quality and quantity of partners' communication. Self-disclosure is a central goal of intimate communication. An understanding of self-disclosure and its role in developing and maintaining intimacy is essential to improving and stabilizing the significant relationships in people's lives.

EXCEPTIONS TO SELF-DISCLOSURE RULES

Two kinds of interactions may appear to violate the rules of developing self-disclosure: brief intimate encounters and "love at first sight." In the first case, a brief interaction with a stranger involves unusually deep self-disclosure. Psychologist Zick Rubin has dubbed this the "Fort Lauderdale phenomenon," for the Florida city that is a popular destination for spring vacation travel. A college student on vacation may feel less inhibited about self-disclosure with others encountered there, because he or she will not see any of these people again. Thus, high levels of self-disclosure are possible because no future relationship is anticipated.

In "love at first sight," two people may become quickly and mutually attracted and communicate intimately with each other with the intention of maintaining their relationship in the future. Altman and Taylor warn, however, that the two individuals have no history of communication, so no trust has been established between them. The risk of conflict is high, and conflict is likely to be more destructive than if the relationship had been established more gradually. Thus, disclosing too much, too fast, can doom a relationship even when disclosure is reciprocal and when both partners have similar motives.

ROLE IN PSYCHOLOGICAL WELL-BEING

The relationship between psychological adjustment and quantity or amount of self-disclosure has been explored by Valerian Derlega and Alan Chaikin in their 1975 book *Sharing Intimacy: What We Reveal to Others and Why*. Derlega and Chaikin suggest that adjustment is a curvilinear (changing) function of self-disclosure, rather than a linear (constant) one. A person's adjustment does not continually increase as the amount that he or she self-discloses increases. Initially, as self-disclosure increases from low to medium levels, adjustment also improves—up to a point. Beyond that optimal point, increasing from medium to high self-disclosure actually reduces psychological adjustment. In other words, disclosing too much can interfere with a person's well-being and relationship success.

Self-disclosure is important to psychological well-being. Friends value being able to talk to and "be themselves" with each other. Intimacy involves more than being honest and revealing secrets, however; it is possible to express oneself about personal concerns without participating in an intimate relationship. For example, one may keep a diary or "confide" in a pet. There are also some relationships that have no expectation of reciprocity. A patient or client must describe personal experiences and feelings to a physician or psychotherapist without expecting him or her to respond in kind. In these contexts, it is helpful to be able to express oneself honestly without fear of rejection or criticism. Research evidence confirms that the process of articulating and confiding one's concerns significantly helps in coping with stress and trauma. Diaries and professional relationships are not a substitute for real intimacy, however; genuine intimacy is an outcome of communication within relationships, not of one-sided expression. Confiding in others who are willing to listen is essential to gaining the benefits of social support.

ISSUES OF INTIMACY

Personal relationships are based on interdependence—the reliance of both parties on joint outcomes. Reciprocity in self-disclosure represents a mutual investment that builds such interdependence. Withholding a confidence at one extreme and overdisclosing at the other are both hindrances to satisfactory intimacy. People who fail to establish and maintain intimacy with others experience loneliness. Loneliness is defined as the experience of inadequate or insufficient relationships. A person feels lonely when he or she has fewer relationships than are wanted or when existing relationships fail to meet his or her needs. A pattern of inappropriate or inexpressive self-disclosure can ultimately lead one to experience chronic loneliness.

Training in social skills may help those who suffer the consequences of unsatisfactory relationships or loneliness. Individuals could be taught, in psychotherapy or support groups, to modify their self-disclosure. Overdisclosers could become selective in choosing their confidants, and low revealers could learn how to express themselves more openly and personally. Like other relationship skills, self-disclosure requires motivation and competence, but contributes to better communication and higher self-esteem.

INFLUENCES AND EVOLUTION OF STUDY

Research on self-disclosure was influenced by the human potential movement of the 1960's and 1970's. Early theorists such as Jourard argued that it is important to be able to reveal aspects of oneself to a few significant others. Work by Altman and Taylor and by Derlega and Chaikin extended the concept of self-disclosure into the context of personal relationships and communication. Work conducted in the 1970's and 1980's explored the ways people choose topics and levels in disclosing to others. Self-disclosure has come to be regarded more as an aspect of interpersonal communication than of self-development. Whether a disclosure is appropriate depends on the relationship of the discloser to the listener and on the expectations of both individuals.

Altman and Taylor's theory of social penetration recognizes that self-disclosure involves changes in both the quantity and quality of intimate communication. Later research has concentrated on identifying the qualities of appropriate and healthy communication. An understanding of how self-disclosure is developed and how it contributes to communication is important in the study of close relationships; identifying problems in self-disclosure can lead to solving those problems. Research on loneliness has led to the development of social-skills training programs. Lonely people can be taught to listen better, ask open-ended questions, and show their attention to those with whom they interact. Similarly, self-disclosure skills can be improved with education based on an understanding of intimate communication.

SOURCES FOR FURTHER STUDY

Adler, Ronald B., Lawrence B. Rosenfeld, and Neil Towne. *Interplay: The Process of Interpersonal Communication.* 7th ed. Pacific Grove, Calif.: International Thomson, 1998. Focuses on the skills and processes at work in effective communication; offers examples and suggestions for improving listening, expressing, and verbal and nonverbal language. The text also reviews the risks and advantages involved in self-disclosure. Very readable and practical.

Altman, Irwin, and Dalmas A. Taylor. *Social Penetration: The Development of Interpersonal Relationships.* New York: Holt, Rinehart and Winston, 1973. This short, very readable book presents the theory of social penetration, describing how self-disclosure varies in breadth and depth over time. Includes helpful illustrations and numerous examples.

Brehm, Sharon S. *Intimate Relationships.* 3d ed. New York: McGraw-Hill, 2001. Brehm's text reviews the major issues and processes in close relationships: attraction, love, sexuality, social exchange, fairness, commitment, power, jealousy, communication, conflict and dissolution, loneliness, the social network, and therapeutic intervention. Aimed at college students, the book is rich with examples and helpful aids to learning.

Derlega, Valerian, Sandra Metts, Sandra Petronio, and Steven Margulies, eds. *Self-Disclosure.* Thousand Oaks, Calif.: Sage Publications, 1993. Essays on the importance of self-disclosure in close relationships and the ways in which people negotiate the process with their partners.

Duck, Steve. *Relating to Others.* 2d ed. Buckingham, England: Open University Press, 1999. Duck, an important influence in the field of close relationships, discusses the stages in the life cycle of a relationship, from first meeting to maintenance to dissolution. Includes research findings and theoretical context, and suggests additional sources. Extremely readable for the college or high school student.

Knapp, Mark L., and Anita L. Vangelisti. *Interpersonal Communication and Human Relationships.* 4th ed. Boston: Allyn & Bacon, 1999. Knapp, a leading communication researcher, explains the nature of interpersonal communication and describes its form in dialogue, ritual, and intimacy. Discusses the important elements in personal communication and how these can be evaluated and developed.

Ann L. Weber

SEE ALSO: Affiliation and friendship; Coping: Social support; Emotional expression; Intimacy; Psychotherapy: Goals and techniques; Rational-emotive therapy; Self; Self-presentation.

Self-esteem

TYPE OF PSYCHOLOGY: Social psychology
FIELDS OF STUDY: Childhood and adolescent disorders; cognitive development; social perception and cognition

Self-esteem research examines how individuals come to feel as they do about themselves. Psychologists seek to understand how self-esteem develops and what can be done to change negative views of the self once they have been established.

KEY CONCEPTS
- attributions
- identity negotiation
- inheritable traits
- self-concept
- self-efficacy
- self-esteem

INTRODUCTION

"Self-esteem" is a term with which almost everyone is familiar, yet it is not necessarily easily understood. Psychologist William James gave the first clear definition in 1892 when he said that self-esteem equals success divided by pretensions. In other words, feelings of self-worth come from the successes an individual achieves tempered by what the person had expected to achieve. If the person expected to do extremely well on an exam (his or her pretensions are quite high) and scores an A, then his or her self-esteem should be high. If, however, the person expected to do well and then scores a D, his or her self-esteem should be low.

This important but simplistic view of self-esteem started a movement toward a better understanding of the complex series of factors that come together to create the positive or negative feelings individuals have about who they are. Once a person has developed a self-concept (a global idea of all the things that define who and what a person is), that person is likely to exhibit behaviors that are consistent with that self-concept. If a young woman believes that she is a good tennis player, then she is likely to put herself in situations in which that factor is important. Once she behaves (in this case, plays her game of tennis), she is likely to receive feedback from others as to how she did. This feedback determines how she will feel about her tennis-playing ability. Over time, these specific instances of positive or negative feedback about tennis-playing ability will come together to create the more global feelings of positivity or negativity a person has about the self in general.

Even though an individual may believe that she is good at tennis, her ability may not live up to those expectations, and she may receive feedback telling her so (for example, losing in the early rounds of a tournament). In this case, the individual may come to feel somewhat negative about her tennis ability. If this continues to happen, she will adjust her view of her ability and come to believe that she is not a good tennis player after all. To the extent that the

person truly wanted to be good, this realization can cause her to feel quite negative about all aspects of her self. When this happens, the person is said to have developed low self-esteem.

ROLE OF ATTRIBUTIONS

The reality of how self-esteem develops, however, is more complicated than this example demonstrates. People do not always accept the feedback that others offer, and they may believe that their failure means nothing more than having an off day. In order to understand the impact that success and failure will have on self-esteem, it is important to understand the kinds of attributions people make for their successes and failures. When a person succeeds or fails, there are three levels of attributions that can be made for explaining the occurrence. First, the individual must decide if the event occurred because of something internal (something inside caused it to happen) or something external (something in the environment caused it to happen). Second, it must be decided whether the event occurred because of a stable factor (since it happened this time, it will happen again) or a temporary circumstance (it probably will not happen again). Finally, it must be decided whether the event occurred because of something specific (this failure resulted because of poor tennis ability) or something global (failure resulted at this undertaking because of lack of ability to do anything).

It is easy to see that the kinds of attributions individuals make for their successes and failures will have a profound impact on how a particular event influences their self-esteem. If a decision is made that a failure at tennis occurred because of something internal (lack of ability), stable (the ability will never be present), and global (lack of any ability), then a failure is going to damage self-esteem severely. Self-esteem is created through the blending of expectations for success, actual levels of success, and the kinds of attributions made for why success or failure occurred.

CYCLIC PERPETUATION

Once positive or negative self-esteem has developed, it will perpetuate itself in a cycle. If a person believes that he is a failure, he may put himself into situations in which he is destined to fail. If he does not think he can succeed, he may not put forth the amount of effort that success would require. Similarly, if a person believes that he is a success, he will not let one little failure cause him to change his entire opinion of his self. Self-esteem, once it is created, is very difficult to change. If a person dislikes who she is, yet someone else tries to tell her that she is wonderful, she probably will not believe that person. More likely, she will wonder what this person could possibly want from her that he or she is willing to lie and be so nice to get it. On the other hand, if the person feels positive about herself, a single instance of failure will be written off as bad luck, poor effort, or a simple fluke. A negative self-esteem cycle, once it gets started, is very difficult to change, and learning how to break this cycle is the single greatest challenge to self-esteem therapists.

UNDERSTANDING NEGATIVE SELF-ESTEEM

Understanding self-esteem has considerable practical importance in daily life. If it is believed that all successes come from external sources (luck or someone's pity), then good things coming from others can be seen as an attempt to degrade the individual or offer a bribe. People feeling this way relate to others in a judgmental way and cause them to turn away. When others turn away, the person takes it as a signal that he or she was correct about his or her unworthiness, and the negative self-esteem level is perpetuated.

If this negative self-esteem cycle is to be broken, it is important to convince the person of the critical point made by George Herbert Mead. According to Mead, self-esteem is a product of people's interpretation of the feedback that they receive from others. A person with low self-esteem often misinterprets that feedback. If someone with low self-esteem is told, "You look really nice today," he or she is likely to misinterpret that to mean, "You usually look terrible; what did you do different today?"

Ralph Turner has said that the self is not fixed and that the person with low self-esteem must be convinced that he or she is not at the mercy of a self: He or she can be, and is, the creator of a self. It helps to put the person into a situation in which he or she can succeed with no possibility for the wrong attributions to be made. If a person cannot read, this failure will generalize to other situations and is likely to be considered a stable and global deficiency. If this person is taught to read, however, even a person with low self-esteem would find it difficult to argue that the success was situational. In this way, the person begins to see that he or she can take control and

that failures need not be catastrophic for the other self-conceptions he or she might hold.

A person with negative self-esteem is extremely difficult to help. It takes more than the providing of positive feedback to assist such a person. Imagine a series of circles, one inside the other, each one getting smaller. Take that smallest, innermost circle and assign it a negative value. This represents an overall negative self-esteem. Then assign negative values to all the outer circles as well. These represent how the person feels about his or her specific attributes.

If positive messages are directed toward a person with negative values assigned to all these layers of self-esteem, they will not easily penetrate the negative layers; they will be much more likely to bounce off. Negative messages, on the other hand, will easily enter the circles and will strengthen the negativity. Penetration of all the negative layers can, however, sometimes be achieved by a long-term direction of positive and loving messages toward the person with low self-esteem. In effect, the innermost circle, that of global self-esteem, will eventually be exposed. Self-esteem can then be improved if enough positive, loving messages can be directed at the level of the person's global self-esteem. This is a difficult process, partly because as soon as the person's negative self-image comes into serious question, confusion about his or her identity results; living in self-hate, although often painful, is still more secure than suddenly living in doubt.

Once the negative signs have been replaced with positive ones, the new self-esteem level will be as impervious to change as the negative one was. Now, when the person enters a situation, he or she will have more realistic expectations as to what he or she can and cannot do. The person has been taught to make realistic attributions about success and failure. Most important, the individual has been taught that one need not succeed at everything to be a worthy person. William James suggested in 1892 that striving does as much to alleviate self-esteem problems as actual success. Once the individual is convinced that setting a goal and striving rather than not trying at all is all it takes to feel good about him- or herself, the person is truly on the way to having high self-esteem.

IMPORTANCE OF CHILDHOOD AND ADOLESCENCE

An interest in self-esteem developed along with interest in psychological questions in general. Early psy-

Feedback from parents plays a crucial role in the development of a child's self-esteem. (CLEO Photography)

chologists such as Sigmund Freud, Carl G. Jung, William James, and others all realized that an important part of what makes individuals think and act the way they do is determined by the early experiences that create their sense of self and self-esteem. A very important aspect of psychological inquiry has been asking how and why people perceive and interpret the same event so differently. Self-esteem and self-concept play a big role in these interpretations. Knowing an individual's self-esteem level helps one to predict how others will be perceived, what kind of other individuals will be chosen for interaction, and the kinds of attitudes and beliefs the person may hold.

An understanding of childhood development and adolescence would be impossible without an understanding of the forces that combine to create a person's sense of self-esteem. Adolescence has often been described as a time of "storm and stress" because the teenager is trying to negotiate an identity (create a sense of self and self-esteem that he or she would like to have). Teenagers' own wishes and desires, however, are not the only things they must

consider. They are receiving pressure from parents, peers, and society as a whole to be a certain kind of person and do certain kinds of things. Only when self-esteem development is fully understood will it be known how to alleviate some of the trials and tribulations of adolescence and ensure that teenagers develop a healthy and productive view of their worth.

Role in Contemporary Society

The role of self-esteem will probably be even greater as psychological inquiry moves ahead. Contemporary society continues to tell people that if they want to succeed, they have to achieve more. Yet economic downturns and increasing competition to enter colleges and careers make it even more difficult for young people to live up to those expectations and feel good about who they are. The role that psychologists with experience in self-esteem enhancement training will play in the future cannot be overemphasized. In order for adults to lead healthy, productive, and satisfied lives, they must feel good about who they are and where they are going. This requires an intimate understanding of the factors that combine to create people's expectations for success and the likelihood that they will be able to achieve that level of success. Self-esteem development must be kept in mind in helping young people create for themselves a realistic set of expectations for success and an ability to make realistic attributions for why their successes and failures occur.

Sources for Further Study

Butler, Gillian. *Overcoming Social Anxiety and Shyness: A Self-Help Guide Using Cognitive-Behavioral Techniques.* New York: New York University Press, 2001. A practical guide to changing negative thought patterns in order to increase self-esteem.

Coopersmith, Stanley. *The Antecedents of Self-Esteem.* Palo Alto, Calif.: Consulting Psychologists Press, 1981. A very well written and informative look at the background factors that influence the development of self-esteem. Includes statistics and figures but is fairly nontechnical, and the comprehensiveness of the book is well worth the effort.

Jones, Warren H., Jonathan M. Cheek, and Stephen R. Briggs. *Shyness: Perspectives on Research and Treatment.* New York: Plenum, 1986. Presents a thorough view of the development of shyness and the impact it has on social relationships. Many individuals with low self-esteem suffer from shyness, and it is difficult to understand one without the other. The writing is technical; appropriate for a college audience.

Kernis, Michael. *Efficacy, Angency, and Self-Esteem.* New York: Plenum, 1995. A collection of papers that challenge existing notions of self-esteem in contemporary therapy or offer suggestions for new areas of research.

Rosenberg, Morris. *Society and the Adolescent Self-Image.* Reprint. Collingdale, Pa.: DIANE, 1999. Although written in the mid-1960's, this is still one of the best books available on self-esteem. Rosenberg's influence remains strong, and the self-esteem scale he included in this book is still widely used to measure self-esteem. Appropriate for both college and high school students.

Randall E. Osborne

SEE ALSO: Affiliation and friendship; Attitude formation and change; Child abuse; Identity crises; Positive psychology; Self; Self-perception theory; Social perception.

Self-perception theory

TYPE OF PSYCHOLOGY: Social psychology
FIELDS OF STUDY: Attitudes and behavior; social perception and cognition

Self-perception theory examines how behavior can affect attitudes. Research stemming from the theory has led to increased understanding of attitude change, persuasion, and intrinsic motivation.

KEY CONCEPTS
- attitude
- attribution process
- counterattitudinal behavior
- foot-in-the-door effect
- induced-compliance paradigm
- intrinsic motivation
- overjustification effect
- self-discrepancy theory
- self-perception

INTRODUCTION

Self-perception theory, which was proposed by psychologist Daryl Bem in 1965, consists of two postu-lates. The first is that individuals learn about their own attitudes, emotions, and other internal states partially by inferring them from observations of their own behavior and the circumstances in which their behavior occurs. The second is that, to the extent that individuals' internal cues regarding their internal states are weak or ambiguous, they must infer those internal states in the same way that an observer would—based on external cues. Thus, the theory proposes that people's knowledge of their own feelings often comes from inferences based on external information rather than from direct internal access to their feelings.

To understand the self-perception process, one must first consider how an individual generally learns about another person's feelings. The person's behavior is observed, and possible external factors that might account for the behavior are considered. If powerful external inducements for the behavior are observed, the person's behavior is likely to be attributed to those external inducements. If, however, compelling external causes of the behavior are not observed, the person's behavior is likely to be attributed to some internal factor in the individual, such as an attitude or an emotion.

For example, if an observer watches a person give a speech supporting a certain political candidate, the observer may infer that the person likes that candidate. If, however, the observer knows that the person was forced to give the speech or was offered a large sum of money to give the speech, the observer is likely to attribute the speech to the external inducement rather than to the person's attitude toward the candidate. This process of determining the causal explanation for a behavior is called the attribution process.

Self-perception theory posits that when internal cues are not particularly informative, people act like observers of their own behavior and engage in this same attribution process. Thus, when people engage in a new behavior and perceive no external factors controlling their behavior, they are likely to infer an attitude that provides an explanation for that behavior. Through this process, an individual's behavior can affect his or her attitude. For example, if an individual eats pistachio ice cream for the first time with no external inducement and is then asked if he likes pistachio ice cream, he is likely to infer his attitude based on how much of the ice cream he ate and how fast he ate it.

The theory specifies two factors, however, that limit the extent to which an observed behavior will affect an attitude. First, if the individual has clear prior internal information regarding his or her attitude toward the behavior, a given instance of the behavior is not likely to affect that attitude. If a person has eaten and expressed a liking for pistachio ice cream many times before, a new instance of eating that ice cream is not likely to effect that person's attitude toward it. Second, if there is a strong external inducement for the behavior, the behavior will be attributed to that external factor rather than to an attitude. If a person was ordered at gunpoint to eat the ice cream or was offered a large sum of money to eat the ice cream, she would not infer from the behavior that she likes pistachio ice cream, but rather that she ate the ice cream because of the external inducement (the threat of punishment or the promise of reward).

RESEARCH SUPPORT

Self-perception theory has been supported by various lines of research. The critical assumption underlying the theory is that individuals sometimes do not have internal access to the causes of their own behavior. This notion has been supported by a variety of findings summarized by psychologists Richard Nisbett and Timothy Wilson. These studies have shown that people often do not have accurate knowledge of why they behave as they do. For example, female participants were asked to choose a favorite from among four pairs of virtually identical stockings hanging on a rack. The position of each pair of stockings was varied, and the researchers found that the rightmost pair (usually the last pair examined) was chosen 80 percent of the time. When the participants were asked to explain their choices, they had no trouble generating reasons; however, none of the participants mentioned that the position of the pair of stockings affected the choice, even though it was clearly a major factor. Similar deficits in causal self-knowledge have been shown in connection with a wide variety of phenomena, including why people feel the way they do about books and films, and what factors affect their moods.

The primary hypothesis derived from self-perception theory is that, when individuals engage in a new behavior that differs from their past behavior and there appears to be little or no external inducement, they will infer an attitude that is consistent with that behavior. Many studies using the induced-compliance paradigm have supported this hypothesis. In the typical study, individuals are led to write an essay expressing an attitude on an issue that is different from their own initial attitude. If the participants perceive that they can choose whether to write an essay and they are not offered a substantial external inducement (for example, a large amount of money) for doing so, their attitudes become more consistent with the attitudes expressed in their essays. If, however, the participants are not given a choice or are offered a substantial external inducement to write an essay, they do not change their attitudes. Thus, the participants in these studies infer their attitudes from their behavior unless their behavior appears to be controlled by a lack of choice or a large external inducement.

ATTITUDE CHANGE

Self-perception theory has implications for the development of attitudes and emotions, persuasion, compliance, and intrinsic motivation. According to Bem, the self-perception process begins in early childhood, when children are taught how to describe their internal states in much the same way that they learn to describe external objects and events. For example, if a child consumes large quantities of grape juice, the parent may tell the child, "You really like grape juice." Similarly, if a child has a temper tantrum, the parent may say, "You're really angry, aren't you?" In this way, children learn how to infer their own attitudes and emotions. The socialization process can thus be viewed as training in how to infer one's attitudes and emotions in a culturally appropriate manner.

Self-perception processes can continue to affect an individual's attitudes throughout his or her life span. Induced-compliance research indicates that, whenever people are induced to behave in a way that is somehow different from their past behavior and do not perceive a strong external inducement for doing so, their attitudes will become more favorable toward that behavior. Thus, by subtly encouraging a change in a person's behavior, one can effect a change in that person's attitude (persuasion).

One application of this notion is to psychotherapy. Various techniques used in psychotherapy encourage the client to behave in new, more beneficial ways; it is hoped that such techniques also lead the client to develop new, more beneficial attitudes. Consistent with this idea, a number of studies have shown that, when participants are induced to write favorable statements about themselves or present themselves to an interviewer in self-enhancing ways and they perceive that they freely chose to do so, they experience an increase in self-esteem.

Self-perception theory has implications for compliance as well as persuasion. Compliance is acceding to a request from another. Research has shown that one way to increase compliance with a particular request is to first gain compliance with a smaller request. This phenomenon is known as the foot-in-the-door effect, a name derived from the door-to-door sales strategy of first getting one's foot in the door. In the first demonstration of this phenomenon, some participants were asked to comply with a small request: to sign a safe-driving petition. All of them agreed to do so. Two weeks later, all the participants were asked to comply with a larger request: to place "Drive Carefully" signs in their front yards. Participants who had been asked to sign the petition were three times more likely to comply with the larger request than those participants who had not been asked to sign the petition. Many subsequent studies have confirmed this effect.

Self-perception theory provides the most widely accepted explanation of the foot-in-the-door effect. Compliance with the initial request is posited to lead individuals to infer either that they like to be helpful or that they like the requester or the type of request with which they have complied. The newly formed attitudes resulting from the initial compliance make the participant more receptive to the second, larger request. This technique is commonly used by salespeople, and it is also employed to increase compliance with requests made by charitable organizations, such as the Red Cross. More generally, the foot-in-the-door effect suggests that each small commitment people make to a personal, organizational, or career goal will lead to a larger commitment to that goal.

INTRINSIC MOTIVATION

All these applications of self-perception theory are based on the notion that, when behavior is not sufficiently justified by external inducements, an individual will infer that he or she is intrinsically motivated to engage in that behavior. Research on the overjustification effect has revealed a complementary ten-

Self-Discrepancy Theory

Self-perception theory describes the tendency to use external information, such as observing one's own behaviors, in order to infer attitudes and beliefs and to gain self-knowledge. However, this self-knowledge does not come without emotional consequences. In 1987, E. Tory Higgins proposed that self-discrepancy theory can predict and explain these affective reactions. Higgins theorized that an individual's self-concept is formed of not just one accurate collection of self-beliefs and attitudes, but that individuals also maintain distinct images of their "ideal" and "ought" selves. Ideal selves encompass all that a person wishes to be (a "perfect" self), and ought selves encompass all that a person feels obliged to be (a "should" self). Self-discrepancy theory posits that incongruencies between an individual's actual self and either the ideal or the ought self lead to negative emotions, and as a result influence future behaviors.

Self-discrepancy research indicates that when people are made aware, either by reflecting upon their own behavior or through social feedback, that a discrepancy exists between their actual self and their ideal self, they experience "dejection" emotions, such as depression and disappointment. Additionally, when a discrepancy is

noted between one's actual and ought selves, "agitation" emotions result, such as anxiety and guilt. The magnitude of these affective reactions are predicated on several factors, such as the size of the discrepancy ("My behavior was in complete opposition to how I should have behaved," or "I acted very closely to my ideal") and the importance and relevance of the discrepant behavior to the individual ("I really should not eat two pieces of cake," as opposed to "I really should not cheat").

Later research suggested the inclusion of another self model, the "undesired" or "feared" self, into self-discrepancy theory. Here, the relationship between self-views and emotions is reversed; a discrepancy between actual and undesired self would lead to positive emotions and a congruency would lead to negative emotions.

The relationship between self-discrepancy judgments and emotions has factored into psychological research on a wide variety of topics. Self-discrepancy theory has helped increase understanding of eating disorders, health maintenance, psychological coping styles, and educational performance.

Michelle Murphy

dency of people to infer that they are not intrinsically motivated to engage in an activity if there appears to be too much external justification for the behavior. From the perspective of self-perception theory, if an individual is initially intrinsically motivated to engage in a behavior but is offered a large external inducement for performing the behavior, the person may infer that he or she is performing the behavior for the external inducement; this attribution will lead the individual to conclude that he or she is not interested in the activity for its own sake. Thus, large external inducements for engaging in a previously enjoyable activity may overjustify the activity, thereby undermining intrinsic interest in that activity.

The classic demonstration of the overjustification effect was conducted by psychologists Mark Lepper, David Greene, and Richard Nisbett. Nursery school children were first given a chance to play with colorful felt-tip markers. The researchers noted the amount of time each child played with the markers and used this as as a measure of intrinsic motivation. Two weeks later, the children were divided into three groups that were approximately equal in their initial levels of intrinsic motivation. Each child in the first group was simply asked to play with the markers. The children in the second group were told that, if they played with the markers, they would receive a "good player award," a gold star, and a ribbon when they were done. The third group of children was not offered rewards for playing with the markers; after they were done, however, the children were given the awards, stars, and ribbons anyway.

Approximately one week later, each child was observed in a free-play period in which he or she could play with the markers or engage in other activities. The group of children that had previously been offered and had received rewards for playing with the markers spent less free time engaged in that activity than the group that received no rewards and the group that unexpectedly received the rewards. Thus, intrinsic motivation to perform the activity was undermined in children who had previously been offered a substantial external inducement to engage in it. Probably because of their reduced intrinsic interest, these same children drew lower-quality pictures with the markers than the children in the other groups. Similar effects have been shown for both children and adults across a wide range of activities. In addition, overjustification effects have been shown to result from external in-

ducements such as deadlines and competition as well as from various types of rewards.

Behaviorists such as B. F. Skinner popularized the strategy of using rewards to reinforce behavior. Based on the overjustification research, the wisdom of this strategy has been challenged. Rewards are commonly used in child-rearing, education, and work settings, yet in all three settings it is harmful to undermine the individual's intrinsic motivation to engage in the desired behaviors. For example, if a child has some intrinsic interest in doing homework, offering a reward for doing the homework is likely to motivate the behavior but is also likely to undermine the child's intrinsic interest in the activity; thus, when the reward is no longer offered, the child may be less likely to engage in the activity than before he or she was ever offered a reward for doing it.

If the individual has no intrinsic interest in the behavior, there is no problem with using rewards, because there is no intrinsic motivation to undermine. In addition, research has shown that rewards do not necessarily undermine intrinsic motivation; they do so only to the extent that the reward is perceived to be a factor controlling the behavior. Thus, if a behavior is subtly rewarded or the rewards are viewed as indicators of the quality of one's performance, they may actually increase rather than decrease intrinsic motivation. The key to the effective use of rewards is therefore to present them in such a way that they are perceived to be rewards for competence rather than efforts to coerce the individual into engaging in the task.

SELF-PERCEPTION THEORY VERSUS COGNITIVE DISSONANCE THEORY

Self-perception theory first gained prominence in 1967, when Daryl Bem argued that the theory could provide an alternative explanation for the large body of evidence supporting Leon Festinger's influential cognitive dissonance theory. From its inception in 1957, cognitive dissonance theory generated considerable supportive research. The theory proposed that, when an individual holds two cognitions such that one cognition logically implies the opposite of the other, the individual experiences a negative tension state, known as dissonance, and becomes motivated to reduce the dissonance; this can be done by changing one of the cognitions or by adding consonant cognitions, which reduces the overall level of inconsistency.

Most of the research on the theory utilized the induced-compliance paradigm. In these studies, participants would be induced to engage in a behavior contrary to their prior attitudes; if the participants engaged in such counterattitudinal behavior while perceiving that they had a choice and had no sufficient external justification for doing so, they were assumed to be experiencing dissonance. Study after study supported the prediction that these participants would change their attitudes so that they would be more consistent with their behavior, presumably to reduce dissonance.

Bem argued that self-perception theory could account for these findings more simply than dissonance theory by positing that, when participants in these studies observed themselves engaging in a behavior with little external inducement, they logically inferred an attitude consistent with that behavior. Thus, Bem offered a cognitive explanation for the most popular motivational theory of the time. Since then, it has virtually become a tradition in social psychology for cognitive theories to be pitted against motivational theories in attempting to account for social attitudes and behavior.

This challenge to dissonance theory was viewed as a major controversy in the field, and it generated much research that attempted to support one theory or the other. Finally, in the mid-1970's, research emerged that resolved the controversy. Evidence was obtained that supported dissonance theory by showing that, when people engage in counterattitudinal behavior with little external inducement, they do experience a negative psychological state, and this negative state does motivate the attitude change following counterattitudinal behavior. It was also found, however, that, when individuals engage in behavior that is different from behavior that would be implied by their prior attitudes but not so different that it is really inconsistent with prior attitudes, an attitude change may still occur; this attitude change is best accounted for by self-perception theory. Self-perception theory is also still considered to be the best explanation for the foot-in-the-door and over-justification effects, effects that do not involve counterattitudinal behavior and therefore cannot be explained by cognitive dissonance theory.

Sources for Further Study

Bem, Daryl J. "Self-Perception Theory." In *Advances in Experimental Social Psychology*. Vol. 6, edited by Leonard Berkowitz. New York: Academic Press, 1972. This chapter is the definitive summation of self-perception theory. Includes discussions of the roots of the theory, research relevant to it, and the theory's place within the field of social psychology.

Cialdini, Robert B. *Influence: Science and Practice*. 3d ed. New York: HarperCollins, 1993. Summarizes what has been learned about techniques intended to influence another's attitudes and behavior and how these techniques work. Includes a discussion of the foot-in-the-door technique and other strategies that capitalize on self-perception processes.

Fazio, R. H. "Self-Perception Theory: A Current Perspective." In *Social Influence: The Ontario Symposium*. Vol. 5, edited by M. P. Zanna, J. M. Olson, and C. P. Herman. Hillsdale, N.J.: Lawrence Erlbaum, 1987. An overview of self-perception theory that places the theory within the context of recent advances in theory and research in social psychology.

Higgins, E. T. "Self-Discrepancy: A Theory Relating Self and Affect." *Psychological Review* 94 (1987): 319-340. Higgins's original introduction to and overview of self-discrepancy theory.

Moskowitz, Gordon B., ed. *Cognitive Social Psychology: The Princeton Symposium on the Legacy and Future of Social Cognition*. Mahwah, N.J.: Lawrence Erlbaum, 2001. Provides an overview of current research on self-perception from a cognitive perspective.

Riding, Richard J., and Stephen G. Rayner, eds. *Self Perception*. Westport, Conn.: Ablex, 2001. This book provides an overview of recent self-perception research from an international perspective, largely focused on the influence of self-perception theory on academic performance. Discusses impact of self-perception on motivation.

Robins, Richard W., and Oliver P. John. "The Quest for Self-Insight: Theory and Research on Accuracy and Bias in Self-Perception." In *Handbook of Personality Psychology*, edited by Robert Hogan and John A. Johnson et al. San Diego, Calif.: Academic Press, 1997. Provides a broad overview of social psychological research and theory in self-perception studies, and specifically addresses the psychological processes involved in self-perception.

Jeff Greenberg;
updated by Michelle Murphy

See also: Attitude-behavior consistency; Attitude formation and change; Causal attribution; Cognitive dissonance; Emotions; Motivation; Radical behaviorism: B. F. Skinner; Work motivation.

Self-presentation

Type of psychology: Social psychology
Fields of study: Social perception and cognition

Self-presentation is behavior with which people try to affect how they are perceived and judged by others; much social behavior is influenced by self-presentational motives and goals.

Key concepts
- impression management
- ingratiation
- intimidation
- power
- self-monitoring
- self-promotion
- social anxiety
- supplication

Introduction

Although they may or may not be consciously thinking about it, people often try to control the information that others receive about them. When they are deliberately trying to make a certain impression on others, people may carefully choose their dress, think about what to say, monitor their behavior, pick their friends, and even decide what to eat. Self-presentation refers to the various behaviors with which people attempt to manage and influence the impressions they make on others. Nearly any public behavior may be strategically regulated in the service of impression management, and people may behave quite differently in the presence of others from the way they behave when they are alone. Moreover, self-presentation is not always a conscious activity; without planning to, people may fall into familiar patterns of behavior that represent personal habits of self-presentation.

The impressions of someone that others form substantially determine how they treat that person. Obviously, if others like and respect someone, they behave differently toward him or her from the way they would if the person were disliked or mistrusted. Thus, it is usually personally advantageous for a person to have some control over what others think of him or her. To the extent that one can regulate one's image in others' eyes, one gains influence over their behavior toward one and increases one's interpersonal power. Self-presentational perspectives on social interaction assume that people manage their impressions to augment their power and maximize their social outcomes.

Impression Management and Strategies

Self-presentation, however, is usually not deceitful. Although people do occasionally misrepresent themselves through lying and pretense, most self-presentation communicates one's authentic attributes to others. Because frauds and cheats are rejected by others, dishonest self-presentation is risky. Instead, impression management usually involves the attempt to reveal, in a selective fashion, those aspects of one's true character that will allow one to attain one's current goals. By announcing some of their attitudes but not mentioning others, for example, people may appear to have something in common with almost anyone they meet; this simple tactic of impression management facilitates graceful and rewarding social interaction and does not involve untruthfulness at all. Over time, genuine, realistic presentations of self in which people accurately reveal portions of themselves to others are likely to be more successful than those in which people pretend to be things they are not.

Nevertheless, because most people have diverse interests and talents, there may be many distinct impressions they can honestly attempt to create, and people may seek different images in different situations. Edward Jones and Thane Pittman identified four discrete strategies of self-presentation that produce disparate results. When people seek acceptance and liking, they typically ingratiate themselves with others by doing favors, paying compliments, mentioning areas of agreement, and describing themselves in attractive, desirable ways. On other occasions, when they wish their abilities to be recognized and respected by others, people may engage in self-promotion, recounting their accomplishments or strategically arranging public demonstrations of their skills. Both ingratiation (a strategy of self-presentation in which one seeks to elicit liking and affection from others) and self-promotion create socially desirable impressions and thus are very common strategies of self-presentation.

In contrast, other strategies create undesirable impressions. Through intimidation, people portray themselves as ruthless, dangerous, and menacing so that others will do their bidding. Such behavior is obnoxious and tends to drive others away, but if those others cannot easily escape, intimidation often works. Drill sergeants who threaten recalcitrant recruits usually are not interested in being liked; they want compliance, and the more fierce they seem, the more likely they may be to get it. Finally, using the strategy of supplication, people sometimes present themselves as inept or infirm in order to avoid obligations and elicit help and support from others. A person who plays sick in order to stay home from work or school is engaging in supplication.

People's choices of strategies and desired images depend on several factors, such as the values and preferences of the target audience. People often tailor their self-presentations to fit the interests of the others they are trying to impress. In one study of this phenomenon, college women were given job interviews with a male interviewer who, they were told, was either quite traditional or "liberated" in his views toward women. With this information in hand, the women dressed, acted, and spoke differently for the different targets. They wore more makeup and jewelry, behaved less assertively, and expressed a greater interest in children to the traditional interviewer than they did to the liberated interviewer.

Individuals' own self-concepts also influence their self-presentations. People typically prefer to manage impressions that are personally palatable, both because they are easier to maintain and because they help bolster self-esteem; however, self-presentations also shape self-concepts. When people do occasionally claim images they personally feel they do not deserve, their audiences may either see through the fraudulent claim and dispute the image or accept it as legitimate. In the latter case, the audience's approving reactions may gradually convince people that they really do deserve the images they are projecting. Because a person's self-concept is determined, in part, by feedback received from others, self-presentations that were once inaccurate can become truthful over time as people are gradually persuaded by others that they really are the people they were pretending to be.

FINESSING PUBLIC IMAGE

Studies of self-presentation demonstrate that people are capable of enormous subtlety as they fine-tune their public images. For example, Robert Cialdini and his colleagues have identified several ingenious, specific tactics of ingratiation. Observations of students at famous football colleges (such as Notre Dame, Ohio State, the University of Southern California, Arizona, Pittsburgh, and Louisiana State) revealed that after a weekend football victory, students were especially likely to come to class on Monday wearing school colors and insignia. If their team had lost, however, such identifying apparel was conspicuously absent. Further laboratory studies suggested that the students were strategically choosing their apparel to publicize their association with a winning team, a tendency Cialdini called "basking in reflected glory." By contrast, they were careful not to mention their connection to a loser. In general, people who seek acceptance and liking will advertise their association with other desirable images, while trying to distance themselves from failure and other disreputable images.

Furthermore, they may do this with precise sophistication. In another study by Cialdini, people privately learned that they had a trivial connection—a shared birthdate—with another person who was said to have either high or low social or intellectual ability. The participants then encountered a public, personal success or failure when they were informed that they had either high or low social ability themselves. Armed with this information, people cleverly selected the specific self-descriptions that would make the best possible impression on the researchers. If they had failed their social ability test, they typically mentioned their similarity with another person who had high intellect but did not bring up their connection to another person with higher social ability than themselves. They thus publicized a flattering link between themselves and others while steering clear of comparisons that would make them look bad. In contrast, if they had passed the social ability test and the researchers already thought highly of them, people brought up their connection to another person who had poorer social ability. By mentioning their resemblance to less talented others, people not only reminded their audiences of their superior talent, but seemed humble and modest as well.

Self-presentation can be ingenious, indeed. In general, if they wish to ingratiate themselves with others, people with deficient images try to find something good to communicate about themselves that does not contradict the negative information the audience already has. If they are already held in high esteem, however, people typically select modest, self-effacing presentations that demonstrate that they are humble as well as talented.

People do not go to such trouble for everyone, however; if people do not care what a particular audience thinks, they may not be motivated to create any impression at all. One experiment that illustrated this point invited women to "get acquainted" with men who were either desirable or undesirable partners. Snacks were provided; the women who were paired with attractive men ate much less than the women stuck with unappealing partners. Because women who eat lightly are often considered more feminine than those who eat heartily, women who wanted to create a favorable impression strategically limited their snack consumption; in contrast, those who were less eager to impress their partners ate as much as they liked.

ROLE IN SOCIAL ANXIETIES

On occasion, people care too much what an audience thinks. One reason that people suffer from social anxieties such as shyness or stage fright is that their desire to make a particular impression on a certain audience is too high. According to theorists Mark Leary and Barry Schlenker, people suffer from social anxiety when they are motivated to create a certain impression but doubt their ability to do so. Any influence that increases one's motivation (such as the attractiveness, prestige, or power of an audience) or causes one to doubt one's ability (such as unfamiliar situations or inadequate personal social skills) can cause social anxiety. This self-presentation perspective suggests that, if excessive social anxiety is a problem, different therapies will be needed for different people. Some sufferers will benefit most from behavioral social skills training, whereas others who have passable skills simply need to worry less what others are thinking of them; cognitive therapies will be best for them.

ROLE OF SELF-MONITORING

Finally, people differ in their self-presentational proclivities. Those high in the trait of "self-monitoring" tend to be sensitive to social cues that suggest how one should act in a particular situation and are ad-

ept at adjusting their self-presentations to fit in. By comparison, low self-monitors seem less attentive and flexible, and tend to display more stable images regardless of their situational appropriateness. High self-monitors are more changeable and energetic self-presenters, and as a result, they create social worlds that are different from those of low self-monitors. Because they can deftly switch images from one audience to the next, high self-monitors tend to have wider circles of friends with whom they have less in common than do low self-monitors. Compared to high self-monitors, lows must search harder for partners with whom they share broader compatibilities. Over time, however, lows are likely to develop longer-lasting, more committed relationships with others; they invest more in the partners they have. High self-monitors are more influenced by social image than lows are, a self-presentational difference with important consequences for interaction.

THEORETICAL ROOTS AND INFLUENCES

The roots of self-presentation theory date back to the very beginnings of American psychology and the writings of William James in 1890. James recognized that the human self is multifaceted, and that it is not surprising for different audiences to have very different impressions of the same individual. After James, in the early twentieth century, sociologists Charles Horton Cooley and George Herbert Mead stressed that others' impressions of an individual are especially important, shaping that person's social life and personal self-concept. The most influential parent of this perspective, however, was Erving Goffman, who was the first to insist that people actively, consciously, and deliberately construct social images for public consumption. Goffman's book *The Presentation of Self in Everyday Life* (1959) eloquently compared social behavior to a theatrical performance staged for credulous audiences, complete with scripts, props, and backstage areas where the actors drop their roles.

As it emerged thereafter, self-presentation theory seemed to be a heretical alternative to established explanations for some social phenomena. For example, whereas cognitive dissonance theory suggested that people sometimes change attitudes which are inconsistent with their behavior in order to gain peace of mind, self-presentation theory argued that people merely report different attitudes that make them look consistent, without changing their real attitudes at all. Nevertheless, despite theoretical controversy, Goffman's provocative dramaturgical analogy gradually became more widely accepted as researchers demonstrated that a wide variety of social behavior was affected by self-presentational concerns. With the publication in 1980 of Barry Schlenker's book-length review of self-presentation research, impression management theory finally entered the mainstream of social psychology.

IMPORTANCE AND CONTRIBUTIONS

The lasting importance of self-presentation theory lies in its reminders that people are cognizant of the images they present to others and often thoughtfully attempt to shape those images to accomplish their objectives. As a result, much social behavior has a self-presentational component. An angry boss may have real problems controlling his temper, for example, but he may also occasionally exaggerate his anger to intimidate his employees. Even people suffering from severe mental illness may engage in impression management; research has revealed that institutionalized schizophrenics sometimes adjust the apparent severity of their symptoms so that they seem well enough to be granted special privileges without seeming so healthy that they are released back into the threatening free world. In this case, self-presentation theory does not suggest that schizophrenics are merely pretending to be disturbed; obviously, most psychotic people are burdened by real psychological or biological problems. Impression management, however, may contribute in part to their apparent illness, just as it does to many other social behaviors. In general, self-presentation theory does not claim to replace other explanations for behavior, but it does assert that much of what people do is influenced by self-presentational motives and concerns.

SOURCES FOR FURTHER STUDY

Baumeister, Roy F., ed. *Public Self and Private Self*. New York: Springer-Verlag, 1986. Extends and refines self-presentation theory with individual chapters written by experts in the field. Difficult reading for a layperson, but essential reading for an advanced student of impression management. Its erudite discussion persuasively demonstrates the fundamental importance of self-presentation in social life.

Brissett, Dennis, and Charles Edgley, eds. *Life as Theater: A Dramaturgical Sourcebook*. 2d ed. New York: Aldine de Gruyter, 1991. A collection of many short papers that illustrate the uses of self-presentation concepts in sociology, political science, anthropology, and communication studies. Meant as a college text; contains a useful bibliography.

Goffman, Erving. *The Presentation of Self in Everyday Life*. Garden City, N.Y.: Doubleday, 1959. This classic work, still in print, coined the term "self-presentation" and almost single-handedly created this field of study. Goffman suggested that people stage dramatic performances for their audiences, carefully selecting their lines and props. The book can be easily read by undergraduates and is still full of fresh insights.

Jones, E. E., and Thane Pittman. "Toward a General Theory of Strategic Self-Presentation." In *Psychological Perspectives on the Self*, edited by Jerry Suls. Hillsdale, N.J.: Lawrence Erlbaum, 1982. Describes and differentiates the strategies of ingratiation, intimidation, self-promotion, and supplication. although written for a college audience, its clever analysis will intrigue most readers.

Leary, Mark R., and Rowland S. Miller. *Social Psychology and Dysfunctional Behavior: Origins, Diagnosis, and Treatment*. New York: Springer-Verlag, 1986. Three chapters of this book use self-presentational concepts to help explain maladaptive behavior ranging from schizophrenia to shyness and stage fright. Accessible to a lay reader. Demonstrates the utility of the self-presentation perspective on problematic behavior.

Schlenker, Barry R. *Impression Management: The Self-Concept, Social Identity, and Interpersonal Relations*. Monterey, Calif.: Brooks/Cole, 1980. A complete and readable introduction to the study of impression management. An excellent, comprehensive source that collects relevant research and theory; it devotes individual chapters to specific self-presentational behaviors such as self-descriptions, expressed beliefs, and personal appearance.

_____, ed. *The Self and Social Life*. New York: McGraw-Hill, 1985. Contains chapters contributed by eminent researchers who explore various applications of the self-presentation perspective. Topics such as excuse making, self-control, detection of deceit, and social power are covered in a scholarly smorgasbord that shows how pervasive impression management is. College audiences will have no difficulty with this collection.

Snyder, Mark. *Public Appearances, Private Realities: The Psychology of Self-Monitoring*. New York: W. H. Freeman, 1987. A very readable, entertaining study of important individual differences in self-presentation. The differences between the social worlds of high and low self-monitors will fascinate most readers.

Weber, Robert. *The Created Self: Reinventing Body, Persona, and Spirit.* New York: W. W. Norton, 2000. Explores the many ways in which people present the self, from psychological structures to physical appearance.

Rowland Miller

SEE ALSO: Attitude-behavior consistency; Self; Self-disclosure; Self-esteem; Self-perception theory.

Selye, Hans

BORN: January 26, 1907, in Vienna, Austria
DIED: October 16, 1982, in Montreal, Canada
IDENTITY: Austrian-born Canadian physician and endocrinologist
TYPE OF PSYCHOLOGY: Stress
FIELDS OF STUDY: Biology of stress; critical issues in stress; stress and illness

Selye, called the founder of the stress field, devoted his entire professional life to the study of stress.

Hans Hugo Selye was born in Vienna and started medical school in 1925 at the University of Prague. While in medical school, he began his research into causes of stress and its effects on the body. He noticed that people undergoing a wide variety of stressors exhibited, in addition to those symptoms associated with the specific stressor, symptoms that were remarkably similar regardless of the type of stress being experienced. In other words, each stressor (for instance, cold) caused its own specific response (shivering) and a nonspecific set of symptoms which he described as "the syndrome of just being sick." He named this collection of nonspecific symptoms the general adaptation syndrome (GAS), also known as the Selye syndrome. These nonspecific symptoms, over time, lead to physical illness and, ultimately, death. In his own words, "Every stress leaves an indelible scar, and the organism pays for its survival after a stressful situation by becoming a little older."

Selye proposed three stages of the GAS: alarm, in which the body prepares for "fight or flight" when challenged by a stressor; resistance, in which the body returns to normal but requires enormous energy to maintain homeostasis; and exhaustion, when continued stress causes symptoms similar to the alarm stage. Because at this point the body's resources are depleted, physical illness ensues. Selye also coined the term "eustress" for the positive, challenging type of stress that helps people grow, and defined "distress" as the negative, destructive type of stress.

In 1936, he published his first scientific paper on the subject of stress. During his lifetime, he wrote thirty-nine books and more than 1,700 scholarly articles on this subject. Two of Selye's best-known works are *Stress Without Distress* (1974) and *The Stress of Life* (1956). *Stress Without Distress* was published in seventeen languages and is still widely available.

In addition to his medical studies in Prague, Selye studied in Paris and Rome, earning M.D., Ph.D., and D.Sc. degrees. He left Europe when he received a Rockefeller Research Fellowship and a position at The Johns Hopkins University in Baltimore, Maryland. In 1932, he became an associate professor of histology at McGill University in Montreal and, in 1945, the first director of the Institute of Experimental Medicine and Surgery at the University of Montreal, where he served until he retired in 1976. With Alvin Toffler, he founded the International Institute of Stress in 1979. Much honored for his scientific work, Selye was granted forty-three honorary doctorates during his lifetime. After his death, the Hans Selye Chair was established in 1989 at the University of Montreal.

SOURCES FOR FURTHER STUDY

Selye, Hans. *The Stress of My Life: A Scientist's Memoirs.* New York: Van Nostrand Reinhold, 1979. Selye's autobiography.

Viner, Russell. "Putting Stress in Life: Hans Selye and the Making of Stress Theory." *Social Studies of Science* 29, no. 3 (June, 1999): 391-410. Discusses the process by which Selye's theories of stress, originally formulated in the 1930's, became accepted in the 1970's.

Rebecca Lovell Scott

SEE ALSO: General adaptation syndrome; Stress: Behavioral and physiological responses; Stress-related diseases.

Sensation and perception

TYPE OF PSYCHOLOGY: Sensation and perception
FIELDS OF STUDY: Auditory, chemical, cutaneous,
and body senses; vision

The study of sensation and perception examines the
relationship between input from the world and the
manner in which people react to it. Through the pro-
cess of sensation, the body receives various stimuli
that are transformed into neural messages and
transmitted to the brain. Perception is the meaning
and interpretation given to these messages.

KEY CONCEPTS
- absolute threshold
- acuity
- attention
- sensory deprivation
- sensory receptors

INTRODUCTION

Although the distinction between sensation and
perception is not always clear, psychologists attempt
to distinguish between the two concepts. Sensation
is generally viewed as the initial contact between organisms and their physical environment. It focuses
on the interaction between various forms of sensory stimulation and how these sensations are registered by the sense organs (nose, skin, eyes, ears, and
tongue). The process by which an individual then
interprets and organizes this information to produce conscious experiences is known as perception.

The warmth of the sun, the distinctive sound of a
jet airplane rumbling down a runway, the smell of
freshly baked bread, and the taste of an ice cream
sundae all have an impact on the body's sensory receptors. The signals received are transmitted to the
brain via the nervous system; there, interpretation
of the information is performed. The body's sensory receptors are capable of detecting very low
levels of stimulation. Eugene Galanter's studies indicated that on a clear night, the human eye is capable
of viewing a candle at a distance of 30 miles (48 kilo-
meters), while the ears can detect the ticking of a
watch 20 feet (6 meters) away in a quiet room. He
also demonstrated that the tongue can taste a tea-
spoon of sugar dissolved in 2 gallons (about 7.5 li-
ters) of water. People can feel a bee wing falling on
the cheek and can smell a single drop of perfume

in a three-bedroom apartment. Awareness of these
faint stimuli demonstrates the absolute thresholds,
defined as the minimum amount of stimulus that
can be detected 50 percent of the time.

SIGNAL RECOGNITION

A person's ability to detect a weak stimulus, often
called a signal, depends not only on the strength of
the signal or stimulus but also on the person's psychological state. For example, a child remaining at
home alone for the first time may be startled by an
almost imperceptible noise. In a normal setting,
with his or her parents at home, the same noise or
signal would probably go unnoticed. Scientists who
study signal detention seek to explain why people
respond differently to a similar signal and why the
same person's reactions vary as circumstances
change. Studies have shown that people's reactions
to signals depend on many factors, including the
time of day and the type of signal.

Much controversy has arisen over the subject of
subliminal signals—signals that one's body receives
without one's conscious awareness. It has long been
thought that these subliminal signals could influence a person's behaviors through persuasion.
Many researchers believe that individuals do sense
subliminal sensations; however, it is highly unlikely
that this information will somehow change an individual's behaviors. Researchers Anthony Pratkanis
and Anthony Greenwald suggest that in the area of
advertising, subliminal procedures offer little or
nothing of value to the marketing practitioner.

ADAPTATION AND SELECTIVE ATTENTION

An individual's response to a stimulus may change
over time. For example, when a swimmer first enters
the cold ocean, the initial response may be to complain about the water's frigidity; however, after a few
minutes, the water feels comfortable. This is an example of sensory adaptation—the body's ability to
diminish sensitivity to stimuli that are unchanging.
Sensory receptors are initially alert to the coldness
of the water, but prolonged exposure reduces sensitivity. This is an important benefit to humans in that
it allows an individual not to be distracted by constant stimuli that are uninformative. It would be
very difficult to function daily if one's body were
constantly aware of the fit of shoes and garments,
the rumble of a heating system, or constant street
noises.

The reception of sensory information by the senses, and the transmission of this information to the brain, is included under the term "sensation." Of equal importance is the process of perception: the way an individual selects information, organizes it, and makes an interpretation. In this manner, one achieves a grasp of one's surroundings. People cannot absorb and understand all the available sensory information received from the environment. Thus, they must selectively attend to certain information and disregard other material. Through the process of selective attention, people are able to maximize information gained from the object of focus, while at the same time ignoring irrelevant material. To some degree, people are capable of controlling the focus of their attention; in many instances, however, focus can be shifted undesirably. For example, while one is watching a television show, extraneous stimuli such as a car horn blaring may change one's focus.

The fundamental focus of the study of perception is how people come to comprehend the world around them through its objects and events. People are constantly giving meaning to a host of stimuli being received from all their senses. While research suggests that people prize visual stimuli above other forms, information from all other senses must also be processed. More difficult to understand is the concept of extrasensory perception (ESP). More researchers are becoming interested in the possible existence of extrasensory perception—perceptions that are not based on information from the sensory receptors. Often included under the heading of ESP are such questionable abilities as clairvoyance and telepathy. While psychologists generally remain skeptical as to the existence of ESP, some do not deny that evidence may someday be available supporting its existence.

FIVE LAWS OF GROUPING

Knowledge of the fields of sensation and perception assists people in understanding their environment. By understanding how and why people respond to various stimuli, scientists have been able to identify important factors which have proved useful in such fields as advertising, industry, and education.

Max Wertheimer discussed five laws of grouping that describe why certain elements seem to go together rather than remain independent. The laws include the law of similarity, which states that similar objects tend to be seen as a unit; the law of nearness, which indicates that objects near one another

tend to be seen as a unit; the law of closure, which states that when a figure has a gap, the figure still tends to be seen as closed; the law of common fate, which states that when objects move in the same direction, they tend to be seen as a unit; and the law of good continuation, which states that objects organized in a straight line or a smooth curve tend to be seen as a unit. These laws are illustrated in the figure on the following page.

USE IN ADVERTISING AND MARKETING

The laws of grouping are frequently utilized in the field of advertising. Advertisers attempt to associate their products with various stimuli. For example, David L. Loudon and Albert J. Della Bitta, after studying advertising dealing with menthol cigarettes, noted that the advertisers often show mentholated cigarettes in green, springlike settings to suggest freshness and taste. Similarly, summertime soft-drink advertisements include refreshing outdoor scenes depicting cool, fresh, clean running water, which is meant to be associated with the beverage. Also, advertisements for rugged four-wheel-drive vehicles utilize the laws of grouping by placing their vehicles in harsh, rugged climates. The viewer develops a perception of toughness and ruggedness.

The overall goal of advertisers is to provide consumers with appropriate sensations that will cause them to perceive the products in a manner that the advertisers desire. By structuring the stimuli that reach the senses, advertisers can build a foundation for perceptions of products, making them seem durable, sensuous, refreshing, or desirable. By utilizing the results of numerous research studies pertaining to perception, subtle yet effective manipulation of the consumer is achieved.

COLOR STUDIES

Another area that has been researched extensively by industry deals with color. If one were in a restaurant ordering dinner and received an orange steak with purple French fries and a blue salad, the meal would be difficult to consume. People's individual perceptions of color are extremely important. Variations from these expectations can be very difficult to overcome. Researchers have found that people's perceptions of color also influence their beliefs about products. When reactions to laundry detergents were examined, detergent in a blue box was found to be too weak, while detergent in a yellow

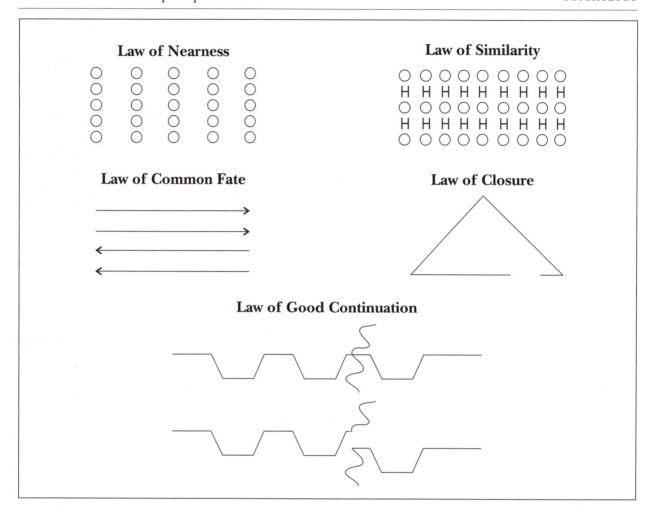

box was thought to be too strong. Consumers believed, based on coloration, that the ideal detergent came in a blue box with yellow accentuation. Similarly, when individuals were asked to judge the capsule color of drugs, findings suggested that orange capsules were frequently seen as stimulants, white capsules as having an analgesic action, and lavender capsules as having a hallucinogenic effect.

Studies have shown that various colors have proved more satisfactory than others for industrial application. Red has been shown typically to be perceived as a sign of danger and is used to warn individuals of hazardous situations. Yellow is also a sign of warning. It is frequently used on highway signs as a warning indicator because of its high degree of visibility in adverse weather conditions. Instrument panels in both automobiles and airplanes are frequently equipped with orange- and yellow-tipped instrument indicators, because research has demonstrated that these colors are easily distinguished from the dark background of the gauges. Finally, industry has not overlooked the fact that many colors have a calming and relaxing effect on people. Thus, soft pastels are often used in the workplace.

USE IN EDUCATION

The field of education has also benefitted from research in the areas of sensation and perception. Knowing how young children perceive educational materials is important in developing ways to increase their skills and motivation. Textbook publishers have found that materials need to be visually attractive to children in order to help them focus on activities. Graphics and illustrations help the young learner to understand written materials. Size of printed text is also important to accommodate the developmental level of the student. For example, primers and primary-level reading series typically have larger print to assist the student in focusing on the text. As the child's abilities to discriminate letters and numbers become more efficient with age, the print size diminishes to that of the size of characters in adult books. Similar techniques continue into high school and college; especially in introductory courses, texts are designed utilizing extensive amounts of color, along with variation in page design. The reader's eyes are attracted by numerous stimuli to pictures, figures, definitions, and charts strategically placed on each page. This technique allows the author to highlight and accent essential points of information.

Early Research

The study of sensation and perception began more than two thousand years ago with the Greek philosophers and is one of the oldest fields in psychology. There are numerous theories, hypotheses, and facts dealing with how people obtain information about their world, what type of information they obtain, and what they do with this information once it has been obtained. None of this information has been sufficient to account for human perceptual experiences and perceptual behavior, so research in the area of sensation and perception continues.

The philosopher Thomas Reed made the original distinction between sensations and perceptions. He proposed that the crucial difference between them is that perceptions always refer to external objects, whereas sensations refer to the experiences within a person that are not linked to external objects. Many psychologists of the nineteenth century proposed that sensations are elementary building blocks of perceptions. According to their ideas, perceptions arise from the addition of numerous sensations. The sum of these sensations thus creates a perception. Other psychologists believed that making a distinction between sensations and perceptions was not useful.

The first psychologists saw the importance of perception when they realized that information from the senses was necessary in order to learn, think, and memorize. Thus, research pertaining to the senses was a central research component of all the psychological laboratories established in Europe and the United States during the late nineteenth and early twentieth centuries.

Applications in Contemporary Society

By studying perceptions, researchers can identify potential environmental hazards that threaten the senses. Studying perception has also enabled people to develop devices that ensure optimal performance of the senses. For example, on a daily basis, one's senses rely on such manufactured objects as telephones, clocks, televisions, and computers. To be effective, these devices must be tailored to the human sensory systems.

The study of sensations and perceptions has also made it possible to build and develop prosthetic devices to aid individuals with impaired sensory function. For example, hearing aids amplify sound for hard-of-hearing individuals; however, when all sounds are amplified to the same degree it is often difficult for people to discriminate between sounds. From the work of Richard Gregory, a British psychologist, an instrument was developed that would amplify only speech sounds, thus allowing a person to attend more adequately to conversations and tune out background noise.

Finally, understanding perception is important for comprehending and appreciating the perceptual experience called art. When knowledge of perception is combined with the process of perceiving artistic works, this understanding adds an additional dimension to one's ability to view a work of art.

Sources for Further Study

Goldstein, E. Bruce. *Sensation and Perception.* 6th ed. Belmont, Calif.: Wadsworth, 2001. Excellent overview of the field of sensation and perception. Chapters focus on subjects dealing with vision, hearing, and touch, but Goldstein also adds chapters on perceived speech and the chemical senses.

Gregory, R. L. *Eye and Brain: The Psychology of Seeing.* 5th ed. Princeton, N.J.: Princeton University Press, 1997. A broad book on vision for the general reader. Beneficial for students in the areas of psychology, biology, and physiology. Includes many illustrations that help to explain complex matters in an understandable fashion.

Matlin, M. W. *Sensation and Perception.* 4th ed. Boston: Allyn & Bacon, 1996. Matlin's book is an introductory text covering all general areas of sensation and perception. Themes carried throughout the text are intended to provide additional structure for the material; these themes reflect the author's eclectic, theoretical orientation.

Schiff, William. *Perception: An Applied Approach.* Boston: Houghton Mifflin, 1980. Schiff's book is concerned with how people can, and do, use their senses to comprehend their world and their relation to it. Interesting chapters cover such topics as social-event perception, personal perception, and individual differences in perception.

Sekuler, Robert, and Robert R. Blake. *Perception.* 4th ed. New York: McGraw-Hill, 2001. Sekuler and Blake attempt to explain seeing, hearing, smelling, and tasting to students of perception. Extensive use of illustrations allows the reader to understand materials more fully. A series of short illustrations is also utilized by the authors to depict additional concepts.

Eugene R. Johnson

SEE ALSO: Advertising; Attention; Depth and motion perception; Hearing; Kinesthetic memory; Senses; Signal detection theory; Smell and taste; Touch and pressure; Visual system.

Senses

TYPE OF PSYCHOLOGY: Sensation and perception
FIELDS OF STUDY: Auditory, chemical, cutaneous, and body senses; vision

Humans process information using at least five sensory modalities: sight, sound, taste, smell, and the body senses, which include touch, temperature, balance, and pain. Because people's sensation and perception of external stimuli define their world, knowledge of these processes is relevant to every aspect of daily life.

KEY CONCEPTS
- cutaneous
- perception
- proximate
- receptor
- sensation
- ultimate studies
- *Umwelt*

INTRODUCTION

Humans have five sense organs: the eyes, ears, taste buds, nasal mucosa, and skin. Each sense organ is specialized to intercept a particular kind of environmental energy and then to convert that energy into a message that the brain can interpret. Together, these two processes are called sensation.

The first step of sensation, the interception of external energy, is done by the part of the sense organ that is in direct contact with the environment. Each sense organ has a specialized shape and structure designed to intercept a particular form of energy. The second step, conversion of the captured energy into signals the brain can understand, is done by cells inside the sense organ called receptors. Receptors are structures to which physicists and engineers refer as transducers: They convert one form of energy into another. Artificial transducers are common. Hydroelectric plants, for example, intercept flowing water and convert it to electricity; then appliances convert the electricity into heat, moving parts, sound, or light displays. Receptors are biological transducers which convert environmental energy intercepted by the sense organ into neural signals. These signals are then sent to the brain, where they are interpreted through a process called perception.

The eye, the best understood of all the sense organs, consists of a lens which focuses light (a kind of electromagnetic energy) through a small hole (the pupil) onto a sheet of cells (the retina). The retina contains the eye's receptor cells: the rods, which are sensitive to all wavelengths of light in the visible spectrum, and three kinds of cones, which are sensitive to those wavelengths that the brain perceives as blue, green, and yellow.

The ear funnels air pressure waves onto the tympanic membrane (more commonly known as the eardrum), where vibrations are transmitted to the inner ear. In the inner ear, receptors called hair cells are stimulated by different frequency vibrations; they then send signals to the brain which are interpreted as different pitches and harmonics.

Taste buds are small bumps on the tongue and parts of the throat which are continuously bathed in liquid. Receptors in the taste buds intercept any chemicals which have been dissolved in the liquid. Molecules of different shapes trigger messages from different receptors. Humans have several kinds of taste receptors which send signals the brain interprets as bitter, at least two kinds of receptors which send signals interpreted as sweet, and one kind of receptor each that sends messages interpreted as salty and sour.

The nasal mucosa, the sense organ for smell, is a layer of cells lining parts of the nasal passageways and throat; it intercepts chemicals directly from inhaled air. Apparently, cells in the nasal mucosa can produce receptor cells (called olfactory receptors) throughout life. This way, people can develop the capacity to smell "new" chemicals which they could not smell before. New olfactory receptors seem to be created in response to exposure to novel chemicals, analogous to the production of antibodies when the immune system is exposed to foreign material. Because of this ability to create new olfactory receptors, it is not possible to list and categorize all the different types of smells.

The skin is the largest sense organ in the human body; its sense, touch, actually consists of several different senses, collectively referred to as the cutaneous senses. Receptors called mechanoreceptors are triggered by mechanical movements of the skin and send signals that the brain interprets as vibration, light or deep pressure, and stretching. Thermoreceptors intercept heat passing in or out of the body through the skin; their signals are interpreted by the brain as warmth and cold, respectively. Receptors which are triggered when skin cells are damaged are called nociceptors; their signals to the brain are interpreted as pain.

ANIMAL SENSES

Some animals have sense organs that humans do not and can thereby sense and perceive stimuli that humans cannot. Many birds and probably a variety of marine creatures can detect variations in the earth's magnetic field; some fish and invertebrates can detect electrical fields. Other animals have sense organs similar to, but more sensitive than, those of humans; they can intercept a broader range of energy or detect it at lower levels. Insects can see ultraviolet light, while pit vipers can sense infrared. Elephants can hear infrasound, and mice can hear ultrasound. The olfactory sensitivity of most animals far surpasses that of humans. Because of differences in sensory apparatus, each animal experiences a different sensory reality; this is termed each animal's *Umwelt*.

BIOENGINEERING USES

One application of the knowledge of sensory modalities is in the field of bioengineering. Knowing that sense organs are biological transducers allows the possibility of replacing damaged or nonfunc-

tional sense organs with artificial transducers, the same way artificial limbs replace missing ones. Today's most advanced artificial limbs can be connected directly to nerves that send information from the motor (movement) areas of the brain; thus, a person can direct movement of the artificial limb with neural messages via thoughts. Similarly, bioengineers are researching the use of small sensors that can be set up to send electrical signals directly to a person's sensory nerves or the sensory cortex of the brain. Researchers have already developed the first version of a hearing aid to help people who have nerve deafness in the inner ear but whose auditory processing centers in the brain are still intact.

HUMAN FACTORS ENGINEERING

Another field which applies the findings of experimental sensory psychologists is called human factors engineering. People who design complicated instrument panels (for example, in jet cockpits or nuclear reactors) must have an understanding of what kinds of stimuli will elicit attention, what will be irritating, and what will fade unnoticed into the background. Using knowledge of how sound is transmitted and how the human brain perceives sound, human factors engineers have designed police and ambulance sirens which make one type of sound while the vehicle is moving quickly (the air-raid-type wailing sound), and another while the vehicle is moving slowly, as through a crowded intersection (alternating pulses of different pitches). These two types of sounds maximize the likelihood that the siren will be noticed in the different environmental settings. Research by human factors engineers has also prompted many communities to change the color of fire engines from red to yellow; since red is difficult to see in twilight and darkness and bright yellow can be seen well at all times of day, yellow makes a better warning color.

Research by human factors engineers and environmental psychologists is also used to improve commercial products and other aspects of day-to-day living, answering questions such as, How loud should the music be in a dentist's waiting office? What color packaging will attract the most buyers to a product? How much salt does a potato chip need? How much light is necessary to maximize production in a factory? Will noise in a domed stadium cause damage in the fans? Research on sensation and perception is applied in almost every setting imaginable.

INFLUENCING ANIMAL BEHAVIOR

Knowledge of sensation and perception can also be used to influence the behavior of other animals. Since people visit zoos during the daytime, nocturnal animals are often housed in areas bathed in only red light. Most nocturnal animals are colorblind, and since red light by itself is so difficult to see, the animals are tricked into perceiving that it is nighttime and become active for the viewers. Knowing that vultures have an exceptionally good sense of smell and that they are attracted to the scent of rotting meat allowed scientists to find an invisible but dangerous leak in a long, geographically isolated pipeline; after adding the aroma of rotting meat into the pipeline fuel, they simply waited to see where the vultures started circling—and knew where they would find the leak.

LEARNING THEORY

The knowledge that sensation and perception differ across species has also influenced the biggest and perhaps most important field in all of psychology: learning theory. The so-called laws of learning were derived from observations of animals during the acquisition of associations between two previously unassociated stimuli, between a stimulus and a response, or between a behavior and a consequent change in the environment. These laws were originally thought to generalize equally to all species and all stimuli. This belief, along with the prevailing *Zeitgeist* which held that learning was the basis of all behavior, led to the assumption that studies of any animal could serve as a sufficient model for discovering the principles guiding human learning and behavior. It is now known that such is not the case.

Although laws of learning do generalize nicely in the acquisition of associations between biologically neutral stimuli, each animal's sensory apparatus is designed specifically to sense those stimuli that are relevant for its lifestyle, and how it perceives those stimuli will also be related to its lifestyle. Therefore, the meaning of a particular stimulus may be different for different species, so results from studies on one animal cannot be generalized to another; neither can results from studies using one stimulus or stimulus modality be generalized to another.

Finally, it is important to note that scientific inquiry itself is dependent upon human understanding of the human senses. Scientific method is based on the philosophy of empiricism, which states that knowledge must be obtained by direct experience using the physical senses (or extensions of them). In short, all scientific data are collected through the physical senses; thus, the entirety of scientific knowledge is ultimately based upon, and limited by, human understanding of, and the limitations of, the human senses.

EVOLUTION OF STUDY

In the late nineteenth and early twentieth centuries, Wilhelm Wundt, often considered the founder of scientific psychology, aspired to study the most fundamental units (or structures) of the mind. Wundt and other European psychologists (called structuralists) focused much of their attention on the description of mental responses to external stimuli—in other words, on sensation and perception. Around the same time, educational philosopher William James developed functionalism in the United States. Functionalists avoided questions about what was happening in the mind and brain and focused on questions about why people respond the way they do to different stimuli.

Today, both the structuralist and the functionalist methodologies have been replaced, but the fundamental questions they addressed remain. Psychologists who study sensation and perception still conduct research into how sense organs and the brain work together to produce perceptions (proximate studies) and why people and other animals have their own particular *Umwelts* (ultimate studies). Results from proximate and ultimate studies typically lead to different kinds of insights about the human condition. Proximate studies lead to solutions for real-world problems, while studies of ultimate functions provide enlightenment about the evolution of human nature and humans' place in the world; they help identify what stimuli were important throughout human evolutionary history.

For example, the human ear is fine-tuned so that its greatest sensitivity is in the frequency range that matches sounds produced by the human voice. Clearly, this reflects the importance of communication—and, in turn, cooperation—throughout human evolution. More specifically, hearing sensitivity peaks nearer to the frequencies produced by female voices than male voices. This suggests that human language capacity may have evolved out of mother-infant interactions rather than from the need for communication in some other activity, such as hunting.

STIMULI ADAPTATIONS FOR SURVIVAL

Knowing what kinds and intensities of stimuli the human sense organs can detect suggests what stimuli have been important for human survival; furthermore, the way the brain perceives those stimuli says something about their role. Most stimuli that are perceived positively are, in fact, good for people; food tastes and smells "good" because without some kind of psychological inducement to eat, people would not survive. Stimuli that are perceived negatively are those that people need to avoid; the fact that rotting foods smell "bad" is the brain's way of keeping one from eating something that might make one sick. To give an example from another sensory modality, most adults find the sound of a crying baby bothersome; in order to stop the sound, they address the needs of the infant. Cooing and laughing are rewards that reinforce good parenting.

SOURCES FOR FURTHER STUDY

Ackerman, Diane. *A Natural History of the Senses*. Reprint. New York: Vintage, 1991. A best-selling rumination on the senses, written by a poet. A remarkable mixture of science and art.

Brown, Evan L., and Kenneth Deffenbacher. *Perception and the Senses*. New York: Oxford University Press, 1979. This text differs from most textbooks on sensation in that it integrates ethological, cross-species information with the traditional coverage of human sensory physiology and psychophysics. Although technical, the book is user-friendly. Each chapter has its own outline, glossary, and set of suggested readings.

Buddenbrock, Wolfgang von. *The Senses*. Ann Arbor: University of Michigan Press, 1958. Easy-to-read descriptions of different *Umwelts*, with many fascinating examples. Since the focus is almost entirely on ultimate explanations rather than sensory mechanisms, new technologies have not made this book outdated.

Gescheider, George. *Psychophysics: The Fundamentals*. 3d ed. Hillsdale, N.J.: Lawrence Erlbaum, 1997. A thorough introduction to psychophysics, focusing on measurement techniques and the theory of signal detection.

Hall, Edward Twitchell. *The Hidden Dimension*. 1969. Reprint. Garden City, N.Y.: Anchor Books, 1990. Written by an anthropologist, this book on cross-cultural differences in use of space includes three chapters on the perception of space as influenced by each sensory modality. These provide good examples of using human factors and environmental psychology to address real-world problems, particularly problems in architecture and interpersonal communication.

Scharf, Bertram, ed. *Experimental Sensory Psychology*. Glenview, Ill.: Scott, Foresman, 1975. Includes an introduction, a chapter on psychophysics, a chapter on each sensory modality, and a postscript on the direction of modern studies. Provides excellent detailed descriptions of sensory mechanisms and psychophysical laws. Includes many diagrams, formulas, and technical terms but is still very readable.

Seligman, Martin E. P. "On the Generality of the Laws of Learning." *Psychological Review* 77, no. 5 (1970): 406-418. The article that triggered the ongoing debate over the generalizability of the results of learning studies across different species and different types of stimuli. Although written for a professional audience, the paper describes the basic assumptions of learning studies, so previous familiarity with learning theory is not necessary.

Stone, Herbert, and Joel L. Sidel. *Sensory Evaluation Practices*. 2d ed. Orlando, Fla.: Academic Press, 1997. Although written for professionals, this text can provide the layperson with insight into the world of product research. Mostly describes techniques for designing studies of the sensory evaluation of food products, but most of the principles are generalizable to other products and industries.

Linda Mealey

SEE ALSO: Hearing; Pain; Sensation and perception; Smell and taste; Touch and pressure; Vision: Brightness and contrast; Vision: Color; Visual system.

Separation and divorce
Adult issues

TYPE OF PSYCHOLOGY: Developmental psychology
FIELDS OF STUDY: Adulthood; coping; interpersonal relations; stress and illness

Marriage is one of the most significant of all adult life structures, and so the experience of separation and divorce is a major change in the psychological life and subsequent development of the adults involved.

KEY CONCEPTS
- acceptance
- anger
- bargaining
- denial
- depression
- divorce
- morbid dependency
- parental alienation syndrome
- preseparation
- separation

INTRODUCTION

Separation and divorce occur when a husband and wife decide to cease living together. In some cases, separation is temporary, allowing a couple to resolve their problems and resume living together. A divorce is a permanent loss and the end of a marriage.

In the United States, divorce is very common, with approximately one divorce for every two marriages in an average year. This is among the highest divorce rates in the world (although rates of marriage and remarriage in the United States are also among the highest). This rate, however, varied considerably over the twentieth century. Factors contributing to these trends include the decreasing significance of religious stigma against divorce; the increasing perception that marriage should be based on love and serve personal growth and self-fulfillment; and the attainment by women of economic self-sufficiency.

Demographically, divorce is more common in couples who married young, who experienced a premarital pregnancy, and who are financially downwardly mobile. Divorce is also more prevalent in couples who come from divorced families or have not resolved attachments or conflicts with their families of origin. Divorce is more frequent in subsequent marriages than in first marriages.

DIVORCE AS A LEGAL AND ECONOMIC REALITY

Divorce, like marriage, is a legal arrangement with significant economic consequences. The major le-

gal issues include division of property, alimony, child support, custody, and visitation. While these issues are settled by the divorcing couple through negotiation or litigation, the courts of each state now have guidelines that specify certain parameters as generally appropriate. How these are handled will have a large impact on the psychological experience of divorce. The legal process establishes and promotes an adversarial relationship for the couple. While this arrangement is to be expected of a jurisprudence system built upon an adversarial pursuit of justice, an essentially combative relationship is profoundly antithetical to the goal of a psychologically healthy divorce. Rather than working together toward a mutually satisfying result, divorcing couples are trained to compete in a distinctly win-lose arena, often with disastrous consequences for both. As an appreciation of the psychological costs of these consequences has grown, mediation has emerged as an increasingly popular alternative way of resolving the legal issues.

THE PSYCHOLOGICAL PHASES OF DIVORCE

When a couple divorces, a great loss is experienced by all family members. This experience is not a momentary event. Its impact continues to unfold over time, as its meaning undergoes various transformations until it is gradually assimilated. There are predictable stages involved in letting go of a marriage and moving on in life. These stages appear in the experience of both members of the couple, regardless of who wanted the separation or divorce. The spouse who decides to live apart usually begins grieving the relationship while the couple is still living together. Although both spouses go through a mourning process, they often go through stages at different times and rates.

Much of the literature in the psychology of divorce has been devoted to mapping these phases. Some recognize that the steps of divorce actually begin in the preseparation period. As Constance Ahrons demonstrated in *The Good Divorce* (1994), divorce is not entered into easily or quickly. Typically, the preseparation phase involves a protracted period of confused tension, and it is during this painfully drawn-out ending that the most serious psychological harm is inflicted on any children. Divorced couples frequently realize, in hindsight, that the marriage should have ended sooner. Sadly, it is this period of painful conflict that often provides the needed momentum for the separation to be enacted as welcome relief.

Craig and Sandra Everett in *Healthy Divorce* (1994), identify three preseparation stages. First, clouds of doubt gather, as one becomes increasingly disillusioned with one's partner and ambivalent about continuing in the marriage. One may become confused with questions about what was initially attractive about one's partner. One becomes increasingly angry and critical, and acts out that unhappiness. These "early warning signs" could lead the couple to make changes to save their marriage, especially with the help of marriage therapy, but the full significance of these signs is usually unrecognized and therapy entered into only later, when it is too late. The second preseparation stage is "the cold shoulder." Warmth and affection are withdrawn, and there is less talk, disclosure, or support as one becomes emotionally unavailable to one's partner. This pulling away is also evident in a declining interest or responsiveness in sexual relations and even in physical withdrawal, as more separate and independent activity is undertaken, excluding the partner. In stage three, fantasies of a life beyond the marriage emerge. Usually they are idealized sexual or romantic liaisons or adventurous escapes. Sometimes a spouse may act out these fantasies through extramarital affairs.

Once the actual physical separation takes place, the couple undergoes a grieving process, an experience of "letting go" of their marriage. As a form of grief work, this process is analogous to the phases people experience when mourning the death of a loved one, or when coming to terms with one's own impending death (a process first identified by Elisabeth Kübler-Ross in 1969). Not everyone goes through all the stages, and sometimes people's grieving varies from the usual sequence. Some people get "stuck" in certain stages of the mourning process and need psychotherapy to help them move on.

STAGES OF GRIEVING

In the first phase, denial, a person may completely deny the marital problem, or, in a more sophisticated form, the person may minimize the import of problem by a sort of magical thinking, an "if only . . . " fantasy ("It could all be resolved if only . . . "). Such a fantasy can be held in one's mind only (safe from any testing against reality), or it may lead to desperate, even self-destructive efforts to resurrect a dead

relationship. In the extreme, this course can become a pathological morbid dependency on the partner. Unable to move on, such a person may remain fixated on their former spouse for many years afterward. Even after it becomes evident that the partner has actually left, a person can still use wishful thinking to minimize the real impact of this rupture. For example, one may tell oneself that the partner will come back once he or she realizes that no one else will be as good for them. The children of divorcing parents are prone to such fantasies of reconciliation as well. They will be very vulnerable to construing parents' words or actions as hopeful indicators of this possibility.

In the second phase, anger, a person tends to blame the breakup on the other. Thoughts such as "If he (or she) were not like this, we could still be married" are very common. Here, unlike the experience of grieving a death, there is an overwhelming sense of personal rejection by one who was loved dearly. It is this profound hurt that underlies the intense feelings of anger. In such a view, the marital breakdown is seen as completely the fault of the other, and one cannot see one's own role in the unsatisfactory state of the marriage. In this phase, one is likely to become outspokenly critical of one's partner to friends and children. Richard A. Gardner has described this "campaign of denigration" and the sad consequences that accrue when one parent successfully induces in the children a directive to carry this anger toward the other parent. Gardner identifies the subsequent withdrawing of affection by the child as the parental alienation syndrome: a loss, sometimes for years, of a close bond with that parent. In another extreme form, such anger can become pathologically overgeneralized. It is directed then to all men or women. Such a negative stereotype will preclude or sabotage any subsequent effort toward an intimate relationship.

In the third phase, bargaining, the reality of the ending is still avoided, now by maneuvers designed to ward it off. Typically, they involve implicit or explicit offers to act differently to better suit one's partner. The "bargain" involves a fantasy that change would eliminate the problem and stop the divorce. Like denial, these typically are formulated as "if only . . . " In the extreme form, the bargain is made with oneself, to enact changes designed to alter the situation. While all these bargaining ploys are unrealistic, their function is something deeper than warding off the divorce, for which they are in-effective. They serve to ward off the subjective experience of the reality and finality of the divorce by remaining focused on how to "fix" it.

In the fourth phase, depression, the reality of the divorce breaks through one's previous efforts to minimize or avoid its emotional impact. The person feels the depressive weight of the loss without the cushioning provided by denial, anger, and bargaining. This initial despair is founded upon a deep sense of shame for having a failed marriage, and so is accompanied by feelings of guilt and low self-esteem. Then the demands of life and fears about the future can become overwhelming. One feels inadequate to handle the roles previously taken care of by the other spouse (such as finances or social arrangements). Self-defeating thoughts further undermine functioning. The person may cry frequently and experience a variety of somatic problems, including changes in appetite (either eating very little or overeating); changes in sleep (either insomnia or excessive sleeping); a marked decrease in level of energy; a tendency to become isolated from social contact; an increased use of addictive substances (such as alcohol, nicotine, television, computers); and a loss of pleasure in things that used to bring joy. These symptoms are manifestations of the crushing sadness that the reality of the divorce now brings as the person begins to experience the true impact of the loss.

Beyond the sense of sheer loss, there is a final phase of this process. In the fifth phase, acceptance, resolution occurs. The person accepts that the marriage has ended and will not be revived and that one can survive and even thrive. The person reorients to a divorced life, incorporating this reality into a new sense of identity and functioning. When this occurs, there is a renewed interest in life; regular patterns of sleeping, eating, and activity resume; and coping mechanisms (such as excessive drinking or television viewing) abate. As anger and guilt are released, the person now can speak about and relate to the former spouse without bitterness. The person does not forget the painful experience of the divorce or the preceding unhappiness in the marriage. Rather, the marital failure is seen as an opportunity for personal growth, an occasion to learn lessons and gain insights to integrate into subsequent relationships.

As negative overgeneralizations about the other gender and about the possibility of intimate relationships are released, the person becomes available to form new interpersonal connections. Typically, divorced couples do remarry, often to others who are themselves divorced. The resulting unions can involve a bewildering array of steprelationships with children of new partners. Their success will depend on whether the new couple has been able to work through the issues from their divorces.

Sources for Further Study

Ahrons, Constance. *The Good Divorce*. New York: HarperCollins, 1994. Sage and simply presented advice on how to keep one's family together when one's marriage falls apart.

Everett, Craig, and Sandra Everett. *Healthy Divorce*. San Francisco: Jossey-Bass, 1994. A simple presentation of fourteen stages of separation, divorce, and remarriage.

Gardner, Richard A. *The Parental Alienation Syndrome*. 2d ed. Creeskill, N.J.: Creative Therapeutics, 1998. A comprehensive depiction of a disorder in children brought about by a divorced parent who alienates the child from the other parent.

Guttman, Joseph. *Divorce in Psychosocial Perspective*. Hillsdale, N.J.: Lawrence Erlbaum, 1993. A good summary of various models of the divorce process, emphasizing a psychosocial approach.

Kaufman, Taube S. *The Combined Family*. New York: Plenum, 1993. A well-presented guide to understanding one's family roles within steprelationships.

Kübler-Ross, Elisabeth. *On Death and Dying*. 1969. Reprint. New York: Charles Scribner's Sons, 1997. The classic study of the stages of coming to terms with impending death.

Margulies, Sam. *Getting Divorced Without Ruining Your Life*. New York: Simon & Schuster, 1992. Advice on making decisions regarding a divorce agreement that works for both partners.

Schaffer, Jill. "A Humanistic Approach to Mediation." *The Humanistic Psychologist* 27, no. 2 (1999): 213-220. A view of mediation as offering the possibility of transforming relationships through mutuality, respect, and dignity.

Christopher M. Aanstoos and Judi Garland

See also: Couples therapy; Family life: Adult issues; Intimacy; Love; Midlife crises; Parental alienation syndrome; Separation and divorce: Children's issues.

MAGILL'S ENCYCLOPEDIA OF SOCIAL SCIENCE

PSYCHOLOGY

COMPLETE LIST OF ENTRIES

CATEGORIZED LIST OF ENTRIES

ABILITY TESTING

Ability tests
Career and personnel testing
College entrance examinations
Confidentiality
Creativity: Assessment

General Aptitude Test Battery
     (GATB)
Giftedness
Intelligence tests
Kuder Occupational Interest
     Survey (KOIS)

Peabody Individual Achievement
     Test (PIAT)
Stanford-Binet test
Strong Interest Inventory (SII)
Testing: Historical perspectives

Brain damage
Breuer, Josef
Coaching
Cognitive dissonance
Community psychology
Consumer psychology
Coping: Chronic illness
Disaster psychology
Dix, Dorothea
Drug therapies
Ego defense mechanisms
Guilt
Horney, Karen
Impulse control disorders
Kraepelin, Emil
Lorenz, Konrad
Media psychology
Misbehavior
Motivation
Observational learning and
    modeling therapy
Obsessive-compulsive disorder
Oedipus complex
Parental alienation syndrome
Phobias
Post-traumatic stress disorder
Prejudice
Profiling
Psychosurgery
Religion and psychology
Religiosity: Measurement
Road rage
Self
Self-perception theory
Separation anxiety
Shyness
Sport psychology
State-Trait Anxiety Inventory
Support groups
Violence by children and
    teenagers
Virtual reality
Watson, John B.

ATTITUDES AND BEHAVIOR
Ageism
Altruism, cooperation, and
    empathy
Attitude-behavior consistency
Attitude formation and change

Behavior therapy
Cooperation, competition, and
    negotiation
Cooperative learning
Coping: Social support
Crowd behavior
Father-child relationship
Group decision making
Groups
Intergroup relations
Mother-child relationship
Observational learning and
    modeling therapy
Parental alienation syndrome
Prejudice
Prejudice reduction
Racism
Sexism
Sibling relationships
Social identity theory
Support groups

BEHAVIORAL AND COGNITIVE
    MODELS
Abnormality
Abnormality: Psychological
    models
Aging: Cognitive changes
Anxiety disorders
Artificial intelligence
Beck, Aaron T.
Behavior therapy
Behaviorism
Brain damage
Cognitive social learning: Walter
    Mischel
Constructivist psychology
Development
Forensic psychology
Motivation
Operant conditioning therapies
Personal constructs: George A.
    Kelly
Piaget, Jean
Radical behaviorism: B. F.
    Skinner
Reinforcement
Rule-governed behavior
S-R theory: Neal E. Miller and
    John Dollard

Skinner, B. F.
Social learning: Albert Bandura
Thorndike, Edward L.

BEHAVIORAL THERAPIES
Aversion, implosion, and
    systematic desensitization
Bed-wetting
Behavior therapy
Biofeedback and relaxation
Brief therapy
Cognitive behavior therapy
Constructivist psychology
Coping: Chronic illness
Coping: Strategies
Eysenck, Hans
Kraepelin, Emil
Mental health practitioners
Observational learning and
    modeling therapy
Oedipus complex
Operant conditioning therapies
Pain management
Parental alienation syndrome
Psychopathology
Psychotherapy: Children
Reinforcement
Speech disorders
Sport psychology
Support groups
Virtual reality

BIOLOGICAL BASES OF BEHAVIOR
Adrenal gland
Aggression
Artificial intelligence
Bipolar disorder
Birth: Effects on physical
    development
Brain damage
Brain specialization
Brain structure
Cannon, Walter B.
Circadian rhythms
Drug therapies
Endocrine system
Endorphins
Evolutionary psychology
Fight-or-flight response
Gonads

Reality therapy
Sport psychology
Support groups
Transactional analysis
Virtual reality

CONDITIONING
Behavior therapy
Behaviorism
Conditioning
Learning
Memory: Animal research
Motivation
Operant conditioning therapies
Parental alienation syndrome
Pavlov, Ivan
Pavlovian conditioning
Radical behaviorism: B. F.
　　Skinner
Reinforcement
Rule-governed behavior
Taste aversion

CONSCIOUSNESS
Artificial intelligence
Attention
Automaticity
Brain damage
Circadian rhythms
Consciousness
Consciousness: Altered states
Coping: Terminal illness
Denial
Dreams
Hallucinations
Hypnosis
Insomnia
Meditation and relaxation
Self
Sleep
Sleep apnea syndromes and
　　narcolepsy

COPING
Aggression
Amnesia and fugue
Anger
Beck Depression Inventory
　　(BDI)
Biofeedback and relaxation

Coping: Chronic illness
Coping: Social support
Coping: Strategies
Coping: Terminal illness
Denial
Disaster psychology
Environmental psychology
Grieving
Health psychology
Impulse control disorders
Media psychology
Midlife crises
Multiple personality
Pain management
Parental alienation syndrome
Religion and psychology
Religiosity: Measurement
Social networks
Stepfamilies
Stress
Stress: Behavioral and
　　psychological responses
Substance use disorders
Support groups

DEPRESSION
Alzheimer's disease
Battered woman syndrome
Beck, Aaron T.
Beck Depression Inventory
　　(BDI)
Bipolar disorder
Children's Depression Inventory
　　(CDI)
Circadian rhythms
Clinical depression
Coping: Chronic illness
Coping: Terminal illness
Dementia
Depression
Disaster psychology
Drug therapies
Grieving
Impulse control disorders
Kraepelin, Emil
Media psychology
Mood disorders
Parental alienation syndrome
Postpartum depression
Psychosurgery

Seasonal affective disorder
Social networks
Suicide
Support groups

DEVELOPMENTAL PSYCHOLOGY
Adolescence: Cognitive skills
Adolescence: Cross-cultural
　　patterns
Adolescence: Sexuality
Ageism
Aging: Cognitive changes
Aging: Physical changes
Aging: Theories
Attachment and bonding in
　　infancy and childhood
Birth: Effects on physical
　　development
Birth order and personality
Career selection, development,
　　and change
Child abuse
Cognitive ability: Gender
　　differences
Cognitive development: Jean
　　Piaget
Death and dying
Denial
Development
Developmental disabilities
Developmental methodologies
Erikson, Erik
Family life: Adult issues
Family life: Children's issues
Father-child relationship
Freud, Anna
Gender-identity formation
Gesell, Arnold
Giftedness
Gilligan, Carol
Helping
Identity crises
Juvenile delinquency
Kinesthetic memory
Mental retardation
Midlife crises
Moral development
Mother-child relationship
Motor development
Oedipus complex

California Psychological
  Inventory (CPI)
Career and personnel testing
Career Occupational Preference
  System (COPS)
Children's Depression Inventory
  (CDI)
Clinical interviewing, testing,
  and observation
College entrance examinations
Confidentiality
Creativity: Assessment
General Aptitude Test Battery
  (GATB)
Intelligence tests
Kuder Occupational Interest
  Survey (KOIS)
Minnesota Multiphasic
  Personality Inventory
  (MMPI)
Peabody Individual
  Achievement Test (PIAT)
Stanford-Binet test
State-Trait Anxiety Inventory
Strong Interest Inventory (SII)
Testing: Historical perspectives
Thematic Apperception Test
  (TAT)
Wechsler Intelligence Scale for
  Children-Third Edition
  (WISC-III)

THOUGHT
Aging: Cognitive changes
Alzheimer's disease
Analytic psychology: Jacques
  Lacan
Bandura, Albert
Beck Depression Inventory
  (BDI)
Behaviorism
Brain damage
Brain structure
Cognitive ability: Gender
  differences
Cognitive psychology
Concept formation
Consciousness
Consumer psychology
Dementia

Dreams
Lacan, Jacques
Language
Linguistics
Logic and reasoning
Media psychology
Nervous system
Piaget, Jean
Psychoanalysis
Psychobiology
Structuralism and functionalism
Thought: Inferential
Thought: Study and
  measurement

TREATMENTS
Adlerian psychotherapy
American Psychiatric
  Association
Analytical psychotherapy
Aversion, implosion, and
  systematic desensitization
Behavior therapy
Behavioral family therapy
Biofeedback and relaxation
Bipolar disorder
Brief therapy
Cognitive behavior therapy
Cognitive therapy
Coping: Chronic illness
Coping: Strategies
Couples therapy
Disaster psychology
Drug therapies
Eysenck, Hans
Feminist psychotherapy
Gestalt therapy
Group therapy
Hysteria
Internet psychology
Kraepelin, Emil
Mental health practitioners
Music, dance, and theater therapy
Nervous system
Observational learning and
  modeling therapy
Operant conditioning therapies
Pain management
Parental alienation syndrome
Person-centered therapy

Play therapy
Psychoanalysis
Psychopathology
Psychosurgery
Psychotherapy: Children
Psychotherapy: Effectiveness
Psychotherapy: Goals and
  techniques
Psychotherapy: Historical
  approaches
Psychotic disorders
Rational-emotive therapy
Reality therapy
Reinforcement
Shock therapy
Speech disorders
Sport psychology
Strategic family therapy
Substance use disorders
Support groups
Transactional analysis
Virtual reality

VISION
Artificial intelligence
Brain damage
Depth and motion perception
Nearsightedness and
  farsightedness
Nervous system
Pattern recognition
Pattern vision
Psychobiology
Sensation and perception
Senses
Synesthesia
Vision: Brightness and
  contrast
Vision: Color
Visual system

WOMEN'S PSYCHOLOGY
Anorexia nervosa and bulimia
  nervosa
Battered woman syndrome
Child abuse
Codependency
Cognitive ability: Gender
  differences
Couples therapy